Introduction
to
Technical Services

Recent Titles in the
Library and Information Science Text Series

Introduction to Technical Services

EIGHTH EDITION

G. Edward Evans,
Sheila S. Intner,
and Jean Weihs

Library and Information Science Text Series

LIBRARIES UNLIMITED

AN IMPRINT OF ABC-CLIO, LLC
Santa Barbara, California • Denver, Colorado • Oxford, England

Library of Congress Cataloging-in-Publication Data

Evans, G. Edward, 1937–
    Introduction to technical services / G. Edward Evans, Sheila S. Intner, and Jean Weihs. — 8th ed.
          p. cm. — (Recent titles in library and information science text series)
    Includes bibliographical references and index.
    ISBN 978-1-59158-889-4 (acid-free paper) — ISBN 978-1-59158-888-7 (pbk. : acid-free paper) — ISBN 978-1-59158-890-0 (ebook)   1. Technical services (Libraries)—United States.   2. Technical services (Libraries)—Canada.   I. Intner, Sheila S.   II. Weihs, Jean Riddle.   III. Title.
    Z688.6.U6E84   2011
    025'.02—dc22   2010036005

ISBN: 978-1-59158-889-4
          978-1-59158-888-7 (pbk.)
EISBN: 978-1-59158-890-0

15   14   13   12   11   1   2   3   4   5

This book is also available on the World Wide Web as an eBook.
Visit www.abc-clio.com for details.

Libraries Unlimited
An Imprint of ABC-CLIO, LLC

ABC-CLIO, LLC
130 Cremona Drive, P.O. Box 1911
Santa Barbara, California 93116-1911

This book is printed on acid-free paper ∞

Manufactured in the United States of America

Contents

Part II: Acquisitions and Serials

Part III: Cataloging and Processing

Preface to the Eighth Edition

The first edition of this book was written in 1970 and had a length of 175 printed pages. This edition is 500 printed pages and reflects the dramatic changes that have transformed technical services over the past 40-plus years. The whats, hows, and wheres related to technical service activities bear only the broadest correlation with the activities of the 1970s.

This edition further emphasizes the rapidly changing environment in which technical services are conducted. There are several new chapters: chapter 4, "Technical Service Issues," includes material related to physical space needs; chapter 8, "E-Resource Issues," examines how the growth of e-materials affects technical service work; chapter 19, "Copy Cataloging," reflects the ever-increasing need to be more efficient and to save limited funds for technical service activities; chapter 13, "Overview and Decisions," addresses the issue of why and how the local OPAC has become a gateway to the universe of knowledge; and finally, chapter 20, "Processing Materials," covers the activities involved in making sure the items that go into a library's collection are properly identified as belonging to the library and determining where the item is physically located in the collection. All of the other chapters have been extensively rewritten and updated to reflect 2010 technical service functions and activities.

We also thank Jay Lucker for providing an excellent section in chapter 4 on planning physical spaces for technical services.

Part I

---◆---

General Background

Chapter

Introduction

Because technical services are usually not purchased by end-users, their value for money (or benefit-cost ratio) cannot be directly measured.

—Philip Hider, 2008

Given this daunting but exciting set of circumstances, there is a future for technical services, but it may take on other names (access management and digital and Internet services are two examples).

—Vera Fessler, 2007

Introduction to Library Technical Services, Eighth Edition, may be the last edition with that title, assuming that Vera Fessler's assessment of the future of technical services is accurate.[1] The chapter epigraphs suggest that in the 21st century there will be major changes in what librarians have been calling technical services. We, the authors, both agree and disagree with Fessler's view. In the broadest sense of information service, the traditional functions—acquisitions and cataloging/indexing—will remain but will probably have new names. The fact that technology is causing significant changes in how libraries deliver their services and what they offer does not fundamentally change the goals of the basic functions. What and how we will perform technical service activities in the future certainly will look very different compared with today. Those differences may be even more profound than how things were done when the first edition of this book appeared in 1970, and technology was a mainframe computer. The basic functions and their labels have remained constant for more than 40 years. Who really knows what changes lie ahead over even the next 10 years?

Some individuals may doubt the viability of libraries in general, not just technical services. Certainly, the popular press makes it appear as if anything worth having access to is freely available on the Web. There is no question that there is an enormous volume of material on the Web; a simple Google search usually returns tens of thousands of hits. A question that is rarely addressed in the press is, "how do you sort out the useful from the totally worthless?" Librarians and teachers understand that many, if not most, young people seek information in a very different way than in the past. What libraries have been, and still are, good at is assessing, acquiring, and organizing important useful information and helping end-users gain access to that information. Essentially, libraries add value to information materials through the basic functions they perform. Much of that value added arises from the activities that we cover in this book—technical services.

Libraries have a long history—almost 5,000 years—of not only providing society with access to information but also being able to adapt to changing technology. That adaptability will likely continue well into the future. Several years ago Ann Okerson wrote about what she considered to be eight "eternal verities" about library collections and services that are still valid today and that will continue to remain so well into the future:[2]

1. Content is selectable.
2. Content is collectable.
3. Libraries retain information for the long term.
4. Collections grow and require some type of space.
5. Long-term retention requires preservation of some type.
6. Libraries expect to be around for a very long time.
7. Libraries exist to meet users' information needs.
8. Today's information is worldwide and so are libraries to help ensure the worldwide preservation of information/knowledge.

We share these beliefs as her points are not tied to the form or manner of performing an activity.

The epigraph from Philip Hider indicates that placing a direct monetary value on technical services activities is very difficult. However, libraries have been making an effort to demonstrate what their return on investment is to those who fund their operations. One such study, from late 2006, reported that a group of public libraries gave evidence that they provide a 4 to 1 return on investment to their service communities.[3] That is to say, the libraries created an annual economic impact on the community that was four times greater than the amount the communities invested in library services. Almost any investor would be pleased with that level of return and would continue to invest in the service. In his conclusion about his survey of a public library in New South Wales, Australia, Hider wrote:

> Results from the CV survey indicated that Wagga Wagga City Library provides good value for money, and that its technical services provide especially good value. Given that the library is often visited for its collections (particularly its physical collection), the importance of the technical services operations might come as a great surprise, but the extent to which these operations add value to the collection, making it worth much more than if it comprised a randomly purchased and randomly arranged set if items, is worth emphasizing.[4]

LIBRARIES AND CUSTOMER SERVICE

We don't argue that libraries are a societal good whose value goes far beyond any measure that can be derived by cost analysis or return on investment. However, it is also true that libraries are under enormous pressures to demonstrate evidence of accountability. As Weingand states,

> Librarians who flinch at the word *customer* are operating out of an outmoded paradigm. This older paradigm portrays the library as a "public good" with as high a ranking on the "goodness" scale as the national flag, parenthood, and apple pie. As a public good, the library "should" receive public support. However, today's library is in increasingly tight competition for declining resources, and unless it adopts and masters the language and techniques of its competitors, it faces a future of declining support and significance.[5]

In their "Top Ten Assumptions for the Future of Academic Libraries and Librarians," the Association of College and Research Libraries Research Committee listed as number seven, "As part of the 'business of higher education,' students will increasingly view themselves as 'customers' of the academic library and will demand high-quality facilities, resources, and services attuned to their needs and concerns."[6] Another rationale, from a public-library perspective, is provided by Walters when she states that "good service will result in customers voting for bond elections, contributing private dollars, and volunteering to support libraries. Poor service will result in lost elections and lost funding. It is as simple as that. Good customer service pays."[7]

CUSTOMER SERVICE PHILOSOPHY

As noted earlier, attracting and retaining customers through programs specifically designed to produce loyalty to an organization's product or service became a popular marketing trend in the 1980s. Every organization needs repeat customers to survive, and libraries are no exception. However, customers tend to remain loyal only as long as they are satisfied with the quality of the service or product provided. If these do not measure up or keep pace with changing customer preferences or needs, then repeat use cannot be ensured. As Jurewicz and Cutler observed, "We have seen it in our own lives that as customer habits have changed, savvy businesses have changed their service strategies in an attempt to anticipate customer needs. . . . Too busy to go to the mall? Buy from a catalog online and we'll send it to your door. Need to know when to update your online auction bid? Sign up for our service and we'll notify you. Want to know where your package is? Check our website and we'll track it for you."[8]

Some people, both inside and outside the library profession, seem to believe only public service personnel need to think about customer service and its quality. Nothing could be further from the truth. Service quality begins in technical services.

This is as good a place as any to insert a word or two about words referring to the individuals who access libraries and their services. Words such as *patron, client, user,* and *customer* appear in library literature as references to such people. The labels have even generated a modicum of heat among the people who use one of the variations.

"Patron" is one of the longest-standing terms; however, some people think that label is demeaning to libraries and their staffs. (One can view patronage as suggesting that something cannot to exist on its own and requires a special person[s] to underwrite its existence). "Customer," although it is in many ways the most appropriate term—as in "customer service"—is viewed by some in the field as too profit-oriented or commercial to use for a public service/good like a library. "Client" also carries a stigma of commercialism for some—lawyers or brokers have clients, not a library. "User," for a few people, suggests a person with some bad habits. So, where does this leave us? Based on our years of library and archival experience, we believe either "customer" or "user" best reflects what library services are all about. After some debate, we have elected to employ "user" in this work to refer to the people who come to the library, or access online, library services.

ROLE OF LIBRARY SERVICES

Libraries have a long history of adapting to change, and one of the keys to their longevity has been their focus on service to the primary and secondary user community. We are not suggesting that today's service philosophy—equal service to all primary users—has been in place all that long. Just as the contents of libraries have changed over time, so has the service philosophy evolved.

For the vast majority of their history, libraries served a very small segment of the people in their societies. The earliest libraries catered to government officers and religious leaders and essentially contained administrative materials (one can imagine how many clay tablets—rarely with more than a few square inches of writing surface—one would need for even a short poem). During the time scrolls were the dominant information technology, the topical range of materials increased (in addition to government data, there were plays, histories, and so on within libraries), as did the number of persons who could read and were given access to libraries. However, that number was still only a small percentage of the total population. The Dark Ages and Middle Ages brought about a narrowing of access—very few people could read, including royalty. Also, books (called a codex)—the new "technology" of the time—were literally chained down in libraries because of their value, both because of their content and because of the cost of producing a handwritten book. Most of the books produced during this time were religious in character. With the arrival of movable type and the printing press, information materials began the explosion that continues to this day.

To understand the importance of excellent library service, you need only go back to the work of S.R. Ranganathan (an Indian scholar/mathematician/librarian) who played a leading role in developing modern librarianship in India. His *Five Laws of Library Science* was, and still is, the most succinct statement about what to consider when creating a collection or service that truly serves the end-user: books are for use, every reader his book, every book its reader, save the reader's time, and a library is a growing organism.[9] These laws have a very clear customer focus and are essential to providing economical services. Since its first publication, time and time again Ranganathan's basic concepts have proven their viability and their applicability to varying areas of the field.

WHAT ARE TECHNICAL SERVICES?

Technical services traditionally handled those tasks associated with bringing materials into the library and making them ready for the general public or service population to use. Public services managed those activities that directly assisted the end-user in gaining access to information in the library's collection as well as from other collections. Later in this chapter we discuss how that pattern is changing. Although the structure is evolving, libraries still need to acquire materials in some manner for the end-user and process the items, be they paper or electronic.

All libraries, regardless of type, perform nine basic functions to carry out their information transfer activities:

1. *Identification:* Locating potentially worthwhile items to add to the collection(s).
2. *Selection:* Deciding which of the identified items to add to the collection(s).
3. *Acquisitions:* Securing the items selected for the collection(s).
4. *Organization:* Indexing and cataloging the items acquired in a manner that will help the end-user locate materials in the collection(s).
5. *Preparation:* Labeling and otherwise making the items ready for storage in a manner that allows for easy retrieval.
6. *Storage:* Housing the prepared items in units that take into consideration the long-term preservation of the items while allowing staff and end-users easy access to the material.
7. *Interpretation:* Helping end-users locate appropriate materials that meet the users' needs.
8. *Utilization:* Providing equipment and space to allow staff and end-users to make effective use of the items in the collection(s).
9. *Dissemination:* Establishing a system that allows for the use of items away from the library.

This book focuses on the first five activities (traditional technical services functions).[10]

TECHNICAL SERVICES BACKGROUND

Over the past 50 years there has been a steady shift in the philosophy underlying technical services. Emphasis is increasingly being placed on the end-user. Cataloging activities, which are the underlying core element in providing access to collections and quality service, are dependent on a complex set of rules and codes difficult for non-cataloger librarians, much less the general public, to fully comprehend. The codes and rules are essential in providing consistency when organizing collections. Financial transactions (acquisitions) are also dependent on a set of codes and rules that are almost incomprehensible to anyone without a background in accounting or bookkeeping. Until relatively recently, end-user consideration or input to how the activities operated played almost no role in technical services. As late as the 1960s and early 1970s the general opinion was that the public card catalog, the means to gain access to the information about the library's collections, was a tool created by librarians for librarians.

Over time, and with a growing focus on attempting to understand end-users' information-seeking behavior and adjusting library processes and procedures to reflect that understanding, there were efforts to make technical services outputs more user-friendly. An example of the shift in thinking is illustrated in an article by Karen Drabenstott, Schelle Simcox, and Eileen Fenton reporting the results of a study of end-user understanding of public catalog subject headings. In their conclusion, they noted, "It is time for the library community to grapple with the difficult questions about its subject access system and make informed decisions about solving the problem of low levels of end-user subject heading understanding."[11]

Libraries have tried a number of organizational structures in the hope of breaking the front room (public services) and back room (technical services) view that prevailed in the past and that may still be encountered in some libraries. As far back as the 1940s, Raymond Swank argued that catalogers and bibliographers were the key staff to create a collection that end-users would find valuable.[12] However, for a variety of reasons, he was ahead of existing practice, and it was almost 10 years before anyone attempted to implement some of his ideas. In the mid-1950s, the University of Nebraska experimented with a subject approach to providing end-user access.[13] The library assigned librarians responsibility for a subject area and for carrying out all the functions outlined in the previous section with the exception of preparation and storage. In theory, a person working directly with the public ought to better understand user needs and behavior, and therefore be able to create collections and access tools tailored to local conditions. Again, the effort was premature, and after a few years the concept was abandoned. The primary reason was that not everyone was equally interested or capable in all areas and end-users suffered the consequences of uneven subject service.

From a practical point of view, there were, and probably still are, issues in applying the concept in the real world. Individuals are usually neither equally skilled nor interested in every functional area of a library, so the person tends to focus on the high-interest areas at the expense of the other areas. As you might expect, that leads to very uneven service within and across subjects. In a statement to the Academic Technical Services Discussion Group session of the American Library Association (ALA), a group devoted to the concept of blending public and technical services responsibilities, Laura Harper correctly noted that you cannot force people to do what they cannot or do not want to do.[14]

A common method for achieving some of the benefits of these ideas about blending the two traditionally distinct areas is to have technical services librarians work some hours at the reference desk. (Note: We are not aware of many instances where public service personnel also work in technical services on a part-time basis. Perhaps the work is too technical for less than three-quarter or full-time work.) Libraries take different approaches to that idea, ranging from voluntary to required desk hours. Such requests may, in fact, be a directive; in other instances compliance is truly up to the individual. In the long run, having individuals who want to do both activities will provide better-quality service to users. At the Loyola Marymount University (LMU) Library in Los Angeles, two newly graduated catalog librarians asked if they could have some reference desk hours when they were hired. Both believed working at the reference desk would help maintain their reference skills and enhance their career options. Fifteen years later, they were still working at the reference desk and had not tested the career development idea. It is likely, if one or both were to leave, that the head of public services would probably want to make desk hours a part of the required duties for their successors, as both catalog librarians have become a true part of the reference team.

There are some disadvantages to consider before implementing such a plan. One is loss of productivity. For example, for technical services personnel an hour spent on the reference desk is an hour not spent on the "real job." When there is a processing backlog, the sense of what is real work becomes even stronger. Reference personnel also lose some productivity because they must train or update the reference skills of the technical service librarians. When reference work drew solely on printed materials this was not a major concern; today, with ever-increasing dependence on constantly changing electronic resources, it can be a significant issue.

Another issue is the quality of service that part-timers are able to provide, especially if desk hours are required. The LMU Library conducted several faculty and student surveys regarding all aspects of library service as part of an assessment program in preparation for an institution-wide accreditation visit. One of the surprise findings was that the reference staff service overall was very highly regarded by both students and faculty. There were, however, numerous written comments about several librarians who only worked a few hours a week (none of the part-timers works more than four hours). Reference staff wore name tags displaying first names, so users had a sense of with whom they worked. Comments indicated that although the part-timers tried to help and sometimes succeeded, the time required was too high and the degree of confidence in the results of the assistance was low from the user's perspective.

A third issue is staff perception. When only technical services librarians are asked to cross over (that is, reference staff are not asked to assist in technical services), this sends a message about values—that of devaluing technical service activities. With some administrative effort you can reduce the sense of devaluation but seldom eliminate it. One method for blending the two areas that is not often used is a modified version of the subject approach. Sometimes this is referred to as "matrix teams," in which several people share a set of duties but allocate their time according to their interest and skill levels. An example might be four persons who share acquisitions, cataloging, reference, and collection development responsibilities for the humanities. They might allocate their work time as illustrated in Table 1.1; notice that both the rows and columns add up to 100 percent.

TABLE 1.1   MATRIX TEAM

	Person A	Person B	Person C	Person D	Total Time
Acquisitions	30%	20%	25%	25%	100%
Cataloging	40%	20%	25%	15%	100%
Reference	15%	15%	25%	45%	100%
Collection development	15%	45%	25%	15%	100%

Clearly, the benefit of this approach is a better use of the skills, knowledge, and interests of each team member. At the same time, team members gain a holistic view of the library's activities and service programs, which in turn should result in improved decision making, at least in terms of end-user needs. It is also clear that a matrix team needs individuals who are not only committed to the concept but also reasonably skilled in all the areas. That type of person is not always available, and developing in-house interest and skills or seeking such breadth during the hiring process takes time.

Knowledge Goals for Staff

The ALA Council adopted a set of core competencies for librarianship in January 2009.[15] Four of the eight competencies identified relate to the areas of interest to this book—information resources, organization of recorded knowledge and information, technological knowledge, and administration/management. Chapters 2 through 11 address information resources, technology, and administration/management. The balance of the chapters examines issues related to the organization of knowledge, technology, and administration/management.

What are some of the specific competencies called for by the ALA? In terms of information resources, there is an expectation that a person understands the basics of information from its creation to distribution and eventual disposal. Also, there is a call for library staff members to have a grasp of the issues associated with creating and managing library collections (all formats) from selection to withdrawal.

For organization of knowledge, a person should know the principles related to ordering and systematically representing knowledge and information. Further, the individuals needs an understanding of the skills required to organize and describe information resources and systems for cataloging, metadata, indexing, and classification of materials. Joy Williams provides excellent information about why all library employees, not just those in technical services, ought to have knowledge of the machine-readable cataloging (MARC) format and its role in online public access catalogs (OPACs).[16]

When it comes to technology it is not surprising to read that everyone needs to understand how technology affects all aspects of library service and its daily work activities. Also essential is the skill to assess the cost-effectiveness and potential of existing and developing technologies for library work. It goes with saying that having basic computer skills with productivity software—word processing and spreadsheet for example—is a minimal requirement.

From the administration/management perspective, there are the obvious expectations that staff members have a grasp of the fundamentals of planning, priority setting, and fiscal matters (in technical services accounting and bookkeeping are examples of the fiscal area). Collaborative skills—from teamwork to working with other libraries and organizations—are also needed. Finally, all libraries and component units, including technical services, must be constantly assessing their activities and demonstrating their accountability.

SUMMARY

The technical services function provides both information resources that end-users need and the means of gaining effective and efficient access to those materials. Technology has played an ever-greater role in changing the way in which technical services departments operate, but it has not changed their basic functions. In addition to technology, general economic conditions have also had a significant impact on the activities performed.

REVIEW QUESTIONS

1. What are the eight "truths" regarding library functions according to Okerson?
2. Describe the relationship between quality service and technical services.
3. Discuss the changing philosophy and nature of technical services work.
4. Describe some of the various organizational structures technical services has tried and the pros and cons of the variations.
5. Describe the areas of competency that all library employees ought to have based on the ALA core competencies.

NOTES

The epigraphs for this chapter are from Philip Hider, "How Much Are Technical Services Worth," *Library Resources & Technical Services* 52, no. 4 (2008); and Vera Fessler, "The Future of Technical Services," *Library Administration & Management* 21, no. 3 (2007).

1. Fessler, "The Future of Technical Services," 139–44, 155.

2. Ann Okerson, "Asteroids, Moore's Law, and the Star Alliance," *Journal of Academic Librarianship* 29, no. 5 (2003): 280.

3. 9libraries, "Economic Benefit Study Released November 29, 2006," http://9libraries.info.

4. Hider, "How Much Are Technical Services Worth," 259.

5. Darlene E. Weingand, *Customer Service Excellence: A Concise Guide for Librarians* (Chicago: American Library Association, 1997), 3.

6. Association of College and Research Libraries, *Environmental Scan 2007* (Chicago: American Library Association, 2008).

7. Suzanne Walters, *Customer Service: A How-To-Do-It Manual for Librarians* (New York: Neal-Schuman, 1994).

8. Lynn Jurewicz and Todd Cutler, *High Tech High Touch: Library Customer Service through Technology* (Chicago: American Library Association, 2003), 2.

9. S. R. Ranganathan, *Five Laws of Library Science* (Madras, India: Madras Library Association, 1931).

10. For information on the four remaining activities, please see G. Edward Evans and Thomas L. Carter, *Introduction to Library Public Services,* 7th ed. (Westport, CT: Libraries Unlimited, 2009).

11. Karen M. Drabenstott, Schelle Simcox, and Eileen Fenton, "End-User Understanding of Subject Headings in Library Catalogs," *Library Resources & Technical Services* 43 (1999): 160.

12. Raymond C. Swank, "The Catalog Department in the Library Organization," *Library Quarterly* 18 (1948): 24–32.

13. Frank A. Lundy, "The Divisional Plan Library," *College & Research Libraries* 17 (1956): 143–48.

14.   Sara Evans Davenport, "The Blurring of Divisional Lines between Technical and Public Services," *Reference Librarian* 15, no. 34 (1991): 49.

15.   American Library Association Council, *Core Competencies of Librarianship* (Chicago: American Library Association, 2009), www.ala.org/ala/educationcareers/careers/corecomp/index.cfm.

16.   Joy Williams, "MARC Data, the OPAC and Library Professionals," *Electronic Library and Information Systems* 43, no. 1 (2008): 7–17.

SUGGESTED READING

Baker, Barry. "Resource Sharing: Outsourcing and Technical Services." *Technical Services Quarterly* 16, no. 2 (1998): 35–45.

Chu, Felix Tse-Hsiu. "Assessing the Infrastructure: Technical Support for Library Services." *Illinois Library Association* 19, no. 4 (2001): 9–11.

Dillion, Dennis. "Fishing the Electronic River: Disruptive Technologies, the Unlibrary, and the Ecology of Information." *Journal of Library Administration* 36, no. 3 (2002): 45–58.

The Economist. "Flat Prospects." 382 (March 17, 2008): 72.

Evans, G. Edward. "Reflections on Creating Information Service Collections." In *The Portable MLIS: Insights From the Experts,* ed. Ken Haycock and Brooke Sheldon, 88–97. Westport, CT: Libraries Unlimited, 2008.

Fain, Margaret, Micheline Brown, and Allison Faix. "Cross-Training Reference Librarians to Catalog." *Technical Services Quarterly* 22, no. 1 (2004): 41–53.

Gordon, Rachel Singer, and Michael Stephens. "Tech Tips for Every Librarian." *Computers in Libraries* 27, no. 5 (2007): 30–31.

Gregory, Joan M., Alice Weber, and Shona Dippie. "Innovative Roles for Technical Services Librarians: Extending Our Reach." *Technical Services Quarterly* 25, no. 4 (2008): 37–47.

Hearn, Stephen. "Comparing Catalogs." *Library Resources & Technical Services* 53, no. 1 (2009): 25–40.

Hirshon, Arnold, and Barbara Winters. *Outsourcing Library Technical Services: A How-to-Do-It Manual for Librarians.* New York: Neal-Schuman, 1996.

Intner, Sheila S. "Putting the Service in Technical Services." *ALCTS Newsletter* 9, nos. 4–6 (1998): 38–39.

Makinen, Ruth. "Scheduling Technical Services Staff at the Reference Desk." *The Reference Librarian* 59 (1997): 139–46.

Marcum, Deanna B. "The Future of Cataloging." *Library Resources and Technical Services* 50, no.1 (2006): 5–9.

Matthews, Joseph R. "Customer Satisfaction." *Public Libraries* 47, no. 6 (2008): 52–54

Polivka, Anne, and Thomas Nardone. "The Definition of 'Contingent Work.'" *Monthly Labor Review* 112 (1989): 10.

Stephens, Michael. "The Promise of Web 2.0." *American Libraries* 37, no. 9 (2006): 32.

Taylor, Arlene G. "Organizing and Representation of Information/Knowledge." In *The Portable MLIS: Insights From the Experts,* ed. Ken Haycock and Brooke Sheldon, 98–111. Westport, CT: Libraries Unlimited, 2008.

Chapter

Technical Services Administration

The technical services manager's most important responsibilities, whether or not he or she delegates any part of the managerial authority to another, are ensuring that library policies are properly interpreted and implemented, that work is fairly distributed, and that all the work that is supposed to be done is done well and in a timely and cost-effective manner.

—Shelia Intner and Peggy Johnson, 2008

[L]ibrary quality has been synonymous with collection size—an assessment of what the library *has* rather than with what the library *does*.

—Peter Hernon and Ellen Altman, 1998

Managing and administration are often used as synonyms, although they have slightly different meanings. In the chapter epigraph, Intner and Johnson identify most of the roles and responsibilities involved in overseeing technical services operations. A slightly more detailed way to view the issue is to think of a manager of technical services operations as someone who is purposeful; makes things happen; accomplishes operations through people; is effective through the use of special knowledge, skills, practice, and experience; is aided by technology but not replaced by it; is accountable for the quality of outputs; and is responsible for the cost-benefits of activities. That is a rather long list, and all the factors are important.

If you had to pick just one of the above factors as the most critical, it would probably be remembering that it takes a team effort (the people factor) to have a successful outcome. Everyone can and should contribute to the outcome, regardless of a person's job description or pay grade. Because there must be some understanding of the managerial aspects of operations for there to be effective team performance, the content of this chapter has value for all categories of staff.

What are the differences, if any, between the terms "administrator," "manager," and "supervisor"? The root meaning of administrator is derived from Latin—*ad* (to) and *ministratio* (give service). Thus, an administrator gives service to her organization. In current usage, the term most often denotes the senior person in an organization or the group of people at the most senior level (the administration). Manager/management generally refers to those who organize and coordinate activities in terms of a set of principles (mission), values, goals, policies, and so on. Supervisors have some of the responsibilities of managers, although at a lower level of accountability. They are responsible for the productivity and actions of a small group of employees. If you think of an organization as consisting of three levels of accountability—top, middle, and bottom—at the top would be administrators and managers, in the middle are the supervisors, and the bottom are the frontline staff.

Given the aforementioned definitions, the head of technical services would be a manager. Depending upon the library's organizational structure, there may be several levels of managers. For example, a library might have a head of technical services and a head of the acquisitions department, a head of cataloging, and perhaps a head of processing or serials or preservation, all of whom would be managers with probably one or two supervisors reporting to them. The foregoing reflects an older organizational pattern, but one often still encountered. Today, quite frequently there is a flattening of the structure—and fewer layers of managers.

The ultimate key to unit and library success is to have everyone working together (teamwork) to achieve the organizational goals. This applies to both the traditional organizational model (each person working more or less independently) and a more formal team structure (more about teams and team building later in this chapter). Shifting from being an administrator, manager, or supervisor to being a leader is a key factor in achieving effective teamwork regardless of the organizational structure. Some years ago, Gleeson and Miller suggested that managers and supervisors in technical services ought to become coordinators rather than directors of their staff if they want to have units that adjust quickly to changing circumstances.[1] That advice is just as valid today as when it was first offered. Although Lihong Zhu focused on advertisements for head cataloging positions in academic libraries, her finding that the positions have become more multifaceted than in the past applies to almost all positions in technical services, not just heads of cataloging.[2] One of the newest aspects is the emphasis on team building.

The Tips sections in this chapter will be useful at some point in your working career, perhaps sooner than expected. As Pat Tunstall commented;

> In these days of reduced funds and staff cutbacks, it is not unusual for people to be moved sideways into supervisory positions or to have a number of library pages suddenly added to their list of responsibilities. It is often the case that these reluctant draftee managers have no previous experience . . . Who can blame them for feeling anxious about how they will handle their new charges?[3]

TIPS FOR EFFECTIVE TIME MANAGEMENT

Managing your time will assist you in more ways than just getting more work done. It can help reduce work stress for your benefit (and sometimes for your colleagues as well). It may also help supervisors and managers delegate activities or reduce the tendency to "put off until tomorrow what you can do today" behavior. These tips are relatively easy to implement; what is more difficult is to follow them long enough to make them habits rather than special activities. Perhaps the least complicated but hardest to follow is avoiding the paper-shuffle game (this also relates to e-mail). In most work situations, there is a steady flow of documents across the desk, via the in basket or e-mail. Some of it is informational in nature and is the easiest to read and toss or delete. Too often, however, there is a tendency to quickly look at such items and think, "I'll get to this later when I have more time," and then set it aside in what becomes an ever-growing pile of "when I have time" reading material. For many people that growing pile (mountain) becomes a source of stress because "when I have time" never seems to come. Reading the material when it arrives and taking the appropriate action—filing it for future reference, passing it on, recycling it, or hitting the delete button—will resolve the problem.

Some material may require a response by a given date. Again, responding right away will save time in the long run. There is a tendency to think, "Oh, this is due in two weeks (or whenever); I'll do this later." If nothing more, handling the matter immediately saves the review time involved in rereading the material when the response is due. In addition, given that many issues arise unexpectedly, having completed an expected project ahead of time allows for more flexibility in responding to rush projects that suddenly appear. Waiting until later may lead to the item getting mislaid or falling so far down the e-mail list it is overlooked until after the date due, and that can cause an even greater expenditure of time and effort. There are items that require some searching for information or just straightforward time to think about before taking action; a useful method for handling such items is to have a filing system based on action time requirements—start tomorrow, the day after, in three days, and so forth. (This approach also helps organize time, as discussed later.)

A few items are complex or difficult projects that may seem overwhelming. One way to handle those items is to establish a finish-by date that is slightly earlier than the required date and break the activity into small, daily actions to maintain a sense of progress and provide a measure of success.

Perhaps the second most common suggestion for managing time is to create to-do lists. Using a file-folder system (either paper based or electronic) is a sound variation of the to-do list. One simple way to do this is to set up a file for each day of the week, one for next week, two weeks, and three weeks, thus covering a month. The files can hold some of the action items that require time to address thoughtfully. Each day just before leaving work, go into the next day's folder and set up the priorities for the items in the folder (the next day's to-do list). It is a good idea to make the first item something of high interest and relatively easy to accomplish; this creates a positive sense of achievement that may carry over into less interesting but necessary activities. At the end of each work week, again at the end of the day, go through the next week's folder and sort the material into the appropriate folders by the day each item should be handled. Certainly setting up such a system takes some time, as does the daily review; however, as one of the authors can attest, it saves a surprising amount of time in the long run.

Interruptions are one of the most common reasons given for not having enough time at work. "If it weren't for all the interruptions I'd be fine," is a lament of many staff members. Interruptions cost time, even when they are warranted, because they fragment one's activities. It always takes a few minutes to get back to where one left off in a task after the interruption. The three most frequent sources of interruptions are the telephone, colleagues dropping by, and checking to see if one has e-mail. Managing the telephone is easier to handle than workmates, but both can be done without offending people.

With telephone calls, batch the necessary ones and spend a few minutes planning each, asking "What do I need to convey or learn." Make a list for each call and stick to it. Use a large pad of paper to keep all the notes and lists together. (Looking for the lunch napkin, business card, or empty envelope with the needed information is a great time waster.) Time management consultants often suggest that a business call should not require more than three minutes.[4] If the matter is too complex or detailed to handle in that time, consider some form of written communication. This is a useful guideline for most business calls, but there are exceptions, especially when developing or maintaining a working relationship with someone in another organization, such as a library vendor or bindery firm. It is also good, if not always possible, to batch return calls. A useful approach to handling incoming calls, at least from other library staff members and those with whom you work, is to tell people "the best time to call me is between x and y." Although this does not and should not stop calls from coming in at other times, it does, in time, lead to batching of many, if not most, incoming calls. During that calling time frame, engage in activities that take less concentration, making the interruptions less of a problem. Additional options to consider would be to automatically forward your phone to voicemail or to screen calls via the caller ID function on your phone, if these features are available, or to find an alternative work location if you are in an open office setting. Although these methods should not be relied upon constantly, they may be helpful during times when interruptions would be extremely counterproductive, such as when you are operating under a critical deadline.

E-mail can become almost as big a time waster as the telephone. To remedy this use the same approach to e-mail as to the telephone. Read and respond to these messages in batches. Don't fall into the pattern of leaving your e-mail active all day or frequently checking to see whether there is mail if you want to make the most effective use of your time.

With colleagues, if at all possible, try to establish time frames when dropping by is welcome and times when dropping by is not welcome. For supervisors, it is a little easier to establish times when staff can come by with questions and some time during the day when the door is closed (even if there is no physical door to close). In smoothly running units, establishing such times for everyone is relatively easy. In times of change or uncertainty, creating such time is problematic, but even in those circumstances having some private work time can be beneficial. However, supervisors need to make it clear that a closed-door time does not mean they are unavailable for unusual or emergency situations.

Sometimes a person likes to engage in small talk before and after getting to the purpose of a visit. Frequently these are also people who, if allowed, will spend more time on the informal and social aspects of the visit than on the issue in question. Setting time limits and sticking to them—"I can give you xx minutes"—is a sound method for any interruption, unless of course the person in question is a supervisor. However, a supervisor should be as concerned about effective time usage as the person interrupted and should take no more time than necessary. Finally, there is nothing wrong with asking people what it is they want to discuss, in a polite way, if they are having trouble getting to the point.

There are many other time management techniques, and several books on this topic are listed in the Suggested Reading section of this chapter.

TIPS FOR MEETINGS

Meetings are related to time management in the sense that they may be effective or a wasteful use of finite work time. Meetings are a given in the workplace. How well the convener structures and runs the meeting determines how useful the meeting will be for the attendees. It is rather common to hear a manager or supervisor say, "All I do is attend meetings." In a formal teamwork environment, that statement might apply to all team members, as team meetings are essential to team success. Thus, having effective meetings is a key component in having unit productivity.

What makes for a useful meeting that does not waste time? Essentially, you should divide meetings into three broad steps—before, during, and ending. The before aspect relates to planning—(consisting of four Ps: purpose, people, place, preparation). First and foremost, consider what is the *purpose* of the meeting? Everyone has experienced mandatory-attendance meetings and left wondering, "What was that all about?" Without a clear purpose, no meeting will be a success; it is likely to start with vague comments, wander in a variety of directions, and end with no one certain why it was called. Who should attend (*people*) is also part of the planning process. Striking the correct balance between having too many attendees (people with little concern or interest in the topic) and too few (missing a key person) can be a challenge. Some people believe they should sit in on every meeting, regardless of topic, while others resist attending all but the most critical meetings. Where to hold the meeting (*place*) is a frequently overlooked element in the planning process. Meetings are very often held in spaces with no thought to how the space may affect its purpose. One obvious impact is the difference between a meeting in the boss's office and a meeting in a conference room. Place considerations can also include whether technology is needed at the meeting (to demonstrate a process or function) and whether the locale convenient to all participants. Also important is the furniture arrangement—one arrangement may be conducive to peer interaction and another may convey a power structure, for example. The final P is *preparation*—preparing an agenda, checking the space and any equipment that may be needed, and so on. When setting the agenda be sure to place the most important topic first and have clearly defined outcome in mind. Too often time is wasted on less important topics just because they are high on the agenda. Another key part of preparation is letting attendees know what they should prepare to discuss.

During the meeting there are four Fs to consider—focus, facilitation, feedback, and fellowship. A convener must keep the group on track (following agenda topics only, or gaining group consensus on how to deal with topics that may pop up). When the group loses its *focus,* time is wasted. Conveners must be *facilitators* and keep the group focused. What this means is to ensure that all attendees become part of the meeting, even if it means calling on them. Presumably, assuming the convener addressed the four Ps, everyone in attendance is there because he has an interest or stake in the discussion. Thus, all voices should be heard. One technique for achieving this, without embarrassing anyone, is to say, "Let's take a moment to see where we stand. Let's go around the room and get everyone's thoughts." Providing positive *feedback* is a hallmark of a good convener. Even if the convener does not agree with an expressed view, she phrases her response in a way that will not crush further discussion. Some examples of how to respond are to say, "Tell me more; how can we sell that to the boss?" or "Let's combine our ideas to get the best solution." Having fun or feeling like a group member (*fellowship*), although not essential in all cases, can often enhance a meeting's outcome. Lighten up meetings with laughter and humor whenever possible. You will be pleasantly surprised how much more effective the meetings become.

The ending portion of the meeting features the four Cs of completion—consensus, closure, critique, and communication. Gaining group *consensus* on the outcome of the meeting (e.g., actions to take, decisions made) is an essential element in successful meetings. Too often a meeting ends with everyone thinking much was accomplished, but shortly afterward the attendees begin to wonder just what the outcome was. Providing a perceived view of the consensus helps everyone leave with a sense of accomplishment; it also gives the group a final chance to know if, in fact, there is consensus. Clearly, if there is to be consensus there must also be an understanding of the next steps (*closure*). Another challenge for many conveners is getting the meeting to end in the allotted time. If the prior four Ps and four Fs were addressed, however, ending on time should be no problem in most cases. It is when some aspects of planning and flow are poorly thought through that the endless meetings occur. Spending some time, with and without the group, going over what worked and did not work with the meeting (*critique*) will pay dividends for future meetings. The last step is to *communicate*. Part of that process is to have a record of what transpired, not word for word, but in broad brushstrokes. Sending a summary of the meeting to group members may bring to light something important that was overlooked. Finally, informing other interested parties about the outcome will build a sense of shared involvement if nothing else.

TIPS FOR TEAM BUILDING

The term *team* is used in a variety of ways, even when referring to a workplace concept. One definition of a workplace team that appears to capture the current work environment is a "work group [that] is made up of individuals who see themselves and who are seen by others as a social entity, who are interdependent because of the tasks they perform as members of the group, who are embedded in one or more larger social systems, and who perform tasks that affect others."[5] Perhaps two more elements ought to be part of the definition—team work groups develop a shared commitment to one another and are empowered to make decisions regarding their activities.

Teams take several approaches in terms of management style—empowered, project, and working are three of the most common types of teams. *Empowered* (or self-managed) teams have a high degree of autonomy in some activity and are more or less permanent in character. An example of such a group might be a retrospective cataloging team, if they have great latitude to determine their work activities. *Project* teams are assembled to carry out a specific task, usually with a target completion date. An example might be a PromptCat implementation team. *Working* teams are developed by supervisors to improve the cooperation or coordination of work activities within their areas of responsibility and to involve the staff in more of the unit's planning and decision-making activities. In the first two types of teams, managers often implement a team-selection process that is designed to bring to the team people with the different skills needed to handle the assigned task. Working teams seldom start with a selection process, but over time the supervisor might adjust job descriptions to bring in new or missing skill sets to improve the team's performance.

No matter what type of team is being considered, most of the elements of good team building apply. Good team building starts with creating two types of matrices: *skills* and *responsibilities.* Even when someone is not in a position to select team members, it is useful to develop a skills matrix to identify the ideal skill sets. That way, if there is an opportunity to select a new person, one can quickly rewrite the appropriate job description. Such a matrix also helps one think about skill sets that exist in the work unit for meeting the existing responsibilities. It may even lead to reassigning duties among the existing staff. Table 2.1 illustrates a simplified responsibility matrix for handling PromptCat.

TABLE 2.1   MINIMAL CATALOGING WITH LIBRARY OF CONGRESS RECORDS

MARC tag	Requirement	Action If Record Not as Required
FF:ELvl	ELvl is blank, 1 or 4. There is no need to check Elvl for Prompt-Cat books—only when cataloging on OCLC.	Refer to cataloger. Record is incomplete.
050	050 call number is present. Second indicator is zero.	Refer to cataloger. Needs verification.
	No explicit la is visible in the 050.	Refer to cataloger. Need to choose/complete call number.
	Call number does not begin with PZ or Z5000+.	Refer to cataloger. Usually needs different call number.
245	245 field matches title on title page exactly, except for punctuation.	Refer to cataloger. Needs adjustment or different record.
	245 lc (if present) matches form of author's name on title page exactly, omitting titles like "Dr." or "The Reverend."	Refer to cataloger. Needs adjustment.
	Title does not begin with an initial article in a foreign language (e.g., La, El, Los, Le, Das, Der, Eine, Une).	Refer to cataloger. Needs added title to index initial article. If in doubt, refer foreign language titles to cataloger.
	Different title on spine, or prominent embedded portion of title on title page, is recorded in a 246 field.	Refer to cataloger. Needs added title field.

(*Continued*)

TABLE 2.1 *(Continued)*

MARC tag	Requirement	Action If Record Not as Required
250	Edition statement (if any) on the cover, title page, page before t-p or back of t-p, is shown in 250 field.	Refer to cataloger. Needs adjustment or different record.
260	Publisher named in 260 lb appears on the cover, title-page, page before t-p or back of t-p.	Refer to cataloger. Needs adjustment or different record.
300	Height of book in 300 lc is less than 29 cm.	Measure book, rounding to next full cm. Adjust 300 lc to match. If 29 cm. or more, make bib loc and item loc "lmlo." If book is labeled for Main Stacks, relabel for Oversize.
440/490	Series title (if any) appearing on the cover, title page, page before t-p or back of t-p is shown in 440 or 490 field.	Refer to cataloger. Needs adjustment or different record.
Screenplays	Item is not a screenplay (TV or movie script).	Refer to cataloger. Needs additional title information and subject headings.

MARC = machine-readable cataloging.

Teams in the workplace have been around for a long time in one form or another. They are not a new concept; however, they are playing an ever-greater role in how organizations get things done. Over the past 20-some years, organizations, including libraries, have undergone a flattening of their structures, resulting in fewer layers of management. In many cases, they experienced downsizing or received no increase in staffing, even with increased workloads. As a result of these events, the staff must be more productive, be flexible, learn new skills, and take on more responsibilities. So far, the 21st century has placed additional pressure on organizations and their personnel to be adept at handling rapid change with reduced resources. All of these factors place a premium on flexibility and having a knowledgeable workforce that is more capable of working independently than in the past.

Supervisors must get the best possible performance from their existing staff, and they must depend on team members to operate and solve problems, often on their own. (Fewer supervisors are available, and if work is to progress in a timely fashion, team members must act without waiting for assistance from higher-level personnel.) Although the management fundamentals—decision making, planning, organizing, and so on—remain unchanged, there is a shift in who engages in these activities when true teams exist.

Some of the differences between a true team environment and a traditional workplace are significant from a supervisor's point of view. Teams call for consensus rather than command and control. They require acceptance of the idea that conflict (both positive and negative) is a normal part of team operations, and those conflicts must be addressed in an open, honest manner. Although not every difference of opinion that occurs in a team will result in negative conflict, time will still need to be spent in meetings to resolve problems or make decisions. Reaching decisions in a team setting tends to be more knowledge based than when it is done on the basis of one person's opinion. In teams, more emphasis must be placed on the whys than on the hows.

Creating a team requires careful thought and an understanding of the work personalities of the potential team members. (Not all workers are comfortable working on a team.) The first step in team creation is determining how big the team should be and whom to select. The second step is to create an environment conducive to teamwork (empowerment and support). Establishing realistic goals is the third step. Providing training and development opportunities for team members is the fourth step—although this step is ongoing in character. The last, and perhaps the most difficult step in using true teams, is for the supervisor/manager to let the team go and only become involved in team activities when asked to do so.

In addition, to setting clear goals and directions and establishing the right team environment, it is important to consider the tasks the team is to perform. The leader must be certain the tasks *require* teamwork. A common mistake, especially in first-time team environments, is creating a team in name only (the team has tasks, yes, but not those requiring teamwork). What happens is an appearance of teamwork, but in reality it is just individuals doing their own independent work. Making this mistake quickly leads to disillusionment on the part of both the team and the manager. Another fairly common mistake is assigning tasks that only occasionally call for teamwork. Although there will likely be times when team members need to work independently to produce a product that is shared by or ultimately benefits the entire team, assigning too many individualized tasks to the team risks sending a mixed message and does not take advantage of the benefits of a team-based structure.

There is also the complex task of assessing team performance. This can be particularly problematic when some staff members, those who are not a team, receive individual performance reviews and team members are on a different system. In the minds of most people, performance reviews and salary increases are closely linked, so some will have difficulty accepting a team assignment knowing the group's efforts will be assessed rather than individual work.

TIPS FOR STAFF MOTIVATION

Motivating staff is an ongoing process, and it seems much more challenging now than in the past. Budget cuts, staff reductions, unit reorganizations, and teams are just a few of the factors making it difficult to keep morale up. Almost any type of change in the work environment can create four stages of staff reactions, depending on the nature of the change:

1. Disbelief, shock, and denial;
2. Anger, rage, and resentment;
3. Emotional bargaining—where anger moves to depression; and finally
4. Acceptance

During the first stage, people are often shocked that changes might or will take place. They believe the changes cannot or will not work, and some staff may actively work against the changes. Involving the staff and allowing them maximum input will help, as will providing honest and forthright explanations about what is involved in the proposed change. Indicating the benefits is also helpful. If there will be staff reductions, this should first be made clear to the staff involved in a private manner. Trying to hide such facts until later will damage credibility with the remaining staff.

In stage two, the initial denial and shock usually shift to anger, especially if there are to be staff reductions that require layoffs rather than normal attrition. That anger is normally focused on the immediate supervisor rather than the actual factor making the changes necessary. During the third stage, staff members likely to be affected by the change begin to start thinking about their options. Occasionally, some resign before there is any final decision. Often, these are the most qualified individuals who are less likely to lose their positions. Others become depressed, and their work quality and quantity begin to fall. Eventually, there is an acceptance that what seemed unthinkable will in fact take place.

Susan Cartwright and Cary Cooper identified 12 of the most common workplace stressors.[6] The technical services environment appears to have the potential to experience all 12 factors from time to time. The stressors are

- loss of identity as organizational size changes;
- lack of information, poor/inconsistent communication;
- fear of job loss or demotion;
- possible transfer/relocation;
- loss of or reduced power, status, and prestige;
- disrupted or uncertain career path;
- change in rules, regulations, procedures, and reporting structure;
- change in colleagues, supervisors, and subordinates;
- ambiguous reporting systems, roles, and procedures;
- devaluation of old skills and expertise;
- personality/workplace culture clashes; and
- increased workload.

Some factors are less controllable than others; for example, workload increases are often difficult to control at least in the short term. (Some of the steps to take to reduce the stress were discussed previously.) Providing more information can be very helpful; the word does not always get out as much as one might think, and what does get out is often less than accurate. Keep the communication process open to feedback; make it clear that questions and expressions of concern are welcome. Be as specific as possible about the whats, whys, whens, and wherefores of events or projects that may be stressful. Involving staff in the process as much as possible helps them have a sense of control over their destiny. Work at developing a team approach, if not actual work teams.

The basics of team motivation do not vary much from that of individual employees. An underlying factor in everyone's motivation to work is self-interest, if nothing more than working as a legal means of securing the money one needs to live. It is of course far more complex than that, but self-interest is a factor. Thus, the first difference in the team environment is the need to keep self-interest to a minimum. Another difference is that the team will likely consist of members from different generations (baby boomers and Generation Xers, for example) who may be more or less inclined toward teamwork.

Monitoring team activities is an essential role for a manager or supervisor. When a team exhibits morale or productivity problems, the manager or supervisor must intervene. If the poor morale is arising from a performance problem as a team, assisting the team with its problem solving to isolate the issue may lead to a solution. That will not resolve the poor morale by itself, but it will stop the performance problem from feeding the morale issue. It may be as simple as the timing of the resources needed for effective teamwork, for example, the flow of material from acquisitions to the catalog department. On the other hand, the issue may be a nonperforming team member. When that is the case, the team may be hard pressed to resolve the matter on its own.

When morale is just starting to decline (moderate to low morale), several things can be done. One step is to model behavior that is positively geared toward success. If a manager can identify coachable areas in need of improvement, it is probably a good time for some serious coaching. Helping the team find one or two small and quick successes almost always boosts morale. Having a team meeting and discussing the vision and its positive values may also make a difference for the better. Demonstrating commitment to the vision and modeling that commitment will help team members buy into that vision. Such discussions may also lead to revelations about what may be causing a decline in morale, assuming you are an effective listener. Listening is a major component in effective communication.

TIPS FOR COMMUNICATION

Given the current work environment, team-based technical services activities that cut across traditional activity lines are more likely to produce positive results and require effective communication. Good teams should have the following characteristics:

- A broad range of skills and cross training
- Strong senior management support
- Greater than traditional latitude in determining work activities
- A commitment to being well-informed

Effective communication—speaking, writing, and listening—is the glue of successful team functionality. Group commitment, decision making, problem solving, conflict resolution, and accountability all rest on the quality of the communication that occurs in the team. Team members who understand and follow four communication rules find themselves, more often than not, on great teams.

- **Rule one: Be open and honest with one another.** This leads to vulnerability; being open and honest almost always generates a greater commitment to one another.
- **Rule two: Be clear and concise.** Trying to show off one's vocabulary tends to turn off listeners and makes the real message harder to identify. Being long-winded does little but eat up valuable team time.

- **Rule three: Maintain consistency.** This does not mean being unwilling to compromise or to admit to being wrong about something. However, constantly changing views or positions raises doubts about a person and may lead to less trust.
- **Rule four: Be civil and courteous and show respect for others and their views.**

Teams that follow these rules in their communication with one another, with the leader, with other units or teams, and with the public are likely to achieve great things.

People often slip into the habit of thinking of communication as a one-way process based on oral and written messages sent and received. To be truly effective, communication must be based on a two-way feedback process to prevent misunderstandings and to clarify points. Even when remembering that communication is two way in nature, people frequently forget the importance of *listening* and thinking *before* providing feedback.

Listening is an art that many people need to practice more than they do and one that some people never seem to develop. One reason is that we tend to forget that we can hear at least four times faster than most people normally speak. so the difference between speaking and listening speeds allows ample time for the listener's mind to wander away from the speaker's message. If in doubt about this difference, take a few minutes to think carefully about the last lecture or speech you attended. Did you really only think about the presentation? Or did you also think about the quality of the presentation? Did you think about what you needed to do after the presentation was over? Did you doodle on the page if you were taking notes? Did you think about the room, the people, or what the weather was like outside? The list could go on and on. The point is that any such thoughts take your attention away from the message and illustrate that listening speed was not taxed to any great extent by the presentation.

Improving listening skills is necessary for effective team performance. Tips for improving listening include (1) thinking about questions the presentation or the speaker brings to mind that need to be raised for clarification; (2) asking for examples or providing paraphrased feedback during the presentation; (3) concentrating on what is new, different, or questionable; and (4) summarizing the key points after the presentation, which is a way of concentrating attention on the message being delivered and not allowing one's mind to wander to other matters.

The communication process has a passive side as well. Nonverbal behavior can be almost as important, if not the most significant part of the communication process. Speakers and listeners both pick up on the nonverbal behaviors or cues and may have very different reactions to those behaviors. Libraries are becoming more and more diverse in terms of staff and the end-users served. Communication is a process highly influenced by cultural and societal factors. Although we are more likely to think about the importance of our word choice in a diverse environment, we sometimes overlook the nonverbal issues.

Three examples illustrate the point about cultural differences and nonverbal behavior. Generally in Western European societies, direct eye contact during a conversation is considered a sign of a listening, open, straightforward, honest person. Lack of such eye contact suggests the opposite. However, in other cultures, direct eye contact is seen as insulting, disrespectful, and even threatening. Likewise, European-based patterns expect some nonverbal signals that the person is listening, such as nodding in agreement. In some cultures, such behavior is not expected or is even viewed as presumptuous on the listener's part. Physical space during a conversation is also a factor. Some societies expect people to be up close and personal, while in others such behavior is viewed as pushy and rude. Knowing something about the expected communication behavior of the various cultures represented in the team or workplace can be beneficial for overall working relationships and productivity. (A note about diversity: The Loyola Marymount University [LMU] Library PromptCat team consisted of 11 members of the cataloging and acquisitions departments. In terms of cultural diversity there were two people from the Philippines, one from India, one from Taiwan, one from Japan, one Chinese American, and one Latino, with the balance from Western European backgrounds. Clearly, to work effectively the team had to address different communication styles.)

There are times when personal influence is not enough, and negotiating will be necessary to achieve the desired results. Negotiating should be, both within the group and with other units, a process of give and take. Before starting negotiations it is advisable to have a clear understanding of what the bottom line is for each party involved, that is, what cannot be modified. In the workplace setting, there are usually at least three bottom lines. First is the institutional goal of what must take place—for example, PromptCat *must* be implemented in a cost-effective manner. Second is a goal the staff desires—for example, any new process *must not* result in added workload but rather be a replacement. A third bottom line is that of the manager or supervisor—the outcome *must* be something he can be comfortable with implementing. Following are some negotiating tips:

- Differentiating between wants, needs, and musts is required for all sides.
- Asking high and giving low is expected, but don't be ridiculous about either end.
- Conceding something, which is necessary if there is to be negotiation, is also expected, but when doing so don't simply give in.
- Winning something and losing something is the goal of negotiations; no side should leave believing it has lost on every issue

Supervising or administering a unit in technical services calls for the same basic management skills and knowledge as any other unit in the library. However, some of those basic skills are being called upon with ever-increasing frequency as libraries try to adjust to a changing external environment. Some of the skills that need to come into play more often are managing change, fostering innovation and creativity, containing costs, building teams, and motivating staff.

THE "MORE" FACTOR

Some years ago Cecily Johns wrote that the motto for cataloging and technical services is and always will be "more, better, cheaper, faster."[7] These are shorthand labels for what administrators of technical services units must constantly address, and they are just as relevant now as when Johns first wrote them.

For most libraries in the 1980s and early 1990s, "more" did not mean a higher volume of books and serials to acquire, catalog, and process. The "more" was the expanding range of material formats that had to be dealt with on a regular basis. A seemingly constantly changing information industry created, and occasionally dropped, new formats for delivering material, which generated pressures on technical services units to keep evolving. Electronic materials quickly demonstrated that libraries had to gear up to handle not only constant change but also very rapid shifts in direction.

As both a library school educator and library administrator for many years, one of the authors, Dr. Evans, has experienced those events from the classroom/conceptual point of view and the "how are we going to deal with this development" practical perspective. The factors noted in chapter 1 as leading to the changing shape of technical services—economic, technological, and financial—make it difficult for practitioners to keep abreast of the shifting landscape of information resources and still get their work done.

Whereas public, school, and community college libraries have a long history of acquiring and building collections of audiovisual and nonbook formats, the same is not true of large academic libraries. With the proliferation of electronic databases, even the largest research libraries are adding formats that 15 to 20 years ago were considered inappropriate for their collections.

THE FASTER/BETTER/CHEAPER FACTORS

Certainly the Internet has contributed significantly to the "more" factor. On the plus side, it has also helped with the faster and better factors. Think of the Internet as just another tool, rather like the machine-readable cataloging (MARC) format, that facilitates more effective use of time and effort.

For example, in the not-so-distant past, libraries often compared working practices and policies by conducting field trips or site visits to neighboring libraries. Although such trips still occur, they are becoming rare. In their place, staff use the Internet, through e-mail systems and discussion lists, to post questions such as, "How do you handle x?" In addition to saving travel time and expenses, responses often come in from around the world, and staff can draw on a much wider range of experience. Furthermore, discussion lists help keep the staff informed about new developments and issues. Technical services librarians and senior paraprofessional staff usually subscribe to several such lists.

Everything covered in this book has one or more Web sites devoted to it. There are URLs throughout the book, but these addresses are likely to have changed by the time you read this—the average life span for a Web site is under 24 months. Still, a good starting point, no matter what library topic is of interest, is the Internet Library for Librarians (http://www.itcompany.com/inforetriever).

Although collection development is of only passing interest for this book, a number of Web sites are useful to both collection development staff and acquisitions personnel. These range from information producer Web sites (an example is the Association of American University Presses at http://aaupnet.org) to general online vendors such as

Amazon (http://www.amazon.com). Looking for an out-of-print title? Try Bibliofind (now a subsidiary of Amazon) at http://www.bibliofind.com. Sites like the last two provide links to reviews and other information and have ordering capabilities. A few offer Boolean searching in addition to the expected author, title, publisher, and International Standard Book Number (ISBN) searches.

A specific example of how technology assists in the faster/better side of acquisitions work is in letting end-users know what new titles are ready for use. Years ago, many libraries—academic, public, and special, in particular—issued some type of recent additions or new titles lists. Producing such lists was labor intensive: collecting the slips for recently processed titles, typing the list, verifying that the information was correct, maintaining a mailing list for interested recipients, and producing and distributing the information. By the mid-1980s such lists were disappearing as libraries struggled with budget and staff reductions. End-users voiced concerns about the loss and questioned the factors that led to dropping the lists.

Such lists are making a comeback thanks to technology. Many systems make it possible to run a management report that lists all the titles added to the database between x and y dates. Most allow downloading of the information into a word-processing program where a staff member can quickly format the data for publication. The end product is often a paper list and an electronic version for posting on the library's Web site. Another step can be to e-mail specific information such as the "item is ready for use" to the requestor and others who have an interest in the topic. This is a return to what was part of a service called selective dissemination of information back when there was staffing available for such activities.

Serial publications have always been a challenge for library staff because of their changing nature. (Years ago they were thought to be *the* challenge, but technology has assumed that mantle.) New titles, changing titles, variations in numbering systems, special issues, delays in publications, suspension of publication, and ceasing to exist are but a few of the challenges serials present to libraries. Keeping up to date in a print-only environment was almost impossible, but the Internet makes it *almost* possible. Anyone with an interest in serials should subscribe to SERIALST (http://www.uvm.edu/~bmaclenn/serialst.html), an open forum for discussing the perplexing world of serials. Because subscribers are from around the world—more than 40 countries are represented—one quickly learns that many, if not most, of the concerns about serials are global rather than local in character. Electronic journals and/or paper-based titles with electronic editions represent another challenge for technical services. Some vendors have records that can be downloaded, assuming that the integrated library system (ILS) allows for that and can make the necessary links. For many libraries, if the process depended solely on manual inputting, there would be many fewer records for electronic resources.

Cataloging departments and catalogers have been online for longer than most others in the library world. A popular discussion list for catalogers is AUTOCAT (http://listserv.syr.edu/archives/autocat.html), initiated many years ago by list owner Judith Hopkins of the State University of New York at Buffalo. Cataloging questions often elicit dozens of responses, sometimes within hours of being posted. Opinions and answers come from all over the world, sometimes with documentation. Some of the most prolific participants work at national libraries, research institutions, or specialized information centers. The Canadian counterpart to AUTOCAT is the Canadian Library Association Technical Services Interest Group Forum, TSIG-L. It can be located via the Canadian Library Association Web site at http://www.cla.ca, or at http://www3.fis. utoronto.ca/people/affiliated/tsig.

Catalogers are frequently able to obtain authoritative information, free cataloging advice, selected tools, and other assistance from Web sites maintained by national libraries and bibliographic networks as well as by commercial vendors of cataloging systems, publishers, and other companies. Some of the most useful government and nonprofit organization Web sites are the Library of Congress Cataloging and Acquisitions Web site (http://www.loc.gov/aba/), the Library and Archives Canada Web site (http://www.collectionscanada.gc.ca/), and the OCLC Web site (http://www.oclc. org). Offerings at these Web sites vary from organization to organization and change over time, but typical features include descriptions of the organization's latest activities and projects, lists of publications and online order forms, and e-mail access to persons responsible for answering inquiries or providing additional information. Occasionally, full text of some documents or methods of downloading them free of charge are posted. Early in 2001, OCLC began giving an online course for a fee on cataloging Internet resources. Since that time, a number of resources for technical services librarians have been made available, such as those found on the OCLC Web-Junction Technical Services resources site (http://www.webjunction.org/technical-services/).

The Internet is a great tool, but it can also present a problem in that the staff can spend a little too much time surfing it. Some control and self-monitoring is necessary to maintain unit productivity. However, allowing some level of surfing may help reduce some of the workplace stress that is so common in the changing technical services environment. Also, staff members need to become comfortable with the electronic databases the library purchases to provide proper service.

RESTRUCTURING TO PROVIDE "FASTER AND BETTER"

Pressure for more, better, faster, cheaper, combined with budget woes and, all too frequently, staff reductions have led to restructuring of technical services units. A buzzword for this is "reengineering." Close inspection of what the gurus of reengineering suggest reveals that the concept has much in common with what was once labeled "operations analysis" and "scientific management." Good management practice calls for ongoing assessment and evaluation of policies, procedures, workflow, and so forth. Unfortunately, in most situations daily demands seem to keep people from doing this on a regular basis.

You don't need to hire an outsider to handle many of the basic techniques of work analysis. If you seriously think about each of the following questions, you will be well on your way to creating an effective and efficient unit:

- What is done?
- Why is it done?
- Where is it done?
- When is it done?

- Who does it?
- How is it done?

An excellent text to help with rethinking operations is Richard Dougherty's *Streamlining Library Services*.[8] The book is a greatly revised and updated version of the classic Dougherty wrote many years ago.

An example of planning and rethinking activities is the implementation of PromptCat, which calls for a planning team of catalogers and acquisition staff. The process is not as complicated as a merge, but it can be more contentious because it often demonstrates that neither unit really understands what the other does.

One challenge that arises when it comes to merging or starting a program such as PromptCat is the question of quality control and what that means in a particular library. In the case of outsourcing copy cataloging (PromptCat), many units have some interest as the data from the outside agency become a part of the library's online public access catalog (OPAC). Often there are staff members who believe no effort should be spared to create an error-free OPAC, while others believe perfection is impossibly expensive and does not serve the end-user in the long run.

STANDARDS

OPACs are the end-user's key to unlocking the library's resources and, in some cases, the resources of other libraries. They play a more prominent role for users than did the card catalogs of years gone by, if for no other reason than that they generally offer more modes of access and are considered quicker and easier to use than their forerunners. Given their importance to quality customer service, it is a good practice to have just one unit responsible for OPAC maintenance.

One long-standing management technique for assigning task responsibility is to give it to the unit or person who most frequently performs the task. The catalog department creates the initial bibliographic record for each new title and item records for additional copies or volumes in a set that ultimately constitutes the core of the database. Thus, it is rather common that the cataloging unit is responsible for maintaining the database content and its quality.

If it is just a matter of initial inputting of data, the task would be of less concern; however, it goes far beyond that. There are ongoing adjustments that must be, should be, or are desirable to make in the existing records. On the "must" side is indicating changes in the location information, say from open stacks to storage. Another must is deleting records for withdrawn or lost items. A "should be" issue is cross-linking different records for works by a single author who has several name variations. One of the most desired adjustments, but one that is not implemented as often as staff would like, is updating subject headings, which seem to change on a regular basis. Handling the changes manually eats up limited staff time. If the ILS does not provide updating capability, some libraries have found it cost-effective to outsource the work. In many ways, the process of deciding what is not an error is difficult. It may require months of discussion before there is agreement on items that can be less than perfect and still go into the OPAC.

TABLE 2.2   RESPONSIBILITY MATRIX

	Head Cataloger	Head of Acquisitions	Cataloging Assistant	Receiving Assistant	Invoice Assistant	Physical Processing
Establish PromptCat profiles and processing requirements with OCLC and vendors.	P	S				
Define cataloging review process, including definition and handling of errors and exceptions.	P		S			
Load PromptCat files into local system.	S	S		P		
Compare books to PromptCat records and approve payment.	S		S	P		
Route errors and exceptions to appropriate staff.	S		S	P		
Pay invoices.		S			P	
Correct errors and exceptions.	S		P			
Relabel books as necessary.			S			P
Provide feedback to OCLC and vendors.	P	P				

P = primary responsibility; S = supporting responsibility.

Standards are a good starting point for anyone thinking about outsourcing. An example of a standard created by a technical services unit is illustrated in Table 2.2. The LMU library uses the chart for handling incoming PromptCat items. The basic concept underlying the chart is that the standards should be clear enough so persons who have no cataloging background can quickly review incoming materials and decide if they are acceptable or require the attention of the cataloging staff. (See chapter 14 for a discussion of MARC tags.)

SUMMARY

The management issues in today's technical services environment are essentially the same as for other areas of the library: too much to do, too few people to do what must be done, and constant pressure to do more with less. Basic management practices are key elements in making the "more, faster, better, cheaper" pressures somewhat more manageable. A host of management resources are available for technical services staffs to consult. This chapter covers only a few of the topics; management of organizations in times of change and stress is the subject of a great many full-length books.

It does not appear likely that the library work environment is going to change much from the present circumstances in the very near future. Concepts of time and stress management are helpful for all staff. Developing ways of sorting out what is essential, desirable, and nice to have with all staff members is also worthwhile. Creating even an informal sense of team membership prevents members from feeling as if they are alone. Working on communication and negotiating skills promotes a work environment that is effective and somewhat, if not completely, comfortable for everyone.

REVIEW QUESTIONS

1. What are some steps to take to better manage your work time?

2. Describe the elements involved in running effective meetings.

3. Discuss the issues that contribute to the pressure on technical services units to do more.

4. Discuss the issues that contribute to pressures to do things faster, better, and cheaper.

5. What steps have technical services taken to address the need to do things faster, better, and cheaper?

6. Teamwork or team projects call for some changes in the way individuals do their work. What are some of those changes?

NOTES

The epigraphs for this chapter are from Peter Hernon and Ellen Altman, *Assessing Service Quality: Satisfying the Expectations of Library Customers* (Chicago, IL: American Library Association, 1998) and Shelia Intner and Peggy Johnson, *Fundamentals of Technical Services Management* (Chicago, IL: American Library Association, 2008).

1. Maureen Gleason and Robert Miller, "Technical Services: Direction or Coordination?" *Technical Services Quarterly* 4, no. 3 (1987): 13–19.

2. Lihong Zhu, "Head Cataloging Positions in Academic Libraries: Analysis of Job Advertisements," *Technical Services Quarterly* 25, no. 4 (2008): 49–70.

3. Pat Tunstall, "The Accidental Supervisor," *Public Libraries* 45, no. 3 (2006): 50.

4. Susan Cartwright and Cary Cooper, *Managing Workplace Stress* (Thousand Oaks, CA: Sage Publications, 1977).

5. Richard Guzzo and Marcus Dickson, "Teams in Organizations," in *Annual Review of Psychology,* ed. James Spence (Palo Alto, CA: Annual Reviews, 1996), 308–9.

6. Cartwright and Cooper, *Managing Workplace Stress,* 34.

7. Cecily Johns, "Technical Services Organization," in *Technical Services Today,* 2nd ed., ed. Michael Gorman (Englewood, CO: Libraries Unlimited, 1988).

8.   Richard Dougherty, *Streamlining Library Services: What We Do, How Much Time It Takes, What It Costs, and How We Can Do It Better* (Lanham, MD: Scarecrow Press, 2008).

SUGGESTED READING

Ahronheim, Judith. "Technical Services Management Issues in the Metadata Environment." *Technicalities* 19, no. 3 (1999): 4–6.

Burke, Leslie, and Stephanie McConnell. "Technical Services Departments in the Digital Age: The Four R's of Adapting to New Technology," *Against the Grain* 19, no. 5 (2007): 58–64.

Canepi, Kitti. "Work Analysis in Library Technical Services." *Technical Services Quarterly* 25, no. 2 (2007): 19–30.

Christopher, Connie. *Empowering Your Library.* Chicago, IL: American Library Association, 2003.

Deeken, JoAnne, Paula L. Webb, and Virginia Taffurelli. "We are All Winners: Training Silents and Millenials to Work as a Team," *Serials Librarian* 54, no. 3/4 (2008): 211–16.

De Jager, Martha. "The KMAT: Benchmarking Knowledge Management." *Library Management* 20, no. 7 (1999): 367–72.

Durrance, Joan C., and Karen E. Fisher. *How Libraries and Librarians Help: A Guide to Identifying User-Centered Outcomes.* Chicago, IL: American Library Association, 2004.

Fessler, Vera. "The Future of Technical Services (It's Not the Technical Services It Was)." *Library Administration & Management* 21, no. 3 (2007): 139–44.

Harer, John B., and Larry Nash White. "Using Stories to Manage Libraries." *Technical Services Quarterly* 25, no. 1 (2007): 39–50.

Hernon, Peter, and Ellen Altman. *Assessing Service Quality.* Chicago, IL: American Library Association, 1998.

Katzenbach, Jon R., and Douglas K. Smith. *The Wisdom of Teams: Creating the High-Performance Organization.* New York: HarperBusiness Essentials, 2003.

Langley, Anne. "Case Study Six: Run with the Meeting." *Against the Grain* 19, no. 4 (2007): 70–71.

LeFasto, Frank, and Carl Larson. *When Teams Work Best.* Thousand Oaks, CA: Sage Publications, 2001.

McGurr, Melanie. "Improving the Flow of Materials in a Cataloging Department." *Library Resources and Technical Services,* 52, no. 2 (2008): 54–60.

Medeiros, Norm. "Factors Influencing Competency Perceptions and Expectations of Technical Service Administrators." *Library Resources & Technical Services* 49, no. 3 (2006): 167–74.

Metzer, Mary C. "Enhancing Library Staff Training and Patron Service Through a Cross-Departmental Exchange." *Technical Services Quarterly* 24, no. 2 (2006): 1–7.

Mosby, Anne Page, and Judith D. Brook. "Devils and Goddesses in the Library: Reflections on Leadership, Team Building, Staff Development, and Success." *Georgia Library Quarterly* 42, no. 4 (2006): 5–10.

Olsgaard, Jane K. "Relocation, Reorganization, Retrenchment." *Library Collections, Acquisitions, and Technical Services* 24, no. 3 (2000): 426–28.

Pritchard, Sarah. "Library Benchmarking: Old Wine in New Bottles?" *Journal of Academic Librarianship* 21, no. 11 (1995): 491–95.

Rodacker, Uwe. "Successful Managers." *Supervision* 67, no. 5 (2006): 8–9.

Slight-Gibney, Nancy. "How Far Have We Come? Benchmarking Time and Costs for Monograph Purchasing." *Library Collections, Acquisitions and Technical Services* 23, no. 2 (1999): 47–59.

Williams, Pauline C., and Kathleen Barone. "Impact of Outsourcing Technical Service Operations in a Small Academic Library." *College & Undergraduate Libraries* 7, no. 2 (2001): 1–9.

Chapter

3

Staffing

The proliferation of e-resources has led to the emergence of new service paradigms and new roles for staff.

—William Curran, 2006

Have the requirements for jobs in technical services changed? What qualifications are necessary to obtain professional positions in technical services?

—JoAnne Deekan and Deborah Thomas, 2006

Most libraries will have limited use for catalogers whose education has focused narrowly on electronic resources and metadata. Unfortunately, recent discussions with library school students and recent graduates suggests that some students may be receiving the impression that there is a significant market for people with just such a restricted focus.

—Janet Swan Hill, 2005

Although a library may have solid funding and a new building, without great people its services will be inadequate. People are the key to a library's success, not the technology, not the collections, and not its physical environment. Certainly, all the latter factors are important, but it is how well the staff members perform their duties that makes users think "their" library is one of the best. What many people, both in and out of the profession, tend to forget is that it is the entire staff that makes the difference, not just those in public services. Quality begins in the back room— technical services.

Gaining the services of the best and brightest people is a process that requires thoughtful planning. When it comes to hiring people who will provide outstanding service, you must think and plan even more carefully. People are the key to providing successful service—people who are thoughtfully selected, people who are given proper support and ongoing training, and most important, people who really do like people.

Hire happy people. That may sound platitudinous and rather silly. However, research has shown that it does in fact make a difference in customer service and satisfaction. "The bigger the employee's smile, the happier the customer. That is the conclusion of new research from Bowling Green and Penn State Universities. . . . If a manager wants employees to deliver service with a smile, they can do better than mandate it. They should create an environment that encourages genuine smiles."[1]

Sometimes those of us working in libraries, forget that our users are our real employers. These are the people who really fund our paychecks. Providing them with the best possible service, within our power, is the least we can do. David Drickhamer suggested that managers who "believe as a matter of faith that if they take care of their employees—offering continuous training, regularly assessing performance, and treat them with the same respect with which they would like to be treated—those employees will help deliver superior performance. Lo and behold, it's true."[2]

STAFFING CATEGORIES

For most of the general public, anyone working in the library is a "librarian." Actually libraries, like most other organizations, utilize several categories of employees. The labels for the categories vary from library to library; however, there are four basic groups:

- Full-time employees who have a master's degree in library and information science (MLS) and/or a subject graduate degree (librarians/professionals/ subject specialists)
- Full-time employees with degrees ranging from high school to postgraduate (paraprofessional, nonprofessional, support staff, library assistant, technical assistant, library media technical assistant, and clerical staff are some of the more common titles)
- Part-time employees with or without a degree (pages, shelvers, interns, student assistants, volunteers)
- Volunteers

Starting in the 1960s, an ever-increasing volume of literature examined the question of library staffing categories, job titles, job duties, and related issues. The interest in the topic has grown substantially since the 1970s. Part of the reason for the increasing coverage arises from the factors discussed in chapter 1 relating to the changing nature of library activities. To a large degree, what has been taking place is summed up in a statement by Michael Gorman: "No librarian should do a job a paraprofessional can do, no paraprofessional should do a job that a clerical staff member can do, and no human being should do a job a machine can do."[3]

The chapter epigraph from William Curran also reflects what is taking place. Budget reductions, downsizing, technology, and changing staffing patterns all create an environment of uncertainty, tension, and often fear. Add to that mix variable beliefs or understandings about the types of work and who should do what, when, and how, and there are bound to be concerns about employment security and what jobs will exist in the future as well as the labels associated with those positions. Liz Lane and Barbara Stewart have correctly noted that "many staff members are being assigned higher-level work which then require an upward reclassification of jobs in the automated technical services environment. Work previously done at lower levels has either become automated, outsourced to a library vendor, or is not done anymore."[4]

Librarians

In the current information world, the differences between a librarian and a paraprofessional are probably most apparent in the human resources (HR) department rather than within the library. The reason for HR's ability to differentiate between the two is that it maintains the job descriptions, position holder's name, and salary classifications. None of these attributes is apparent on a daily basis in the library. On the floor, especially for the users, it is almost impossible to know who holds what job title. William Curran indicated that three-quarters of the libraries in his survey reported that the need for paraprofessionals to perform tasks once done by librarians had increased over the previous five years, and that they also expected the trend would continue for at least five more years. Curran noted, "A redefinition of roles and expectations is needed. The level of competencies in information technology as well as the constant upgrading of equipment create expectations on the part of library users and invite professional and paraprofessional staff into a new routine of duties and responsibilities."[5]

People holding positions designated as "librarian" generally have an MLS. "Generally" is an important word in the preceding sentence. School libraries, when they have a librarian, usually require that person to hold a teaching certificate with some coursework in librarianship. Many large research libraries have bibliographic or subject librarians or administrators who may hold a graduate degree in their assigned subject area. Finally, some librarians may have satisfied a frequent phrase in position advertisements—"MLS or equivalent required." Just what is "equivalent" varies from institution to institution. However, the vast majority of librarians do in fact have an MLS degree.

In 1992, Paula Kaufman noted that the categories used to classify library employees "can create problems, tensions, and conflicts between library nonprofessional and professional staffs."[6] These tensions, at least in technical services, go back to at least the mid-1960s and the movement to create computerized processing centers.

Paraprofessional/Support Staff

If the definition of librarian appears rather vague, deciding on a label and required background for those holding nonlibrarian positions in libraries is even fuzzier. Years ago Elin Christianson reported on the various labels used to designate nonlibrarian personnel and attitudes about those labels.[7] The list included clerk/clerical, library aide, library associate, library assistant, library clerk, library technician, nonprofessional, paraprofessional, supportive/support, and subprofessional. The only label that did not elicit at least a few negative responses from those holding such positions was library technician. Paraprofessional had only a few negative comments, and today there would likely be none, given the rise of groups such as paralegals, paramedics, and so on.

A journal for people in these ranks was *Library Mosaics,* and its editorial staff consistently used the label paraprofessional. (We were saddened to see it cease publication at the end of 2005. However, its back files have a wealth of information for anyone interested in this field.) Perhaps the Council on Library/Media Technicians (COLT; http://colt.ucr.edu) and/or the American Library Association's (ALA) Library Support Staff Interests Round Table (LSSIRT; http://www.ala.org/ala/lssirt) will fill in the void left by the passing of *Library Mosaics.* Clearly, there is still no consensus as to what the label for nonlibrarian positions should be. This is probably due to a lack of agreement about what training/education is required to hold such positions. We prefer either paraprofessional or support staff.

Support staff members are the backbone of library services. Without them, few libraries could offer the variety and quality of services that they do. "According to the 2004 statistics from the National Center for Education Statistics (NCES) 230,843 workers are employed in U.S. academic and public libraries. Of these, 160,150 (69%) are library support staff."[8] The total number of support staff is even greater when one adds those in school and special libraries.

What type of background is called for to fill nonlibrarian positions now that those employees often perform duties and carry responsibilities that were once the sole domain of MLS holders? Like so many questions, the answer is, it depends. Ideally, individuals who perform such work would have, and many do have, extensive education, training, and library experience. Without a doubt, having a degree from a program that focuses on library and information services, in all their forms, is very valuable. Someone who has the ability, interest, and desire to grow and learn on the job can also fill such positions in time. Although having a supervisor who encourages and trains people is a wonderful asset, a person can independently gain the requisite knowledge and skills through workshops, online opportunities, and formal classes. (Note that some entry-level positions require no prior library experience or knowledge, are clerical in nature, and should not carry the label paraprofessional or library technician.)

People usually think of their work in one of two ways—as a job or as a career. Job-oriented individuals only focus on the assigned duties. They often perform those responsibilities at an extremely high level and are a very valuable organizational resource. However, when their work shift ends, so does their interest in the organization. They have more important interests. Career-oriented people, on the other hand, have a strong interest in their organization and an interest in the field in general. They are quick to volunteer to take on new tasks, especially those that offer an opportunity to learn a new skill or gain new knowledge. Because of their interest in the organization, they offer suggestions for improvements and accept committee assignments willingly. Career-oriented individuals form the core of paraprofessional ranks. Note, however, that career-oriented persons, when overworked and undersupported, can quickly become job oriented. This is something all good supervisors attempt to avoid and try to point out to more senior managers when they observe such mistreatment.

For the career-oriented person, the LSSIRT has created the *Task Force on Career Ladders.*[9] This document, and the companion *Continuing Education & Training Opportunities* publication,[10] are useful to review and should be thoughtfully considered. As the *Career Ladders* work indicates, "career development shifts the responsibility to the individual and away from the organization."[11] It goes on to point out that libraries have an obligation in this area as well, such as providing opportunities for skill development, promotions, and the chance to put new skills to use.

A key point was made in the LSSIRT Training statement: "Although there has been rapid development of electronic databases, the Internet, and other resources, there has not been nearly enough training for the staff who must use these resources."[12] The authors go on to suggest that "there should be standard core competencies for all levels of support staff."[13] The Support Staff Section of the Connecticut Library Association developed such a competency list—both for all staff and for some areas of service, for example public services (http://ctlibraryassociation.org/archive/class.html). Many of their general staff competencies are ones you would expect to find in any list of desirable staff traits—positive attitude toward users, being open to change, having good communication skills, and being willing and able to work independently. Below are the 11 competencies for public service staff:

- Ability to introduce users to all library services
- Ability to use the entire library collection to satisfy user requests
- Knowledge of library's circulation system and public access catalog
- Knowledge of fine and fee policies, and cash and security procedures
- Knowledge of basic reference and information resources and referral procedures
- Knowledge of available community resources
- Knowledge of library copyright requirements
- Knowledge of library classification system with the ability to do shelving and shelf reading
- Familiarity with reader's advisory issues and resources
- Familiarity with ILL [interlibrary loan] procedures
- Ability to deal with disruptive patrons and emergency situations

As of 2008, the ALA is undertaking a certification program for support staff. Learn more about this program at the Library Support Staff Certification Program Web site (http://ala-apa.org/lssc/).

Other Full-Time Staff

There are a variety of full-time employees who work in libraries but do not fall into the previous two categories. The most obvious are clerical staff, such as receptionists and secretaries. These are job categories that only require general office skills—a person does not need to have any prior background in library operations to carry out the job functions. Other clerical positions might include processing and mailing notices to users (overdue and document delivery information, for example) or maintaining order in the current magazine and newspaper area.

A library may also employ a bookkeeper, whose only special library knowledge is likely to be the concept of encumbrance; but even that is not unique to the library environment. Someone with a general background in bookkeeping can quickly step into a library administrative office and handle the budget record-keeping activities. Only if the person is to handle the financial records for the acquisitions department would she need to understand the principles of encumbering funds. In larger libraries, there may be some information technology staff that handle networking/server maintenance and the like, and who have no responsibility for specific library technologies. The very largest libraries are likely to have other professional positions, such as fund-raising specialists, training officers, marketing and public relations people, or HR personnel who may or may not have an MLS. (We cover part-time and volunteer personnel later in this chapter.)

Shannon Hoffman suggested that clerical staff provide general office skills, while shelvers (or part-time personnel) perform a variety of very routine but essential tasks.[14] She further proposed that "paralibrarians" would be a preferable term for those with library training but less than an MLS. "This title is a title that would command respect and understanding by the public. Now is the time for the librarians to give more support to paraprofessionals and establish them with an appropriate title. By this means librarians can project themselves forward in the quest for professionalism."[15]

One reason for covering all library staff in this discussion is technology or information communication technology (ICT). Over the years this book has been available (1971 to the present), there has been a profound shift in staffing patterns, as technology has become an ever more dominant feature in the daily work patterns of library staff. In fact, ICT has become so integrated to the work flow that when the system has problems, or goes down, work almost comes to a complete stop. ICT has changed work requirements, skills, and who does what. It has also made the case for cross-training and/or teamwork crystal clear, thus, further blurring job distinctions. Libraries are their increasing use of empowered teams that are composed of a variety of job categories. (Empowered teams have decision-making powers.) ICT and other factors have resulted in a flattening of the traditional hierarchy of library organizations.

One impact of a changing economic picture and new technologies is that library staff sizes have remained relatively constant in spite of increased user demands and expectations. Technology allows public-service personnel to handle changing and, in a few cases, increased, workloads without additional people. Occasionally, it has allowed some libraries to shift positions from technical to public services.

Libraries require a much wider variety of skill sets than they did even 5 or 50 years ago. Budget restraints in turn create situations in which public service staff must be able to fill in for one another (cross-training). Technology also brings with it the need for constant training, as it seems to change every day.

STAFFING PROCESS

Selecting appropriate staff, regardless of category—full-time, part-time, and even volunteers—requires significant time, planning, and effort. Although few libraries have an HR unit, library staff do become involved in the HR process on an operational level, so this chapter includes a short discussion of the major HR issues. During a library career, a person is likely to be involved in all of the issues covered from time to time. Understanding some of the key points of the recruitment and selection process is useful when you are looking for a job and when you are asked to serve on a search committee.

A supervisor needs to have a sense of what goes into a job description, how to orient and train new people, and how to handle the inevitable performance appraisal process.

Human resources departments expect and require library staff involvement, to some degree, in a number of key steps in the staffing process. Those steps are some variation of the following:

- Needs determination/succession planning
- Job design
- Recruitment
- Selection
- Orientation and training
- Evaluation
- Coaching and discipline
- Resignation and termination

Determining staffing needs is usually the responsibility of senior managers. Typically, staffing needs fall into one of two lists. The first is a wish list of positions that would be wonderful to have, if only funding were available; it is often a long list, and it is a special occasion when a new full-time employee (FTE) is finally funded. The second, and shorter, list covers expected vacancies—retirements, promotions, and resignations. It is up to the library to keep HR informed of expected vacancies. Knowing in advance what positions may become vacant and the timing may help HR do some combination recruiting for several units, which should stretch limited advertising dollars and generate a stronger pool of candidates.

It almost goes without saying that the job design or description is the foundation for getting the best and brightest people. The U.S. Department of Labor suggests a process for developing job descriptions and deciding on the proper selection of instruments such as appropriate paper or hands-on tests. The suggested process starts with the library's organizational goals that a particular job is to assist in fulfilling. (Note: every staff member holds a separate position; however, several people may hold the same job—for example, document delivery assistant.) Designing a job requires answering questions such as "What activities are necessary to accomplish organizational goals?" Answering this apparently simple question is usually more complex than one might expect. It requires detailed information in order to be useful. The goal is to be as comprehensive as possible in listing the tasks. Being too brief or too broad creates more work later in the process. For example, a task for a circulation service point position should be more than "check out materials." The job description should cover all aspects of the work, such as checking the user's borrowing status, providing answers to questions about item availability or items the person could not locate, and deactivating security tags. Such detail is essential for developing sound job descriptions as it helps you identify the necessary skills and knowledge to successfully perform the work.

Another step is establishing job success criteria (JCS), which are the keys to selecting the right person for the right position. This is also the most difficult and subjective of the steps in the model. While the goal of the process is simple to state—"What distinguishes successful from unsuccessful performance in the position?"—it is difficult to carry out. What constitutes success will vary from library to library and from time to time as the work changes. For example, being courteous to users is always important, but what if a person is courteous while providing incorrect information? What about a person who is great with users but is unwilling or unable to work well with other staff members? Thinking through the JSCs makes it much easier to select the right person for the position. JSCs allow you to develop the best questions to ask the candidates, those that most accurately reflect the skills and knowledge needed for success.

Job specifications (JS) are the skills, traits, knowledge, and experience that, when combined, results in successful performance. JSs are the requirements typically listed in job descriptions and advertisements, such as the educational background or degree required, years of experience, and a list of the specific skills sought. From a legal point of view, these items must be bona fide occupational qualifications (BFOQ). Merely saying they are will not satisfy a court, if you are challenged. You might have to be able to prove that they are the skills, knowledge, and experience a person ought to possess to succeed. For example, you might like to have someone with a high school diploma, but can you prove that it is essential to succeed in the work? If you can't, don't make it a requirement; make it something desirable.

Having completed the aforementioned steps, you can decide what instruments you should use to help decide which applicants to call in for an interview. Some instruments you likely know well—application forms, names of references, and letters of interest. Others that are less common are various tests of basic required skills—such as a certain level of error-free keyboarding. Library skills tests, such as alphabetizing or putting call numbers in order, are handled by the library. Whatever instruments you select, you must have a clear link back to the JSC and JS and in the event that you are challenged in court.

Recruitment

Once you develop the job description (JD), HR can commence the search for suitable applicants. Many large libraries conduct national searches for librarian and other professional positions while drawing on the local labor market for paraprofessional and clerical positions. Advertisements for openings ought to provide the basic job description information and indicate where and when a person should apply.

The search often begins as an internal process; that is, an announcement of a vacancy goes to the library's staff. In some organizations, the policy is to interview any internal candidates before going outside. More often, the search is both internal and external—with any internal applicants having the advantage of knowing more about the nature of the open position and being a known quantity to the employer (often, but not always, a good thing). In the United States, employers must place advertisements or recruit in places where persons in the protected categories (according to civil rights acts) are likely to see position announcements.

Selecting the Pool

Most recruiting efforts generate a larger pool of applicants than it is feasible to interview. Deciding whom to interview draws on information produced by the selection instruments you identified. The most common place to begin the sorting process is the application form and cover letter (when you apply for a position, keep this fact in mind; how carefully you prepare these documents often decides your chances of getting interviewed). Some of the factors to look for are if the person has the required skills, how carefully materials are presented, and if the person supplies all the required information. A rough sorting of applicants just using basic issues such as those listed previously will usually reduce the pool by a substantial number. A further reduction, if necessary, can be done by asking how many of the desirable skills/abilities the applicant possesses. Having a final interview pool of three to six people is likely to produce a person to whom you would like to make an offer. Because the selection process involves a substantial amount of subjectivity, having developed sound JSCs and JSs will help keep the process as objective as possible.

Interviewing

The interview process will come into play when you are applying for a position and when you serve on a search committee. In both instances, it requires an understanding of the process and a good deal of practice to become an effective interviewee or interviewer. What follows applies to both sides of the interview table.

A sound interview process has six important elements. First, there is the need to plan the process. Beyond the obvious—such as timing and place—some of the key planning issues are the length of the interview, whom to involve in the interview, the questions to ask, if there should be a tour, and how much time to devote to answering candidates' questions. As a candidate, you should also plan your questions about the position and institution.

The second element, and perhaps the most critical in a legal sense, is to carefully review the interview questions for their compliance with antidiscrimination laws; this is an area where HR staff can be of great assistance. Having consistency and comparability of information about each candidate is also important. Maintaining consistency in the questions and the structure of the entire process for all the candidates is critical when it comes time to assess each one and make a final selection. Questions must be job related. If you can't link each question to the job description, don't ask it. Asking a few open-ended questions gives candidates an opportunity to respond more fully and demonstrate some of their skills.

Below are a few examples of legal open-ended questions that could apply to a variety of vacant library positions:

- What do you think your (current or former) supervisor would tell a friend about you?
- What are some of the special skills you would bring to this job?
- Tell me about who and what has motivated your work efforts in the past.
- Have you performed the work entailed by this position before? If so, when? Do you see any significant differences between then and now?
- Give the candidate a real-life situation and ask how the person would handle it. (The situation ought to relate to the work the person would be doing.)
- What things do you like the most about your current position? What do you like the least?
- Tell me about one of your major accomplishments in your present position.
- Tell me about the goals you set for yourself in terms of work.
- What does the term "service" mean to you?

- What are some new work skills or knowledge that you believe would improve your performance on the job?
- What are your current career plans? Do you see them changing in the next three years? What do you envision for yourself over the long term?

The third element is having a segment of time when the candidate is given a clear sense of what he would actually do in the available position and an overview of the library's operation and mission. Also, having some time to explain the relationship of the library to its parent body helps candidates make an informed decision should an offer be made. It is also the time for the candidate to ask the search committee questions.

A fourth element in the process is the personal impact of the candidate and the interviewers on one another. Creating a relaxed and friendly atmosphere at the outset helps candidates become less nervous and thus more effective during the formal interview. Such things as tone of voice, eye contact, personal appearance and grooming, posture, and gestures on the part of candidate and interviewer influence both parties. Keep in mind, in a culturally diverse community, the meanings of these things may be very, very different. For example, lack of eye contact does not always mean a person is the "shifty-eyed character" of English novels.

The fifth element, which is related to impact, is how the interviewer responds to the applicant. Interviewers must be careful to control any nonverbal behavior that may encourage or discourage the applicant in an inappropriate way. Not showing an interest in what the candidate is saying will discourage the person from expanding on her thoughts, and this may well carry over to the remainder of the interview. Anyone with extensive interviewing experience understands just how difficult controlling those two behaviors can be at times.

The final element is to assess the interview data fairly and equitably for all the interviewees. Following are some of the issues that can cause unfair processing:

- Stereotyping the type of person that would be right for the position
- Allowing different members of a search committee to use different weights for various attributes
- Overusing visual clues about the candidate that are not job related
- Not recognizing "contrast effects"—that is, when a strong candidate follows a very weak candidate, the contrast makes the stronger applicant look even stronger than he may be.

Here are some suggestions to keep in mind when you are being interviewed:

- Take some time to research the library and its parent organization ahead of time; their Web sites can tell you a great deal about them.
- Generate a few questions about the library based on your research and your own interests.
- If you did not receive a full position description, don't be shy about asking for one; take time to think of questions about the position.
- Spend some time thinking about the answers you might give to questions that are likely to be part of the interview (for example, what interests you about

this particular position? What do you consider your strengths and your weaknesses? What does the term "service" mean to you?).

- Dress appropriately.
- Be on time.
- Be certain to have the name and its correct pronunciation for the chairperson of the interview committee.
- Remember that your body language also reflects your interest and attentiveness.
- Taking time to think before answering complex questions is appropriate—thinking before speaking is always a good idea.
- When asked a multipart questions, be sure to cover all the parts; asking the interviewer to clarify or repeat such questions is appropriate.
- Asking how any personal or potentially illegal question(s) relate to job performance is appropriate; however, be sure to ask in a nonconfrontational manner.
- Thank the interviewer(s) for the opportunity to interview for the position.
- Asking about the anticipated time frame for the hiring decision is appropriate.
- To learn from each interview experience, jot down a few post-interview notes about some of the high and low points of the interview.
- Even if you decide during the interview process that this is not the position for you, send a follow-up thank-you note to the chair of the search committee, supervisor for the position, or head of HR (whichever is most appropriate), thanking them for their time and for giving you an opportunity to meet with them

What should you do if you are asked inappropriate questions, and is this likely to happen? An article by Marilyn Gardner indicates that it happens more often than one would expect, especially with small and medium-sized organizations, in part because people are not aware they are doing anything wrong. In her article Gardner quotes John Petrella, an employment lawyer, "It happens all the time. . . . It's really easy for employers to get in trouble. It's really easy to run afoul of the antidiscrimination laws."[16] The article goes on to address what to do if you are asked improper questions and offers different approaches to consider before you respond to such questions. First, ask yourself, and perhaps the interviewer, "Is this question related to the position I'm applying for?" Remember, the question could be appropriate if it is clearly job related. At the same time you might want to consider, "Do I really want to work for an organization that asks such questions?" You do have the choice of not answering the questions, knowing that it might mean you will not get an offer. You can, of course, answer the question and then inquire as to the relevance of the question to the position. There is a reasonable chance that you will have to deal with this issue at some point in your career, as an interviewee (try not to do it when you are the interviewer).

STAFF DEVELOPMENT, TRAINING, AND RETENTION

Once a person has been selected and has accepted the position, the next step is to develop a plan for orienting her to the position and the library. Sometimes people forget that the first few days on a job sets a pattern that can be either negative or positive. Those first few days are especially critical to the person's fitting in and the person's views about the library and its long-term training/development program. A well-thought-out orientation, including the training required for the position, will make it more likely that you will retain the person. Yet too often the first days focus only on the activities of the position. That is natural as in most cases the position has been vacant for a month or more and work has stacked up, but falling into this trap may result in a higher turnover than anyone would like.

Generally, the first week should be equally divided between position training and learning about the library and its parent organization. For most people, the first days on a new job are stressful and confusing. The common practice of taking the new employee around to meet everyone, assuming there are more than a dozen people to meet, leaves the new employee with a blur of faces, a few names (rarely connected to the right face), and a vague sense of what others do. Breaking the process up over several days gives the new person a better chance to absorb information and make meaningful connections. Starting with the home unit and working out through units that feed into and receive output from the home unit allows the new employee to gain a sense of where her position fits in the scheme of things and how it is important to library operations. After that you can move on to other units to allow the person to gain an overall picture of operations. Linking a new employee to someone at his level in the work group (a mentor) provides a personal connection for clarification or for questions the new employee might be afraid to ask his supervisor, lest he be thought of as silly. It also helps the mentors by giving them recognition and the motivation to check over those points that the mentor may have been taking for granted. One institution with a well-thought-out orientation program is the University of Washington (http://www.washington.edu/admin/hr/pod/newemp/).

Retention

A major concern for organizations is retaining their best people. Nora Spinks offered some interesting thoughts about how generational differences affect retention: "If you were a child in the 50s (a Boomer), you saw that working hard was a strategy that led to success. Loyalty was rewarded with long-term employment through to retirement. However, if you were a child in the 70s or 80s (a Nexus), you saw adults working hard and getting laid off, downsized or reengineered out of a job anyway. Employment tenure was out of your control, employers offered you a job as long as they felt you were of value, then let you go."[17]

For many employers, their lack of loyalty to long-term staff is coming back to haunt them. "Why should I have any loyalty to the organization if it has none for me?" is a question in the minds of many workers. For many, all it takes is a hint of staffing changes—real or imagined—or something perceived to be a threat, and people start looking for other employment and in many cases actually leaving. They have experienced or heard of organizations that announce staff reductions and say in effect to the staff, "We don't need you but fully expect you to give a 100 percent work effort until the day you are terminated." When that happens, the outcome is what you would expect—performance declines and people leave as quickly as possible. Although the pattern is primarily seen in for-profit organizations, staff reductions in force are not unheard of in libraries.

Another retention factor that is gaining the attention of researchers is new-job regrets, which about 25 percent of newly hired people experience.[18] All too often the regrets arise from the employer overselling the nature of the position or some other aspect of the environment. If you properly followed the steps outlined earlier and the new hire had a copy of the job description before accepting the offer, there should be few problems related to the nature of the work. Where you may unknowingly oversell is when you really need to fill the position and fall into the trap of making the institution, opportunities, benefits, and so forth appear better than they actually are. In the long run, overselling or misrepresenting the position makes for very unhappy people—both the new hire and yourself. When the remorse is very strong, the probability that the person will quit is extremely high.

Training and Development

One key method for gaining and retaining staff loyalty, is to have programs that give ample opportunities for staff to grow and develop. Without a doubt this will help with the long-term retention of the best and brightest people. You have two basic training/development areas to consider—specific job-related skills and career-development competencies and opportunities.

Libraries face a rapidly changing technological environment. Keeping staff current with the changes related to their activities is a major challenge, especially when budgets are static. It is also crystal clear that failing to maintain staff skills will result in users receiving poorer service, which in turn leads to user dissatisfaction. Technology carries with it two financial challenges—acquiring and upgrading requisite technology and funding staff training.

Certainly training and development go beyond technological issues. Some of the other major areas include training for people moving into supervisory positions and training designed to keep staff up-to-date on changing professional standards. In technical services, staying current with standards is critical, and too often, limited travel funds for staff lead to long-term performance problems for the staff and the library.

Professional associations can and do provide excellent training opportunities. Annual conventions often have workshops and other continuing education programs. Unfortunately, there are very few such organizational opportunities for support staff; this seems to be changing, at least with the ALA, where the annual conference started a "conference within a conference" for support staff. (The primary reason for the lack of programs is that there is limited financial assistance for support staff travel. In addition, their salaries are substantially lower, making it difficult for many of them to pay for such opportunities on their own. Thus, groups such as COLT have difficulty attracting enough people to a workshop to make the effort worthwhile.) As more educational institutions and professional bodies extend the range of distance education programs, training opportunities are increasing for support staff—particularly via "Webinars" and video conferencing. Notable examples of these training opportunities are the SirsiDynix Institute's (http://www.sirsidynixinstitute.com/) "Soaring to Excellence" series and the programs available through the Online Computer Library Center's WebJunction (http://www.webjunction.org).

In addition to concerns about funding, libraries face the problem of limited staffing, at least in most services. When staff is limited, it becomes difficult to have employees away at training programs for any length of time. Some jurisdictions are so shortsighted that they refuse to give time off to attend training programs even when the staff member is willing to pay for the program—shortsighted because in time the staff member's services will become less and less effective if training is not kept current .

Singer and Goodrich outlined five critical factors for retaining and motivating library staff.[19] These are principles for a supervisor to exemplify and to help employees perform as well.

- Focus: employees know what they need to do and what is expected of them
- Involvement: people support most what they help create
- Development: opportunities for learning and growth are encouraged
- Gratitude: good performance is recognized (formally and informally)
- Accountability: employees are responsible for their performance or lack thereof

PERFORMANCE APPRAISAL

Singer and Goodrich's last point regarding accountability directly links to performance appraisal. Performance assessment takes two forms—ongoing daily review with occasional corrective action and an annual overall assessment.

In terms of corrective action, an employee's poor performance should be discussed as situations arise. Trying to avoid unpleasant interactions regarding performance and letting problems slide only hurts everyone in the long run. Being told that something was or is amiss during the annual performance review, when it is too late to take corrective action, causes anger, frustration, and poorer performance down the road. Furthermore, other employees will notice the lack of any corrective action, and they are likely to conclude that supervisors don't really care about quality performance. When that happens, they are likely to let their work performance slide. By the time that happens, the situation is highly complex situation and will be difficult to resolve. Finally, service to users also suffers, and that in turn can lead to a serious lack of user support.

Following certain steps when corrective action is needed can help make the process as effective as possible. Start by stating the purpose of the session; even if the situation has the potential for confrontation, speak calmly. Plan on letting the employee talk as much as possible. *Listening* is the key to having a successful session. Too often, there is a tendency to start planning one's response rather than listening and trying to *hear* what the person is saying. Silence, even a long one, serves a good purpose—it lets both parties think about what is taking place. Setting a time limit for the session can defeat the purpose of the session; it may take time to get to the central issue(s). Expect the employee to be unhappy, upset, and probably argumentative, and there is the possibility that she may engage in a personal verbal attack on you. It is important, if difficult, not to take the attack very personally; above all, do *not* respond in kind. Total resolution is not the only indication of a successful session. Sometimes it takes a series of sessions to reach a complete resolution. Try to end the session on a positive note and, if appropriate, schedule a follow-up session.

The goal is to be as consistent as possible in your evaluations. Standards should not shift from one week to the next or, worse yet, vary from one employee to another. Remember you should be evaluating outcomes rather than the process (as long as the process does not cause trouble or problems for others). You shouldn't hold a new employee as closely accountable for an error as an older, more experienced person. This does *not* mean that you ignore the newcomer's problem. Naturally, a person lacking the skill to do a task needs additional training rather than criticism. If the training does not work, then other adjustments will be necessary, including the difficult but occasionally necessary step of termination.

Something to consider before taking corrective steps is to think about personal biases that might color your judgment of people and their performance. When it is clear something should be done, think about the timing of the next appraisal (keeping in mind any and all personal biases), and then begin the counseling process. Keep in mind this may require further serious steps, especially if a person has had a negative review for two years in succession. It is always wise to work collaboratively with HR in these situations.

Annual performance reviews are something that most people endure and almost never look forward to, much less enjoy. Neither the givers nor the recipients have great faith in the process or that much good will come out of what many view as an ordeal.

Probably the biggest challenge, and where the difficulty lies, is in the dual nature of the review process. Although most HR departments attempt to keep it to a single purpose, performance enhancement, the reality is that there is sometimes an unofficial but real link to salary increases. The dual purpose is well documented, but most clearly articulated by Saul Gellerman.[20] The single process attempts to handle behavioral issues (work performance) and administrative issues (compensation and occasional promotions). The two purposes are almost diametrically opposed in character. To be effective in improving performance, the process should be open and candid. From an administrative perspective the process should be closed and secretive. Trying to accomplish both in a single process is a challenge to say the least. Almost every employee believes the salary aspect is the dominant factor.

If you give constant honest feedback throughout the year—both praise and correction—the annual review will be as painless and stress free as possible. There is no way to remove the salary component, however, as long as the parent organization, directly or indirectly, uses reviews as part of its salary deliberations/considerations.

In spite of your best efforts, there will be times when disciplinary action must take place. Needless to say, such action should only follow after a number of counseling sessions have failed to resolve the issue. In the United States, HR units label the process "progressive discipline." The process consists of a series of steps that become progressively more severe and can end with termination. Most of the time, the process never reaches the termination stage as the parties resolve the issue earlier. The sooner you address performance issues, the less likely it is you will have to go through the stress of a formal grievance procedure.

PART-TIME STAFF

The literature tends to pay little attention to part-time staff. This is unfortunate as the work of part-timers is often critical to quality public service—just think about those who reshelve collections materials, or handle physical processing of materials duties for the collections, most of whom are part-time people, and the impact of those tasks on quality of service.

Although you will encounter part-time people in almost any job category, two part-time groups are very common in libraries—student assistants and volunteers. These two groups, especially students in educational library settings, may come close to the equivalent of full-time staff in terms of hours worked. (A 2005 survey by the Association of Research Libraries noted that the average number of student workers exceed, by a slight margin, the average number of full-time personnel in public services. See Association of Research Libraries, *ARL Statistics Interaction Edition*, http://www.fisher.lib.virginia.edu/arl.) For many libraries, quality service would not be possible without the aid of part-time students and volunteers. The work such individuals perform should receive the same attention and thought given to full-time positions.

Students

Almost all libraries associated with educational institutions make extensive use of student labor. No matter what type of library—college, school, or university—the students have, or should have, the proper handling of their studies as their primary objective. Working in the library, even for pay, is much lower priority and the fact must be kept in mind when using student labor. Many public libraries also use students for positions such as pages or stack maintenance personnel. In technical services, they perform a variety of duties that are necessary but not challenging for a person to do full-time. At public libraries, unlike at academic institutions, part-time student workers are viewed as any other part-time staff members, except that perhaps they are given a little slack in scheduling during exam periods.

The early literature about using students as employees gives the impression that student workers are too much trouble and not worth the effort. The focus then was on the limitations and problems of employing students. Such an emphasis may have been necessary to work out the issues, but part of the problem likely did and can lie in not spending enough time on preplanning and developing true job descriptions for what the students will do. In any event, what is clear is that educational libraries are very dependent on such labor.

Beyond the obvious benefit of having valuable work accomplished at a modest cost, students bring several benefits to the library. One benefit is that as peers/classmates, they are often viewed as more approachable than the full-time staff. This is especially true when the student body's cultural composition and that of the full-time staff is markedly different. Student employees are much more likely to have a sound idea of what technologies students use and how and when they use the technologies. Such information can be of great value when planning a new service or a different approach to an old one. Yet another benefit is that students can help full-time staff understand where the students are coming from—they relate more effectively to the primary service population. Finally, they are the pool from which to recruit individuals to librarianship.

Certainly, you need to recognize the generational differences regarding work expectations and the workplace when adding students to the staffing mix. There are only a few "traditionalists" (those born before 1945) still working in libraries, and most are working as volunteers rather than as paid staff. The traditionalists worked in highly structured workplaces for almost all their careers and are comfortable with a hierarchical system. They believe in hard work, commitment, and loyalty.

Baby boomers (those born 1946–1964) are the largest generation in the workplace and in the population. They are now mostly in the senior positions in libraries. When they entered the workforce, there was great competition for available jobs; further, they faced a highly competitive work environment for much of their careers. Generally, they are less inclined to teamwork in the sense of the term today. They were also the first generation to experience significant layoffs, which often reinforced their need to be competitive and independent.

Generation X (those born 1965–1980) is a much smaller cohort. These are the people who will begin to fill the senior positions in libraries as baby boomers retire—a process that is now under way. They grew up pretty much on their own— latchkey children with two working parents or in a single-parent home. Generally, they are very independent and have strong doubts about authority and loyalty. Often they value their free time more highly than doing extra work to earn more money, even when that work might lead to a promotion. They are much more comfortable with self-managed teams than are the baby boomers.

Millennials (those born 1981–1999), the most recent group to enter the workforce, are even fewer in number than Generation X. This generation will not face strong competition for positions given their small numbers; in fact, it is likely the employers will be the ones competing for employees. Millennials were the first generation to grow up in a technology-filled world—technology was not new; it was just the way the world was. Technology is something they are comfortable with; they expect it to work properly and on demand. Their expectation of a quick response often carries over into their workplace expectations. Employers are finding that millennial-generation employees have little patience when it comes to waiting for promotions and are quick to leave organizations. Teams have been a natural part of their growing up in school and in highly structured group activities such as sports, so work teams do not seem unnatural to them.

When there is a mix of generations in the workplace, as in most libraries, there are motivation challenges to address. Large numbers of student workers adds to the complexity. Supervisors will probably need to use different approaches with students than with the older full-time staff.

Just as you want to retain full-time staff, you also want to retain student workers for as long as possible. There is the obvious built-in student turnover as they graduate; however, keeping the best workers for as long as possible lowers training costs and some supervision costs. One step to take, even if it is not well implemented with the full-time staff, is to create student work teams. As noted, millennials are team oriented and need little assistance fitting into team duties and responsibilities. Consider building teams around a set of duties rather than scheduled work times. In the past, a duties approach was difficult at best and often impossible. With texting, cell phones, e-mail, and the like, students are in touch all the time making it easier to implement a duties system. A team that seldom has more than one member on duty at any time can still be very effective in a technological environment.

Teams need leaders, and this provides opportunities for promotion and rewards. With multiple work schedules, there may also be opportunities for assistant leaders. Such a structure may also allow you to create a student career ladder with appropriate pay differentials.

Regardless of how you structure the work, students should be held just as accountable for the quality of their work as full-time staff. (This also applies to volunteer workers.) Having different standards of accountability can and probably will lead to major morale problems and low-quality overall performance for the library.

Sound mentoring is effective in recruiting people to librarianship. Students tend to be open to mentoring when it focuses on issues they perceive as relevant. If for nothing more than helping them to learn appropriate work behavior and dress, this is useful activity. This section has touched on only a few of the benefits of using student workers. We highly recommend you spend some time reviewing Kimberly B. Sweetman's *Managing Student Assistants*.[21] Although its primary focus is on academic libraries, it has much to offer anyone thinking about or using student employees.

Volunteers

Library volunteers play a growing role in daily operations. They are likely to become even more common as more and more of the baby boomer generation retires. Many small libraries (rural, school, and church) are totally dependent on volunteers, with perhaps a retired person with library experience taking a lead role. Other libraries may be less dependent on volunteer assistance, but still use such services for important tasks.

During the late 1990s, there was a major effort to increase volunteerism in the United States. Although there is less government emphasis now, volunteer service hours grow steadily.

No matter what values you place on the work, as of 2009, many granting agencies currently allow libraries to use an $18.21 per hour rate for valuing volunteer service, and the annual contribution is in the billions of dollars. While volunteer work is increasing, there is concern about being able to retain volunteers. Daniel Kadlec reported that "Nearly 38 million Americans who had volunteered in a nonprofit in the past didn't show up last year [2005] . . . That is a waste of talent and desire."[22] Organizations cannot waste such potential people power. As baby boomers retire, they take with them a vast amount of experience and, perhaps more importantly, institutional memory that is very valuable. The professional literature frequently has stories about library staff members retiring and then returning as volunteers. Losing such people because the volunteer activities have not been properly planned would be very sad.

There is a vast pool of talented energetic, and motivated volunteers to tap into and, one hopes, retain. Volunteers can become highly committed to a library's organizational goals, given the proper environment, even if they have never worked in a library. Part of that environment is thinking about volunteers as being just as important to quality service as any paid staff member.

Begin your thinking and planning for volunteers by considering a few basic questions:

- Should we use volunteers? (A very key question to ponder)
- Where could we use volunteers?
- How would we use them?
- Would the tasks be meaningful for volunteers?
- Who would supervise the volunteers?
- Would we have one person in charge of the overall program?
- Do we have or can we create meaningful volunteer rewards?

Dale Freund explored the question of whether volunteers should be used in libraries.[23] He believed that when done properly and for the right reasons, the answer is yes. Success hinges on your thinking through questions such as the aforementioned and creating a plan.

There are three major volunteer categories to think about in the United States. One is the short-term volunteer. These are the people who will work on special projects or events but have no interest in a regular commitment, such as coming in one day per week for a few hours. Some library examples are an annual book sale, disaster recovery efforts, or a capital fund-raising campaign. A second category is the commitment volunteer. These are people who have a strong interest in the area in which they seek volunteer opportunities. They expect to gain gratification, knowledge, and useful skills as well as a sense of accomplishment from the work they perform. For most libraries, these are the people who form the backbone of a successful long-term volunteer program. They are also the group that requires the most careful planning and needs the most meaningful work to perform.

Finally, there are volunteers who engage in the activity because of some outside pressure rather than any personal desire. You may be able to transform some of these people into committed volunteers, but only through careful planning. Two significant sources of outside pressure are the workplace and school. Many for-profit organizations, while not making volunteering mandatory, make it very clear that they expect employees to engage in some form of volunteer work. Such organizations normally have a very broad definition of what constitutes volunteer work and how that activity counts in the performance review process. A few colleges and universities have gone so far as to make volunteer work a graduation requirement. Most don't go that far, but they do encourage students to volunteer, often through such means as adding it to the student's transcript, offering credit for the approved activities. These approaches have been rather successful; for example, in 2005, more than 3.3 million college students engaged in service to some nonprofit organization and averaged just under 100 hours per student.[24]

Where do you begin your search for volunteers? Your recruiting efforts will not take place in the same venues as for paid staff. There are five major places to explore; each requires a somewhat different approach to the message and where to place that message:

- Retirees
- Students

- Homemakers
- Employed people
- Unemployed people (most hope to gain a marketable skill or perhaps secure a paid position with the organization)

Reaching out to students, the employed, and the unemployed is relatively easy as there are organizations that will help get your message out. Retirees are a little more challenging; however, senior centers and other locations that offer senior programs are a good starting point. Homemakers are the biggest challenge; in this case school libraries have an inside track on getting great volunteers.

The best way to develop a cadre of committed volunteers is to start with job descriptions, using the same method as for paid staff positions. Doing this provides a solid base for everyone about the whats and hows of the positions. Surprises such as "I don't want to make photocopies" are much less likely when the person had an opportunity to review a JD indicating photocopying was part of the job. As with paid positions, the JD should outline duties and experience/skills sought. (Note: after preparing the descriptions it is wise to consult the HR department to explore any issues such as injury or liability coverage for volunteers.)

When it comes to volunteers, there is rarely a pool of applicants to interview—you are happy to have someone interested in the position. That notwithstanding, the interview is just as important for volunteers as it is for paid staff. This is the opportunity for both parties to assess skills, motivation, and the nature of the work.

Generally, volunteers require more initial training and development than paid staff. This is particularly true when the volunteer has retired from a somewhat similar paid position—for example, a retired school librarian volunteering in an archive. Volunteers often need time to unlearn years of past practices and/or modify beliefs about how things should be done. Too often the supervisor's assumption is that such people have done this before and therefore need very little training. It may be a while before it becomes apparent that this was a poor assumption and work must be redone.

There is no doubt that volunteers provide wonderful assistance to thousands of libraries, however, there are a few areas in which tension can arise between volunteers and paid staff.[25] One obvious area is a fear or concern about job security, especially where funding is tight or hiring freezes are in place. Paid staff may harbor unstated worries that their jobs may be in jeopardy, especially if some of the volunteers have prior library experience. We are unaware of any documented case where paid staff lost their jobs because of the availability of volunteers. However, we do know of instances where layoffs took place because of funding problems and sometime later the organization restarted a service based on volunteer help. When starting a volunteer program, you should address this concern openly and honestly with the paid staff.

Another challenge is when volunteers and paid staff perform the same tasks, which is something to avoid whenever possible. When it does happen, performance assessment becomes a significant issue. There may be strong resentment of the volunteers' apparent freedom to come and go with little or no notice and the appearance that they are held to a lower work standard. Paid staff may also think the volunteers are receiving encouragement or praise for work they believe is less than standard, or at least a lower standard than they are expected to deliver. Your managerial creativity and ingenuity will face great challenges when you try to provide that extra level of encouragement to volunteers and retain their services, while not undermining staff morale.

SUMMARY

Many years ago John D. Rockefeller is supposed to have said, "I will pay more for the ability to deal with people than any other ability under the sun." Whether he said that or not, the sentiment is the key to having quality library services: hire top-notch people and retain their services and loyalty. To be able to do that you need to follow sound people-planning practices and thoughtfully design their work activities.

It may not seem likely right now that you will need much of the information in this chapter; however, we anticipate that paraprofessionals will play an ever-growing role in quality library services. Those roles will call for greater involvement in personnel matters, from how to select the right person, to how to supervise and motivate team members, whether they are full time, part time or volunteers.

REVIEW QUESTIONS

1. What are the typical employee categories in most libraries?

2. Which label do you prefer for nonlibrarian positions in libraries? Explain your preference.

3. What are the major steps in the staffing process?

4. Why is the job description such an important document?

5. In what ways do student workers differ from other library employees?

6. Do you think volunteers are more valuable to libraries? Explain your position.

NOTES

The epigraphs for this chapter are taken from William Curran, "The 8Rs and Training Needs," *Argus* 35, no. 2 (2006): 29–33; JoAnne Deekan and Deborah Thomas, "Technical Service Job Ads," *College & Research Libraries* 67, no. 2 (2006): 136–45; and Janet Swan Hill, "Analog People for Digital Dreams," *Library Resources & Technical Services* 49, no. 1 (2005): 14–18.

1. "Service With a Very Big Smile," *Harvard Business Review* 85, no. 5 (2007): 24.

2. David Drickhamer, "Putting People First Pays Off," *Materials Handling Management* 61, no. 6 (2006): 42.

3. Michael Gorman, "Innocent Pleasures," in *The Future Is Now: The Changing Face of Technical Services,* proceedings of the OCLC symposium, ALA Midwinter Conference, Los Angeles, February 4 (Dublin, OH: OCLC, 1994), 40.

4. Liz Lane and Barbara Stewart, "The Evolution of Technical Services to Serve the Digital Academic Library," in *Recreating the Academic Library: Breaking Virtual Ground,* ed. Cheryl LaGuardia (New York: Neal-Schuman, 1998), 156.

5.   Curran, "The 8Rs and Training Needs," 30.

6.   Paula Kaufman, "Professional Diversity in Libraries," *Library Trends* 41, no. 4 (1992): 214.

7.   Elin Christianson, *Paraprofessional and Nonprofessional Staff in Special Libraries* (New York: Special Library Association, 1973).

8.   American Library Association, Library Support Staff Certification Project, 2008, http:/// www.ala-apa.org/certification/supportstaff.html.

9.   American Library Association, *Task Force on Career Ladders,* Library Support Staff Interests Round Table.

10.   American Library Association, *Continuing Education & Training Opportunities*. Library Support Staff Interests Round Table.

11.   American Library Association, *Task Force on Career Ladders,* 4.

12.   American Library Association, *Training Statement,* Library Support Staff Interests Round Table, 4.

13.   American Library Association, *Training Statement,* 5.

14.   Shannon L. Hoffman, "Who Is a Librarian," *Library Mosaics* 4, no. 4 (1993): 8–11.

15.   Ibid., 10.

16.   Marilyn Gardner, "Job Interviewers: What Can They Legally Ask?" *Arizona Daily Sun,* July 29, 2007, D1.

17.   Nora Spinks, "Talking About the Generation," *Canadian Healthcare Manager* 12, no. 7 (2005): 11.

18.   Marilyn Gardner, "New Job Regrets: Should You Go or Stay?" *Arizona Daily Sun,* August 12, 2007: D1, D4.

19.   Paula Singer and Jeanne Goodrich, "Retaining and Motivating High Performing Employees," *Public Libraries* 45, no. 1 (2006): 62–63.

20.   Saul Gellerman, *Management of Human Resources* (New York: Holt Rinehart, 1976).

21.   Kimberly B. Sweetman, *Managing Student Assistants* (New York: Neal-Schuman, 2007).

22.   Daniel Kadlec, "The Right Way to Volunteer," *Time* 168, no. 10 (2006): 76.

23.   Dale Freund, "Do Volunteers Belong in the Library?" *Rural Libraries* 25, no. 1 (2005): 19–41.

24.   Justin Pope, "College Volunteers Skyrocket," *Arizona Daily Sun,* October 16, 2006, A1.

25.   Sue W. McGown, "Valuable Volunteers," *Library Media Connection* 26, no. 2 (2007): 10–13.

SUGGESTED READING

Armstrong, Sharon, and Madelyn Applebaum. *Stress-Free Performance Appraisals.* Franklin Lakes, NJ: Career Press, 2003.

Bazirjian, Rosann, and Nancy Markle Stanley. "Assessing the Effectiveness of Team-based Structures in Libraries." *Library Collections, Acquisitions and Technical Services* 25, no.2 (2001): 131–57.

Bliss, Elizabeth S. "Staffing the Small Public Library," *Rural Libraries* 26, no. 1 (2006): 7–28.

Cervera, Barbara. "There Is Life After Technical Services." *Technicalities* 21, no. 3 (2001):10–11.

Davenport, Thomas. *The Care and Feeding of Knowledge Workers.* Boston: Harvard Business School Press, 2005.

Division of Library Development, Connecticut State Library. *Guidelines for Using Volunteers in Libraries,* 1997. http://www.cslib.org/volguide.

Driggers, Preston, and Eileen Duma. *Managing Library Volunteers.* Chicago: American Library Association, 2002.

El-Shervini, Magda. "Copy Catalogers and Their Changing Roles at Ohio State University." *Library Management* 22, nos. 1/2 (2001): 80–85.

Evans, G. Edward. *Performance Management and Appraisal: How-to Do-It.* New York: Neal-Schuman, 2004.

Giesecke, Joan, and Beth McNeil. *Fundamentals of Library Supervision.* Chicago: American Library Association, 2005.

Goodrich, Jeanne. "Staffing Public Libraries: Are There Models or Best Practices?" *Public Libraries* 44, no. 5 (2005): 277–81

Holcomb, Jean M. "The Annual Performance Evaluation: Necessary Evil or Golden Opportunity?" *Law Library Journal* 98, no. 3 (2006): 569–74.

Hurt, Tara Ludlow, and Deborah Stansbury Sunday. "Career Paths for Paraprofessionals: Your Ladder to Success," *Library Mosaics* 16, no. 1 (2005): 8–11.

Intner, Sheila S. "Job-Hunting in Technical Services." *Technicalities* 28, no. 5 (2008): 1, 17–19.

Kennan, MaryAnn, Patricia Willard, and Concepción Wilson. "What Do They Want? A Study of Changing Employer Expectations of Information Professionals." *Australian Academic Research Libraries* 37, no. 1 (2006):17–37.

Kutzik, Jennifer S. "Are You the Librarian?" *American Libraries* 36, no. 3 (2005): 32–34.

McCune, Bonnie. "Diversity and Volunteers." *Colorado Libraries* 31, no. 3 (2005): 43–44.

Mestas, Marie. "San Bernardino Valley College Library Technology Program." *Mosaics* 16, no. 1 (2005): 16–17.

Miller, Corey E., and Carl L. Thornton. "How Accurate Are Your Performance Appraisals?" *Public Personnel Management* 35, no. 2 (2006): 153–62.

Morrison, Douglas. "In the Name of Service." *American Libraries* 39, no. 6 (2008): 51.

Oblinger, Diana. "Boomers, GenXers & Millennials: Understanding the New Students," *EDUCAUSE Review* 38, no. 4 (2003): 37–47.

Osa, Justlina, Sylvia Nyana, and Clara Ogbaa. "Effective Cross-Cultural Communication to Enhance Reference Transactions," *Knowledge Quest* 35, no. 2 (2006): 22–24.

Parsons, Martha. "Are Library Support Staff Up to the Challenge?" *Library Mosaics* 16, no. 3 (2005): 18–19.

Reed, Sally G. *Library Volunteers—Worth the Effort: A Program Manager's Guide.* Jefferson, NC: McFarland, 1994.

Ruschoff, Carlen. "Competencies for 21st Century Technical Services." *Technicalities* 27, no. 6 (2007): 1, 14–16.

Shin, Sunney, and Brian Kleiner. "How to Manage Unpaid Volunteers in Organizations." *Management Research News* 26, nos. 2–4 (2003): 63–70.

Stanley, Mary J. *Managing Library Employees.* New York: Neal-Schuman, 2008.

Todaro, Julie, and Mark L. Smith. *Training Library Staff and Volunteers to Provide Extraordinary Customer Service.* New York: Neal-Schuman, 2006.

Tucker, James Cory. "Getting Down to Business: Library Staff Training." *Reference Services Review* 32, no. 3 (2004): 293–301.

Tunstall, Pat. "The Accidental Supervisor," *Public Libraries* 45, no. 3 (2006): 50–57.

Uchitelle, Louis. *The Disposable American: Layoffs and Their Consequences.* New York: Knopf, 2006.

Chapter

Technical Services Issues

The economic benefit of consortia lies in the ability of libraries to take their budgets further, spending less and getting more.

—Catherine Maskell, 2008

A critical underlying perspective is the expected outcome of the assessment process: evaluation for accountability or for continuous improvement. . . . The strategies undertaken to demonstrate accountability fall along a continuum of "we do it because we have to" to "we do it because it is a tool in helping the institution review, evaluate, and improve efficiency and effectiveness."

—Robert Dugan, 2006

There have always been challenges and issues facing technical services, just as there have for other library units. However, in the current environment, new challenges seem to appear just as soon as you think you've addressed one or more of them. Some of the issues we cover in this chapter are long-standing while others are of more recent origin. Certainly, the most critical issue facing every person and organization as we prepared this book is the serious downturn in the world economy—with the U.S. leading the way. That overarching issue has and will continue to have an impact on all aspects of the issues we cover in this chapter:

- Technology
- Outsourcing
- Cooperative/consortial activities
- Quality assurance (assessment and accountability)
- Fiscal/budgetary
- Physical work space

TECHNOLOGY

Many people are unaware that it was cataloging that originally brought computers and networking into libraries on a large scale many years ago. The Integrated Library System (ILS; computer systems and programs that link library operations in an almost seamless manner) grew out of libraries' efforts to provide cost-effective handling of acquisitions, cataloging, and other technical services activities. Few people who began their careers in technical services at that time ever dreamed that these efforts would lead to the current library technology. Today's systems handle all of the traditional technical services functions and so much more. Technology has accelerated the performance of activities and improved consistency throughout the library; perhaps the area where this is most evident is technical services. You can see the impact of technology in almost all libraries. In terms of technical services, the Loyola Marymount University (LMU) library is probably a representative example of how technology affected technical services activities.

In 1987, the LMU library had four OCLC terminals in the cataloging department and no other computers. The acquisitions budget at that time was just under $400,000, and the library cataloged and processed between 3,500 and 4,000 items per year. By 1990, an ILS was in place and computers or terminals were available on about two-thirds of the staff desks. As of 2008/2009, the acquisitions budget was more than $3.6 million, and processing exceeded 20,000 items. Although the dollar amount and production output grew during this time period, what is impressive is that the staffing actually *declined* by one full-time equivalent (FTE). This result was made possible only by taking advantage of advances in technology, primarily the capabilities of the ILS.

Productivity gains from an ILS come about in several ways. One of the most significant arises from the ability to share files at the desktop level throughout the library. One of the great challenges for architects designing a new library facility in pre-ILS days was that almost every staff member wanted to be adjacent to the public card catalog in order to make the workday easier. Exacerbating those demands was the fact that the end-users had to have access to the catalog as well. Obviously, satisfying all of the wishes was impossible. The Online Public Access Catalog (OPAC), a key element in an ILS, allows remote access from almost anywhere and often on a 24/7 basis for anyone with a network connection. (Statewide networks such as OhioLINK and California's LINK+ further enhance the quality of service to end-users and provide real-time information to technical services staff about collections in other libraries. We will explore in more depth later in this chapter.)

Sharing files electronically reduces staff time spent walking to and from their desks to shared paper-based files. Some of the shared files for technical services, both in the past and present, include on order, in processing, serials check-in, shelflist, and of course, the public catalog. Both technical and public services staff require access to information contained in such files from time to time; in pre-ILS times, staff walked for a good part of their workday. Also, some of these files contained basically the same information, but were arranged differently. Creating and maintaining the files also required substantial staff time, especially when there were hundreds, and often in large libraries, thousands of slips of paper. (A traditional format in U.S. libraries was, and still is to some degree, a 3- × 5-inch [approximately 8- × 13-cm] card or paper slip.) Maintaining paper-based files was a challenge for every technical services unit. Misfiled slips were a constant issue and could cost the library money. For example, if a book was already on order but the order slip was in an incorrect location, a second unneeded copy might be ordered because of the filing error.

An ILS generally provides keyword searching of a variety of fields in the electronic bibliographic record. (Information about fields and bibliographic records is in chapters 13, 14, and 15.) Keyword searches provide a more complete view of collection content than does a traditional subject search based on a set of standardized subject headings. This is because a keyword search scans multiple fields, such as title, subtitle, and notes, not just the subject heading field. Libraries have found, after installing their first ILS, that users comment that they are surprised at how much more they find when using keyword searches.

Many ILS systems offer staff members and end-users the opportunity to browse the collection electronically. That is, a person can view all the bibliographic records in the database regardless of the item's status—on order, in process, checked out, missing, and at the bindery, for example.

One of the attractions of journals and newspapers for readers is the currency of the information. A frequent user question is, "Has the latest issue of XX arrived yet?" In pre-ILS days, such queries required a telephone call or a trip to the serials check-in file, usually located in technical services, to provide the answer. Most ILSs automatically display data on the latest issue processed through the OPAC. Even on-order information is often available to end-users in some systems, which is particularly useful in academic institutions where faculty requests are key to building the collections and faculty want to know the status of their requests.

Another reason for increased productivity is that a single electronic record can serve many purposes. With paper-based systems, technical services staff often had to re-create the same information in a slightly different arrangement or attempt to use multiple carbon-copy forms and then arrange the copies in the desired order. Anyone who has worked with multiple-copy order forms can recall how faint the images are on the fourth, fifth, or sixth copy. Not having to re-create records and having the computer rearrange information has freed up a considerable amount of staff time. There is also greater consistency and accuracy in the files, assuming that the original data entry was correct.

Overall, the ILS has given libraries a strong incentive to review what, how, and who does what. Technical services units have taken advantage of the opportunities and made numerous adjustments in their workflows and staffing patterns (see chapter 2 and chapter 3). There is every reason to believe that the ILS will continue to evolve and provide further opportunities for improvements in productivity.

The opening paragraph to this chapter mentioned how just when you think you've resolved one challenge, things change. Providing end-users with ever-greater access to useful information through such features as keyword searching and 24/7 remote access to the OPAC and other databases seemed like good solutions—and they were—but technology keeps changing. We now know more adjustments are necessary if we are to effectively serve our various stakeholders. Beth Camden wrote, "Once considered the crowning jewel of libraries the integrated library system (ILS) has lost its luster as our users have moved to Web search engines as their primary research tools."[1] In a follow-up article, Carlen Ruschoff discussed some of the factors that will force significant changes on the next generation ILS. She noted that the Web search engines, "developed *outside* of the ILS, created a 'discovery layer' that is able to search across databases and files of information. Essentially what happened is that one very important feature has been removed from the ILS."[2] Her comments about how designers must think about a new ILS reflect the fact challenges are never over:

> As we begin conceptualizing the ILS of tomorrow, we have to be very conscious of the work we will be doing five or more years from now, as well as the work we will *not* be doing. We need to be bold enough to re-examine the ways in which we do our work now, and imagine how it might be done differently.[3]

That next generation ILS is highly unlikely to be less expensive than the current systems, which are not cheap. Finding the necessary funding to acquire such systems will be a major challenge unless there is a quick turnaround in the economy.

Certainly the impact of technology now goes far beyond the ILS. The Internet and Web 2.0 applications have had a substantial impact on library activities. Vendors, especially those handling books or journals, are providing more of their services through the Web. Following are two examples of ways in which vendor Web services influence technical services. First, importing OCLC or Library of Congress bibliographic data has been a staple activity in libraries for many years. What has changed and is changing is that it is becoming easier to download files from vendors into the ILS and then modify the files to meet local needs. In the not-too-distant past, the best one could expect was to make modifications of files in the bibliographic utilities' or vendor's database and then import the file. The supplier also determined the amount of modification or manipulation that could be made. In general, they allowed limited modification. Another change is the ability to order materials and pay invoices electronically, which makes for faster service and, assuming the electronic data are correct, fewer errors.

An important element in the area of electronic influences is *metadata* (see chapter 19), which is the generic term for cataloging and indexing for electronic documents. Web sites are a mixed bag of information ranging from the worthless, or even dangerous, to the authoritative. Libraries have been engaging in electronic collection development of Web resources for a number of years by attempting to sort out the good from the bad and the ugly. The idea is to identify worthwhile and reliable electronic resource sites and provide end-users with access to those sites. A serious issue for libraries is how to go about describing such locations in the library's OPAC or on its Web page. Metadata (information about information) is a term used to identify this concern. The Dublin Core (http://www.dublincore.org) is an example of an effort to reach agreement on a standardized method for describing Internet/Web resources. Another such effort began in July 2000, when OCLC and hundreds of cooperating libraries launched the Cooperative Online Resource Catalog (CORC) project, a service that allowed libraries around the world to retrieve and describe outstanding Internet resources. This program was incorporated into OCLC *Connexion* service in 2002 (Archived Projects, OCLC, http://www.oclc.org/research/projects/archive/default.htm).

Libraries are using technology to empower their users to shop for services. Libraries are using the Internet and their Web sites as a major part of their information-delivery systems. Library Web sites have gone from simply linking to their OPAC to offering online reference services, blogs, RSS feeds, wikis, meeting room reservations, digital newsletters, subject guides to information, and links to various commercial and in-house databases, among other things.

Michael Stephens lists some of the uses libraries are making of Web 2.0 social software tools "in creating conversations, connections, and community":

- *Openness.* Libraries use weblogs to generate dialogue and tell the human story of the library.
- *Ease of use.* Libraries use instant messaging to perform virtual reference instead of hard-to-use proprietary platforms.
- *Innovation.* Libraries create subject-based wikis where users can suggest resources and ask questions.
- *Social interaction.* Comment-enabled weblogs allow users to get involved with library planning and programs.
- *Creation of content.* A library offers space and digital tools to create audio and video presentations, stories and more. (See the Public Library of Charlotte and Mecklenburg County's "ImaginOn" program for a good example: http://www.imaginon.org/index.asp).
- *Sharing.* A library feeds RSS content from various sources to other Web pages within the local community.
- *Decentralization.* A librarian creates a Google Maps mash-up of the routes of library delivery vehicles.
- *Participation.* The library begins a wiki for its strategic plans, inviting all staff and users to participate in a vision for the future.
- *Trust.* Librarians release control of their data and utilize radical trust with their users and each other. Staff members blog freely and informally.[4]

Allowing users into library resources that were formerly the exclusive domain of library staff is not without controversy. Some argue that there is a danger of deprofessionalizing libraries by allowing too much creative participation by users. Web 2.0 technology is most effective if viewed as supplementing, not replacing, traditional library expertise. For example, allowing users to tag entries in the OPAC with their own descriptors, comments, reviews, and ratings does not replace the cataloging expertise required to assign controlled vocabulary subject headings. Tagging does, however, offer an additional means for customers to discover the contents of libraries' OPACs and improves their utility. (For an example of tagging in action, see the University of Pennsylvania's PennTags at http://tags.library.upenn.edu/.) Using Web 2.0 tools is a customer-centered paradigm that seeks to reduce barriers to information, increase library knowledge of customer wants and needs, and improve customer satisfaction with library services and resources.

Providing access to Web 2.0 productivity tools (for example, Google Docs and Spreadsheets) has a dual advantage for libraries, especially small libraries. Online productivity software allows library users to write resumes, create newsletters, share documents, and do other tasks usually performed by Microsoft Office or Apple suites. The online software allows them to create, store, access, and share their documents online for free, anywhere they can access a network connection. Empowering people to customize their own Web-based services in this way can be an important step to lessening the technology gap between the haves and the have-nots and will certainly create a loyal base of library supporters who utilize these services. Offering online productivity software is also an advantage for the library. It can be expensive to keep up with new versions of commercial office productivity software (e.g., Microsoft and Apple), both the software and hardware requirements, and providing access to, and training in, the alternative free software can allow the library to provide user services they could not otherwise afford.[5]

OUTSOURCING

Outsourcing means having some service or activity performed by persons or organizations (called "third parties") that are not part of a library or library system. When looking at the professional literature of the past 10 years for discussions about the concept, a newcomer to the field might think outsourcing is a new phenomenon in libraries. That impression is only partially correct. Technical services units have been outsourcing activities for a great many years: using jobbers for ordering books rather than purchasing directly from the publisher; using serial vendors to place the bulk of subscriptions rather than going directly to the publishers; and using outside companies to bind and repair materials for the collection. (We will examine the foregoing topics in the chapters that follow.) Somewhat new are efforts to use outside agencies for other activities and even overall library operations. In the case of overall operations, U.S. government agencies have used such services for their library programs for many years, as have some corporations. What is happening late in the first decade of the 21st century is serious reductions in service locations and even closing of some public and special libraries as economic conditions worsen. As a result, if funding bodies are looking to reduce costs they are not looking to outsource activities but rather to cut or close down the activity.

Recent emphasis on outsourcing started in the for-profit sector in the 1980s and 1990s—at the same time topics such as reengineering and downsizing were popular. Like libraries, businesses had employed the concept for many years without media attention. The difference in coverage was that the idea was often linked with staff reductions. Another term that came into play at the time was *contingent workforce.* Anne Polivka and Thomas Nardone defined this concept as

> a wide range of employment practices, including part-time work, temporary work, employee leasing, self-employment, contracting out, and home-based work. As a result, the operational definition of a contingent job has become an arrangement that differs from full-time, permanent, wage, and salary employment.[6]

"Contracting out" is a synonym for outsourcing. Karen Jette and Clay-Edward Dixon discussed contingent work in libraries in an article in *Library Administration & Management,* noting that libraries have also employed that concept for many years.[7] Their article has a sound section on the pros and cons of such work, including outsourcing.

As a cost-reduction tactic, outsourcing may be correct and effective in the short run but may have unexpected long-term consequences. No matter what one does, certain coordination costs will always be present. Reducing those coordination and monitoring costs results in long-term quality-control issues. Expertise that will be needed later may also be lost, and the cost of re-securing that expertise can be high. There may also be unexpected salary implications, if the activity outsourced involves staffing changes.

Despite these drawbacks, there is substantial potential for using outsourcing as another tool for helping to control costs and supplement or expand services. This is how libraries have effectively employed the concept in the past without labeling it "outsourcing." Two examples from acquisitions and one from cataloging illustrate the point that outsourcing has a long tradition in libraries. As mentioned previously, using a book or a serials jobber is not absolutely essential for libraries. A library could place all its orders for books or journals directly with the publishers. For very small libraries that may be a reasonable option. However, as the volume of orders increases, the work involved in maintaining address files, credit terms, discount information, and so forth from hundreds or even thousands of publishers becomes prohibitive. Years ago, acquisitions librarians saw the value of placing a single order with a jobber or wholesaler for the items needed from various publishers. (Placing one order for 100 books from 35 different publishers instead of placing 35 orders with the individual publishers saves staff time in order preparation alone.) The idea was not to reduce staff or cut costs; it was to make the most effective use of existing staff and control costs as much as possible.

Another example, and one that is not often mentioned as outsourcing, is the use of approval plans in academic libraries. In these plans, the vendor identifies items that match a list of subject areas that the library wants to collect and ships various materials that fall into the category to the library for review and/or automatic inclusion into the collection. Thus, the library outsources the identification function, one of the basic library functions. Some approval plans allow for materials to arrive "shelf ready"—that is, with spine labels already affixed, thus reducing the need for staff time devoted to processing such materials.

Cataloging departments have an equally long, if not longer, history of using outsourcing. For example, until widespread implementation of the ILS most libraries made extensive use of catalog cards produced by commercial companies and the Library of Congress (which started selling its cards in 1901). Certainly there was even greater use of the *National Union Catalog* (NUC) and *Canadiana* in creating cards for public catalogs. (One of this book's authors well remembers his days as a cataloger with the responsibility of overseeing the duplication of LC/NUC and local copy for use in the library's public catalog and shelflist.) No one thought of this as outsourcing; at best it may have been regarded as resource sharing (although libraries were depending on third parties to provide the product and did pay for the services and cards). By the 1960s, there were efforts to create shared processing centers. These efforts resulted in bibliographic utilities such as OCLC. This form of outsourcing is an accepted and very valuable service.

A common first response to suggestions of using outsourcing for a library activity, especially cataloging, is the lack of quality control on the part of third parties. Local catalogers are known to "correct mistakes" made by the Library of Congress, and many have grave doubts that bibliographic records from other libraries can possibly be as accurate as ones produced in-house. Obviously doubts about a third-party source (whether another library or a for-profit entity) are even greater. One of this book's authors noted that the goal of the perfect catalog record and perfect public catalog is akin to seeking the Holy Grail—a worthy idea but, at least in the case of cataloging, highly unrealistic and costly in many ways for the library.[8] Certainly there are quality concerns, but they exist no matter where the work is done or by whom, and the reality is that perfection is highly unlikely to exist anywhere at a reasonable cost to the library and end-users. Quality of third-party work therefore should not be a limiting factor in deciding to move ahead with an outsourcing project; it should just be one of many issues that must be addressed.

COOPERATIVE/CONSORTIAL ACTIVITIES

Libraries have engaged in cooperative activities for a long time—well over 100 years. Thus, you would expect that they would have mastered the process. Overall they know what is necessary for achieving a successful cooperative venture. They have also learned that each new effort will bring with it some new challenges. They also know that truly successful programs must change with the changing times.

The Library of Congress's distribution of cataloging information is one the very oldest of U.S. library cooperative programs. As mentioned previously, the program began late in 1901 with the distribution of catalog cards. Over the years it changed the manner of distribution (from card stock to online and individual title information within the publication—called "cataloging in publication") and expanded the number of libraries that contribute data. As Martha Yee wrote:

> This [ingenious] scheme, by which a shared cataloging program to lower cataloging costs produced the equivalent of a national bibliography at the same time, has become the envy of the rest of the world. This approach is now very much taken for granted in the United States, but could not have happened without the conjunction of a number of economic, political, and social factors.[9]

Outside factors often play a key role in motivating cooperative/consortial activities to begin and affect the way in which they operate and change over time.

Another highly successful and long-standing endeavor is OCLC (close to 50 years old as we prepared this edition). During the 1960s, U.S. librarians engaged in a variety of efforts to create cooperative or centralized technical services centers. Some projects focused on a type of library, such as academic or public. Later efforts focused on multi-type regional or statewide programs. The results of those efforts are OCLC, Inc., and state and regional networks (such as Lyrasis or OCLC Western) that go well beyond offering technical services activities.

There have been major expansions of consortial activities in the recent past. We will explore some of these expansions in the chapter on electronic resources (chapter 8). Briefly, one of the more recent efforts are resource sharing networks such as Ohio-LINK (http://www.ohiolink.edu/) and California's LINK+ (http://csul.iii.com/). Such networks are built and operate on the basis of libraries' collection databases, which are generated by their technical services units.

Most of the early efforts focused on internal library operations; certainly, they led to service improvements or reduced library costs, but they were not directly visible to the users. Many of today's projects are something users see and appreciate. Shirley Kennedy reflected on the visibility aspect when she wrote:

> Up until a couple of months ago I had not set foot in a public library in more than five years. . . . But one day, a colleague passed along some information about the county public library cooperative upgrading its online system, and I had to take a look. It's awesome. . . . What is cool is that we have the Pinellas Automated Library System, which lets you browse or search through the collections of all 15 member libraries, select or reserve materials, and have them sent to a library convenient to you.[10]

We will cover systems like the two mentioned above in the chapters on e-resources and services (chapters 7, 8, and 9). (For an overview of older cooperative ventures, see chapter 4 of the last edition of this book view it online at http://lu.com/bookext.cfm, as a supplement to this edition, along with additional illustrations of technical services activities.)

The line between cooperative activities and consortia efforts is not sharp and never has been. Perhaps it easiest to think of cooperative ventures as less formalized. Generally, a consortia has some type of legal status (a nonprofit corporation for example). One of this book's authors (Evans) had extensive experience with an operation that slowly grew from a small urban informal cooperative into a statewide nonprofit corporation (SCELC—first as Southern California Electronic Library Cooperative and later as the Statewide California Electronic Library Consortium; http://scelc.org/).

Regardless of the label, the bottom line is that it is all about libraries working together to stretch funding, expand services, and share workloads or some other desired outcome. To be successful there must be trust and compromises and there must be true teamwork.[11] Technical services unit heads may or may not have a direct representation on the group that actually makes decisions regarding the venture, even though such decisions may affect the workload. Generally, the members of the controlling board are library directors. There is a practical reason for this; there must be the authority to commit a library to new program elements or modifications of a program element. However, there must be thoughtful, meaningful, and ongoing consultation with technical services personnel for there to be success in any cooperative effort.

Magda El-Sherbini and Amanda Wilson in writing about alternative methods to distribute library resources, noted:

> By eliminating the middle steps of creating, accessing, and retrieving information via intermediaries such as regional consortia, OCLC, and costly OPACs, libraries might realize substantial savings that could be diverted to enrich bibliographic records that form the foundation of the current bibliographic structure.[12]

Whether they are correct in their view that cutting out such cooperative activities will save money or better serve users seems to be a debatable point. What is clear is that consortia provide visible and appreciated services to end-users who might well be unhappy about the loss of a valued program.

QUALITY ASSURANCE

Accountability and assessment are interrelated and are an important part of library operations. Certainly, accountability goes well beyond assessment; however, assessment is one of the key elements in demonstrating accountability. Those who provide funds for library operations, be they public agencies or private individuals, expect value for their funds. Not too many years ago funders started asking for more than statistics about how the monies were expended. They want proof that the funds actually had a valuable outcome (outcome assessment).

Libraries also undertake assessments/evaluations of their programs in order to publicize their worth to the public. Libraries and library staff have generally done a less than stellar job of educating their publics about the libraries' contributions to society. Joan Durrance and Karen Fisher stated the problem succinctly: "The truth is that librarians have failed to explain to those outside the field what contributions they and their institutions actually make to society at large."[13] Experts, legislators, and decision makers often ignore the vital role libraries play in supporting learning and developing an informed citizenry. This is seen no more clearly than in the perennial struggles for funding faced by public, school, and academic libraries, particularly in times of budget constraints.

What is known now as assessment began in most libraries with the collection and compilation of statistics about inputs and outputs (total dollars spent on how many books, for example). Initially, libraries developed the statistics primarily for internal reasons and secondarily for use in budget presentations. They wanted to use the information gathered to improve library efficiency or effectiveness. Internally, the increasing complexity and cost of library operations, along with increasing demand for services, requires good information for planning and evaluation purposes. There was a need for objective, standardized data on which to base decisions. The statistics provide *some* insight into current performance and allow the staff to see where improvements may be called for. They also help managers allocate resources, plan operations and services, and make better decisions. The data also help to assess the success of new programs and services.

Quantity rather than quality was the focus of most such initial data collection efforts, which ultimately told the staff, funding bodies, and public little about the value of the spending activities. Circulation counts and the number of reference questions asked, books purchased, and items cataloged and processed are perhaps mildly interesting, but they provide no insight into their ultimate value. More recently, a shift has occurred toward measuring the quality of a library and its services. Despite this shift, traditional inputs and outputs are still valuable measures for determining if a library is functioning effectively and efficiently. They can be especially useful when enabling a library to compare its program to professional standards and to benchmarking data provided by other libraries.

Assessment and planning are intertwined. You cannot assess something until you know what the goal is for the activity being assessed. To be meaningful, the activity should be apart of plan. To be effective, plans must be long- and short-term in focus. This is not the place to review the planning process. However, basic institutional planning begins by defining the organizational mission and then developing long- and short-term objectives and goals. Assessment and quality assurance draws on the planning process by

- establishing clear, relevant, and slightly stretching goals/targets;
- designing and implementing activities to reach the goals;
- evaluating if and how well the goals are achieved; and
- revising or creating new activities to better achieve the desired outcome.

Essentially, quality control and assessment help the library and its funders gather information about how well it is achieving the agreed-upon goals.

Because technical services activities do not usually involve direct contact with the end-users, the challenges of assessment can be rather substantial. Libraries are required to develop strategic plans and to review them annually, keeping a strong focus on the outcomes of all their activities. Identifying appropriate goals that relate to user outcomes can be challenging. However, it is an area that technical services staff must address.

BUDGETARY ISSUES

Budget considerations have played a significant role in determining all aspects of library services, not just technical services, over the past 30 years. They will be even more so in light of the economic downturn that began in 2008. All of the usual economic and financial suspects appear on the following list of influences:

- Overall economic conditions
- Reluctance of taxpayers to raise taxes (and in some cases rolling them back)
- Shifting allocation priorities by funding authorities
- Increasing prices of collection materials, perhaps not as rapidly as in the past but still rising
- Rapidly changing technology and the constant need to upgrade systems.

We are likely to see phrases such as "small is beautiful," "less is more," "downsizing," and "reengineering" become commonplace once again. They all reflect the idea that organizations could be more effective, often with fewer staff. For libraries, the approaches represented by these expressions resulted in major changes in services, staffing, and collections in the past and will do so again.

Government officials understand that voters want certain services maintained regardless of economic conditions. Police, fire, sanitation, and road maintenance services are high priorities. Services such as schools, libraries, museums, and parks have to struggle for a share of the small amount of funding that remains after top-priority services are almost fully funded. Often the best a library can hope for is funding at the same level as the previous year.

While addressing these challenges, libraries also face the need to install a variety of technologies and then maintain them at an appropriate level, if the library is to remain a viable player in the information society. Technology changes rapidly, and it is often impossible not to move forward with those changes if one hopes to receive support for the technology. Upgrading always seems to cost more than expected, which puts an additional strain on the budget.

All of these factors, and others, create an environment in which libraries face difficult financial and service choices. Initially, some libraries thought reducing service hours might prompt end-users to demand that authorities increase funding to restore service levels, but this seldom happens. Another approach that almost every library tries is to reduce its collection-building activities. One change is to reduce one-time purchases—books and media formats—to maintain current journal subscriptions. However, year after year of double-digit price increases in serial prices force libraries to engage in serial and/or database cancellation projects while also trying to maintain or increase book purchases as those collections began showing serious signs of aging.

One of the other frequently seen outcomes of the overall reduction or minimal growth in the library budget is changes in staffing patterns. Sometimes this takes the form of hiring freezes (not being allowed to fill a staff vacancy) for long periods of time or furloughs (unpaid leave). At other times it involves losing a position when a staff member resigns (staff attrition). Occasionally, it is outright staff reductions through voluntary or involuntary terminations (called "reductions in force," "riffing," or "redundancy" depending on location). Not surprisingly, having fewer one-time purchases and fewer serial titles to process, as well as seeing an overall drop in the number of materials to catalog, means technical services faces pressure to reduce its staff. It also means that there is pressure to look at alternative methods for handling the workload. One such method is outsourcing, as discussed earlier.

SPACES FOR TECHNICAL SERVICES

Currently, there is a debate about the role of the library as "place," although most of this is focused on how end-users and, to a lesser extent, how collections are accommodated. In all of the ongoing efforts to make library buildings more accessible, more user-friendly, more technologically sophisticated, and more energy efficient, less attention has been paid to the spaces assigned to technical services operations. This is not to say that technical services is neglected in the planning of new and renovated buildings, but rather that most of what has happened in the way of change turns out to be more of a by-product of the larger set of issues confronting space planners.

The following are among the most significant factors affecting space planning for technical services:

- The ubiquitous use of computers as an essential component of almost all activities. This includes the use of fixed workstations and the use of portable laptops and other small devices. The widespread use of wireless technology has expanded libraries' flexibility in deploying this technology.
- The increased use of commercial processing services—outsourcing—principally in public libraries, has certainly had an impact on the amount of space required in-house.
- On the other hand, for libraries that do their own processing, the wider range of materials being acquired and processed (e.g., CD, DVD, computer software, kits) requires space and furnishings that are more varied than in the time when libraries had to deal only with books and journals.
- The overall decrease in the number of paper subscriptions received by libraries of all types.
- The greater attention being paid to issues of ergonomics, lighting, air quality, and green buildings than ever before.

- The Americans With Disabilities Act, which has enormous implications not only for public spaces in libraries but also for staff workplaces.
- The recognized need for flexibility of space to meet future needs as well as for these spaces to respond to current requirements.
- The more varied nature of many technical services staff positions in terms of work components, which often brings with it the need for access to more kinds of space and equipment.

Some Key Issues

Significantly more library building projects involve interior renovations and rearrangements than the construction of new buildings. This has been the case for decades, and it is extremely unlikely that the situation will change for the foreseeable future. The issues outlined here are applicable to both existing and new spaces, but clearly, in large academic and public libraries, the relocation of technical services departments, while possibly desirable, is much more difficult.

Historically, technical services operations were situated with major concern about their proximity to the card catalog, printed bibliographic tools, materials receiving and delivery, and, in small public libraries, to their service points. In today's environment a number of these relationships have become less critical, and this provides an opportunity to rethink where technical services might be located. The impact of requiring processing operations to meet the several requirements listed above inevitably led to most of the departments being on the main (entry) level because that is usually where the catalog and the reference collection were located. There are fewer constraints about location now that the traditional card catalog is gone and most major bibliographic tools are available online. It is also clear that good vertical access to receiving and delivery via elevator are an appropriate alternative to being close to the loading dock.

A recent trend, especially among large academic research libraries and large urban public libraries, is to move all or part of technical services offsite. Although such remote locations existed in the past, for example at the California State University–Northridge in the late 1960s and 1970s, technology has significantly accelerated the practice. The rationale for this has been primarily to increase the amount of space available for public services and collections. Critics of the separation of technical services have cited as downside effects the loss of collegiality with the rest of the staff, the inconvenience for faculty and students who may need to visit technical services, and the additional costs associated with materials delivery. However, it appears likely the trend will continue.

Planning Issues

The emancipation of technical services from its physical proximity to the public catalog permits space planners to consider a variety of locations within the building. The factors that should influence the location include:

- The need for convenient access to receiving and delivery areas. As noted earlier, this does not mean that technical services departments need to be adjacent to the loading dock. It does mean that there should be horizontal or vertical access that ideally does not involve extensive travel through public areas of the library.

- Libraries in which faculty and others have to review approval plan materials or items being considered for transfer to storage or withdrawal need space within their technical services area where these activities can be conducted. These areas need to be accessible to the public. While they do not have to be front and center, it does suggest the need to be on a major traffic route with a visible entry. Having visitors on a regular basis also brings with it the need to design the interior space to ensure that materials in process are secure.

- Technical services departments clearly need to be accessible to other library staff. This is especially true where the collection development function is not part of technical services. This is also important where there is a separate preservation/conservation unit.

- In smaller libraries, especially small public libraries, processing operations are often staffed by people who have other responsibilities, including working with the public. This needs to be considered in deciding where to locate the backroom functions.

A series of planning questions will inevitably arise in looking at existing technical services spaces and in planning areas in new or renovated buildings. Whatever the situation, the key factors that should influence interior design include future flexibility; the efficient movement of people and materials; the security of materials in process; and a comfortable, ergonomically effective, and inviting space for those who work in the area. It may be obvious but should be said that many library staff spend seven to eight hours within the building, primarily during the daytime, yet in many buildings they do not have adequate access to natural light. Reader spaces are often given higher priority to windows even though much use of that space takes place after the sun goes down.

In looking at how best to organize and arrange spaces for technical services, planners should be concerned about the following:

- Will the space work better as one large, open space or as a series of connected departmental areas? How important is it to retain the identity of acquisitions, serials, cataloging, and so on? Will the current organizational structure be around in 5 to 10 years? If change is anticipated, how can this best be accommodated? Is it conceivable that technical services space could become public space? How does this influence location and design?

- What is the basis for providing enclosed office space versus open workstations? It is feasible to create a spacious, comfortable, and efficient work area without erecting floor-to-ceiling walls. The use of partitions and office landscaping can provide a sense of privacy and separateness without incurring the additional costs for lighting and air supply and return. Many libraries have given up the concept of private offices, even for department heads and supervisors, and rely instead on having a number of enclosed spaces that can be used when needed on a sign-up basis. If private offices are to be included, they should be designed as generically as possible so that changes in administrative responsibility and organizational structure can be accommodated.

- The organization of space should reflect the efficient flow of materials within the department.
- Individual work spaces should provide sufficient space for the variety of activities taking place. This includes space for computers, tabletop work surfaces, book trucks, file cabinets, and shelving.
- It is highly desirable to centralize as many service functions as possible within the larger space, including copiers, scanners, printers, fax machines, and supply cabinets.
- Recognize that materials in process often do not have security devices, so there should be good perimeter security—doors and windows—and lockable storage for valuable materials. Every staff member should likewise have a secure space for personal items.
- Space should be provided for staff meetings. This can be accommodated by a variety of mechanisms—meeting space within an enclosed office, open meeting space in a common area, a closed meeting room within the technical services area, or use of meeting spaces elsewhere in the building.
- Space should also be provided for training current and new staff. This may be accomplished by using facilities elsewhere in the library (e.g., computer labs or classrooms), but large technical services departments probably need a dedicated training space.
- Shelving should be designed and located to provide convenience and flexibility. The use of movable compact shelving should be considered for storing items that do not have to be immediately accessible (e.g., arrearages, incoming gifts, exchange stock, materials awaiting bindery pickup). There also needs to be shelving appropriate for the storage of nonbook items, such as CDs, DVD, and archives. Art books and music may also require customized shelving.
- Technical services areas need to be planned with consideration of current and future technological requirements. Attention should be paid to power and network connectivity, including wireless access. It is critical that the space be able to adapt to changes in equipment and operations.
- Carpeting is recommended for all spaces except shipping and receiving; this will enhance noise control.
- The amount of space to be allocated should reflect the number of staff to be housed and the amount of material that is moving into and through the department. In general, technical services departments require between 100 and 150 square feet per staff member.
- Space should be provided for all of the book trucks that are being used.
- Space requirements for some specific spaces within technical services departments:

  - Enclosed office: 120–150 square feet
  - Open staff workstation: 80–100 square feet
  - Student workstation: 50–60 square feet
  - Work table (3 feet × 8 feet)   100 square feet

- Technical services staff need convenient access to restrooms and the staff lounge,

- Libraries that use volunteers to help process materials and provide other support need to make sure there are appropriate and sufficient workspaces for these people.

Administrative offices and workstations should be located to provide both visibility and privacy. Conference rooms and/or meeting spaces also require privacy. There also needs to be accommodation for support personnel and for a reception area.

The kinds of activities that could be accommodated in a shared area within technical services include:

- Mail opening and sorting
- Staff mailboxes
- Staff restrooms
- Sink
- Kitchen

A mail-opening area requires a number of spaces: sorting tables, mailboxes, trash receptacles, and a counter if outgoing mail is also involved. There needs to be shelving for incoming books and books in process. If there is an approval area, there should be shelving that is easily accessible along with chairs and tables. There also needs to be separate shelving for books being reviewed for weeding or relocation, shelving or file cabinets for publisher's catalogs, and part-time and student workstations.

Although the mail/receiving function is not necessarily part of technical services, it has a critical relationship with that area. Some of the planning issues that often arise include:

- How to monitor mail delivery if the area is not staffed
- The need for storage space for incoming supplies and equipment
- The need for a separate, secure storage space for special collections and archives
- The need for convenient access to elevator
- The need to have no building air supply intake anywhere near the loading dock
- The need for a canopy or other weather protection
- The need for double-width doors leading from the loading dock into the building

The question of enclosed versus open offices for cataloging personnel is a common planning issue. The work is more detail oriented than most of the other technical services activities and having a relatively noise free work environment is important. The challenge for the planning team is how to achieve the necessary work environment for catalogers without creating resentment on the part of the technical services staff that do not have private offices. If end-processing takes place here, there needs to be space provision for label printers and for the substantial amount of supplies that are used. Cataloging of nonprint material, including microforms, requires viewing equipment and appropriate work space.

Planning new or renovated space for technical services operations requires careful consideration of both current practice and potential changes. While these areas are not as visible as an information commons or a reading room, they still need to be designed to provide for maximum efficiency and flexibility and for the well-being of those who work there.

SUMMARY

Technical services units are facing a great many issues. Without question, technology is an ongoing issue for libraries, not just technical services. Staying reasonably current is expensive. Training staff and helping them stay up-to-date with technological developments is a constant challenge. Even the library's OPAC is undergoing changes as users apparently now go first to the Web when seeking information. As budgets become tighter and tighter, libraries will turn to even greater use of cooperative efforts and consortia to stretch limited funds. That type of shift will present some additional issues in terms of accountability and assessment for the individual institutions and their funding bodies as they become increasingly dependent upon actions of other libraries. Certainly the current economic environment is not conducive to asking for budget increases; the fight is to keep something close to recent past allocations. The situation is likely to remain tight for some time to come, at least for libraries. The final issue touched on in this chapter was physical space for technical services activities. Given the current economic downturn, it is likely that the best technical services can hope for is an occasional influx of funding to upgrade/remodel existing spaces. Those units that do have the opportunity to design a new area will be very, very fortunate.

REVIEW QUESTIONS

1. What are some of the reasons libraries try to assess their performance?
2. Give an example of an "input" and an "output."
3. What does accountability mean in terms of library performance?
4. How does accountability change the way libraries assess themselves?
5. Discuss what is new and old about the concept of outsourcing technical services.
6. Discuss the ways in which integrated library systems (ILSs) have had an impact on technical services activities and organization.
7. What are some of the other ways technology affects technical services?
8. Discuss how the economy has influenced technical services.
9. Discuss what is new and not new about the concept of outsourcing technical services.
10. List the significant factors in planning technical services work spaces.

NOTES

The epigraphs for this chapter are taken from Robert E. Dugan, "Assessment Strategies for Institutional Accountability," in *Revisiting Outcome Assessment in Higher Education,* ed. Peter

Hernon, Robert Dugan, and Candy Schwartz, 97–116 (Westport, CT: Libraries Unlimited, 2006) and Catherine A. Maskell, "Consortia: Anti-competitive or in the Public Good?" *Library Hi Tech* 26, no. 2 (2008): 164–83.

1. Beth Picknally Camden, "OPAC—Going, Going, Gone!" *Technicalities* 28, no. 5 (2008): 1.

2. Carlen Ruschoff, "The Integrated Library System: Are You Ready for the Next Generation ILS?" *Technicalities* 28, no. 6 (2008): 1.

3. Ibid., 13.

4. Michael Stephens, "The Promise of Web 2.0," *American Libraries* 37, no. 9 (2006): 32.

5. Rachel Singer Gordon and Michael Stephens, "Tech Tips for Every Librarian," *Computers in Libraries* 27, no. 9 (2007): 48–49.

6. Anne Polivka and Thomas Nardone, "On the Definition of 'Contingent Work,'" *Monthly Labor Review* 112, no. 12 (1989): 10.

7. Karen Jette and Clay-Edward Dixon, "The Outsourced/Contingent Workforce: Abuse, Threat, or Blessing?" *Library Administration & Management* 12, no. 3 (1998): 220–25.

8. Sheila S. Intner, ed., "Copy Cataloging and the Perfect Record Mentality," in *Interfaces: Relationships Between Library Technical and Public Services,* 154–59 (Englewood, CO: Libraries Unlimited, 1993).

9. Martha M. Yee, "'Wholly Visionary': The American Library Association, the Library of Congress, and the Card Distribution Program," *Library Resources & Technical Services* 53, no. 2 (2009): 68.

10. Shirley Duglin Kennedy, "True Confessions," *Information Today* 25, no. 9 (2008): 18, 19.

11. G. Edward Evans, "Management Issues of Co-operative Ventures and Consortia in the USA—Part One," *Library Management* 23, nos. 4/5 (2002): 213–26; G. Edward Evans, "Management Issues of Consortia—Part Two," *Library Management* 23, nos. 6/7 (2002): 275–86; Lisa German, "It's All About Teamwork: Working in a Consortial Environment," *Technicalities* 28, no. 3 (2008): 1, 12–15.

12. Magda El-Sherbini and Amanda J. Wilson, "New Strategies for Delivering Library Resources to Users," *Journal of Academic Librarianship* 33, no. 2 (2007): 241.

13. Joan C. Durrance and Karen E. Fisher, How *Libraries and Librarians Help: A Guide to Identifying User-Centered Outcomes* (Chicago: ALA, 2005): 4.

SUGGESTED READING

Adams, Katherine C. "Separate Means Unequal: Decrying the Marginalization of Technical Services." *American Libraries* 40, no. 4 (2009): 29.

Antelman, Kristin, and Mona Couts. "Embracing Ambiguity . . . Or Not: What the Triangle Research Libraries Network Learned About Collaboration." *College & Research Libraries News* 70, no. 4 (2009): 230–233.

Badertscher, Amy E. "Is There a Future for Technical Services?" In *Defining Relevancy: Managing the New Academic Library,* ed. Janet McNeil Hurlbert, 213–20. Westport, CT: Libraries Unlimited, 2008.

Barton, Hope, Michael Wright, and Randy Roeder. "It Never Ends . . . Technical Services and Planning in a Changing Environment." *Against the Grain* 19, no. 5 (2007): 46–52.

Boock, Michael. "Changes in Responsibilities, Organization and Staffing Within Technical Services Departments." *Technical Services Quarterly* 25, no. 3 (2008): 71–75.

Burke, Leslie, and Stephanie McConnell. "Technical Services Departments in the Digital Age: The Four R's of Adapting to New Technology." *Against the Grain*19, no. 5 (2007): 58–64.

Canepi, Kitti. "Work Analysis in Library Technical Services." *Technical Services Quarterly* 25 no. 2 (2007): 19–30.

DeVoe, Kristen. "Look How Far We've Come: Changing Technical Services Workflows." *Against the Grain* 19, no. 5 (2007): 1–16.

Greever, Karen E., and Debra K. Andreadis. "Technical Services Work Redesign Across Two College Libraries." *Technical Services Quarterly* 24, no. 2 (2006): 45–54.

McGurr, Melanie. "Improving the Flow of Materials in a Cataloging Department." *Library Resources & Technical Services* 52, no. 2 (2008): 54–60.

Medeiros, Norm. "The Catalog's Last Stand." *OCLC Systems & Services: International Digital Library Perspectives* 23, no. 3 (2007): 235–37.

Robertson, Sharon, and Anita Catoggio. "Strategic Procurement of Public Library Collections." *Australasian Public Libraries and Information Services* 20 no. 1 (2007): 20–27.

Rupp, Nathan, and Lisa Mobley. "Use of Technology in Managing Electronic Resource Workflow." *Against the Grain* 19, no. 5 (2007): 18–22.

Sanchez, Elaine. *Emerging Issues in Academic Library Cataloging & Technical Services.* New York: Primary Research Group, 2007.

Steele, Tom. "The New Cooperative Cataloging." *Library Hi Tech* 27, no. 1 (2009): 68–77.

Stump, Sheryl, and Rick Torgerson. "Keeping Your Plates Spinning: Technical Services Tasks from Delta State's Perspective." *Mississippi Libraries* 70, no. 2 (2006): 30–32.

Youngman, Daryl C. "Process Flow Analysis in Academic Libraries." *Technical Services Quarterly* 24, no. 1 (2007): 37–44.

Part II

◆

Acquisitions and Serials

5   Acquisitions—Overview

Acquisitions forms a vital link in the cycle of publishing, selection, request, and providing materials for use. The imperatives for acquisitions staff are to find and acquire material as quickly as possible, while offering an efficient and responsive service.

—Liz Chapman, 2004

The definition of "acquire" has also evolved far beyond purchasing, subscribing, and licensing. Acquisitions activities now include—and in the future will increasingly include—issues of rights management.

—Vera Fessler, 2007

The whats and hows of acquisitions work have probably changed more than other technical function during the 40-plus years this title has existed. Although our opening quotation from Liz Chapman could well have stood as opening to the chapter on acquisitions in the first edition of this book, how those basic roles currently play out is vastly different from the past. Vera Fessler's quotation suggests, in broad strokes, just what some of the changes entail.

The contribution of the acquisitions department to the library's public service function consists primarily of handling the business of ordering and receiving the materials selected for inclusion in the collection. Not all additions to the collection are the result of purchases; some are gifts or exchanges. The term "collections" goes far beyond physical objects. Much of the information libraries provide access to is electronic and most of those data are Web-based.

The acquisitions department is usually responsible for handling all the financial aspects associated with the library being able to legally make the information (print or electronic) available to the public. Most of the work requires some knowledge of computers, the Internet, and search techniques. Support staff does a large portion of the work in this department because very little of it requires graduate-level education. In some libraries, the acquisitions department does not have even one librarian staff member. Library acquisitions work only covers the procedures used in buying or otherwise acquiring materials for the collection. Acquiring office supplies and library equipment, such as computers, desks, or book trucks, is seldom part of the acquisitions department's duties.

A common misconception is that acquisitions departments determine what materials are in the library's collections. Decisions regarding what to add to a collection are rarely made in acquisitions, although even this is changing. The usual practice is that some other group (usually the collection development or selection staff) makes such decisions and passes the request on to the acquisition staff to secure the item.

COLLECTION DEVELOPMENT AND ACQUISITIONS

A library's mission, regardless of type, is to serve the information needs of its end-users. The purpose of collection development is to select materials to serve the information, educational, and/or recreational needs of its primary service community. However, broad objectives such as these are difficult to interpret because one person's recreation may be another's education. Each type of library—academic, public, school, or special—has a set of specific service objectives designed to support the community's activities. Selection officers must know the community and its information needs. They devote time gaining an understanding of the community or institution they serve as well as learning what materials are available to satisfy a given need. Limited financial resources mean most libraries can only acquire a percentage of the relevant and desired material during a budget cycle; thus, selection officers must decide which needs and items are the highest priority.

Selection policies help reduce some of the problems of making such decisions. In all but the smallest libraries, several individuals normally share the responsibility for selecting materials. Naturally, the involvement of several people in the selection process increases the need for coordinating and understanding selection procedures. Policies usually include all of the following:

- A statement regarding who has the authority to select materials. Often the director has this authority but delegates it to staff members. In such cases, this must be clearly stated.
- A statement concerning who is responsible for selecting materials.
- A statement of the library's goals and objectives for its collections.
- A list of the criteria for selecting materials.
- A list of review sources used in selecting materials.
- An outline of the procedures for handling problems (complaints about having or not having certain items).
- Guidelines for allocating available funds for the collections.

Collection development and acquisitions have always been closely coordinated, if not integrated, in libraries and information centers with successful programs. In an increasingly electronic environment, that coordination is vital. Joyce Ogburn noted:

> Managing an acquisitions program calls for a special set of skills and activities: assessment, prediction, control, choice, validation, and quantification. Libraries assess the risk and feasibility of acquisition, the availability of the resources, and the chances of success, control the system and methods needed, the choice of the source, the supporting services, and the resources themselves; and quantify the resources, work, and costs involved to conduct the business of acquisitions and measures of success.[1]

Such skills and activities are a constant, but today's libraries may need to draw upon the expertise of a number of staff members to acquire the desired electronic resources. Two of the factors that generate this need are that most e-resources are leased not purchased (legal contracts are the norm) and that many may be paid for through a consortia that may often have very different requirements for handling the acquisition process than a local library (more about both issues in later chapters).

Beyond the obvious purpose of supporting overall library objectives, the acquisitions department has both library-wide goals and departmental goals. Library-wide goals can be grouped into five broad areas of purpose:

- Develop a knowledge of information producers operations
- Help in the selection and collection development process
- Process requests for items to be added to the collection
- Monitor the expenditure of collection development funds
- Maintain all required records and produce reports regarding the expenditure of funds

By disseminating materials from the various information producers and vendors, the acquisitions department aids in the selection process, even if there is a duplication of information. Because most information producers are uncertain about who in the library makes purchasing decisions, they frequently send multiple copies of their promotional material to a library. This is not surprising, as producers buy a number of mailing lists to use when promoting a new or revised product, resulting in several copies of the promotional literature being received by a single staff member. However, a librarian should not assume that a promotional piece of no interest did, in fact, reach the appropriate staff member.

Acquisitions departments gather information regarding changes in publishing schedules, new producers, and new services from existing producers/suppliers. Many acquisitions departments serve as clearinghouses for this type of information for the library. Indeed, in larger libraries, the department sometimes operates a limited selective dissemination of information (SDI) system by routing information to selectors based on each individual's subject or area of responsibility. Despite the changing technological environment, there is no particular reason to change the location of such activities unless there is a major reorganization. Figure 5.1 illustrates the basic functions of an acquisitions department.

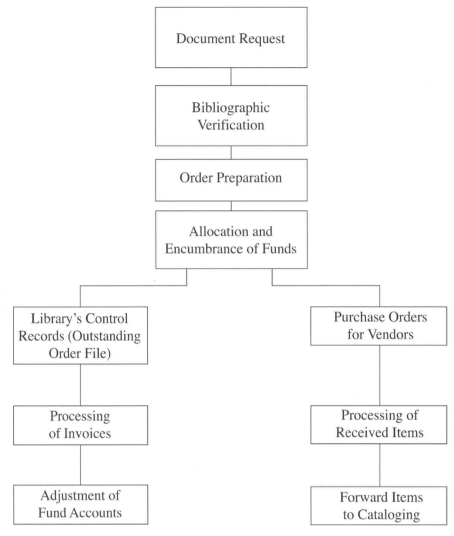

Figure 5.1. Acquisition process.

Acquisitions departments also have internal goals. Following are four common goals:

- Acquire materials as quickly as possible.
- Maintain a high level of accuracy in all work procedures.
- Keep work processes simple to achieve the lowest possible unit cost.
- Develop close, friendly working relationships with other library units and vendors.

Speed is a significant factor in meeting end-user expectations and determining their satisfaction, a key issue in how they assess the library's quality. A system that requires three or four months to secure items that are available in local bookstores will create a serious public relations problem. However, a system that is fast but error prone increases operating costs and wastes the time and energy of departmental staff and vendors. By keeping procedures simple and periodically reviewing workflow, the department can help the library provide top-quality service.

Speed, accuracy, and thrift should be the watchwords of acquisitions departments. Certainly online ordering, electronic invoicing, and credit-card payments greatly enhance the speed with which the department can handle much of the traditional paperwork. What has not changed much is the speed with which items actually arrive. The label "snail mail" is still all too often appropriate for the shipping speed, unless one is willing to pay a premium price for faster service.

As of 2010, the American Library Association (ALA) had four published standards/guidelines relating to acquisitions:

- *Guide to Performance Evaluation of Serial Vendors*
- *Guide to Selecting and Acquiring CD-ROMs, Software, and other Electronic Publications*
- *Guide to Handling Approval Plans*
- *Guide to Preservation in Acquisition Processing*

ALA has a number of other guidelines/standards for library activities that may have implications for acquisitions departments depending on the type of library and the service population. (To review the many options to consider, see the American Library Association Web site at http://www.ala.org/ala/aboutala/offices/ors/standardsa.)

TYPES OF MATERIALS ACQUIRED

Print Materials

Books and printed materials still represent a significant percentage of library purchases. Publishers in the United States still produce more than 30,000 new titles each year and more than 10,000 new editions. Even if libraries devoted all their acquisitions funds to buying print items, few could (and would want to) buy the total output. Large book jobbers, dealing only in English-language books, have hundreds of thousands of titles in stock. Out-of-print materials dealers have millions of English language titles for sale. Adding in books in all other languages the number is in the tens of millions. Almost any of these titles could be of interest to some library.

In addition to books, thousands of periodical and serial titles appear in print every year. Government documents—national, state, local, and international—are another category of printed material acquired by libraries of all sizes, although more and more of these items are in a being issued in digital format (see chapter 9). Further, many scholarly publications, dissertations, theses, and publications of learned societies primarily appear in print. Atlases, sheet maps (topographic maps; county highway maps; maps of national parks, forests, and recreation areas; aviation charts; and navigational charts), folded maps (highway maps), raised relief maps, and globes are staples in many library collections.

Printed music is another category of material that should be familiar to acquisitions department personnel. Piano-vocal scores, miniature scores, and monumental sets are in larger library collections. Pamphlets and ephemera of all types (broadsides, house organs, personal papers, and documents) are also part of material the acquisitions department orders and receives.

An unfolding issue at the time we prepared this chapter (in 2010) is the Google book-scanning project. The project and all its implications is much too complicated to cover in this book. However, if the courts uphold an agreement reached in 2008 between copyright holders and Google, the way libraries approach collection development may well change. Google has and is scanning millions of books housed in research libraries across the United States. Many of the books included in project are covered by copyright. Google plans on selling access to its scanned materials and has set aside money to compensate rights holders of titles still under copyright but not commercially available. One aspect that does not appear clear yet is whether "commercially available" includes the out-of-print dealers. In any event, the final court decision is likely to affect acquisitions work to some extent.

Nonbook Materials

Popular media formats are audiotapes (books on tape, for example), music CD recordings, and DVDs. Most libraries (medium-sized or larger) have at least a small audio collection. Public and school libraries tend to have larger media collections, and DVDs are among the most circulated items in many public libraries. Libraries face a number of challenges in acquiring these items, but many of the steps used to order a book apply to these other media as well (see chapter 10).

A format that is a crossover between paper and media is the microformat. Microfilm and microfiche are the two most common forms. They were a very common medium that saved shelf space for large quantities of relatively low-use print materials such as newspapers or collections of rare books. Many libraries still have legacy collections of microforms, and some out-of-print titles are only available in a microformat.

Electronic Resources

Electronic resources also come in a variety of forms: CDs, tape loads, and Web resources. Many of the products are variations of print-based materials, such as encyclopedias, indexes, and abstracting services. Others are the full text of print-based publications, such as books and journals. Still others are original publications in an electronic format. More and more products are appearing that are multimedia in character, including text, sound, and graphics. Each variation has some special features that must be taken into consideration at the time of acquisition. There are also special legal issues with electronic resources that do not arise with print-based items. These points are explored in chapter 7.

A library's collection exists to achieve certain objectives: education, information, aesthetic appreciation, recreation, and research. Each objective requires a different mix of formats. Aesthetic appreciation often requires recorded music, dramatic readings, and visual and graphic materials of various types. Research objectives often require acquiring report literature and conference papers and proceedings. The acquisition of these materials requires in-depth knowledge about the materials and suitable sources of supply.

GENERAL PROCEDURES

Staffing patterns vary in acquisitions departments, but a librarian is almost always the department's ultimate supervisor. As the workload increases, the library may divide the work into several subunits. Generally, support staff members have the supervisory responsibility for the subunits. A very large library might have separate units for verification, ordering, bookkeeping, receiving, bindery preparation, and gifts and exchange. Most verification activities are the responsibility of library support staff or part-time help.

Request Processing

The first step in the acquisitions process is to organize the incoming requests. Requests to purchase an item arrive in the department in a variety of forms, especially if nonlibrary staff are allowed to request material; they may range from oral requests to a scrawled note on a napkin, a completed request form, and everything in between. Department staff organize all requests to a standard format so they can carry out their work efficiently. Each library will have its own request form, generally in a paper version and an electronic version somewhere on the library's Web site, if the public may submit requests.

Commercially produced request cards cover all the following categories of information that suppliers need to accurately fulfill an order: author, title, publisher, date of publication, edition, International Standard Book Number (ISBN) or International Standard Serial Number (ISSN), Standard Address Number (SAN), price, and number of copies. Many forms provide space for other information that is of interest only to libraries, such as requester's name, series, vendor, funding source, and approval signature. Sample request forms are illustrated in Figures 5.2 and 5.3.

Order No.	Author:	L.C. No.
Dealer	Title	
Requested by:	Publisher: Year: Edition: Vols:	
Fund Chgd.	No. Copies:	List Price

Figure 5.2. Book request form.

```
┌─────────────────────────────────────────────────────────────────────┐
│                    SERIAL/PERIODICAL REQUEST CARD                     │
│   TITLE_____  │
│                                                                       │
│   _____ ISSN NO._____  │
│                                                                       │
│   VOL./YEAR REQUESTED _____ BACKSET _____  │
│                                                                       │
│   PUBLISHER _____ PLACE _____ PRICE_____     │
│                                                                       │
│   PRIORITY:_____CORE _____RELATED_____RESEARCH          │
│                                                                       │
│   COURSES IT WOULD SUPPORT (COURSE NO.): _____    │
│                                                                       │
│   REQUESTED BY _____ DATE _____    │
│                                                                       │
│   APPROVEDBY _____    │
│                                                                       │
│                                                                       │
│   PLEASE JUSTIFY THE SUBSCRIPTION TO THIS TITLE IN THE LIGHT OF OUR    │
│   VERY LIMITED BUDGET FOR NEW SERIALS.                                │
│   ACA/SER/01/10 rev.                                                  │
│                                                                       │
└─────────────────────────────────────────────────────────────────────┘
```

Figure 5.3. Serials request form.

Note that problems may arise with the request forms. For example, users sometimes request items already in the collection because they do not know how to use the public catalog effectively, or people occasionally combine or confuse authors' names, titles, publishers, and so forth. Therefore, verification work is normally the first step in acquisitions process.

Liz Chapman provided a good six-point checklist for designing or selecting a request form:

- Is it easy for users to fill in?
- Does it provide a logical checking route for library staff?
- Does the checked form reflect the order in which data will be input to the order system or put onto an order form?
- Does it provide an accessible format for checking during the stage *after* the book has been ordered but *before* it has arrived?
- Does it provide an efficient format for checking that the book you receive is the one you ordered?
- Will it be able to move with the book from acquisitions through cataloging and processing?[2]

Verifying

Verifying or searching consists of two steps: establishing the existence of a particular item and determining whether the library needs to order the item. In the first case, the concern is with identifying the correct author, title, publisher, and other necessary ordering data. In the second step, the process determines the library's need for the item: Is it already in the collection? Is it on order? Is it received but not yet represented in the public catalog? Is there a need for a second copy or multiple copies? These are a few examples of why the step is necessary. The ILSs make this latter step quick and easy, except for determining the need for additional copies. Many systems have the capability of displaying order and received status in the OPAC, which reduces the number of duplicate requests. (Most ILSs provide two modes of operation—staff and public. The library has options of how much information is displayed and in what form it will be available, such as the MARC record, in the public mode.)

Where to begin the process? The answer depends on the library's collection-development system. If the forms are filled out by experienced selection personnel, then determining the need is generally the most efficient way to start. A study by Karen Schmidt of incoming requests and the cost of preorder searching indicated that between 30 and 40 percent of nonlibrarian requests are incorrect or for items already in the collection.[3] When a large percentage of the requests are from users, it is advisable to start with determining the existence of the title requested.

Corporate authors (see chapter 15), conference papers, proceedings, or transactions are the most troublesome to search. Fortunately, keyword searching has eased, but not eliminated, the challenge. Titles do not change after publication and are easier to search. Main-entry searching requires a greater knowledge of cataloging rules, which, in turn, requires more time for training searchers and more time spent searching.

One area where technical services work can become challenging may arise at this stage. The question is who should establish the main entry? Certainly, it will save staff time if the data start off in the ILS in the desired form, and that will save time in the cataloging process. However, doing so requires more knowledge of cataloging on the part of the verification staff than was common in the past. Also, unless there was or is some rethinking of workload requirements the acquisitions department may find it difficult to take on new duties. Electronic capabilities make the determination relatively easy, however, if one understands the basics of cataloging.

There are some common problems to be aware of when doing verification work. One obvious problem is variant spellings of an author's name, both first and last, such as the last names Smith, Smythe, Johnson, or Johnsen or a first name such as Gail, Gale, or Gayle. Another problem is variations of the author's name that appear in a publication, for example, Ed Evans, Edward Evans, Edward G. Evans, G. Edward Evans, Gayle Edward Evans, or Gayle E. Evans. Each of these variations has appeared on at least one of Evans's publications. Corporate author entries provide even bigger challenges to the searcher's imagination and ingenuity (see chapter 15). Collected works and joint authors also present challenges for searchers. They must use their imagination when working with problem requests. Some libraries maintain a name-authority file (see chapter 15 for details), especially libraries with online catalogs, which can be of great assistance with variant forms of a name.

There are several files to check when establishing the library's need for an item; this is true whether the files are paper or electronic. The most obvious starting point is the OPAC. Starting with a title search is a sound approach; titles rarely change after publication. In some libraries, even if there is an online public catalog, there may be several other paper-based public catalogs to search, for example, special collections or a media catalog, and all should be part of the checking process, if appropriate. Audiovisual materials, government documents, serials, and collections in special locations often may not be fully represented in the OPAC because their records are not yet in digital form. Other public service files that searchers need to examine are those for lost, missing, or damaged items (replacement files). The searcher would not examine all of these files for all items, but merely for those requests for items found in the OPAC but not marked "added copy" or "replacement."

Online systems are available in many libraries to speed preorder checking. *Books in Print* is available in both a print and online version. Other commercial bibliographic selection aids are also available in electronic formats. Networks such as OCLC have large bibliographic databases that ease verification work. Integrated automation systems have eased the workload on some aspects of acquisitions. For example, it is possible to download bibliographic data from networks or from other libraries. With some systems, the staff can use the downloaded data to prepare a computer-generated order form, provide an online status report, and create the basis for local cataloging work. In some libraries, a person responsible for preorder activities may be able to do 90 percent or more of the work at one terminal merely by moving between the ILS and Internet.

Verification work can be quickly carried out employing the catalogs of the Library of Congress (LC; http://www.loc.gov), Library and Archives Canada (http://www.amicus.collectionscanada.ca/, which includes holdings of more than 1,300 Canadian libraries), the British Library (http://www.bl.uk/reshelp/), or the National Library of Australia (http://catalogue.nla.gov.au/). The LC search offers 14 options:

- Keyword
- Title keyword
- Author/creator keyword
- Subject keyword
- Name/title keyword
- Series/uniform title keyword
- Expert search
- Title begins with
- Author/creator browse
- Subject browse
- Call number browse (LC classification numbers)
- Call number browse (other shelving numbers)
- Number search (Library of Congress Control Number [LCCN], ISBN, ISSN)
- Author/creator sorted by title browse

The page also offers tips on how to best use each option. OCLC's WorldCat offers a basic and advanced search option. With the advanced option one can include keyword, title, and author, language, format, content, and audience—and limit by date—in a single search. Needless to say these sites cut down verification time dramatically. They can also supply cataloging data.

One of the authors (Evans) looks after a modest-size library (200,000+ items) and archives with the assistance of eight volunteers. In 2006, the library purchased a computer-based library system, ResourceMate. One of the attractions of the system is its modest cost and surprising capabilities. The software allows the user to go to the Library of Congress catalog, find the desired record, and import the MARC record into the local database. The program inserts the data in the proper fields and allows for importing of MARC data from a number of other libraries. The electronic capabilities make the limited amount of staff time much more productive for verification and cataloging work.

Verification, the first step in the acquisitions procedure, is perhaps the most interesting and challenging duty in this department. The attempt to establish an item's existence when there is very little information is similar to detective work.

Ordering

Today, most libraries use computer-generated orders and store the data electronically, thus reducing the volume of paper associated with ordering activities. A few libraries generate no paper order form for current trade books and handle the entire order process electronically, storing the transaction in both the library's and the supplier's computers. In the future, this may be the way all libraries place their orders; however, for thousands of libraries, the paperless order is not yet a reality.

Some years ago vendors and libraries agreed upon a set of guidelines for placing orders. (*Guidelines for Handling Library Orders for In-Print Monographic Publications,* 2nd ed. [Chicago: American Library Association, 1984]. Although no longer listed by ALA as an active guideline, almost all libraries implemented its key elements.) One suggestion is that libraries use the American National Standards Institute (ANSI) Committee Z39 single-title order form, which measures 3×5 inches (about 8×13 centimeters), a size that has been common for years in technical services units.

Regardless of the method used to order material, the vendor must receive enough information to ensure shipment of the proper item: author, title, publisher, date of publication, price, edition (if there are various editions), number of copies, order number, and any special instructions regarding invoicing or methods of payment. Also, more suppliers are asking for the ISBN or ISSN. In time, International Standard Numbers (ISNs) may be all the library needs to send, because ISNs are unique numbers representing a specific journal or a specific edition of a specific title. Other uses of these numbers are in cataloging, data processing, and public service activities, so it is important to understand ISBNs and how they work.

One important characteristic of ISBNs is that there is a unique ISBN for each edition of a book and for paper and hardbound versions. For example, the number for the first edition of this book was 0-87287-029-4; the second edition was 0-87287-125-8. The number for the hardbound version of the seventh edition was 1-56308-918-1 and the paper edition was, 1-56308-922-X. The number(s) before the first hyphen represents the country of origin; the second set of numbers is for the individual publisher; the third set represents the title, edition, and format; and the last number is a "check digit." Recently, a three-digit prefix has been added—either 978 or 979. The ISSN is an eight-digit number that identifies the publisher and title for periodicals. As with the ISBN, the last digit serves as the control. The ISBNs and ISSNs were both developed in the expectation of extensive computer use in book distribution.

From the point of view of some acquisitions departments, the ISBN is the *only* information needed to order a book from a jobber because it identifies the specific edition and binding. Ordering by ISBN could be a major time-saver: no more keying in of author, title, publisher, place, date, or price. However, mistakes might arise from just using the ISBN (e.g., transposed numbers, errors in copying). If the library provides author, title, and publisher, for example, the jobber may be able to provide the desired item despite a typographic error. Nevertheless, serious consideration should be given to using only the ISBN.

The ISBN is one of several ways to search for bibliographic data in an electronic environment. When one is searching hundreds of titles a day, saving 10 to 20 seconds per search is important.

Acquisitions department staff need to realize that because the ISBN *is* unique, it should only be used in conjunction with other search techniques to verify information about a title, not to determine if the library already has a copy of a particular book. A reprint of a particular title will have a different ISBN than the original; perhaps the requester does not know that the library already has the originally published edition. Further, if a book is published simultaneously in the United States and in Europe, each edition will have its own ISBN. Acquisitions department staff should be very careful that one person isn't ordering a particular book using the U.S. ISBN when another has just ordered the same title using the British or Canadian ISBN.

An article by Audrey Eaglen outlined other issues related to using ISBNs. Though Eaglen was writing in 1989, those same issues are still problems today. First, she noted that publishers sometimes use the number for inventory control, getting a new number for each reprinting of the title and using the number to track the number of copies sold from that print run. Second, publishers often only give part of the ISBN, usually the third element (title/edition) in their ads and promotional literature. A third problem she noted is that review media, when they include ISBNs, often do not list the correct number. She stated that, "Approximately ten percent of the ISBNs given in its (*PW*) 'Forecasts' reviews are simply incorrect."[4] These problems, combined with the fact that a book published in both cloth and paperback formats by different publishers in the United States and the United Kingdom can have four different ISBNs, illustrate the limitations of the system.

Another standard of ANSI Committee Z39 is the SAN. Like the ISBN, the SAN is a unique seven-digit number that identifies each address or organization doing business in the U.S. and Canadian book trade. For example, the SAN of the Loyola Marymount University's library is 332-9135, Brodart is 159-9984, Libraries Unlimited is 202-6767, and Thomas Allen & Son is 115-1762. Perhaps eventually all that will be necessary to order a title electronically will be three sets of unique numbers: the ISBN or ISSN and the SANs for the supplier and the buyer. Keys to SANs appear in a variety of sources, such as the *American Library Directory,* which includes library SANs in its entries.

Reporting

We mentioned speed of acquisitions as one measure users take into consideration when judging library quality, assuming they are allowed to submit requests. It is true that some of the desired titles may be available at local bookstores, but most are not. Also, when there is a special reason for doing so, a staff member can go to the store to purchase the title. (In the past, when there was a true independent bookstore with a strong stock, some libraries used bookstores as their primary jobber. It helped the local economy and generally led to faster delivery of desired titles. Today there few such stores' most bookstores are part of national chains that tend to focus on titles appealing to the mass market.)

Typically a 30-day window for delivery is standard for vendors, after which the library may reasonably start a claiming process. Paul Orkiszewski did a comparative study of Amazon.com and a library vendor and found that Amazon's average delivery time was two weeks while the major vendor's average was four weeks.[5] However, Amazon's cancellation rate was more than twice that of the vendor; further, of the 5,134 titles in the study sample, 327 were not available for ordering through Amazon. (We discuss Amazon and the above study in the next chapter.)

Vendors are supposed to report the status of titles not yet delivered upon receipt of a claim. Most integrated library system acquisitions modules have the ability to generate claim forms based on the order date and the expected delivery that the department establishes. Vendors should respond with a meaningful report within a reasonable period. One less than helpful report that vendors occasionally use is "temporarily out of stock." How long is "temporarily"? What has the vendor done to secure the item? Poor or inaccurate reporting costs the library money, as Audrey Eaglen pointed out in "Trouble in Kiddyland: The Hidden Costs of O.P. and O.S."[6] In periods of rapid inflation, each day a library's funds remain committed but unexpended erodes buying power because producers and suppliers may raise prices without notice. Recommended status descriptions on vendor reports are "not yet received from publisher"; "out-of-stock, ordering"; "claiming"; "canceled"; "not yet published"; "out-of-stock, publisher"; "out-of-print"; "publication canceled"; "out-of-stock indefinitely" (treat this one as a cancellation); "not our publication" (NOP); "wrong title supplied"; "defective copy"; and "wrong quantity supplied." After staff members learn how long, on average, a vendor takes to supply titles reported in one of the recommended categories, it is possible to make informed decisions regarding when to cancel and when to wait for delivery.

When dealing with U.S. publishers, allowing for the normal snail-mail time, it is reasonable to send a second claim 60 days after the first claim, if there has been no status report. Many order forms carry a statement reading "cancel after *x* days." Although such statements are legally binding, most libraries send a separate cancellation notice. (Note: The order slip is in fact a legal contract committing the library to pay for the item upon delivery.) Cancellation should not take place until after the normal response time passes, unless there are unusual circumstances. The most common occurrence is unexpected budget cuts; unfortunately, such cuts occur with some frequency. Most vendors are cooperative about making the adjustments. By establishing a regular cancellation date, libraries that must expend funds within a period of time (usually 12 months) can avoid or reduce the last-minute scramble of canceling outstanding orders and ordering materials that the vendor can deliver in time to expend the funds. (Budgets, timeframes, accounting, and expenditures are explored in greater detail in chapter 12.)

Before placing an order, the staff must make three important decisions:

- Which acquisition method to use.
- What vendor to use.
- What funding source to use.

Receiving Orders

When the boxes of ordered items arrive the department has a receiving process that must be followed if the library is to satisfy accountability requirements and ensure that funds are effectively spent.

The process commences with careful unpacking. Shipments arrive with a packing slip that should reflect every item in the shipment. A shipment may be one box or dozens; no matter how many boxes there are, there will be only one packing slip for the entire shipment. In a large library, there may be several shipments each day from different vendors or even the same vendor who sent an order in two shipments. It is very important to keep each shipment separated from the others as not doing so will make the following steps more complex than need be.

Step two is finding the packing slip for each shipment. Generally, this is easy as the shipper has attached a plastic envelope marked "packing slip" to one of the boxes, but that is not always the case. Sometimes the packing list is inside a box, even in the bottom of a box under a cardboard liner. Why all the bother about a packing slip? The slip is supposed to accurately reflect all the items in a shipment, which the vast majority of the time it does. However, when it does not match there could be problems between the vendor and library over completion of an order. Typical issues are an item is listed as part of the shipment but isn't there or items are in the shipment that were not ordered. (Note: It is useful to have available a copy of the order during the checking process.) Another common issue is too many or too few copies of an ordered title were shipped; again having the original order provides the correct information. (You can imagine the complexity of this seemingly simple activity if multiple shipments are intermixed.) Normally the packing slip will indicate if it is partial or complete order fulfillment. Some libraries also do a quick check of books to identify any obvious defects—missing or blank pages, or upside down text for example. Unfortunately, security is also an issue. When the material arrives there is no indication of who owns the item (almost all libraries "property mark" items in their collections). Commercial outlets refer to "shrinkage"—items that go missing—for libraries there is shrinkage both before and after items are added to the collections. The time between unpacking and property marking is a vulnerable period. Often there is insufficient time to fully process all of a day's shipments; leaving the material exposed is an invitation for some people to take something. The danger is particularly true for approval items (see later sections) when items remain, unmarked, in a location where selectors can look through the items *before* the library decides to acquire the title. Vendors are usually very accommodating about shipment errors, budget problems, defective copies, and so on, but generally are not willing to accept a title for return that has been "stamped, folded, stapled, and mutilated" as someone once referred to library property-marking activities. Media such as DVDs and audio recordings seem to be particularly prone to shrinkage.

The remainder of this chapter explores the methods of acquiring materials. Chapter 6 discusses vendors: when and how to use them and what to expect from them. Chapter 12 covers the fiscal side of acquisitions work.

ACQUISITION METHODS

Essentially, there are eight standard methods of acquisition—firm order, standing order, approval plans, blanket order, subscriptions (for serials departments), leases, gifts, and exchange programs. A *firm order* (orders in which desired items are individually named) is the usual method for titles that the library *knows* it wants. For most current items, a firm order is the only logical method to use. It is often the best method for the first volume in a series, even if the selectors believe they are likely to order the entire series. While it is possible to order directly from the producers, doing so takes substantially more time than placing an order for a number of titles from different producers with a jobber/wholesaler. The major drawback of this method is the time it takes to prepare the individual orders.

Standing orders (an open order for all titles fitting a particular category) are best for items that are serial in character and the library is confident it wants all the publications as they appear. Some examples are a numbered or unnumbered series from a publisher that deal with a single subject area. Another broad category is the irregular publications of a professional society—memoirs and special commemorative volumes, for example. The library places the order for the series or items rather like it places a journal subscription. The supplier (vendor or producer) automatically sends the items as they appear along with an invoice. There is a distinction between "thinking about" and "planning on" when considering series items. When the selector knows that the reputation of the publisher or editor of the series is sound, it is probably best to place a standing order. *If* the library knows it wants all the items, then a standing order will save staff time and effort due to the automatic shipments. However, especially in academic libraries, standing orders are often the result of a faculty member's request, and if the library does not periodically review its standing orders it may find that the requester left the institution years before or there is no longer an interest in the series' subject. The result is money spent on less useful items. If there is some question about suitability or content of the series, a firm order or approval copy order for the first volume is the better choice. Not all publisher's series are in fact quality titles, and in some cases they are almost, if not in fact, fraudulent. For example, in 1993 there were a number of e-mail messages on one of the collection development discussion lists regarding an article in *Lingua Franca* about a publisher that appeared to be a vanity house but that marketed books as part of a series.[7] (A vanity publisher simply prints any person's book as long as the individual pays all of the production costs.) Getting to know publishers and editors is an important activity for acquisitions department staff.

The greatest drawback to standing orders is their unpredictable nature in terms of numbers and cost. Certainly, there is no problem about numbers for the regular series, but their cost per item may vary. When it comes to publishers' series or irregular series, a library may go years without receiving a title, then receive several in one year. This is one of the areas where Joyce Ogburn's prediction skills come into play, as one must guesstimate how much money to set aside at the start of the budget year to cover standing order expenses.[8] Looking at past experience and using an average amount is a safe approach; however, the library is seldom able to set aside exactly the right amount. Committing (encumbering) too much money for too long may result in lost opportunities to acquire other useful items. Committing too little can result in not having the funds available to pay invoices when they arrive. Standing orders are a valuable acquisition method, but one that requires careful monitoring throughout the year.

Approval plans are, in a sense, a variation of the standing order concept. They involve automatic shipment of items to the library from a vendor along with automatic invoicing, after the library accepts the item. The differences are that the approval plan normally covers a number of subject areas and the library has the right to return titles it does not want. Approval plans can save staff time and effort when properly implemented. They can also be costly when not thoughtfully established and carefully monitored. Another advantage is the right to return unwanted items; the underlying assumption is that collection development staff can make better decisions about an item's appropriateness by looking at the item before committing to its purchase. However, there is research evidence that indicates the approval plan can result in a substantially higher number of very low or no-use items being added to the collection.[9]

The key element in making the approval plan a cost-effective acquisition method is creating a sound profile with the plan vendor. A profile outlines the parameters of the plan and covers issues such as subjects desired, levels of treatment (e.g., undergraduate, graduate), languages/countries coverage, no reprints, no collections of reprinted articles, and so forth. The more time devoted to defining the profile, as well as monitoring the actual operation of the plan and making adjustments, the greater the value of an approval plan to the library and the acquisitions department. Monitoring operations and actually reviewing the item are also obvious keys to success. Given the staffing situation in most libraries, there is a real danger that the plan will shift from approval to blanket order, simply because the staff has to attend to many pressing duties, leaving them little time for the task of reviewing approval titles.

A *blanket order* is a combination of a firm order and an approval plan. It is a commitment on the library's part to purchase all of something, usually the output of a publisher, or items in a limited subject area, or items from a particular country. In the case of a subject area or country, there is a profile developed between the library and the blanket-order vendor. The materials arrive automatically along with the invoice, thus saving staff time. Another advantage, for country blanket order plans, is that they ensure that the library acquires a copy of limited print runs. (It is not uncommon to have very limited print runs of scholarly items in many countries. If the library waits for an announcement or a listing in a national bibliography before ordering, there may be no copies available to purchase.) Like the standing order, the major drawback of blanket-order plans is predicting how much money the library will need to reserve to cover the invoices. There is even less predictability with blanket-order plans because there are more variables.

Subscriptions, for journals, newspapers, and many other serials, are a combination of standing and blanket orders. A library may enter a subscription for a given time frame just as an individual does for personal magazines. However, rather than going through an annual renewal process, many libraries enter into an agreement with a serials vendor to automatically renew subscriptions until the library requests a cancellation (called "'til forbidden orders"). This saves the library and vendor staff time and paperwork and is a cost-effective system for titles the library is *certain* are of long-term interest to end-users.

Leases are now commonplace for handling electronic resources, especially those that are Web based. The decision to lease is almost always in the hands of the supplier rather than the library, although sometimes a library can buy the product, usually at a substantially higher price. The difference between buying and leasing has significant implications for the library and its users. In short, the library pays for *access* to the information for as long as it pays the annual fee. At the end of a lease the library generally loses all access to the material it was paying for, although some suppliers will provide long-term access to the material that was available during the lease period.

Chapters 7 and 8 provide more information about this and other issues related to electronic resources.

Frequently, the acquisitions department is the library's designated recipient of unsolicited *gifts* of books, serials, and other materials (sometimes accompanied by a variety of molds and insects) that well-meaning people give to the library. Solicited and unsolicited gifts can be a source of important out-of-print materials for replacement, extra copies, and the filling of gaps in the collection. The collection-development policy statement on gifts will help acquisitions personnel process the material quickly. A good article outlining all aspects of handling gifts is Mary Bostic's "Gifts to Libraries: Coping Effectively."[10] Another excellent survey of both gift and exchange programs is by Steven Carrico; it covers all management aspects of the work.[11]

Reviewing gifts is important, as a library cannot afford to discard valuable or needed items that arrive as gifts. However, the library must keep in mind the fact that it should not add unnecessary items just because they were free. Processing and storage costs are the same for a gift as for a purchased item. Older books require careful checking, as variations in printings and editions may determine whether an item is valuable or worthless. (Usually, a second or third printing is less valuable than the first printing of a work.) Persons with extensive training and experience in bibliographic checking must do the searching.

Steven Carrico provides an excellent summary of the advantages and disadvantages of gift programs:

Positive Points of Gifts

1. Gifts can replace worn and missing items in a library.
2. Out-of-print desiderata often surface from gift donations.
3. Gifts can foster communication and goodwill in a library community.
4. Gifts may become heavily used or important research additions to a collection.
5. Some titles that are not available by purchase are available as gifts.
6. Worthwhile gift material not selected for a library collection can be put in a book sale, sold to dealers, or given away to underfunded libraries and institutions.

Negative Points

1. Gifts require staff time and are costly to process.
2. Dealing with even well meaning gift donors is frequently an aggravation to staff.
3. Gifts take up precious space in a library.
4. Many collection managers give gifts low priority, so they may sit on review shelves for a long time.
5. A large percentage of most gifts are not added to a collection, which creates disposal problems.
6. Overall, since most gift books added to a collection are older editions, they will be less frequently used by library patrons.[12]

There are some legal aspects about gifts, at least in the United States, that staff must understand. One Internal Revenue Service (IRS) regulation relevant to libraries has to do with gifts and donations to a library or a not-for-profit information center. Any library, or its parent institution, that receives a gift in-kind (books, journals, manuscripts, and so forth) with an appraised value of $5,000 or more must report the gift to the IRS. A second regulation forbids the receiving party (in this case the library) from providing an estimated value for the gift in-kind. A disinterested party or organization must make the valuation. The latter requirement grew out of concern that recipients were placing unrealistically high values on gifts. The donor received a larger tax deduction than was warranted, and it did not cost the receiving organization anything to place a high value on the gift. Normally, an appraiser charges a fee for valuing gifts, and the donor is supposed to pay the fee. Most often, the appraisers are antiquarian dealers who charge a flat fee for the service unless the collection is large or complex. If the appraisal is complex, the appraiser either charges a percentage of the appraised value or an hourly fee.

Typically, with gifts thought to be worth less than $4,999, the library may write a letter of acknowledgment indicating the number and type of items received. For gifts of less than $250, the IRS does not require a letter. The donor can set a value on the gift for tax purposes. (The best practice is to provide a letter for any accepted gift.) If asked, the library can provide dealer catalogs for the donors to see retail prices for items similar to their donation. However, the final value of the gift is established by the donor and his tax accountant.

To meet IRS requirements, a letter must contain the library's name, the date of the contribution, the location/place of the gift (even if it is the library), and a description of the gift. At a minimum that description should provide number and kind of gift (for example, 100 mass-market paperbacks, 40 hardcover books, six complete and unbound volumes of *National Geographic*). More information regarding these regulations can be found in the IRS publications *Charitable Contributions* (IRS Publication No. 526) and *Charitable Contributions—Substantiation and Disclosure* (IRS Publication No. 1771). Both are available online at http://www.irs.gov/formspubs/index.html.

Donations and gifts also present an acquisitions option that can be appropriate at times. Sometimes a library user or board member donates personal books or magazines on a regular basis, making it unnecessary to order the item if there is no immediate demand for the material. Occasionally, an appropriate series or set costs so much a library cannot buy it with regular funding sources. Seeking a donor to assist with funding or to pay for the purchase is not unheard of, but again, there may be substantial delays in acquiring the item. Most often, this takes place with rare books and special collections items. An active (and well-to-do) Friends of the Library group may be the answer to a special purchase situation. Friends groups, used judiciously, can significantly expand the collection and stretch funds.

Deciding to use the gift method of acquisition will almost always result in a long delay in receiving the desired item. This is also true of the deposit method of acquisition. Verification may establish that an item is a government publication that may be part of the library's depository program, or it may be a new government series that is expected to become part of the program. In either case, the acquisitions staff would not issue a firm order but would notify the requester so that she can decide what to do.

The final acquisition category is the *exchange* method. There are two basic types of exchange activity: the exchange of unwanted duplicate or gift materials and the exchange of new materials between libraries. Usually, only large research libraries engage in exchange of new materials. In essence, cooperating institutions trade institutional publications. Tozzer Library (Harvard University's anthropology library) has exchange agreements with several hundred organizations. These organizations send their publications to Tozzer, which, in turn, sends them Peabody Museum publications. Often, this method is the only way a library can acquire an organization's publications, especially from countries with a developing book trade.

Occasionally, libraries use this system to acquire materials from countries in which there are commercial trade restrictions. Where government trade restrictions make buying and selling of publications from certain countries difficult or impossible, the cooperating libraries acquire (buy) their local publications for exchange. Exchanges of this type are complex and difficult to manage, and this is a method of last resort. Libraries can exercise better quality control when they trade for known organizational series or titles than when the choice of publications from the organization is more or less left to chance. Exchanges of this type exist on the basis of formal agreements between the cooperating organizations. They play an important role in developing comprehensive subject collections.

The Canadian Book Exchange Centre (CBEC), a service operated by the Library and Archives Canada, is a redistribution center and a clearinghouse for the exchange of materials in all formats between libraries. The service is free, although participating libraries must pay shipping charges. Individuals can donate items to the centre but cannot receive items in exchange. Details about CBEC's activities can be found at www.nlc-bnc.ca/6/10/index-e.html.

Libraries normally add only a small percentage of unsolicited gifts to the collection. This means the library must dispose of many unwanted items. In some libraries, a separate unit, usually is called the exchange department, handles unneeded material. In most cases, the gift unit handles the disposal work.

Disposition of unwanted gift materials is an activity that almost every library engages in at some time. One method is to list the unwanted items and mail the list to exchange units in other libraries, and the first library to request an item gets it for the shipping cost (usually media rate postage). This method is time-consuming and takes up scarce shelf space in many libraries. Another method is to arrange with an out-of-print dealer to take the items, usually as a lot rather than for a per-item price. It is unusual to receive cash, however; instead, the dealer gives the library a line of credit. The library then uses the credit to acquire materials from the dealer. This system works well when the library has specialized materials the dealer wants and when the dealer stocks enough useful material so that the library can use its credit within a reasonable time (18 to 24 months).

Holding a book sale is yet another method of disposing of unwanted material, one that is gaining in popularity as dealers resist the credit-memo system. However, this is not a free venture, as staff must select the items for sale, establish a fair price, find a suitable location, and monitor the sale. Depending on the volume of gifts, annual, semiannual, or monthly sales are appropriate. Sales can be an excellent Friends of the Library project that can save some staff time. A few libraries use an ongoing sale tactic, especially when they have limited staff and space and a high volume of unwanted gifts. There is a Web site devoted to listing book sales in the United States, including library book sales (http://www.book-sales-in-america.com).

SERIALS PROCESSING

Users and librarians often want to know the library's exact holdings for a journal or magazine. Are some issues missing? What is the latest issue? When did the library last pay for the subscription? How often does the library bind the issues? What is the publication's format? Where can the library subscribe to a particular periodical? The ILS serials software can easily supply such information and can even display the latest issue received information in the OPAC, but without careful data entry much of the software's capability is lost.

Most librarians agree that serials control constitutes one of the major record-keeping headaches in technical services. The basic method is to employ a control record for each title. This can be a page in a notebook, a 3- × 5-inch (about 8- × 13-centimeter) card file, a card in a visible file (see Figures 5.4 and 5.5), or a computer record. A single record should contain all information for a given title, such as when the subscription began, its acquisition source, renewal frequency, and binding information.

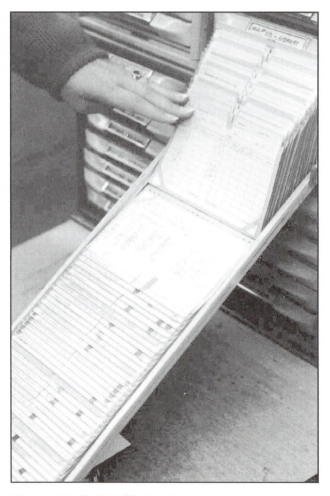

Figure 5.4. Visible file check-in system.

Figure 5.4—*Continued*

PUBLISHERS ADDRESS						ORDER NO.	
						DATE	
						FUND	
SOURCE						BIND	

YEAR & VOL.	INVOICE NO.	COST	CLAIM RECORD	YEAR & VOL.	INVOICE NO.	COST	CLAIM RECORD

ACME VISIBLE CROZET VIRGINIA #88055-6

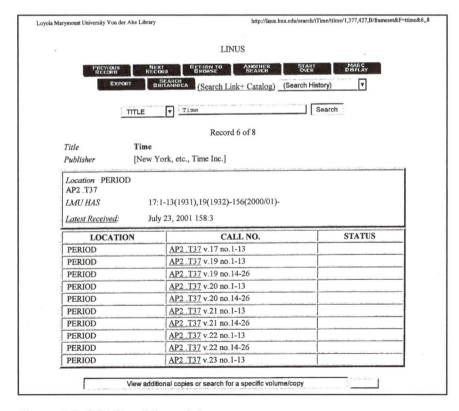

Figure 5.5. OPAC public serials screen.

Figure 5.5—*Continued*

```
 C1041435            Last updated: 09-27-01 Created: 09-29-94 Revision: 488
 TITLE        Time
 LOCATIONS    lmlp                 CALL #      AP2 .T37
 NOTE         Library keeps both formats (mfm & print)

Boxes 1 to 84 of 84
|    Jul 3|    Jul 10|    Jul 17|    Jul 24|    Jul 31|    Aug 7|    Aug 14|
| BOUND    | BOUND    | BOUND    | BOUND    | BOUND    | BOUND    | BOUND    |
| 05-18-01 | 05-18-01 | 05-18-01 | 05-18-01 | 05-18-01 | 05-18-01 | 05-18-01 |
|156:1    1|156:2    1|156:3    1|156:4    1|156:5    1|156:6    1|156:7    1|
|    Aug 21|    Aug 28|    Sep 4|    Sep 11|    Sep 18|    Sep 25|    Oct 2|
| BOUND    | BOUND    | BOUND    | BOUND    | BOUND    | BOUND    | BOUND    |
| 05-18-01 | 05-18-01 | 05-18-01 | 05-18-01 | 05-18-01 | 05-18-01 | 06-26-01 |
|156:8    1|156:9    1|156:10   1|156:11   1|156:12   1|156:13   1|156:14   1|
|    Oct 9|    Oct 16|    Oct 23|    Oct 30|    Nov 6|    Nov 13|    Nov 20|
| BOUND    | BOUND    | BOUND    | BOUND    | BOUND    | BOUND    | BOUND    |
| 06-26-01 | 06-26-01 | 06-26-01 | 06-26-01 | 06-26-01 | 06-26-01 | 06-26-01 |
|156:15   1|156:16   1|156:17   1|156:18   1|156:19   1|156:20   1|156:21   1|
|    Nov 27|    Dec 4|    Dec 11|    Dec 18|         |    Win 01|    Jan 8|
| BOUND    | BOUND    | BOUND    | BOUND    | BOUND    | BOUND    | BOUND    |
| 06-26-01 | 06-26-01 | 06-26-01 | 06-26-01 |Dec25/Jan1|Life issue| 09-27-01 |
|156:22   1|156:23   1|156:24   1|156:25   1|156:26   1|156:27   1|157:1    1|
|    Jan 15|    Jan 22|    Jan 29|    Feb 5|    Feb 12|    Feb 19|    Feb 26|
| BOUND    | BOUND    | BOUND    | BOUND    | BOUND    | BOUND    | BOUND    |
| 09-27-01 | 09-27-01 | 09-27-01 | 09-27-01 | 09-27-01 | 09-27-01 | 09-27-01 |
|157:2    1|157:3    1|157:4    1|157:5    1|157:6    1|157:7    1|157:8    1|
|    Mar 5|    Mar 12|    Mar 19|    Mar 26|    Apr 2|    Apr 9|    Apr 16|
| BOUND    | BOUND    | BOUND    | BOUND    | BOUND    | BOUND    | BOUND    |
| 09-27-01 | 09-27-01 | 09-27-01 | 09-27-01 | 09-27-01 | 09-27-01 | 09-27-01 |
|157:9    1|157:10   1|157:11   1|157:12   1|157:13   1|157:14   1|157:15   1|
|    Apr 23|    Apr 30|    May 7|    May 14|    May 21|    May 28|    Jun 4|
| BOUND    | BOUND    | BOUND    | BOUND    | BOUND    | BOUND    | BOUND    |
| 09-27-01 | 09-27-01 | 09-27-01 | 09-27-01 | 09-27-01 | 09-27-01 | 09-27-01 |
|157:16   1|157:17   1|157:18   1|157:19   1|157:20   1|157:21   1|157:22   1|
|    Jun 11|    Jun 18|    Jun 25|    Jul 2|    Jul 9|    Jul 16|    Jul 23|
| BOUND    | BOUND    | BOUND    | BOUND    | ARRIVED  | ARRIVED  | ARRIVED  |
| 09-27-01 | 09-27-01 | 09-27-01 | 09-27-01 | 07-03-01 | 07-10-01 | 07-18-01 |
|157:23   1|157:24   1|157:25   1|157:26   1|158:1    1|158:2    1|158:3    1|
|    Jul 30|    Aug 6|    Aug 13|    Aug 20|    Aug 27|    Sep 3|    Sep 10|
| ARRIVED  | ARRIVED  | ARRIVED  | ARRIVED  | ARRIVED  | ARRIVED  | ARRIVED  |
| 07-24-01 | 08-07-01 | 08-14-01 | 08-22-01 | 08-30-01 | 09-07-01 |
|158:4    1|158:5    1|158:6    1|158:7    1|158:8    1|158:9    1|158:10   1|
|    Sep 17|    Sep 11|    Sep 24|    Fal 01|    Oct 1|    Oct 8|    Oct 15|
| ARRIVED  | ARRIVED  | ARRIVED  | ARRIVED  | ARRIVED  | EXPECTED | E        |
| 09-11-01 |Special is|Special is|Special is| 09-24-01 | 10-10-01 | 10-17-01 |
|158:11   1|158:12   1|158:13   1|158:14   1|158:15   1|158:16    |158:17    |
|    Oct 22|    Oct 29|    Nov 5|    Nov 12|    Nov 19|    Nov 26|    Dec 3|
| E        | E        | E        | E        | E        | E        | E        |
| 10-24-01 | 10-31-01 | 11-07-01 | 11-14-01 | 11-21-01 | 11-28-01 | 12-05-01 |
|158:18    |158:19    |158:20    |158:21    |158:22    |158:23    |158:24    |
|    Dec 10|    Dec 17|    Dec 24|    Dec 31|    Jan 7|    Jan 14|    Jan 21|
| E        | E        | E        | E        | E        | E        | E        |
| 12-12-01 | 12-19-01 | 12-26-01 | 01-02-02 | 01-09-02 | 01-16-02 | 01-23-02 |
|158:25    |158:26    |159:1     |159:2     |159:3     |159:4     |159:5     |
```

SUMMARY

Acquisition work is detail oriented and moderately complex; it is also interesting and challenging at times. It calls for knowledge of information producers. It also involves a number of legal issues, for example, a firm order slip is a contract, electronic products come with contracts and lease forms, and even gifts may have legal implications. Technology helps acquisitions staff members keep up with an ever-increasing volume of work; however, it is still the individuals who take the time to really understand the information trade that make the process work as well as it does.

REVIEW QUESTIONS

1. Identify the major purpose(s) of library collections.

2. Discuss the basic elements and purposes of book selection policies.

3. How is materials selection handled in public libraries? How does this differ from selection in educational institution libraries?

4. Discuss the factors that require close cooperation between selectors and acquisitions department.

5. What are the typical kinds of materials a library acquires?

6. Discuss the three broad categories of acquisitions work.

7. What are the steps in preorder work? Discuss each.

8. What are the three special numbers associated with the book trade and acquisitions work that save time?

9. Discuss the various vendor reports that libraries receive regarding the orders they place.

10. What are the three key decisions that the acquisitions department makes about acquiring an item?

11. List and discuss each of the methods of acquisitions. What are the advantages and disadvantages of each?

12. Discuss the legal issues associated with gifts to U.S. libraries.

13. Discuss the steps in the receiving process.

14. What challenges do e-serials present in terms of receipt?

NOTES

The epigraphs for this chapter are from Liz Chapman, *Managing Acquisitions in Libraries and Information Services* (London: Facet Publishing, 2004) and Vera Fessler, "The Future of Technical Services," *Library Administration & Management* 21, no. 3 (2007): 141.

1. Joyce L. Ogburn, "T2: Theory in Acquisition Revisited," *Library Acquisitions* 21, no. 2 (1997): 168.

2. Chapman, *Managing Acquisitions.*

3. Karen Schmidt, "Cost of Pre-order Searching," in *Operational Costs in Acquisitions,* ed. J. Coffey (New York: Haworth Press, 1990).

4. Audrey Eaglen, "The ISBN: A Good Tool Sorely Misused," *Collection Building* 10, no. 1 (1989): 76.

5. Paul Orkiszewski, "A Comparative Study of Amazon.com as a Library Book and Media Vendor," *Library Resources & Technical Services* 49, no. 3 (2005): 204–9.

6. Audrey B. Eaglen, "Trouble in Kiddyland: The Hidden Costs of O.P. and O.S.," *Collection Building* 6, no. 2 (1984): 26–28.

7. Warren St. John, "Vanity's Fare: The Peripatetic Professor and His Peculiarly Profitable Press," *Lingua Franca* 3, no. 5 (1993): 1, 22–25, 62.

8.   Ogburn, "T2: Theory in Acquisition Revisited."

9.   G. Edward Evans, "Book Selection and Book Collection Usage in Academic Libraries," *Library Quarterly* 40, no. 3 (1970): 297–308; and G. Edward Evans, "Approval Plans and Collection Development in Academic Libraries," *Library Resources & Technical Services* 18, no. 1 (1974): 35–50.

10.   Mary Bostic, "Gifts to Libraries: Coping Effectively," *Collection Management* 14, nos. 3/4 (1991): 175–84.

11.   Steven Carrico, "Gifts and Exchanges," in *Business of Acquisitions,* 2nd ed., ed. K. Schmidt (Chicago: American Library Association, 1999).

12.   Ibid., 210.

SELECTED WEB SITES AND DISCUSSION LISTS

025.2 Acquisitions (AcqLink), http://bubl.ac.uk/link/linkbrowse.cfm?menuid=1026

AcqWeb, http://www.acqweb.org/

ALCTS Publications Acquisitions Bibliography, http://www.ala.org/ala/mgrps/divs/alcts/resources/index.cfm

SERIALST Discussion Forum, http://www.uvm.edu/%7ebmaclenn/serialst.html

SUGGESTED READING

Barnes, Matt, Jon Clayborne, and Suzy Szazz Palmer. "Book Pricing: Publisher, Vendor, and Library Perspectives." *Collection Building* 24, no. 3 (2005): 87–91.

Fowler, David, and Janet Arcand. "Monographs Acquisitions Time and Cost Studies." *Library Resources & Technical Services* 47, no. 3 (2003): 109–24.

Furr, Patricia. "Electronic Acquisitions: How E-Commerce May Change the Way That Your Library Buys Books." *Mississippi Libraries* 70, no. 2 (2006): 26–27.

Ward, Judith. "Acquisitions Globalized: The Foreign Language Acquisitions Experience in a Research Library." *Library Resources & Technical Services* 53, no. 2 (2009): 86–93.

6

Distributors and Vendors

Vendors are liaisons among content providers, the vendor, and librarians—a task that requires diplomacy as well as solid communications skills.

—Carol Tenopir, 2005

During my regular work day, I spend a lot of time contacting vendors to resolve problems, claim missing serial issues, order replacements, set up new standing orders and subscriptions, obtain price quotes, sort out billing questions, and track down problems with online access. No two vendor customer service operations are alike and many of them are slowly driving me up a wall.

—Anne Myers, 2009

"Select the vendor," is a simple phrase that belies the complexity and importance to a library's quality of service and, in part, its financial condition. Without the assistance of vendors and distributors, libraries would need to vastly increase technical services staffing to handle the increased workload. Or they simply would not be able to make available all the resources they currently offer because the existing staff would be overloaded with work. As the Tenopir epigraph states, vendors are in the middle between content creators and providers and the library. They provide a consolidation point for acquisitions work. They offer services that are substantially lower in cost than what the library could and often offer services requiring skills that do not exist among the library staff.

All units in technical services use some form outsourcing (binding of materials for example) or vendor services (purchasing books for example). Vendors come in a variety of forms—for-profit (subscription agencies and retail outlets are two such types) and nonprofit (consortia and Library of Congress are examples). Most libraries use one or more vendors of each type. In terms of acquisitions work, some vendors are broad based (offering a variety of formats, books, audio recordings, and videorecordings) while others are highly specialized such as scientific, technical, and medical (STM) firms. One advantage of using a vendor for purchasing collection items is that one order to a vendor can supply material from a variety of producers. There is a trade-off, however, between one-stop shopping convenience and the possibility of receiving a larger discount by going directly to the producer. Thus, in making that simple act of selecting the vendor, the staff must understand what vendor is the best choice for the particular need and whether it would be more advantageous to deal directly with the producer.

MAKING THE SELECTION—FACTORS TO CONSIDER

Much of the following applies to almost all vendors that a library might go to for a product or service. The following material focuses on vendors who support the library's acquisition functions. Six broad categories usually come into play in making a selection: what is commonly carried (normal stock), the firm's technological capability, how quickly the firm is likely to deliver materials (order fulfillment), the firm's financial condition and discounts offered, the range of services available, and customer service. It is essential to remember that in most instances there will be a contract, with all the legalities that entails, once a choice is made. The contract will specify all the terms and conditions, many of which could have serious financial consequences for the library should the library wish to cancel or otherwise modify the agreement.

What the Firm Stocks

When looking for a source for collection items a key concern is what the company usually carries in stock. Vendors' Web sites often claim "Over xxx million items in our warehouse" or something very similar. That is not useful information; it could mean there are many copies of a few thousand titles. What is useful is having a list of all the producers and publishers the firm regularly carries in its warehouses and what series, producers, and publishers they do *not* carry—such a list may be surprisingly long and have unexpected names. What are the vendor's specialties, if any? For example, Baker & Taylor specializes in public and school library markets while Midwest Library Service's primary focus is academic libraries. Sales representatives often say the firm can supply *any* title from *any* publisher, with only minor exceptions. While it may be possible for a general (primarily mass-market titles) book supplier to secure STM titles, the delays in delivery may be excessive. Knowing which publishers the vendor does not handle helps maintain good working relations in the long run, although securing that information may prove to be challenging.

Vendor Technological Capability

In this category, probably the key question is, does the firm's system have an interface that will work effectively with the library's integrated library system (ILS)? If the answer is yes, may the library have a free test period to determine those capabilities prior to signing a contract? Other technology concerns include whether the firm offers free online preorder checking, electronic ordering, invoicing, payments, claiming, technology support/troubleshooting, and hours of availability. Today the technological issues are almost as important as the firm's stock.

Speed of Delivery

As mentioned several times, speed of fulfillment of requests is one measure by which the user community judges the quality of service. Thus, it is not surprising that vendor speed of fulfillment is a factor in making a final decision about which vendor to employ. Information about the average delivery time from the vendor ought to be cross-checked with some of the vendor's current customers. (There should be no hesitation on the vendor's part in supplying a list of current customers. It also often pays to contact customers not on the list as a further cross-check.)

Many ILS systems are capable of producing a report similar to the one shown in the Vendor Performance Statistics chart. Thus, libraries can reasonably quickly tell you what their actual experience with the firm has been.

VENDOR PERFORMANCE STATISTICS—DELIVERY TIME
PROCESSED RECORD # : 1583591 TO 1984433
COUNT ORDERS PLACED IN PERIOD 06-01-09 TO 04-20-10

	Avg Del Time	02 wks	04 wks	08 wks	12 wks	16 wks	17+ wks
1 a&e	7.7	0	2	5	0	0	1
2 abc	10.3	21	323	3020	1506	369	622
3 abca	0.0	5208	1	3	1	0	1
4 abcc	3.1	115	3	11	0	1	7
5 aber	6.2	1	8	10	3	1	1
6 aip	3.0	0	1	0	0	0	0
7 ala	0.6	54	1	1	1	1	0
8 alss	6.7	1	1	5	2	0	0
9 ama	0.0	1	0	0	0	0	0
10 amazc	3.4	10	3	5	1	0	0
11 amb	13.5	9	31	1194	831	252	370

Vendor Performance Statistics—Percentages Processed Record No.: 1583591 to 1984433 Count Orders Placed in Period 6/01/09 to 4/20/10

Each row in the report represents a firm that a hypothetical library uses to secure its collection material. This type of report capability is highly useful for evaluating vendor performance (more about this activity later in this chapter).

Many vendors promise 24-hour shipment of items in stock. Do they make good on such claims? Generally, yes; however, the key phrase is *in stock*. Frequently, there can be delays of three to four months in receiving a complete order because one or more titles are not in stock. For the library and the vendor, such delays are problematic. Generally, the acquisitions department cannot authorize payment for anything less than a completed order. A delay of several months beyond the normal lag time in payment (see later in the chapter) can cause a financial burden for the vendor. One way around the issue is to cancel those items that will take extra time to deliver (so the current order is then completed) and reorder them when they are in stock. That approach is time consuming for the library. Addressing such issues prior to signing a contract is in everyone's best interest.

Financial Considerations

There is more to consider in this category than what, if any, the discount may be; however, the discount rate is a topic acquisitions departments frequently discuss when they get together. Certainly, the discount rate is important, but what is equally important is to what percentage of the items that discount rate applies and whether there are classes of material that carry service charges rather than a discount. There is also the possibility the rate will be dependent upon the contracted dollar amount spent with the firm within a specified period (the greater the amount spent, the higher the discount).

Discounting, especially in the book trade is something of a maze. The discount the library may receive is dependent upon the discount the vendor receives from the producers or publishers. Because vendors buy in volume, they receive a substantial discount from producers. When they sell a copy of the highly discounted title to the library, the library receives a discount off the producer's list price. However, that is substantially lower than the discount the vendor received. Clearly, there must be a profit margin for the firm to stay in business. For example, if the vendor received a 40 percent discount from the producer, the discount given the library will be 15 to 20 percent. If the library ordered the title directly from the producer, there is a slight chance the discount may be about the same level (10 to 20 percent). The advantage for the library of going with a vendor rather than with the producer directly comes about from staff savings. That is, being able to send the vendor one order for titles from dozens of producers rather than creating dozens of orders for each producer.

Book-trade discounting is particularly complex. Every publisher's discount schedule is slightly different, if not unique. Some items are *net* (no discount); usually these are textbooks, STM titles, or items of limited sales appeal. *Short discounts* are normally 20 percent; these are items the producers expect will have limited appeal but that have more potential than the net titles. *Trade discounts* range from 30 to 60 percent or more; items in this category are high-demand items or high-risk popular fiction such as first time authors. Publishers believe that by giving a high discount for fiction, bookstores will stock more copies and thus help promote the title. Vendors normally receive 40 to 50 percent discounts, primarily because of their high-volume orders (hundreds of copies per title rather than the tens that most libraries and independent bookstore owners order).

One important financial issue is how the firm handles invoicing, especially how long the library has to make the payment without incurring a late charge. For most libraries anything less than 60 days will pose a serious problem. Very few libraries have authority to issue a payment; what they have is the authority to indicate to the parent institution's (city, school district, academic institution, or company) business office that the invoice should be paid. The process of moving the invoice through the system and getting the check or voucher drawn up and in the hands of the vendor almost always takes more than 30 days. An occasional rush payment is usually possible, but the occasions must be few and far between not the norm. For smaller vendors the time lag may be more than it can handle on a regular basis.

Some vendors will order a single title from a publisher when it is not in stock in order to fulfill the order in a timely manner. Others, however, may wait until they have received multiple requests for the item before placing the order. By placing a multiple-copy order, the vendor receives a higher discount. It may take several months before the vendor accumulates enough requests to generate the discount level it believes makes the transaction profitable. The impact of this practice may or may not be serious depending on where the library is in its budget cycle and inflation rates. Some vendors will place a single-copy order, but at a much lower discount than the library's usual discount or impose a service charge.

Another financial concern is with the firm's financial stability. Like everyone else vendors have encountered financial problems during the current recession. Some publishers are requiring prepayment or have placed vendors on a pro forma status. Pro forma status requires prepayment, and suppliers extend credit on the basis of the current performance in payment of bills. Much of the credit and order fulfillment extended by publishers depends on an almost personal relationship with the buyer. That in turn affects the vendor's ability to fulfill orders as quickly as it did in the past. Thus, libraries must select a vendor with care. It is not inappropriate to check a prospective vendor's financial status (through a rating service, such as Dun and Bradstreet).

Vendors' Services

Many major vendors offer a variety of services that go beyond supplying items for the collection. They offer almost one-stop technical services, from preorder checking to cataloging to shelf-ready (processed) material.

Some of the larger U.S. library book vendors are Baker & Taylor, Brodart, Follett, Blackwell North America, and Midwest Library Service. Two large Canadian book wholesalers are National Book Service and United Library Supply. EBSCO is probably the largest U.S. serials vendor. In addition, there are smaller firms that provide good-quality service to libraries and information centers. However, as discussed later, their numbers are decreasing. Most countries with an active book trade have similar organizations. Libraries often use a vendor in countries where they buy large quantities of materials. As a general rule a vendor in the country of origin has a better chance of locating a desired item than does one from another country. There also are specialized vendors, such as Majors, a leading firm for STM books, and French Language Resources, a Canadian firm that provides French-language books for schools and classrooms.

Baker & Taylor, Brodart, and Follett focus on public and school library needs. Blackwell North America and Midwest Library Service handle the academic library market primarily. Almost all vendors offer some combination, if not all, of the following in addition to the basic order fulfillment service:

- Preorder searching and verification—many allow a search and direct downloading into an order form.
- Selection assistance, such as access to reviews of items from major review journals—many public and school libraries require any purchased title to be selected on the basis of published reviews.
- More than one type of format (printed books, e-books, audio/video recordings, for example).
- Electronic table of contents and/or book jacket art for ordered titles—academic libraries like the table of contents service as it becomes searchable in the online public access catalog (OPAC) and is a valued service by researchers. For a public library the cover art, attached to OPAC record, helps attract a reader to the item, rather like bookstores displaying many titles with the jacket facing out rather than having the spine showing.
- Cataloging and shelf-ready processing—cataloging can take the form of downloading a machine-readable cataloging (MARC) record into the library's ILS for catalogers to modify as necessary or having the vendor actually do the cataloging and forwarding the final record. Shelf ready means the items arrive with labels and any necessary book pockets, property stamps, date due slips, and so on in place and ready to go into the collection.
- Customized management data—see the discussion that follows.

In addition to materials, Brodart is a major resource for library furniture and equipment (e.g., book trucks, step stools, shelving units) and supplies (e.g., bar codes, date due slips).

Brodart also offers a rental service, the McNaughton Plan, which is designed to help solve the problem of providing an adequate number of high-demand titles for books and audio recordings. Most public libraries face the challenge of having a high demand for popular titles; however, that high demand only lasts a short time. The challenge is how to meet the demand and yet not spend too much money on short-term interest items. One solution libraries employ is to buy two or three copies and set up a reservation or request queue for those wishing to read or listen to the item. The public understands the challenge but still does express frustration with the reservation system. McNaughton offers another alternative: rent multiple copies for the duration of the title's popularity and return the unneeded copies. Brodart describes the plan as a *leasing* program. The plan offers high-demand items that Brodart's staff selects. A library cannot order just any book; it must be on Brodart's list of high-demand titles. Some financial savings occur as there are no processing costs because the books come shelf-ready and the leasing fee is substantially lower than the item's purchase price. Further, users are happy because of shorter waiting times for the latest bestseller. All in all, anyone involved in meeting recreational reading needs will find the program worth investigating.

Acquisitions departments generate a variety of reports from their ILS about the unit's activities, as illustrated later in the chapter. Vendors can also supply some management data for the department that are drawn from outside sources. One type of data that is very useful for budget planning purposes is the average cost of materials. The following is an example of pricing information from a vendor for a library:

**UNIVERSITY PRESS PUBLICATIONS ANALYSIS
BY SUBJECT FOR THE PERIOD 5/1/08 TO 4/30/09
REPORT DATE 5/3/09**

LC Classification #	Description	Number of Titles	Total Price	Average Price
AC 1-195	Collections of monograph	2	54.95	27.48**
AG 1-90	Dictionaries. Minor encyc.	2	38.90	19.45**
AM 10-101	Museography. Individual	1	32.50	32.50**
AM 111-160	Museology. Museum methods	1	25.00	25.00**
AS	Academies & learned soc.	4	322.00	80.50**
AZ	History of scholarship	2	55.00	27.50**
	A'S SUBTOTALS	12	528.35	44.03**
B	Philosophy (General)	7	409.90	58.56**

Customer Service Considerations

As the second chapter epigraph suggests, customer service is no small issue for libraries. The list of topics described in Myers's quotation as being customer service–related is long but is still not a complete listing of all the challenges that arise and that require staff interaction between the library and vendor. Long-term relationships are the result of respectful dealings by both parties as well as taking some time to learn about the other party's challenges and needs. Such relationships are also based on having realistic expectations of one another.

Acquisition departments have a right to expect that a vendor will provide

- a large inventory of titles in appropriate formats,
- prompt and accurate order fulfillment,
- prompt and accurate reporting on items not in stock,
- personal service at a reasonable price,
- prompt technical support for problems with shared technology, and
- timely correction of faulty services such as incorrect cataloging or incorrectly processed shelf-ready items.

Most vendors are reasonably good at meeting those expectations once they become aware of the library's specific issues. Getting them become aware is sometimes a challenge, however. Telephone trees are a bane for almost all customers, not just library staff. E-mail and "contact us" boxes often seem to lead to black holes rather than service. In defense of the vendors, current economic conditions cause them as many staffing issues as libraries face. Layoffs, furloughs, and frozen vacant positions force organizations to employ technology to help address some of the personnel shortfalls. Patience is a key to maintaining civil working relationships.

Vendors also have a right to expect the following from libraries:

- A reasonable time to gain an understanding of the library's needs,
- Cooperation in placing orders using the firm's system rather than complaints that "we did it this way with our former vendor,"
- Keeping paperwork to a minimum and attempting to streamline library operations,
- Prompt payment for services, and,
- That customers will not require too many exceptions to the firm's normal processes.

Libraries sometimes employ practices that are somewhat outmoded and reflect an attitude of "we always do it this way" and expect the vendor to change its practices to conform to the library's approach. Unless there is a parent institutional requirement involved, the library should be open to at least considering modifying its practices. Being open about the average invoice payment cycle, ability to authorize partial payments, and similar matters from the start will also create a more positive relationship.

One action for libraries to avoid is dumping their problem orders on vendors and ordering easy items directly from the publishers to maximize its discount. This is a shortsighted practice. Without the income from easy, high-volume items, no vendor can stay in business. Someone has to handle the problem orders, and most vendors will try to track down the difficult items, especially for good customers. However, libraries should give vendors easy orders as well. Many of the problems facing vendors involve cash flow. Lack of cash has been the downfall of many businesses, and it becomes critical for vendors if they are expected to handle too many problem orders; staff expenses go up, but income does not.

Vendors provide a valuable service to libraries. Given a good working relationship, both parties benefit. But where does a library learn about vendors and their services? Beyond attending library association conferences and word-of-mouth suggestions from peers, several guides are available. General publications such as *Literary Market Place, International Literary Market Place, International Subscription Agent,* Quill & Quire's *Canadian Publishers Directory,* or specialized lists by format, region of the world, and subject matter will provide a long list of possibilities. One can also post questions about vendor experiences on acquisitions discussion lists, such as AcqWeb, see list of useful Web sites at the end of the chapter.

One question for a library to answer is how many vendors to use. There are pros and cons for consolidating business with only one or two vendors just as there are for using a number of vendors for the same type of product. Consolidation usually means the vendor gains a better sense of the library's requirements, perhaps provides a better discount, and may even offer some free services. Having several vendors for a type of product may provide a higher discount, at least when there is a degree of competition for the library's business. One drawback is that the service may not be as good and perhaps the vendors will not have the resources to invest in newer technology. The primary concern should be service followed by financial strength—it is not unheard of for major vendors to have serious financial problems.

VENDOR EVALUATION

Acquisitions departments should engage in ongoing monitoring of vendor performance. In the past, monitoring vendors was time-consuming and difficult, and it still is if a library is working with a manual acquisitions system. However, automated acquisitions systems can produce a variety of useful management and vendor reports very quickly and in various formats. Knowing what to do with the quantity of data the systems can produce is another matter.

Acquisitions staff undertake two types of evaluation. One is monitoring vendor performance with an eye to identifying small concerns that left unnoticed could become a major issue. The other is a formal assessment of the vendor with an eye toward changing vendors or renewing a contract.

One obvious issue that arises in the evaluation process is which vendor performs best on a given type of order (examples are conference proceedings, music scores, or video recordings). The first step is to decide what *best* means. Highest discount? Fastest delivery? Most accurate reports? Highest percentage of the order filled with the first shipment? All of the above? The answer varies from library to library depending on local needs and conditions. Once the library defines *best,* it knows what data to get from the system. Following are other evaluation issues:

- Who handles rush orders most efficiently?
- Who handles international orders most effectively—a dealer in the country of origin or a general international dealer?
- Are specialty dealers more effective in handling their specialties than are general dealers?
- Who handles claims the quickest?

Following are sample system reports illustrating several years' performance of some book vendors for a hypothetical library. The first example illustrates claim performance of 11 vendors.

CLAIMS PERFORMANCE FISCAL YEAR 2008–2009

Total Claims	# Orders	Avg Est Price/ Order	Avg Est Price Recd Order	Avg Amt Paid/ Order	% Orders Recd	% Orders Cancld	% Orders Claimed	
1 a&e	11	$27.68	$33.70	$32.63	72.72	9.09	0.00	0
2 abc	6687	$45.96	$46.81	$41.75	87.64	1.85	0.00	0
3 abca	5226	$162.50	$47.78	$139.94	99.77	0.09	0.00	0

(Continued)

CLAIMS PERFORMANCE FISCAL YEAR 2008–2009 (*Continued*)

Total Claims	# Orders	Avg Est Price/ Order	Avg Est Price Recd Order	Avg Amt Paid/ Order	% Orders Recd	% Orders Cancld	% Orders Claimed	
4 abcc	144	$57.74	$59.59	$104.72	95.13	0.69	0.00	0
5 abcr	24	$43.52	$43.52	$48.57	100.00	0.00	0.00	0
6 aip	2	$0.00	$0.00	$259.06	50.00	0.00	0.00	0
7 ala	58	$32.48	$32.48	$42.66	100.00	0.00	0.00	0
8 alss	10	$249.50	$253.88	$295.88	90.00	0.00	0.00	0
9 ama	1	$0.00	$0.00	$0.00	100.00	0.00	0.00	0
10 amazc	21	$25.44	$27.59	$26.71	90.47	4.76	0.00	0
11 amb	3399	$41.32	$41.56	$40.74	79.05	1.26	0.20	7

The next example shows data about cost of items from the same 11 vendors.

VENDOR PERFORMANCE STATISTICS—AMOUNTS
FISCAL YEAR 2008–2009

	Est Price Orders	Est Price Recpts	Est Price Cancls	Est Price Ords	Amt Paid
1 a&e	$304.50	$269.60	$0.00	$34.90	$261.04
2 abc	$307,399.34	$274,411.86	$80.00	$32,907.48	$244,698.59
3 abca	$849,246.70	$249,134.80	$150,000.00	$450,111.90	$729,696.37
4 abcc	$8,315.96	$8,165.01	$0.00	$150.95	$14,347.08
5 abcr	$1,044.66	$1,044.66	$0.00	$0.00	$1,165.90
6 aip	$0.00	$0.00	$0.00	$0.00	$259.06
7 ala	$1,883.91	$1,883.91	$0.00	$0.00	$2,474.81
8 alss	$2,495.00	$2,285.00	$0.00	$210.00	$2,662.97
9 ama	$0.00	$0.00	$0.00	$0.00	$0.00
10 amazc	$534.31	$524.31	$0.00	$10.00	$507.54
11 amb	$140,458.35	$111,693.47	$0.00	$28,764.88	$109,479.45

The final example illustrates a summary report on a year's acquisitions transactions. The estimated price is the amount the department encumbered (more about encumbrance in chapter 12) and "paid amount" reflects the actual cost (estimated cost minus actual discount, if any).

VENDOR PERFORMANCE STATISTICS—TOTAL
FISCAL YEAR 2008–2009

Average Estimated Price per Order:	$2,517,010.67 / 39060 = $64.43
Average Paid Amount of Receipts:	$2,235,412.84 / 35270 = $63.38
Average Estimated Price for Received Orders :	$1,682,515.20 / 35270 = 47.70
Average Delivery Time as days:	219988034 / 35270 = 6237
% Orders Received in 2 weeks:	2663 / 35270 = 35.90 %
% Orders Received in 4 weeks:	3839 / 35270 = 10.88 %
% Orders Received in 8 weeks:	10920 / 35270 = 30.96 %
% Orders Received in 12 weeks:	4700 / 35270 = 13.32 %
% Orders Received in 16 weeks:	1341 / 35270 = 3.80 %
% Orders Received in 17+ weeks:	1807 / 35270 = 5.12 %
% Cancelled:	577 / 39060 = 1.47 %
% Claimed:	9 / 39060 = 0.02 %
Average Claims per Claimed Order:	9 / 9 = 1.00
Average Claims per Order:	9 / 39060 = 0.00

In addition to generating system reports based on normal operating procedures, a library can conduct some experiments by placing a random sample of a type of order with several vendors to assess their performance. When doing a test or experiment, be certain that each vendor receives approximately the same mix of titles, that no vendor receives more or fewer easy or hard-to-handle items. Often, the normal procedure data reflect the use of a particular vendor for only one type of order. This makes comparing vendor performance rather meaningless because one is not comparing like groups. The library can use the test method to select a vendor for a particular type of order and use the operating data approach to monitor ongoing performance.

Checking on the performance of serials vendors is more difficult. Most libraries use only one domestic serials vendor and perhaps a second firm that specializes in journals from other countries. A library that is just establishing a current subscription list, or starting a large number of new subscriptions, might consider splitting the list between two or more vendors for several years to determine which would be the best sole source for the long term.

A limited amount of checking is possible through comparisons with other libraries. Often, this type of checking is done in a casual manner, that is, by merely asking a colleague in another library, "Do you use vendor X? How do you like them?" or "How much is your service charge?" To make valid and useful comparisons, a library needs to know the other library's title mix.

One way to compare serials vendors is to investigate a sample of commonly held titles. Factors to examine include the service charges on those titles, the effectiveness of claims processing, and other issues like vendor follow-up and handling of credit memos.

In any vendor evaluation, keep in mind some of the problems vendors have with producers:

- Changes in title, or not publishing the title;
- Not being informed when publishing schedules change or when publishers suspend or cease publication;
- Incorrect International Standard Book Numbers (ISBNs) or International Standard Serial Numbers (ISSNs);
- Producers refusing to take returns;
- Producers refusing to sell through vendors;
- Producers reducing discounts or charging for freight and handling, when those were free in the past;
- Poor fulfillment on the producer's part;
- Constantly changing policies on the producer's part; and
- Producer price increases without prior notice.

References to several models for conducting vendor evaluation studies are included in the Suggested Reading section of this chapter.

Several years ago, a student in one of the author's (Evans) courses asked during a discussion of vendors, "Why are you so pro-vendor? They are our enemies, with all their high prices and low discounts." Perhaps Evans's work experience in bookstores, publishing, and libraries is a factor in his not being highly critical of vendors. However, it is not a matter of being "so pro-vendor," but rather recognizing that there are at least two sides to most stories. Libraries depend on vendors; they offer services that save libraries time, effort, and staffing. Libraries need vendors and need to understand their problems.

That said, libraries must monitor vendor performance, question charges, and challenge charges that seem inappropriate. Maintaining good relations is everyone's business. If librarians, vendors, and producers take time to learn about one another's business, working relationships will be better.

RETAIL OUTLETS

The book distribution system in the United States is cumbersome and frequently adds to the cost of books. A simplified system would benefit everyone. Perhaps the best illustration of the complexity of the system is in the area of discounts, returns, billings, and so forth. Each year the American Booksellers Association publishes a 500-page guide, *ABA Book Buyer's Handbook*.[1] Pity the poor bookseller who, confronted with all of the other problems of a bookstore, must also work through a mass of legal forms and sales conditions for purchasing from various publishers. This process creates extra work for the bookseller and publisher, and they undoubtedly pass their costs on to the buyer.

In general, bookstores can be a valuable means of acquiring new books. Carrying out visual inspection of local stores and discussing the library's needs with bookstore owners can forge an important link in the selection and acquisition program. Libraries in large metropolitan areas generally have good bookstores nearby, but many libraries are lucky if there is one bookstore in the community. Although most libraries will spend only a small portion of the materials budget in such stores, the possibility is worth exploring. Most bookstores have limited potential as a major source of supply for acquisitions departments, but when a general bookstore exists nearby, the library ought to talk to the owner to determine what, if any, business relationship might be possible. It may take time for the relationship to fully develop, but it can prove mutually beneficial. The large U.S. national chains, such as Borders and Barnes & Noble, operate very differently from local stores and are not likely to be able to accommodate library needs beyond occasionally allowing a corporate or educational discount on some of the titles they carry.

Quebec libraries must purchase their books from at least three accredited bookstores. Such bookstores must be based in Quebec and owned by a Quebecer. Some libraries, however, are able to buy books directly from distributors because they have private funding also.

A reasonable question to pose at this point is, "what about Internet bookstores?" Is Amazon.com a retailer or a wholesaler? An early 2001 check of Yahoo's Books page had links to more than 490 online stores (both new and out-of-print [OP] sources). Today such a search generates thousands of hits. Certainly these stores are popular, but not always the quickest means of getting a book in hand, at least during holiday periods.

Amazon.com is a resource for libraries for the purchase of some popular items. One challenge for libraries is developing a workable means of payment. The online shopping sites are based on credit card payments. Libraries and their parent organizations operate on a purchase order or invoice system. Although the situation is changing, many libraries cannot get a credit card or the necessary approval for a line of credit due to regulations or reluctance on the part of the library's parent organization. Some departments will use a personal card and go through a reimbursement process; however, this is not a long-term or high-volume solution. One of the authors, Evans, worked at an academic library where, after a significant passage of time and effort, it was able to secure a corporate account with Amazon. Overall, the effort was of only marginal value to the acquisitions department.

Monica Fusich wrote a brief article on the use of Amazon.com and other e-stores that appeared in *C&RL News*.[2] She outlined several services she found useful as a collection development officer who has other duties as well. Being a reference librarian or having some other full-time assignment as well as having selection responsibilities is very common in the current library environment. Fusich mentioned the following features:

- Cumulated book reviews (one must remember some of the reviews are from the general public)
- Search and browsing capability
- Size of the database(s)
- Coverage of in-print and OP titles and nonbook media
- Notification services (a rather limited selective dissemination of information service as of mid-1999)

A more recent assessment of Amazon as a library vendor was Paul Orkiszewski's comparative study of Amazon and a traditional library book and media vendor. He found that on average the Amazon discount was lower (8.75%) than that of the traditional vendors (15.24%). One of his conclusions was, "Libraries interested in using Amazon should find it useful for trade and popular press books, DVDs, and book and media items that are needed quickly."[3] Although e-stores are not *the* answer to the challenges facing busy acquisition departments, they can be of assistance and should not be dismissed out of hand.

OUT-OF-PRINT, ANTIQUARIAN, AND RARE BOOK DEALERS

Retrospective collection building is one of the most interesting and challenging areas of acquisitions work. Libraries buy retrospectively for two reasons: to fill in gaps in the collection and to replace worn-out or lost copies of titles. There has been a steady decline in retrospective buying on the part of libraries over the past 20 years because limited budgets and the need to increase purchases of nonprint and electronic resources. Another factor in the decline has been the proliferation of bibliographic databases such as OCLC, which make locating a copy of an OP title to borrow through interlibrary loan much easier. As a result, acquisitions staff and selectors have decreasing experience to draw upon when they need to work in this field. Dealers in this field are a special breed unlike other vendors with which the library has more experience.

One outcome of the decline is that the field, which has always been very dependent on collectors, is even more driven today by collector interests than by library needs. Allowing for overlap, there are two broad categories of OP dealers. (It should be noted that most of these individuals dislike the label "secondhand dealer.") One category focuses primarily on general OP books, that is, on buying and selling relatively recent OP books. Often, these books sell at prices that are the same as, or only slightly higher than, their publication price. The other category of dealer focuses on rare, antiquarian, and special (for example, fore-edge painted, miniature, or private press) books. Prices for this type of book can range from around U.S. $10 to several thousand dollars per item.

The face of this field is changing. Margaret Landesman provided an excellent, detailed outline of the current dealer categories[4]:

- Book scouts that work part-time or full-time to search out desirable books and sell them to dealers and collectors. Such individuals are one of the primary reasons one gets so many hits when searching the Web for OP titles. They carry little or no stock.
- Operators of neighborhood stores that have limited service hours, often only one or two days a week. Stores are in low-cost areas. Today, many operators only use the facility as a storage unit and depend on selling through the Web and a few very loyal customers rather than walk-in trade. Their stock is generally recent materials and covers a variety of subject areas.
- Specialized dealers that often issue catalogs in addition to their Web postings and do searching in their specialty. Their stock is limited in scope, but successful dealers have depth of coverage in their specialties.
- General out-of-print dealers that have a substantial store and a rather large stock in varied areas are what most people think of when thinking about OP dealers. With the Web, searching for titles is a common service and a few issue catalogs.

- Mixed in-print and OP stores—often a store that was an independent new bookshop that is trying to survive the competition from the superstores by diversifying. A good example of a mixed store is Powell's City of Books in Portland, Oregon (http://www.powells.com/).
- Academic library book vendors that also offer OP search services.
- Rare book dealers that specialize in rare and expensive titles. Most established rare book dealers do not handle the more ordinary scholarly OOP titles, but many general OP dealers also handle some rare books.

Most of such dealers have small shops in low-rent areas or operate out of their homes. Because of this diversity, it is difficult to make many generalizations about this group.

Most libraries have occasion to use the services of these dealers. Acquisitions departments that handle purchases for large research collections tend to spend much of their time (or at least they did in the past) engaged in retrospective purchasing activities. Public libraries also buy from OP dealers, especially for replacement copies and occasionally for retrospective collection building. School libraries make limited use of this distribution system for replacement copies. Scientific and technical libraries rarely need to worry about acquiring retrospective materials.

Many acquisitions librarians and book dealers classify OP book distribution services into three general types: (1) a complete book service, (2) a complete sales service, and (3) a complete bookstore. The first two may operate in a manner that does not allow, or at least require, customers to come to the seller's location. All contact is by e-mail, telephone, and occasionally by regular mail. The owner may maintain only a small stock of choice items in a garage or basement. In a *complete book service,* a dealer actively searches for items for a customer, even if the items are not in stock. In the past this was the standard approach for serious retrospective collection development. Today with several OP Web search sites many libraries handle all the work themselves.

A *sales service* is just what the name implies: A dealer reads the wanted sections of book trade Web sites and publications and sends off quotes on items in his stock. Such services seldom place ads or conduct searches for a customer. The *complete bookstore* is a store operation that depends on in-person trade. Stores of this type often engage in book service and sales service activities as well. They are also becoming an endangered species.

Since 2000, the OP trade has become very dependent upon the Web, and there are thousands of OP dealers with a Web presence. To some degree the Web has kept prices down, or slowed their increase. Checking prices through a site such as Abebooks (http://www.abebooks.com) is very easy. (This site is the digital version of what was the standard U.S. journal for the OP trade—*AB Bookman's Weekly.* The site was established in 1995 and has no direct connection with the journal.)

An example of the power of Web searching for OP titles is one done in August 2009 for Charles Dickens's books. A general search turned up 77,000+ copies ranging in price from U.S. $1.00 to tens of thousands of dollars. Narrowing the search to first editions dropped the number of hits to 1,837. Again, the lowest price was $1.00; however, item 1,837 was a collection of five volumes of Dickens's Christmas stories—each a first edition first printing—for a mere U.S. $42,500. Sellers were from many countries (a total of 21—for example, Australia, Canada, Denmark, India, Norway, Scotland, and the U.K.) and cities across the United States.

When Henry Fairfield Osborn's two-volume set *Proboscidea: A Monograph of the Discovery, Evolution, Migration and Extinction of the Mastodons and Elephants of the World* (American Museum of Natural History, vol. 1, 1936 and vol. 2, 1942), an example of a title that might reflect the interest of a science library, was searched only three sets turned up on abebook.com and bookfinder.com. One set was available from a dealer in Edinburgh, Scotland, and two sets were available from U.S. dealers—in Ithaca, New York, and Iowa City, Iowa—and prices ranged from US$4,179.60 to US$5,800. Before OP online searching was possible such a search or want listing could have gone for years before there was success. Now, in a matter of minutes, definitive results are available. If you don't get a hit, in most cases dozens of hits, you can be reasonably sure the item is not available or you are lacking some critical data about the title. One reason for suspecting the item is not available is that sites such as abebooks.com and bookfinder.com have listings from tens of thousands dealers worldwide and the Web has become their major source of business.

As with dealer's catalog descriptions, one must be careful to read the description with a critical mind, at least for rare-book purchases. Despite the need for caution, the Web has indeed changed the nature of retrospective collection development. Dealer descriptions and condition statements can be very idiosyncratic and one must read them with a degree of caution. There are no official standards for such information. Some years ago *AB Bookman's Weekly* put forward some suggested terms and their definition. What follows can only be thought of as broad meanings to help assess what a dealer may be describing.

Two of the top-level condition terms you may see are *as new* and *fine.* Presumably an "as new" implies a flawless item—the identical condition as when published—including a perfect dust jacket, if that was part of the original publication. Sometimes a dealer will use *mint* for this state. "Fine" is a slightly less perfect state; perhaps there is a little evidence of shelf wear and use but of a very minor nature. *Very good* and *good* are conditions that most libraries find acceptable for general collection replacement copies—there is evidence of wear. *Fair* and *poor* condition states probably are not suitable for libraries except when nothing else is available and the need is very strong as they imply some defects in the item. *Ex-library,* as the term indicates, means the copy has the usual stamping, perforations, spindling, and other mutilations that libraries use to property mark an item.

A library may assume that most OP dealers sell their stock as described or "as is." If there is no statement about the item's condition, it should be in good or better condition. A common statement in catalogs is "terms—all books in original binding and in good or better condition unless otherwise stated."

One requisite that a library ought to use is the OP dealer's reputation for honesty, service, and fair prices. To gain such a reputation requires a considerable period of time in this field. In a Web-based environment, this issue is a challenge for libraries. If one is only purchasing a $20 or $30 replacement copy, the risks of dealing with an unknown dealer are not all that high. For higher-priced materials there are real risks. The risks were there in the pre-electronic environment as well, but the ease of posting an item for sale on the Web has magnified the opportunities for less than honest sellers to make a sale.

When you search for a title on a site such as abebooks.com, your result appears as a listing of sellers, prices and a brief description of the book's condition. While it is possible to order directly from the result pages it is advisable to follow the available link to the seller's page and, if there is one, the home page for the seller. One the best assurances of a reputable dealer is membership in one the bookseller associations such as Antiquarian Booksellers Association of America. That is not to say that not being a member is necessarily a negative sign, but its presence is a positive one. Also, going to the seller's pages provides important information about terms and conditions, as well as contact information where you can attempt to clarify issues and perhaps try to negotiate the price. (Yes, it is possible to try to get a better price—you will not get one if you don't ask. It is probably not worth the time to try this with inexpensive items though.)

One element in the OP trade is very mysterious to the outsider and even to librarians who have had years of experience with these dealers: How do dealers determine the asking price? (The rule of thumb of paying one-third or less of the expected sales income is probably ignored more than it is practiced. The "or less" is the key.) The markup is at least 100 percent, but how much more? One may find a book in an OP store with no price on it, take it to the salesperson (often the owner), ask the price, and receive, after a quick look, the answer, "Oh, yes. That is X dollars." Sometimes the amount is lower than one expects, other times much higher, but most of the time it is close to the price the library is willing to pay. Some salespersons seem to be mind readers and know exactly how much a customer is willing to pay. Sol Malkin summed up the outsider's feeling about pricing in the OP trade: "Many new book dealers think of the antiquarian bookseller as a second-hand junkman or as a weird character who obtains books by sorcery, prices them by cannibalistic necromancy, and sells them by black magic."[5]

As amusing as Malkin's theory may be, prices are in actuality based on a number of interrelated factors:

1. How much it costs to acquire the item
2. The amount of current interest in collecting a particular subject or author
3. The number of copies printed and the number of copies still in existence
4. The physical condition of the copy
5. Any special features of the particular copy (autographed by the author or signed or owned by a famous person, for example)
6. What other dealers are asking for copies of the same edition in the same condition

In the past it might have appeared that magic is the essential ingredient in successful OP operations—getting the price right. To a large degree, dealers set prices after they know the answers to the questions of supply and potential sales. Without question, the current asking price is the major determining factor—given equal conditions in the other five areas. The ability to search online to determine how many copies are available and what their asking price is has simplified pricing for both the dealer and the buyer.

Working in this area can be fun and frustrating at the same time. Clearly, there is a need for experience with dealers to know if their descriptions of their offerings are good enough for the library. There is also the nagging question of fair-market price for what is often a one-of-a-kind offering, at least at that moment. Commercial guides can help with evaluating the asking or quoted price, such as *Bookman's Price Index, American Book Prices Current,* and *Book-Auction Records.*[6]

SUMMARY

The distribution system for books and other library materials is varied and complex and must be understood and appreciated by acquisitions staff. This chapter provides highlights of what the library needs to know; and it portrays just the beginning of a long, challenging, but enjoyable learning process. Jobbers, book dealers, and media vendors are more than willing to explain how they modify their operations to accommodate library requirements, when they know that a librarian has taken time to learn something about their operations.

REVIEW QUESTIONS

1. What are the typical discounts on books and to which category of books do they *normally* apply?

2. List four important questions to ask any vendor.

3. Identify seven key factors to consider when selecting a vendor.

4. What do vendors expect from libraries?

5. Identify some important factors to examine when assessing vendor performance.

6. List the seven types of OP sources and describe what is special about each one.

7. Pricing OP materials is complex. What are the factors dealers take into account when setting a price?

NOTES

The epigraphs for this chapter are from Carol Tenopir, "Working for a Vendor," *Library Journal* 130, no. 12 (2005): 29 and Carol Myers, "Lament for Lost Customer Service," *AALL Spectrum* 13, no. 7 (2009): 3–4.

1.   American Booksellers Association, *ABA Book Buyer's Handbook* (New York: American Booksellers Association, 1947–).

2.   Monica Fusich, "Collectiondevelopment.com: Using Amazon.com and Other Online Bookstores for Collection Development," *C&RL News* 59, no. 11 (1998): 659–61.

3.   Paul Orkiszewski, "A Comparative Study of Amazon.com as a Library Book and Media Vendor," *Library Resources & Technical Services* 49, no. 3 (2005): 208.

4.   Margaret Landesman, "Out-of-Print and Secondhand Market," in *The Business of Library Acquisitions,* ed. K. A. Schmidt (Chicago: American Library Association, 1990).

5.   Sol Malkin, "Rare and Out-of-Print Books," in *A Manual on Bookselling* (New York: American Booksellers Association, 1974), 208.

6.   *Bookman's Price Index* (Detroit: Gale Research, 1964–), *American Book Prices Current* (New York: Bancroft-Parkman, 1930– , annual), and *Book-Auction Records* (London: W. Dawson, 1902– , annual).

SELECTED WEB SITES

AbeBooks, http://www. abebooks.com

Alibris, http://www.alibris.com

Antiquarian Booksellers Association of America, http://www.abaa.org

Bookfinder.com, http://www.bookfinder.com

Books.com, http://www.books.com

International League of Antiquarian Booksellers, http://www.ilab.com

Internet Bookshop, http://www.bookshop.co.uk/

UMI Book Vault, http://www.UMI.com/ph/Support/BOD/bkvault.htm

SUGGESTED READING

Allen, Sydney K., and Heather S. Miler. "Libraries on the Book Buying Merry-Go-Round: Internet Booksellers vs. Library Book Vendors." *Against the Grain* 12, no. 1 (2000): 1, 16–22.

Anderson, Rick. *Buying and Contracting for Resources and Services.* New York. Neal-Schuman Publishers, 2003.

Anderson, Rick. "How to Make Your Book Vendor Love You." *Against the Grain* 10, no. 8 (1998): 68–70.

Brown, Lynne C. "Vendor Evaluation." *Collection Management* 19 (1995): 47–46.

Edelmn, Hendrik, and Robert B. Holly. *Marketing to Libraries for the New Millennium: Libraries, Vendors, and Publishers.* Lanham, MD: Scarecrow Press, 2002.

Gammon, Julia A. "Partnering with Vendors for Increased Productivity." *Library Acquisitions* 21, no. 2 (1997): 229–35.

Gray, David, and Malcolm Brantz. "Out of the Box and Into the Bookstore: Nontraditional Use of the Bookstore." *Against the Grain* 15, no. 3 (2003): 36, 38, 40, 42.

Hirko, Buff. "Get Vendor Savvy." *Library Journal Net Connect* Spring (2004): 12–13.

Hoffert, Barbara. "Who's Selecting Now?" *Library Journal* 132, no. 14 (2007): 40–43.

Hubbard, William J., and Jodi Welch. "An Empirical Test of Two Vendors' Trade Discounts." *Library Acquisitions* 22, no. 2 (1998): 131–37.

Kuo, Hui-Min. "Comparing Vendor Discounts for Firm Orders: Fixed vs. Sliding." *Technical Services Quarterly* 18, no. 4 (2001): 1–10.

Kuo, Hui-Min. "Flat or Float? A Study of Vendor Discount Rates Applied to Firm Orders in a College Library." *Library Acquisitions* 22, no. 4 (1998): 409–14.

Lugg, Rick, and Ruth Fischer. "Many Vendors, One Face." *Library Journal Net Connect* Spring (2005): 4–8.

McDowell, Nicola, and G. E. Gorman. "Relevance of Vendor's Usage Statistics in Academic Library E-Resource Management." *Australian Academic Research Libraries* 35, no. 4 (2004): 322–43.

Nardini, Robert F. "Issues in Vendor/Library Relations—The Sales Call." *Against the Grain* 13, no. 6 (2001): 88–89.

Nardini, Robert F., and John Abbott. "Issues in Library/Vendor Relations: Will Amazon Wal-Mart the Books Vendors?" *Against the Grain* 13, no. 1 (2001): 72–74.

Pomerantz, Sarah, and Andrew White. "Re-modeling ILS Acquisitions Data to Financially Transition from Print to Digital Formats." *Library Collections, Acquisitions, & Technical Services* 33 (2009): 42–49.

Rendell, Kenneth. "The Future of the Manuscript and Rare Book Business." *RBM* 2, no. 1 (2001): 13–33.

Somsel. Larisa. "Buying Books Online Is No Mystery." *Collection Management* 29, nos. 3/4 (2004): 41–52.

Stamison, Christine, Bob Pershing, and Chris Beckett. "What They Never Told You About Vendors in Library School." *Serials Librarian* 56, no. 1 (2009): 139–45.

"Vendor Connections: Relations with School Media Specialists." *School Librarian's Workshop* 17 (1997): 1–2.

Walther, James. 1998. "Assessing Library Vendor Relations: A Focus on Evaluation and Communication." *Bottom Line* 11, no. 4: 149–57.

Wirth, Andrea A. "ticTOCs: A New Service for 'Keeping Current.' " *Collection Management* 34 (2009): 229–33.

Chapter

Print and Digital Books

The book is not dead. In fact, the world is producing more books than ever before. According to Bowker, 700,000 new titles were published worldwide in 1998; 859,000 in 2003 and 976,000 in 2007. Despite the Great Recession of 2009 that has hit hard the publishing industry so hard; one million new books will soon produced each year.

—Robert Darnton, 2009

Creating an e-library is an ambitious project for any library, because the process attempts to recreate the library collection and the library services—in virtual space. In its simplest form an e-library is a collection of Web-accessible information resources from a variety of resources, including freely available Web sites and fee-based Web accessible databases.

—Dianne K. Kovacs and Kara L. Robinson, 2004

Paper-based books are dead! Long live the paper-based book! For the better part of 40 years various pundits have predicted the imminent demise of the book as well as the coming of the paperless office. Neither prediction has yet come true. They both probably will occur sometime in the future; however, neither is likely during the lifetime of this edition of *Introduction to Library Technical Services.* As a result, libraries will continue to acquire at least some, if not a sizable number of, paper-based books, magazines, newspapers, and other documents until that time arrives. If you have doubts, spend some time in your local bookstore and public library and observe the number of people buying, reading, and utilizing paper-based items.

Acquisitions departments probably could function without knowing very much about the producers of the product they purchase. However, the departments will be more effective and more efficient when the staff understands something about the production side of the information cycle: creation, production, distribution, access/storage, and usage. Understanding the factors that enter into the costs and discounts of the products a library purchases assists in the business activities it undertakes (better vendor relations) and end-user interactions (better public relations).

In the past, information producers could be categorized by their products: (1) those who produced printed matter (books, periodicals, newspapers, and the like) and (2) those who produced other media, such as sound recording or videos. It was rare for a producer to work in both areas. Today the situation is different. Although some companies still focus on one information format, most major publishers make material available in both broad categories. Even scholarly and university presses have moved into electronic publishing, including offering titles solely available on CDs or in other digital formats.

The following sections provide an overview of how the items that libraries acquire come into being. It also provides some useful information that will make working with producers and vendors more effective.

WHAT IS PUBLISHING?

Publishers and producers supply the necessary capital and editorial assistance required to transform an author's manuscript/ideas into a book or electronic product. (Two exceptions to this are vanity and subsidy presses, which are discussed later in this section.) Generally, publishers and producers perform six basic functions:

- Tap sources of materials (manuscripts) by contracting with authors.
- Raise and supply the capital to produce books or e-products.
- Aid in the development of the manuscript by working with the authors and providing editorial assistance.
- Contract for the manufacturing (printing, binding, formatting) of the materials for sale.
- Distribute the materials and promote and advertise the titles.
- Maintain records of sales, contracts, and correspondence relating to the production and sale of materials.

Producers usually have five basic organizational units: administration, editorial, design/production, marketing, and fulfillment. Administration ensures that there is adequate capital and coordination between the functional units.

It is in the editorial area that producers face their biggest challenge. They must have a strong backlist of titles (items released in years past) and an annual output of new material. Acquisitions and managing editors discuss and review ideas for new titles or articles in the case of magazines/journals. They develop a list (a combination of prior publications, manuscripts in production, and titles under contract) that they hope will achieve a profit while avoiding unnecessary competition with other producers.

Securing and reviewing manuscripts is a time-consuming activity for most editors. An educated guess is that editors reject approximately nine-tenths of all unsolicited manuscripts after the first examination. After the first complete reading, still more manuscripts are rejected. Even after a careful review by several people, all of whom having favorable reactions, the editor may not accept the manuscript. Three common reasons for the rejection are that (1) the title will not fit into the new list, (2) the sales potential (market) is thought to be too small, and (3) the cost of production would be too high.

Librarians and readers sometimes complain that commercial producers are exclusively, or at least overly, concerned with profit and have little concern for quality. What these people forget is that publishing houses are businesses and must show a profit if they are to continue to operate. Barbara Fister, in an article that compared the views of a publisher's editor and a librarian about the publishing industry, wrote this about book quality from the editor's perspective;

> I don't want to publish schlock. I'd much rather publish quality books, and I fight really hard to get attention for my authors, but we have to publish what people want. The fact is, seven out of ten books don't recoup their costs. It's the best sellers and the steady sellers on the back list that pay the bills.[1]

Even the not-for-profit producers such as university presses have to attempt to break even each year. Such presses know that not every title released will sell well enough to recover its production costs. Thus, some titles must do well enough to generate the income that allows for a break-even year. In good economic times, the university maybe willing to cover any losses in a year as part of its obligation to scholarship; however, in difficult times it may not be able to underwrite a series of losing years.

Librarians also complain that the producers are not releasing enough titles on this or that topic. Again, the issue goes back to the producers' need to at least break even to stay in business. It would be difficult for most producers to stay operational for very long if all they could depend upon were sales to libraries. This is not to say library purchasing is insignificant, it is—libraries spent more than $2 billion in 2003.[2] Even the American Library Association's publication program is not solely dependent on library sales—there is an expectation that there will be at least some sales to individuals and perhaps even some sales as textbooks. Commercial publishers that have product "lines" that focus on librarianship spread their focus among several markets, especially on textbooks. Editors must make their decisions, at least in part, the sales potential for a title not just the content.

Production/design and marketing join with the editorial team to make the final decisions regarding production details. Most publishers can package and price publications in a variety of ways. Some years ago, the Association of University Publishers released an interesting book, *One Book Five Ways*,[3] which provides a fascinating picture of how five different university presses would handle the same project. In all five functional areas, the presses would have proceeded differently, from contract agreement (administration), copyediting (editorial), physical format/design (production), pricing and advertising (marketing), to distribution (fulfillment).

Production staff consider such issues as page size, typeface, number and type of illustrative materials, and cover design, as well as typesetting, printing, and binding. Their input and the decision made regarding the physical form of the item play a major role in how much the title will cost. Although electronic and desktop publishing are changing how and who performs some production activities, the basic issues of design, layout, use of illustrations, and use of color remain unchanged.

Marketing departments are responsible for promoting and selling the product. They provide input about the sales potential of the title. Further, this unit often decides how many review copies to distribute and to what review sources. (Reviews are a key element in libraries' and the publics' making a purchase decision.) The marketing department decides where, when, or whether to place an advertisement for a title; ads play little role in a library's decision to or not to acquire a title, however. All of these decisions influence the cost of the items produced. Many small publishers use direct mail (catalogs and brochures) or e-mail to market their books. Small presses present some challenges for acquisitions departments—see the section on small presses later in this chapter.

One activity for which most marketing units are responsible is exhibits. For library personnel, conventions are one of the best places to meet publishers' representatives and have some input into the publishing decision-making process. From the publishers' point of view, if the conferees go to the exhibits, conventions can be a cost-effective way of reaching a large number of potential customers in a brief time. Library staff members should also remember that the fees exhibitors pay help underwrite the cost of the convention.

Publishers use a variety of distribution outlets, selling directly to individuals, institutions, retailers, and wholesalers. Distribution is a major problem for publishers and libraries because of the number of channels available and the implications for acquiring a specific publication. Each channel has a different discount, and they are accessed through different sources. Production and distribution of information materials, whether print or nonprint, consist of several elements, all interacting with one another. Writers and creators of the material can and do distribute their output in several ways: directly to the community or public, to agents who in turn pass it on to producers, or directly to the producers. Producers seeking writers often approach agents with publication ideas. Figure 7.1 illustrates the complexity of the system by depicting the variety of channels publishers use to distribute their publications to the consumer.

Fulfillment activities are those needed to process an order and those connected with the warehousing of the materials produced. In many ways, fulfillment is the least controllable cost factor for a publisher. As noted earlier, a publisher's distribution system is rather complex (see Figure 7.1). Libraries and information centers sometimes add to the cost of their purchases by requiring special handling of their orders. Keeping special needs to a minimum can help keep prices in check. Speeding up payments to publishers and vendors will also help slow price increases, because the longer a publisher has to carry an outstanding account, the more interest has to be paid. Ultimately, most increases in the cost of doing business result in a higher price for the buyer, so whatever libraries can do to help publishers control their fulfillment costs will also help their acquisitions budgets.

For various reasons, despite strong marketing efforts, some publications do not sell as well as expected. When this happens, sooner or later the publisher has to dispose of the material; often these become remaindered items. A decision by the U.S. Internal Revenue Service (*Thor Power Tool Co. v. Commissioner of Internal Revenue*, 439 U.S. 522 [1979]) has influenced the size of press runs in the United States and

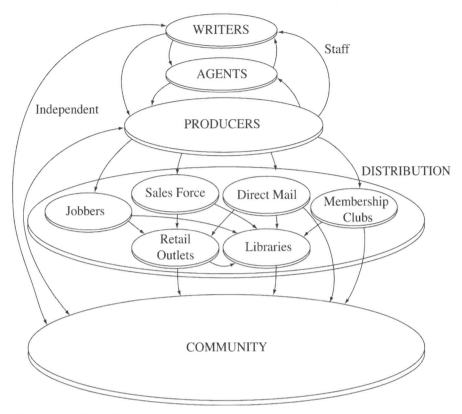

Figure 7.1. Distribution system.

the speed with which publishers remainder slow-moving warehouse stock. Remaindered items sell for a small fraction of their actual production costs. Prior to the *Thor* decision, businesses would write down the value of their inventories, or warehouse stock, to a nominal level at the end of the tax year. The resulting loss in the value of the inventory (which was, by and large, only a paper loss) then became a tax deduction for the company, thereby increasing the profit margin. Since *Thor,* publishers can only take such a deduction if the material is defective or offered for sale below actual production costs. Under the previous method, publishers could find it profitable to keep slow-selling titles in their warehouses for years. At first, the ruling increased the number of remaindered books, but now most publishers have cut back on the size of their print runs in an attempt to match inventories to expected sales volume. More often than not, this means higher unit costs and retail prices. The decision also means the idea of putting off the purchase of a book title for several years in order to maintain funding for journal subscriptions may mean the only option for securing the title is through the out-of-print trade.

What is a typical return for a 250-page trade book selling for U.S. $25.00? Following are costs for a hypothetical first press run:

Suggested Retail Price	$25.00
Printing/binding	−2.00
	23.00

Warehouse/distribution	*–2.00*
	21.00
Discount to retailer	*–12.50*
	8.50
Overhead (including editorial)	*–2.00*
	6.50
Marketing	*–1.50*
	5.00
Author royalty (10–15%)	*–1.25**
Profit	$ 3.75

*Most royalties are based on the net sales income, not the list price. Also, neither publishers nor authors receive any income from resales.

Anyone concerned with acquisitions budgets must make use of statistical data about publishing output and pricing in order to develop intelligent budget requests and work plans. Statistical data about the number of new titles available as paperbacks, reprints, and so forth can be useful in planning the workload for the next fiscal year. Knowing the pricing patterns over a period of years and the expected acquisitions budget allows libraries to project workload. The two most accessible sources of publishing statistics for the United States are *Publishers Weekly* and *The Bowker Annual.* Data in these resources, and almost all other statistical data about publishing, come from the American Book Producers Association (ABPA). It is also important to understand that not all publishers belong to that group; in fact, many of the small regional publishers are not members. If the library tries to acquire many of its regional publications, it will not have as useful projection by just using ABPA data.

This brief overview outlines the most basic elements of publishing. Its purpose is to start a technical services novice thinking about the trade.

TYPES OF PUBLISHERS

The publication *Book Industry Trends* (from the Book industry Study Group) employs a 10-category system for grouping the book publishing industry in the United States:

- Trade
- Mass market
- Book clubs
- Mail order (including e-mail)
- Religious
- Professional
- University presses
- Elementary and high school (El-Hi) textbooks
- College textbook
- Publisher/distributor

Because *Book Industry Trends* is primarily interested in economic and statistical data and publishers can and do have several lines, their grouping is slightly different from the one used in this book. (Note: Publishers often have several lines or divisions that handle a specific type of publishing such as trade books, college textbooks, and mass-market paperbacks.) The following discussion provides an overview of the above and two additional types of publishing firms, some of which mirror the categories used by *Book Industry Trends,* and some that are more specific to the library world. Some are identified by different names.

Trade publishers produce a wide range of titles, both fiction and nonfiction, that have wide sales potential. HarperCollins; Alfred A. Knopf; Doubleday; Macmillan; Little, Brown; Thames & Hudson; Random House; and McClelland & Stewart are typical trade publishers. Many trade publishers have divisions that produce specialty titles, such as children's, college textbooks, paperback, and reference. Trade publishers have three markets: bookstores, libraries, and wholesalers. To sell their products, publishers occasionally employ sales representatives to visit prospective buyers in each of the markets. The goal is not only to sell titles but also to gather information about topics of interest that the publisher is considering issuing one or more titles about. Discounts for trade titles tend to be higher than for many other types of publications.

Specialty publishers restrict output to a few areas or subjects. Facts on File is an example of a specialty publisher in the field of reference titles. Specialty publishers' audiences are smaller and more critical of the material than are trade publishers' audiences. The categories of specialty publishers include reference, paperback, children's, microform, music, cartographic, and subject areas such as librarianship. Discounts tend to be low for titles in this category.

Textbook publishers, especially those that target the primary and secondary schools (El-Hi), occupy one of the highest-risk areas of publishing. Most publishers in this area develop a line of textbooks for several grades, for example, a social studies series. Preparation of such texts requires large amounts of time, energy, and money. Printing costs are high because most school texts feature expensive color plates and other specialized presswork. Such projects require large, up-front investments that must be recouped before a profit can be realized. If enough school districts adopt a text, profits can be substantial, but failure to secure adoption can mean tremendous losses. Larger textbook firms, such as Ginn or Pearson Scott Foresman, produce several series to help ensure a profit or to cushion against loss. Given the extreme volatility of this venue, the question remains, "why would a company take this risk?" During the 1990s, U.S. El-Hi publishers faced increased pressure to change the content of their publications from a variety of special-interest groups. This pressure adds yet another element of risk to textbook publishing. Discounts are rare for El-Hi titles, except in very large quantities, and low for college-level materials.

Subject specialty publishers share some of the characteristics of textbook houses. Many have narrow markets that are easy to identify. Focusing marketing efforts on a limited number of potential buyers allows specialty publishers to achieve a reasonable return with less risk than a trade publisher takes on a nonfiction title. Specialty houses exist for a variety of fields; examples include art (e.g., Harry N. Abrams), music (e.g., Schirmer), science (e.g., Academic Press), technical (e.g., American Technical Publishers), law (e.g., West Publishing), and medical (e.g., W. B. Saunders). Many specialty books require expensive graphic preparation or presswork. Such presswork increases production costs, which is one of the reasons art, music, and science, medical, and technology titles are so costly. Another factor in their cost is their smaller market compared with the market for a trade title. A smaller market means the publisher must recover production costs from fewer books. Although the risk level is greater for specialty publishing than for trade publishing, it is much lower than that for El-Hi publishers. Discounts for such items are low to nonexistent.

Vanity presses differ from other publishing houses in that they receive most of their operating funds from the authors who pay to have their manuscript published. Two examples of such presses are Outskirts Press and iUniverse. Vanity presses always show a profit and never lack material to produce. They offer editing assistance for a fee, and they arrange to print as many copies of the book as the author can afford. Distribution is the author's chore. Although providing some of the same functions as other publishers, they do not share the same risks. Many authors who use vanity presses donate copies of their books to local libraries, but such items frequently arrive with no indication that they are gifts. Books arriving in the acquisitions department without packing slips or invoices create extra work for the staff as they attempt to determine why the item arrived. By knowing vanity publishers, acquisitions department staff can make their work easier.

Private presses are not business operations in the sense that the owners do not always expect to make money. Most private presses are an avocation rather than a vocation for the owners. Examples are Henry Morris, Bird, and Poull Press. In many instances, the owners do not sell their products but give them away. Most private presses are owned by individuals who enjoy fine printing and experimenting with type fonts and design. When an owner gives away the end product (often produced on a hand press), only a few copies are printed. In the past, many developments in type and book design originated with private presses, and some of the most beautiful examples of typographic and book design originated at private presses. Large research libraries often attempt to secure copies of items produced by private presses.

Scholarly publishers, as part of a not-for-profit organization, receive subsidies. Most are part of an academic institution (University of California Press), a museum (Museum of Northern Arizona), a research institution (Battelle Memorial Institute), or a learned society (American Philosophical Society). Scholars established these presses to produce scholarly books that would not be accepted by most for-profit publishers. As such, most scholarly books have limited sales appeal. A commercial, or for-profit, publisher considering a scholarly manuscript has three choices: (1) publish it and try to sell it at a price to ensure that costs are recovered; (2) publish it, sell it at a price comparable to commercial titles, and lose money; or (3) do not publish the item. Because of economic factors and a need to disseminate scholarly information regardless of cost (that is, even if it will lose money), the subsidized (by tax exemption, if nothing else) not-for-profit press exists. As publishing costs have skyrocketed, it has been necessary to fully subsidize some scholarly books, almost in the manner of a vanity press.

The role of the scholarly press in the economical and open dissemination of knowledge is critical. Every country needs some form of this type of press. Without scholarly presses, important works with limited appeal do not get published. Certainly there are times when a commercial house is willing to publish a book that will not show a profit because the publisher thinks the book is important, but relying on that type of willingness will, in the long run, mean that many important works will never appear in print. Discounts for scholarly press titles are normally modest at best. Like their for-profit counterparts, scholarly presses are making ever-greater use of electronic publishing techniques.

Government presses are the world's largest publishers. The combined annual output of government publications—international (UNESCO); national (U.S. Government Printing Office and Canadian Government Publishing); and state, provincial, regional, and local (Los Angeles or state of California)—dwarfs commercial output. In the past, many people thought of government publications as being characterized by poor physical quality or as uninteresting items that governments gave away. Today, some government publications rival the best offerings of commercial publishers and cost much less. (The government price does not fully recover production costs, so the price can be lower.) Most government publishing activity goes well beyond the printing of legislative hearings or actions and occasional executive materials. Often national governments publish essential and inexpensive (frequently free) materials on nutrition, farming, building trades, travel, and many other topics. (See chapter 10 for more detailed information about government publications.)

Paperback publishers produce two types of work: quality trade paperbacks and mass-market paperbacks. A trade publisher may have a quality paperback division or may issue the paperbound version of a book through the same division that issued the hardcover edition. The publisher may publish original paperbacks, that is, a first edition in paperback. Distribution of quality paperbacks is the same as for hardcover books. Mass-market paperback publishers generally, but not always, issue reprints, or publications that first appeared in hardcover. Their distribution differs from that of other books. Their low price is based, in part, on the concept of mass sales. Therefore, they sell anywhere the publisher can get someone to handle them. The paperback books on sale in train and bus stations, airline terminals, corner stores, and kiosks are mass-market paperbacks. These books have a short shelf life compared with hardcovers.

Books with paper covers are not new. In some countries all books are published with paper covers, and buyers must bind the books they wish to keep. The major difference is that most people think of only the mass-market paperback as a "paperback." The emphasis on popular, previously published titles issued in new and colorful covers and sold at a low price is apparent. Those are the elements of the paperback revolution, not the paper cover or even the relatively compact form. Nor has the paperback created a whole new group of readers, as some overenthusiastic writers claim. It has merely tapped an existing market for low-cost, popular books.

Contrary to popular belief, using a paper cover rather than a hard cover does not reduce the unit cost of a book by any significant amount. Original paperbacks incur the same costs, except for the cover material, as a hardcover title, which is why their cost is so much higher than that of reprint paperbacks. The reason the price of paperbacks is so much lower than hardcovers is that most first appeared as hardcovers. The title already sold well in hardcover, or there would be no reason to bring out a paper version, so the book has probably already shown a profit. This means the publisher has already recovered almost all of the major production costs, thus making it possible to reduce the price. In addition, releasing a paperback version of a hardcover title allows the publisher to benefit from marketing efforts expended on the hardcover version. Marketing efforts for the hardcover carry over to the paperback, which further reduces publishing costs. Economies of scale, or high sales volume and low per-unit profits, also reduce the price. Discounts for original titles in paperback are similar to those for hardbacks, while mass-market discounts tend to be higher.

Small presses are important for some libraries. Some people, including librarians think of small presses as literary presses. Anyone reading the annual "Small Press Round-Up" in *Library Journal* could reasonably reach the same conclusion. The reality is that small presses are as diverse as the international publishing conglomerates. Size is the only real difference; in functions and interests small presses are no different from large trade publishers.

A good guide to the output of small presses is *Small Press Record of Books in Print* (*SPRBIP*, Dust books). The *SPRBIP* is the definitive record of books in print by the small-press industry, listing more than 40,000 titles from more than 4,600 small, independent, educational and self-publishers worldwide and is available on a CD-ROM (http://www.dustbooks.com/sr.htm). Many small presses are one-person operations, a sideline from the publisher's home. Such presses seldom publish more than four titles per year. The listings in *SPRBIP* show the broad range of subject interests of small presses and that there are both book and periodical presses in this category. Some people assume that the content of small-press publications is poor. This is incorrect, for small presses do not produce proportionally, any more poor-quality titles than do the large publishers. Often, it is only through the small press that one can find information on less popular topics.

Another factor that sets small presses apart from their larger counterparts is economics. Large publishers have high costs and need substantial sales to recover their costs, but small presses can produce a book for a limited market at a reasonable cost and still expect some profit. Small presses can also produce books more quickly than their larger counterparts.

From an acquisitions point of view, small presses represent a challenge. Tracking down new releases can present a variety of problems. Locating a correct current address is one common problem. Another is learning about a small-press title before it goes out of print. *SPRBIP* tries to provide current information. However, waiting for the annual *SPRBIP* may take too long, because small presses frequently move about and their press runs are small, that is, only a limited quantity of books are printed.

Acquisitions departments interested in small presses have had some commercial help. Quality Books, Inc. (a vendor that in the past was known primarily as a source of remainder books) has become active in the distribution of small-press publications. Although it stocks books from only a small percentage of the presses listed in *SPRBIP* (about one-fifth), the fact that it does stock the items is a major feature. Like most other distributors, it has a Web presence (http://www.quality-books.com/).

Serial (newspaper and periodical) *publishers* are a different class of publisher. Usually, book publishers depend on persons outside their organization to write the material they publish. Newspaper and periodical publishers have staff reporters or writers. Of course, there are exceptions to the exception. For instance, some popular (and most scholarly) periodicals consist of articles written by persons not employed by the organization that publishes the journal. In general, in newspaper or periodical publishing, one finds the same range of activities found in book publishing. In other words, there are commercial publishers of popular materials, specialty publishers, children's publishers, scholarly or academic publishers, and government publishers.

All subcategories share the characteristics of their book publishing counterparts, and some are divisions of book publishing organizations.

Publishers/distributors are an important part of the publishing industry in Canada. Because Canada's small population is stretched over a very large country, distribution costs are higher and production runs are lower than in the United States. Many Canadian publishers, such as Thomas Allen and Fitzhenry & Whiteside, also function as distributors or agents of foreign publishers to supplement their publishing activities. A list of Canadian publishers is found in *Canadian Publishers Directory,* published semi-annually by International Press Publications, Inc. (http://www.ippbooks.com/store/).

ELECTRONIC PUBLISHING

There is no doubt that the world of publishing has changed and will continue to change as a result of technology. Like libraries, technology has caused producers to adjust and change the way they conduct their day-to-day activities, but at present the underlying functions remain stable. In many ways, what has taken place in publishing over the past 20-plus years is rather similar to the events that occurred in the 1440s with the invention of the printing press. Just as it took time for the printing press to become the transforming force of Western European society, so it will take time for us to realize the full potential of e-publishing. As noted by Jenkins:

> E-books are considered the third wave of electronic publishing. The first wave included the conversion of indices from secondary publishers to searchable online databases such as Dialog developed in the 1970s. The second wave came when the internet became popular and journals began converting articles to Portable Document Format (PDF) and including Standard Generalized Markup Language (SGML) to allowing users to link out to references for further study. E-books followed providing many of the benefits of their earlier counterparts, particularly 24/7 remote access.[4]

Two major factors about the two technologies have had implications for society. First, both technologies changed the manner in which people communicate with one another and the speed of the process. Second, both technologies also generated unintended consequences; none of the 15th-century printers foresaw what having more and more people able to read, write, and communicate would mean. Societies change along with their changing circumstances; however, in general, societies make adjustments rather slowly with something of a trial-and-error modifications process. Unlike the printing press in Western Europe, the digital revolution is a worldwide phenomenon. That in turn means a host of societies are attempting to assimilate the electronic environment and the speed with which people can and do communicate around the world. We are in the very early stages of what will probably be a very different world years from now.

Publishers still find the Web world something of a challenge and are struggling to find a satisfactory manner to use it and generate an adequate income stream to remain profitable. Some have tried issuing "born digital" titles (material not first released in a paper format) with less than great success. Most can offer other firms, such as Amazon and Barnes & Noble, e-versions of titles they release in paper. Finding the proper pricing structure for this approach is still very much up in the air. Perhaps the type of e-readers on market in 2010 and beyond (such as Amazon's Kindle, Sony Reader, and Barnes & Noble's Nook) will overcome the proprietary issues that caused earlier e-readers to fail.

E-Readers

While it has certainly been possible for some time to read and review books on laptop and desktop computer Web browsers through such services as NetLibrary, personal e-readers are becoming more and more popular as a convenient means of accessing e-titles. The current generation of e-readers will likely have greater staying power than their earlier predecessors, in part because there will continue to be a steady and varied supply of titles to download given the companies now offering the hardware. There is also a strong probability that the current single-function units will morph in some manner with the existing multifunction cell phones and MP3 players.

For libraries, e-readers present some new challenges for service models and acquisitions budgets. First, there is a question of just how many individuals will be willing to pay the cost for an electronic device that is a single-function proprietary device? Many librarians will remember the days when the VHS and Beta videocassettes competed for dominance—a battle that lasted for many years with Beta finally the loser. However, before the battle was over many libraries had invested considerable sums in acquiring Beta cassettes. Although the situation is somewhat different today, there is still the memory of what happened with the video formats and what happened to libraries that jumped on the e-reader bandwagon after the first e-readers came on the market not too long ago.

Assuming that a library does consider entering into a service related to the new e-readers, there are still questions regarding which platforms to support, how much money to commit to the service, whether users should pay some or all of the costs, and perhaps most importantly how to handle the increased workload (see below for examples) that e-readers would create for the staff. Also, libraries must decide whether or not to try to address both types of e-books. There are digitized e-books that libraries can provide access to online and there are titles intended for downloading onto a reader. In 2007, Connaway and Wicht reported that e-books represented only 5 percent of academic library collections, just over 2 percent of public library collections and between 15 and 60 percent of special library collections. Most of the holdings were for e-titles made available online rather than downloaded to a reader.[5] As identified by Connaway and Wicht, there are currently at least four barriers to widespread library adaptation of e-books:

- Lack of standards for software and hardware
- Usage rights (single user) tend go against libraries' operating philosophy (open access)
- Pricing models are rather unrealistic for library budgets, especially during lean economic times
- Lack of a library-based discovery system (titles are currently available only through online public access catalogs [OPACs] that for young users do not match the ease of use of Google and Yahoo).

So far, as of late 2010, efforts to get e-readers into the education market have been more or less a research and development activity than one geared to market penetration. Anne Behler reported on a joint project between Sony and the Penn State University Libraries to test 100 of Sony's e-book readers for general-use lending and in classroom settings.[6] One of the libraries' issues was that the Sony Reader is designed for a single user, or at best a family (the usage terms are for no more than five readers for a single download)—which represent serious cost and workload considerations. The project's major finding, in terms of library usage, was that "Unfortunately, the current hardware dependent-technology model is not scalable to a larger academic setting, particularly a library-supported one."[7] One of the significant factors in reaching that conclusion, and one that seems applicable to any size library, was the considerable staff time that was required to create numerous separate logins, passwords, and alias e-mail accounts, and to load books onto e-readers. The e-readers did not fare much better in the classroom setting.

E-resources present something of a conundrum for publishers and libraries. As Algenio and Thompson-Young noted, "Publishers want to sell books to customers and libraries want to lend books to users. E-books challenge both of these goals, since one e-book could be accessed by multiple library users at a time or could be protected by software that requires payment per view."[8] Just how e-readers and library service will play out is impossible to accurately predict; however, libraries have effectively dealt with a variety of information-delivery systems in the past and they will likely do so again.

TECHNOLOGY AND INFORMATION PRODUCERS

As was true of promises of cost savings from using technology in libraries, producers have *not* found that technology has reduced their cost of doing business. Perhaps part of the reason for not realizing cost savings is that the producers have not modified their approach to doing business. However, just as libraries found that they did not save money through the use of technology but were able to do more with existing resources, publishers are finding it possible to do more without increasing their personnel. For both producers and consumers the question is, "What is the correct balance between traditional and electronics at what cost?"

One area where the expected cost savings for consumers has not materialized is college textbooks. The Digital Scholarship and Publishing Center noted that despite student and faculty hopes, e-textbooks have not actually reduced end-user's expenses:

> Publishers' electronic textbooks do tend to cost less than the print versions, but the lower initial cost can be deceiving. Because publishers maintain control over digital textbooks, they can restrict how they are used and distributed. A student using an electronic textbook cannot sell that book back to the bookstore to recoup some of the cost, nor can other students buy cheaper versions of electronic texts. A 2008 study by the Student Public Interest Research Group found that on average, electronic textbooks cost the same as print versions bought and sold back to the bookstore.[9]

One factor that makes digital formats a success lies in the capability to quickly search vast quantities of text such as via Project Gutenberg and Pandora or via a commercial database like *American Poetry Database.* Another major plus for digital materials is having full-text journal articles available online. Speed, search ability, and remote access are the primary pluses of digital. On the other hand, costs and preservation are long-term concerns regarding digital formats that must be addressed by libraries—usually by technical services and/or information technology staff. Costs such as encoding (e.g., SGML, XTML) large files to increase search ability, and issues of long-term maintenance of the digital material, intellectual property rights, and data accuracy and integrity are among the more pressing issues facing libraries when it comes to digital materials.

As attractive as e-resources have become, some sense of the staying power of print is found in such sources as *Books in Print.* A check of booksinprint.com in late 2009 indicated that there were more than 7.5 million English language titles in the database. (Note: These numbers are based on unique International Standard Book Numbers [ISBNs]; thus, many titles would be double-counted if there were both hardcover and paper versions in print. Some popular titles might even be triple-counted, if there an audio version were also available.) Certainly, electronic products are being produced, but as of late 2009 they had not noticeably displaced the production of print materials. The 2003–2004 edition of *Books in Print* listed 203,000 *new* titles; Darnton noted that 976,000 new books were released worldwide in 2007.[10]

ACQUISITIONS AND E-RESOURCES

Acquisition of e-resources presents some significant differences from their paper counterparts. From a distribution perspective, there are three sources for e-materials—directly from the publisher (e.g., ABC-CLIO's eBook Collection at http://www.abc-clio.com/ProductTours/Default.aspx?tourid=18), from a vendor for e-publishers (e.g., EBSCO's Electronic Book Collections, at http://www2.ebsco.com/en-us/ProductsSer vices/ebooks/Pages/index.aspx), and from an e-book database (e.g., ebrary, at http://www.ebrary.com/corp/). No matter how the material is distributed, libraries must work through such issues as what type of reading software is required and what access model the distributor imposes. Realistically, ordering is handled directly from either the publisher or the e-book vendor. Since 2007, many publishers and e-vendors have been partnering with paper-based library book vendors to better market their products; two examples are NetLibrary (http://www.netlibrary.com/) partnering with OCLC, and EBook Library (EBL; http://www.eblib.com/?p=about) partnering with both publishers and distributors. A comprehensive article surveying the e-book vendor landscape and worth reviewing is by Vasileiou, Hartley, and Rowley,[11] who present key characteristics of 20 major e-book companies—both publishers and aggregators.

Without question, the biggest difference between print and digital book acquisition lies in what the library receives for the monies paid. "Purchased" is generally an inappropriate term for the digital book acquisition process. More often than not the e-vendor will initially offer what amounts to a lease to have access to the material under consideration. The agreement typically allows access only for as long as the library pays fees, and the library loses access should it have to cancel what is a form of subscription. (There are two major types of e-resources—serials and books/reports/government documents. For reports and government documents, access is often free and online. Serials and e-books generally require payment before access is available.)

Early successes in e-resources, from the producers' point-of-view, were with serials. For the producers, the paper-based subscription pricing models worked well and because of that early success they have moved over into the developing e-book arena. (We will explore the issues of licensing and negotiation in the serials chapter.) A few e-vendors do offer packages that become a permanent part of the library's collection after payment; however, that practice is not all that widespread yet. At the time this volume was prepared only two e-vendors offered perpetual multiple-user packages: Books 24–7 (http://books24-7.com/en/) and the aforementioned EBL. Similarly, three firms offered a single-user perpetual package—EBL, ebrary, and NetLibrary. As you might expect, the various packages have very different costs and conditions, which makes the coordination between collection development and acquisitions personnel very important. Silberer and Bass suggested that in terms of perpetual e-book pricing that, "the future of this type of pricing is probably cover price plus a premium for multiple users and perpetual ownership (i.e., 1.25 or 1.50 times the list price plus access fees based on FTE."[12] (FTE is a reference to full-time equivalent and a reflection of an academic library environment.) Another pricing option for which whose popularity and durability remains to be seen is patron-driven acquisition. Sue Polanka describes this approach in her 2009 article, "Off the Shelf: Patron-Driven Acquisition."[13]

THE GOOGLE BOOKS LIBRARY PROJECT

Electronic collections are not limited to those purchased from commercial vendors for viewing on e-readers or via Web browsers. As noted by Kovacs and Robinson, "Some digital collections are preservation projects designed to ensure that fragile historical materials are available for future generations. Libraries participate in many local history projects and preservation projects."[14] Two examples of such collections include the American Memory project, sponsored by the Library of Congress (http://memory.loc.gov/ammem/index.html), and Digital Collections@UM at the University of Maryland Libraries (http://www.lib.umd.edu/digital/). However, there is one digitization project that has gained far more press and attention than any other: the Google Books Library Project (http://books.google.com).

Although at the time we prepared this edition the final outcome of Google Books Library Project had not been decide by the courts, we believe it will exist in some form and thus should be covered. The project started around 2003 when Google approached the Library of Congress with a proposal to digitize all the books in the library. When the Library of Congress offered a counterproposal that would only include public domain (i.e., those no longer covered by copyright) books, Google did not follow up. Rather, Google turned to other major research libraries, such as those at the University of Michigan, Oxford University, and Harvard University, and the New York Public Library with some success.

The notion that a company would be allowed to make digital copies of copyrighted works got the attention of many rights holders who sued Google in 2005.

The case was complex and took until October 28, 2008, before a proposed settlement was reached. (An overview of the settlement is available from the American Library Association Washington Office Web site: http://wo.ala.org/gbs/. Google's report on the settlement may be viewed at http://books.google.com/googlebooks/agreement/.) What Google has been doing is scanning material and creating an electronic index available free of charge to users to search the database. In the case of public-domain items, users may view or download the entire text. Copyrighted works are available in small segments, which Google offers as downloadable files for a fee in the case of "orphan works" (copyrighted works that are still covered, but owner of rights not located) and copyrighted works that are not commercially available. The settlement had not yet been approved by a federal judge as of late 2010.

An article in the September 5, 2009, issue of the *Economist* reported, "Now Google and its former antagonists are seeking judicial approval for the deal they reached last year to settle the class-action suit. Among other things, this would allow the company to scan millions of out-of-print books, including orphan works, without seeking permission from individual copyright holders."[15] As part of the settlement, Google would set aside funds from sales of digitized works in a special fund (a "book-rights registry") to presumably pay copyright holders a share of the sales income. One impact of the agreement between Google and the research libraries be to "in effect create a legally sanctioned cartel for digital-book rights that could artificially inflate the price of library subscriptions."[16]

Marybeth Peters, U.S. Register of Copyright, in a statement to the U.S. House of Representatives Judiciary Committee on September 10, 2009, noted that, "Under the proposed settlement, the parties have crafted a class that is not anchored to past or imminent scanning, but instead turns on the much broader question of whether a work was *published* by January 5, 2009. As defined, the class would allow Google to continue to scan entire libraries, for commercial gain, into the indefinite future. The settlement would bind authors, publishers, their heirs and successors to these rules, even though Google has not yet scanned, and may never scan their works."[17]

It should come as no surprise that authors and publishers voiced great displeasure about the proposed settlement as they were not part of the settlement process nor were they contacted in any manner. Other countries put forward strong objections as well, and by September 2009, Google, at a hearing convened by the European Commission to attempt to answer some of the European concerns, reported that it had already digitized 10 million books both public domain and copyrighted books (without the copyright owners specific permission).[18]

How will the Google project affect libraries in the long term? That remains to be seen. (A reminder, the courts had yet to rule on the settlement when this book went to press, and the courts can accept or reject any part, or all of, the proposed agreement. Thus, what follows is based on what is in the settlement as it stands.)

On the "good for society" side, the digitized materials will be searchable using the Google search software—providing searching depth that is impossible in a paper version without great expense. It means that anyone with a computer who can connect to Google will, for the present, have free access to a wealth of information that has been vetted by the standard quality-control process of publishing, unlike the content that anyone can post on the Web without regard for accuracy. Teskey went so far as to identify three possible negative impacts, should the settlement and project ultimately fail:

(1) Publishers and authors will forfeit a major opportunity to create new commercial value for millions of out-of-print books. (2) There will be a continuing "chill" for organizations or institutions planning digitization projects, and possible lawsuits if one includes an orphan work by mistake. (3) Those with print disabilities lose the promise of a vast accessible digital collection.[19]

There several components to the service side of the proposal (free service for all users, fee-based service for all users, free public-access service for public libraries and not-for-profit academic institutions, and institutional subscriptions). The "at present" aspect previously mentioned is particularly noteworthy as Google clearly expects to generate a revenue stream from more than posting advertisements on the displayed pages. The public-access service component will be available to public and nonprofit academic libraries/institutions upon request on a one-terminal basis. A public library system would be allowed one such terminal in each building in its system. Academic libraries would be eligible for terminals based on institutional full-time equivalent employees. Although the settlement mentions the possibility of free or fee-based expansion beyond one terminal, it does not address when or at what cost such expansion might occur. (Note: Schools [kindergarten through 12th grade] and special libraries are not mentioned in the settlement.)

What could a person do at a free library-based Google terminal? All the books in the institutional subscription database would be viewable. The institutional subscription database would include all public domain and all copyrighted, but not commercially available titles. Users could print pages from the title at a reasonable per-page charge, the rate to be set by Google in conjunction with its partners. Users could not cut-and-paste text from the material. With an institutional subscription, the user could do all of this and could cut and paste up to four pages at a time and thereby, using multiple cut-and-paste operations, copy the entire title. Similarly, a person could use multiple commands to print the entire text.

Clearly, the project would have a marked impact on library retrospective collection development. It is rather unclear what the drafters of agreement had in mind by the phrase "not commercially available." Are books for sale by out-of-print dealers commercially available? It seems the dealers would say so, and much of their stock consists of titles that are in the public domain. There is no indication that there was anyone from that field at the table when the proposed settlement was reached in 2005. The bottom line is that we will have to await the court's judgment before we can realistically assess the impact of the project on library services, library budgets, and acquisitions activities. Associated Press reported on November 10, 2009, that "The Justice department has warned it would probably try to block the current agreement from taking effect because antitrust regulators had concluded it threatened to thwart competition and drive up prices."[20]

SUMMARY

Today, with products like Kindle, Sony Reader, and Barnes and Noble's Nook, many people read both paper-based and e-books, subscribe to paper-based magazines, read full-text journal articles through library databases, and buy or have home-delivered newspapers while also occasionally checking the news on the Internet. In other words, people make use of both formats depending upon physical circumstance and need. Just as radio did not destroy newspapers and television did not kill motion pictures, both print and digital information formats will likely coexist for some time to come.

This chapter briefly outlined the history and development of publishers that produce the materials libraries acquire, catalog, and process to create the collections for their user communities. It described how these businesses function and some of the major types of material they produce. It also noted how the various types of businesses differ and how those differences affect the cost of the materials acquired. It provided some background about the nature and issues related to producers efforts to remain viable in an ever-growing digital environment , and reviewed the background of the Google Books Library Project, a case all librarians should monitor, not just those in technical services.

REVIEW QUESTIONS

1. How does understanding the production of information resources benefit a person working in acquisitions?

2. What role do publishers play in the information/communication cycle?

3. Describe the typical publishing functions.

4. Discuss the factors that go into determining the price of publications.

5. Describe the major categories of publishers.

6. In what ways has the digital age affected information producers and acquisitions departments?

7. Discuss the issues related to e-readers that libraries must consider before entering this service area.

8. What are the current pricing models for e-resources?

9. Discuss the implication of Google's Book Project for libraries and copyright holders.

NOTES

The epigraphs for this chapter are from Robert Darnton, "On the Ropes? Robert Darnton's Case for Books," *Publisher's Weekly,* September 14, 2009, 18, http://www.publishersweekly.com/article/CA6696290.html and Diane K. Kovacs and Kara L. Robinson, *The Kovacs Guide to Electronic Library Collection Development* (New York: Neal-Schumann, 2004).

1. Barbara Fister, "Publishers & Librarians: Two Cultures, One Goal," *Library Journal* 134, no. 8 (2009): 24.

2. Evan St. Lifer, "Your Impact on Book Buying," *School Library Journal* 50, no. 9 (2004): 11.

3. Association of University Publishers, *One Book Five Ways* (Los Altos, CA: William Kaufmann, 1977).

4.   Alanna Jenkins, "What is Inhibiting the Proliferation of E-books in the Academic Library?" *Scroll* 1, no. 1 (2008), https://jps.library.utoronto.ca/index.php/fdt/article/viewArticle/4905/1764.

5.   Lynn Silipigni Connaway and Heather L. Wicht, "What Happened to the E-Book Revolution: The Gradual Integration of E-Books into Academic Libraries," *Journal of Electronic Publishing* 10, no. 3 (2007), http://quod.lib.umich.edu/cgi/t/text/text-idx?c=jep;cc=jep;q1=33 36451.0010.3*;rgn=main;view=text;idno=3336451.0010.302.

6.   Anne Behler, "E-readers in Action," *American Libraries* 40, no. 10 (2009): 56–59.

7.   Ibid., 57.

8.   Emilie Algenio and Alexia Thompson-Young, "Licensing E-Books: The Good, the Bad, and the Ugly," *Journal of Library Administration* 42, nos. 3/4 (2009): 113–28.

9.   Digital Scholarship and Publishing Center, *Frequently Asked Questions About Open Textbooks,* 2008, http://www.lib.ncsu.edu/dspc/opentextsfaq.html.

10.   Darnton, "On the Ropes?" 18.

11.   Magdalini Vasileiou, Richard Hartley, and Jennifer Rowley, "An Overview of the E-Book Marketplace," *Online Information Review* 33, no. 1 (2009): 173–92.

12.   Zsolt Silberer and David Bass, "Battle for eBook Mindshare: It's All About Rights," *IFLA Journal* 33, no. 1 (2007): 29.

13.   Sue Polanka, "Off the Shelf: Patron-Driven Acquisition," *Booklist* 105, nos. 9/10 (2009): 121.

14.   Kovacs and Robinson, *The Kovacs Guide to Electronic Library Collection Development,* 53.

15.   "Tome Raider," *The Economist* 392, no. 8647 (2009): 72.

16.   "Google's Big Books Case," *The Economist* 392, no. 8647 (2009): 18.

17.   Marybeth Peters, "Statement of Marybeth Peters, The Register of Copyrights, Before the Committee on the Judiciary," *Hearing on Competition and Commerce in Digital Books: The Proposed Google Book Settlement,* September 10, 2009, http://judiciary.house.gov/hearings/pdf/Peters090910.pdf.

18.   See http://judiciary.house.gov/hearings/pdf/Peters090910.pdf.

19.   John Teskey, "The Google Settlement," *Feliciter* 55, no. 5 (2009): 185.

20.   Associated Press, "Deadline in Google Book Deal Extended to Friday," *Arizona Daily Sun,* Tuesday, November 10, 2009, A8.

SUGGESTED READING

Bailey, Charles W. *Google Book Search Bibliography.* 2009. http://www.digital-scholarship.org/gbsb/gbsb.htm.

Band, Jonathan. *A Guide for the Perplexed: Libraries and the Google Library Project Settlement.* American Library Association, Association of Research Libraries, 2008. http://www.arl.org/bm~doc/google-settlement-13nov08.pdf.

Hiott, Judith, and Carla Beasley. "Electronic Collection Management: Completing the Cycle—Experiences at Two Libraries." *Acquisitions Librarian* 17, nos. 33/34 (2005): 159–78.

Kenney, Brian. "The Trouble with Google: Why Are School Libraries Being Left Out in the Cold?" *School Library Journal* 55, no. 4 (2009): 11.

McCargar, Victoria. "Kiss Your Assets Goodbye: Best Practices and Digital Archiving in the Publishing Industry." *Seybold Report* 7, no. 16 (2007): 5–7.

Morris, Carolyn. "Issues in Vendor/Library Relations—Buying eBooks: Does Workflow Work? Part I." *Against the Grain* 20, no. 4 (2008): 85–87.

Morris, Carolyn. "Issues in Vendor/Library Relations—Buying eBooks: Does Workflow Work? Part II." *Against the Grain* 20, no. 6 (2008/2009): 76–77.

Mullen, Laura Bowering. "Publishers and Librarians: New Dialogues in Changing Times." *Issues in Science and Technology Librarianship* no. 56 (2009): 6. http://www.istl.org/09-winter/viewpoint.html.

Munro, Bruce, and Peter Philips. "A Collection of Importance: The Role of Selection in Academic Libraries." *Australian Academic & Research Libraries* 39, no. 3 (2008): 149–70.

Robertson, Sharon. "Strategic Procurement of Public Library Collections." *Australasian Public Libraries and Information Services* 20, no. 1 (2007): 20–27.

Shelburne, Wendy Allen. "E-book Usage in an Academic Library: User Attitudes and Behaviors." *Library Collections, Acquisitions, and Technical Services* 33, nos. 2/3 (2009): 59–72.

Slater, Robert. "E-books or Print Books, 'Big Deals' or Local Selections—What Gets More Use?" *Library Collections, Acquisitions, & Technical Services* 33, no. 1 (2009): 31–41.

Teel, Linda M. "Applying the Basics to Improve the Collection." *Collection Building* 27, no. 3 (2008): 96–103.

Ward, Judith. "Acquisitions Globalized: The Foreign Language Experience in a Research Library." *Library Resources & Technical Services* 53, no. 2 (2009): 86–93.

Wolf, Martin. "Going E-Only: A Feasible Option in the Current UK Journals Marketplace?" *Acquisitions Librarian* 19, nos. 1/2 (2007): 63–74.

Chapter

E-Resource Issues

One major factor differentiating electronic from printed information is the shift from product to service.

—David Ball, 2006

The exchange of a print license tends to be initiated by the vendor. Since it already reflects the vendor's business model, it is up to the library to negotiate for the terms that meet the library's requirements.

—Emilie Algenio and Alexia Thompson-Young, 2005

Many experienced librarian negotiators agree: one of the biggest mistakes librarians make is underestimating the power they hold as possible negotiators.

—Jill E. Grogg, 2008

Chapter 7 concluded with some coverage of e-books and a brief discussion of some issues related to e-resources in general. In this chapter, we take a more in-depth look at how e-collection development differs from paper-based collecting and the general implications for acquisitions activities. E-collections are becoming an increasing percentage of a library's collections.

It has taken centuries for libraries to create a reasonably effective system for handling print resources. When audiovisual materials (such as recorded music and videos) became widely available to the public, it took some years for such items to become standard features in library collections. E-resources seem to have gone from a dream to an essential element in a library's service program in a flash. That adoption speed still causes some confusion for the library staff and users. The field is still working on how to create a highly effective, cost-efficient, and seamlessly integrated information collection. The number of resources that have become available electronically has grown exponentially in the recent past. However, the time may not yet be right for an "e-only" library. For a discussion of an e-only initiative attempted by the Stanford University Meyer Library, see Johanna Drucker's "Blind Spots" article, in the April 3, 2009, issue of the *Chronicle of Higher Education.*[1]

What constitutes a library's e-resource collection? An e-collection might consist of a core set of databases, a collection of links to Web sites embedded in OPAC records, and one or more terminals connected to service sites. The most familiar component is a core of databases usually containing full-text journal articles (Proquest, and EBSCOHost are two examples). E-books (NetLibrary is one such vendor) and "born digital" journals (*portal: The Library and the Academy* is one example) and books are another element of library e-collections. Embedded Web site links may be to service sites such as Ancestry Plus or to information sites like the OCLC's WorldCat or Kelly's Blue Book. At some point in the near future there is likely to be a dedicated terminal for Google Books in most public and academic libraries (at the time this chapter was being prepared there was no clear indication that school libraries would be part of the Google settlement).

DIFFERENCES BETWEEN E-RESOURCE AND PRINT COLLECTION BUILDING

There are several differences between how selection and acquisition decisions are made when it comes to e-resources. Selection of these resources builds on the criteria used when selecting paper-based titles. The quality of the material, such as accuracy, currency, and usability, are just as much factors for e-resources as they are for print items. E-resources must also reflect the information needs and wants of the library's service community. Both require at least some cost-benefit consideration. Maintaining subject/topical balance is equally important for both formats. There are, however, some significant differences, which we will cover in the next few sections.

Ownership Issues

Perhaps the most significant difference between a print and an e-resource is that a library rarely owns a physical product for the e-material. Rather, it has access rights. Many, if not most, e-resource products are only available through a license. The standard license for a product often contains some limitations regarding access and usage of the material, which can be problematic for the library.

Some of the issues that arise are (1) restrictions that may limit or forbid the use of the content for interlibrary lending, (2) limits on the number of individuals who may access the material at the same time (simultaneous users), (3) restrictions on the use of the material by nonlibrary cardholders (any user group not identified as part of the license), (4) availability of remote access (proxy server issues and in-library usage), and (5) even restrictions making the library liable for how an individual makes use of the information gathered after leaving the building. Depending on the content of the license, the library may wish to negotiate with the vendor regarding such limitations.

The license is a legal document, and institutional attorneys may have to become involved in the negotiations. Some libraries have at least considered, if they have not actually done so, spending funds on having the library's legal counsel draw up a basic license that reflects the library's starting point for the negotiations. Mark Watson explored the question of whether a library needs a legal consultant to address licensing issues. He said, "It is simply a fact of licensing life that where librarians care about the content, interface, or ability to perform interlibrary loan, the lawyers are looking for assurance that the university will not be subject to unlimited indemnification provisions, or that obligations for attorney fees will be subject to the limitations and conditions of the state constitution. . . . To sum up, I think the forces shaping our libraries today make employing a library lawyer a good, forward thinking idea."[2]

There are three basic types of licenses for digital products libraries are interested in making available to their users. First, there is the compulsory agreement. Under such licenses a library, after accepting the contract, may use the material freely as long as it pays any associated fees and complies with copyright regulations. Shrink-wrapped licenses are familiar to anyone who has purchased a software package from a store (in an online transaction, it is called a "click-on" agreement or license). The first two types are not negotiable; the third type is negotiable and is the type associated with the vast majority of digital material of interest to libraries.

Negotiating the License

The concept of negotiating a license may seem daunting. However, it is important to remember that everyone negotiates every day, even if they do not realize they are doing so. If nothing else, one interacts with family members and coworkers, and brings both parties to agreement over everything from who waters the office plants to who prepares dinner. This is negotiation in action, and as Jill Grogg wrote, we participate in a "myriad of negotiations that each of us conducts every day—in both our professional and our personal lives."[3] She also noted that for many librarians, negotiations fall into the category of business activities in which they would rather not have to engage. Further, she commented that "If librarians felt more comfortable with the specifics of contract law, copyright, and intellectual property as well as with negotiation in general, we would be better stewards for our resources and better representatives for our users."[4]

Negotiation is about resolving a matter in such a way that all parties involved achieve some gain rather than all or nothing. The "I Win! You Lose!" approach (also known as zero-sum outcomes) is not what is needed if libraries and vendors are to succeed in achieving their long-term goals. What are a few of the most common goals for libraries and vendors to achieve in the negotiation process?

Library Goals

- Secure the highest-quality content appropriate for its service community.
- Ensure reliable/stable electronic access.
- Expend available funds as prudently as possible.
- Provide maximum usage rights for the service population.
- Reduce staffing costs associated with the product's usage as much as possible.
- Avoid any limitations on existing or traditional services (such as interlibrary loan).

Vendor Goals

- Realize a maximum profit from its products.
- Improve or expand its products.
- Protect its intellectual property rights and content.
- Offer products that customers want and need.
- Retain a satisfied customer base.
- Secure positive customer recommendations through quality customer service and support.

To have a mutually beneficial negotiation, certain elements must be present on both sides of the negotiation table. First and foremost, there should be no hidden agendas. There must be open and honest exchanges of information regarding the party's positions. Everyone must be willing to listen and learn what the other side's views are and make serious efforts to understand those positions. If everyone can maintain control of what they know are their hot-button statements or words, the prospect for a good resolution is greatly improved. Finally, and most important, there must be a willingness to compromise; having a set of "never change" positions may well lead to an impasse.

Group Decision Making

Another significant difference between print and e-resource acquisitions decisions is that many, if not most, libraries employ a team or committee to select e-materials. This approach is necessary as there are both technical and content issues to think about and very often the product under consideration contains multiple titles that frequently cut across disciplines. Brian Quinn made the point that "Decisions regarding titles that represent a substantial investment, such as databases, or that involve an ongoing investment, such as subscriptions to journals, are commonly made in a group context. Important collection development decisions are made by groups whose members often consist of various stakeholders . . . all of whom are involved in developing the collection."[5] For the newcomer to the process, having an understanding of the library and its service community can be vital to being an effective advocate for a position to acquire or not acquire a product or title.

When it comes to library collections, the decision-making process can have three stakeholders—personal selection decisions, internal groups (selection committees and teams), and/or external groups (such as consortia). Although most of the basic elements of personal decision-making (such as risk and uncertainty) also apply to group decision-making, several special group-process issues are also in play. If anything, group decision-making is even more complex than personal decision-making. Many e-resource decisions are a combination of two group decisions—an internal group and an external group or consortium in which the individual library has but one voice or vote. It is also a situation in which the external decision may override or change local desires or decisions.

One important aspect of group decisions is how the group views the process—is the group searching for the best answer or trying to make the case for a particular decision. While this process is a factor for individual decisions, it becomes critical in the group setting, especially when there is both an internal and external decision involved. When a group views the process as advocacy, there is often a sense of competition to see whose view will prevail. Such an atmosphere does not lend itself to sound decision making or at least not a decision that is very rapid. Strong views or values and hidden agendas get in the way of meaningful and open exchanges.

Groups can easily fall into the trap of groupthink. Two factors frequently play a role in groupthink. Perhaps the most common is the desire to keep the process moving along. This often results in a too quick decision without much effort to develop, much less assess, multiple options. The second common factor is the desire to be a team player; this too can reduce options and very likely limit thoughtful critical assessment or idea generation. (A good article that provides guidance on group and team decision-making is H. Frank Cervone, "Making Decisions: Methods for Digital Library Project Teams," *OCLC Systems & Services* 21, no. 1 [2005]: 30–35.)

Libraries increasingly face consortial decision-making in terms of full-text journal databases. While all the above elements and issues are in play, some other issues further complicate the matter. First, and foremost, unlike internal group decisions there is rarely a single person in charge of the decision (which is especially important in the case of an impasse). Thus, accountability is very vague at best. Also, a library's choices for action are limited when it comes to consortial decisions—reject, accept, accept and hope for the best, fight to change the decision, or go on alone.

Generally, consortia decisions are ones in which two Cs—concessions and consensus—are key factors in the final outcome. Another C for consortial decision-making is consideration—a library may not always get what it would like, if the group is to succeed. A final C, one that is often the most significant, is the presence or absence of coalitions. In many ways, the existence of coalitions can help move matters forward as coalitions normally reduce the number of variables in play with a large group.

A major challenge for such groups is determining what is best. The number of bests is substantially greater in a consortial environment than for a single library. There are the bests for each institution, the bests for coalitions, and, of course, the bests for the group as a whole.

Building trust is always a factor in group decision-making, but it becomes more of a challenge for consortial members as they have less time together than individuals who work together on a daily (or even monthly) basis. Time is a key factor in creating trust and it is in limited supply in such situations. A related factor is that, more often than not, institutional representatives at such meetings are a senior, if not the senior, manager. Generally, such people are not used to having their ideas or views openly challenged, as may happen in a consortial setting. Time together, trust, concessions, and consensus are the key elements for successful consortial decision-making. (An outstanding article, if complex for those uncomfortable with qualitative methods, is Robert M. Hayes, "Cooperative Game Theoretic Models for Decision-Making in the Context of Library Cooperation," *Library Trends* 51, no. 3 [2003]: 441–61.)

Trials

For many of the e-products that libraries consider making available to their users, there is a trial period before a final agreement is implemented. There are several reasons for this:

- The relatively high cost of e-products
- The variety of search techniques available from vendor to vendor

- The actual content of the database or product
- The ease of use in terms of staff and users
- The technical requirements that need to be met to make the product available given a library's infrastructure.

In one sense, the trial is somewhat like the approval process for books. The library staff and users are able to take the product for an extended test drive. Often the trial is for consortial members only and involves strict time limits. The final acquisition decision may rest on what the membership as a whole decides. Thus, not only do the local staff members have an opinion, but so do other libraries and the local service community. As one might guess, this can add complexity to making a decision for individual libraries.

Purchase Price

To some degree, acquiring access to an e-resource is akin to purchasing a new car. At the outset, the library is not certain what the purchase price will be. Certainly, like a new automobile, there is a suggested retail price; however, just as with a new car the suggested retail price is rarely the final price. If the vendor is a firm with which the library has done a substantial amount of business over a number of years, there may be a discount for the library going it alone. When the library is part of a consortia the final price is often not settled until well after the trial period ends.

Two major factors cause the consortial price to vary. One factor is that the final price may be dependent upon the number of members who decide to participate in the deal. Generally, the more members that join, the lower the per-library price becomes. Based on the authors' experience, getting to the final cost may take several months. For example, a library that initially thought it did not want the product because of budget constraints learns that the cost is dropping as more libraries sign on and decides it would like to acquire access as well. That in turn may cause the vendor to recalculate the price—it almost always results in a lower figure but does extend the timeline. Another cost variable, especially for academic libraries, is that the vendor may set the price based on the size of the potential user population—for example, the charge might be based on the number of full-time students. As the number of users increases the price per user drops in some incremental manner. Again, as more institutions join, there is a chance that a library may decide the cost has become affordable and the final cost is once again adjusted.

What this means for the acquisitions department is there may be some extended period during which it does not know how much money should be set aside (encumbered) to pay the expected invoice. Occasionally, by the time the invoice arrives the final cost is different than anticipated—higher or lower. In either case, the change can present problems for the department, depending upon where the library is in its fiscal year (FY). If the change takes place in the first quarter of a FY, it is easier to make adjustments in the funding allocations. When such a change takes place in the final quarter, however, there may be serious problems. One might wonder why a lower price offered at any time of the year would present a problem for the department. When such an event takes place in the final quarter, the library might lose money that it may have been able to use on a different resource. (See chapter 12, on fiscal management, for a full discussion of encumbrance and fiscal-year cycles.)

Also, like a new car, products may offer optional extras or upgrades; this is especially true of journal full-text databases. Usually the base product offers access to articles from the current issue to some point back in time. For example, base coverage may be for the previous ten years; however, the journals in the database may have existed for much longer than that. The vendor may offer back-issue coverage at an additional cost. Some break down the back files into increments of 10 to 15 years, each at an added charge. It might seem obvious that a library with an interest in certain titles might well have the back issues in paper form and there would be no need to purchase access to a digital format as well. That is often the case; however, more and more users are becoming accustomed to having 24/7 remote access to journals, and they pressure the library to have key titles available in digital format as far back as possible.

Staff and User Issues

Ease of use is another consideration regarding e-resources. Would the product require staff training? How easy will it be for the public to use, or will users require staff assistance? In terms of Web sites, there is also an issue of selecting and maintaining links and deciding how to handle that ongoing task (there is some evidence that a Web address only remains active for 18 to 24 months before the owner makes some change to the address as the site is updated).[6] A source for reviews of potential Web sites that a library may wish to provide links to is the Internet Reviews Archive (http://www.bowdoin.edu/~samato/IRA/), which is the archive for the *College & Research Library News* section that lists Web sites for various subject areas.

Technical Issues

A key technical issue is where the content will reside. Will it exist on the library's server or the vendor's server? Or is it otherwise Web based? Servers have maximum limits for access, after which response time begins to decline, and in extreme cases, shuts down. Thus, having a sense of how great the load is on the library's server becomes critical to reaching a decision on whether to acquire a product that would reside on the vendor's server. Another technical consideration is the robustness of the library's information communication technology infrastructure. Certainly, both server and infrastructure can be improved, but it will increase overall costs.

There is also a question of how much technology support is needed and/or available from library staff. For smaller libraries, staffing issues are always a challenge, and committing any significant amount of time to maintaining or supporting a new product is problematic. Knowing what would be required beforehand is essential for making an informed purchase decision.

Similarly, clarifying what, if any, special equipment or software will be needed is an important issue. Also, the question of accessing the content must be fully understood. Options range from users needing a password for access, having access IP secured, or by barcode access (such as the code on a person's borrower card), or through a proxy server. An increasing concern is whether or not the resource allows for remote access, or if it can be accessed only from within the library. Each option has different library staffing implications.

Cancellations

When a library cancels a paper-based subscription, it still retains the paper copies it paid for and may keep those items indefinitely. With e-resources there is a question regarding what, if any, rights the library has to long-term access to the content that existed during the time it paid for access. (In the days when subscriptions consisted mainly of CD-ROM products that were loaded locally, normally the disks had to be returned or destroyed by the library upon termination of a subscription.) A related concern that may arise in terms of cancellations is whether the library should cancel subscriptions to paper journals if the titles are included in the e-package and/or withdraw books when they become available online. Especially with journals, the issue can be more complex than it might appear. Some publishers link the cost of the e-journal to maintaining a paper subscription—they raise the price of the e-only subscription if the library drops the paper subscription.

ASSESSMENT OF E-RESOURCES

Assessment involves several issues—content of the product, ability to select portions of the product, and statistical data regarding usage. When considering a journal database, knowing what titles are included is a factor in the selection decision. A sales pitch that the database provides full text for 3,000 journals is not at all helpful. What needs to be known are what titles, what time period they cover, whether full text mean all graphics are included, whether the graphics are part of the article's file or must be viewed or downloaded separately, and to what degree the titles replicate current paper subscriptions. These are a few of the key questions that the vendor and the library must answer.

If an e-product or e-service under consideration could or would replace paper-based items, some assessment of how great an improvement the e-version would provide is reasonable. The e-product will almost always cost more than its paper-based version, thus some form of cost benefit analysis is in order, especially in times of tight budgets. Essentially, there is a need to justify the additional costs.

Related to the cost-benefit analysis is the possibility of canceling the paper-based titles in order to reduce the overall cost of the e-title in terms of the library's budget. As noted earlier, some libraries in the early days of e-journal databases thought about and did cancel the paper subscriptions to keep within their budget only to find there were problems. For example, full-text article databases generally only include advertisements if both text and ads are on the same page. For some academic departments, the advertisements are important to their research and teaching. A more critical problem is that some publishers place an embargo on when an e-version of a journal issue may appear. The publisher's goal is to maintain its paper subscription base and may hold off on an e-version for as much as one year. For many people, such a delay is critical to their work, which means the library must maintain the paper version in addition to the electronic copy or pay interlibrary loan fees for a requested article that falls within the embargo period.

When it comes to large database products, very often they are available through one or more consortium to which the library belongs. The question then becomes, what will the package cost? It is not uncommon for the cost of the product or service to vary from consortium to consortium. This is due to that fact the consortium's price is often based on how many of its members take part in the deal. Many e-products base their academic pricing on the basis of institutional student full-time equivalents (FTEs). The rate is xx cents per student FTE, and as the total number of FTEs increases at institutions in the consortium that lease the product the rate drops. Thus, determining the library's final cost can take some time.

Statistics

While circulation and processing statistics have long been kept for print library materials, e-materials can present unique challenges when it comes to quantifying their use. Such challenges were succinctly described by Martha Whittaker, who observed

> On the face of it, keeping track of usage in the digital environment should be much easier than in the print environment. . . . Computers are good at counting things. It is not easy, however, because there are so many variables in the way people access and use digital materials. We cannot just look at circulation statistics or scan the unshelved books and journals on tables at the end of the day for accurate usage information.[7]

Inherent challenges or not, given that some libraries expend up to 51 percent of their materials budget on electronic resources,[8] this means that once an e-resource is purchased, it generally needs to be scrutinized much more closely than its print counterpart. As noted by Bertot, McClure, and Ryan, "Without the development, collection, analysis, and reporting of electronic resource and service measures . . . libraries are misrepresenting their overall service usage and potentially damaging their ability to compete for scarce funding resources in their communities."[9]

Luckily, initiatives have been developed in recent years in response to the need for gathering statistics for online resources. These include Project COUNTER (Counting Online Usage of NeTworked Electronic Resources, http://www.projectcounter.org/), and the International Coalition of Library Consortia's (ICOLC) "Guidelines for Statistical Measures of Usage of Web-Based Information Resources" (http://www.library.yale.edu/consortia/2001webstats.htm).[10] Project COUNTER was launched in 2002 as a means of setting standards for "recording and reporting of online usage statistics in a consistent, credible and compatible way," and operates through the publication of a series of Codes of Practice, which are designed to specify guidelines for the production of vendor reports. The ICOLC Guidelines, on the other hand, established consistent "boundaries" for what should be included in vendor statistical reports, without compromising user privacy or confidentiality.

COUNTER and ICOLC address statistics from the vendor side of the equation. Additionally, the implementation of a local Electronic Resource Management System (ERMS) allows libraries to track acquisitions, usage data, and licensing efforts. ERMSs are largely credited to the work of Tim Jewell at the University of Washington and the Digital Library Federation.[11] Vendors currently offering such systems include Innovative Interfaces (ERMS) and Ex Libris (Verde). Unfortunately, such systems can be cost prohibitive for some institutions. However, low-cost alternatives are available, ranging from open-source products,[12] to Web 2.0 applications[13] or the use of simple spreadsheet software.[14]

SUMMARY

As Kyrillidou and Bland noted, "Not only have electronic materials expenditures grown sharply in the past decade, they have grown at a rate far exceeding that of library materials expenditures overall. . . . In every year of the last decade electronic materials expenditures have grown sharply, anywhere between two and ten times faster than other materials expenditures have."[15] Whether or not this rate of growth can be sustained in times of economic downturn remains to be seen. However, this statistic still highlights the need for technical services staff to understand several of the unique issues surrounding the acquisition and maintenance of e-resources, including licensing issues, purchase prices, and consortial efforts to secure such resources for library collections.

A number of initiatives have been developed to help libraries analyze usage of e-resources. These include Project COUNTER, the ICOLC Guidelines, and the ARL New Measures Initiative (http://www.arl.org/stats/newmeas/newmeas.html), which includes an e-metrics component. Such initiatives have greatly facilitated the way e-resources can be analyzed. However, there is a continued need for refinement of such measures, as indicated by Blecic, Fiscella, and Wiberley, who reported that continuing "innovations in electronic resource functionality will necessitate advances in electronic resource usage measures to describe use meaningfully."[16]

REVIEW QUESTIONS

1. What are the primary components of a library's e-collection?

2. Identify the major differences between selecting and acquiring print materials and e-materials.

3. What are the typical goals for the library and for the vendor in terms of e-products?

4. Explain why it is advisable to consult legal counsel before signing a licensing agreement.

5. Discuss common reasons why vendors offer e-resource trials.

6. List several factors complicating the process of setting the purchase price for an e-resource.

NOTES

The epigraphs for this chapter are taken from Emilie Algenio and Alexia Thompson-Young, "Licensing E-Books: The Good, the Bad, and the Ugly," *Journal of Library Administration* 42, nos. 3/4 (2005): 113–28; and David Ball, "Signing Away Our Freedom: The Implications of Electronic Resource Licences," *Acquisitions Librarian* 18, no. 35/36 (2006): 7–20.

1. Johanna Drucker, "Blind Spots," *Chronicle of Higher Education* 55, no. 30 (2009): B6–B7.

2.   Mark Watson, "Licensing Electronic Resources: Is a Lawyer in Your Future?" *Technicalities* 28, no. 4 (2008): 13.

3.   Jill E. Grogg, "Negotiation for the Librarian," *Journal of Electronic Resources Librarianship* 20, no. 4 (2008): 210.

4.   Ibid., 211.

5.   Brian Quinn, "The Psychology of Group Decision Making in Collection Development," *Library Collections, Acquisitions, & Technical Services* 32, no. 1 (2008): 10.

6.   Wallace Koehler, "Web Page Change and Persistence—A Four-Year Longitudinal Study," *Journal of the American Society for Information Science & Technology* 53, no. 2 (2002): 162–71; Carmine Sellitto, "The Impact of Impermanent Web-located Citations: A Study of 123 Scholarly Conference Publications," *Journal of the American Society for Information Science and Technology* 56, no. 7 (2005): 695–703; and Mary F. Casserly and James E. Bird, "Web Citation Availability: A Follow-up Study," *Library Resources & Technical Services* 52, no. 1 (2008): 42–53.

7.   Martha Whittaker, "The Challenge of Acquisitions in the Digital Age," *portal: Libraries and the Academy* 8, no. 4 (2008): 443.

8.   Martha Kyrillidou and Les Bland, *ARL Statistics: 2007–2008* (Washington, D.C.: Association of Research Libraries, 2009), http://www.arl.org/bm~doc/arlstat08.pdf.

9.   John Carlo Bertot, Charles R. McClure, and Joe Ryan, *Statistics and Performance Measures for Public Library Networked Services* (Chicago: American Library Association, 2001).

10.   International Coalition of Library Consortia, "Guidelines for Statistical Measures of Usage of Web-Based Information Resources," 2001, http://www.library.yale.edu/consortia/2001webstats.htm.

11.   Timothy D. Jewell, *Selection and Presentation of Commercially Available Electronic Resources* (Washington, D.C.: Digital Library Federation and Council on Library and Information Resources, 2001), http://www.clir.org/pubs/reports/pub99/pub99.pdf; and Timothy D. Jewell, Ivy Anderson, Adam Chandler, Sharon E. Farb, Kimberly Parker, Angela Riggio, and Nathan D.M. Robertson, *Electronic Resource Management: Report of the DLF ERM Initiative* (Washington, D.C.: Digital Library Foundation, 2004), http://www.diglib.org/pubs/dlf102/.

12.   William Doering and Galadriel Chilton, "ERMes: Open Source Simplicity for Your E-Resource Management," *Computers in Libraries* 29, no. 8 (2009): 20–24.

13.   Adam Murray, "Electronic Resource Management 2.0: Using Web 2.0 Technologies as Cost-Effective Alternatives to an Electronic Resource Management System," *Journal of Electronic Resources Librarianship* 20, no. 3 (2008): 156–68.

14.   Mary Walker, "E-Resource Statistics: What to Do When You Have No Money," *Journal of Electronic Resources Librarianship* 21, no. 3 (2009): 237–50.

15.   Kyrillidou and Bland, *ARL Statistics,* 18.

16.   Deborah D. Blecic, Joan B. Fiscella, and Stephen E. Wiberley Jr., "Measurement of Use of Electronic Resources: Advances in Use Statistics and Innovations in Resource Functionality," *College & Research Libraries* 68, no. 1 (2007): 42.

SUGGESTED READING

Albitz, Becky. *Licensing and Managing Digital Resources.* Oxford: Chandos Publishing, 2008.

Best, Rickey D. "Issues on the Selection of Electronic Resources." In *Handbook of Electronic and Digital Acquisitions,* ed. Thomas W. Leonhardt, 91–126. Binghamton, NY: Haworth Press, 2006.

Brown, Kincaid C. "Tactics and Terms in the Negotiation of Electronic Resource Licenses." In *Electronic Resource Management in Libraries: Research and Practice,* ed. Holly Yu and Scott Breivold, 174–93. Hershey, PA: IGI Global.

Cervone, H. Frank. "Managing Digital Libraries: The View From 30,000 Feet: Strategic Analysis for Digital Library Development." *OCLC Systems & Services* 25, no. 1 (2009): 16–19.

Cervone, H. Frank. "Managing Digital Libraries: The View From 30,000 Feet: Working Through Resistance to Change by Using the 'Competing Commitments Model." *OCLC Systems & Services* 23, no. 3 (2007): 250–53.

Collins, Maria D.D., and Patrick L. Carr. *Managing the Transition from Print to Electronic Journals and Resources: A Guide for Library and Information Professionals.* New York: Routledge, 2008.

Chou, Min, and Oliver Zhou. "The Impact of Licenses on Library Collections." *Acquisitions Librarian* 17, nos. 33/34 (2005): 7–23.

Cole, Louise. "The E-Deal: Keeping Up to Date and Allowing Access to the End User." *The Serials Librarian* 57, no. 4 (2009): 399–409.

Conger, Joan E. "Negotiation for the Rest of Us." *Serials Librarian* 50, nos. 1/2 (2006): 105–17.

Farrelly, Michael Garrett. "Revisiting the Digital Divide." *Public Libraries* 48, no. 5 (2009): 22–23.

Feick, Tina. "Electronic Journal Subscriptions: The Agent's Perspective." *Against the Grain* 17, no. 6 (2005): 42–45.

Gedye, Richard, and Fytton Rowland. "Usage Factors." *Serials* 22, no. 3 (2009): 233–34.

Gregory, Vicki L., and Ardis Hanson. *Selecting and Managing Electronic Resources: A How-to-do-it Manual for Librarians,* rev. ed. New York: Neal-Schuman, 2006.

Harris, Lesley Ellen. "Licenses and Legalities: Know Your Rights—And Obligations—When Using Licensed Electronic Content." *American Libraries* 40, nos. 6/7 (2009): 58–60.

Harris, Lesley Ellen. *Licensing Digital Content.* Chicago, IL: American Library Association, 2002.

Hiott, Judith, and Carla Beasley. "Electronic Collection Management: Completing the Cycle—Experiences at Two Libraries." *Acquisitions Librarian* 17, nos. 33/34 (2005): 159–78.

International Coalition of Library Consortia (ICOLC). *Statement on the Global Economic Crisis and Its Impact on Consortial Licenses,* 2009. http://www.library.yale.edu/consortia/icolc-econcrisis-0109.htm.

Ives, Gary, and Steve Fallon. "Stung If You Do, Stung If You Don't—The Good and the Bad of the Big Deal." *Serials Librarian* 56, no. 1–4 (2009): 163–67.

Joshipura, Smita. "Selecting, Acquiring, and Renewing Electronic Resources." In *Electronic Resource Management in Libraries: Research and Practice,* ed. Holly Yu and Scott Breivold, 48–70. Hershey, PA: IGI Global, 2008.

Kinman, Virginia. "E-Metrics and Library Assessment in Action." *Journal of Electronic Resources Librarianship* 21, no. 1 (2009): 15–36.

McMullen, Susan, Patricia B.M. Brennan, Joanna M. Burkhardt, and Marla Wallace. "Collection Development Strategies for Online Aggregated Databases." In *Handbook of Electronic and Digital Acquisitions,* ed. Thomas W. Leonhardt, 61–90. Binghamton, NY: Haworth Press, 2006.

Shipe, Timothy. "Travels into Several Remote Corners of the Information Universe: A Voyage to the Department of the Houyhnhnmists, or, Licensing Issues and the Integrated Collection." *Acquisitions Librarian* 17, no. 33/34 (2005): 25–34.

Strader, C. Rockelle, Alison C. Roth, and Robert W. Boissy. "E-Journal Access: A Collaborative Checklist for Libraries, Subscription Agents, and Publishers." *Serials Librarian* 55, no. 1/2 (2008): 98–116.

Torbert, Christina. "Collaborative Journal Purchasing Today: Results of a Survey." *Serials Librarian* 55, no. 1/2 (2008): 168–83.

Tucker, Cory. "Benchmarking Usage Statistics in Collection Management Decisions for Serials." *Journal of Electronic Resources Librarianship* 21, no. 1 (2009): 48–61.

Chapter

9

Serials—Print and Electronic

Love e-journals or hate them, one thing a library cannot do is ignore them.

—*Margaret Sylvia, 2005*

Within the next ten years or so, we predict that many more major magazine and newspaper publications will be going all-digital. In that environment, should we continue to provide a format-based area of the library (the periodicals room)?

—*Michael Porter and David Lee King, 2009*

There is some validity to having older magazines as they are primary source material, serving as a window to the past.

—*School Librarians Workshop, 2009*

For some people serials are the most frequently consulted library resource. In the not-too-distant past, it was print-based serials, and today it is a combination of print and digital that many people expect and want. People still subscribe to paper-based newspapers and magazines. Professional associations still issue information in paper but also release it in an e-format. How long this dual process will last is an open question. However, it seems likely it will exist for the lifetime of this edition of *Introduction to Library Technical Services*. Thus, we will discuss both formats although there will be a greater emphasis on the digital side.

A shift to electronic serials, or e-serials, is an ongoing process in most libraries, as they secure the necessary funding or are able to leverage the price advantages of consortia pricing of publishers' or aggregator's packages. Some academic libraries have established a policy that electronic versions of serials are the first choice rather than paper. However, there are some reasons beyond cost that would lead many libraries to continue to retain paper titles, perhaps in addition to an e-version. Any library that of-fers recreational reading materials is likely to keep subscriptions to paper versions of the most popular serials—magazines and newspapers. There are still people who enjoy sitting and reading the entire issue of a magazine or newspaper. Although it is possible to do this with electronic publications, the process is cumbersome, time consuming, and not all that pleasant. From a library point of view, having a user monopolize a computer for an hour or more while reading all of the articles in a journal is rarely practical, as few libraries have sufficient machines to allow more than a limited time per user.

There are also individuals who enjoy looking at the advertisements, which are gen-erally omitted in the e-version. Another factor is many people do not have home access to high-speed broadband network connections. Downloading even a relatively small PDF containing modest graphics with a dial-up connection takes a very long time. An-other factor is the escalating cost of subscriptions, even for individuals, which translates into people depending on libraries for access to some of their lower-interest journals and magazines.

Currency is very important for those who use serials on a regular basis. Serial update intervals can be very short, daily in the case of many newspapers. Articles in a serial are short (compared to book-length treatments of the same topic) and focus on a fairly narrow subject. Readers with very specific information needs frequently find that serials provide the desired data more quickly than books. Finally, serials are often the first printed source of information about a new subject or development. People use serials as a source for learning about new things while using books to gain a broader or deeper knowledge of a subject they may have first encountered in a serial. Also, the sheer volume of new information appearing in serials far exceeds that of books.

Technology has modified almost every aspect of library operations; its impact on many activities, if not most, has been in how we do something rather than what we do. With serials, at least for the electronic versions (or e-serials), the "what is done" is very different now (a few examples being the elimination of: check-in, labeling issues, insert-ing security strips, shelving and reshelving, searching for missing issues, gathering up issues to go to the bindery, or shifting of bound copies to make room for new volumes). Obviously, while these advances are major changes in the way serials work is done—all those steps do still apply to paper-based serials in the vast majority of libraries.

WHAT IS A SERIAL?

Customers and librarians frequently use the words *journals, magazines, periodi-cals,* and *serials* interchangeably, with no great misunderstanding resulting from the im-precise usage. Thomas Nisonger, in his book on serials management, devoted more than six pages to how different groups have attempted to define the material that is covered in this chapter.[1] As noted earlier, the electronic world is changing the nature of serials and the way libraries process them. The Internet has even changed what a library should consider a serial. T. Scott Plutchak suggested that "The serial as defined by the librar-ians is an anachronism in the digital age, and will not survive for long. . . . This matter of definitions bedevils us all, and I'm sure you've had the same kinds of discussions in your institutions that we've had in mine as we try to figure out how to shoehorn these new information resources that we're dealing with into the same old categories."[2] For our purposes, the following definition will suffice: a serial is a publication issued as one of a consecutively numbered and indefinitely continued series.

Plutchak's point is well taken, that is, the library focus has been, and still is to a large extent, on the physical format rather than content. However, at present the old definitions still exist and are widely used in libraries. What are those definitions? Some years ago, Fritz Machlup and Kenneth Leeson developed an 18-part classification system for serials.[3] Their system covered all types of serials, including serials "not elsewhere classified." (We have yet to encounter a serial that does not fit into one of the other 17 categories.) Each of the major categories has some special features that have implications for the acquisitions staff.

Institutional reports are annual, semiannual, quarterly, or occasional reports of corporations, financial institutions, and organizations serving business and finance. Academic libraries serving business and management programs frequently need to acquire this type of serial. Corporate libraries actively collect this category. Most of the reports available to libraries and information centers are free for the asking.

Some organizations will add a library to their distribution list, but others will respond only to requests for the current edition. Collecting in this area is labor intensive, because it requires maintaining address and correspondence files, especially if a library collects much beyond the large national corporations. Thanks to online resources, such as EDGAR Online (from the Securities and Exchange Commission), filings are now available from a number of sources.

Yearbooks and proceedings are annuals, biennials, and occasional publications, bound or stapled, including yearbooks, almanacs, proceedings, transactions, memoirs, directories, and reports of societies and associations. Many libraries collect these serials, especially academic, special, and large public libraries. The more libraries that collect a particular society's or association's publications, the more likely it is that a commercial vendor will handle a standing order for the material. Although it is possible to secure some of these serials through a vendor, a significant number must be obtained directly from the society or association. Again, this category normally requires setting up and maintaining address and correspondence files, which is only slightly less labor intensive than doing the same for annual reports of organizations.

Superseding serials fall into one of two categories, both of which are labor intensive in their paper-based format. One group consists of the superseding serial services (each new issue superseding previous ones). These include publications such as telephone directories and product catalogs. The second group consists of the non-superseding serial services, many of which were print-based loose-leaf publications that provided information such as changes in accounting rules or government regulations. In the past, both groups often required careful filing of new material and the removal of other (older or superseded) material. Most of the services are now available online, reducing most of the staffing and training issues. Most of these publications are only available from the publisher. Examples of such services are the *Labor Relations Reporter* from the Bureau of National Affairs, the *Standard Federal Tax Reporter* from Commerce Clearing House, and *Ontario Annotated Reports* from LexisNexis Canada.

Non-superseding serials are less of a problem, and some are available from serial jobbers. However, the materials in this class tend to be expensive, and many must be ordered directly from the publisher. Indexing and abstracting services fall into one of these two classes. All types of libraries need a few of these reference serials. As the serial collection grows, there is an increasing demand from users for more indexing and abstracting services.

Newspapers are one of the obvious serials that libraries acquire in both print and electronic formats. Serial jobbers handle subscriptions to major domestic and international newspapers for libraries. At the time the order is placed for a paper subscription for nonlocal newspapers, the library must establish the value of the newspaper's content for its user community. That is, how critical is it to have the latest issue in the shortest possible time? For example, *The London Times* can be ordered in a variety of delivery packages, each with a different cost: daily airmail edition by air freight, daily airmail edition by airmail (the most expensive option), daily regular edition by air freight, daily regular edition in weekly packets (the least expensive option), or microfilm edition. *The New York Times* offers an even wider variety of editions: city edition, late city edition, national edition, New York edition, large-type weekly, same day, next day, two day, weekly packets, microfilm, and others. Clearly, each variation has cost and workload implications.

Almost all major newspapers are now somewhat available online; we say somewhat because at the time this was written, newspapers were struggling with the issue of staying in business. They are trying to develop a workable model for generating income to replace revenue lost due to rapidly declining paper subscriptions. As a result they often allow free access to a limited version of a story and provide access to the full story when a reader pays a fee—per-story fee, monthly fee, and annual fee are some of the models in use in 2010. Libraries can also provide online access through several database vendors such as NewsBank; some of the serials databases include some newspaper coverage as well, for example EBSCO*host*.

Newsletters, leaflets, news releases, and similar materials are a form of serial that some libraries actively acquire. Corporate libraries are the most active in gathering material in this category, especially those supporting marketing, lobbying, and public relations activities. Many of the items in this class are free; all a library needs to do is ask to be placed on the distribution list. Other items, especially newsletters containing economic or trade data, can be exceedingly expensive. (A number of U.S. services cost in excess of $20,000 for quarterly newsletters of only a few pages. It is at that point that one can begin to fully appreciate the difference between the cost of the information and the cost of the package in which it comes.) Whether a service is free or subscription based, someone must put in the time and effort to identify the sources and get on the appropriate mailing lists or enter the subscription.

Magazines are the most common serials and the category that most often comes to mind when thinking about serials. Machlup and Leeson defined magazines as mass-market or popular serials and divided them into five subgroups. These are the titles that almost any serial jobber will handle for a library. Following are the five subgroups:

- Mass market serials and weekly or monthly news magazines (such as *Newsweek* or *Macleans*)
- Popular magazines dealing with fiction, pictures, sports, travel, fashion, sex, humor, and comics (such as *Sports Illustrated* or *Toronto Fashion*)
- Magazines that popularize science and social, political, and cultural affairs (*Smithsonian* or *Canadian Geographic*)

- Magazines focusing on opinion and criticism—social, political, literary, artistic, aesthetic, or religious (examples are *Foreign Affairs* or *This Magazine*)
- Other magazines not elsewhere classified. An example of such a title is an organization publication (governmental or private) that is really a public relations vehicle, sometimes called a "house organ." These publications often contain general-interest material, but there is usually some clearly stated or implied relationship between the subject covered and the issuing organization (e.g., *Plain Truth* or *On Patrol*). Another type of publication in the "other" category is the magazine found in the pocket of airline seats.

Libraries may receive a substantial number of house organs because their publishers give them away. Vendors seldom handle this type of magazine.

Journals are, in the Machlup system, titles that are of interest to a narrower segment of the user population, sometimes referred to as "informed laypeople," and researchers and scholars. This category has four subcategories, with one subcategory divided into two smaller units:

- Nonspecialized journals for the intelligentsia who are well-informed on literature, art, social affairs, politics, and so on (*Science* and *Equinox* are examples)
- Learned journals for specialists—primary research journals and secondary research journals (*American Indian Culture and Research Journal* and *The Canadian Historical Review,* for example)
- Practical professional journals in applied fields, including technology, medicine, law, agriculture, management, library and information science, business, and trades (*RQ* or *Canadian Journal of Emergency Medicine*, for example)
- Parochial journals of any type but addressed chiefly to a parochial audience— local or regional—(*Kiva* or *Toronto Life*).

Most titles in these categories are available through vendors, although the library must place direct orders for some of the more specialized learned journals. Most parochial journals must be purchased directly from the publisher; local history and regional archaeological publications are examples of this class of serial. Sometimes a library must join an association to obtain its publications.

The final serial category identified by Machlup consists of "government publications, reports, bulletins, statistical series, releases, etc. by public agencies, executive, legislative and judiciary, local, state, national, foreign and international." Because this group is covered in chapter 10, no discussion is included here.

With these variations in serials in mind, it is clear why there is confusion about terms and why there are challenges in collecting and preserving them. Each type fills a niche in the information dissemination system. Although they do create special handling procedures and problems, they are a necessary part of any library's collection. Patrick Carr opened his article with the following:

The literature of serials librarianship published in 2006 and 2007 reveals a field in rapid transition. The changes occurring range from the shifting nature of serial collections to evolving models, initiatives, and management strategies used to acquire and administer access to these collections.[4]

The remainder of this chapter looks at some of the long-standing issues related to serial management and many of the transition issues alluded to in the Carr quotation.

ISSUES AND CONCERNS

Aline Soules explored the issues of the changing nature of the concept of serials in the digital world and the challenges facing both the producers and consumers of the information such publications make available. She concluded her article by stating; "The older, established concept of a serial served as the basis for the new, more flexible concepts of continuing and integrating resources."[5] The key word in the foregoing is "continuing." The following issues and concerns relate to serials, whether print or electronic, in their current forms. How they may change over the next 5 to 10 years is impossible to predict accurately. What is certain is that the issues and concerns will continue to evolve and change.

A serial, by definition, usually implies that the library will have an ongoing commitment to acquire the title. That commitment raises issues of staffing and budget concerns. From a technical services workload point of view, print subscriptions require annual renewal and attention. E-serials, at least those in a vendor's package of serials, require somewhat less staff attention; however, such packages ought to be reviewed annually. Most serial vendors have a system that allows for automatic renewal, thus reducing some of the staffing concerns. Such automatic renewal options should not stop the staff from annually reviewing the renewal list to ensure that all the titles and databases are still of interest to the user community.

Cost and Pricing

A long-term commitment to a serial results in subscription costs becoming a fixed feature of the budget. With rapidly rising prices and small budget increases, each year serials take up an increasing proportion of the total materials budget. Chapter 12 (on fiscal management) provides more information about this problem, but in general, serial prices have been increasing at a much faster rate than general inflation. Thus, each year the amount of money required to maintain the present serials subscriptions increases at a rate greater than many libraries are able to sustain.

One important difference between print and electronic serials, from the library perspective, is that e-serials pricing is very opaque compared with print. Print prices are basically fixed, though there may be a discount for placing a multiple-year subscription. Perhaps there is a discount if the library subscribes to several titles from the same publisher. A serials jobber may give a discount to a library when the total value of the subscriptions reaches a certain level. In such cases, it is based on the total list of titles not any one title.

When it comes to pricing e-versions of titles, the picture is rather murky. Some of the factors that complicate the situation are

- pricing based on being a component of a bundle or deal,
- pricing that links paper and digital versions of a title,
- pricing based on the concept of "site" (frequently, branches of a library each count as an independent unit rather than as part of a single system),
- pricing based on the number of simultaneous users (maximum number of readers allowed at one time),
- pricing based on a license for a single library versus one obtained through a consortium, and
- pricing based on receiving the current title only or including both the current issues and backfiles.

Essentially, one is never completely certain what the cost will be until the invoice arrives.

Publishers have employed a dual pricing model for some time for print titles—one price for individual subscribers and another for institutions and libraries. The rationale behind the model was that the institutional subscription provided access for many readers, some of whom might be individual subscribers if it were not for the institutional subscription. For electronic serials, some publishers and vendors employ a somewhat similar tiered model. This model is based on some range of factors, such as the size of the library's acquisition budget or the number of potential readers/users. Most of the tiered schedules have multiple tiers, such as using the acquisitions budget example (under $100,000, $100,001 to $250,000, and so forth) as price points or tiers. Tiered pricing is rather common for consortia purchases, and the final cost for a library becomes a function of how many libraries decide to participate in the deal. (We discussed this issue in chapter 8.)

Some publishers allow free online access when a library or individual places an order for a print subscription. An example is *The Economist,* which allows for online access to back issues, additional material for a story in the print issue, and access to additional news stories. One reason for providing the access for libraries is that it appears to maintain a subscriber base, which is a factor in how the publication is able to charge advertisers—more subscribers equals a higher advertising fee. The extra material available online becomes a bonus for the library users.

Some years ago Kristin Gerhard suggested that there are nine pricing models for e-serials:[6]

1. General price-for-value
2. Clarity or firmness
3. Number of simultaneous users
4. Type of users
5. Location of seats
6. Amount of use
7. Unit priced
8. Timing of payments
9. Division of pricing

By price-for-value, she was suggesting a relationship from the library perspective between readers to cost—many readers for a high-price publication could be viewed as inexpensive, while a low-priced title with only one or two readers would be considered expensive. The model also includes extra features that become part of the subscription, such as online access to additional material. Her clarity or firmness model related to how much flexibility there was in the price—if a discount was available or not and if negotiation was possible, for example. (We touched on simultaneous users in the preceding paragraphs.) Type of users related to such factors as total institutional full-time equivalents, student majors in a discipline, or business type in nonacademic environments. Location of seats is a variation of the site pricing covered earlier. Amount-of-use models include pay per page viewed, pay for amount of time, or unlimited usage. Unit pricing relates to a charge per article, per issue, or per journal—current and/or backfile. Timing of payments is more like financing payments—one time, quarterly, or other some other option—of course with some interest costs associated, and/or possible maintenance fees. The final model is a consortia model in which the total package price is divided equally among members.

The bottom line is that the proliferation of e-serials has not reduced the cost of acquiring and maintaining a serials collection—an early hope of librarians. Publishers have realized little in terms of cost savings from moving from print to digital formats; nor has the greater than Consumer Price Index (CPI) price increase spiral slowed much. The e-format has not changed the amount of library staff time that must be devoted to managing serials—the work is rather different, but the time commitment is just as great. What e-serials have done is provide more readers with more information more quickly than was ever possible in the print-only environment.

Acquisition

Electronic serials have created new challenges for acquisitions departments. Perhaps one of the biggest challenges is calculating price increases. As we will discuss in chapter 12, having sound estimates of the coming year's price increases is very important for the acquisitions department and the library. Print journals have a long history of double-digit annual price increases. As a result, the profession and serial vendors developed several annual reports that provide some rather accurate estimates of the potential jumps in price. The reports break prices down into various subject/topical/library-type categories, making it possible to make predications. That system has not worked very effectively for e-titles, however, at least for the producer and vendor packages, because of the number of variables in how a library acquires access to such packages.

The so-called "Big Deal" packages of e-journals have created the most difficulty for predicting cost increases year to year for even a class of libraries. Carlson and Pope noted that the Big Deals offered a library a large number of titles for a flat annual license fee.[7] Publishers and other vendors (sometimes referred to as aggregators) put forward packages. In the case of publishers, the package usually included all of their titles; aggregators offered packages of titles from a variety of publishers. Some libraries negotiated a license independently, while many more acquired access through a consortium. To complicate estimating e-price increases, various consortia worked out a price based on its membership, which could change from year to year. The result has been rather great price variations.

Another outcome of the Big Deal is that many of the packages are just that, a package. A library either gets all the titles or does not get the package. That means a library may, or likely will, have to handle a number of titles that are irrelevant for its service population. As noted earlier, there are many issues associated with handling e-titles, and having extra work related to titles almost no local user is interested in just adds to the staff workload with no tangible benefit for the library. David Ball noted that with Big Deals in place, "we no longer take the decisions on developing our collections that we have been used to. . . . We shall increasingly decide on content not at the journal level but at the publisher level."[8] Users are interested in content not the journal title or who publishes the information. Packages of serials shift the focus away from a fundamental tenet of collections development—meeting user needs. Big-deal costs can be so high as to reduce available funds to the point that a library must start canceling individual subscriptions or dramatically cut back on book and media purchases. A counterpoint view regarding the value of big packages was expressed by Donald Taylor, who noted that newly available titles could be used by researchers: "Although this analysis is only a snapshot of activity, the increase in citations in 2004 and 2005 to articles from Big Deal journals previously unavailable to SFU [Simon Fraser University] Library demonstrates that SFU researchers are making use of these previously unavailable journals in their research."[9]

By early 2010, the economic picture for libraries had radically changed from what it was when Big Deals first were being offered. As a result, stagnant or declining financial resources have forced a rethinking of the overall value of such packages. Certainly, some libraries have sharply reduced their use of package deals. Some have been working with vendors and publishers to modify packages—tailoring the package to reflect just titles the library needs and thereby reduce the cost of the package. In late 2009, David Fowler suggested that,

> The next twelve months to two years will be critical to the future of libraries as they look to new ways to acquire and present materials in a time of declining budgets, but with an ever-demanding user base. Full or partial divestment of Big Deal packages is an inevitable element of this transition. The full impact of how libraries will cope is yet to be known, but it seems inevitable that the publishing landscape will look much different in 2011 and beyond than it does in 2009.[10]

As is true of most aspects of e-serials, managing them is complex. One small example are open-access titles (discussed more fully later in this chapter), which may or may not pass through the acquisitions department because they are free. Such titles raise the issue of who will be responsible for ensuring that such titles are available in the same manner as paid-for titles. Another question is, who in the library is responsible for the various licenses? When it comes to a new package license, the matter may be straightforward; however, just as serial prices increase every year, many licensors make small adjustments to their agreements from time to time. Tracking such modifications and assessing their implications can present a challenge.

Because of the complexity of managing electronic resources, most ILS vendors and other vendors offer serials management software. Most of the available packages have three special features:

- The system links or shows the relationship of each e-title, package, license, and how the library makes the material accessible to users.

- The system is able to track each of the above for each title.
- The system provides the capability to generate a variety of reports and can export data about each, all, or a subset of titles.

The following list of items these system do, or ought to, track suggests just how complicated the process is. Some factors apply to managing either print or electronic titles and some apply to e-serials only.

Factors that apply to print and electronic titles:

- Title
- Purchase order number
- Fund charged
- Date ordered
- Vendor/publisher
- Annual subscription cost
- Renewal date
- Coverage dates

Factors that apply only to e-serials:

- Information if both print and e-versions
- Consortia source, if applicable
- Usage statistics (from online sources)
- URL of title in library
- Limitations on access, if any
- License restrictions
- Date license was reviewed
- Person signing license
- Cataloging notification
- Webmaster notification
- Administrative user name and password
- Technical support information

Processing

Another fixed element of serials is processing. Both print titles and e-serials require regular maintenance and updating. When ordering and receiving a monograph, the library incurs a one-time cost. but serials have ongoing costs regardless of format.

Checking in and claiming missing issues is a normal part of maintaining print serials collections. A staff member records each issue when it arrives in the library. When a person notes a missing item, the library contacts the publisher or subscription agent to request the missing material—this is known as *placing a claim.* Acting promptly is important because publishers generally print only slightly more copies than the number of subscribers. Serial publishers know a certain percentage of issues do go astray in the mail, and they print extra copies to cover expected claims. There are times when the number of claims is greater than the number of available copies. When that happens, some unlucky libraries receive out-of-print notices. The closer the claim is made to the publication date, the greater the chances are of receiving the wayward issue. ILS serial modules assist in all aspects of serials work, including providing automatic claiming. Clearly, each new serial adds to the workload on an ongoing basis.

Work routines for electronic publications, as mentioned earlier, are different. The Digital Library Federation has developed a set of flow diagrams that reflect a type of best practices for acquiring electronic journals (http://www.diglib.org/pubs/dlf102/dlf102.htm#dlfermi0408appb). (We urge readers to review this document to fully grasp the complexity of the process. Many of the items on the chart are activities that must also be handled for print titles.)

Processing e-journals and e-serials, from selection to access, is a complex process as the aforementioned flow charts illustrate. We touched on the issue of knowing the final cost of e-materials earlier. Another question is, how many times does a library need to provide access to the same material? And, how much money might be saved if the title were available in only one database? We cannot say much about the cost factor of title duplication; however, there is clear evidence regarding the actual duplication concern.

The following is a small example of title duplication in aggregator databases using two librarianship titles. *Library Resources & Technical Services* is available full text electronically from the American Library Association, Wilson's *Omnifile* and *Library Literature and Information Science Full Text, ProQuest Central* and *ProQuest Research Library,* and EBSCOhost's *Academic Search Complete. Library Journal* has even greater duplication—in addition to its availability in the EBSCO, ProQuest, and Wilson databases, it is also found in ABI/*Inform, LexisNexis Academic,* and *MasterFILE Premier.*

Most libraries have limited acquisition funds, so licensing access to the same title multiple times does cost more than necessary at times—each aggregator pays the publisher a fee for each title in the database. Although the amount of money may be small, there is additional work for the library. The challenge is that not all the databases are equal in their coverage and the end-users need to know what is covered where and when in order to decide which product to start searching. (Using *Library Journal* as an example, EBSCO covers 1976 to date, ABI and ProQuest databases have 1989 onward, Wilson coverage starts in 1998, and LexisNexis coverage starts with 2001.) Most aggregate databases contain thousands of titles. Someone on the library staff must identify the all titles and the coverage in all the databases and ensure the accuracy of the information on an ongoing basis. We explore additional issues of access in the next section of this chapter.

Another factor that creates work challenges and cost concerns for the library is that occasionally a publisher will decide to enhance the digital revenue stream for a title by auctioning off the digital rights to a single aggregator. When that happens, assuming the title in question is very important to the library's user community, it may mean licensing a database that contains that title and hundreds or even thousands of titles of little or no interest.

Access

Gaining access to serial content is also a concern. In a print environment, users have little interest in searching through issue after issue to locate needed material, especially in light of the ease of employing the Boolean search capabilities of online databases.

An entire industry has developed around providing access to print serials. A variety of indexing and abstracting services provide services that help people locate information in serials. Naturally, most of these services are expensive and represent a further concern when maintaining a useful serials collection. There are also access issues related to digital serials, although of a very different type. Earlier, we mentioned the issue of what happens to access to articles in e-titles when the library cancels its subscription. At least with print issues, the library retains the issues it paid for; continuing access to such e-issues may or may not be possible depending on the license terms the library agreed to when it started the subscription.

One important reason users want access to serials is their currency. Digital versions of print-based titles may or may not be as current as the print version. There are two aspects to this issue—who creates the digital version and when that version is released. Converting the print material to a digital format takes some time, perhaps just a matter of a few hours between when the print and digital forms are available to users; however, when the publishers outsource the digitization work, the delay can be weeks or even months. The second factor is an embargo placed on the release of the electronic version. That is, the publisher, in an effort to retain the paper subscription base, withholds the release of digital version for a period of time. The length of that time frame varies; a frequent embargo period is until the next print issue is released. Other publishers may employ a fixed period, such as two or more months regardless of when the next issue appears. (Yearlong embargoes of full-text content in aggregator databases are not uncommon.)

A rarely discussed access issue, at least in the professional literature, is the completeness and reliability of the digital version compared with the print version. A print version is not subject to modification of its content. Digital versions can be and are easily modified, and not just for correcting an author error of fact. Yes, publishers do issue corrections and errata sheets from time to time; however, those do not modify the text that first appeared.

There are occasions when e-content was there yesterday and then—poof—it's gone today. Such disappearances arise most often from a court decision or legal settlement. One major example, which is still not fully resolved, started in 2001 (*New York Times v. Tasini*). The original Supreme Court decision revolved around the question of when is "revised collective work" actually a revision or a new work and, in the case of freelance writers, who owns copyright. What the court ruled was, when a user of a digital version of the material sees an independent article and perceives it to be independent (i.e., it is not in the original context of the publication, including advertisements) such material is not a revised work and the author retains all rights. The result was that database vendors and publishers either had to locate the author and negotiate a new contract or remove the digital material. As result, thousands of articles disappeared from databases.

The court also suggested that the parties attempt to reach a settlement to resolve matters. In 2009, the court rejected a proposed settlement that would have created a method for handling material for which the publisher could not locate the author. Once again thousands of digital articles were in jeopardy of disappearing. As Adam Liptak wrote, "With no comprehensive settlement in place, the brief added, the publishers and databases will have no choice but to search for and delete whole swaths of freelance works from their digital archives, or risk repetitive litigation over the same dispute the parties sought to settle in this case."[11]

Another type of disappearance, perhaps less common, is the removal of controversial material as the result of a legal settlement or verbal agreement. One such example was when *The Economist* reported it withdrew part of an article from its digital archive on June 7, 2003, page 67. In this instance, it was part of a defamation agreement. It is difficult to assess just how often all or parts of digital articles are modified as a result of threats of legal action, ethical reasons, political correctness, and other reasons. Such changes are easy to carry out in the digital world. From a scholarly and historical point of view, having the original and modified version available for study could shed light on changing values and views.

Providing access to digital journals is not a simple matter of mounting a database. *Q.7* It is far more complex than labeling and placing a paper issue on the shelf in the public service area. Libraries have several options for providing end-user access—Web pages, through the OPAC, through online course systems such as Blackboard, and through in-house reserve systems. No matter which options are selected, the library must maintain such things as operable pathways, checking that any links are up to date and that the expected material is still active on the site. Beyond this, the library must work to make the access as transparent and user-friendly as possible. Activities such as the foregoing require staff time and effort; thus, e-serials have not reduced the serials workload, merely changed its nature.

Most libraries maintain a separate database for their serials. When that is the case a number of questions ought to be considered and reviewed from time to time. A sampling of such questions includes the following:

- How much information should the library provide to end-users regarding each title?
- Should the library establish a priority listing for titles that appear in more than one database?
- Should the library limit the number of hits that come up on a search? This may be important in school and smaller public libraries.
- Should the library attempt to identify peer-reviewed journals for end-users?
- Should there be information about embargoes associated with hits from embargoed titles?

Each question has implications for staff workloads, generally those of technical services staff.

To close this section, we should mention the concept of open access, which is a business model that allows end-users to have access to journal content without paying a fee. In short, the model hopes that donations and advertising will generate enough income to allow the publication to continue. The notion that somehow material gets on the Web with no cost involved is a myth. If nothing more, there are time costs involved with getting anything ready to go on the Web. From a scholarly journal point of view, even in the print environment, large amounts of time are volunteered by peer reviewers; that does not change in the digital world. Generally, journal editors are compensated, perhaps modestly, but nonetheless they are paid something for the time they devote to putting together an issue. Again, that is unlikely to change in the e-environment, at least in the long term. The reality is, as Steve Black noted, "Open Access has two faces, if you will, the philosophical, mission-driven decision to maximize availability to potential readers, and business models of how to pay the bills without subscription revenue."[12]

Preservation

Long-term preservation of information is one of the responsibilities of the nation's large research libraries. To some extent all libraries engage in preservation activities for shorter or longer periods of time. In the not very distant past, libraries committed a significant portion of their collection storage space to housing serials. While indeed currency of information is the major attraction of serials for end-users, serials also provide a record of past events that researchers and students can and do draw upon. Thus, there is a need for libraries to think about how to preserve the information contained in serials, and they have a responsibility to take on this preservation role.

Most print serials arrive in successive issues as paperbacks. If the library maintains print serials indefinitely or a title receives relatively heavy use, the library usually repackages the serial for more convenient handling or preservation. One method is to store the loose issues in a cardboard or metal container (sometimes referred to as a Princeton File) that keeps a limited number of issues together in a vertical position. This makes it easier to shelve the loose issues alongside bound materials.

The most common long-term storage treatment of paper-based serials is binding. Bindery operations are usually part of technical services and are associated with serials activities. Several labor-intensive steps are involved in processing serial binding activities. Someone must decide how quickly to bind a completed volume of a journal. (A journal with a relatively low number of pages per volume and that receives relatively low usage might not go to the bindery until several volumes have arrived. At the other extreme are weekly publications that receive very heavy use; such journals may go to the bindery several times in a year.) Normally, current issues of journals are in open stacks where users have easy access. When it is time to bind a title, someone must collect the appropriate issues, prepare bindery instructions that indicate the color of the binding, the journal title that is to appear on the spine of the binding and, if the library classifies its serials, the classification, volume number, and year or years included. Upon the return of a bindery shipment, someone must review each physical volume to ensure that the instructions were carried out properly. This describes the ideal situation, which does not always occur; sometimes a needed issue is not on the shelf. Perhaps a user has it, perhaps someone left it on a table or in a study carrel, or perhaps it has gone missing. Sorting out the problems takes time, and when the issue is missing, the library must decide if or how to replace the missing material (some firms specialize in selling back issues of journals).

A third preservation alternative for print titles is microformat storage. Microformats save large amounts of collection space and rarely go missing. However, users generally dislike the format. The format also requires equipment to read the material, and more often than not equipment that has scanning or printing capabilities, all of which require servicing, staff training, funding, and floor space. In addition to the foregoing, there are questions regarding format—microfilm or microfiche, positive or negative images, standard or archival quality, and what reduction ratios to use.

Today's digital world raises questions about the need to retain long runs of journals that occupy valuable floor space. (Some libraries have ceased binding titles that they have available in a digital format.) An interesting article looking at print journal retention in a medical library environment, where access to older research information is often important, is by Kaplan, Steinberg, and Doucette. The study examined two concerns—the need for information older than 15 years and the chronic library problem of lack of collection storage space. The authors concluded:

> Citation analysis and ILL statistics clearly indicate that the current literature is used predominately and that use of older journal literature drops dramatically after the current fifteen years. . . . The authors and the majority of survey respondents think that the tide is slowly shifting away from maintaining large, costly retrospective collections toward the concept of access instead of ownership with a fresh approach to the library as place.[13]

Librarians are well aware of end-users' preference for online or digital access to information. However, before making a decision regarding long-term retention of print journals, the library ought to engage in some serious review of the issues of the long-term viability of digital data. While long-term binding of print serials takes time and money, the process is not that complex. When it comes to e-serials, the situation is far more problematic, and it appears likely to be far more expensive long term.

First, and foremost, print retention decisions have almost always been the library's sole responsibility or purview—at least for the vast majority of libraries. (Again, the large research libraries and organizations such as the Center for Research Libraries do have a concern with maintaining at least one copy of all books and journals somewhere in the country.) Digital preservation decisions involve at least two other players—publishers or authors and digital database vendors. In terms of scholarly communication, end-user interests and needs ought to also factor into the decision-making process.

Digital preservation covers all information formats, regardless of how they originated—print and digital, print to digital, or "born digital." There are two basic technical issues for digital preservation—how the data are stored (e.g., hard drive, server, CD, DVD) and the retrieval-equipment capabilities (e.g., hardware, operating systems, and application software). Both are complex and subject to rather rapid change. "Here today and gone tomorrow" has to be in the forefront of thinking when considering digital preservation and its technologies. (Try opening a Word 3 document with current equipment and software and compare the results to the original document if one has doubts about the challenges.) Beyond these issues lie such things as who controls the material and the purpose of the control (revenue generation, for example). While scholars are still able to interpret ancient clay tablets and scrolls, opening readable digital files stored just 10 years ago is almost impossible today. The fact of the matter is that highly acid paper has a longer life span than the uncertain life span of digital files.

None of the existing digital preservation methods can guarantee fully readable files beyond a decade or two without someone monitoring changes in technology and migrating the preservation files to the new technology. Some U.S. government agencies, such as NASA, have found that even when using the appropriate procedures for storing data, such as tapes, information is lost. One technique that avoids software and platform issues is saving digital material as American Standard Code for Information Interchange (ASCII) files. Even that option has two long-term concerns. The most obvious is the fact that ASCII strips out all formatting—for example font differences and justification. The second concern is the possibility, and given the nature of technology, perhaps one with a high probability of occurring, that ASCII will cease to be the accepted baseline of digital activities. Clearly, digital preservation is more complex than paper-based preservation, both in the short and long term.

Answering the question about who should be responsible for digital preservation is not easy. Four main players should have some responsibility. The originators of the content have a vested interest, but few of them have resources to do much beyond making backup copies of their work and rarely have time to migrate the material from platform to platform.

The groups with the greatest resources are the publisher and the vendors who package and sell access to the information. Because most of them are for-profit entities, their focus is on revenue generation (and even not-for profits generally have to break even financially), and they have little incentive to retain material that fails to produce income. The reality is that long-term storage of very-low-use material will do almost nothing positive for the bottom line of such organizations.

Individual libraries and cooperative library efforts are the other two groups with a strong interest in long-term preservation. In the past, these two groups handled preservation activities and neither originators nor sellers took much notice, but information and intellectual property have taken on a significant financial value. As a result, publishers and vendors generally no longer sell the material but rather lease it to libraries and place limits on what a library can and cannot do with material—including long-term preservation.

For digital serials that are subscriptions, that is, not part of a publisher or vendor package of serial titles, a library might be allowed to create a "dim" or "dark" archive on its server of material for which it paid the subscription price. (A digital dark archive is one that allows no public access to the stored information except under the most exceptional circumstance—a trigger event—such as the publisher going out of business. A dim archive allows some limited public access under less drastic circumstances— such as an extended period where online access is otherwise unavailable.) According to Kenney and colleagues, "what librarians really want, in short, is at least a dim archive— though the level of dimness can vary."[14] If the activity falls to individual libraries, there will likely be costly duplication and probably great holes in the coverage.

The best option, and one has been emerging over the past 10 years or so, is cooperative projects; some just with libraries and a few as partnership of libraries and producers. Following are four of the more long-standing cooperatives:

- JSTOR—More than 6,000 organizations worldwide participate in JSTOR (short for Journal Storage), which was founded in 1995 and archives scholarly high-quality academic journals in the humanities, social sciences, and sciences, as well as monographs and other materials valuable for academic work. The archives are expanded continuously to add international publications. In 2009, JSTOR merged with and became a service of Ithaka, a not-for-profit organization helping the academic community use digital technologies to preserve the scholarly record and to advance scholarship and teaching in sustainable ways. Libraries pay a rather substantial annual fee—tens of thousands of dollars—to participate in the program. See http:// www.jstor.org/page/info/about/organization/ for more details.

- LOCKSS (Lots of Copies Keep Stuff Safe), based at Stanford University Libraries, is an international community initiative that provides libraries with digital preservation tools and support so that they can easily and inexpensively collect and preserve their own copies of authorized e-content (http://lockss.stanford.edu/lockss/How_It_Works). As of early 2010, 116 U.S. and 12 Canadian colleges and universities, as well as institutions throughout Europe, Asia, the Middle East, and Latin America, were taking part in the program. This program is based on local libraries storing the digital content. Hundreds of publishers have also elected to use LOCKKS as their digital preservation and post-cancellation partner.
- OCLC—The OCLC Digital Archive is one of many services and products offered by OCLC. It is also a local library digital preservation system (http://www.oclc.org/digitalarchive/default.htm).
- PubMed Central—The National Library of Medicine/National Institutes of Health provides a free digital archive of biomedical and life science journal literature (http://www.ncbi.nlm.nih.gov/pmc/).

Although beyond the scope of this book, we should mention the concept of institutional repositories. These are primarily academic library undertakings intended to collect and preserve locally produced scholarly material, which is sometimes referred to as "gray literature"; this includes, for example, drafts of reports and conference papers that scholars distribute to each other and are rarely published in the traditional meaning of the term. Some libraries are embarking on long-term preservation of locally generated scholarly material; a process that may soon change the nature of scholarly journal publishing.

Finally, we suggest that the reader consult Benjamin Abrahamse's two articles that address cataloging issues related to digital preservation.[15]

Backfiles

What is meant by the term "backfiles"? Serial backfiles are the collections of previously published volumes/numbers of the library's current and past subscriptions. Such collections have always been a significant part of modern academic libraries' overall collections. For public, corporate, and school libraries, the size and time frame of such collections are generally smaller and shorter in duration, rarely more than a few years.

When an academic library starts a subscription to a journal sometime after volume 1, number 1, appeared, it must decide how necessary it is to acquire the older (back) issues. If there is a perceived need, the library must determine where to acquire the material and at what cost. Some serial publishers have full runs available, and many Web-based packages offer access to older material for an extra annual fee for the oldest material. Backfiles of print titles may be available from reprint houses in bound or unbound forms. Such material tends to be expensive; they certainly take up valuable shelf space and often receive very little use. Libraries also cannot assume that vendors handling online full-text serials will maintain backfiles or make them available for all titles. Back-issue dealers are also very important when it comes to acquiring copies of missing issues that were unavailable from the publisher when claimed and issues that go missing before a volume can be bound. One source for more popular back issues is UsedMagZ.com (http://usedmagz.com).

What a library decides to do about print-journal retention is often influenced by what exists in digital form and how secure that availability may be long term. Library staff members are well aware of the fact that users' preferences are for e-resources (ease of access and speed are two major factors in this preference). They are also aware that, at present, the e-environment is in a state of constant change, and files available through producers or other vendors may not always be there—see the earlier discussion regarding preservation. In 2006 and 2007, Laura Kane McElfresh wrote about libraries going e-only for serials.[16] Her academic library decided to move to e-only for subscription titles (this did not include titles in multi-title databases). Even with the goal of dropping paper titles, the library had a concern with keeping backfiles of the publication available to its users for the periods for which it had paid subscriptions.

Christina Torbert reported that in her survey of library acquisition of electronic backfiles, "One of earliest concerns about purchasing journal in electronic-only format was a lack of paid-for, tangible backfiles that were guaranteed to remain accessible if the current subscription were to be canceled."[17] She noted, when it came to making the acquisition decision that, "While there is no published literature specific to choosing packages of electronic backfiles, there is a body of literature about purchasing packages of electronic journals. It might be supposed that similar criteria and decision-making patterns would be followed for purchasing electronic backfiles."[18]

Changing Nature

Serials change over time as new editors, governing boards, or owners make major and minor shifts in the content and orientation. From the acquisitions department point of view, a change in a print title is yet another workload issue. It is very important for cataloging and the OPAC that there be a clear trail from former to current title whether print or electronic.[19]

For some journals there is a long history of title changes, which can be confusing for end-users who may not know of the changes over time and may think the library has fewer holdings than it actually does. Steve Black succinctly summed up the library view regarding the changing character and titles of serials, noting "Since changes in title create work for librarians and confusion for patrons, librarians want title changes to occur only for compelling reasons."[20] Although his comment focused on titles, other changes also create the issues he mentioned—such as frequency of publication, scope of coverage, and, in the case of scholarly journals, even splitting into two titles with slightly different coverage.

Assessment and Evaluation

Assessing or evaluating library collections is, or ought to be, an ongoing activity, especially for serials that are expensive to acquire and manage. The reality that e-resources represent an ever-growing component of the collection and the library's budget has made e-resource evaluation very important. As Borin and Yi noted, "there is no 'single' correct way to evaluate collections in today's complex and changing environment."[21]

For e-resources, several methods are available for assessment. Like other aspects of collection assessment, there are both internal and external reasons for conducting an evaluation. Perhaps the most common assessment indicator, which can satisfy internal or external needs, is value for monies spent. Such issues as usage per title, usage per unit cost, and impact on ILL activities apply to both print and e-titles. Some e-title questions relate to frequency of downloading versus viewing, e-title impact on print usage, and, in the case of package deals, usage of previously unavailable e-titles.

Print serial assessment is straightforward and completely in the hands of the library staff. How often and what method of data collecting to employ takes time and effort; however, when the task is done the library can have a high degree of confidence that the data reflect the reality. The situation is less clear-cut in terms of e-titles.

What are some of the issues that make assessing e-usage somewhat murky? The following list represents a *sample* of the factors that cause e-usage data to be suspect from time to time and make comparisons problematic.

- Vendors/publishers do not all supply usage data for their product/titles.
- Data that are reported vary from vendor/publisher to vendor/publisher.
- Some vendors only report cumulative data when the product is a consortia lease.
- User behavior—double clicking, moving from an html to a PDF copy of an article for example—can skew the usage data depending on how a vendor/library counts use.
- It is unclear how to count a "no hit" search and determine whether it was user error or no data.
- It is difficult to determine how long usage data will be retained and whether the library can download the data and retain it as long necessary.
- Product upgrades may or may not retain early usage data.
- System crashes often result in lost data.

To some extent, libraries can create their own system for measuring usage if they have the technological capability. Transaction and Web log analyses can compile data about user activity at a Web site or electronic resource the library makes available. Network-usage analysis is a broader-scale assessment that focuses on network or terminal usage. A library can also create a means through which the user can assess a resource—for example, a pop-up box that allows the user to comment on the product at the time of use. (This is an online version of a long-standing library assessment method—the user survey.)

Because of the many challenges to gathering meaningful data about e-resources, there has been an effort to bring about some consistency in what vendors and publishers supply to libraries. The effort, labeled COUNTER (Counting Online Usage of Networked Electronic Resources), was launched in March 2002 and "is an international initiative serving librarians, publishers and intermediaries by setting standards that facilitate the recording and reporting of online usage statistics in a consistent, credible and compatible way" (http://www.projectcounter.org/).

Following are some other groups that have also been working on improving the quality of e-resource assessment:

- ARL New Measures Initiative (http://www.arl.org/stats/initiatives/emetrics/index.shtml). The ARL (Association of Research Libraries) New Measures Initiative was established in response to the following two needs: increasing demand for libraries to demonstrate outcomes and impacts in areas important to the institution, and increasing pressure to maximize use of resources. Of particular interest is the work associated with the E-metrics portion of this initiative (http://www.arl.org/stats/initiatives/emetrics/index.shtml), which is an effort to explore the feasibility of defining and collecting data on the use and value of electronic resources.
- ICOLC Guidelines for Statistical Measures of Usage of Web-based Information Resources (http://www.library.yale.edu/consortia/2001webstats.htm). The International Coalition of Library Consortia (ICOLC), which has been in existence since 1996, is an international, informal group currently comprising more than 200 library consortia in North America, Australia, Asia, and Africa. ICOLC has developed a set of Guidelines for Statistical Measures of Usage of Web-based Information Resources. Revised in 2001, the guidelines specify a set of minimum requirements for usage data and provide guidance on privacy, confidentiality, access, delivery, and report formats.
- NISO/SUSHI (http://www.niso.org/workrooms/sushi/). NISO is the National Information Standards Organization of the United States and SUSHI (Standardized Usage Harvesting Initiative) is a protocol (Z 39.93–2007) developed to facilitate the automated harvesting and consolidation of usage statistics from different vendors.[22]

Assessment of collections, as well as all other library activities, is a component of the library's ability to demonstrate to its various stakeholders its accountability for the resources it has been given. Efforts such as those listed in this chapter should be encouraged and supported by libraries everywhere.

SUMMARY

Serials have a long history of being a high-demand component of any library's collection. One element in their popularity is their currency of information. Another aspect of serials, whether print or electronic, is they represent a major part of a library's collection-development expenditures.

Serials, both print and electronic formats, require a significant amount of staff time to process, manage, and conserve. Each of the areas have different elements depending upon format; however, e-titles generally are more complex to manage. For example, preserving print titles is (usually) solely an internal library issue; e-serial preservation on the other hand usually involves several other parties (authors, publishers, and vendors).

At present both print and electronic serials play a role in library service. However, given the popularity of the e-format with users print titles will probably play less and less of a role in the future.

REVIEW QUESTIONS

1. What is a serial and how is the concept of serial changing?

2. List the serial categories developed by Machlup and their implications for the acquisitions department's workload.

3. In what ways do serials subscriptions differ from orders for other formats?

4. Discuss some of the trends that are changing the nature of serials distribution and library functions and activities related to serials.

5. Cost is a recurring theme for serials. Discuss this issue and its impact on acquisitions departments.

6. Discuss the issues of preserving serials, both print versions and electronic versions, for the long term.

7. What are the basic issues related to providing access to both print serials and e-serials?

8. Discuss the interrelationship between access, preservation, and backfiles for both print serials and e-serials.

9. What are three significant issues related to the changing nature of serials?

10. Discuss the complexities of e-serials acquisitions and management.

11. Describe four initiatives designed to improve e-resource assessment.

NOTES

Epigraphs for this chapter are from Margaret Sylvia, "E-Serials How Tos," *Library Journal* 130, no. 7 (2005): 128; Michael Porter and David Lee King, "Magazines Going Digital," *Public Libraries* 48, no. 2 (2009): 20–21; and "Putting Periodicals in Their Place," *School Librarians Workshop* 30, no. 1 (2009): 11.

1. Thomas Nisonger, *Management of Serials in Libraries* (Englewood, CO: Libraries Unlimited, 1998).

2. T. Scott Plutchak, "What's a Serial When You're Running in Internet Time?" *Serials Librarian* 52, nos. 1/2 (2007): 81.

3. Fritz Machlup and Kenneth Leeson, *Information Through the Printed Word* (New York: New York University, 1978).

4. Patrick L. Carr, "From Innovation to Transformation: A Review of the 2006–7 Serials Literature," *Library Resources & Technical Services* 53, no. 1 (2009): 3.

5. Aline Soules, "The Enduring Serial," *Serials Librarian* 51, no. 1 (2006): 113.

6. Kristen H. Gerhard, "Pricing Models for Electronic Journals and Other Electronic Academic Materials: The State of the Art," *Journal of Library Administration* 42, nos. 3/4 (2005): 7–8.

7. Amy Carlson and Barbara Pope, "The 'Big Deal': A Survey of How Libraries Are Responding and What the Alternative Are," *Serials Librarian* 57, no. 4 (2009): 381.

8. David Ball, "Signing Away Our Freedom; Implications of Electronic Resources Licenses," *Acquisitions Librarian* 18, nos. 35/36 (2006): 17.

9.   Donald Taylor, "Looking for a Link: Comparing Faculty Citations Pre- and Post-Big Deal," *Electronic Journal of Academic and Special Librarianship* 8, no. 1 (2007): "Conclusions," http://southernlibrarianship.icaap.org/content/v08n01/taylor_d01.htm.

10.   David Fowler, "The Bundling and Unbundling of E-Serials," *Serials Librarian* 57, no. 4 (2009): 352.

11.   Adam Liptak, "Supreme Court to Revisit a Case on Breach of Copyright," *New York Times,* March 3, 2009, Late Edition, sec. B. For a further discussion of the impact of the Tasini decision, see Barbara Quint, "Where Have All the Archives Gone?" *Information Today* 26, no. 7 (2009): 1–2, 38–39.

12.   Steve Black, "Editors' Perspectives on Current Topics in Serials," *Serials Librarian* 57, no. 3 (2009): 207.

13.   Richard Kaplan, Marilyn Steinberg, and Joanne Doucette, "Retention of Retrospective Print Journals in a Digital Age: Trends and Analysis," *Journal of Medical Librarianship* 94, no. 4 (2006): 392.

14.   Anne R. Kenney, Richard Entlich, Peter B. Hirtle, Nancy Y. McGovern, and Ellie Buckley, *E-Journal Archiving Metes and Bounds: A Survey of the Landscape* (Washington, D.C.: Council on Library and Information Resources, 2006), http://www.clir.org/pubs/reports/pub138/pub138.pdf.

15.   Benjamin Abrahamse, "Cataloging Matters for Digital Preservation," *Serials Librarian* 57, nos. 1/2 (2009): 48–50; and Benjamin Abrahamse, "Cataloging Matters for Digital Preservation—Part 2," *Serials Librarian* 57, no. 3 (2009): 190–93.

16.   Laura Kane McElfresh, "The E-Only Experience: 'Moving Beyond Paper'." *Technicalities* 26, no. 4 (2006): 1, 11–13; and Laura Kane McElfresh, "Going E-Only: Coming Soon, the Deluge," *Technicalities* 27, no. 2 (2007): 1, 11–13.

17.   Christina Torbert, "Purchasing of Electronic Backfiles: Results of a Survey," *Serial Librarian* 57, no. 4 (2009): 410.

18.   Ibid., 412.

19.   See Julian Everett Allgood, "Serials and Multiple Versions, or the Inextricable Trend Towards Work-Level Displays," *Library Resources & Technical Services* 51, no. 3 (2007): 160–78, as well as a discussion of the issue in chapter 14 on cataloging.

20.   Black, "Editors' Perspectives on Current Topics in Serials," 200.

21.   Jacquelin Borin and Hua Yi, "Indicators for Collection Evaluation: A New Dimensional Framework," *Collection Building* 27, no. 4 (2008): 141.

22.   For a more complete discussion of the development of the SUSHI standard, see Arthur Hendricks, "SUSHI, Not Just a Tasty Lunch Anymore: The Development of the NISO Committee SU's SUSHI Standard," *Library Hi Tech* 25, no. 3 (20007): 422–29.

SUGGESTED READING

Allgood, Julian Everett. "Serials and Multiple Versions, or the Inextricable Trend Towards Work-Level Displays." *Library Resources & Technical Services* 51, no. 3 (2007): 160–78.

Best, Rickey D. "Is the 'Big Deal' Dead?" *Serials Librarian* 57, no. 4 (2009): 353–63.

Botero, Cecilia, Steven Carrico, and Michele R. Tennant. "Using Comparative Online Journal Usage Studies to Assess the Big Deal." *Library Resources & Technical Services* 52, no. 2 (2008): 61–68.

Cole, Louise. "The E-Deal: Keeping Up to Date and Allowing Access to the End User." *Serials Librarian* 57, no. 4 (2009): 399–409.

Corbett, Lauren E. "Serials: Review of the Literature 2000–2003." *Library Resources & Technical Services* 50, no. 1 (2006): 16–30.

Crothers Stephen, Margaret Prabhu, and Shirley Sullivan. "Electronic Journal Delivery in Academic Libraries." *Acquisitions Librarian* 19, nos. 1/2 (2007): 15–45.

Davis, Roger. "A Web-Based Usage Counter for Serials Collections." *Serials Librarian* 57, nos. 1/2 (2009): 137–48.

Feick, Tina, and Gary Ives. "Big E-Package Deals: Smoothing the Way Through Subscription Agents." *Serials Librarian* 50, nos. 3/4 (2006): 267–70.

McElfresh, Laura Kane. "When a Journal Isn't a Journal," *Technicalities* 27, no. 1 (2007): 1, 11–13.

McMenemy, David, and Paul F. Burton. "Managing Access: Legal and Policy Issues of ICT Use," in *Delivering Digital Services,* ed. Alan Paultez, 1–34. London: Facet Publishing, 2005.

Millard, Scott. *Introduction to Serials Work for Library Technicians.* New York: Haworth, 2004.

Pesch, Oliver. "ISSN-L A New Standard Means Better Links." *Serials Librarian* 57, nos. 1/2 (2009): 40–47.

Pike, George H. "Revisiting Tasini." *Information Today* 25, no. 1 (2008): 17, 20.

Stamison, Christine, Bob Persing, and Chris Beckett. "What They Never Told You About Vendors in Library School." *Serials Librarian* 56, nos. 1/4 (2009): 139–45.

Waller, Andrew, and Gwen Bird. "'We Own It': Dealing With 'Perpetual Access' in Big Deals." *Serials Librarian* 50, nos. 1/2 (2006): 179–96.

White, Sonya, and J. Eric Davies. "Simplifying Serials Sourcing: A Case Study in Decision Support for Managing Electronic Journals Access." *Bottom Line* 18, no. 1 (2005): 7–13.

Chapter

Government Information

A popular Government without popular information, or the means of acquiring it, is but a Prologue to a Farce or a Tragedy; or perhaps both. . . . And a people who mean to be their own Governors, must arm themselves with the power which knowledge gives.

—James Madison, 1822

For more than 150 years, the United States Government Printing Office (GPO), along with its Federal Depository Library Program (FDLP), has supported an informed citizenry and democracy by ensuring access and preservation to a broad swath of federal government information.

—John A. Schuler, Paul T. Jaeger, and John Carlo Bertot, 2010

Although nearly 200 years have passed since James Madison wrote his letter regarding the need for an informed citizenry, the need for citizens to be informed about their government has not diminished. In fact, the need is probably greater today than at any time in the past. However, the way people gain access to such information has changed dramatically in the past 10 to 15 years. Libraries have always played a role in helping people gain such access, and it seems likely they will continue to do so.

An example of the importance of accurate information regarding government actions was the confusion, misinformation, and misinterpretation of what was actually proposed in the federal 2010 healthcare reform legislation. At more than 2,000 pages, it is no wonder people had trouble understanding its content much less its potential impact on themselves and U.S. society. Another example of confusion over fact versus fiction occurred after the events of 9/11. Some of the fallout of 9/11, in terms of government information, will be covered later in this chapter.

Clearly, interest in and concern about society's access to government information has had a long history in the United States, as evidenced in the epigraph by James

Madison. The issue of open access to government information is a national and a worldwide concern.

Government information has been, and to large extent still is, a mysterious and frequently misunderstood part of the information world. Because government publications arise out of government action or a perceived need to inform citizens about some matter, and appear in either print or digital form, these materials can confuse library staff and user alike. Much current information is accessible through the Web, although older materials may only be available in a print copy. Online searches, regardless of the search engine used, produce thousands of hits for most queries. Where government information will appear in the search results is a matter of the search engine's relevance algorithm and the search terms used. Regardless of perceived limitations in locating the materials, government information constitutes an important, current, and vital part of having an informed citizenry.

Government information and publications provide a surprising wealth of information on almost any topic. People use various labels for this type of material, such as *government publications, government information, official documents, federal documents, agency publications, legislative documents,* and *executive documents.*

Government information comes in a variety of sizes, shapes, and formats: books, technical reports, periodicals, pamphlets, microforms, posters, films, slides, photographs, CD-ROMs, online databases, audio recordings, and maps. Because such publications are the product of many diverse branches and agencies of government, they have no special subject focus and usually reflect the concerns of the agency that produced them. Predictably, a document produced by the U.S. Department of Agriculture (USDA) probably deals with a subject related to agriculture, such as livestock statistics, horticulture, or irrigation. However, the relationship may be less direct, because the USDA also publishes information about nutrition, forestry, and home economics. As remote as the connection may seem, most government publications have some connection to the issuing agencies' purpose.

Libraries store government print and media materials in several ways, ranging from a separate collection containing nothing but government publications to complete integration into the general collection. When the material is segregated from the general collection, usage tends to be lower than for material integrated into the collection with like topics. In an online environment, it is much easier to access government materials. It is interesting that several studies of the use of government information as reflected in citations have shown usage remaining constant, even in an Internet world—"despite this increased visibility and access, the use of physical documents collections and citation patterns indicate that government material is not being used or cited more frequently today than it was in the 1980s."[1]

How the library stores these materials affects their technical services processing; they may be fully cataloged, partially cataloged, or uncataloged. Documents may be classified according to the system used for the other collections (such as the Dewey Decimal System or Library of Congress Classification system) or one designed by the national government for organizing its publications (in the United States the system is the Superintendent of Documents [SuDocs] classification system).

Access to these materials varies from special manual indexes to full online public access catalog (OPAC) representation. Adding to the confusion created by their diverse management, the hard-copy items have only one common trait: they are all official products of some government or international body. Thus, many have corporate rather than personal author entries (see the cataloging chapters for a discussion of the differences), which makes it more difficult for users to know how to search for desired material. If the material is included in an OPAC, with subject or keyword search capability, end-users identify and use more government information than they will if the information is only in manual files.

The inherent diversity of government agencies and their publications, combined with the diverse library management techniques concerning print government documents, has created something of a bibliographic schizophrenia. However, this immense body of information, available at a modest cost or free through the Internet, makes government publications and services a worthwhile library information resource, even if they are a challenge at times to handle. Making both print and digital versions of government information equally accessible to end-users is an ongoing challenge.

BACKGROUND

In 1813, Congress selected a few U.S. libraries to become part of a system that evolved over time into what is now called the Federal Depository Library Program (we cover FDLP later in the chapter). The initial program only covered congressional materials. By 1857, the program had expanded to cover items produced by the executive branch. The depository program grew over the next 130 years both in types of material distributed and in the number of libraries receiving all or some of the available material.

At some point, in small steps, the U.S. government decided that citizens not only needed access to information about government activities but also needed information that would improve the economy or enhance their daily lives. Thus, how-to publications on topics such as gardening and carpentry became part of the government's publishing program, and a second purpose of the government publication program evolved: helping people improve the quality of their lives.

It is unlikely that the founders of the depository system envisioned that the federal government eventually would become the country's largest publisher or would debate which documents should be available to the public. Today, there is a debate about what information should be available and the role the government should play in producing such publications, and the debate has had some impact on libraries. Morton summarized the situation as follows:

> The first information obligation of the government of the United States is to produce the information it needs to effectively govern, and in so doing provide accurate information about its activities for itself and so it can be held accountable to, and by, its constituents.
>
> To accomplish this, the government, libraries, and the press all must, and do, play important roles. The government, however, is neither obliged (nor should it feel so) to produce, let alone provide it, based on the needs of the researchers who occupy the nation's libraries. One neither disputes the needs of these researchers nor their researches.[2]

By the early 1980s, there were more than 1,300 U.S. government document full and partial depository libraries. During President Ronald Reagan's first term in office, the Office of Management and Budget (OMB) received authorization to develop a federal information policy as the result of the passage of the Paperwork Reduction Act of 1980 (Public Law No. 96–511). The OMB was given the responsibility to minimize the cost of collecting, maintaining, using, and disseminating information.

One of the OMB's initiatives supported the concept of disseminating federal information as raw data in an electronic format. Certainly the OMB's role in shifting the emphasis from paper to electronic means of dissemination was significant. In 1996, Congress began debating the Government Printing Reform Act of 1996, the core concept of which was to provide easy access to government information by electronic means.

Today, documents such as Congressional hearings and legislation are available in both print and digital formats. Government agencies at all levels have a Web presence; for example, there are more than 30,000 federal Web sites. When one thinks about all the state and local government agencies in existence, there are potentially tens of thousands of governmental Web sites available, all providing access to information and services. A popular press label for this phenomenon is "e-government."

E-GOVERNMENT

More and more governments, at all levels, are moving toward e-government, and libraries, especially public libraries, are playing a role in making e-government more of a reality. Donna Blankinship reported on a recent study, funded by the Bill and Melinda Gates Foundation, of computer use and libraries. She noted that the study "confirms what public librarians have been saying as they compete for public dollars to expand their services and high speed Internet access: library computer use by the general public is widespread and not just among poor people."[3] The usage is certainly wide ranging, and some of the usage is for gaining access to government information.

E-government refers to how almost all levels of government are now attempting to more actively engage their citizens in the governance process through the use of the Internet and technology. Government agencies use the Web to disseminate information and provide services. Rose and Grant noted, "As the scope of E-Government capabilities has grown and the concept has evolved, the definition of E-Government has evolved with it. E-Government is no longer viewed as a simple provision of information and services via the internet, but as a way of transforming how citizens interact with government."[4]

The Economist published an 18-page supplement entitled "The Electronic Bureaucrat: A Special Report on Technology and Government." The introductory essay to the supplement ends with the following:

> Although hopes have been high and the investment has been huge, so far the results have mostly been disappointing. That reflects a big difficulty in e-government (and in writing about it): it touches on so many other things.

What exactly is it that public organisations are trying to maximise, and how can it be measured?[5]

The report raises several questions: What is the role and purpose of government information and e-government? And what role can and should libraries play? It turns out that libraries, especially public libraries, are playing a significant role in making the e-government concept a reality.

Although technical services departments are less and less involved in digital government information than when all the information was paper based, they still have some role in creating and maintaining links and providing information to users through the OPAC. Also, at present, libraries still acquire some paper-based government publications.

The reality is that more libraries are probably more actively engaged in the government information dissemination process than at any time in the past. When it was just a print world, FDLP libraries were the primary source for government information (many of which were academic libraries), and a person had to visit the library to gain access. Today, Internet searches provide government information alongside other sources of information. What has also changed is that public libraries are now the most active in providing people with access to government information. This is largely due to the limits academic libraries must place on outside users when it comes to online access—their primary service population consists of their students, faculty, and institutional staff. Almost by default, public libraries, because of the open access to their facilities and services, have become a major interface between citizens and government information.

As government agencies began shifting some of their services to the Web, in some cases making it the only means of gaining access to a service, libraries have found themselves under growing pressure and absorbing new costs. The costs are for the staff time and training that are required to effectively assist users, time that is reallocated from other library activities, and expenses related to the equipment and Internet connectivity. Bertot and colleagues made the following observation about the new costs and e-government: "Yet libraries are increasingly challenged, even as they have stepped up to meet the increasing demands for Internet access and services."[6] Along the same lines, in 2009, Jennie Burroughs stated,

> The strong momentum toward a primarily digital government information system has created a new set of challenges for libraries. . . . Information seekers are finding and using government information through more pathways than ever before. In many cases, users clamor for improved digital access and mainstream findability. On other occasions, users may value traditional services and tangible collections. Information seekers' research skills, subject interests, learning styles, and technological proficiency are extremely diverse, which makes it difficult to meet all needs.[7]

Although Burroughs's article focused on an academic library, her points about the users' diversity of skills and interests apply to all libraries. In a public library setting, this diversity becomes very pronounced. When a library provides users with assistance, such as selecting the proper government form, liability concerns quickly come to the forefront of the library's thinking about just how much e-government services to provide.

CATEGORIES OF GOVERNMENT INFORMATION

It is not as easy as one might think to define what government information is. Clearly, legislative body material or documents produced by the executive branch of government, regardless of its level—national to local, are items most people would agree fit the concept of government information. However, are reports prepared by non-governmental organizations (NGOs) but required by a government agency truly government publications? What about the publications produced by short-term and long-term multi-jurisdictional groups? Usually discussions of government information include materials published by the United Nations (UN), which is clearly not a government body in the usual meaning of the term. Rather, countries contribute funds to operate the UN, including their information and publications program. For our purposes we take the broad view that any information that has government involvement, with or without direct government funds, falls into the category of government information.

U.S. Documents

The executive, judicial, and legislative branches, as well as executive cabinet-level agencies and independent agencies, all issue documents. Presidential commission reports belong to this class of publications, as do the budget documents. Cabinet-level departments (e.g., the USDA or the Department of the Interior) include administrative units, such as agencies and bureaus. Most of these units issue reports, regulations, statistics, and monographs; many issue educational and public relations materials as well. In addition to cabinet-level agency publications, many independent agencies release a range of information. The Tennessee Valley Authority, Federal Reserve Board, and Central Intelligence Agency are examples of independent agencies that also publish documents.

Judicial documents (aside from case-law reports) are not as numerous as those from the other two branches of government. The best known and most important title is the *Supreme Court Reports,* which contains Supreme Court opinions and decisions. (Note: Private commercial publishers issue the decisions of lower federal courts; these are not normally considered government documents.) Although large legal libraries must have a set of the *Supreme Court Reports,* other libraries may also find them useful for historical and political reasons. As a result, many larger public and academic libraries acquire a set for the general collection, even when there is a good legal library nearby.

Congressional publications are second in number and popularity only to executive publications. In addition to the text of proposed and passed legislation, these publications include materials documenting House and Senate deliberations. Floor debates appear in the *Congressional Record;* assessments of the need for legislation are available in congressional committee reports; testimony before congressional committees appears in documents that bear the words *Hearings of* or *Hearings on;* and there are also several important reference books, such as *Official Congressional Directory, Senate Manual,* and *House Rules.* The *Congressional Record* provides a semi-verbatim transcript of the proceedings on the floor of each house of Congress (semi-verbatim because it is possible for a congressperson to add or delete material in the *Congressional Record*. Thus, it is not a completely accurate record of what actually transpired on the floor of Congress). Many libraries, including large public libraries, find that there is a strong demand for access to the *Congressional Record*. Luckily, online access to recent issues of the *Congressional Record* is available through the Library of Congress's THOMAS system (http://thomas.loc.gov/home/cr_help.htm).

The Government Printing Office (GPO, http://www.gpoaccess.gov) as noted earlier provides the largest range of U.S. government information.

State and Local Governments

Several differences exist between state and federal information in the United States. One difference, as of 2010, is that there is a stronger print orientation at the state and local level, although the most state governments have at least some Web presence. A second, and often overlooked, difference is that states can and frequently do copyright their publications. Some shared characteristics between state and federal information are the diversity of subject matter, relatively low purchase price, and increasing difficulty in identifying what is an official publication.

Like the federal publishing program, most state programs now produce materials mandated by law; that is, they record government activities and release a variety of statistical data and general information about the state. Many of the federal statistical publications are compilations of state data, which means the most current information, by as much as two or three years, is in the state publications. The volume of general information and how-to publications from states is low compared with federal output.

Access to, and identification of, state and local publications was difficult in the past. Today it is much easier as sites such as GovEngine.com (http://www.govengine.com) provide links to state and local information online, which has greatly enhanced access. The Library of Congress (http://www.loc.gov/rr/news/stategov/stategov.html) also provides links to state government Web sites and some local government sites. Yet another service is the State and Local Government on the Net Web site (http://www.statelocalgov.net/).

Depository practices and requirements differ from state to state. The statutes of any particular state will provide the frequency and the statutory framework of the depository program. The state library can provide more detailed information about its state depository program, including a list of depositories, sales and acquisition information, and information about which materials are available from a central source and which are available only from individual agencies.

In the past, it was a major challenge for libraries to provide much access to local government information, even for the library's own local government. With Web access, a person can not only find a surprising amount of information about her home town government but can also compare what is happening locally with what is happening with other local governments.

Public libraries still make an effort to collect and preserve local government information, at least when it is available in a print format. The challenges of preserving the digital material is usually well beyond the technological and staffing resources of a local library.

Canadian Government information

Types of government documents in Canada are similar to those in the United States. Canadian Government Publishing is the official publisher of federal documents (http://canada.gc.ca/publications/publication-eng.html or http://publications.gc.ca/). For many years the annual, quarterly, and weekly listings of federal government publications appeared in book format. However, in the 1980s and early 1990s the annual and the quarterly lists disappeared, leaving the weekly lists, which now are found both in a paper format and on the aforementioned government Web site.

Provincial governments also list their publications on their Web sites. In addition, many provinces have bookstores where their publications can be purchased or designate independent bookstores to sell their publications.

Documents from Other Countries

In many countries, the government publication programs are similar to the Canadian and U.S. programs in terms of volume and complexity. The good news is that these large-scale programs generally have an agency, like the U.S. GPO, that is the primary distributor of the publications. Very few countries offer a depository program to libraries in other countries. Only the large research libraries actively collect such documents because few users need the material.

International documents, especially UN publications, however, do have a wider appeal. Intergovernmental organizations (IGOs) are the major source of international publications and information. An IGO may be defined as a group of three or more member countries working together on one or more long-term, common interests. Without doubt, the largest IGO is the UN. NGOs such as the World Health Organization (http://www.who.int/en/) also issue publications and information of interest to a fairly large number of library users.

The UN has an extensive publications program and, like other government bodies, is beginning to issue material in electronic formats. The UN Web site provides a broad range of information about the organization (https://unp.un.org/), which includes ordering information. The site also has a listing of all UN depository libraries worldwide. For most libraries that have some UN documents, the material is part of the regular collection, circulating or reference, rather than being held in a separate document area, simply because they do not acquire very many titles.

Although very few countries offer depository arrangements for libraries in other countries, some do allow libraries to establish a deposit account. Variations in exchange rates, however, often cause problems about how much money is available in an account. One method that works, if a library wishes to buy a substantial number of publications from a country, is to have a book dealer or vendor in the country purchase the documents.

Library staff members who work regularly with government information believe better and more frequent use of print government material would benefit most users. They believe that if people understood the broad range of information and subjects available, usage would increase.

Two factors work against increased usage. First, in depository collections, the lack of full cataloging for all received items means users interested in accessing such items often cannot find them using the OPAC. The high volume of material received is a major factor in not fully cataloging depository items. Second, if depository items are not fully cataloged, libraries normally establish a separate area to house the items. Frequently, government documents collections reside in a corner or basement of the library with the lowest volume of traffic. The old saying "out of sight, out of mind" is all too true about government documents. The Library and Archives Canada, however, provides cataloging copy in its free AMICUS service (http://www.collectionscanada.gc.ca/amicus/index-e.html) for all items chosen for depository. This cataloging is completed by the time the items are distributed.

ACCESS TO GOVERNMENT INFORMATION

Suzanne Piotrowski's book on government and its services suggests that there are four primary means by which people gain access to government information:

- From agency press releases, documents posted online, or through libraries/depositories,
- Through responses to formal user requests, often based on the Freedom of Information Act process,
- From leaks or whistle-blower statements, and
- Through town hall meetings and other public hearings.[8]

In this chapter the focus is just on the first category.

In the not-too-distant past, print documents provided critical information and libraries filled two roles: acquiring government material and providing assistance in accessing the information. Today, there is a vast universe of such information available through the Internet. A significant difference exists between the two means of access.

Since 9/11, the U.S. federal government has rethought what and how much government information ought to be available to the general public. With paper documents, you may not have the most current information, but you know that what you are looking at has not been modified by some unknown, perhaps third nongovernment party. Also, a paper document is not likely to vanish in the blink of an eye. Neither is true of the digital format. Kathy Dempsey's editorial entitled "The Info Was There, Then ____ Poof" sums up the issue of permanence and digital information. Her editorial prefaced a themed issue dealing with government information, in which she highlighted a key concern; "Where do you draw the line between which data should be public and which should be kept private?"[9] We might add "and who should make that critical call?" Dempsey related how one of the articles intended for that issue went "poof" when the White House requested a final review process. (The authors of the article in question worked in a federal information center and their piece was to describe the factors that determine what information is deemed classified.) In another article, Klein and Schwal discussed the delicate balance society must achieve between maintaining free access to information and security, if its citizens are to effectively participate in a meaningful democracy.[10]

When it was just a print world, the process of gaining access to government information was complex and often painfully slow. Libraries and their staff were an essential part of the process. Something that is frequently overlooked in the debate about security and access is the fact that depository libraries (the largest holders of print government publications) do not *own* the material. Although they invest significant sums of money in the long-term storage of the material and in staff effort to servicing the collections, they do not have ownership. The government can and has at various times withdrawn material from depository collections—that process is not just a post-9/11 phenomenon. Further, it can do so without consultation and libraries have no recourse.

Klein and Schwal (who themselves are federal government employees) in their concluding section made the following points; "Newly generated government information will be evaluated against established criteria for review for public release, the same as always. There is no core group making these decisions, although there may be a tendency on the part of those responsible to err on the side of caution."[11]

Accessing U.S. Government Information

One of the early efforts to provide digital access to U.S. federal government documents was the Government Information Locator Service (GILS). GILS was created in 1994 to provide a user-oriented system that would help users identify digital federal information. The system was not just a GPO system; as a result, more than 30 GILS servers were located across government agencies. The system was shut down in September 2008, and the U.S. Government Accountability Office plans to have all the old records (from December 7, 1994 through September 2, 2008) converted to the new system, called the Federal Digital System, or FDsys, some time in 2010. (For more details about GILS and materials contained in the system, see http://www.gils.net. Information about FDsys may be found at http://www.gpo.gov/fdsys/search/home.action.)

Currently, what is perhaps the most user-friendly site for accessing U.S. Federal government information is the portal USA.gov, which is called the "U.S. Government's Official Web Portal" (http://www.usa.gov). In addition to the expected search box at the top of the page, the home page offers an Explore Topics tab listing a set of broad topical selections (such as "Consumer Guides" and "Health and Nutrition") that provide links to government information on the topic from any agency. There is also a Find Government Agencies tab that has links to the three main branches of government and their agencies, to online sites for the states and U.S. territories, local jurisdictions, and tribal governments. The state, local, and tribal pages also offer more search options than federal government–generated information.

Preservation of Government Information

Preservation issues for government information are the same as for the general collection. Paper-based government publications are just as likely to be on acidic paper as their commercial cousins. There was, in 1990, a congressional resolution to encourage, if not require, all publishers to use acid-free paper for important publications. Nonprint government materials also suffer from the same problems as their commercial counterparts, for example, poor processing—especially microformats—and poor bonding of the emulsion layer to the carrier film base in photographs and motion picture film. All of these materials need the same care in handling by staff and users as well as the appropriate environmental controls (temperature and humidity) as those items discussed in other chapters.

Like their digital serial counterparts, e-government documents face challenges related to how to and who should ensure long-term preservation of the material. As would be expected, national libraries and archives undertake almost all of the work related to national government–generated material. When it comes to state and local jurisdictions, however, the issue is much less clear. All levels of government are currently facing major budgetary challenges. Neither academic nor public libraries are funded or staffed at a level for anyone to realistically expect them to take on the work of preserving government-generated e-documents.

One example of a province-focused project to preserve e-material is from Ontario, Canada. Rea Devakos and Annemarie Toth-Waddell describe a joint effort by the Ontario Legislative Library and the Ontario Council of University Libraries to preserve electronic government documents using the D-Space system.[12]

The challenge of preserving state, local, and multi-jurisdictional e-material grows greater each day. How society and its libraries will resolve the issue remains to be seen.

FEDERAL DEPOSITORY LIBRARY PROGRAM

As noted earlier, the concept of a national system of libraries holding government documents has a long history. Certainly, there has been success in getting government information into libraries across the nation where the public has reasonably convenient access to the material. There are two types of depository libraries, full and selective. A full depository agrees to accept all items available to FDLP participants (essentially those materials handled by the GPO; selective institutions take only a portion of the material). The selective libraries are encouraged to take at least 15 percent of the items available—the depository program does *not* include all publications issued by federal agencies and organizations. A list of member libraries is available from the GPO Web site (http://catalog.gpo.gov/fdlpdir/FDLPdir.jsp).

At one time there were 1,365 depository libraries in the United States, but as of 2010 the number had dropped to 1,250. The number has been declining over the past 15 years because many libraries that were selective members dropped out of the program as collection space and staffing problems grew and electronic access increased.

The composition of the FDLP is heavily weighted toward academic libraries (50%), with public libraries a distant second (20%). The balance consists of academic law libraries (11%), community college libraries (5%), 5 state and special libraries (5%), federal and state court libraries (5%), and federal agency libraries (4%). Many people view academic libraries as intimidating, so the growing number of public libraries offering e-government access should increase usage of government information as people are often more comfortable in a public library setting.

A thoughtful reader may wonder about the costs associated with being a depository library. A study by Robert Dugan and Ellen Dodsworth indicated that the Georgetown University library expended $217,970 in direct, support, and overhead costs on its depository program.[13] One can only wonder what the costs would be in 2010. For smaller depository programs, the dollar costs would be much smaller, but the proportions of depository costs to total operating expenses would likely be very similar. There is no question that there are substantial dollar and staff costs associated with depository status. For at least some selective depositories, those costs and related issues caused them to rethink the value of being a selective depository, especially in terms of technical services staff time and steadily shrinking collection storage space.

As the federal government moves toward increasing dependence on electronic dissemination of information, the following types of questions are being raised:

- Is the FDLP still necessary?
- Is the FDLP a remnant of the 19th century?
- Is the FDLP the best way to get information to people in the 21st century?
- Is there a way to change the system to make it more cost-effective?

Peter Hernon and Laura Saunders, in writing about the future of the FDLP concluded, "Finally, by 2023, there might be a new future that involves a decentralized network of libraries."[14]

At the same time the Hernon and Saunders article appeared, the Depository Library Council released a draft strategic plan covering 2009–2014. That document made the point, "At the same time, any strategic vision needs to embrace new ways of collaboration and partnership among depositories and with GPO. This cooperation may include ways of building and sustaining future digital collections of published Federal information sources, but it also must include the deliberative preservation of significant paper and print collections of Federal information."[15] One of the concluding points of the strategic plan was that, "The successful model will be a careful blend of the program's traditional accessibility and technological innovation."[16] As of 2010, it appears that the FDLP program will continue for some years, but in a very different form. How the changes will affect technical services activities related to government information remains to be seen.

A reminder: any depository library, partial or full, *must* allow anyone access to the federal documents, regardless of the library's policies about public use of its other collections. (The U.S. Code, Title 44, § 1911 [1944] states, "Depository libraries shall make government publications available for free use of the general public.") The federal depository library system has developed the *FDL Handbook* (http://www.fdlp.gov/ administration/handbook), which includes guidelines for access to materials (http:// www.fdlp.gov/administration/handbook/116-chapter4?start=2). If the library restricts public access to its general collections and few people request access to the documents collection, staff members, especially new staff, may unknowingly deny legally required access.

Another depository requirement is that there is a library staff member primarily responsible for handling the depository material. Very often when there is just one person, the staff member is part of the technical services section because of the high volume of record keeping and processing associated with maintaining a documents collection. FDLP members have an obligation to promote their federal information collections and services. The *FDL Handbook* states that when it comes to promotion, the outreach "should be ongoing and increase visibility of the depository, depository resources, and depository services" (http://www.fdlp.gov/administration/handbook/116-

chapter4?start=5). As a result, the library's primary service population may not be the target group the GPO is interested in reaching.

Another aspect of the depository program is mandated retention. Adequate collection space is a chronic problem in most libraries. One method for gaining space is deselecting material from the collection. A traditional weeding or deselection technique is to remove the lowest-use items and store them in less expensive space or discard the material. Government publications more often than not fall into the very low-use category; nevertheless, the depository may not be as quick to remove these items as it might be with low-use purchased materials. All depository libraries must retain items for at least five years after receipt. Regional (i.e., full) depositories *must* retain their collections, and selective depositories must offer items identified as discards to the regional library and local partial depositories before discarding them (http://www.fdlp.gov/administra tion/handbook/392-chapter5?start=14). On the plus side, periodic reviews of the documents collection may also encourage a review of the general collection low-use items that also occupy valuable shelf space.

CANADIAN DEPOSITORY PROGRAMS

There are 271 full and selective depositories for Canadian federal government documents in Canada, and one each in 38 countries around the world. The Depository Services Program Web site describes the system as follows:

> Full depository status is granted to Canadian libraries that are nominated and approved by a Committee consisting of representatives of the National Library of Canada and the Depository Services Program. This status is granted as either English, or French, or bilingual, depending on the clientele of the library in question. Full Depository Libraries automatically receive a shipment of *all* publications listed for distribution by the Program in the *Weekly Checklist* of Canadian government publications for that week.
>
> All other depositories have the status of selective depository. Selective depository libraries use the *Weekly Checklist* to *choose* those items they are entitled to order. Selective depository status is granted to Canadian public libraries and libraries of Canadian educational institutions which are open to the general public or clientele at least twenty hours per week and have at least one full-time employee. (http://dsp-psd.pwgsc.gc.ca/Depo/table-e.html)

Canadian provincial governments also provide depository programs. For example, Ontario only has selective depositories. Ontario used to publish a weekly checklist but now publishes its checklist on its Web site under the heading "New Releases."

ACQUISITION OF GOVERNMENT INFORMATION

Even if a library is a full depository, it will still need to acquire some paper-based government documents in the traditional manner as not all material is available through GPO. Documents librarians have always known that FDLP does not provide complete coverage of federal material. A U.S. General Accounting Office report, *Information Management: Electronic Dissemination of Government Publications,* found that 50 percent of all the federal documents published in 1996 were not indexed, cataloged, or disseminated to the depository libraries (http://www.gao.gov/new.items/d01428.pdf). A more recent study has not been conducted; however, it seems probable that the problem persists. Thus, a substantial amount of acquisitions work is still required, at least for FDLP members.

Many documents are available free from issuing agencies and congressional representatives. They are also available as gifts or exchanges from libraries that have held them for the statutory period and wish to dispose of them or from other libraries with extra nondepository copies. Another common method of acquisition is purchase through the agency's official sales program. The agency may or may not offer a standing order program. Some commercial jobbers and bookstores deal in government documents, and some booksellers, especially used or rare booksellers, may stock some government documents.

To locate GPO federal material, the source to consult is the Catalog of U.S. Government Publications (http://catalog.gpo.gov) the successor to the *Monthly Catalog*. Another resource is GPO's Online Paper Store (http://www.gpo.gov/customers/store.htm).

One large commercial vendor of government documents is Bernan Associates of Maryland. As noted on its Web site:

> Bernan is a leading distributor of essential publications from the United States government and intergovernmental organizations, and a respected publisher of critically acclaimed reference works based on government data. The two businesses are intertwined; for ease of description, we will describe them as distinct activities.
>
> Bernan offers easy, one-stop access to a world of government and international agency books, journals, and CD-ROMs for academic and public libraries in the U.S., as well as law and corporate libraries. (http://www.bernan.com/General/About_Bernan.aspx)

Bernan Associates handles federal documents and offers several standing-order programs.

Through the UN Publications Web site (https://unp.un.org/), a library may acquire items issued by such entities as the UN Educational, Scientific and Cultural Organization (UNESCO), as well as other UN and international organization publications. While offering no depository plan, it does have a deposit account service for libraries allowed by their parent organization to establish an account of this type:

> Any customer, non-account or account holder, wishing to establish a deposit account should submit their request in writing. A minimum initial deposit of US$500.00 should be maintained. Upon receipt of your deposit, an account number will be assigned. . . . All prices are quoted in US dollars, prices are subject to change without notice. Shipping and handling fee will be added to each order. Special shipping instructions can usually be accommodated

and these will be charged on an individual basis. Discounts are offered to wholesalers, retailers and agents. (https://unp.un.org/Librarians.aspx)

Standing order and subscription services are also available. In addition, some titles are available online. A full listing of agencies that release their publications through this program is available online (https://unp.un.org/Agency.aspx).

Some U.S. congressional publications, such as hearings and committee reports, and a few agency publications, may be obtained by contacting the local or Washington, D.C., offices of congressional representatives. Obviously, this is not an appropriate acquisitions technique for large quantities or standing orders, but it can be quite effective for current issues or special subject publications. It is especially effective for acquiring information about current legislation or information covering a wide range of subjects. School and media centers should take advantage of this source of free government documents. The best method for acquiring recently out-of-print or nonsales publications is to contact the issuing agency directly. The annual *United States Government Manual* (http://www.gpoaccess.gov/gmanual/browse.html) provides a list of addresses, telephone numbers, and e-mail addresses for the major and minor agencies of the federal government. Individual contact can produce copies of many federal documents, often free of charge.

SUMMARY

Government information is an important element in any library's collection or service program. It is important for citizens to have such information easily available, even if people do not use it heavily. All types of libraries can acquire useful information from government agencies at a reasonable cost. However, securing and processing the desired material can present significant challenges for technical services units.

REVIEW QUESTIONS

1. How has the Internet changed access to government information?

2. What role do public libraries play in helping citizens interact with their governments?

3. What are some of the issues related to the need to maintain the delicate balance between security and access?

4. What types of information can you locate on the Internet about your home town government? How does that compare to what you can find out about you state government?

5. Where would you look for information about UNESCO programs on the Internet? The World Health Organization's publication program?

6. What do you see as the future of the FDLP? How will changes in the FDLP affect other libraries?

NOTES

The epigraphs for this chapter are from James Madison, 1822, "Letter to W. T. Barry, August 4," in *The Writings of James Madison,* ed. Gaillard Hunt, vol. 9 (New York: G.P. Putnam's Sons, 1910), 103; and John A. Schuler, Paul T. Jaeger, and John Carlo Bertot, "Implications of Harmonizing the Future of the Federal Depository Library Program Within E-Government Principles and Policies," *Government Information Quarterly* 27, no. 1 (2010): 9–16.

1.   Debra Cheney, "Government Information Collections and Services in the Social Sciences," *Journal of Academic Librarianship* 32, no. 3 (2006): 303.

2.   Bruce Morton, "The Depository Library System: A Costly Anachronism," *Library Journal* 112, no. 15 (1987): 53.

3.   Donna Blankinship, "Library-Computer Use Common," *Arizona Republic,* March 28, 2010, A23.

4.   Wade R. Rose and Gerald G. Grant, "Critical Issues Pertaining to the Planning and Implementation of E-Government Initiatives," *Government Information Quarterly* 27, no. 1 (2010): 26.

5.   "The Electronic Bureaucrat: A Special Report on Technology and Government," *The Economist* 386, no. 8567, supplement (2008): 4.

6.   John Carlo Bertot, Paul T. Jaeger, Lesley A. Langa, and Charles R. McClure, "Drafted: I Want You to Deliver Government [Information]," *Library Journal* 131, no. 13 (2006): 34.

7.   Jennie M. Burroughs, "What Users Want: Assessing Government Information Preferences to Drive Information Services," *Government Information Quarterly* 26, no. 1 (2009): 203.

8.   Suzanne J. Piotrowski, *Governmental Transparency in the Path of Administrative Reform* (Albany: State University of New York Press, 2007): 7–8.

9.   Kathy Dempsey, "The Info Was There, Then _____ Poof," *Computers in Libraries* 24, no. 4 (2004): 4.

10.   Bonnie Klein and Sandy Schwal, "A Delicate Balance: National Security vs. Public Access," *Computers in Libraries* 25, no. 3 (2005): 16–23.

11.   Ibid., 23.

12.   Rea Devakos and Annemarie Toth-Waddell, "Ontario Government Documents Repository D-Space Pilot Project," *OCLC Systems and Services* 24, no. 1 (2008): 40–47.

13.   Robert E. Dugan and Ellen M. Dodsworth, "Costing Out a Depository Library: What Free Government Information?" *Government Information Quarterly* 11, no. 3 (1994): 267.

14.   Peter Hernon and Laura Saunders, "The Federal Depository Library Program in 2023: One Perspective on the Transition to the Future," *College & Research Libraries* 70, no. 4 (2009): 366.

15.   Depository Library Council, *Federal Depository Library Program Strategic Plan, 2009–2014* (Washington, D.C.: Government Printing Office, 2009), 3, http://www.fdlp.gov/component/docman/doc_download/37-fdlp-stratigic-plan-2009–2014-draft-3?ItemId=45.

16.   Ibid., 9.

SUGGESTED READING

Cantello, Gillian, and John Stegenga. "Government Web Content in Canada: A National Library Web Archive Perspective." *IFLA Conference Proceedings* (2008): 1–19. http://www.ifla.org/en/ifla-publications.

Chapman, Bert, and John A. Shuler. "Letters to the Editor." *College & Research Libraries* 70, no. 5 (2009): 419–20. (Comments regarding the Hernon and Saunders survey referred to in the chapter.)

Church, Jim. "International Documents Roundup: The 'Official Record Only' Option: The UN Official Documents System and the Archival Role of UN Depository Libraries." *DttP* 33, no. 3 (2005): 11–13.

Englert, Tracy. "Biz of Acq—'Free' Access to Subscription Databases Through the FDLP: Government Documents and Acquisitions." *Against the Grain* 21, no. 5 (2009): 66, 68.

Garvin, Peggy. "The Government Domain: FirstGov becomes First in Government Search." Law and Technology Resources for Legal Professionals Web site, 2006, http://www.llrx.com/columns/govdomain13.htm.

Jacobs, James A., James R. Jacobs, and Shinjoung Yeo. "Government Information in the Digital Age: The Once and Future Federal Depository Library Program," *Journal of Academic Librarianship* 31, no. 3 (2005): 198–208.

Jaeger, Paul T. "Building E-government into the Library and Information Science Curriculum: The Future of Government Information and Services." *Journal of Education for Library and Information Science* 49, no. 3 (2008): 167–79.

Missingham, Roxanne. "Access to Australian Government Information: A Decade of Changes 1997–2007." *Government Information Quarterly* 25, no. 1 (2008): 25–37.

Priebe, Ted, Amy Welch, and Marian MacGilvray. "The U.S. Government Printing Office's Initiatives for the Federal Depository Library Program to Set the Stage for the 21st Century." *Government Information Quarterly* 25, no. 1 (2008): 48–56.

Rossmann, Brian. "Legacy Documents Collections: Separate the Wheat from the Chaff," *DttP* 33, no. 4 (2005): 8–9.

Rossmann, Brian. "Legacy Government Documents Collections in the Digital Age." *Against the Grain* 18, no. 5 (2006): 48–52.

Rossmann, Brian. "Promote Your Documents Expertise," *DttP* 34, no. 1 (2006): 5–6.

Schuler, John A. "Citizen-Centered Government." *Journal of Academic Librarianship* 29, no. 2 (2003): 107–10.

Schuler, John A. "New Economic Models for the Federal Depository System." *Journal of Academic Librarianship* 30, no. 1 (2004): 243–49.

Selby, Barbie. "Age of Aquarius—The FDLP in the 21st Century." *Government Information Quarterly* 25, no. 1 (2008): 38–47.

Chapter

11

Media

Banks of CDs for borrowing may slowly disappear from libraries in the years ahead, but the idea of lending music to patrons is still very much alive.

—American Libraries, 2008

Playing games in today's public and school libraries is a profoundly social experience for library patrons both young and old.

—Dale Lipschulz, 2009

It appears that we are beginning to enter what some have called the "post-literate age." Jones-Kavalier and Flannigan noted, "Prior to the 21st century, *literate* defined a person's ability to read and write, separating the educated from the uneducated. With the advent of the new millennium and the rapidity with which technology has changed society, the concept of literacy has assumed new meanings."[1] Doug Johnson has suggested that a post-literate society is one in which a person can read and write but chooses to gather information and learn through "audio, video, graphics, and gaming."[2] Allan Rough, in writing about nonprint media services at the University of Maryland, noted that the Bantu of Africa employ a single word, *kunzwa*, to mean "to see, to hear, to understand."[3] He used the translated meaning as the motto for his new media services facilities and placed it on the wall just inside the entrance.

One interesting challenge for society and libraries is the fact that students, from preschool to postgraduate work, are being taught by teachers who, on average, are very much less literate than their students in terms of today's digital technologies. The students have grown up in a world in which digital technology is just there; it is not something they had to try to learn about later in life. The students are what Prensky calls "digital natives," and their teachers and other elders are "digital immigrants" who are trying to become literate in the new systems of communication and learning.[4]

Johnson suggested that we need to recreate our libraries for the needs of the post-literate society: "The term 'postliterate library' may appear to be an oxymoron at first glance, but it is not true. Our best libraries are already postliterate, increasingly meeting the needs of users who communicate, play, and learn using media other than print."[5] Indeed libraries have been adding nonprint items to their collections for many years. It is highly unlikely that 20 years ago many of the advocates for media in libraries were thinking about a post-literate society, but they did recognize that many people learn and communicate more effectively through nonprint means.

For some time there were two schools of thought within the profession regarding media's role, or lack thereof, in libraries. Some librarians held that that media formats distract libraries from their primary mission—the promotion of lifelong reading—especially the reading of quality literary titles. Further, such collections drain essential resources from print material. Essentially, such people viewed libraries as being in the "book" rather than the "information" business. Will Manly suggested that, "Videos are the 'Twinkies' of library collections."[6]

Others, Sally Mason for example, held the view that media formats are as central to collections as print materials; "Clearly, the visual media will only become more important to library service in the future. . . . It is not enough for librarians to 'capitulate' on the issue of visual media. We must become leaders and advocates . . . helping the public to learn what is available, to sort through multiple possibilities, and offering guidance in the use of media to obtain needed information."[7] Likewise, Myra Brown suggested, "It is counterproductive to stigmatize one format while deifying print. We dilute our energy by imposing such artificial distinctions."[8]

Regardless of differences in philosophy, various nonprint formats have been present in libraries for the better part of 100 years. (Music recording were one of the first nonprint items added to library collections.) Media resources have been an interesting, varied, and challenging component of collections. In today's digital environment, they remain interesting and challenging, if perhaps not as varied as in the past.

Today, almost all academic, public, and school libraries have at least some small collection of nonprint items. There is also a general recognition that other media play an important role in having an informed society. Anyone reading *Publishers Weekly* (*PW*) or shopping on Amazon.com knows that publishers and booksellers no longer limit themselves to just books and magazines. They see themselves as being in the information business. Regular columns in *PW* on audio and video releases indicate that producers and vendors view this field as an important market. The use of computerized typesetting and scanning equipment, which produces a record of the text in a digital format, opened up a number of options for delivering the information, such as the Kindle and Nook e-readers.

All one has to do is think about the growth of Web 2.0 and sites like MySpace and YouTube to realize the importance of visuals and interaction to youth. Social media or social networking is a tool for sharing one's personnel experiences through text, visuals, and sound. A library of any type that ignores social media does so at its peril, at least from a long-term point of view. For effective outreach, libraries need to focus their communication on "people like us" rather than the traditional top-down organizational format. Digitization has to a large degree made some of the old media formats less significant. However, for the near term, libraries will have legacy media collections that contain material that is not available in a digital form.

The bottom line is that technology has reduced media to its basic of visual and audio, but from the staff perspective, it has done so in more complex ways than in the past. As Howard Story wrote, "Many of us long for the way we were or what we think were simpler days. Phonograph records, audio cassettes, film, color television, video cassettes, all at one time were classified as new technology and during their introduction caused someone great anxiety. Digital technology is no different."[9]

MEDIA ISSUES

Media formats present several challenges for the library and its acquisitions department budget. Unlike print materials, in most cases media formats require some type of equipment in order to access their content. Thus, there is the both the cost of buying the equipment and the cost of maintaining it on an ongoing basis. Failure to maintain the equipment will damage the medium used with it, which is much more fragile than paper-based content. There is also, at times, an issue of equipment compatibility when ordering new titles (such as DVD or Blu-ray).

Because media items are generally used with equipment, they wear out or are damaged more quickly than print materials, especially when the public may check them out for home use. Replacement costs are substantial for many formats; for example, libraries circulating video formats expect to get fewer than 25 circulations before the title is too worn to remain in circulation.

Also, unlike print, some media, such as video, often have restrictions on how they may be used, especially where the material may be used in a public setting. There is a concept called "performance rights" that does impact library usage—more about this later in the chapter.

One ongoing issue for libraries and acquisitions budgets is the speed of technological change. Those working with end-users have to keep pondering the question, "How many times must we purchase a copy of Beethoven's Fifth Symphony or the movie *Gone With the Wind*?" Since the 1960s, the music recording collections have moved from vinyl disks (in several different sizes and speeds) to cassettes (in several variations) to CDs. A similar series of changes took place in terms of motion pictures—film (16mm and 8mm) to cassette (VHS and Beta) to DVD and now Blu-ray. Changes in technology leave libraries with legacy collections of items many users view as dinosaurs. Moving too quickly into a format (for example Beta) that does not last is a waste of funds, yet waiting too long can also be costly, if for no other reason than losing users' goodwill and support.

Long-term preservation of media is not a significant issue for most libraries—the material wears out quickly and the equipment changes very fast as well—but there are short-term issues related to wear, damage, and security. Those concerns will be touched on later in the chapter.

CURRENT MEDIA FORMATS

As stated previously, a given in media services is changing formats, which will keep your work life interesting. The pace of change of 40 years ago now seems slower than a snail's, while today's pace seems to be light speed. Alan Kaye wrote, "Now picture and sound seem to having their way with computers and the Internet. Multimedia information has become almost native to computers, collapsing the market for analog formats and creating a digital world."[10] He went on to discuss how libraries like his have already eliminated or are in the process of eliminating filmstrips, slide sets, 16mm and 8mm films, Super 8mm films, and all phonograph records and music audiocassettes. Not all libraries have gone that far, and many still have some legacy collections. Thus, we briefly mention such formats in what follows; if you are interested in more information about such formats, consult the previous edition of this book.

Motion Pictures and Video

Most libraries have weeded or are weeding their film collections in terms of 16mm and 8mm formats. About the only environment in which such films are found are special collections and archives. Like many of the other formats covered in this chapter, film content has migrated to a digital form (DVDs and increasingly to streaming video). Videocassettes (VHS) are still in collections and are available for purchase, primarily because much of the content is not yet available in a digital form.

Format battles in the video field have been ongoing for some years now. One well-known battle was between Beta and VHS, with VHS the winner. A more recent struggle was between DVD, Blu-ray, and HD-DVD. By 2008, the HD-DVD format had fallen out of the contest. Libraries are once again caught in the middle of a commercial battle where they must bet on a winning side or spend limited funds duplicating the same content in competing formats. The issue is that a DVD player cannot play a Blu-ray disk; however, most Blu-ray players can play the older DVD format. Although prices for Blu-ray players have fallen, less than 10 percent of U.S. households had a Blu-ray player by late 2009,[11] so there was not too much demand from users for libraries to offer titles in this format.

Notwithstanding the Blu-ray issue, most libraries have substantial collections of VHS material and DVDs. According to Norman Oder in late 2005, many libraries were still purchasing VHS cassettes in large numbers.[12] By 2007, DVDs had overtaken VHS, at least for feature film titles. "Part of the growth in the DVD era comes down to simple economics. They can buy more movies with their budgets than they could in the VHS era."[13] Most of the video circulation comes from movies in the public library setting while curriculum-related videos dominate educational library usage. However, the acquisitions patterns vary greatly as some public libraries believe they compete with local video rental outlets if they offer movie titles, as do the rental stores. Another factor is that DVDs require even less shelf or storage space per title.

Given the quick release of DVDs after a film is in theaters, DVD collections generate some of the same issues as best-seller books. Everyone wants it now, not next month after all the talk has faded. In terms of circulation, feature-film videos beat nonfiction videos hands down; theatrical films represent roughly 68 percent of the collections, 72 percent of the expenditures, and 80 percent of the circulations.[14] Unfortunately, as of the 2010, there was no DVD equivalent of the McNaughton book-rental plan where a library may lease multiple copies of a popular title for a short time and return all or some of the copies after the demand has died down. Some libraries attempt to establish a ratio of copies to requests (holds). The problem with purchased multiple copies, print or not, is that they occupy valuable storage space after the demand has died off, and scarce money has been expended on the same content. However, not having the material available when the demand is high can have negative consequences in the form of unhappy users.

Perhaps a solution is on the horizon: downloadable video. Downloadable e-video was being tested by some larger public libraries as of 2007. They use services such as OverDrive (audio books, movies, and concert videos, http://www.overdrive.com/re sources/mediaformats/). The Denver Public Library reported that they had more than 1,200 downloads of their "e-Flicks" though they had only 82 titles available.[15] Content available for downloading was limited in 2010, but will probably increase rapidly as the demand grows. One appealing aspect of the service is that people can download the movies from their homes. Yes, titles are limited, and most of what is available are indies (independent productions) or special interest, but the major studios are not likely to miss an opportunity to increase revenue and from controlled sites.

Cost containment is an issue for most of the libraries offering this type of service. Vendors charge the library a fee based on the community's population. Another concern may be monitoring who is doing the downloading; to address this, some libraries have restricted e-movie files to residents of the service area only. Finally there are often fees to collect from users of the service—in late 2007 they ranged from $2.99 to $49.00 for libraries that do charge a fee.[16] Sometimes, as we will discuss in the next chapter, getting user fees into the library's budget can be a challenge, much less getting them into the acquisitions department budget.

The Arizona Universities Library Consortium (AULC) started an on-demand service for accessing streaming video that may prove to be a workable model for groups of educational libraries.[17] In 2008, the group partnered with Film for the Humanities and Sciences Films Media Group to allow students and faculty members access to all 6,300 educational videos available from the company. The service, Films On Demand, is available at http://ffh.films.com/digitallanding.aspx. The University of Arizona, Arizona State University, and Northern Arizona University libraries provide on- and off-campus students with access to the films; when any title has been accessed three times AULC purchases the perpetual streaming rights for that title. The AULC is also allowed to host the file on an AULC server.

One of the educational usage issues with video is that an instructor often only wants to use a segment from several videos in a class session. While it is possible to have several video players available, having all the equipment present and having all the videos properly queued is a nuisance and a distraction. With streaming video it is possible to select the desired segments and put them together in the desired sequence. An example might be demonstrating how different actors or directors interpret a scene for a Shakespeare play. With video streaming it is possible to

- select segments for an entire class or an individual student,
- select segments for student or teacher presentations,
- bookmark segments for future use,
- control the video the same as on a player (play, pause, rewind, and fast forward), and
- use selected elements in student assignments.[18]

Video streaming is reaching all levels of education from kindergarten to Harvard's Business School. School media centers and academic libraries can use programs such as Windows Media Player, RealTime, or Quicktime to deliver the material to the classroom. The difference between streaming and downloading is that with streaming one has the ability to immediately view images as they arrive rather than waiting for an entire download to be completed before viewing anything. (Maximizing teaching time is a factor for instructors.) Some educational video content providers offer video-streaming services and occasionally material from other producers who are not yet offering such service. Generally, the charge for the streaming service is an annual fee based on school enrollment.

Movie Ratings and Libraries

One concern, especially for public libraries, is the potential for complaints about or censorship challenges to its video collections. Public libraries usually address movie ratings in their collection-development policy statement. School library media centers have somewhat less exposure to challenges because of the instructional nature of the collections; however, even in these libraries it is possible to have a parent complain about a video, such as one dealing with evolution. Very often the complaint will raise the question about the suitability of certain titles for young viewers and the need for "protecting the children." This was the major factor in the creation of the movie rating system. Acquisitions department staff members need some understanding of the rating systems (for movies and games) as some items may have more than one version.

The Motion Picture Association of America (MPAA) has a rating system for its releases—the familiar G, PG, PG-13, R, and NC-17 one sees in the movie section of the newspaper. The Classification and Rating Administration (CARA) within MPAA establishes each film's rating. While these ratings have no legal force and, in fact, are based on the somewhat subjective opinion of the CARA rating board, the general public accepts them as appropriate. The key is the content of each film in terms of its suitability for children.

The unfortunate fact is that even a collection of G- and PG-rated titles does not ensure that there will be no complaints. One possible way to handle the situation, although it is not always easy to accomplish, is to create two sections for video, one in the children's/young adult area and another in the adult area. Again, this will not forestall all complaints, but it could help.

The Indianapolis–Marion County Library developed a video policy after several people expressed concerns about "potential effect on minors."[19] The library formed a Community Video Task Force to review the existing policy and make recommendations, if any, for changes. Their report concluded that the policy should retain the parent's right to restrict a child's borrowing to the juvenile videos, and that the staff should continue to receive training in the current policy. The basic policy is that anyone can borrow any video, unless it is a child with a card stamped "JV," which indicates a parental restriction. The person who raised the issue wanted the policy to require the parents to give written permission for a child to borrow anything but juvenile titles. You might want to check the video polices of some other libraries such as those for the Weyauwega Public Library (http://www.wegalibrary.org/VideoPolicy.asp) or the Oscoda County Library (http://www.oscoda.lib.mi.us/video.html)

Video and Copyright

Videos are an important source of programming for public libraries, although such programming can be something of a problem because of performance rights, which are a component of the copyright law. For libraries in educational settings, performance can be an even more significant issue.

Although there are a considerable number of substantive copyright questions relating to print material, copyright issues are even trickier when it comes to nonprint, especially in academic and school libraries. A full discussion of copyright is not possible or appropriate in this book, but some discussion is relevant to this chapter as it is important to know what rights are acquired at the time of purchase. (Note: What follows *is not legal advice;* it is merely a brief review of the issues and the American Library Association's guidelines and position regarding copyright. When in doubt about what is or is not legal, get legal counsel.) Copyright holders can, do, and have enforced their rights in court.

The purpose of copyright is to promote the development and distribution of information while ensuring that the individual or group that developed the idea or information has exclusive rights to profit from that activity. In addition, society reserves for itself the right to use the material developed within limits without violating the copyright holder's right, through its copyright laws. The labels for the concept vary; in the United States it is called "fair use," in the United Kingdom it is "fair rights," and in Canada it is "fair dealing." The challenge is determining what is fair.

Section 107 of the U.S. Copyright Law (Public Law 94–553, Title 17 of the *U.S. Code*), while legally establishing the doctrine of fair use, is short and fairly nonspecific. The doctrine relates to copying, reproduction (multiple copies), and actual use. It indicates that use for criticism, comment, news reporting, teaching, scholarship, and research are reasonable and fair purposes. Further, it specifies four criteria to consider in determining if the use is fair:

1. The purpose and character of the use, including whether such use is of a commercial nature or is for nonprofit educational purposes;
2. The nature of the copyrighted work;
3. The amount and substantiality of the portion used in relation to the copyrighted work as a whole;
4. The effect of the use upon the potential market for or value of the copyrighted work.

Clearly there is room for interpretation and argument. Guidelines developed by educators, publishers, and authors provide some indication of what various parties believe is reasonable for fair use. The guidelines are not part of the statute, but they were part of the House Judiciary Committee's report on the copyright bill. They are *Guidelines for Classroom Copying in Not-for-Profit Educational Institutions* and *Guidelines for Educational Uses of Music.*[20] It is important to remember that copyright protection extends to literary works; dramatic works; pantomimes and choreographic works; pictorial, graphic, and sculptural works; motion pictures and other audiovisual works; and sound recordings (Sec. 102).

Some of the media discussed in this chapter are specifically covered in several sections of the copyright law. Following are a *few* of the items and relevant sections of the law.

Audiovisual	108 (f) (3)
Audiovisual work other than news	107, 108 (h)
Book	107, 108
Graphic work	107, 108 (h)
Importing copies from abroad	602 (a) (3)
Instructional transmission	107, 110
Motion picture	107, 108 (h)
Musical work	107, 108 (h)
Periodical article	107, 108
Pictorial work	107, 108 (h)
Public broadcasting program	107, 108 (d) (3)
Sound recording	107, 108, 114.

Libraries providing classroom media support face significant copyright questions. Teachers and professors may want to use a personal tape they made in class using the school's equipment. Is that legal? The answer depends on many factors. A key issue is, when did the taping occur? Few tapes the teachers want to use are home videos; most are copies of a broadcast program the teacher made using a personal video recorder. Such off-air recordings may be legally used if they are 45 days old or less and played in the classroom with a teacher present. The tapes must be erased after 45 days to comply with the guidelines.

The issue is too complex to explore in this book, but performance rights are part of the mechanism by which all the people involved in the production of the video receive compensation. The easiest way to think about it is in terms of book royalties: each new copy sold means a small payment is due the author. For performance rights each performance should mean a small payment is due to each of the participants involved in the production of the video or film. To cover such costs the producer or distributor of a video may or may not include performance rights in the price. (Essentially performance rights pertain when there is a presentation to a number of people at the same time, such as a children's program in the library.) The best approach is to acquire videos with performance rights; this will almost always mean a higher price than listed, unless it is clearly stated that the price includes performance rights.

Other Image Formats

As mentioned earlier, many libraries, because of space, maintenance, and low user interest, are disposing of their collections of reel film, filmstrips, slides, and flat pictures. (We hope they do so with care and don't discard items of long-term value societal value solely because of storage space concerns.) Most filmstrips were designed as instructional material and required special projectors, but many of the items are now digitized and available online. The same is true of many of the slide sets. Flat pictures have always presented challenges in organization and access. Scanning images is an approach to keeping pictorial materials in order and increasing access, especially if available via the library Web site, assuming there are no outstanding copyright issues. However, it does little to improve access, unless you engage in a significant amount of indexing. (It is possible to create a Word file of terms and use the "Find" capability to create a very simple digital search function. The process of scanning is more complicated than placing the item on a scanner and clicking "scan." One needs to verify that there is a match been the scanned and original image. Images also require substantial amounts of disk memory and high-end computers (and occasionally printers) to make effective use of them.

Maps

Maps are a form of pictorial material, and most libraries have traditionally held at least a small collection, in addition to atlases in the reference collection. Internet map sites, such as MapQuest, Google Maps, or Multimap, have significantly reduced the demand for road maps in libraries. Information found on such sites provides what most people were seeking when they came to the library "looking for a map"—street and highway information.

Maps actually come in a variety of forms and content. Large public libraries, academic libraries, and many business and industrial libraries have extensive collections. Maps take the form of graphic representations of such things as geological structures, physical features, economic data, and population distributions. They may be in a variety of forms—folded, sheets, raised relief, globes, and even aerial or satellite images. Any major map collection must determine its scope and define what to collect. Although most collections would incorporate aerial photographs, including satellite photographs, should they also house the remote sensing data from satellites? Are raised relief maps worth including, or are they a commercial product of no real informational value? Clearly the users' requirements will determine the answers to these and many other questions about the collection.

Depending on the collection's purpose, maps may be organized in a simple geographic-location sequence or by some more complex system. When someone asks, "Do you have a map of X?" it may (and usually does) mean a map showing streets, roads, and other cultural features. However, it could also mean a topographic map, which provides elevation information in addition to cultural features. Or maybe the person want a soils map to get information for agricultural or construction purposes. Most map users who want a contour map, however, will ask for "the topo map of X." Normally, the person with specialized map needs is knowledgeable about maps and will be precise in her request. In a large collection, it is common to keep types of maps together, for example, topographic, cultural, political, and geologic maps. In addition to content, factors such as projection and scale may be important in the organization and storage of maps. Staff working with large map collections will need special training to handle this format properly.

A relatively new service in some larger academic and public libraries is Geographic Information Services (GIS). Rhonda Houser outlined some of the types of user queries a GIS program might assist with:

- Identifying a specific geographic data set,
- Creating a map or image from a spatial data set,

- Converting spatial data from two or more formats to a single form,
- Cropping spatial data to generate a new map,
- Creating data and applying it to a map,
- Taking Global Positioning System (GPS) data and creating a map,
- Creating a map from tabular data,
- Linking an image to a GIS using geographic coordinates, and
- Performing spatial data analysis.[21]

Audio Recordings

Returning to a widely held format, audio recordings, again, there is great diversity and incompatibility, at least in terms of the legacy collections found in many libraries. Sound recordings were among the first nonprint formats collected by libraries. In public libraries, the recordings are usually part of the circulating collection. For educational libraries the purpose is usually instructional, with limited, if any, use outside the library. This is the media category that most clearly reflects the long-term influence of a changing technology on a library collection.

Audiobooks are the most common audio-recording purchase in libraries. The widespread use of Internet audio streaming, iPods, and other electronic gear has made music recordings low use in most libraries. Many libraries retain their older recordings because often the performance has not yet migrated to a digital form. These can take the form of 78, 33⅓ rpm phonograph records, cassettes, and CDs. Naturally, each format requires special playing equipment. Usually someone who is interested in hearing such material has some familiarity with the equipment, so assisting them is not a great problem. A few libraries are purchasing relatively low-cost equipment and software that allows one to convert phonograph records to an MP3 format, though the library must be careful to do this in compliance with copyright laws.

For public libraries, audiobooks have become almost as important as the video collection. Automobile players and portable handheld DVD players have created a significant market for audiobooks. Even reading a small paperback on a crowded subway or bus can be difficult. Listening to a pocket-sized player with a headset allows the listener to close out the noise, to some degree, and enjoy a favorite piece of music or listen to a best seller. The same is true for those commuting in their cars or just out for a power walk. Another value of audiobooks is providing those with vision impairments additional opportunities to enjoy print material that goes beyond those available through the National Library Service for the Blind and Physically Handicapped.

Books-on-tape cassettes and CDs as well as digital audiobooks (DABs) are very popular. The cassette still has a small niche in the audio collection for commuters whose vehicle CD player does not provide dependable playback (road bumps can translate into sound bumps, perhaps skipping the key information in a whodunit). Tape decks do not suffer from this problem, but fewer and fewer vehicles have them as a standard feature.

Many libraries are forming collaborative DAB services. Some examples of existing programs in early 2010 include Illinois Kids Zone (www.ilkidszone.info), ListenOhio (www.listenohio.org), and the Midwest Collaborative for Library Services (http://www.mlcnet.org/cms/sitem.cfm/databases__econtent/digital_books/). Unlike the digital music field, DAB is much more stable and does not, at least in 2010, face the copyright issues of music. In 2010, four major vendors offered DAB products—Audible (www.audible.com), OverDrive (www.overdrive.com), netlibrary/Recorded Books (www.oclc.org/audiobooks/purchase/default.htm), and TumbleBookLibrary (www.tumblebooks.com). Tom Peters and colleagues provided an overview of the differences between the services.[22] There are other smaller services that offer very few titles, but as they grow they may well become significant market players.

Many libraries offer two options for accessing their DAB service—a link from the title's MARC record or a link on the library's Web site. Almost all impose a loan period and limits on the number of titles a person may have at any one time. At the time we prepared this chapter, the major issue was DAB incompatibility with the iPod.

There are major advantages to having DABs as part of a library's audio service program. Most notably, DABs

- are available 24/7,
- are never lost or damaged (at least for the library),
- require no processing,
- require no shelf space,
- never require overdue notices or fines (files automatically delete at the end of the loan period),
- provide the visually impaired with another means of access to popular titles,
- allow for simple weeding,
- allow for easy collaboration, and
- offer easily obtainable usage data from the vendors.

One of the drawbacks of audiocassettes, whether spoken word or music, is that they have a relatively short life span, five to six years, even under optimal usage conditions. They are also small objects that have few places upon which a library can attach a security device, so their loss rate ("shrinkage" in retail terms) can be rather high. Nor, for that matter, is there much room to apply bar codes or other property markings. Replacing lost items can be costly. From the public's and the staff's point of view, the fact that an unabridged audiobook can have as many as four to six cassettes means that keeping everything sorted in its proper order can be a problem. Certainly the staff must check each title that has multiple cassettes each time it is returned. If in fact a person is listening to the cassettes in the car and there is more than one title, there is a very good chance a cassette will end up in the wrong container. No one wants to have the ending of a whodunit delayed because the last cassette is for Shakti Gawin's *Creative Visualization Meditations*.

Games

Should libraries acquire games? Are they actually Will Manley's "Twinkies"? This is not the place to review the pros and cons of gaming and libraries. The reality is that public and school libraries have ever-growing collections of games—educational and recreational in character. Even academic libraries, including at least one large research library, are beginning to collect games.[23] The year 2008 saw the fourth annual academic Games, Learning, and Society conference and the second American Library Association–sponsored Games, Learning, and Libraries symposia. "Twinkies" or not, games are a growing segment of library collections.

Games are among the most complex items to select, acquire, and support of all the media formats in a collection. Two of the major reasons for the complexity are the fact that there are multiple platforms (each widely owned by users) for playing games and that there are often multiple releases for a title. Certainly both issues exist, to some extent, for video titles. However, as of 2010 there are at least 10 platforms for game playing. Although the platforms compete for market share, the competition has not focused on whose standards or technology will win; rather, it is whose games attract and hold players' attention longest and money spent on products for a given platform. Following are the 10 game platforms available on retail store shelves in 2010:

- Nintendo DS
- Nintendo Game Cube
- Playstation 2
- Playstation 3
- Game Boy Advanced
- PC/MAC based games
- Xbox
- Xbox 360
- PSP
- Wii

When such a variety of platforms is combined with cross-platform releases of a title, one can see where there would be serious acquisitions budget issues and possible ordering pitfalls. Acquiring games is more labor intensive than acquiring many of the other collection items. Few traditional library vendors handle games, and at the time of this writing there was no source for placing a standing order. One method to ease the workload is to develop a strong working relationship with a local game store. In the not-too-distant past, in an almost solely print environment, many public and academic libraries established such relationships with a local bookstore. This often helped with rush orders and strengthened the bookstore's income, which in turn expanded the range of titles the store stocked. With a strong local bookstore, library selectors had a form of approval plan without the amount of work for the acquisitions that arises from traditional approval plans.

Cataloging is another challenge for games as the format is relatively new in collections. As a result, assuming that games will be represented in the online public access catalog (OPAC), a great deal of original cataloging is required for games.

Game Ratings

Like motion pictures, games have a rating system. Most video games released in North America carry a rating from the Entertainment Software Rating Board (ESRB), a nonprofit, self-regulatory, third-party entity formed in 1994 by what is now the

Entertainment Software Association. ESRB ratings consist of two parts: a rating symbol on the front of the box addressing age appropriateness, and one of more than 30 different content descriptors (e.g., alcohol reference, blood and gore) on the back of the box elaborating on elements that may be of interest or concern to users and/or their guardians.[24]

The seven ratings on the box front are EC, early childhood; E, everyone six and up; E10, everyone ten and up; T, teen thirteen and up; M, mature seventeen and up; AO, adults only eighteen and up; and RP, rating pending. The rating system complexity and the need to provide information about system requirements exemplify the types of challenges that face acquisitions and cataloging departments in libraries that are collecting games. Games also raise some serious policy issues, in particular how to monitor who uses what rating.

Realia

Teaching realia, test kits, and models can range from samples of materials, such as rocks or insects, to working models and large, take-apart anatomical models. Scientific and technical supply houses offer a variety of large-scale models for use in the classroom. Because the models are expensive, few teachers can afford to buy them, so the instructional media center is the usual source for these, except where there is a large biology or physics department that acquires the items. Even in the case of large departments, students get better service if the models are also in the media center where they can examine the material any time.

With replicas the acquisitions department staff must check for the degree of accuracy that is being requested. Fossils and anatomical replicas are available in differing levels of detail from very few (a general representation) to highly detailed (useful in advanced instruction or basic research). Not all replicas come in different levels of detail, which further compounds the challenge of acquiring the desired item without committing undue staff time to the ordering and receiving process.

Microforms

Paul Negus opened his paper on the future of microfilm by stating, "Microfilm use has declined significantly over the past ten years as digital technologies have been adapted more widely. This seems to be the general feeling and understanding of the microfilm industry, but what is the reality?"[25] He concluded his essay with, "Microfilm is not only alive and well but may well turn out to be the missing Digital Preservation 'Holy Grail' that has alluded [sic] the Archive for the last 20 years."[26]

Although most libraries currently acquire little in the way of microforms, some still do. and a great many more have substantial legacy collections containing information that is still sought by users and is not readily available in any other format. Although it is possible to digitize microforms, few libraries have the funds to undertake such work. Also, few commercial firms find it a profitable activity because of low demand. One of the major factors behind the microformat was its ability to store large volumes of low use information in very little space. The bulk of the material contained in a microformat is either backfiles of serials or rare or ephemeral information. One reason libraries acquired microforms was that they save collection storage space, especially for low-use materials. Thirty years of back issues of a journal, occupying 25 feet of shelving, can be reduced to three reels of microfilm, which, in their cardboard storage boxes, require less than one foot of space.

Microforms may also provide access to primary research material or to items that are very rare and may only be available, in their original form, in one or two libraries in the world. Thus, while many librarians and most of the public view microforms with some degree—or a great deal—of displeasure, they have served a useful function in providing access to materials that might not otherwise be available locally.

Microforms are still in use and are still being acquired by libraries, especially large academic libraries. ProQuest-UMI Microfilm is one of the largest vendors of microform in the marketplace. One example of the products that are available is their American History and Culture set of 8,000 microfiche, which is described as follows: "Since 1930 the National Park Service has sponsored or acquired thousands of archaeological, architectural, ethnographic, museum collections management and historical research reports exploring the riches of the American heritage. Few have been available even at the largest libraries and research institutions."[27] From a technical services point of view, the bad news is the fiche set does not have MARC records available for in putting into the library's OPAC. In a very real sense, thousands of fiche in cabinets without an effective means of accessing individual titles within the set may be a marginal acquisition at best or the catalog department is faced with a very large, probably original, cataloging project.

The two most common microform formats in libraries are reel film and fiche. Reel formats are the older of the two and were widely used for newspapers and serials. Reel microfilms are long strips of film on the appropriate-size reel and have traditionally been available in several sizes: 16mm, 35mm, and 70mm. The film can be positive (i.e., clear with black text) or negative (i.e., dark with white text). Acquisition staff members need to know about these different types because different microfilm readers have different capabilities—the greater the machine's flexibility in handling film size, negative or positive images, and reduction ratios the higher the cost. Few libraries are able to purchase the top-of-the-line reader/printers and therefore select more affordable but more limited models. That in turn means the acquisitions department must know what type of microform to order. Most libraries try to confine the microfilm collection to one or two sizes (such as 35mm and 70mm) and one type (positive or negative). With any large-scale collection, however, more variety is inevitable, because the information needed by the library may only be available in a particular size and type of microfilm.

Microfiche are sheets of film with the images of the original document arranged in columns and rows. Fiche are primarily employed for materials that might have a number of simultaneous users of the collection/title, such as college catalogs or telephone directories. Like other media, microfiche came in a variety of sizes and reduction ratios. Common sizes are 3 by 5 inches, 3 by 6 inches, and 6 by 7 inches, and reduction ratios range from 12 to more than 200. The greater the reduction ratio the more information the producer can fit on a single fiche. Many commercial publications are 48x (the "x" equals the reduction ratio), but the other relatively common ratio is 16x.

Although microforms are becoming more and more a legacy collection format, acquisitions and cataloging staff must have some knowledge of the variations in the format that makes their work just a little more challenging.

PRESERVATION

Throughout the preceding sections we mentioned variations in size and shape of the media formats. This variety has implications for storage, access, and long-term preservation. Although it is possible to use standard library bookcases to house these materials, even with adjustable shelves such storage wastes space. Library equipment and supply houses offer a wide range of cabinets and storage units designed for the different formats and, in more expensive models, to help create better environmental conditions for preservation purposes. Two media formats, microforms and videos/films, have special storage considerations we will touch on briefly.

DVDs present two different and significant challenges for libraries—damage and security. Damage to DVDs is very high. In responding to Oder's survey, one librarian said "[DVDs] are used for coasters and Frisbees."[28] One obvious factor in the damage is that, unlike a cassette, the operating surface is fully exposed during handling the disk. Scratches, chips, and even warping are problems. Thus, the expected circulation life of a popular DVD is low. Many libraries think they are lucky if they get 15 to 20 circulations. Replacement cost can become significant. A few libraries have taken the step of buying one noncirculating copy of titles deemed significant for the library and placing it in their special collection or archive as a means of preservation.

Because of their small size, theft is a much greater problem for DVDs than for VHS cassettes. Determining how to display available titles is also a challenge. Some libraries put out empty cases. Others have tried using locked display cases similar to those used in commercial outlets. A few display color copies of the cases in their OPAC or on a bulletin board, keeping the disk at a service desk. Oder reported that one library had experienced losses in excess of $90,000 in less than five years of offering DVDs.[29] Until someone comes up with an effective solution, library staff, both in technical and public services will spend a significant amount of time dealing with DVD preservation and security matters.

Microforms

Microfiche may or may not be stored inside a protective cover, such as an envelope or a notebook. Unnecessary handling increases the chances of damaging the fiche. Microforms, like many of the other media formats discussed in this chapter, are physically made up of a series of layers. That is, there is a relatively thick, strong carrier base, often acetate or polyacetate, with a very thin surface layer that contains the image. The surface layer is very susceptible to damage. The two common types of fiche are diazo and silver halide. Silver halide is archival quality, but very easy to scratch. Diazo, although not considered a permanent film, is harder to damage, but it is still susceptible to scratching. Most damage occurs during the filing and refiling process. Damage to a corner of the fiche can put a scratch down the entire surface of the fiche behind it. Depending on the film's reduction ratio, the amount of information lost may be little or great (the higher the ratio, the more data will disappear).

Film and Video

Standard library shelving can house films and videos and make them more available for browsing, but it wastes space. Library equipment vendors sell storage cabinets designed to store various types and sizes of media material. The depth, length, and width of video cabinet drawers are such that three or four rows of cassettes will fit into a drawer. A storage problem arises, however, with a mixed collection of VHS, Beta, three-quarter-inch cassettes and DVDs.

In terms of care of these materials, someone should rewind and inspect each video-cassette and film (if film is still in the collection) at least once every six months, even if it is unused. In an environment where there is high temperature (over 80 degrees Fahrenheit) and humidity (65 percent and higher), the thin image-bearing layer (emulsion layer) becomes soft and somewhat sticky. Films and videos left in such conditions for long periods, without use, become so sticky that the image-bearing layer pulls off when use finally occurs.

SUMMARY

One given of media collections is that they will change at almost the same speed as technology in general. Keeping updated with development is a challenge, especially for staff who have more than enough work to occupy their attention. It seems rather likely that media services will play an ever-growing role in the overall service program of most libraries.

REVIEW QUESTIONS

1. What role do media play in library service programs?

2. What are the common problems for media use?

3. What special problems do videos present for the staff?

4. In what ways has technology changed media services over the past five years?

5. Legal use of media is circumscribed by the copyright law. List the major issues.

6. Discuss your views regarding the appropriateness of game collections in libraries. What challenges do they produce?

7. How do long-term preservation issues for media differ from those for print and digital materials?

8. In what manner do media represent special challenges for the cataloging department?

NOTES

The epigraphs for this chapter are taken from "Music Downloading Looks to Big Labels," *American Libraries* 39, no. 5 (2008): 33, and Dale Lipschulz, "Gaming @ Your Library," *American Libraries* 40, nos. 1/2 (2009): 40–43.

1. Barbara R. Jones-Kavalier and Suzanne I. Flannigan, "Connecting the Digital Dots: Literacy of the 21st Century," *Teacher Librarian* 35, no. 3 (2008): 13.

2. Doug Johnson, "Libraries for a Postliterate Society," *Media and the Internet@ Schools* 16, no. 4 (2009): 20.

3. Allan C. Rough, "Nonprint Media Services at the University of Maryland," *College and University Media Review* 12, no. 2 (2006): 47.

4. Marc Prensky, "Digital Natives, Digital Immigrants," *On the Horizon* 9, no. 5 (2001): 1–6.

5. Johnson, "Libraries for a Postliterate Society," 21.

6. Will Manley, "Facing the Public," *Wilson Library Bulletin* 65, no. 6 (1991): 89.

7. Sally Mason, "Libraries, Literacy and the Visual Media," in *Video Collection Development in Multitype Libraries,* ed. G. P. Handman (Westport, CT: Greenwood, 1994), 12.

8. Myra Michele Brown, "Video Libraries: More Than a Lure," *American Libraries* 26, no. 11 (2006): 41.

9. Howard Story, "The World Is Going Digital! How Do I Cope?" *Library Mosaics* 15, no. 2 (2004): 12.

10. Alan Kaye, "Digital Dawn," *Library Journal* 130, no. 9 (2005): 62.

11. Jeff T. Dick, "Bracing for Blu-ray," *Library Journal* 134, no. 19 (2009): 33–35.

12. Norman Oder, "The DVD Predicament," *Library Journal* 130, no. 19 (2005): 35–40.

13. Jennifer Netherby, "Slow to Become a Shelf Staple, DVD Is Still Growing," *Library Journal* 132, supplement (2007): 5–6.

14. Oder, "The DVD Predicament," 40.

15. Ann Kim, "The Future Is Now," *Library Journal* 131, no. 9 (2006): 62.

16. Cindy Spielvogel, "Libraries Lead the Way to Movie Downloads," *Library Journal* 132, no. 10 supplement (2007): 12.

17. Deg Farrelly, "Use-Determined Streaming Video Acquisition: The Arizona Model for FMG *On Demand,*" *College & Universities Media Review* 14 (2008): 65–78.

18. Linda Redden, "Videostreaming I-in K-12 Classrooms," *Media & Methods* 42, no. 1 (2005): 15.

19. Pat Lora, "Public Library Video Collections," in *Video Collection Development in Multitype Libraries,* ed. G. P. Handman (Westport, CT: Greenwood, 1994), 25.

20. U.S. House. 94th Cong., 2d sess., H. Rept. 1476, *Omnibus Copyright Revision Legislative History* (Washington, D.C.: GPO, 1976).

21. Rhonda Houser, "Building a Library GIS Service," *Library Trends* 55, no. 2 (2006): 318–20.

22. Tom Peters, Lori Bell, Diana Sussman, and Sharon Ruda, "An Overview of Digital Audiobooks for Libraries," *Computers in Libraries* 25, no. 7 (2005): 7–8, 61–64.

23. Mary Laskowski and David Ward, "Building Next Generation Video Game Collections in Academic Libraries," *Journal of Academic Librarianship* 35, no. 3 (2009): 267–73.

24. Shawn McCann, "Game Ratings Rundown," *Library Journal* 134, no. 3 (2009): 85.

25. Paul Negus, "The Future of Microfilm," 1, http://www.microfilm.com/pdf/future_of_microfilm_presentation.pdf.

26.   Ibid., 4.

27.   ProQuest-UMI Microfilm, *American History and Culture,* http://www.proquest.com/en-US/catalogs/collections/detail/American-History-and-Culture-224.shtml.

28.   Oder, "The DVD Predicament," 39.

29.   Ibid.

SUGGESTED READING

Allmang, Nancy. "Audiobooks on iPods." *College & Research Libraries News* 70, no. 3 (2009):173–76.

Behler, Anne, Beth Roberts and Karen Dabney. "Circulating Map Collections at Pennsylvania State University," *DttP* 34, no. 4 (2006): 33–36.

Caron, Susan. "Transiting to DVD," *Library Journal* 129, no. 9, supplement (2004): 4–5.

Fling, R. Michael. "Tips on Acquiring Music." *Notes* 63, no. 2 (2006): 279–88.

Gritten, Tim. "Providing Community Outreach Through the Nintendo Wii." *Indiana Libraries* 27, no. 2 (2008): 10–15.

Jeske, Michelle. "Tapping into Media." *Library Journal* 133, no. 15 (2008): 22–25.

Johnson, Suanne. "Comparing Online Streaming Video Sources." *Library Media Connection* 23, no. 6 (2006): 58–60.

King, David Lee. "Video on the Web: the Basics." *Multimedia & Internet @ Schools* 16, no. 1 (2009): 14–16.

Lee, Scott, and Carolyn Burrell. "Introduction to Streaming Video for Novices," *Library Hi Tech News* 21, no. 2 (2004): 20–24.

Mastel, Kristen, and Dave Huston. "Using Video Games to Teach Game Design: A Gaming Collection for Libraries," *Computers in Libraries* 29, no. 3 (2009): 41–44.

Smith, Angel, and Claudene Sproles. "Don't Get Lost: The Basics of Organizing a Library's Map Collection," *Kentucky Libraries* 68, no. 2 (2004): 22–27.

Snow, Maryly. "Learning From Lantern Slides, 1979–2004," *Visual Resources Association Bulletin* 31, no. 1 (2004): 45–50.

Stoltenberg, Jaime, and Abraham Parish. "Geographic Information Systems and Libraries," *Library Trends* 55, no. 2, special issue (2006).

Taylor, Leslie. "DVDs at Public Libraries: For a Fee or Free?" *Feliciter* 55, no. 4: (2009): 165–66.

Chapter

Fiscal Management

There seems to be little doubt that more and more library administrators are beginning to hear officials raising questions such as, "What are the benefits the campus receives for its investments in the library?"

—Richard M. Dougherty, 2009

I used the pie in describing my library budget to an information vendor. My library book and computer research budget is a pie—for me to give you some more of my pie I must make another information vendor's piece smaller.

—Mark E. Estes, 2009

It is impossible for many libraries to fulfill all their patrons' needs and wants. So they'll have to be prudent, keep watch on local priorities, and remind funders of the library's value as they navigate a challenging future.

—Norman Oder, 2010

Accountability is a term one hears in reference to almost all types of libraries. All organizations, profit or nonprofit, are under increasing pressure to demonstrate their value, show that they employed their resources effectively, and prove that they are responsive to the needs and wants of their stakeholders. Although the chapter epigraph from Richard Dougherty relates to academic libraries, the basic message—what value do we get from funding your library operations—is very common in today's tight economic times.

Fiscal accountability is one of the most significant accountability concerns on the part of those who fund an organization and those who use its services. Libraries are no exception to this fact of organizational life. If anything, the recent recession has magnified the importance of proper fiscal management practices for libraries both for accountability reasons and to ensure that available funds are used in the best possible manner, as the epigraph from Norman Oder suggests.

The management concept of return on investment (ROI) relates to the question of value for any type of organization. Libraries have employed the concept from time to time; however, few have used it on a consistent, ongoing basis for budget-request purposes. Larry White made the case for a wider regular use of the concept:

> ROI as an assessment or valuation tool is a valuable asset for the library to possess in addressing customer accountability inquiries. Applying ROI in potentially new applications within the library organization would provide library administrators with a wider scope and effectiveness to report their organization's activities in terms of performance/value/impact and a strategic competitive advantage in the knowledge economy.[1]

Given that a library's materials budget is usually the second-largest component of its budget, acquisitions departments are clearly in the forefront of any effort to demonstrate value and what the funding authorities' ROI may be.

ROI is essentially a ratio of gains and losses resulting from the resources expended to achieve the gain or loss. A positive ROI represents more value gained than resources expended, something that almost every organization hopes to achieve. The unit typically used to measure ROI is money, although other units can and have been tried with rather mixed results. One of the challenges for libraries using ROI is the fact that much of a library's outcomes are more or less intangible, thus making the assignment of dollar and cents difficult and open to wide interpretation. What is the value or worth of a very satisfied reader who has enjoyed dozens of novels over the past 12 months? What is the value or worth gained by a young student who received excellent assistance with a class assignment from the library staff? Whether or not it is difficult to do, libraries must begin to be more proactive in making use of techniques such as ROI to demonstrate their value to society.

Libraries never seem to have enough money to do everything they would like to or should accomplish. Acquisitions departments play an essential role in the effective use of the funds that are available. Library fiscal management is a joint activity involving everyone who participates in the process: selectors, acquisitions staff, and senior management. Controlling expenditures and securing adequate funding are two key activities. Monies spent on materials for the collection constitute the second-largest expense category for most libraries and information centers. Traditionally, in U.S. and Canadian libraries, salaries represent the largest percentage of the total budget, followed by the materials ("book") budget, and finally, all other operating expenses. That sequence still holds today, but the percentage spent on materials has decreased as salaries have risen and the overall budget has increased slowly, if at all. Although percentages vary, the order remains the same in any type of library environment or any size collection. Most of the literature on the topic of collection budgeting reflects a large research library orientation. However, the same issues exist in other libraries.

For some time now there has been a constant pressure on the materials budget of most libraries, which has resulted in a decline in the percentage of the total budget spent on acquiring items for the collection. The almost yearly double-digit inflation of serials prices has further skewed the traditional balance in collection fund allocations. In many libraries in the United States, serials expenditures exceed monographic purchases, even in institutions that have traditionally emphasized book collections. Over the past 15-plus years, budgetary needs for electronic resources have increased dramatically. In some libraries such expenditures predominate, exceeding the combined acquisitions costs of all other collection formats. As we will discuss in the section on fund allocation, the challenges grow for libraries when they attempt to balance competing, yet equally valid, collection format needs.

Comparing the total dollar amount expended on materials 30 years ago with the current funding levels, today's total is considerably higher; but the total expenditures do not tell the entire story. Looking at the number of items acquired for the money spent reveals that the increase in titles acquired is not proportional to funding increases. Libraries are spending more and acquiring less. Since the 1970s, many libraries, along with many other organizations, have dealt with budgets that some call "steady state," others call "zero growth," and still others call "static." At best, budgeting of this type uses the previous year's inflation rate as the base for the next fiscal year's increase. An average inflation rate, like all averages, contains elements that increase at both above and below the average rate. For libraries this is a problem, because the inflation rate for information materials has been running well ahead of the overall inflation rate.

PROBLEMS IN FISCAL MANAGEMENT

Over the years, collection development staffs in the United States and Canada have faced several problems. Book and journal prices have generally increased, and continue to increase, at rates well above the average inflation rate as measured by the Consumer Price Index (CPI). During this same time, serials prices increased even more rapidly than did monograph prices. To maintain serial subscriptions, libraries took monies from book funds, thus further reducing the number of monographs acquired. Eventually, libraries started canceling subscriptions. Thus, differential inflation rates and the use of national average rates as the basis for calculating budgets have contributed to declining acquisition rates for many libraries. As noted in the chapter on serials, the change to digital has not and probably will not solve the greater than CPI price increases for library materials.

A second problem was, and still is, that the materials budget is vulnerable in periods of tight budgets. Expenditures on materials are discretionary in that (in theory) a library could wait to buy an item until the next fiscal year. Institutions set staff salaries on an annual basis, and staff reductions are rare during the middle of a fiscal year, unless the organization faces a major financial crisis. Salaries are usually the last item organizations cut when attempting to save money. Without heat, light, and water (utility bills), the physical facility cannot remain open, so those expenditures are generally not cut. Some operating expenses are discretionary: pens, pencils, paper, printer cartridges, and so forth (i.e., office supplies). Professional development and travel reimbursements may be frozen in an attempt to save funds. Institutions may achieve small savings, in terms of percentage of the total budget, by cutting back in such areas. Institutions with relatively large library collections view the materials budget as one of the largest available pools of funds that can easily be cut in an emergency. Further, the reality is that the monograph materials budget is the only place where significant cuts are easy to make because the material is not purchased on an ongoing basis. All too often, the long-term impact of such decisions does not receive enough consideration, and the other choices appear, at least in the short run, to be even less acceptable. These issues are institutional and apply to corporate and special libraries as much as to publicly funded libraries.

Norman Oder's article, quoted in one of the chapter epigraphs, reported on *Library Journal*'s annual survey of public library budgets. Results of the survey, not surprisingly, showed a downward trend—with a 2.6 percent reduction in the overall average budget, a 3.5 percent decrease for the materials budget, and, for the first time in several years, a 1.6 percent decline in the per capita expenditure.[2] The percentage decreases on overall and collections funding, while not dramatic, have been on a downward slope for some time now. The cumulative impact of year after year reductions is beginning to show in ways service communities are noticing.

One of the survey questions reported in Oder's article asked about what coping strategies the libraries had implemented for addressing the shortfalls. Following were the top six responses:

- Cutting travel and training funds—51 percent
- Freezing salaries—41 percent
- Seeking more outside funding (grants, donations)—36 percent
- Cutting or reducing programming activities—28 percent
- Reducing service hours—26 percent
- Increasing use of volunteers—26 percent[3]

When asked about which cuts or reductions users would probably miss the most, the vast majority of libraries expected service-hour changes to be the most common concern (74%), followed by fewer new titles added (14%), and then reductions in services (12%).[4] Making do with less has become a fact of life for most Canadian and U.S. libraries, and it seems likely to continue to be the case, at least in the short-term. Thus, understanding the issues of financial control and making the most effective use of the available funds is critical. With collection funds usually being the second-largest component in a library's budget, acquisitions staff must commit themselves to handling the funds properly and thoughtfully.

LIBRARY FUND ACCOUNTING

Most libraries and information centers are part of not-for-profit (NFP) organizations. Being NFP affects how the library maintains its financial records, particularly in contrast to for-profit organizations. For libraries that are part of a government jurisdiction, most revenues are received through an annual budget. The funding authorities review the budget requests and authorize certain levels of funding for various activities. The three most common forms of income for libraries are appropriations (monies distributed by the governing body to its agencies to carry out specific purposes), revenue generated by the library as a result of service fees and fines, and endowments and donations.

Because of the nature of the financial activities, certain accounting terms and concepts are different for NFP organizations than for for-profit organizations. However, some general accounting rules and practices do apply. One special term for NFP accounting is *fund accounting.* (Fund accounting has been defined as a set of self-balancing account groups.) Another difference is that whereas the profit-oriented book-keeping system equation uses the terms *assets, liabilities,* and *equity,* NFP accounting uses assets, liabilities, and *fund balance.* One of the equations for NFP bookkeeping is that assets must equal liabilities plus the fund balance; another is that the fund balance is the difference between assets and liabilities. Substituting "equity" for "fund balance" would make the equation apply to for-profit organizations. (A difference between these equations is that an increase in fund balance carries no special meaning, whereas an increase in equity is a positive signal in a for-profit organization.) Other terms, such as *debit, credit, journalizing, posting,* and *trial balance,* have the same meaning regardless of the organization's profit orientation. Balance sheets are discussed in greater detail later in this chapter.

Accounting is the process of identifying, measuring, and communicating economic information to permit informed judgments and decisions by users of the information. Several groups or individuals in the library use accounting information (the term *accounting* includes bookkeeping activities). Selectors need to know how much money they have to spend. The head librarian needs data to maintain control over the library's operation. The business office must have information to ensure that the library handles its funds properly. It is the acquisitions department that provides this information, at least about that portion of the library's budget used for building the collections. Usually there is a support staff member who handles the accounting activities. This person needs to have training and experience in accounting and bookkeeping. Anyone interested in a career as a support staff member in acquisitions might consider taking coursework in accounting, because such work expands employment opportunities (in seeking both a position and promotions).

The bookkeeping unit usually handles all of a library's accounting work (payroll records, accounts payable/receivable, purchasing, inventory control, and some cost accounting). Frequently, this unit is part of the acquisitions department. When this is not the case, that unit must work very closely with the acquisitions department because a large percentage of the accounting work involves both units. Consequently, everyone in acquisitions must have some basic understanding of accounting and bookkeeping, even those not directly involved in those activities.

Although library bookkeeping requires some variations from standard practice, it is important for the library staff handling the internal books to understand standard accounting procedures. The library bookkeeper, for example, must reconcile library records with those of the business office. Because the results concern many people, it is important to understand the business office's records and what they represent.

ACCOUNTING

The term accounting covers several activities that many people view as separate fields:

1. *General accounting* deals with the process of recording fiscal data (this includes bookkeeping).

2. *Cost accounting* determines business costs (most frequently, unit costs).
3. *Tax accounting* determines liability for taxes, especially income and Social Security taxes.
4. *Auditing* is the process of verifying the accuracy of financial records.
5. *Budgetary accounting* is the preparation of systematic forecasts of operations in fiscal terms.
6. *System building* is the development and installation of the appropriate financial records in an organization.
7. *Governmental accounting* deals with maintaining financial records for governmental units.

Library accounting takes in the first four fields and the last; the fifth and sixth fields seldom apply to library situations.

Balance Sheet

One important element in accounting and bookkeeping is the balance sheet, which indicates the institution's financial condition at any given time. Although the library may not always have a balance sheet, its parent or funding body will have one, and the library's expenditures must fit into that larger fiscal picture. Thus, having some basic knowledge of the balance sheet helps the staff understand some of the requirements of the funding authorities. The funding authorities are also usually accountable to other agencies that frequently require financial audits. There is more about audits later in this chapter.

A balance sheet shows the amounts and nature of assets, liabilities, and proprietorship of an organization. The balance sheet is the statement of the basic equation of accounting: assets = liabilities + proprietorship. Assets are anything of value owned; liabilities are obligations to pay (money or other assets) or to render service to persons or organizations now or in the future; proprietorship is the difference between assets and liabilities. A library has proprietorship only when it derives a portion of its funds from endowments. (Normally there is an annual distribution of endowment income. Otherwise, the term "fund balance" may be substituted for "proprietorship.")

No uniform format exists for the balance sheet. However, two very common methods of presenting a statement of financial condition are the account form (horizontal form) and the report form (vertical form). Account forms list assets on the left-hand side of a page and liabilities and proprietorship on the right-hand side. The final totals of the columns are equal. The report form lists all assets, then all liabilities, and finally the proprietorship. A great many variations exist on these basic forms, but the important point to remember is that the assets must equal the liabilities and fund balance/proprietorship.

Accounts and Ledgers

Every business transaction has dual elements (a part of the dual-entry system described later). Every financial entry in the journals and ledgers in the acquisitions department is a business transaction of some type. The dual elements arise because each transaction is an exchange of values: Something of value is given up for something else, presumably of equal value. The bookkeeper must record both elements. As these factors change, they change the value of the assets, liabilities, and fund balance. Thus, it is important to have a recording system that will show the changes with a minimum of space, effort, and error.

Most ILS systems provide a short, accurate method for recording transactions, separating the increases from the decreases for each amount. This means balancing assets against liabilities and fund balance. An account records the effects of a transaction. An acquisitions department uses as many accounts as necessary to provide adequate detailed information. Usually, there is one account for each fund in the department, and once a month the bookkeeper assembles the data in these accounts into a balance sheet. The conventional method of handling accounts places additions to assets on the left side of the account and additions to liabilities and fund balance on the right.

Two terms used in recording changes in value are *debit* (Dr.) and *credit* (Cr.). Debit refers to the left side of an account (assets). Credit refers to the right side (liabilities). Thus, a debit is an entry on the left, and a credit is an entry on the right. The idea of debits tied to assets and credits to liabilities can be very confusing to beginners and to anyone not acquainted with accounting terminology. Perhaps the best way to keep the relationships in mind and to remember how the terms affect the balance is to use a chart like the following:

"Debit" Indicates That	**"Credit" Indicates That**
Assets increase	Assets decrease
Liabilities decrease	Liabilities increase
Fund balance decreases	Fund balance increases
Income decreases	Income increases
Expenses increase	Expenses decrease

A basic rule of accounting is that for every debit there must be a credit. This does not mean that the number of debit and credit entries must be equal, but rather that the debit and credit amounts must be equal.

The name for a group of accounts is the *ledger*. This is a derived record presenting in an analytical form the total effect of all transactions. Data are taken from the books in which the bookkeeper made the original entries (called journals, discussed shortly). Normally, there is only one account on a page of the ledger. In the past, a loose-leaf ledger was very common because it was flexible. Automated systems have made the paper-based ledger a thing of the past, although some acquisitions departments maintain a paper-based shadow system in case the computer system goes down. Accounts can be arranged and rearranged in whatever order works for the department.

Once a month, the bookkeeper prepares a *trial balance*. This is a listing of ledger accounts showing debit and credit balances. The object is to determine whether the debits and credits are equal, or in balance. A trial balance serves several purposes:

1. It provides a partial check on the accuracy of bookkeeping by proving the equality of total debits and credits.
2. It provides a way to more quickly detect errors and their sources.

3. It provides a condensed picture of each account and a summary of all accounts.
4. It is often the basis for preparing financial statements.

Trial balancing uses three columns. One column is for the account total, and the other two are for the account debits and credits. Bookkeepers use two techniques to show the amounts for each account on the trial balance. One technique is to list only the balance of each account; this approach reduces the initial amount of work. The other method is to list the amounts in the debit and credit columns for each account, which provides more detailed information.

The trial balance is an essential accounting tool, but it does not reveal some kinds of errors. It indicates whether debits and credits are equal, but not whether compensating errors have occurred on both sides of the account. An item may be properly posted—that is, the right amounts are on the debit and credit sides—but to the wrong account. A trial balance does not reveal a mistake in classifying information in the journal. Of course, an unrecorded ledger transaction will also go undetected during a trial balance. Therefore, even if the trial balance appears to be correct, there may be a number of errors in the system. This is one of the reasons that it is necessary to have the books audited.

Journal

As just indicated, the ledger is not a complete record of transactions. For a number of reasons, it is desirable to have a preliminary record in which one records transactions in chronological order with an explanation of the nature of each entry. In an acquisitions department, sequential order numbers constitute, in part, such a primary record. The order file used to be a part of what accountants called the "daybook," an informal record of the day's activity. Most organizations do not use a daybook any more but make entries directly into the electronic *journal*. The journal is the book of original entry, with transactions recorded in chronological order. Entries to the journal come from whatever records now substitute for the daybook (e.g., invoices, orders, sales slips, cash-register tapes). A journal may be more than just a book or electronic file with account numbers, debits, credits, and a brief explanation about the transaction. Often associated with it are files of documents or other media (backup material explaining the transaction). Following are the important features of the journal:

1. It is a day-to-day record of each transaction.
2. It is the point at which the debit and credit aspects of all transactions can be analyzed. This very important activity can cause a great many problems if done improperly.
3. It is the point at which a transaction becomes a series of numbers. The explanation of the transaction may not be extensive. However, it must be adequate to direct someone from the journal entry to the proper backup file to find a full explanation.

The term used to indicate recording entries in a journal is *journalizing.* Most libraries (if not all) now use one of several computer-based spreadsheet programs to handle this task. Journals and ledgers are the basic items in what accountants call the *double-entry* accounting system. Double-entry simply means recording each transaction in both the journal and the ledger. The journal is the original chronological record; the ledger is a secondary analytical record. Perhaps the most important difference between the journal and the ledger is that because the journal contains the first entries, it usually carries greater weight as legal evidence.

In most libraries, the major fund is the operating fund. Other funds may be endowment and physical plant funds. The operating funds are the group of accounts used to handle the day-to-day activities of the library for a given time, usually 12 months, and covering such items as salaries, materials purchases, and utility bills. Within the operating fund there may be two categories of accounts: restricted and unrestricted.

Restricted accounts require using the monies only for specific purposes. Collection development and acquisition staffs often work with such accounts (frequently referred to as *funds* in the monetary rather than the accounting meaning of the term). More often than not, these accounts are the result of donations by individuals who have expressed definite ideas about how the library may spend the money.

Some libraries have endowments that are a combination of individual and corporate or foundation gifts. Sometimes gifts are for current use, and sometimes they are for an endowment. Endowments should generate income for the library indefinitely. The normal procedure for endowments is to make available some percentage of the interest earned. The balance of the interest is returned to the endowment to increase its capitalized base. Private libraries, and an increasing number of publicly funded libraries, have one or more endowments. Often, the donor's restrictions are narrow. When the restrictions are too narrow, it is difficult to make effective use of the available monies. Most collection development officers prefer *unrestricted* accounts (used for any appropriate item for the collection) or broad-based restricted accounts.

The purpose of the accounting system is to ensure the proper use of monies provided and to make it possible to track expenditures. That is, one must record (charge) every financial transaction to some account, and a record exists of what the transaction involved. With a properly functioning fund accounting system, it is possible to tie every item acquired to a specific account and to verify when the transaction took place. With a good accounting system, one can easily provide accurate reports about all financial aspects of collection development activities. Furthermore, it is a great planning aid. It takes time to understand accounting systems, but librarians must understand them if they wish to be effective and efficient collection development officers.

A good book to consult for accounting information is G. Stevenson Smith's *Managerial Accounting for Libraries and Other Not-for-Profit Organizations,* 2nd edition. Another good resource is Anne M. Turner's *Managing Money: A Guide for Librarians.*[5]

ESTIMATING COSTS

Several factors influence the funding needs for collection development and thus the amount of money the acquisitions department must handle. Changes in the composition of the service community may have an important impact in either a positive or a negative manner. Another factor is changes in collecting activities, such as the scope or depth desired in a subject area. These factors do not arise very often. The two cost factors that do come up year in and year out are the price of materials and inflation.

From time to time, libraries encounter problems establishing the credibility of collection-building funding requirements. Although a good accounting system will assist in justifying budget requests, additional data about material expenditures are often necessary.

One example of the problems caused by inflation, stable budgets, and rapidly rising prices for materials (and perhaps limited credibility) is what has happened to the expenditures and acquisition rates for U.S. academic libraries. Between 1993 and 1998, monograph prices rose just over 25 percent. For serials, the data were almost shocking: between 1986 and 1996, prices rose 169 percent. Although the total amount of money expended was higher in 1998 than in 1993, the number of monographs purchased fell by 14 percent.[6]

Data about price increases have been available for some time. In the 1970s, U.S. librarians made an all-out effort to create useful library price indexes to measure rates of change. A subcommittee of the American National Standards Institute, the Z39 Committee (1974), was able to develop guidelines for price indexes. By the early 1980s, it was necessary to revise the guidelines, which were later published as Z39.20.[7] Another group effort was that of the Library Materials Price Index Committee (formed by the Association for Library Collections & Technical Services, a division of the American Library Association [ALA]). The committee has produced a price index for U.S. materials and some international publications (available at the ALA's Web site, http://www.ala.org/ala/mgrps/divs/alcts/resources/collect/serials/spi.cfm). These efforts provide consistent data on price changes over a long period, which, when averaged, is as close as anyone can come to predicting future price changes.

The most recent U.S. data are in journals; historical data appear in *The Bowker Annual.* Using *The Bowker Annual* may be adequate for some purposes, but one needs to be aware that the information that appears in the current volume is almost two years old. Preliminary data for books published during a calendar year appear in *Publishers Weekly* (often in late February or early March). Final data appear some months later (September or October). The major problem with the published indexes is that when preparing a budget request, up-to-date information may not be readily available.

Vendors can sometimes provide more current data. Some vendors will provide custom pricing information, and others may provide a general set of data based on their experience. A sample of what an acquisitions department might request or receive from a book vendor is illustrated in Figure 12.1. It is also possible to obtain information about serials subscriptions from a vendor. Figure 12.2 presents a small segment of the data the department might receive from a vendor such as EBSCO.

Just as libraries prepare budget requests at different times of the year, pricing data appear at various times during the year in a variety of sources. The challenge is to find the most current data, which may determine whether the library receives requested funding.

Libraries that purchase a significant number of foreign publications need to estimate the impact of exchange rates. Volatile exchange rates affect buying power almost as much as inflation. For example, in January 1985, the pound sterling was at US$1.2963; in January 1988 it was up to US$1.7813; in 1992 it was US$1.7653; by January 1994 it was down to US$1.4872, and in March 1999 had moved up to US$1.6064.

	Jan. 2008–Dec. 2008		Jan. 2009–Dec. 2009		
	No. of Titles	Average List Price	No. of Titles	Average List Price	Price Variance
Abbeville	69	$48.66	72	$46.01	–5.45%
ABC-CLIO	67	$67.94	47	$83.29	22.59%
Abrams	147	$47.87	161	$45.88	–4.16%
Addison Wesley Longman	499	$38.90	598	$42.41	9.02%
American Chemical Society	103	$125.92	46	$105.22	–16.44%
American Library Association	26	$50.46	61	$38.66	–23.38
Baker Book House	125	$19.33	73	$22.73	17.59%
Ballantine/Fawcett/Del Rey	125	$17.50	258	$19.52	11.54%
Bantam Doubleday Dell	394	$21.09	409	$20.82	–1.28%
Bernan Associates	106	$40.82	52	$49.29	20.75%
Blackwell	227	$60.28	205	$63.69	5.66%
George Braziller	15	$28.31	21	$28.37	0.21%
David Brown Book Co.	43	$46.31	33	$46.37	0.13%
Butterworth-Heinemann	392	$52.78	413	$51.29	–2.82%

Figure 12.1. Average price changes for trade and professional titles.

	Average # of Titles	2005 Average Cost Per Title	2006 Average Cost Per Title	Percent Change 2005-2006	2007 Average Cost Per Title	Percent Change 2007-2008	2008 Average Cost Per Title	Percent Change 2007-2008	2009 Average Cost Per Title	Percent Change 2008-2009
U.S. Titles	2,413	$51.76	$54.79	3.85%	$56.94	3.92%	$58.90	3.44%	$60.61	2.98%
Non U.S. Titles	105	$164.46	$174.05	5.83%	$185.97	5.97%	$196.37	5.59%	$207.49	5.66%
All Titles	2,518	$57.55	$59.90	4.08%	$62.47	4.29%	$64.79	3.71%	$66.91	3.23%

Typical Cost of Subscription List for a Public Library

2005	$151,753.60
2006	$157,954.38
2007	$164,725.29
2008	$170,859.93
2009	$176,429.77

Figure 12.2. Sample of serial vendor's price estimates for public libraries (adopted from EBSCO data).

During the same period, the Canadian dollar went from US$0.6345 to US$0.7693, then to US$0.7913, down to US$0.736, and then to US$0.5199. Although it is impossible to accurately forecast the direction and amount of fluctuation in the exchange rates for the next 12 months, some effort should go into studying the previous 12 months and attempting to predict future trends. (One source for historic data is the Federal Reserve Board's Web site, at http://www.federalreserve.gov/releases/g5a/.) It is important to have good data about the amounts spent in various countries during the previous year. The country of publication may be less important than the country in which the vendor is located. For example, if the library uses the vendor Harrassowitz, prices will be in euros regardless of the country of origin of the items purchased. After collecting the data, the budgeter can use them as factors in estimating the cost of continuing the current acquisition levels from the countries from which the library normally buys.

ALLOCATION OF MONIES

A reader would be correct to think dividing up the materials budget is a rather complicated process. There are usually three broad slices to the materials budget "pie" Mark Estes referred to in one of the chapter epigraphs—monographs, serials, and electronic resources. And, just as in Estes's vendor scenario, when one slice increases in size, more often than not one or both of the other slices get smaller.

If there were only three slices, the process would not be very complicated; although the people in charge of the three areas, assuming more than one person, might well disagree about the size of their respective slices. In most libraries, however, there are several other slices to consider. While there may always be some disagreement about who gets how much money for materials, today's stable or shrinking materials budget can make for interesting debates regarding who should or must get what. Essentially, it a question of whose oxen gets gored.

Ordinarily, the method of allocation selected reflects, at least to some degree, the priorities in the library's collection development policy statement. If the library uses a collecting-intensity ranking system in the collection development policy, it is reasonable to expect to find those levels reflected in the amount of money allocated to the subject or format. Almost all allocation methods are complex, and matching the needs and monies available requires that the library consider several factors.

From the funding authority's point of view, it has no interest in how the library decides to allocate the funds provided as long as the library purchases material for the collection. However, except in the smallest library, there are usually several staff members who would like to have a voice in the allocation discussion. Each person will come to the table with a case for why this year his area should be given a bigger slice of the pie. Just as the library's budget request to the funding authority is partly a political process, so is the internal budget-allocation process for materials.

Each library will have its own categories for allocation, but following are some of the more common categories:

- Adult monographs (fiction/nonfiction)
- Adult media

- Adult serials
- Children's books
- Children's magazines
- Children's media
- Reference department
- Replacement items
- Rental/lease titles
- Young adult (YA) books
- YA magazines
- YA media

This list reflects, more or less, a public library environment. When it comes to academic and school libraries, the list of categories becomes even more complex.

Educational libraries not only have to address the three broad categories of monographs, serials, and electronic resources and some items on the previous list, such as reference and replacements, but they also have teaching departments and faculty members lobbying for a slice of the ever-smaller pie, as discussed later.

Among the issues that factor into the allocation process are past practices, differential publication rates, unit cost and inflation rates, level of demand, and actual usage of the material. Implementing a formal allocation system takes time and effort. Yet some professionals question whether it is worthwhile allocating the monies. Opponents to allocation claim that it is difficult to develop a fair allocation model, and it is time-consuming to calculate the amounts needed. Certainly allocations add to the workload in the acquisitions department as staff have to track more expenditure categories. Those opposed to the process also claim that, because the models are difficult to develop, libraries tend to leave the allocations in place too long and simply add in the next year's percentage increase rather than recalculating the figures annually. They suggest that selectors may not spend accounts effectively because there is too much or too little money available. Finally, they argue that it is difficult to effect transfers from one account to another during the year. Proponents of allocation claim that it provides better control of collection development and is a more effective way to monitor expenditures.

A good allocation process provides at least four outcomes. First and foremost, it matches, or should match, available funds with actual funding needs. Second, it provides selectors with guidelines for how they should allocate their time. That is, if someone is responsible for three selection areas with funding allocations of US$15,000, $5,000, and $500, it is clear which area requires the most attention. (In many cases, it is more difficult to spend the smaller amount, because one must be careful to spend it wisely.) Third, the allocation process provides a means of assessing the selector's work at the end of the fiscal year. Finally, it provides the service community with a sense of collecting priorities, assuming that the allocation information is made available to them. The library can communicate the information in terms of percentages rather than specific monetary amounts if there is a concern about divulging budgetary data.

The allocation process should be collaborative, with input from all interested parties. Two things are certain, regardless of whether the library uses a formal or informal approach to gaining input: the process has political overtones, and the outcome will invariably disappoint an individual or a group. This is particularly true when introducing a revised allocation when the budget is static. Those who receive more money will be happy, but those who lose funds will object to the method used to reallocate the funds. Unfortunately, sometimes the objectors are influential enough to get the allocations changed, which defeats the purpose of the process—matching funds to needs. Virginia Williams and June Schmidt's article on book-fund allocation provides a good review of the various allocation formulas libraries, especially academic and school libraries, employ as well as the pros and cons of each.[8]

Which allocation method the library selects is influenced, in part, by internal library practices, institutional needs, and extra-institutional requirements (such as those of accreditation agencies). Internal factors include operational practices that determine what type of information is readily available to those making the allocation decisions (e.g., vendor's country of origin, number of approval titles versus firm orders, format and subject data, and use). How the library organizes its services—centralized or decentralized—also plays a role. Other internal factors affecting which allocation method is used include past practices for allocation and the purpose of allocation (that is, its use as a control mechanism or guideline). Institutional factors, in addition to the obvious importance of the institution's mission and goals, include the type of budget control it uses, its organization, and its overall financial condition. Extra-institutional factors are the political atmosphere (for example, the degree of accountability), economic conditions, social expectations and values regarding information services (such as equal access and literacy levels), and outside agencies (such as accreditation bodies or governmental bodies) that monitor or control the institution.

Allocation methods can be regarded as a continuum, with "impulse" at one end of the scale and "formula" at the opposite end. Between the two extremes are several more or less structured methods. *Impulse allocations* can take the form of allowing active selectors to have greatest access to available funds or, in a slightly more structured approach, to allocate on the basis of perceptions of need. History of past use and some annual percentage increase for each allocation area is a little more formal; it is probably one of the most widely used methods. Allocating on the basis of organizational structure (main and branch units) is still more formal (often, the allocation is a fixed percentage of the fund pool). Adding to that method some incremental funding based on workload (such as circulation data) moves the library closer to the formula end of the continuum. Also, somewhere in the middle of the continuum is the *format allocation method* (such as funds for books, serials, media, electronic resources, and reference).

Most libraries that use a format allocation system use several approaches. Many small libraries, including most school media centers, use the format system, with monographs, serials, and audiovisuals being the broad groupings. The library divides these funds by subject (e.g., language arts), grade level (e.g., fifth grade), or user group (e.g., professional reading).

Occasionally, libraries divide monograph funds into current, retrospective, and replacement categories. In libraries using approval, blanket-order, or standing-order plans, it is normal practice to set aside monies for each program before making any other allocations. A typical approach would be to set aside an amount equal to the prior year's expenditure for the category with an additional amount to cover expected inflation. The reason for setting aside these funds first is that they are ongoing commitments.

Formula allocations have become more and more popular, especially in large libraries. Librarians have proposed many formulas over the years; however, no formula has become standard. Each library must decide which, if any, formula is most appropriate for its special circumstances. An article by Ian R. Young describes a project that compared seven formulas.[9] His results showed that, although each formula used one or more unique variables, there were no statistically significant differences among the formula results in terms of a single institution. He concluded that there was a high degree of similarity among the seven formulas, at least when applied to his institutional setting. Based on our experience with formulas and the selection of a formula in several institutional settings, we would say that the library selects the formula that contains all the variables necessary to satisfy all the interested parties. (Thus, political rather than practical considerations dictate which formula is used.) Only quantifiable factors (for example, average price, number of titles published, and use data) can be used as variables in formulas. This does not mean that subjective judgments do not play a role, but the allocation process as a whole depends on weightings, circulation data, production figures, inflation and exchange rates, number of users, and so forth. Figure 12.3 illustrates the allocation formula used at a university library and a small sample of the outcome of applying such a formula to three teaching departments.

Department	Use	Average Cost	Cost-Use	Percent Cost-Use	Formula Allocation	Present Allocation
Psychology (BF & RC 435-577)	4,674	$38.55	180,183	0.07	$12,693	$15,033
Sociology (HM-HX)	5,311	$37.85	201,021	0.09	$14,542	$6,587
Theater Arts (PN 1600-1989, 2000-3310)	144	$38.14	5,492	0.003	$361	$3,908
Theology (BL-BX)	6,503	$36.49	237,294	0.1	$16,258	$7,409
Totals			2,491,436		$181,342	$180,652

Use = Circulated use of the class numbers associated with the department.

Average Cost = Price listed as average for that discipline in *Choice*.

Cost-Use = Average cost times use for the field.

Percent Cost-Use = Percentage of library's total cost-use for the field.

Formula Allocation = Amount of new allocation under new formula.

Percent Allocation = Amount of current allocation.

Figure 12.3. Sample of an allocation table.

The ALA's *Guide to Budget Allocation for Information Resources* lists six broad allocation methods: historical, zero based (no consideration of past practice), formulas, ranking (a variation of formulas), percentages, and other modeling techniques.[10] The book also outlines some of the variations in formulas by type of library. For example, academic libraries might consider enrollment by major or degrees granted in a field. Public libraries might factor in differences in the service communities being served, the ratio of copies per title of bestsellers to general titles, or the demand (in terms of use or requests) in popular subject fields. Special libraries use such factors as delivery-time expectations of the clients, service charge backs, and the number of clients or departments served. Many school media centers use factors like changes in curriculum, number and ability of students by grade level, and loss and aging rates of various subject areas in the collection. The guide provides a starting point for librarians thinking about changing the allocation process their library uses.

Allocating funds is an involved process, and changing an existing method is almost more difficult than establishing a new one. Often, past practices and political issues keep the process from moving forward or evolving. In the case of serials, how much to allocate to current materials and how much to allocate to retrospective purchases is related, in part, to the serials inflation rate. If the decision is to maintain serials at the expense of monographs, in time there will be a significant need for retrospective buying funds to fill gaps in the monograph collection. Subject variations also complicate the picture. Science materials are very expensive; social science materials are substantially less costly but are more numerous. Electronic access, rather than local ownership, also clouds the picture, especially because electronic access often involves cost at the individual level, something with which allocation models have not dealt. Although allocation work frequently involves political issues and occasionally involves upset individuals, in the long run careful attention to this process will produce a better collection for the organization the library or information center serves.

ENCUMBERING

One aspect of accounting and financial management in collection development that differs from typical accounting practice is the process of *encumbering*. This is a process that allows the library to set aside monies to pay for ordered items. When the library waits 60, 90, or 120 days or more for orders, there is some chance that the monies available will be over- or underspent, if there is no system that allows for setting aside monies.

The following chart shows how the process works. Day 1, the first day of the fiscal year, shows the library with an annual allocation of $1,000 for a particular subject area. On day 2, the library orders an item with a list price of $24.95. Although there may be shipping and handling charges, there will probably be a discount. Because none of the costs and credits are known at the time, the list price is the amount a staff member records as encumbered. Some departments add a fixed percentage of the list price to the total amount encumbered to more closely match what the invoice price will be. The unexpended column reflects the $24.95 deduction, with zero showing in the expended category. Sixty-two days later, the item and invoice arrive; the invoice reflects a 15 percent discount ($3.74) and no shipping or handling charges. The bookkeeper records the actual cost ($21.21) under expended and adds the $3.74 to the unexpended amount. The amount encumbered now is zero.

	Unexpended	Encumbered	Expended
Day 1	$1000.00	0	0
Day 2	$975.05	$24.95	0
Day 62	$978.79	0	$21.21

This system is much more complex than the example suggests, because libraries place and receive multiple orders every day. With each transaction the amounts in each column change. *Neither the acquisitions department nor the library knows the precise balance, except on the first and last day of the fiscal year.* If the funding body takes back all unexpended funds at the end of the fiscal year (a *cash accounting* system), the acquisitions department staff must know the fund(s) balances as they enter the final quarter of the year.

Several factors make it difficult to learn the exact status of the funds, even with the use of encumbrance. One factor is delivery of orders. Vendors may assure customers that they will deliver before the end of the fiscal year but fail to do so. Such a failure can result in the encumbered money being lost. With a cash system, the acquisitions department staff must make some choices at the end of the fiscal year if there are funds in the encumbered category. The main issue is determining if the items still on order are important enough to leave on order. An affirmative answer has substantial implications for collection development.

Using the foregoing example and assuming that day 62 comes after the start of a new fiscal year and the new allocation is $1,000, on day 1 of the new fiscal year, the amount unexpended would be $975.05 ($1,000 minus $24.95), encumbered $24.95, and expended zero. In essence, there is a reduction in the amount available for new orders, and the library has lost $24.95 from the prior year's allocation. (One of the authors once took over as head of a library on June 25, and the system's financial officer reported that the entire acquisitions allocation was encumbered for the coming fiscal year, starting July 1. To have some funds for collection development over the next 12 months, it was necessary to cancel 347 orders.) With an *accrual system,* the unexpended funds carry forward into the next fiscal year. Under such a system, using the previous example, the day 1 figures would be unexpended $1,000, encumbered $24.95, and expended zero.

The staff also needs to consider how reliable the vendor or producer is, because occasionally an item never arrives. How long should the library wait? The answer varies from producer to producer and country to country. If the library buys substantial amounts from developing countries, waiting several years is not unreasonable. Because print runs tend to be very close to the number of copies on order, the chance of never being able to acquire the item makes it dangerous to cancel the order.

There is a problem in leaving funds encumbered for long periods under either system, especially when there is rapid inflation or exchange rates are unfavorable. The latter are two reasons why setting a firm but reasonable date for automatic cancellation of unfilled orders is important.

Other factors making it difficult to know the precise fund balance during the year are pricing and discounts. Prices are subject to change without notice on most library materials, particularly online resources, which means the price may be higher on delivery than when ordered. In addition, discounts are unpredictable. Because of the uncertainty, most libraries encumber the list price without freight charges and hope the amount will be adequate. Exchange rates enter the picture for international acquisitions, and the question of when the rate is set can be a critical issue. Certainly, the rate is not firm on the date the order is placed, but is it firm at the time of shipment, the date of the invoice, the date the library receives the invoice and items, the date the financial office issues the check, or even the date the supplier deposits the check? With international orders, libraries can expect four months or more to elapse between order placement and delivery. In periods of rapid rate changes, even a four-month difference can significantly affect the amount of money available for purchases.

Shipping and handling rates and taxes on items purchased have also taken a toll on collection development funds. Vendors that in the past paid for shipping now pass the cost to customers. The U.S. Postal Service has reduced the difference between postal rates such as the book rate and parcel post. In 1970 it cost $0.18 to ship a two-pound book; in 1980 it cost $0.80; by 1999 the rate was $1.54; by 2001 the cost had risen to $2.38, and as of early 2010 the price was $2.77 with an additional increase scheduled for later in the year. All the charges on the invoice (postage, handling, shipping, taxes, and so forth) must come from the acquisitions budget. As these charges mount there is less money to acquire new items.

The point of all this work is to allow the library to spend all the materials funds available in a timely manner without over-ordering. Remember that an order is a legal contract between the library and the supplier. Certainly, most suppliers who have a long-standing relationship with libraries will understand an occasional overcommitment of funds, but they have a legal right to full, prompt payment for all orders placed. One way they allow libraries to handle the problem is to ship the order on time but hold the invoice until the start of the next fiscal year.

A major problem confronting a bookkeeper in the acquisitions department is the number of accounts with allocations. In some libraries, the number may run over 200. Restricted funds are especially problematic because the library may charge only certain types of materials to the account. Although the bookkeeper's job may be to assign charges to the various accounts, that person must also know approximately how much money remains as free balance, as encumbered, and as expended. As the number of accounts goes up, so does the bookkeeper's workload.

Moving monies back and forth, especially in a manual system, can lead to errors, so the acquisitions department must have a good bookkeeper. Automated accounting systems speed the recording activities and provide greater accuracy, as long as the data entry is correct. Despite the uncertainty that exists with the encumbering system, it is still better than just having unexpended and expended categories, because without it libraries would not know how much of the unexpended balance was actually needed for items on order.

VOUCHERS

Most government accounting methods, as well as the methods used by many other organizations, use a voucher system. A *voucher* provides verification of all transactions involving expenditures and the authorization for such expenditures. It is a form that both summarizes an expenditure and carries the signatures vouching for its correctness. Further, it authorizes entry into the books and approves payment of charges. Libraries do not usually issue vouchers as such; however, the requirement of the librarian's signature on a purchase order and on invoices is part of the voucher system of the library's parent organization (e.g., city, university, school district).

Without a voucher, there will be no payment to a vendor. Because it takes a long time for a voucher to make its way through a government system, a substantial amount of correspondence can occur between the library and vendors regarding when payments will take place. This points to the need for accurate bookkeeping records and close cooperation between bookkeepers in the acquisitions department and the authority that finally issues the checks or voucher.

ORDER AND INVOICE CONTROL

Bookkeepers control the vendor's compliance with the fiscal regulations of the library's governing agency. For example, they are responsible for checking invoices for all the required information: signature, purchase order number, and so forth. If materials on prepaid orders do not arrive by the end of the fiscal year, the library will request a refund because the vendor may want to hold the money as a credit for future orders. As noted previously, it is very convenient to work with the same vendors, because they become familiar with the library's payment procedures. Whenever a library selects a new vendor, it is wise to send a letter explaining the library's financial arrangements and why it may take up to three months to receive payment.

RECONCILIATION OF ACCOUNTS

One difficulty facing the bookkeeper is knowing precisely where the library stands financially. The encumbered amount is always greater than the amount expended because some items have discounts but not others. Some monthly routines are part of the acquisitions department's bookkeeper workload, such as reconciling the library's estimate of its financial status with that of the supervising agency. The agency that oversees the library's expenditure of funds will probably not list all of the separate funds used internally. Rather, it will show only the amount allocated to the library to buy library materials. How the library distributes the funds is of no interest to the agency, as long as the monies actually go for materials for the collection. The agency's concern is with two categories of funds: expended and unexpended. The library has a third category of money—encumbered funds—that makes reconciliation complex. As part of the reconciliation process, the bookkeeper normally creates for each library fund a statement of its unencumbered balance, encumbered funds, and liquidated or expended funds. When selectors have budgetary responsibility, monthly statements go to them so they know their available balance, or they may have the ability to view (but not necessarily revise) entries in the online ordering system used by the institution to see real-time balances in their account(s). The final reconciliation sheet shows when the library received an invoice, the dealer's invoice number, the amount of money encumbered, and the discount received. The next column (net) indicates the amount actually paid to the dealer for the items; the tax column represents the tax on the monies expended.

The library must also carry out a number of end-of-fiscal-year routines, and the bookkeeper is responsible for many of these. The library is normally on a one-year fiscal cycle (a cash accounting system, as mentioned earlier). That is, any money remaining in the library's budget at the end of the fiscal year reverts to the funding agency. Libraries are seldom able to carry any unexpended funds forward into the next fiscal year, including encumbered funds. Therefore, several months prior to the end of the fiscal year, it is necessary to check with the vendors on outstanding orders to determine whether they will make delivery in time. If they are unable to deliver the items before the fiscal year ends, libraries usually cancel the order and place one for something that is available or will be available before the end of the fiscal year. This year-end exercise can create bookkeeping nightmares.

The bookkeeper's primary duty is to ensure that the library neither overspends nor underspends its budget. Because discounts and cancellations are unknown quantities up until the moment the invoice arrives, it becomes a challenge for the bookkeeper to estimate accurately just where the library stands financially.

AUDITS

Are audits really necessary in libraries? Must libraries remember how, where, when, and on what it spent every cent? (An enjoyable short poem by Robert Frost entitled the "Hardship of Accounting" addresses the issue of accounting and audits; see http://varietyreading.carlsguides.com/forwards/hardship.php). Unfortunately, the answer is *yes* when it comes to library funds. Some years ago, Herbert Snyder and Julia Hersberger published an article outlining embezzlement in public libraries. The article makes it clear why regular financial audits are necessary.[11]

There are three basic audit types. *Operational audits* examine an organization's procedures and practices, usually with the goal of making improvements. *Compliance audits* examine how well an organization is following procedures established by some higher-level body. An example might be to determine if the acquisitions department has followed the procedures for funds received through a federal government Library Services and Construction Act grant. A *financial audit* is what comes to people's minds when they hear the word "audit." It is often a yearly event for the acquisitions department wherein its records are examined by nonlibrary personnel to assure the funding authority and other parties that the monies were in fact expended in the expected way and that the records of those transactions comply with standard accounting practices and guidelines. One aspect of having the power to manage and expend substantial amounts of money is fiscal accountability. The amount of money does not need to be substantial if it involves public or private funds. For acquisitions departments, the auditor's visit is probably second only to the annual performance appraisal process in terms of worry and stress on the staff's part. The worry is not that they have done something wrong, but rather their not being able to find some type of documentation that an auditor wishes to check.

A legalistic definition of an *audit* is the process of accumulating and evaluating evidence about quantifiable information of an economic entity to determine and report on the degree of correspondence between the information and established criteria. More simply put, it is the process of ensuring that the financial records are accurate and that the information is presented correctly using accepted accounting practices, and making recommendations for improvements in how the process is carried out. The basic questions and required records relate to whether the purchase was made with proper authorization, was received, and was paid for in an appropriate manner, and whether the item is still available. (If the item is not still available, there should be appropriate records regarding its disposal.) With automated acquisitions systems, undergoing an audit is less time consuming than in the past, where the paper trail was in fact a number of different paper records that had to be gathered and compared. At least now the computer system can pull up the necessary information fairly quickly.

SUMMARY

Financial management, bookkeeping, and a basic understanding of how trained bookkeepers do their work is important in an acquisitions department. Libraries are accountable for the funds they receive, and the acquisitions department is one of the few places in the library where library funds are committed to obligations. For most libraries, the two largest segments of the budget are staff salaries and monies to build the collections. Only the collection development funds are actually available for the staff to expend. It is important for the staff to understand and use proper bookkeeping methods. This chapter covers only the most elementary aspects of accounting, but the concepts and terms that technical services staff should be familiar with include *account, balance sheet, credit, daybook, debit, double-entry accounting, journalizing, ledger, posting, encumbering, trail balance, voucher, account reconciliation,* and *audit.* Additional resources are listed in the Suggested reading section.

Libraries must be constantly aware of changes in prices and invoicing practices to gain the maximum number of additions to the collection. Watch for changes, and demand explanations of freight and handling charges, inappropriate dual-pricing systems, or other costs that may place additional strain on the budget. By understanding basic accounting principles and using the reports and records generated by the library's accounting system, the library will be better able to monitor the use of available monies and use them effectively to meet the needs of the public.

REVIEW QUESTIONS

1. What are some of the economic issues facing today's libraries and what must they do to prove their value to society?

2. Who in the library needs accounting information, and why?

3. What is the primary function of the bookkeeping department in a library, and what are the three basic steps in bookkeeping?

4. Define *accounts, balance sheet, credit, debit, journal, ledger, posting, trial balance,* and *voucher.*

5. Define *encumber.*

6. Name one monthly routine and one yearly routine that the bookkeeper performs.

7. Describe the purpose of an audit.

8. What are some of the coping mechanism available to the library to help address budget shortfalls?

NOTES

The epigraphs for this chapter are from Richard M. Dougherty, "Assessment + Analysis = Accountability," *College & Research Libraries* 70, no. 5 (2009): 417–18; Mark E. Estes, "Slicing Your Pieces of the Pie," *AALL Spectrum* 13, no. 4 (2009): 1; and Norman Oder, "Permanent Shift?" *Library Journal* 135, no. 1 (2010): 44–46.

1. Larry Nash White, "An Old Tool With Potential New Uses: Return on Investment," *Bottom Line* 20, no. 1 (2007): 8.

2. Oder, "Permanent Shift?" 44.

3. Ibid., 46.

4. Ibid., 44.

5. G. Stevenson Smith, *Managerial Accounting for Libraries and Other Not-for-Profit Organizations,* 2nd ed. (Chicago: American Library Association, 2002) and Anne M. Turner, *Managing Money: A Guide for Librarians* (Jefferson, NC: McFarland & Company, 2007).

6. Barbara Hoffert, "Book Report, Part 2: What Academic Libraries Buy and How Much They Spend," *Library Journal* 123, no. 18 (1998): 145.

7. National Information Standards Organization, *Criteria for Price Indexes for Printed Library Materials: An American National Standard* (Bethesda, MD: NISO Press, 1999).

8. Virginia Kay Williams and June Schmidt, "Determining the Average Cost of a Book for Allocation Formulas," *Library Resources & Technical Services* 52, no. 1 (2008): 60–70.

9. Ian R. Young, "A Quantitative Comparison of Acquisitions Budget Allocation Formulas Using a Single Institutional Setting," *Library Acquisitions* 16, no. 3 (1992): 229–42.

10. Edward Shreeves, ed., *Guide to Budget Allocation for Information Resources,* Collection Management and Development Guides, no. 4 (Chicago: American Library Association, 1991).

11. Herbert Snyder and Julia Hersberger, "Public Libraries and Embezzlement: An Examination of Internal Control and Financial Misconduct," *Library Quarterly* 67, no. 1 (1997): 1–23.

SUGGESTED READING

Anderson, Colleen D. "Accounting and Auditing Resources." *College & Research Libraries News* 69, no. 2 (2008): 96–100.

Brent, Gerry, and Linda Porter. "Community Partnerships Help Finance Library Growth." *Florida Libraries* 51, no. 2 (2008): 14–15.

Canady, Denise. "Libraries Get Creative, Involve Communities to Raise Funds." *Indiana Libraries* 27, no. 2 (2008): 76–77.

Cox, Marge. "10 Tips for Budgeting." *Library Media Connection* 26, no. 4 (2008): 24–25.

DiMattia, Susan S. "Getting the Money You Need: Relationships and Fundraising." *Online* 32, no. 1 (2008): 22–26.

Linn, Mott. "Budget Systems Used in Allocating Resources to Libraries." *Bottom Line* 20, no. 1 (2007): 20–29.

Malhotra, Deepak, and Max H. Bazerman. "Investigative Negotiation." *Harvard Business Review* 85, no. 9 (2007): 72–78.

Pearson, Peter. "Fundraising and Advocacy in Tough Times." *Public Libraries* 48, no. 4 (2009): 21–24.

Steele, Kirstin. "Trying to Thrive: Making Do Without Making Waves." *Bottom Line* 21, no. 1 (2008): 17–19.

Steele, Kirstin. "Are Budget Limitations Real? Perspective, Perceptions, and a Plan." *Bottom Line* 21, no. 3 (2008): 85–87.

Umbach, Judith. "Planning in Hard Times." *Feliciter* 55, no. 1 (2009): 10.

Part III

Cataloging
and Processing

Overview and Decisions

Our present practices are not based on "by guess and by golly." They are based on centuries of pragmatic experience, culminating in the ISBD [International Standard Bibliographic Description] selection and order of elements. The data needed to identify a resource changes little whether the resource is incunabula or a remote electronic resource, nor whether the data is on a 3 × 5 in. card or is electronic.

—J. McRee (Mac) Elrod

Until the middle of the 20th century, local library catalogs were valuable solely as guides to individual library collections, establishing the presence or absence of materials wanted by people using a library. As Charles Cutter put it, the purpose of a library catalog was

1. To enable a person to find a book when one of the following is known:

   a. the author
   b. the title
   c. the subject

2. To show what the library has

   d. by a given author
   e. on a given subject
   f. in a given kind of literature

3. To assist in the choice of a book

   g. as to the edition (bibliographically)
   h. as to its character (literary or topical)[1]

Until the advent of computers in the latter half of the 20th century, all a catalog record revealed was that the title it represented was once purchased by the library and assigned a place on the shelves. The answer it could not give was "Can I have this material now?" By the end of the 20th century, when online catalogs were linked to order files and borrowing files, the availability of materials could also be determined using the catalog, greatly enhancing search results. In the 21st century, local library catalogs have become gateways to a much larger universe of knowledge than is held by any individual library. This expanded reach, however, does not obviate the need for good cataloging at the local level. It makes the work done at local levels more important than ever, because it is the foundation for a wider range of bibliographic services to clients far from and near to the local library.

THE RATIONALE FOR GOOD CATALOGING

As stated in chapter 1, quality user service is a high-priority goal of technical services. Catalogs, which were once considered tools intended primarily for librarians, now serve a broad range of library users, including children and adults, scholars and students, well-read searchers and searchers with little reading experience, as well as librarians assisting people in person, online, or via telephone reference service. Catalogs must be navigable by all of these varied constituencies, and able to give them easy-to-obtain, accurate information that is sufficiently complete to answer their questions and facilitate their use of library collections.

Collection size has changed dramatically over time. The Library of Congress's (LC) collection, which was destroyed during the War of 1812, was reestablished with the acquisition of Thomas Jefferson's library, totaling almost 7,000 volumes. At the time, Jefferson's was an unusually large personal library, and had grown under LC stewardship to more than one million volumes by the turn of the 20th century. Nowadays, small libraries (as defined by the publishers of cataloging tools intended for their use, such as *Sears List of Subject Headings* and the *Abridged Dewey Decimal Classification*) might hold as many as 20,000 volumes;[2] libraries in colleges and small universities, large towns, and small cities might be expected to have collections of 250,000 to 500,000 volumes or more. Libraries in research universities and large cities often number their holdings at more than a million volumes. Looking for one wanted title among so many possibilities on the shelves requires orderly, well-thought-out arrangements to make them readily available for use. It could take a person a long time spent examining each volume one at a time to learn whether desired materials are present.

All borrowers may not able to visit the library in person. In the 21st century, more and more members of a local library's public are virtual visitors. They need to find out whether the library has the materials they want before they go to it in person. Some are unable to visit the library in person, but can obtain its analog materials through shared borrowing services, such as interlibrary loan (ILL), and its digital materials through electronic delivery systems. To do this, however, they must know if the materials they want are part of the collection and available. Therefore, one of the most important services libraries can provide to the people that use them is accurate, up-to-date bibliographic information.

Both of these modern-day library features—the large size of local collections and the increasing numbers of people who can use the materials without coming to the library building in person—make having effective bibliographic services worthwhile.

Libraries can provide both *direct* and *indirect access* to the materials in their collections. For analog materials physically stored in a library's collection, direct access is provided through an efficient shelving system that groups materials on the same subjects. Direct access is also known as *physical* or *shelf access,* because people can go directly to the physical objects that make up the collections. Direct access to electronic documents can be accomplished by means of virtual shelving systems that facilitate locating and retrieving desired materials.

Indirect access leads people to substitutes or surrogates for the materials—the catalog records stored in library catalogs—that can be manipulated and searched more quickly and easily than the materials themselves. (In the electronic world, catalog records are known as *metadata.*) Indirect access is also known as *bibliographic access, intellectual access,* or *catalog access.* If a search of the catalog establishes that the desired material is part of the collection, the surrogate will show how to retrieve it, either from the library's shelves or an electronic collection. This is how libraries make finding individual items easy and fast, even when they are part of extremely large collections.

CATALOGING AND CLASSIFICATION PROCESSES

Cataloging, in broad terms, is the process of preparing surrogate records for the materials in local library collections. Filed together in catalogs under the headings that Cutter suggested—authors, titles, and subjects—these surrogates enable a person to find the materials by "letting their fingers do the walking," to paraphrase the Yellow Pages slogan. Classification is part of the process of arranging the materials in an orderly fashion by subject on shelves—whether physical or virtual shelves—making it quick and easy to obtain the materials themselves. Cataloging and classification add to public service by saving people time and effort in getting materials from their libraries.

Information that identifies materials in catalog records may begin as part of an order record. When a title is acquired, technical services staff members document the transactions, such as placing orders for the materials, receiving them, and paying for them. Cataloging operations begin with the basic information used for the order. In many instances this is downloaded from a supplier's database derived from a larger catalog, such as the LC's machine-readable cataloging (MARC) database or the Online Computer Library Center's (OCLC) WorldCat network database. Local library catalogers edit or add to this basic information to produce a complete, accurate record for the material known as a *bibliographic record* or *"bib"* record, for short. When the information is not derived from a national library or a network database, catalogers match the data with the material and add missing data to ensure that the bib record is complete and correct. Bib records include a full description of the material and its content, and an assigned call number (shelf address) that tells where the material is stored in the library's stacks, storage facilities, digital files, or elsewhere.

Rules govern the kinds of data that appear in bib records, how they are recorded, which elements are used for retrieving the records from the file (known variously as headings, access points, and tracings), and how the retrieval elements are formatted. In addition to Cutter's three retrieval elements—authors, titles, and subjects—catalogs can be searched by call numbers; keywords; unique numbers such as International Standard Book Numbers (ISBNs), International Standard Serial Numbers (ISSNs), and network control numbers; and combinations of these elements with languages, physical formats, and dates. The software that governs catalog systems can make almost every word in catalog records retrievable through keyword searching, although this is not a typical feature.

The completed bib records, arranged by call number, are the basis for inventory control, to which more information is added: where and when items originated and were made part of the library collection, how much they cost, and where they were assigned to be stored. The circulation system adds still more information to these records, such as whether the items are in their assigned location or not, and, if not, who has borrowed them and when they are due back at the library. Thus, the catalog is simultaneously a reference tool for library users and staff seeking to find materials as well as for collection managers seeking to keep track of the library's stock.

DECISIONS

Local libraries must make choices about what kinds of cataloging and classification systems they will adopt in giving access to their collections, both direct access if collections are stored in open shelves and users are able to visit the building, and/or indirect access via a public catalog if shelves are closed or users cannot visit in person. In the 21st century, few libraries make these decisions in isolation. They are influenced by what other libraries in their area do, what peer libraries serving similar kinds of constituencies do, and what they have done in the past. The most basic decision, however, might well be to follow library-wide standards that govern cataloging and classification. Standards aim to ensure quality. Standard methods can be less costly than customized ones, even when the customized method appears to be simpler. For one thing, products available in the marketplace are geared to standards and are likely to be familiar to the people who are going to use them.

A second important overall decision is whether new catalog records will be prepared in the library or purchased in finished form from outside sources. Advantages of preparing catalog records in-house are that local librarians can control the operations in a manner that serves their local needs and priorities, implement variations from the standards if they believe them to be important, and utilize staff and budget resources as they see fit. Purchasing finished catalog records from outside sources puts control of both the operations and the products in the hands of outside organizations, which might or might not be good for the local library in terms of cost, quality, and speed. This does not need to be an either-or decision—some catalog records might be purchased and others prepared in-house—and either choice involves more decision making.

Buying finished catalog records requires finding a reliable source that will supply the records needed by the library at least as quickly as they can be prepared in-house, and do so at cost and quality levels equal to or better than library-produced records. If a local library has an operating catalog department, its products, turnaround time, and costs can be compared with alternative sources, and decisions made on the basis of the actual performance of each source. A decision to buy finished catalog records requires negotiating a contract with the source organization that ensures the performance of both the seller (preparing quality records detailing the library's specific needs at agreed-upon prices in an agreed-upon time frame) and the buyer (paying the seller according to the agreed-upon schedule and keeping to the agreed-upon services), and protects both parties from departures from the agreement.

A decision to prepare records in the library is not the final one. Library catalog departments can operate in different ways. Few departments prepare every record themselves from scratch. Most libraries divide their catalog operations into materials for which source records are readily available that can be used as the basis for finished records, called "copy" cataloging, and materials that have no such data and must be prepared from scratch, called "original" cataloging. Many libraries buy cataloging data to use in preparing their records in-house. Sources for cataloging data include free Cataloging-in-Publication found in books and some other library materials, subscriptions to LC's MARC records, or the databases of bibliographic networks such as OCLC and AMICUS, or to other kinds of shared cataloging organizations.

No matter where and by whom catalog records are prepared, decisions about the details of cataloging products are important and include the following:

- How much information should be given in bibliographic descriptions?
- Which subject authority(ies) should be the source(s) for subject descriptors?
- What classification system should be used as the basis for shelf addresses?
- Will the library maintain a local authority file for the headings used in its catalog?

Bibliographic Levels

Descriptive cataloging rules, which will be covered in chapter 14, permit three distinct models for standard bibliographic description, called bibliographic levels. Libraries may choose the simplest style, level 1, if they have no need for much detail. This level does not require selected elements of information, such as subtitles and other title details, secondary publishers and distributors, or information about the series to which materials belong. Level 1 is the model for records in national bibliographic networks that can be called standard even though they contain less data than that needed to qualify as full-level cataloging. Bibliographic level 2 requires more information. It is the model used by national bibliographic networks for full-level cataloging. The third and most complex bibliographic level is not widely used; it requires the inclusion of all the data that result from applying every rule relevant to the materials being cataloged. These three levels are demonstrated in Figure 13.1.

The choice of bibliographic level should be made according to the following criteria: the size of the catalog; the number of materials likely to have similar bibliographic data; the knowledge levels of the people using the catalog; and the desired value of the catalog for research purposes. The larger the catalog, the more likely it is that greater detail is needed to distinguish similar materials and the more likely the collection it represents contains larger numbers of materials that are so similar they can be confused. Small catalogs representing general collections might be expected to avoid such problems by having fewer materials that are enough alike to cause confusion. However,

This example is an illustration of:
- uniform title (in 3rd level cataloging)
- multiple statements of responsibility (in 2nd and 3rd level cataloging)
- descriptive illustration statement (in 2nd and 3rd level cataloging)
- bibliography note (in 2nd and 3rd level cataloging)
- edition and history note (in 2nd level cataloging)
- contents note (in 3rd level cataloging)
- Library of Congress subject headings
- personal name added entries (in 2nd and 3rd level cataloging)
- added entry for title
- Library of Congress CIP data found on the colophon
- 3 levels of cataloging

1st level cataloging

```
Laubier, Guillaume de.
  The most beautiful libraries in the world. -- Harry N. Abrams,
2003.
   247 p.

   ISBN 0-8109-4634-3.

   1. Libraries.  2. Library buildings -- Pictorial works.
I. Title.
```

2nd level cataloging

```
Laubier, Guillaume de.
  The most beautiful libraries in the world / photographs by
Guillaume de Laubier ; text by Jacques Bosser ; foreword by James
Billington ; translated from the French by Laurel Hirsch. -- New
York : Harry N. Abrams, 2003.
   247 p. : chiefly col. ill. ; 29 cm.

   Originally published as Bibliothèques du monde.
   Includes bibliographical references.
   ISBN 0-8109-4634-3.

   1. Library buildings.  2. Library architecture.  3. Libraries.
4. Library buildings -- Pictorial works.  5. Library architecture
-- Pictorial works.  5. Libraries -- Pictorial works.  I. Bosser,
Jacques.  II. Title.
```

Figure 13.1

Figure 13.1—*Continued*

```
3rd level cataloging

Laubier, Guillaume de.
   [Bibliothèques du monde]
   The most beautiful libraries in the world / photographs by
Guillaume de Laubier ; text by Jacques Bosser ; foreword by James
Billington ; translated from the French by Laurel Hirsch. -- New
York : Harry N. Abrams, 2003.
   247 p. : chiefly col. ill. ; 29 cm.

   Includes bibliographical references.
   Contents: National Library of Austria, Vienna -- The
Benedictine Abbey Library of Admont, Austria -- The Herzogin Anna
Amalia Library, Weimar, Germany -- The Benedictine Abbey Library
of Metten, Germany -- The Monastic Library at Wiblingen, Ulm,
Germany -- The Vatican Library, Rome -- Riccardian Library,
Florence -- The Institute Library, Paris -- The Mazarine Library,
Paris -- The Senate Library, Paris -- The Cabinet des livres of
the Duc d'Aumale, Chantilly, France -- The Abbey Library of Saint
Gall, Switzerland -- The John Rylands Library, Manchester,
England -- Bodleian Library, Oxford, England -- Wren Library,
Trinity College, Cambridge, England -- Trinity College Library,
Dublin -- The Library of the Mafra National Palace, Portugal --
National Library, Prague -- The Library of the Royal Monastery of
El Escorial, San Lorenzo del Escorial, Spain -- The Athenaeum,
Boston -- The Library of Congress, Washington, D.C. -- The New
York Public Library -- National Library of Russia, St. Petersburg
-- Bibliography.
   ISBN 0-8109-4634-3.

   1. Library buildings.  2. Library architecture.  3. Libraries.
4. Library buildings -- Pictorial works.  5. Library architecture
-- Pictorial works.  5. Libraries -- Pictorial works.  I. Bosser,
Jacques.  II. Billington, James.  III. Hirsch, Laurel.  IV.
Title.
```

small catalogs representing specialized collections might have records for many similar materials and, thus, require more detail to identify them uniquely.

When the people who search library catalogs are experts, they can be expected to understand and use added bibliographic information in catalog records. If the catalog is used for research purposes, such details as specific editors and translators, publishers and distributors, casts, illustrative matter, bibliographies and indexes are likely to play a role in the selection and use of materials. Bibliographic level 1 would not furnish enough data to satisfy their needs. For most institutions, level 2 is chosen to satisfy the needs of expert researchers. However, in some instances, even bibliographic level 2 might not be sufficient, warranting the additional detail mandated by level 3.

Subject Authorities

At one time, local libraries chose one general subject authority as the source for subject descriptors, such as *Sears List of Subject Headings* (Sears) or *Library of Congress Subject Headings* (LCSH). The choice was usually made on the basis of library type and size; small school and public libraries used Sears, though some used LCSH and its subset of descriptors for children's materials (formerly known as Annotated Card headings, now renamed Children's and Young Adults' Cataloging Program; see chapters 16 and 17). Other libraries (larger school and public libraries, academic libraries, and special libraries) generally used LCSH, though they sometimes also used its Children's and Young Adults' Cataloging Program for the children's catalogs. In the 21st century, however, use of multiple subject authorities has become commonplace.

Specialized vocabularies for art, medicine, literary and film genres, and other subjects can be used together with a general vocabulary, most often LCSH. The first decision by general libraries about subject authorities continues to be a choice between Sears and LCSH, but it may not be the only decision to be made. Libraries with collections in specialized subject areas often make a second and/or third decision to use specialized subject vocabularies for materials in those fields. Rather than conflict with the general descriptors, the specialized descriptors augment a catalog's retrieval vocabulary and enhance search success for the specialized materials to which they are applied.

Classification Systems

Most general libraries choose to arrange their materials on the shelves using call numbers based on the Dewey Decimal Classification (DDC) or the Library of Congress Classification (LCC). For the most part, school and public libraries use DDC and academic libraries use LCC, although there are many exceptions to this rule of thumb. Specialized libraries might use DDC or LCC, but they might also prefer a classification designed for their subject area, such as the National Library of Medicine (NLM) Classification for medical materials or the Los Angeles County Law Library Classification for legal materials.[3] Specialized classifications have been developed for music, art, engineering, and other subject fields as well as for medicine and law. In some libraries, a specialized system may be used solely for materials in the special subject area, while DDC or LCC is used for materials in all the other areas. This is what is done at the NLM. It uses NLM Classification for medical materials and LCC for the rest.

Classification numbers alone do not provide enough detail for shelving purposes. Standard practice in all types of libraries is to add shelf marks to classification numbers to create addresses known as *call numbers* for materials. Shelf marks identify elements of materials other than their subject matter, such as authors' names, publication dates, and titles. Among the shelf marks, cutter numbers—coded versions of a word from the most important descriptive heading—are usually the first to be assigned. Cutter numbers usually consist of an initial letter followed by one or more digits representing letters of the word. Lists of Cutter numbers representing author surnames are available for this purpose,[4] or the numbers can be derived from the application of a few simple rules, described in chapter 18. Cutter letters—a simpler form—may be preferred in which only an initial letter or the first few letters of the word are given.

Large libraries add more shelf marks, such as dates and title letters, to distinguish among large numbers of materials bearing the same classification number. Small libraries with fewer materials on the same subject may use only one type of shelf mark and give it in simplified form. Nothing requires that a library give each material a unique call number, although such is the practice at LC and other libraries. In some libraries, several different materials can share a single call number.

Another kind of decision involving shelf arrangements is whether material will be deployed by call number in one sequence or several, depending on the physical format of the materials, the age of the materials, their donors, departments, or other factors. The list of shelving practices that deploy materials in more than one shelf sequence is long. Separate shelf sequences for reference and circulating materials are common, as are multiple sequences for books, audiovisuals, music, recordings, and so on. Sometimes the physical format–related sequences involve the use of different classification systems for selected media. Some public libraries exclude most (but not all) fiction materials from the classification, arranging them by author surname unless the material includes criticism and/or editorial notes in addition to the work itself. In the latter event, they are classified and shelved in the regular sequence. Similarly, some libraries place biographies in a separate section arranged by the subjects' surnames. Some libraries divide fiction into genres, with separate shelves for novels, mysteries, westerns, science fiction, short stories, and so on. Some libraries shelve periodicals alphabetically by title in a periodicals unit, regardless of their subject matter.

Other common shelving practices exclude recent acquisitions from the main sequence of shelving, placing them in prominent locations near entrances or circulation desks and arranging them by title or author, or, if only a small number are involved, in random order. Many libraries maintain local history collections, excluding these materials from the rest of the history sequence in DDC or LCC and placing them in unique arrangements in separate rooms or alcoves. Because of the difficulty of cataloging older historical materials, some libraries do not catalog them at all, relying instead on researchers browsing the shelves to find what they want. All of these shelving anomalies make discovery by browsing the main classification sequence difficult, if not impossible. Fortunately, maintaining a good-quality catalog helps people achieve greater success in finding desired materials under these circumstances.

CATALOG DISPLAYS

The technologies used for library catalogs have changed over time. Until the end of the 19th century, library catalogs resembled bibliographies or publishers' catalogs in that the catalog records were written or printed in book-like volumes in which several lines of text were devoted to identifying and describing each title. For economy's sake, book catalogs sometimes gave only one listing per title under a single heading, although multiple listings for author, title, and/or subject headings could be made if a library wished to invest in a bigger, more elaborate, book catalog. Some book catalogs were beautifully made. Librarians seeking to obtain valuable materials as gifts from wealthy owners used such catalogs to show potential donors how an elegantly made book catalog listing their contributed titles could give donors lasting recognition as collectors and philanthropists.

From the end of the 19th century and into the first part of the 20th, card technology was introduced and quickly became popular. Cards were the principal catalog technology for almost a century. The catalog records, printed on 3- × 5-inch cards, were filed in drawers designed to hold hundreds of cards per drawer. Card technology had a number of advantages: the cards were inexpensive to produce; cards for individual titles could be duplicated easily to create multiple headings; and card files were hospitable to changes as new materials were added and old ones removed, whereas book catalogs had to be completely reprinted to reflect any change made after an edition went to press.

The principal disadvantages of card technology were limitations on the amount of information a 3- × 5-inch card could hold and the difficulty of duplicating entire catalogs. These problems were not so important in the early 20th century when people were expected to go to their local library in person and could browse through materials if the catalog records did not give them enough information to determine the usefulness of a particular material.

In the middle of the 20th century, the term "card catalog" was a synonym for "library catalog," but the increasing output of new books and journals from publishers and infusions of money for new materials from government sources made it difficult for catalog departments to keep up with the workload. It was not unusual for large academic and public libraries to have backlogs of unfiled cards large enough to keep filers working for years and equally daunting backlogs of materials awaiting cataloging. Interest in using newly developed computers to speed cataloging operations was keen. Efforts to translate bibliographic records to digitized entries proceeded throughout the 1950s and early 1960s, culminating in the establishment of the MARC database at LC in the 1960s. In 1967, the newly established OCLC[5]—the first shared cataloging network—adopted MARC and soon launched its operations.

Both the LC and OCLC databases were initially programmed to produce cards. OCLC's cards were not printed as elegantly as LC's, but they had the distinct advantage of arriving with added entries already printed on them, all arranged in alphabetic order. In contrast, LC cards came as "unit cards" requiring library staff to add all the headings but the main entry and, then, alphabetize the groups of cards before they could be filed. Not until the 1980s did the advent of microcomputers bring the cost of computers down to levels that libraries of all sizes and types could afford, and allow the shift to fully computerized catalogs to gain momentum.

Ten years later, the computer revolution was close to complete. Card files were superseded by online public access catalogs (OPACs) following a decade of instability during which computer-produced cards were superseded by hybrid technologies such as computer-produced microfilm catalogs and batch-loaded CD-ROM catalogs. These were followed by online catalogs connected to their hosts by telephone lines and, eventually, by Internet-connected networks.

Pioneers in a few university libraries such as those at Stanford, Northwestern, and Brigham Young, developed local OPAC software based on database management system programming. Some succeeded in broadening and refining the software package so other libraries could use it and offered it for sale.[6] At the same time, some commercial suppliers developed proprietary OPAC software and offered these products in the marketplace. The library automation marketplace that began developing in the late 1970s has fluctuated ever since as new vendors enter the field and veterans drop out or merge.

OPAC systems continue to evolve as computer technology evolves. As a result, different OPAC systems have varying display capabilities. Most provide for brief and full displays as well as displays with eye-readable tags (e.g., title, author, edition) or codes (MARC content designators, discussed in chapter 19). Some provide a choice of card style entries with data grouped into paragraphs, as on cards, or into field-by-field displays with one data element per line. Some can accept input and display catalog records in multiple scripts with many symbols and diacritics, while others are limited to the roman alphabet and have only a small selection of the most popularly used symbols and diacritics (for example, those found on a QWERTY keyboard). Libraries might want their OPAC to have all these options or only some, determined by local needs and/or the costs of obtaining them. Libraries might select one set of display options for catalog stations in public areas and a different set for staff-only areas. In addition, changes to catalog databases are usually made only by staff, requiring a system of authorization to thwart accidental or deliberate tampering. Figure 13.2 illustrates several OPAC screen styles.

```
This example is an illustration of:
    •   other title information
    •   edition statement (in full record cataloging)
    •   publication date not listed, copyright date given
    •   detailed pagination
    •   edition and history note
    •   bibliography note (in full record cataloging)
    •   title added entry
    •   ISBN qualified (in MARC record)
    •   Dewey decimal classification
    •   three types of display
    •   2nd level cataloging
```

Brief record screen display

```
Eats, shoots & leaves : the zero tolerance
  approach to punctuation, by Lynne Truss.   2004

Call no. 428.2 TRU
```

Full record screen display

```
Personal Author:   Truss, Lynne.
Title:             Eats, shoots & leaves : the zero tolerance
                   approach to punctuation / Lynne Truss.
Edition            1st American ed.
Publication info:  New York : Gotham Books, c2004. Originally
                   published in Great Britain in 2003 by Profile
                   Books.
Physical descrip:  xxvii, 209 p. ; 20 cm.
Bibliography note: Includes bibliographical references.
Subject:           English language -- Punctuation.
ISBN:              1592400876 (acid-free paper)
Call number        428.2 TRU
```

MARC record

```
003     DLC
020     1592400876 (acid-free paper)
008     040302s2004nyu b 000 eng
082 00  $a 428.2 $2 22
092 0   $a 428.2 $b TRU  $2 22
100 1   $a Truss, Lynne.
245 10  $a Eats, shoots & leaves : $b the zero tolerance approach
to punctuation / $c Lynne Truss.
260     $a New York : $b Gotham Books, ; $c c2004.
300     $a xxvii, 209 p. ; $c 20 cm.
500     Originally published in Great Britain in 2003 by Profile
Books.
504     $a Includes bibliographical references.
650  0  $a English language $x Punctuation.
740  0  $a Eats, shoots, and leaves.
```

Figure 13.2

Figure 13.2—*Continued*

Eats, Shoots & Leaves

The Zero Tolerance Approach to Punctuation

LYNNE TRUSS

GOTHAM BOOKS

GOTHAM BOOKS
Published by Penguin Group (USA) Inc.
375 Hudson Street, New York, New York 10014, U.S.A.
Penguin Books Ltd, Registered Offices: 80 Strand, London WC2R 0RL, England
Penguin Books Australia Ltd, 250 Camberwell Road,
Camberwell, Victoria 3124, Australia
Penguin Books Canada Ltd, 10 Alcorn Avenue,
Toronto, Ontario, Canada M4V 3B2
Penguin Books (NZ) Ltd, Cnr Rosedale and Airborne Roads,
Albany, Auckland 1310, New Zealand

Published by Gotham Books, a division of Penguin Group (USA) Inc.

Originally published in Great Britain in 2003 by Profile Books, Ltd.
First American printing, April 2004

13 15 17 19 20 18 16

Copyright © 2003 by Lynne Truss
Foreword copyright © 2004 by Frank McCourt
All rights reserved

Gotham Books and the skyscraper logo are trademarks of Penguin Group (USA) Inc.

LIBRARY OF CONGRESS CATALOGING-IN-PUBLICATION DATA
has been applied for.

ISBN: 1-592-40087-6

Printed in the United States of America

This book is printed on acid-free paper. ∞

A WORD ABOUT THE FIGURES AND EXAMPLES

Most of the figures in chapters 14 and 15 that highlight descriptive cataloging rules are done in the format used in cataloging-in-publication (CIP) records usually found on the versos of title pages, because CIP is frequently the basis on which catalog records are built and because it is easier to demonstrate cataloging principles without the distraction of computer encoding. All of the figures include "tracings," that is, the subject headings and additional descriptive headings that are added to the records in the course of normal cataloging procedures, and some of the figures also include suggested classification numbers. A student can refer back to these examples when using the chapters dealing with subject headings and classification numbers. In chapter 18, "MARC Format and Metadata," illustrative catalog records contain standard MARC coding. The subfield codes in these records have been separated from the terms by a space to make the coding more understandable to the beginning cataloger.

Some of the figures highlight the difference between LC and the Sears lists of subject headings and between the DDC and the LCC schemes. Students can find these particular figures by consulting the index.

Double hyphens (--) have been used in place of dashes in the subject headings because it is easy for beginners to confuse single hyphens and dashes.

No textbook can supply all the practice students might want or need to polish their cataloging and classification skills. A graduate cataloger will learn the needs of a library's system on the job. The authors believe it is not difficult to do high-quality, standard cataloging. It just takes the right knowledge, a little confidence, and practice.

SUMMARY

The goal of cataloging is to provide public service. Traditionally seen as a tool for librarians, today all kinds of people search the catalog themselves to find material quickly and easily in ever-larger local library collections. Catalogs have long been recognized as the keys to library collections. In the 21st century, catalogs are essential tools for people who cannot visit the library in person. A growing proportion of borrowers are external users—faculty and students at remote campuses of a university or at other universities, people living beyond town or city borders, or students in unaffiliated schools and school districts—that borrow local materials through interlibrary loans and other cooperative programs. External users rely on catalog data to find what they need.

Individual libraries must make policy decisions about their catalogs and the data that go into them. The most important decision is to conform to library-wide standards, because doing so enables local libraries to benefit from many cataloging products and programs. Adopting standard rules and tools used in preparing catalog records from scratch requires corollary decisions about how much data to include, which options for specific kinds of materials to adopt, which subject authorities and classification systems to use, and what should be added to classification numbers to create call numbers. Classified materials may be deployed in one sequence or several. In addition, local libraries need to make choices about the kinds of catalogs they provide and how cataloging information is displayed. Computer catalogs require encoding systems for data entry.

Another basic decision that needs to be made by local libraries is whether to prepare catalog records within the library or obtain them from outside organizations. Chapter 19 discusses hybrid operations "copy cataloging," in which local catalogers start with data obtained from outside sources, but employ it in their in-house workflow.

REVIEW QUESTIONS

1. Discuss two reasons why catalogs are particularly important in the 21st century.

2. Discuss the difference between direct and indirect access to materials.

3. Define what a surrogate is in cataloging terms, and why it is useful.

4. Identify two basic cataloging policy decisions and discuss their importance.

5. Define "bibliographic levels" and discuss the criteria a local library uses to determine an appropriate level.

6. What kinds of shelf marks are added to classification numbers to form call numbers? Discuss their importance.

7. Name two catalog technologies that preceded OPACs and discuss the advantages and disadvantages of each one.

NOTES

1. Charles A. Cutter, *Rules for a Dictionary Catalog,* 4th ed. (Washington, D.C.: Government Printing Office, 1904), 12.

2. A "volume" is defined here informally as an item represented by one catalog record. It could be a book, a run of a periodical, a map, a set of slides, a videorecording, and so on.

3. OCLC's *Bibliographic Formats and Standards* lists 30 separate indicator combinations representing 30 specialized classifications for its 098 call number field. In addition, indicator combinations 31–99 may be defined in the future to accommodate additional classifications.

4. See Charles Ammi Cutter, *Two-Figure Author Table* (Chicopee Falls, MA: H. R. Huntting, 1969–); Charles Ammi Cutter, *Three-Figure Author Table* (Chicopee Falls, MA: H. R. Huntting, 1969–); *Cutter-Sanborn Three-Figure Author Table,* Swanson-Swift rev. (Westport, CT: Libraries Unlimited, 1969). Cutter tables are also available online.

5. When the network expanded to include members from beyond the state of Ohio, the official meaning was deleted and the acronym became as the network's sole name. Later, responding to members' requests, it was changed to mean Online Computer Library Center.

6. Stanford University's BALLOTS software became the basis for the Research Libraries Information Network. Northwestern University's NOTIS software was spun off into a commercial organization. Brigham Young University's data storage backup software was the basis for the DYNIX Integrated Library System.

SUGGESTED READING

Anderson, James D., and José Pérez-Carballo. *Information Retrieval Design: Principles and Options for Information Description, Organization, Display, and Access in Information Retrieval Databases, Digital Libraries, Catalogs, and Indexes.* St. Petersburg, FL: Ometeca Institute, 2005.

Chan, Lois Mai. "Information Resource Management: Description, Access, Organization." In *Cataloging and Classification: An Introduction,* 3rd ed., 3–41. Lanham, MD: Scarecrow Press, 2007.

Guidelines for Standardized Cataloging for Children [draft prepared by] Joanna F. Fountain, for the Association for Library Collections & Technical Services, Cataloging and Classification Section, Cataloging of Children's Materials Committee. http://www.ala.org/ala/mgrps/divs/alcts/resources/org/cat/ccfkch1.cfm.

Intner, Sheila S., with Peggy Johnson. *Fundamentals of Technical Services Management.* Chicago, IL: American Library Association, 2008.

Miksa, Shawne D. "You Need My Metadata: Demonstrating the Value of Library Cataloging." *Journal of Library Metadata* vol. 8, no. 1 (2008): 23–36.

Sleeman, Bill, and Pamela Bluh, eds. *From Catalog to Gateway: Charting a Course for Future Access: Briefings from the ALCTS Catalog Form and Function Committee.* Chicago, IL: American Library Association, 2005.

Tappeiner, Elisabeth, and Kate Lyons. "Library 2.0 and Technical Services: An Urban, Bilingual Community College Experience." In *More Innovative Redesign and Reorganization of Library Technical Services,* ed. Bradford Lee Eden, 107–22. Westport, CT: Libraries Unlimited, 2009.

Taylor, Arlene G. "Part VI: Administrative Issues." In *Introduction to Cataloging and Classification,* 10th ed., 471–508. Westport, CT: Libraries Unlimited, 2006.

Chapter

Description—Identifying Materials

14

Bibliographic description: [T]he aspect of cataloging concerned with the bibliographic and physical description of a book, recording, or other work, accounting for such items as author or performer, title, edition, and imprint as opposed to subject content.

—Dictionary.com

Building a standard cataloging record from scratch usually begins by describing the material according to an accepted set of rules. At this writing, those rules are the *Anglo-American Cataloguing Rules,* second edition, 2002 revision, 2005 update (AACR2-2005).[1] After a description is completed, author and title access points derived from it are selected and put into appropriate form. The choice and form of these access points are also governed by rules in AACR2-2005. Later, other tools are used to select and assign subject descriptors, a classification number, and shelf marks that complete a shelf address for the material. This chapter describes the first part of the process: creating bibliographic descriptions.

AACR2: PAST AND PRESENT

AACR2-2005, the current standard, is available in two forms: in print and online. The print version is sold as unbound, prepunched pages that owners of a previously issued AACR2 loose-leaf binder edition can put in the old binder or in any other binder of sufficient size (new AACR2 binders are no longer available). The online edition is part of the Library of Congress's (LC) *Cataloger's Desktop* product, available by subscription from LC.[2] The online AACR2-2005 is completely indexed, enabling catalogers to search by any word in the text or by rule numbers. Search words can be truncated and combined using AND, OR, and NOT. Users can bookmark and highlight items, and they can annotate the text. Links help users move through the text quickly, and multiple windows can display different pages of text simultaneously. In addition, *Cataloger's Desktop* contains hundreds of valuable reference tools, including LC Rule Interpretations and Library and Archives Canada (LAC) Rule Interpretations, *Subject Cataloging Manual: Subject Headings,* OCLC's *Bibliographic Formats and Standards,* machine-readable cataloging (MARC) 21 and other MARC tables, ALA-LC Romanization tables, *Library of Congress Filing Rules,* the LC Classification Outline, the *Art & Architecture Thesaurus,* and many more important cataloging tools, which save time when catalogers have them at their fingertips.

Anglo-American cooperation goes back to 1908, when the first international code of cataloging rules was issued jointly by British and American librarians. The meeting of minds from opposite sides of the Atlantic Ocean was disrupted during and after World War II, when the American Library Association unilaterally published a new code of rules for access points in 1949. Joint efforts resumed soon after the war's end. In 1961, due in large part to the effort of the Library of Congress's Seymour Lubetzky, an International Conference on Cataloguing Principles was convened in Paris. The meeting resulted in a statement of principles on which cataloging rules were to be based, known as the Paris Principles.[3]

Efforts following the Paris conference to forge a new Anglo-American cataloging code resulted in the publication of the *Anglo-American Cataloging Rules* (AACR1) in 1967. All the differences between British and North American librarians could not be resolved, so AACR1 was published in two versions: one for the British and another for North Americans. Even their titles differed: the British text used the "u" in *cataloguing;* the North American text did not.

AACR1 was designed for use in large research libraries and did not address the concerns of other kinds of libraries. Catalogers in these other libraries wanted more flexibility in the standard, more effective rules for new materials, more examples to aid in applying the rules, and recognition of the way computers were affecting descriptive cataloging. In 1974, AACR1's publishers formed the Joint Steering Committee for Revision of AACR and charged it with being the final authority on the rules. The result of their efforts was a second edition (AACR2) published simultaneously in 1978 by the American Library Association, the Canadian Library Association, and the United Kingdom's Library Association (now called the Chartered Institute of Library and Information Professionals). The second edition has been officially revised four times, in 1988, 1998, 2002, and 2005, and the various versions have been updated many times to incorporate revisions into one text.

Beginning in 1978, AACR2's rules applied to all materials, incorporating the International Standard Bibliographic Description (ISBD) sponsored by the International Federation of Library Associations and Organizations (IFLA). The ISBD mandated a uniform outline consisting of eight bibliographic elements, a system for punctuating them, the order in which they should appear, and the sources to be consulted for the data. The same structure applied to all materials, thereby producing catalog records that could be integrated into one catalog. The punctuation—called confusing and superfluous by critics—made catalog records from different countries understandable and identifiable for computer entry or for use by catalogers who did not know the language in which the record was written. AACR2 also included numerous examples and provided for three levels of detail in catalog records, furnishing the flexibility that small libraries and libraries catering to a nonscholarly audience wanted. Figure 13.1 (pages 250–51) illustrates the differences.

Rule revision continued throughout the 1980s and 1990s. In 1997, a conference on cataloging principles similar to the 1961 Paris conference was convened in Toronto to help the Joint Steering Committee determine whether fundamental change was needed and, if so, what its nature and direction should be.[4] Participants from ten nations recommended adding statements of the principles and functions of a catalog, reorganizing the rules to follow the ISBD model, considering greater internationalization of the rules, and wording rules plainly so that catalogers would not have to depend on expert guidance to apply them. A new cataloging code, titled *Resource Description and Access* (RDA), is in the final stages of release as an online publication in 2010.[5] RDA's rules are organized by descriptive element and include some differences from equivalent rules in AACR2, but they ask catalogers to follow similar processes in identifying materials (called "resources" by RDA) and they produce compatible descriptive data. Testing in the field continues and implementation is expected in 2011. The transition from AACR2 to RDA should be smoother than the one from AACR1 to AACR2. This chapter explains current practice at this writing, with added comments about RDA.

ORGANIZATION OF AACR2-2005

AACR2-2005 is divided into two main sections. The first section covers description of materials; the second covers their retrieval. Rules for retrieval involve the choice and form of headings, called "access points," based on the description. The chapters in the first section are numbered in the ordinary way, from 1 to 13. The chapters in the second section begin with an introductory chapter numbered 20. Subsequent chapters are numbered consecutively from 21 to 26.

The AACR2-2005's chapter 1 contains general rules applying to all materials, supplements, items made up of several types of materials, and reproductions. Chapters 2 to 11 each cover a group of materials, as shown in the following list. Chapter 12 covers materials issued continuously in parts, now called "continuing resources," and chapter 13 covers descriptions for part of a material containing multiple parts, known as "analysis" or "analytical" cataloging. Catalogers speak of "analytics" in referring to title headings made for parts of materials being cataloged, such as each short story from a book of short stories or each symphony from a recording containing several symphonies.

The rules in AACR2-2005 bear mnemonic numbers that help catalogers navigate through the code: the first digit stands for the chapter number; the second stands for the element of description. After that, letters of the alphabet stand for subelements and roman numerals for subdivisions of subelements. Rules relating to physical description (the fifth element of description) are numbered x.5, where x is the chapter (e.g., maps are covered in chapter 3 and videorecordings in chapter 7, so rules for map physical description are numbered 3.5, and similar rules for videos are numbered 7.5). Rule numbers are shorthand for individual rules.

Under AACR2-2005, the first question to ask is, "Is this material made up of one part or more than one?" If there is one part, the next step is to determine which group it belongs to, according to the following choices:

Chapter 2: Books, pamphlets, and printed sheets
Chapter 3: Cartographic materials
Chapter 4: Manuscripts (including manuscript collections)
Chapter 5: Music
Chapter 6: Sound recordings
Chapter 7: Motion pictures and videorecordings
Chapter 8: Graphic materials
Chapter 9: Electronic resources
Chapter 10: Three-dimensional artefacts and realia
Chapter 11: Microforms
Chapter 12: Continuing resources
Chapter 13: Analysis

Chapter 1 is used to describe all materials, together with the chapter or chapters matching the media or publication group(s) to which a material belongs. To catalog an Oscar statue, for example, the rules in chapter 1 and chapter 10 are applied, because the statue is a three-dimensional material. To catalog a serially issued sound recording, videorecording, or electronic resource, three chapters are used: chapter 1; the chapter for the appropriate physical format; and chapter 12, the chapter for serials. RDA's sections are not divided by physical format, but by cataloging entities and, within the sections for description, by attributes (descriptive elements). Variations in the way certain elements are recorded for different media are provided as appropriate.

If the material consists of more than one piece (except continuing resources), catalogers must ask: "Are all the pieces in one format?" Examples of items in one format are multidisc sound recordings and CD-ROMs and multivolume books. If the answer is yes, proceed in the same way as described previously. Choose the appropriate chapter for the medium and begin. If the answer is no, ask: "Is one of the pieces more important than the rest?" If so, the item is cataloged using the chapter for that piece, called the *predominant* piece. All the other pieces are considered accompanying material, subordinate to that piece. If the answer is no, or if at least two pieces in different formats are equal in importance, the item is cataloged as a kit (or, if using the British interpretation of the rules, as a multimedia material), applying rule 1.10 (from chapter 1) and other chapters appropriate to the formats involved.

Judging importance and predominance is subjective. A useful rule of thumb to determine whether one part of a material is predominant is to consider how the content of the item is conveyed. If each piece conveys the whole content, none is predominant and the item is a kit (or multimedia). If none of the pieces conveys the whole content and these pieces must be used together, there is no predominant piece and the item is a kit. But if one piece conveys the whole content and the others only add to it, that piece is predominant and the catalog record should be made for it alone, with the other pieces treated as accompanying materials. Figure 14.1 shows a book and sound recording set in which the book is considered predominant because it includes both the words and pictures, while the recording only includes the words. This item is cataloged as a book with an accompanying sound recording. However, if this item is to be used to teach English to foreign speakers, it might be catalogued as a sound recording with accompanying text. Figure 14.2 shows a sound cassette, response sheets, a post test, and a teacher's guide set. None of the parts conveys the whole content. There are references in the sound cassette to the response sheet and vice versa; the post test needs both to be understood; and the teacher's guide contains more information on the topic. This set is cataloged as a kit.

```
This example is an illustration of:
     •  adaptation
     •  book with accompanying sound disc (first record)
     •  sound disc with accompanying book (second record)
     •  general material designation (second record)
     •  three statements of responsibility
     •  colored illustrations
     •  accompanying material
     •  series statement with subseries and number
     •  summary
     •  contents note (first record)
     •  ISBN qualified
     •  Library of Congress adult and children's subject headings
     •  name-title added entry (bibliographic form of personal
        name)
     •  title added entry
```

2nd level cataloging for a children's collection

```
Thompson, Cheryl.
  Five children and it / E. Nesbit ; retold by Cheryl Thompson ;
illustrated by Chiara Fedele. -- Genoa : Black Cat Publishing,
2006.
  63 p. : col. ill. ; 24 cm. + 1 sound disc (43 min., 5 sec.) :
digital ; 4 ¾ in. -- (Green apple. Starter, CEFR A1)

  Summary: In a gravel pit near where they live, five siblings
discover a sand fairy who grants them wishes.
  Understanding the text: p. 60-63.
  ISBN 9-978-88-530-0475-8 (pbk. and CD).

  1. Fairies.  2. Wishes.  3. Brothers and sisters.  I. Nesbit,
E. (Edith), 1858-1924. Five children and it.  II. Title.
```

2nd level cataloging for English as a second language collection

```
Thompson, Cheryl.
  Five children and it [sound recording] / E. Nesbit ; retold by
Cheryl Thompson ; illustrated by Chiara Fedele. -- Genoa : Black
Cat Publishing, 2006.
  1 sound disc (43 min., 5 sec.) : digital ; 4 ¾ in. + 1 book
(63 p. : col. ill. ; 24 cm.) -- (Green apple. Starter, CEFR A1)

  Summary: In a gravel pit near where they live, five siblings
discover a sand fairy who grants them wishes.

  ISBN 9-978-88-530-0475-8 (pbk. and CD).

  1. English language -- Sound recordings for foreign speakers.
2.  English language -- Textbooks for foreign speakers.
3.  Readers (Elementary).  I. Nesbit, E. (Edith), 1858-1924. Five
children and it.  II. Title.
```

Figure 14.1

Figure 14.1—*Continued*

CHIEF SOURCE OF INFORMATION
(Title Page)

(Information on Verso)

Illustrated by Chiara Fedele

COMPACT DISC LABEL

Information on back cover of book

Starter CEFR A1

This example is an illustration of:
- kit
- general material designation
- publication and copyright dates unknown, century certain
- summary
- Library of Congress and Sears subject heading the same
- Dewey decimal classification
- two levels of cataloging

2nd level cataloging

George, Miriam H.
  Reference books [kit] / author, Miriam H. George. -- Baltimore
: Media Materials, [19--]
  1 sound cassette, 30 identical response sheets, 1 post test, 1
teacher's guide ; in container 29 x 23 x 4 cm.

  Summary: The difference between abridged and unabridged
dictionaries and the use of cross-references in information
searches are explained and specialized reference books
introduced.

1st level cataloging

George, Miriam H.
  Reference books [kit]. -- Media Materials, [19--]
  1 sound cassette, 30 identical response sheets, 1 post test, 1
teacher's guide.

Tracing for both levels
  1. Reference books. I. Title.

Recommended DDC for both levels: 028.7

INFORMATION ON TEACHER'S GUIDE (THE UNIFYING PIECE)

TITLE REFERENCE BOOKS

AUTHOR   Miriam H. George, B.S.Ed.

APPROXIMATE LESSON TIME
   40-45 minutes

PERFORMANCE OBJECTIVES

-Show students that dictionaries and encyclopedias
 have many uses.
-Practice in using guide words and cross
 references.
-Introduce students to the wealth of information
 found in atlases, Readers' Guide, World Almanac,
 Dictionary of American History, Dictionary of
 American Biography, Current Biography, Who's Who
 in America, Twentieth Century Authors, and Familiar Quotations.

SUMMARY

The difference between the abridged and unabridged dictionary is shown. The use of
guide words in dictionaries and encyclopedias
is stressed. The use of cross references in
the card catalog, the Readers' Guide, and in
encyclopedias is explained. Specialized reference books are introduced.

The container is a standard box used for all this firms materials. The unifying piece for this kit is the teacher's guide. All contents have title: Reference Books.

Figure 14.2

Games (including handheld games with computer chips), puzzles, and dioramas are exceptions to the definition of kits. Although usually comprising many pieces in different media, they are considered single units for cataloging purposes and follow chapter 10's rules.

DESCRIPTIVE STRUCTURE AND DATA SOURCES

The ISBD structure for description has eight elements called *areas of description:*

Area 1: Title and statement of responsibility
Area 2: Edition
Area 3: Material specific details (used for selected materials)
Area 4: Publication, distribution, etc.
Area 5: Physical description
Area 6: Series
Area 7: Notes
Area 8: Standard number and terms of availability

All the areas of description do not apply to every material being cataloged; for example, when no edition information appears on material, the edition statement is left out of the description. This also is true of notes, most of which are optional. Material specific details are used only for serially issued materials, electronic resources, maps, and music. (RDA does not have an attribute called "material specific details." It has an attribute called "numbering and dating of serials" that contains the same kind of data for serials.) Many materials have no standard numbers.

Descriptive cataloging is like a puzzle with eight blank spaces, some or all of which are filled in according to information that appears on the material being cataloged. There may be more or less information than needed, or there may be competing sources of information. Rules in AACR2-2005 help catalogers handle these matters. The rules also help them choose the same information sources for cataloging purposes if more than one source is present. These rules are numbered with a zero (x.0) because they precede the areas of description, which are numbered one through eight (x.1–x.8). For example, rule 7.0B covers information sources for motion pictures and videorecordings, rule 9.0B covers information sources for electronic resources, and so on.

At the start of each chapter, all recognized information sources for that media group are discussed. One is designated the *chief* source for that format; the rest are considered *prescribed* sources. Area 1 data must come from the chief source. It is the most important piece of information, and people using the catalog record should be able to assume that it came from the chief source. If, for some reason, it does not—for example, because a book does not have a title page or a visual image has no textual information, catalogers alert the user to this fact by putting information supplied from other sources into square brackets and listing the source of the information in the notes (area 7). The source of title note is especially important for serially issued continuing resources. The first issue is designated as the chief source, but if it is unavailable and another issue (the earliest available) is used instead, it must be noted.

Each area of description has specific sources prescribed for it. Only area 1 must come from the chief source. Data for all the other areas may be taken from any of several sources. Areas 5, 7, and 8 may come from *any* source, including personal knowledge. Information from sources other than the prescribed sources is enclosed in square brackets to identify it. Notes are given to explain the sources of bracketed data, as in Figures 14.4 and 14.5.

The general principle followed by AACR2-2005 about information sources is to *prefer information from the material itself over information from more distant locations.* If a chapter covers a media group that requires hardware (e.g., viewers, projectors, recorders, computers) to see or hear the material itself, alternatives are provided for catalogers who lack equipment. Some materials have multipart chief sources, such as a set of sound discs with labels pasted permanently on each disc or a videorecording with opening and closing credits screens. Practical guidelines for choosing among them are given. If an alternative to the preferred chief source for the format is chosen, it becomes the chief source, and information from it does not have to be bracketed, but the alternative must be explained in a note.

Another general principle followed by AACR2-2005 is to give bibliographic information that is *readily available.* Few, if any, descriptive elements mandate giving information available only from sources outside the material being cataloged that would require time-consuming research to obtain, for instance, counting numerous unnumbered pages or leaves in a book. When desired information is absent from the material being cataloged, it is either omitted (for example, an International Standard Book Number [ISBN]) or estimated (for example, a date of publication).

ISBD PUNCTUATION

IFLA's experts devised a system of punctuation that distinguishes each element and subelement of a catalog record. This helps a cataloger who is unfamiliar with the language of a record to understand and use it. Unfortunately, when punctuation rules are read together at the beginning of each section, they seem very complicated. It is easier to put in the punctuation after the descriptive elements are assembled. Practice also helps a cataloger do this mechanical part of preparing catalog records faster. Figure 14.3 illustrates the punctuation for a typical level 2 description. It can be imitated provided all the same data elements are present, but if any element or subelement is missing, the punctuation changes. Basic punctuations used are described in the sections that follow. Others may be found in AACR2-2005, which gives all the correct marks.

In the style of record shown in Figure 14.3, if an area of description begins a paragraph, there is no designated punctuation that precedes it. If one area of description follows another in the same paragraph, a period-space-dash-space (. –) precedes it. In North America, it has been customary to combine areas 1–4 in one paragraph, areas 5 and 6 in a second, and each note in its own paragraph, but this is changing to a style in which each area of description has its own paragraph. Area 8 is also given a separate paragraph. In some countries, all elements of description appear in one paragraph, so it is useful to have the period-space-dash-space punctuation to define them.

Colons (:), semicolons (;), slashes (/), and commas (,) are used for several kinds of identification; an equals sign (=) denotes the same data in another language; and a

```
This example is an illustration of:
    • joint authors
    • other title information; three periods changed to prevent
      confusion with marks of omission (in 2nd level
      cataloging)
    • detailed pagination (in 2nd level cataloging)
    • index note (in 2nd level cataloging)
    • Library of Congress and Sears subject headings compared
    • personal name added entry
    • title added entry
    • Library of Congress CIP
    • two levels of cataloging
```

1st level cataloging

```
Mortenson, Greg.
  Three cups of tea / Greg Mortenson and David Oliver Relin. --
Penguin Books, 2007.
  349 p., [16] p. of plates.

  ISBN 978-0-14-303825-2.
```

2nd level cataloging

```
Mortenson, Greg.
  Three cups of tea : one man's mission to promote peace--one
school at a time / Greg Mortenson and David Oliver Relin. -- New
York : Penguin Books, 2007.
  349 p., [16] p. of plates : ill., maps ; 21 cm.

  Includes index.
  ISBN 978-0-14-303825-2.
```

Tracing with Library of Congress subject headings

```
  1. Girls' schools -- Pakistan.  2. Girls' schools --
Afghanistan.  3. Humanitarian assistance, American -- Pakistan.
4. Humanitarian assistance, American -- Afghanistan.
5. Mortenson, Greg.  I. Relin, David Oliver.  II. Title.
```

Tracing with Sears subject headings

```
  1. Girls -- Education -- Pakistan.  2. Girls -- Education --
Afghanistan.  3. American foreign aid -- Pakistan.  4. American
foreign aid -- Afghanistan.  5. Mortenson, Greg.  I. Relin, David
Oliver.  II. Title.
```

Publication statement for Canadian libraries
New York ; Toronto : Penguin Books, 2007.

Figure 14.3

Figure 14.3—*Continued*

CHIEF SOURCE OF INFORMATION
(Title Page)

THREE CUPS OF TEA

ONE MAN'S MISSION TO PROMOTE PEACE . . .
ONE SCHOOL AT A TIME

GREG MORTENSON

and

DAVID OLIVER RELIN

PENGUIN BOOKS

(Information on Verso)

PENGUIN BOOKS
Published by the Penguin Group
Penguin Group (USA) Inc., 375 Hudson Street, New York, New York 10014, U.S.A.
Penguin Group (Canada), 90 Eglinton Avenue East, Suite 700, Toronto, Ontario,
Canada M4P 2Y3 (a division of Pearson Penguin Canada Inc.)
Penguin Books Ltd, 80 Strand, London WC2R 0RL, England
Penguin Ireland, 25 St Stephen's Green, Dublin 2, Ireland (a division of Penguin Books Ltd)
Penguin Group (Australia), 250 Camberwell Road, Camberwell, Victoria 3124, Australia
(a division of Pearson Australia Group Pty Ltd)
Penguin Books India Pvt Ltd, 11 Community Centre, Panchsheel Park,
New Delhi – 110 017, India
Penguin Group (NZ), 67 Apollo Drive, Mairangi Bay, Auckland 1310,
New Zealand (a division of Pearson New Zealand Ltd)
Penguin Books (South Africa) (Pty) Ltd, 24 Sturdee Avenue,
Rosebank, Johannesburg 2196, South Africa

Penguin Books Ltd, Registered Offices:
80 Strand, London WC2R 0RL, England

First published in the United States of America by Viking Penguin,
a member of Penguin Group (USA) Inc. 2006
Published in Penguin Books 2007

17 18 19 20

Copyright © Greg Mortenson and David Oliver Relin, 2006
All rights reserved

THE LIBRARY OF CONGRESS HAS CATALOGED THE HARDCOVER EDITION AS FOLLOWS:
Mortenson, Greg.
Three cups of tea : one man's mission to fight terrorism and build nations—one school
at a time / Greg Mortenson and David Oliver Relin.
p.   cm.
Includes index.
ISBN 0-670-03482-7 (hc.)
ISBN 978-0-14-303825-2 (pbk.)
1. Girls' schools—Pakistan. 2. Girls' schools—Afghanistan. 3. Humanitarian
assistance, American—Pakistan. 4. Humanitarian assistance, American—Afghanistan.
5. Mortenson, Greg.
I. Relin, David Oliver. II. Title.
LC2330.M67   2006
371.82209549—dc22
2005043466

Printed in the United States of America
Set in Stempel Garamond • Designed by Elke Sigal

Except in the United States of America, this book is sold subject to the condition
that it shall not, by way of trade or otherwise, be lent, resold, hired out, or otherwise
circulated without the publisher's prior consent in any form of binding or cover
other than that in which it is published and without a similar condition
including this condition being imposed on the subsequent purchaser.

The scanning, uploading and distribution of this book via the Internet or
via any other means without the permission of the publisher is illegal and
punishable by law. Please purchase only authorized electronic editions,
and do not participate in or encourage electronic piracy of copyrighted
materials. Your support of the author's rights is appreciated.

plus sign (+) identifies accompanying materials (area 5). In area 1, colons separate the title proper from the rest of the title; in area 4, they separate the place of publication from the name of the publisher; and in area 5, they separate the extent and specific material designation from other physical details. Slashes identify statements of responsibility in areas 1, 2, 6, and 7. Within statements of responsibility, commas usually separate names when the responsibilities are the same but are shared by more than one person or corporate body, and semicolons separate names when responsibilities differ. This pattern is followed to identify multiple places and names of publishers and distributors, dates of publication, paging sequences, illustration types, and so on. Following are some examples:

1. A book written by one person, illustrated by another, and edited by a third party, in which all the words given appear on the title page as shown below:

   / by James B. Smith ; illustrated by Gloria Green ; edited by Paul Robert Jones.

2. A book written by all three, where the word "by" appears on the title page, with the names listed underneath:

/ by James B. Smith, Gloria Green, Paul Robert Jones.

3. A book written by two people and edited by a third, where the words "by" and "and" appear on the title page, but the words "edited by" do not appear and are supplied by the cataloger to explain Jones's contribution to the book:

/ by James B. Smith and Gloria Green ; [edited by] Paul Robert Jones.

Whenever colons, semicolons, slashes, and equals signs are used in ISBD punctuation, a space is put both before and after the mark. Commas and periods (called "full stops") only have spaces after the marks, not before them, and parentheses and square brackets are spaced as they would be in any text. In most instances, it is the extra spaces that give librarians a clue that the punctuation is intended for identification of an element rather than for grammatical purposes.

Catalogers working in libraries with English-language collections need not worry much about punctuation errors; most patrons do not notice them, and they rarely affect retrieval. However, IFLA created ISBD punctuation to help catalog users understand the bibliographic records for materials in all languages and in nonroman scripts; therefore, libraries that contain foreign language materials should exercise more care in punctuating their catalog records correctly.

The ISBD punctuation marks precede the elements they identify for the same reason statements in a computer program tell the computer what kind of data it is going to receive before sending it (for example, online public access catalogs [OPACs] often instruct searchers to enter search statements such as "ti=hamlet" or "au=shakespeare" in which the requested title or author is preceded by an identifying word or phrase). If a descriptive element or subelement is missing, the ISBD punctuation that precedes it is also omitted.

CREATING THE DESCRIPTION

Area 1: Title and Statement of Responsibility

The first information in any description is the main title, called the *title proper*, which is chosen from the chief source. Title words are transcribed *exactly as they appear* on the material as to their order and spelling, even if they are wrong. The reasoning behind precise transcription is to ensure that a catalog record can be matched to the item it represents, especially when several versions of a title or similar-sounding titles exist.

The layout and typography of the words on the chief source of information are used to determine where a title proper begins and ends. AACR2-2005's rules aid in determining titles proper in special cases that are encountered frequently, for example, if two separate versions of Charles Darwin's voyage appear in the two ways shown in Figures 14.4 and 14.5, rules in Chapter 1 direct the cataloger to transcribe them as given. When there is no rule to determine what should be done, follow your instincts and decide.

This example is an illustration of:
* optional addition of dates to personal name
* edition statement taken from outside prescribed sources (many libraries place such an edition statement in the note area, sometimes as a quoted note)
* multiple places of publication
* publication date not listed, century uncertain
* note regarding edition statement
* Library of Congress subject headings
* title added entry
* Dewey Decimal and Library of Congress classifications compared

2nd level cataloging for a Canadian library

Darwin, Charles, 1809-1882.
   Journal of researches during the voyage of H.M.S. "Beagle" / by Charles Darwin. -- [2nd ed. rev.] -- London ; Toronto : T. Nelson, [19--?]
   543 p. ; 16 cm.

   Edition statement from preface.

2nd level cataloging for a U.S. library

Darwin, Charles, 1809-1882.
   Journal of researches during the voyage of H.M.S. "Beagle" / by Charles Darwin. -- [2nd ed. rev.] -- London ; New York : T. Nelson, [19--?].
   543 p. ; 16 cm.

   Edition statement from preface.

Tracing for both

   1. Beagle Expedition (1831-1836). 2. Natural history.
3. Geology. 4. Voyages around the world. 5. South America -- Description and travel. I. Title.

Recommended DDC: 578.09
Recommended LCC: QH11.D2 1900z or QH31.D2 1900z

CHIEF SOURCE OF INFORMATION
(Title Page)

JOURNAL OF
RESEARCHES
DURING THE
VOYAGE OF H.M.S. "BEAGLE"

BY
CHARLES DARWIN

Thomas Nelson and Sons Ltd.
London Edinburgh New York
Toronto and Paris

(The verso is blank)

Figure 14.4

```
This example is an illustration of:
     •  optional addition of dates to personal name
     •  edition statement taken from outside prescribed sources
        (many libraries place such an edition statement in the
        note area, sometimes as a quoted note)
     •  publication date not listed, copyright date given
     •  numbered series statement
     •  note regarding edition statement
     •  index note
     •  Library of Congress subject headings
     •  title added entry
     •  series added entry
     •  Dewey Decimal and Library of Congress classifications
     •  2nd level cataloging
```

```
Darwin, Charles, 1809-1882.
   The voyage of the Beagle / by Charles Darwin with introduction
and notes. -- [2nd ed.]. -- New York : Collier, c1909.
   547 p. : ill. ; 20 cm. -- (The Harvard classics ; v. 29)

   Edition statement from dedication.
   Includes index.

   1. Beagle Expedition (1831-1836).  2. Natural history.
3. Geology.  4. Voyages around the world.  5. South America --
Description and travel.  I. Title.  II. Series.
```

```
Recommended DDC: 578.09
Recommended LCC: Q11.D2 1909
```

CHIEF SOURCE OF INFORMATION
(Title Page)

THE HARVARD CLASSICS

EDITED BY CHARLES W. ELIOT LL D

⚘

THE VOYAGE OF THE BEAGLE

BY CHARLES DARWIN

WITH INTRODUCTION AND NOTES

VOLUME 29

P F COLLIER & SON COMPANY

NEW YORK

(Information on verso)

Copyright, 1909
By P. F. Collier & Son

Manufacturered in U. S. A.

Figure 14.5

Capitalization and punctuation of titles proper are not transcribed as they appear on the chief source. Capitalization of all parts of the description follows standard rules contained in AACR2-2005's Appendix A. For English-language titles, usually only the first word and subsequent proper nouns are capitalized. Different rules govern capitalization for other languages. Punctuation marks that are the same as those used in ISBD punctuation are not transcribed as they appear, because they might be confused with ISBD punctuation. Instead, catalogers insert appropriate ISBD punctuation and ignore what is given on the material.

Marks of omission, space-three periods-space (. . .), are used to indicate words found on the title page that are omitted from the bibliographic record. In Figure 14.3 the three periods that are part of the title on the title page have been changed to a dash in the bibliographic record to avoid misunderstanding.

Sometimes an item is published in two (or more) languages and has titles in both of them. Both are considered part of the title proper. A bilingual title does not always mean the material is a bilingual work. In Figure 14.6, despite the presence of a bilingual title on the title page, the book is not written in two languages. (ᓄᓇᕗᑦ is pronounced "Nunavut" and translates into English as "Our land."). Many cataloging departments do not have the syllabic typeface to list the Inuktitut title as required for second-level cataloging, so first-level enriched cataloging—defined as more data than required by level 1, but not as much as required by level 2—may be a simple, practical solution for materials bearing titles in nonroman alphabets.

After the title proper, the rules offer an option to give a *general material designation* (gmd) that alerts the catalog user to the item's physical format. The AACR2-2005 has two lists of permissible general material designations (gmds), one for use by British catalogers, the other for catalogers in Australia, Canada, and the United States. Gmds are optional. In libraries consisting mostly of books, the gmd for books, *text,* usually is omitted and only gmds for other formats are used. If books are not a library's primary material, catalogers may decide to use *text* along with all the others. Libraries that use gmds put them immediately after the title proper.

Following the gmd (or following the title proper if a gmd is not used) the rest of the title appears; this is called *other title information* in AACR2-2005. (This part of area 1 is not required for level 1 descriptions.) Figure 14.6 presents an example of other title information given after title proper. Lengthy other title information can be given in the notes, as shown in Figure 14.7.

Some books have *alternate titles,* which are almost always preceded by the word "or". Alternate titles are considered to be part of the title proper. For example, in Figure 14.8, "The confessional of the black penitents" is an alternate title and "a romance" is other title information.

The last part of area 1 is the *statement of responsibility.* Here, the name(s) of the author(s), composer(s), artist(s), programmer(s), or other people or groups responsible for the overall content of the item are given, *provided* the names appear "prominently" on the item being cataloged. Some catalogers interpret "prominent" as appearing on the chief source or outer covering; others include only those names that appear in large print or that are identified as being important contributors to the work. Some catalogers choose not to give the names of translators or writers of forewords, no matter how they are displayed. If no names appear on the item, this element is omitted.

```
This example is an illustration of:
    •  bilingual title in a nonroman script
    •  publication date not listed, copyright date given
    •  unnumbered series statement
    •  series other title information
    •  contents note
    •  title added entry
    •  series added entry
    •  Dewey Decimal classification
    •  1st level cataloging enriched


Weihs, Jean.
    Nunavut : our land. -- M.O.D. Publishing, c1999.
    32 p. -- (Our country : provinces & territories)

    Glossary of English and equivalent Inuktitut words in roman
alphabet and in syllabics with pronunciation guide: p. 29.
    ISBN 1-89446109-6.

    1. Nunavut.  I. Title.  II. Series.


Recommended DDC: 917.19
```

CHIEF SOURCE OF INFORMATION
(Title Page)   (Information on Cover)

NUNAVUT: OUR LAND

ᓄᓇᕗᑦ

Jean Weihs
Illustrated by Cameron Riddle

M.O.D. Publishing
Mississauga, Ontario

(Information on Verso)

© 1999 Jean Weihs

ISBN: 1-89446109-6

OUR COUNTRY:
PROVINCES & TERRITORIES

NUNAVUT

Figure 14.6

This example is an illustration of:
* main entry under compiler
* bibliographic form of name taken from cataloging-in-publication (CIP)
* edition statement
* publication date not listed, copyright date given
* more than one place of publication
* other title information given as a note
* Library of Congress subject headings
* additional title added entry
* Dewey Decimal and Library of Congress classifications
* Library of Congress and British Library CIPs
* 2nd level cataloging

Prytherch, Raymond John.
  Harrod's librarians' glossary and reference book / compiled by Ray Prytherch. -- 10th ed. -- Aldershot, England ; Burlington, VT : Ashgate, c2005.
  xi, 753 p. ; 24 cm.

  "A directory of over 10,200 terms, organizations, projects and acronyms in the areas of information management, library science, publishing and archive management"—T.p.
  ISBN: 0-7546-4038-8.

  1. Library science -- Dictionaries. 2. Information science -- Dictionaries. 3. Publishers and publishing -- Dictionaries. 4. Book industries and book trade -- Dictionaries. 5. Archives -- Administration -- Dictionaries. 6. Bibliography -- Dictionaries. I. Title: Librarians' glossary and reference book. II. Title.

Recommended DDC: 020.3
Recommended LCC: Z1006.H32 2005

CHIEF SOURCE OF INFORMATION
(Title Page)

(Information on Verso)

HARROD'S LIBRARIANS' GLOSSARY

AND REFERENCE BOOK

A Directory of Over 10,200 Terms,
Organizations, Projects and Acronyms
in the Areas of Information
Management, Library Science,
Publishing and Archive Management

Tenth Edition

Compiled

by

RAY PRYTHERCH

ASHGATE

Published by
Ashgate Publishing Limited
Gower House
Croft Road
Aldershot
Hants GU11 3HR
England

Ashgate Publishing Company
Suite 420
101 Cherry Street
Burlington, VT 05401-4405
USA

Ashgate website: http://www.ashgate.com

British Library Cataloguing in Publication Data
Harrod's librarians' glossary and reference book : a
  directory of over 10,200 terms, organizations, projects and
  acronyms in the areas of information management, library
  science, publishing and archive management. - 10th ed.
  1.Library science - Dictionaries 2.Information science -
  Dictionaries 3.Publishers and publishing - Dictionaries
  4. Book industries and trade - Dictionaries 5.Archives -
  Administration - Dictionaries
  I.Prytherch, Raymond John II.Harrod, Leonard Montague
  III.Librarians' glossary and reference book
  020.3

Library of Congress Cataloging-in-Publication Data
Prytherch, Raymond John.
  Harrod's librarians' glossary and reference book : a dictionary of over 10,200 terms,
organizations, projects and acronyms in the areas of information management, library
science, publishing and archive management / by Ray Prytherch.--10th ed.
  p. cm.
  ISBN 0-7546-4038-8
  1. Library science--Dictionaries. 2. Information science--Dictionaries. 3.
Publishers and publishing--Dictionaries. 4. Book industries and trade--Dictionaries.
5. Archives--Administration--Dictionaries. 6. Bibliography--Dictionaries. I. Title:
Librarians' glossary and reference book. II. Title.

Z1006. H32 2005
020'.3--dc22

ISBN 0 7546 4038 8

2004026891

Typeset by P. Stubley, Sheffield

Printed and bound in Great Britain by MPG Books Ltd, Bodmin, Cornwall

Figure 14.7

This example is an illustration of:
- fiction book
- bibliographic form of author's name taken from the Library of Congress authority file
- alternative title
- other title information
- two statements of subsidiary responsibility
- multiple places of publication
- detailed pagination
- series statement
- contents note
- 2 ISBNs
- Library of Congress fiction subject headings
- personal name added entry
- title added entry
- 2nd level cataloging

```
Radcliffe, Ann Ward.
   The Italian, or, The confessional of the black penitents : a
romance / Ann Radcliffe ; edited by Frederick Garber ; with an
introduction and notes by E.J. Clery. -- Oxford ; New York :
Oxford University Press, 1998.
   xxxviii, 423 p. ; 20 cm. -- (Oxford world's classics)

   Includes bibliographical references.
   ISBN 978-0-19-2832542. -- ISBN 0-19-283254-9.

   1. Inquisition -- Fiction.  2. Kidnapping -- Fiction.
3. Monks -- Fiction.  4. Naples (Italy) -- Fiction.  I. Garber,
Frederick.  II. Title.


The publication/distribution area in a Canadian catalog would
read:

Oxford ; Toronto : Oxford University Press, 1998.
```

CHIEF SOURCE OF INFORMATION
(Title Page)

OXFORD WORLD'S CLASSICS

▬

ANN RADCLIFFE

The Italian

or the

Confessional of the
Black Penitents

A ROMANCE

▬

Edited by
FREDERICK GARBER

With an Introduction and Notes by
E. J. CLERY

OXFORD
UNIVERSITY PRESS

(Information on Verso)

OXFORD
UNIVERSITY PRESS

Great Clarendon Street, Oxford OX2 6DP

Oxford University Press is a department of the University of Oxford.
It furthers the University's objective of excellence in research, scholarship,
and education by publishing worldwide in

Oxford New York

Athens Auckland Bangkok Bogotá Buenos Aires Calcutta
Cape Town Chennai Dar es Salaam Delhi Florence Hong Kong Istanbul
Karachi Kuala Lumpur Madrid Melbourne Mexico City Mumbai
Nairobi Paris São Paulo Singapore Taipei Tokyo Toronto Warsaw
with associated companies in Berlin Ibadan

Oxford is a registered trade mark of Oxford University Press
in the UK and in certain other countries

Published in the United States
by Oxford University Press Inc., New York

© Oxford University Press 1968
Chronology © Terry Castle 1998
Biography, Introduction, Note on the Text, and Notes © E. J. Clery 1998

The moral rights of the author have been asserted
Database right Oxford University Press (maker)

First published by Oxford University Press 1968
First published as a World's Classics paperback 1981
Reissued as an Oxford World's Classics paperback 1998

All rights reserved. No part of this publication may be reproduced,
stored in a retrieval system, or transmitted, in any form or by any means,
without the prior permission in writing of Oxford University Press,
or as expressly permitted by law, or under terms agreed with the appropriate
reprographics rights organizations. Enquiries concerning reproduction
outside the scope of the above should be sent to the Rights Department,
Oxford University Press, at the address above

You must not circulate this book in any other binding or cover
and you must impose this same condition on any acquirer

British Library Cataloguing in Publication Data
Data available

Library of Congress Cataloging in Publication Data
Data available

ISBN 978–0–19–2832542
ISBN 0–19–283254–9

8

Printed in Great Britain by
Clays Ltd, St Ives plc

Figure 14.8

Names that are important to the library but are not prominently displayed on the material being cataloged can be given in area 7 (the note area) to form the basis for headings. Any name used as an access point must be given somewhere in the catalog record. If the name has not appeared in areas 1 through 6, a note is given to provide the basis for the access point. Some computerized catalogs have the capacity to search all fields of the record, so putting a name in the note field provides access even if a separate access point is not made. In Figure 14.9, A.J. Casson, an important Canadian painter, is the book's designer. Usually book designers are not given in the catalog record, but an art school might want to provide access to all Casson's work in its collection.

(Level 1 descriptions give only the first statement of responsibility and that only if it differs from the item's main heading, or if there is no personal name main entry heading.)

Area 2: Edition Statement

If an edition is stated on the prescribed sources of information for this area, it is transcribed as it appears in the second area of description. The words of the statement must be given in the same order as they appear, since "second revised edition" is not the

```
This example is an illustration of:
    • main entry under corporate body
    • other title information
    • responsibility not attributed in chief source of
      information
    • edition statement taken from outside prescribed sources
      (Many libraries place such an edition statement in the
      note area, sometimes as a quoted note)
    • publication date not listed, copyright date given
    • work consisting mostly of illustrations
    • credits note
    • edition and history note
    • added entry for designer
    • added entry for author of a part of the work
    • optional addition of full form of given names
    • additional title added entry
    • Dewey Decimal and Library of Congress classifications
    • prime mark in Dewey Decimal Classification
    • 2nd level cataloging


McMichael Canadian Collection.
   A heritage of Canadian art : the McMichael collection. -- [Rev.
and enl. ed.]. -- Toronto : Clarke, Irwin, c1976.
   198 p. : chiefly ill. ; 27 cm.

   Designed by A.J. Casson; biographies by Paul Duval.
   Previous ed. published in 1973 under title: A vision of Canada.
   ISBN 0-7720-1209-1.

   1. McMichael Canadian Collection -- Catalogs.  2. Painting,
Canadian -- Ontario -- Kleinburg -- Catalogs.  3. Art,
Canadian -- Ontario -- Kleinburg -- Catalogs.  4. Artists --
Canada -- Biography.  I. Casson, A.J. (Alfred Joseph).  II.
Duval, Paul.  III. Title.  IV. Title: A vision of Canada.


Recommended DDC: 759.11'074
Recommended LCC: N910.K5712 A56 1979
```

Figure 14.9

Figure 14.9—*Continued*

CHIEF SOURCE OF INFORMATION
(Title Page)

A HERITAGE OF CANADIAN ART

The McMichael Collection

Clarke, Irwin & Company Limited, Toronto, Vancouver

(Information on Verso)   (Information on Book Jacket)

A Heritage of Canadian Art

Designed by A. J. Casson, LL.D., R.C.A.
Photography Hugh W. Thompson
Portraits of Artists by Joachim Gauthier, A.R.C.A., O.S.A.
Produced by Sampson Matthews Limited, Toronto

an enlarged and revised study of
The McMichael Canadian Collection

Design by A. J. Casson

This new book about the famous McMichael
Canadian Collection in Kleinburg carries all the
impact of its highly acclaimed predecessor,
A Vision of Canada. A completely new chapter
on the Woodland Indians has been added, and

(Information on page 16)

sections on other indigenous Canadian cultures have been considerably expanded. A new

ACKNOWLEDGMENTS

introduction covers more fully the philosophy

Paul Duval, well-known author of many books on Canadian
art, contributed to the text for the introduction and is the
author of each of the biographies. His assistance in the preparation of this book has been invaluable.

and history of the collection, and the works of art
contained in it.

We are indebted to Bernhard Cinader F.R.S.C., an eminent
Canadian scientist who prepared the text, *Woodland Indian
Art.* He was among the first to recognize the aesthetic value of
the contemporary art of the Woodland Indian, and to organize
two of the first exhibitions of their work.

Vital Indian and Eskimo creations are presented alongside the work of the Group of
Seven and their contemporaries. Masks and
totems from the West Coast, stone carvings
from the Arctic, magnificent landscapes of the

After eight trips to the Arctic to expand her special

Canadian wilderness, all combine to provide a
rich record of our artistic heritage.

© 1976 McMichael Canadian Collection
ISBN 0 7720 1060 X
Printed in Canada

The book contains 1076 reproductions in black
and white and 126 in full colour. Each facet of

16

the collection is described by an expert, and
sixteen individual biographies with full colour
portraits of each artist by Joachim Gauthier
supplement the text   *(continued on back flap)*

---

same as "revised second edition" or "second edition, revised." A revised edition is not the same as an updated edition, a second edition, or an expanded edition. Words in an edition statement should be abbreviated if any of the words being transcribed are listed in AACR2-2005's Appendix B (words) or C (numbers). Thus, the several examples in this paragraph would be recorded in a catalog record as follows:

Rev. 2nd ed.
2nd rev. ed.
Rev. ed.
Updated ed.
2nd ed.
Expanded ed.

Area 3: Material Specific Details

Three kinds of materials require use of area 3: cartographic materials, printed music, and serial continuing resources in all formats. Each type of material has its own information for this area, hence the name *material specific*. RDA includes rules for serial-related and map-related details as separate descriptive elements.

Cartographic items use area 3 to record the scale and, when found on the item, the projection and, optionally, a statement of coordinates and equinox. Figure 14.10 shows this information for a map. While a statement of scale is required for area 3, given as a representative fraction expressed as a ratio (1:)[6], the other technical specifications are optional and need not be given unless the information is readily available from the item. (Level 1 cataloging only requires giving the scale.)

Printed music often contains a statement of the kind of musical presentation it represents, such as "piano-vocal score" or "miniature score." Statements found on the chief source of the manifestation being cataloged are recorded here, as shown in Figure 14.11.

```
This example is an illustration of:
        •  map
        •  general material designation
        •  main entry under corporate body
        •  same organization listed in statement of responsibility
           and as publisher
        •  statement of scale, projection, and coordinates
        •  open entry
        •  nature and scope of item note
        •  language note
        •  source of title note
        •  physical description note
        •  2nd level cataloging


Ordnance Survey (Ireland).
   Discovery series 1:50,000 [cartographic material] / compiled,
printed and published by the Director of the Ordnance Survey
Office. -- Scale 1:50,000 ; transverse Mercator proj.(W 11° 00'/W
5°30'--N 51°10').-- Dublin : Ordnance Survey of Ireland,
[c1993]-      .
      map : col. ; on sheets 103 x 80 cm. or smaller.

   Relief shown by contours, hyposometric tints, and spot heights.
   Legend and marginal information in English, Gaelic, French, and
German.
   Title from panel.
   Description based on sheet no. 1, Straith Eolais.
   Geographic coverage complete in 89 sheets.
   Each sheet individually titled and numbered.

   1. Ireland -- Maps, Topographic.  I. Title.
```

Figure 14.10

Serially issued continuing resources use area 3 to record the numbering and dating of the first issue. If the first issue is not available and the material is being cataloged from a subsequent issue, area 3 is left blank and the numbering and dating of the earliest available issue is given in a note (see Figure 14.12). Numbering and dating in area 3 are followed by a hyphen and spaces to indicate that the area is unfinished. If the publisher stops issuing the title, data for the final issue can be added in the spaces, as in the following examples:

The first issue of a magazine says "Issue No. 1"

Area 3: Issue no. 1- .

The last issue of the same magazine says "Issue No. 101"

Area 3: Issue no. 1–101.

The first screen of an electronic periodical says "Volume 1, number 1, 2001"

Area 3: Vol. 1, no. 1 (2001)- .

```
This work does not have a title page.
- - - - - - - - - - - - - - - - - - - - - - - - - - - - - - -
The caption states:
    Symphony No. 4
    for Orchestra
    Jean Sibelius, Op. 63.
- - - - - - - - - - - - - - - - - - - - - - - - - - - - - - -
The cover states:
    Miniature Score Edition
    JEAN SIBELIUS
    SYMPHONY No. 4
    in A minor
    Op. 63
    British & Continental Music Agencies Ltd.
    125 Shaftesbury Avenue, London, W.C.2
    Printed In England
- - - - - - - - - - - - - - - - - - - - - - - - - - - - - - -


This example is an illustration of:
    •  musical score
    •  uniform title
    •  optional addition of dates to personal name
    •  optional placement of general material designation at end
       of title proper
    •  musical presentation statement (optional area 3)
    •  publication and copyright dates unknown, century certain
    •  Library of Congress and Sears subject headings compared
    •  2nd level cataloging


Sibelius, Jean, 1865-1957.
   [Symphonies, no. 4, op. 63, A minor]
   Symphony no. 4 in A minor, op. 63 [music] / Jean Sibelius. --
Miniature score. -- London : British & Continental Music
Agencies, [19--].
   1 miniature score (68 p.) ; 18 cm.

   1. Symphonies. Library of Congress subject heading)
                         or
   1. Symphony. (Sears subject heading)

Recommended DDC: 784.2
Recommended LCC: M1001.S52 1900z
```

Figure 14.11

The first screen of an electronic periodical says "Volume 1, number 1, January 1999"
    Area 3: Vol. 1, no. 1 (Jan. 1999)- .

The rules assume that the original numbering style will not change over the life of a serial, but occasionally it does. Sometimes a publisher begins by numbering issues sequentially, but, later on, prefers to supply both volume and issue numbers. This happened with *Library Hi-Tech*, which displays both its old and new numbering systems (see Figure 14.13).

Nonbook titles issued serially may require two kinds of information in two separate area 3 statements. One statement will be for the numbering and dating; one statement will give the relevant medium-related data.

Area 3 is required for level 1 cataloging, but optional subelements are omitted.

Area 4: Publication, Distribution, etc.

For published materials, area 4 gives information about the publishers or other issuing agencies. (For cataloging purposes, all remote-access electronic resources, including all Internet materials, are considered published.) Publishers are responsible for issuing books and other printed materials, although distributors may also issue them. Entities issuing motion pictures, videorecordings, and other recorded materials are generally known as distributors or releasing agencies. Sometimes two publishers or both a

```
This example is an illustration of:
     • online serial
     • main entry under corporate body
     • general material designation
     • open entry
     • system requirements note
     • mode of access note
     • frequency note
     • type of file
     • source of title note
     • availability note
     • Library of Congress subject heading
     • 2nd level cataloging


Louisiana State University (Baton Rouge, La.). College of
     Education.
   Alumni newsletter [electronic resource]. -- Baton Rouge, La :
LSU College of Education

   System requirements: Adobe Acrobat Reader.
   Mode of access: World Wide Web.
   Annual.
   PDF file format.
   Description based on 2006 (viewed on Jan. 13, 2010).
   http://worldcat.org/oclc/301745136/viewonline.

   1. Louisiana State University (Baton Rouge, La.) College of
Education. -- Periodicals.
```

Figure 14.12

ISSN 0737-8831

Consecutive Issue 5; Vol. 2, No. 1/1984

LIBRARY
HI TECH

PUBLISHER
C. Edward Wall

EDITOR-IN-CHIEF
Nancy Jean Melin

ASSOCIATE EDITORIAL DIRECTOR
Thomas Schultheiss

MANAGING EDITOR
Linda Mark

EDITORIAL ASSISTANTS
Karen Bell
Susan Gooding
Jon Hertzig

ADVERTISING
Eileen Parker, *Advertising Manager*
Mary Beth Bimber, *Advertising Assistant*

PRODUCTION
Peggy Cabot, *Production Supervisor*
Bronwyn Beeler, *Production/Layout*
Rebecca McDermott, *Production Assistant*

DESIGN
Bronwyn Beeler
Eileen Parker

Library Hi Tech © Copyright 1984 by the Pierian Press, Inc. Published quarterly: Spring (published April); Summer (published July); Fall (published October); Winter (published January).
    Subscriptions are $39.50 per year; $36.00 per year for each additional subscription, same customer; Foreign subscriptions (including Canada and P.U.A.) are $46.50 per year. Single issues, $12.50; individuals may subscribe for $19.50 per year.* Combined subscriptions to Library Hi Tech Journal and Library Hi Tech News (11 issues per year) are $90.00 per year. Individuals may purchase a combined subscription for $54.00 per year.* Send all subscription orders, changes of address, and claims to Pierian Press, P.O. Box 1808, Ann Arbor, MI 48106: (313) 434-5530.
    *(Individual subscriptions must be paid by personal check or money order and deliverable to home address only.)
    LHT accepts advertising for products or services applicable to libraries/information centers or of interest to those involved with information management. LHT reserves the right to reject any advertisement which is deemed inappropriate to the advertising profile of the periodical or which, in view of the Editors, features misinformation, distortion of facts, or exaggerated claims. Direct advertising correspondence to Eileen Parker, P.O. Box 1808, Ann Arbor, MI 48106. Rates upon request. (313) 434-6409.
    Reader letters and queries may be forwarded directly to the Editor at 42 Grandview, Mt. Kisco, NY 10549, or call 914/666-4099. Editorial specialists are identified at the back of the journal and should be consulted for matters relating to potential and submitted manuscripts as appropriate.
    Library Hi Tech is unique as a current guide to all available and forthcoming technologies applicable to libraries and information centers; as a single source reviewing related literature in periodicals, books, reports, studies and conference proceedings; as a major journal of practical articles related to all available and forthcoming technologies. LHT evaluates, describes, and reports on the selection, installation, maintenance, and integration of systems and hardware. Library Hi Tech is indexed in *Current Index to Journals in Education.*

Figure 14.13

publisher and distributor (or other entity) are named. Occasionally, the place, name, and year of the material's manufacture is given when publication and distribution information is not readily available or in addition to it.

No matter how many entities are named, three pieces of information are given for each: the city in which it is located, its name, and the year it issued the material (see

Figure 14.14). This information is to be given as succinctly as possible, provided it identifies the entity uniquely. (Level 1 records only require information about the first-named publisher.)

Unpublished materials have no entities responsible for their issue, so no issuers' locations and names are given here. Unpublished objects made by people do have dates when they were created, and those dates are given here (see Figure 14.15). Area 4 is omitted entirely for naturally occurring objects that have not been packaged for commercial distribution, such as a shell or geode.

For published serials, the date on the first issue is given in area 4 but is left open by adding a hyphen and spaces following the year with the intention of filling in a closing date should the serial cease publication. When an issue after the first is used as the basis of cataloging, no date is given in area 4. (Level 1 records for serials require only the first publisher's name and date, with the date left open.)

If a publisher has several locations, the first-named city is always given, but, if another is listed more prominently, it also is given. If neither the first-named city nor a more prominently named city is located in the cataloger's home country, but a city in the home country is also listed, it, too, is given. In Figure 14.16, four places of publication are listed on the title page. The first of these—Melbourne—must be given in the catalog record. The second—Oakland—is given in a catalog record for U.S. libraries

```
This example is an illustration of:
     •  game
     •  general material designation
     •  subsidiary responsibility
     •  distributor
     •  publishing date not supplied; copyright date given
     •  other title information in note area
     •  accompanying material
     •  Library of Congress and Sears subject headings compared
     •  title added entry
     •  contradictory and incorrect information given by
        publisher
     •  2nd level cataloging


Hepburn, Rae.
   Tea leaf fortune cards [game] / Ray Hepburn ; illustrated by
Shawna Alexander. -- Boston : Journey Editions ; North Clarendon,
VT : Tuttle Publishing, distributor, c2000.
   200 cards ; col. ; 9 cm. in diameter in box 18 x 18 x 3 cm. + 1
manual (89 p. : ill. ; 17 cm.)

   Other title information on side of box: an innovative system.
   ISBN 1-885203-76-4.

Tracing with Library of Congress subject headings
   1. Fortune-telling by tea leaves.  2. Fortune-telling by cards.
I. Title.

Tracing with Sears subject headings
   1. Fortune telling.  I. Title.


Publication statement for Canadian libraries:
Boston : Journey Editions ; Vancouver : Raincoast Books
distributor, c2000.
```

Figure 14.14

Figure 14.14—*Continued*

(Information on Front of Box)

Information on back of box

Information on side of box

The box has been chosen as the chief source of information
because it holds all the parts. The manual's title page has
slightly different wording. The front of the box states the
manual has 72 pages, the back of the box 96 pages. There are
actually 89 pages.

because it is the first-named place in the home country, but Oakland is not given in a Canadian record.

Production of nonbook items is not synonymous with the publication of books. For films and videos, production means creation, and belongs in area 1. Nonbook items may be released instead of published. The releasing agent and/or distributor is named in area 4, and is equivalent to a book's publisher, as in the following examples:

[S.l.] : Dupuis Frères ; distributed in North America by Langlois, [200-?].

[Brisbane?] : Boolarong Publications in association with Queensland Aboriginal Creations, [19--]

If published material being cataloged does not list places or names of publishers or distributors, catalogers can substitute the abbreviations [S.l.] and [s.n.] in square brackets, meaning *sine loco* (without a place) and *sine nomine* (without a name) for the missing information. RDA eliminates these and other abbreviations, preferring to use words catalog users understand more easily.

The publication or distribution date—the third element of information included in this area—must always be given, with two exceptions: dates are not given to naturally

```
This example is an illustration of:
      •  a handmade item, maker unknown
      •  model
      •  title main entry with supplied title
      •  general material designation
      •  source of title note
      •  first subject heading from Canadian Subject Headings
      •  2nd level cataloging

[Newfoundland mummer] [model]. -- 2007.
  1 model : cotton, wool, and wood ; 24 cm. high, in box 26 x 17
x 10 cm.

  Title supplied by cataloger.

  1. Mummers -- Canada.  2. Newfoundland and Labrador -- Social
life and customs.
```

Figure 14.15

---

occurring objects and serials for which the date of the first issue is unknown. Various kinds of dates are found on materials, including publication (or distribution) dates, copyright dates, printing dates, production dates, manufacture dates, and more. The preferred date for area 4 is *publication* or *distribution,* not copyright, printing, production,

```
This example is an illustration of:
      •  multiple places of publication
      •  work containing only one type of illustration
      •  series statement
      •  contents note
      •  Library of Congress and Sears subject headings the same
      •  National Library of Australia CIP
      •  Dewey decimal classification
      •  2nd level cataloging
```

2nd level cataloging for a U.S. library

```
Kerr, Alex.
  Lost Japan / Alex Kerr. -- Melbourne, Victoria ; Oakland,
Calif. : Lonely Planet, 1996.
  269 p. : maps ; 20 cm. -- (Lonely Planet journeys)

  Glossary: p. 264-269.
  ISBN 0-86442-370-5.
```

2nd level cataloging for a Canadian library

```
Kerr, Alex.
  Lost Japan / Alex Kerr. -- Melbourne, Victoria : Lonely Planet,
1996.
  269 p. : maps ; 20 cm. -- (Lonely Planet journeys)

  Glossary: p. 264-269.
  ISBN 0-86442-370-5.
```

Tracing for both

```
  1. Japan -- Civilization, 1945-.  2. Japan -- Description and
travel.  I. Title.  II. Series.
```

Recommended DDC: 952.04
Recommended DDC: 952.04

Figure 14.16

Figure 14.16—*Continued*

CHIEF SOURCE OF INFORMATION
(Title Page)   (Information on Verso)

LOST JAPAN

ALEX KERR

Lost Japan

Published by Lonely Planet Publications
    Head Office: PO Box 617, Hawthorn, Vic 3122, Australia
    Branches: 155 Filbert St, Suite 251, Oakland, CA 94607, USA
                   10 Barley Mow Passage, Chiswick, London W4 4PH, UK
                   71 bis rue du Cardinal Lemoine, 75005 Paris, France

Published 1996

Printed by SNP Printing Pte Ltd, Singapore

Translated and adapted from *Utsukushiki Nippon no Zanzo* (Shincho-sha, Tokyo, 1993). © Alex Kerr 1993

Author photograph by Philip Gostelow
Map by Trudi Canavan
Calligraphy by Alex Kerr

LONELY PLANET PUBLICATIONS
Melbourne • Oakland • London • Paris

National Library of Australia Cataloguing in Publication Data

Kerr, Alex, 1952-
Lost Japan

ISBN 0 86442 370 5.

1. Kerr, Alex, 1952-
2. Japan – Civilization – 1945-
3. Japan – Description and travel.
I. Kerr, Alex, 1952 – Utsukushiki Nihon no zanzo
II. Title. III. Title: Utsukushiki Nihon no zanzo.

952.04

(Information on Cover)

Text © Alex Kerr 1996
Map © Lonely Planet 1996

or manufacture dates. If there are several dates, all publication or distribution dates, the one that matches the edition statement in area 2 should be chosen to give in area 4.

When no publication or distribution date appears on the item, the next best choice for area 4 is the copyright date. Nonbook materials may be copyrighted long before they are released, so some care should be exercised in selecting old copyright dates for new distributions, for example, a 1990s video production of a 1940s film. It is better to make an educated guess about when the video was released than to use a copyright date from the 1940s for a video that could not have been made or distributed during that decade. The guessed date may be given in one of the following ways, depending on the degree of certainty that it is correct:

[2009]—the year is not in doubt, but the source is not one of those prescribed
[2009?]—the year is in doubt; the cataloger guesses it is 2009
[200–]—the exact year is in doubt, but the cataloger knows it is in the 2000s
[200–?]—the exact year is in doubt; the cataloger guesses it is in the 2000s, but is not
    certain about it

    A copyright date is identified by a "c" or, in the case of some sound recordings, a "p" ("phonogram") immediately preceding the year. The copyright letter and year should be transcribed from the material. If copyright and publication dates differ, both may be given in this area, publication date first, or, the copyright date may be given in a note.

    In the absence of either a publication/distribution date or a copyright date, the date of manufacture may be given in area 4, but it must be identified as such (for example, "1959 printing"). When no dates appear on the item, the cataloger must guess, based on whatever information is available. The cataloger may look up the item in a reference work, consider the technology, or glean clues from the item itself. As shown earlier, AACR2-2005 suggests many ways to express an approximate date, depending on the cataloger's degree of certainty and the time span.[6]

    Figure 14.17 illustrates how research and common sense help approximate a date of publication for a book lacking dates of any kind on it. The preface is dated 1932 and the book's verso says it is a wartime book. To what war does it refer? World War II is a logical assumption. Reference sources reveal that C. H. Best, a well-known scientist who helped discover insulin, was active then. The book was printed in the United States, which entered the war in December 1941, making 1942–1945 the likely range of years in which it was published.

Area 5: Physical Description

    Physical description includes counting the number of physical pieces in which material being cataloged appears, called the *extent of item,* and naming the kind of pieces, called the *specific material designation* (smd). A physical description is not given to electronic resources accessed online unless the online version of the document has page numbers. RDA devotes its section 3 to describing carriers, that is, the physical aspects of the resource, as well as facsimiles, reproductions, and multicarrier resources.

    For some recordings, the duration of the material when played back or projected is given in parentheses after the smd, as shown in Figure 14.18. Other parts of the physical description include other physical details; dimensions; and accompanying materials, if there are any. Accompanying materials are added pieces of material physically separate from what is being cataloged, such as an optical disc issued as an adjunct to a textbook or a separate libretto tucked into the jewel case of an opera recording. Extent, physical details, and dimensions vary by physical form, but accompanying materials are treated the same way for all materials. (Level 1 records require giving only the extent.)

This example is an illustration of:
- joint responsibility
- other title information
- edition statement taken from outside prescribed sources (many libraries place such an edition statement in the note area, sometimes as a quoted note)
- estimated date of publication
- both black and white and colored illustrations
- source of edition note
- publication note
- index note
- Library of Congress and Sears subject headings the same
- Dewey Decimal and Library of Congress classifications
- 2nd level cataloging

```
Best, C.H.
   The human body and its functions : an elementary text-book of
physiology / by C.H. Best and N.B. Taylor. -- [Special ed.]. --
New York : H. Holt, [1942-1945]
   371 p. : ill. (some col.) ; 20 cm.

   Edition statement from spine.
   "A wartime book"--Pref. dated 1932.
   Includes index.

   1. Physiology.  2. Human anatomy.  I. Taylor, N.B.   II. Title.
```

Recommended DDC: 612
Recommended LCC: QP34.B47

CHIEF SOURCE OF INFORMATION
(Title Page)

(Information on Verso)

THE HUMAN BODY
AND ITS FUNCTIONS

AN ELEMENTARY TEXT-BOOK OF PHYSIOLOGY

BY

C. H. BEST, M.A., M.D., D.Sc. (Lond.), F.R.S. (Canada),
F.R.C.P. (Canada)
Professor of Physiology and Director of the Department, Associate
Director of the Connaught Laboratories, Research Associate
in the Banting-Best Department of Medical Research,
University of Toronto

AND

N. B. TAYLOR, M.D., M.R.C.S. (Eng.), L.R.C.P. (Lond.),
F.R.C.S. (Edin.), F.R.C.P. (Canada)
Professor of Physiology, University of Toronto

NEW YORK
HENRY HOLT AND COMPANY

(Information on Spine)

Title Proper

Author's Surnames

Special Edition

A WARTIME BOOK

THIS COMPLETE EDITION IS PRODUCTS IN
FULL COMPLIANCE WITH THE GOVERN-
MENT'S REGULATIONS FOR CONSERVING
PAPER AND OTHER ESSENTIAL MATERIALS

PRINTED IN THE
UNITED STATES OF AMERICA

Figure 14.17

The smd is the "carrier" of the intellectual or artistic content of something that is cataloged. Carriers come in many forms, the most familiar of which are books. Because books have long appeared solely as printed codexes (that is, pages protected by covers), the codex is rarely thought of as a carrier, but if libraries collected texts on papyrus scrolls and cuneiform blocks, the idea of the codex as a text carrier would be clear.

For books, extent is given as the number of pages, leaves (pages with text on only one side), or volumes. The general rule is to give the last numbered page (or leaf) as the total; or, if a book consists of several sequences of numbers, the last numbered page in each sequence. Plates in a book are a special case. By definition, plates are separate pages bound in with a text after it is prepared. They are considered a separate part of the extent and are counted and listed after the regular pagination, shown in Figure 14.3 on page 270.

Electronic resources contained in or on physical carriers, sound recordings, and videorecordings are described in terms of the number of discs, cartridges, cassettes,

```
This example is an illustration of:
    • videorecording
    • collective title
    • title main entry
    • item emanating from a corporate body
    • general material designation
    • place of publication not stated but known
    • probable publication date
    • accompanying material
    • cast note
    • edition and history notes
    • contents note
    • personal name added entries
    • corporate body added entry
    • name/title added entries
    • additional title added entries
    • 2nd level cataloging
```

```
The casebook of Sherlock Holmes [videorecording] / Granada
    Television. -- [Orland Park, Ill.] : MPI Home Video, [2004?].
    3 videodiscs (ca. 6 hr., 30 min.) : sd., b&w ; 4 3/4 in. + 1
descriptive pamphlet.

    Cast: Jeremy Brett (Sherlock Holmes); Edward Hardwick (Dr.
Watson).
    Originally broadcast on television in 1991.
    Based on the novels by Sir Arthur Conan Doyle.
    Contents: disc 1. The disappearance of Lady Frances Carfax. The
problem of Thor bridge. Commentary track with director John
Madden -- disc 2. Shoscombe old place. The Boscombe Valley
mystery -- disc 3. The illustrious client. The creeping man.
Daytime live : an interview with Jeremy Brett and Edward
Hardwicke. Sherlock Museum short. Production notes.

    I. Brett, Jeremy. II. Hardwicke, Edward. III. Madden, John.
IV. Granada Television. V. MPI Home Video. VI. Doyle, Arthur
Conan, Sir. The disappearance of Lady Frances Carfax. VII.
Doyle, Arthur Conan, Sir. The problem of Thor bridge. VIII.
Doyle, Arthur Conan, Sir. Shoscombe old place. IX. Doyle, Arthur
Conan, Sir. The Boscombe Valley mystery. X. Doyle, Arthur Conan,
Sir. The illustrious client. XI. Doyle, Arthur Conan, Sir. The
creeping man. XII. Title: The disappearance of Lady Frances
Carfax. XIII. Title: The problem of Thor bridge. XIV. Title:
Shoscombe old place. XV. Title: The Boscombe Valley mystery.
XVI. Title: The illustrious client. XVII. Title: The creeping
man.
```

Figure 14.18

Figure 14.18—*Continued*

The title screen has no additional information from that found on the disk.

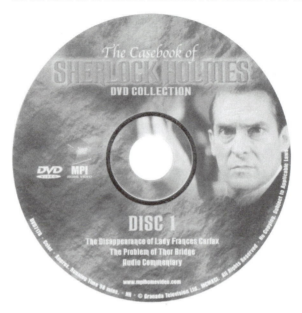

(Information on Container Liner)

reels, or other carrier types. Motion pictures are usually described in terms of the number of reels, although carriers other than reels are occasionally encountered. Microforms, like motion pictures, may be described as reels of film, but they can also be fiches and other microformats. It is not always possible to anticipate development of new physical formats, so rules in several chapters of AACR2-2005 allow catalogers to create appropriate smds whenever necessary.

Other physical details vary by physical format. For books, the most obvious added detail is illustrations. The abbreviation "ill." is given whenever photographs, drawings, or other visual images appear in printed materials and their reproductions. Tables, illustrated title pages, and minor illustrations are not considered "ill." Optionally, specific types of illustrations such as maps, diagrams, genealogies, and so on, can be named in addition to "ill."[7] This option has been adopted for the figures and examples in this book.

Typical physical descriptions for selected formats of materials covered by AACR2-2005 are listed in Figure 14.19. Notice that magnetic disks (the computer floppy disk) are spelled with a "k," whereas optical discs are spelled with a "c."

Area 6: Series

AACR2-2005 defines a series as a group of separate items that contain both individual titles for each item and a common or collective title applying to the group as a whole.[8] If an item belongs to a series, the name of the series is given in this area. (Level 1 records omit the area entirely.) The main title (or, title proper) of a series is transcribed exactly as it appears on the item, even if the cataloger intends to make a heading for the series that differs from the transcription. In addition, if the item being cataloged has a number within the series, it is recorded. If it is important for identification, a statement of responsibility associated with a series may be given. Otherwise, statements of responsibility are omitted. When an International Standard Serial Number (ISSN) for the series is on the item, it is included also (see Figure 14.20). Some items regularly bear both ISBNs and ISSNs, so catalogers can treat them either as serials or monographs.

```
1 videodisc (95 min.) : sd., b&w ; 4 ¾ in.

2 computer disks : col. ; 3 ½ in.

1 CD-ROM : col. ; 4 ¾ in.

1 model (4 pieces) : green and yellow ; 10 x 8 x 4 cm., in box 11
x 9 x 5 cm.

3 microfiches : col. ill., maps

1 flip chart (10 sheets) : double sided, b&w ; 24 x 20 cm.

1 sound disc : digital, stereo. ; 4 ¾ in.
```

Figure 14.19

Area 7: Notes

Notes generally are optional at all bibliographic levels, although there are some important exceptions. These exceptions are clearly stated in rules for other areas of description that instruct catalogers to make specific notes, for example, giving the source of the title proper if it does not come from the chief source. "Title supplied by cataloger" and "Title from cover" explain many bracketed titles proper. For electronic resources, notes explaining the source of the title proper and the system requirements are mandated at all levels.

The rules of AACR2-2005 prescribe the order in which notes should appear. They follow the order of descriptive elements, with notes relating to titles given before notes relating to editions, notes relating to editions before notes relating to publication, distribution, and so on. AACR2-2005 makes it possible for an important note to be put first, out of the usual order. Such changes must be approved by the Joint Steering Committee to become part of AACR2; for example, the frequency of continuing resources is given as the first note. Sometimes, catalogers in an individual nation change the order of notes to conform to policies and practices of its national library.

Two kinds of notes can be made: formal or informal. Informal notes are brief sentences, such as "Title from cover" or "Includes index." Formal notes are formatted in a particular way beginning with an introductory word such as "Summary" or "Contents" followed by a colon and the data, sometimes in a prescribed style (see the Contents note in Figure 14.18). Notes may be combined if it seems appropriate. Among the most familiar combined notes are the bibliography and index notes for books, which use the following standard language: *Includes bibliographical references and index.* Examples

```
This example is an illustration of:
    • other title information
    • detailed pagination
    • descriptive illustration statement
    • numbered series statement with statement of responsibility
    • ISSN for series
    • bibliography and index note
    • Library of Congress subject headings
    • title added entry
    • corporate body added entry
    • series added entry different from series statement
    • National Library of Australia CIP
    • 2nd level cataloging


Price, Helen.
   Stopping the rot : a handbook of preventative conservation for
local studies collections / Helen Price. -- Sydney : Library
Association of Australia, New South Wales Branch, 1988.
   vii, 48 p. : ill., forms ; 29 cm. -- (Occasional paper /
Library Association of Australia, New South Wales Branch, ISSN
0155-5472 ; no. 10)

   Includes bibliography and index.
   ISBN 0 86804 067 3.

   1. Library materials -- Conservation and restoration.
2. Libraries -- Special collections -- Local history.  3. Local
history -- Bibliography -- Methodology.  4. Australia -- History,
Local -- Bibliography -- Methodology.  I. Title.  II. Series:
Occasional paper (Library Association of Australia, New South
Wales Branch) ; no. 10.
```

Figure 14.20

Figure 14.20—*Continued*

Stopping the rot:

a handbook of
preventive conservation
for local studies
collections

Helen Price

Occasional Paper No. 10
Library Association of Australia
New South Wales Branch
Sydney 1988

(Information on Verso)

Published by the Library Association of Australia
New South Wales Branch

National Library of Australia

Cataloguing-in-publication data

ISSN   0155 - 5472.

Price, Patricia Helen, 1931-
Stopping the rot : a handbook of preventive
conservation for local studies collections.

Bibliography.
Includes index.
ISBN   0   86804   067   3.

1.   Library materials - Conservation and
restoration.   2.   Libraries - Special collections
- Local history.   I.   Library Association of
Australia. New South Wales Branch.   II.   Title.
(Series : Occasional paper Library Association
of Australia. New South Wales Branch; no. 10).

Printed by the University of Sydney Printing Service on 85gsm
Challenge Hi-bulk paper produced by APM using an alkaline process.

of notes are included in many places in this book. To find a particular one, readers should consult the index to figures and examples.

Notes that are particularly important to make include the following:

1. *Source of the title proper:* If the preferred chief source for bibliographic information is not available, whatever alternative to it that is chosen to serve as chief source is noted. This note is mandated for all electronic resources, even when the preferred chief source is used, and in some instances it is also used for other types of materials.

2. *Physical description:* Books and other formats can benefit from the added information this note provides, for example, informing searchers a book is chiefly photographs, describing the shape of an object, or the colors of a multicolored visual image.

3. *System requirements:* For videorecordings, this is the place to include information about needed hardware. Two different kinds of system requirements notes are mandated for electronic resources. Resources physically

held in a library are given a systems requirements note. Electronic resources accessed from remote sources, which have no physical existence in local libraries, are given a note that describes how users gain access to them, called a "mode of access" note. This note includes the material's electronic address or Uniform Resource Locator (URL), and the date the item was viewed for cataloging purposes should be added as the final note in the catalog record.

4. *Contents notes:* These notes should be made when an item contains more than one work, such as a book containing two or more novels or a sound recording containing two or more symphonies. This enables catalogers to make added entries for the analytic title for the individual works. Limits on the number of titles to include in a contents note are hard to set. Between the extremes of very few and too many, catalogers must use judgment. The decision should rest on an estimate of how often people want only one of the works, not the whole collection, and whether they can find it another way.

5. *Summaries:* Summaries should always be made for materials unavailable for browsing or that have very little eye-readable information to help a browser decide if they are what he wants, unless the rest of the catalog record describes them clearly. In recent years, increasing numbers of searchers must rely on catalog records to decide if an item is what they want, so summary notes have gained greater importance, even for materials that can be browsed on-site. For many years, the Library of Congress has given summary notes in bibliographic records for children's materials (see chapter 17.)

6. *Details of the library's copy:* This is the place in the catalog record to note torn pages, autographs, unique features, or other details present only in the cataloging library's copy of a material.

7. *Numbers on the item:* Numbers *other than* the ISBN or ISSN that appear on an item, such as Library of Congress Control Numbers or Universal Product Code numbers are given in this note. (ISBNs and ISSNs are given in area 8, see the next section.)

Special notes for continuing resources include the frequency of issue, which AACR2-2005 mandates is given as the first note. Another note gives details of the relationships of the title being cataloged with other titles, such as earlier and later titles, mergers and splits, absorptions, supplements, and so forth.

Area 8: Standard Numbers and Terms of Availability

The eighth and last area of description is optional and is used for a material's standard number, defined solely as the ISBN (for monographs) or ISSN (for serially issued continuing resources). Numbers other than ISBN or ISSN are given in area 7 (see the previous section). Area 8 is also the place to give the purchase price, rental fee, or other terms of availability for material. If no standard number appears on the material being cataloged, area 8 is left blank or only terms of availability are recorded, if desired.

Terms of availability is frequently interpreted as the retail price printed on materials. In practice, however, libraries rarely pay the retail price and prices change over time. In recent years, replacements often cost more than the original material; thus, prices in a catalog record have dubious accuracy. Local policy may be to omit this information even if it is readily available.

For serially issued continuing resources, the key-title, an identifier of the International Serials Data System (ISDS), is entered here. ISDS is an international program of serials identification similar to ISSN sponsored by the United Nations Education, Scientific, and Cultural Organization (UNESCO); ISSN is sponsored by IFLA.

Data describing book bindings and paper, if the paper was treated to reduce acidity, may be added in parentheses following the number; for example, ISBN 0-8389-7809-6 (pbk.) or ISBN 0-8389-0624-9 (alk. paper).

RULE INTERPRETATIONS

National cataloging agencies that implement AACR's rules—generally national libraries—interpret the rules and make decisions on its options that become standard for their countries, because catalogers in local libraries look to them for direction. In the United States, that agency is LC; in Canada, it is LAC. Their rule interpretations and decisions are issued as policy directives called rule interpretations or "RIs" for their catalogers. RIs are made available to outside agencies through online announcements and publications such as LC's *Cataloging Service Bulletin, Cataloger's Desktop,* and the LAC Web site (http://www.collectionscanada.gc.ca/6/18/s18-204-e.html). Rule interpretations are not as authoritative as the rules themselves, but they carry the weight of the largest and most important originators of catalog records in their countries. More importantly, national bibliographic networks conform to them and ask their members to do so, making them standard practice.

SUMMARY

Building a bibliographic description is not as easy a task as it seems at first glance, because publishers of library materials are extremely inventive when it comes to identifying their products. The proliferation of sophisticated material formats and information-delivery systems complicates how catalogers find and prepare bibliographic information completely enough that one material is not mistaken for another. AACR, incorporating the ISBD standard sponsored by IFLA, asks catalogers to seek information for catalog records from the same sources, divide it into the same eight areas of description, and arrange and present the information in the same order. In this way, bibliographic data is understood and can be used or shared around the world. RDA makes some changes in these processes, but includes the same elements in approximately the same order, elaborating on some and applying relaxed application of others. The result is very similar bibliographic descriptions for the resources being cataloged.

In cataloging, all materials have prescribed sources of information, one of which is designated the chief source. Catalog records for all materials begin with title statements (descriptive area 1) and then provide edition data (descriptive area 2), if applicable. Following the edition data, a few material formats add data specific to their type (descriptive area 3). All the other material formats follow edition data with information about publication and distribution (descriptive area 4). Each material format has its own set of rules for describing the physical form of the material (descriptive area 5). One format that lacks physical attributes—remote electronic resources—omits the description of physical form, describing instead in notes (descriptive area 7) how one gains access to the materials. Following the physical description, information about series to which materials belong is given (descriptive area 6), followed by notes that explain features of materials that have not yet been adequately described (descriptive area 7). Finally, ISBNs or ISSNs of materials are given, along with their terms of availability (descriptive area 8).

The next step in the cataloging process is to select headings that can be used as search terms for retrieving specific materials from the catalog. Because the headings are also known as access points, the process of selecting and formulating them is called "access." It is covered in the next chapter.

REVIEW QUESTIONS

1. How long have catalogers from the United States, Canada, and the United Kingdom cooperated in issuing rules for bibliographic description, and has their cooperation ever been interrupted?

2. What international standard is incorporated into the *Anglo-American Cataloguing Rules,* second edition (AACR2), and what does it prescribe?

3. Which areas of description are transcribed and which are constructed according to rules in AACR2?

4. Name three notes that are important to give in a catalog record and explain the importance of each one.

5. In what instance(s) may a date be omitted from a bibliographic record?

6. What data about a series is essential to include in a catalog record?

7. What should a cataloger do when desired information is not on the material being cataloged?

NOTES

1.   *Anglo-American Cataloguing Rules,* 2nd ed., 2002 revision, 2005 update. Prepared under the direction of the Joint Steering Committee for Revision of AACR. Chicago: American Library Association, 2005.

2.   *Cataloger's Desktop* (Washington, D.C.: Library of Congress, Cataloging Distribution Service), http://desktop.loc.gov/.

3.   For a brief report on the conference and the principles, see *Reader in Classification and Descriptive Cataloging,* edited by Ann F. Painter (Washington, D.C.: NCR-Microcard Editions, 1972).

4.   Jean Weihs, ed. *The Principles and Future of AACR: Proceedings of the International Conference on the Principles and Future of AACR, Toronto, Ontario, Canada, October 23–25, 1997* (Ottawa: Canadian Library Association, 1998).

5.   *RDA Toolkit* (Chicago: American Library Association, 2008), http://www.rdatoolkit.org/.

6.   AACR2-2005, rule 3.3B1, 3–11.

7.   AACR2-2005 names nine types of illustrations in rule 2.5C2.

8.   AACR2-2005, Appendix D-7.

SUGGESTED READING

AACR

"The Anglo-American Cataloguing Rules." *National Library of Canada Bulletin* 2, nos. 7/8 (July/Aug. 2000): 11–12.

IFLA Study Group on the Functional Requirements for Bibliographic Records. *Functional Requirements for Bibliographic Records: Final Report.* Munich, Germany: K.G. Saur, 1998.

Maxwell, Robert L. *Maxwell's Handbook for AACR2, Explaining and Illustrating the Anglo-American Cataloguing Rules through the 2003 Update.* Chicago, IL: American Library Association, 2004.

Schottlaender, Brian E.C., ed. *The Future of the Descriptive Cataloging Rules.* Chicago, IL: American Library Association, 1998.

Weihs, Jean. "Interfaces: Will the Toronto Tenets Replace the Paris Principles?" *Technicalities* 17, no. 5 (May 1997): 1, 6–7.

Weihs, Jean, ed. *The Principles and Future of AACR: Proceedings of the International Conference on the Principles and Future Development of AACR, Toronto, Canada, October 23–25, 1997.* Chicago, IL: American Library Association, 1998.

RDA

IFLA Study Group on the Functional Requirements for Bibliographic Records. *Functional Requirements for Bibliographic Records: Final Report.* Munich: Saur, 1998. http://www.ifla.org/en/publications/functional-requirements-for-bibliographic-records.

Joint Steering Committee for Development of RDA. "RDA FAQ." http://www.rda-jsc.org/rda faq.html.

Maxwell, Robert L. *FRBR: A Guide for the Perplexed.* Chicago: American Library Association, 2008.

Oliver, Chris. *Introducing RDA: A Guide to the Basics.* Chicago: American Library Association, 2010.

Taylor, Arlene G. *Understanding FRBR: What It Is and How It Will Affect Our Retrieval Tools.* Westport, CT: Libraries Unlimited, 2007.

Tillett, Barbara. *What Is FRBR? A Conceptual Model for the Bibliographic Universe.* Washington, DC: Cataloging Distribution Service, Library of Congress, 2004. http://www.loc.gov/cds/downloads/FRBR.PDF.

Bibliographic Description

Association for Library Collections & Technical Services, Committee on Cataloging: Description and Access. *Guidelines for Bibliographic Description of Reproductions.* Chicago, IL: American Library Association, 1995.

CONSER Cataloging Manual, 2005 Revision. Washington, D.C.: Library of Congress, Cataloging Distribution Service, 2005–

Ferguson, Bobby. *Blitz Cataloging Workbooks.* Englewood, CO: Libraries Unlimited, 1999–2000. (See volumes on nonbook materials and AACR2/MARC.)

Genereux, Cecilia, and Paul D. Moeller, eds. *Notes for Serials Cataloging,* 3rd ed. Santa Barbara, CA: ABC-CLIO/Libraries Unlimited, 2009.

Hartsock, Ralph. *Notes for Music Catalogers: Examples Illustrating AACR 2 in the Online Bibliographic Record.* Lake Crystal, MN: Soldier Creek Press, 1994.

Intner, Sheila S., Joanna F. Fountain, and Jean Weihs, eds. *Cataloging Correctly for Kids.* 5th ed. Chicago, IL: American Library Association, 2010.

Mangan, Elizabeth, ed. *Cartographic Materials: A Manual of Interpretation for AACR2, 2002 Revision.* 2nd ed. Chicago: American Library Association, 2003.

Olson, Nancy B., with the assistance of Robert L. Bothmann and Jessica J. Schomberg. *Cataloging of Audiovisual Materials and Other Special Materials.* 5th ed. Westport, CT: Libraries Unlimited, 2008.

Smiraglia, Richard P. *Describing Music Materials.* 3rd ed. Lake Crystal, MN: Soldier Creek Press, 1997.

Source of Title Note for Internet Resources. 3rd revision. Created by the Subcommittee on the Source of Title Note for Internet Resources, Cataloging Policy Committee, Online Audiovisual Catalogers. Buffalo, NY: OLAC CAPC, 2005. www.olacinc.org/drupal/?q+node/20.

Visual Resources Association. *Cataloging Cultural Objects: A Guide to Describing Cultural Works and Their Images.* Chicago, IL: American Library Association, 2007.

Weitz, Jay. *Cataloger's Judgment: Music Cataloging Questions and Answers from the Music OCLC Users Group Newsletter.* Westport, CT: Libraries Unlimited, 2004.

Welsh, Anne, and Sue Batley. *Practical Cataloging: AACR, RDA, and MARC21.* New York: Neal-Schuman, 2010.

Yee, Martha M. *Moving Image Cataloging: How to Create and How to Use a Moving Image Catalog.* Westport, CT: Libraries Unlimited, 2007.

Chapter

15

Access Points—
Retrieving the Record

A name, term, code, etc., under which a bibliographic record may be searched and identified.

—Anglo-American Cataloguing Rules, *2nd ed.,*
2002 revision, 2005 update

Creating headings for the description is the next step in the cataloging process. Rules for headings appear in Part II of the *Anglo-American Cataloguing Rules,* second edition, 2002 revision, 2005 update (AACR2-2005). (RDA's section 5 covers this aspect of cataloging.) Catalogers refer to headings by a variety of terms, among them *access points, entries, headings, search terms,* and *authorities.* Because AACR2-2005 prefers the term *access point,* it is used in this chapter. The chapter covers only *descriptive* access points—names of parties responsible for the materials and titles by which materials are known or to which they are related. Access points related to the subject content of materials are not included here. They are discussed in chapters 16–18.

Following AACR2-2005's chapter 20, which introduces Part II, Chapter 21 provides rules that instruct the cataloger how to select elements from the description for access points. When searched in the catalog, inputting the chosen names, titles, or combined names and titles retrieves the record. Chapters 22 through 25 provide rules for putting the chosen headings into proper form. Chapter 22 explains how to construct headings for personal names; chapter 23 for geographic names; chapter 24 for entities made up of named groups of people acting together, known as *corporate bodies*[1] and chapter 25 for conventional titles assigned to works called *uniform titles.* (Dates and control numbers are not mentioned as access points in AACR2, because searching under such numeric elements as well as physical formats is a feature enabled by computers, not a result of applying the rules.)

The final chapter, chapter 26, describes references that help catalog users find material even if they use search terms other than the ones AACR2-2005 prefers. These include *see, see also, name-title,* and *explanatory* references, and how to make them for names of persons, places, corporate bodies, and uniform titles. The chapter also discusses references to added entries (secondary access points) for series and serials and the use of references in place of added entries.

MAIN AND ADDED ENTRIES

Descriptive access points are divided into two kinds: *main entries* and *added entries.* The difference between them is that the first and most important access point chosen is designated the "main" entry; all others are added entries. There are at least two reasons for designating main and added entries. Some libraries maintain single-entry, staff-access-only, official catalogs that are more efficient to search than their multiple-entry public catalogs. The single-entry catalogs are usually main-entry listings. Second, shelf marks—the additions to classification numbers that form call numbers—are derived from main entries. Without them, new rules for creating shelf marks would be needed.

In the Anglo-American cataloging tradition, creators are generally considered the primary identifying features of their works; thus, the rules of AACR2-2005 usually, although not always, instruct catalogers to make creators the main entries of materials being cataloged. Titles are an alternative choice for main entries. Only one creator or one title can be a main entry, however. There are no "joint" main entries. If an item being cataloged has two coequal creators, one is chosen as main entry and the other is automatically an added entry. Similarly, if material bears more than one title (e.g., parallel titles, subtitles, abbreviated titles), and catalogers determine it should have a title main entry, only one is chosen as main entry. The other title can be an added entry.

Authorship (that is, creation) of materials is considered the most important starting point for access. In the distant past, it was assumed that only people could create content and be considered authors, but in modern times, it is not unusual for groups of people working together to produce content. Are these groups equivalent to people? Earlier cataloging rules said yes to this question, provided the groups were named in the materials they created. Such groups are called *corporate bodies.* Corporate bodies for cataloging purposes should not be confused with the legal entities called corporations, although corporations are also considered corporate bodies. As long as a group of people work together and have a name, they qualify as a corporate body.

When a corporate body causes materials to be created, the materials are said to "emanate" from it, even if individuals actually do the writing, composing, programming, compiling, painting, or whatever creative activities are involved in producing the materials. A debate arose in cataloging circles over whether corporate bodies were the same as personal authors. The matter has been decided in different ways over time; however, AACR2, in all its versions, limits the authorship role of corporate bodies, considering them equal to individuals in the creation of only a few types of materials.

Determination of the main entry for material being cataloged is usually a matter of identifying the creator, if there is only one, or the principal creator, if there is more than one. When no such creator is found, the title is the fallback choice for the main entry.

SELECTING THE MAIN ENTRY

The first step in selecting a main entry is to eliminate the possibility that material can be assigned a corporate-body main entry. The cataloger must ask if material emanates from a corporate body and, if so, if it is one of the types of content given a corporate-body main entry. Items emanating from corporate bodies do not automatically get corporate-body main entries. First, the corporate body must be named the "author" on the chief source of information (see Figure 15.1). Second, rule 21.1B2[2] limits assignment of corporate body main entry to six specific types of documents:

- Documents of an administrative nature dealing with the corporate body itself, such as the catalog of a library or an information center, or the membership directory of an association.
- Specified kinds of legal, governmental, and religious documents, primarily laws, court rules, regulations, treaties, and similar materials.
- Documents that represent the collective thought of the body, such as the minutes of meetings, reports of a committee, annual reports, and so on.
- Material representing the collective effort of a voyage, expedition, or a conference meeting the definition of a corporate body when the event is named in the item. Events that have no official names are not defined as corporate bodies.

```
This example is an illustration of:
      • named conference
      • entry under corporate body
      • two other title information statements
      • joint editors
      • publication date not listed, copyright date given
      • edition and history as a quoted note
      • bibliography and index note
      • International Standard Book Number (ISBN) qualified
      • Library of Congress subject headings
      • added entries for editors
      • additional title added entry
      • Library of Congress CIP
      • 2nd level cataloging


North American Serials Interest Group. Conference (17th : 2002 :
    College of William and Mary)
   Transforming serials : the revolution continues : proceedings
of the North American Serials Interest Group, Inc. 17th Annual
Conference, June 20-23, 2002, the College of William and Mary,
Williamsburg, Virginia / Susan L. Scheiberg, Shelley Neville,
editors. -- New York : Haworth, c2003.
   365 p. ; 21 cm.

   "Co-published simultaneously as The serials librarian, v. 44,
nos. 1/2 and 3/4 (2003)".
   Includes bibliographical references and index.
   ISBN 0-7890-2282-6 (pbk. : alk paper).

   1. Serials librarianship -- Congresses.  2. Libraries --
Special collections -- Electronic journals -- Congresses.  3.
Electronic journals -- Congresses.  I. Scheiberg, Susan.  II.
Neville, Shelley.  III. Serials librarian.  IV. Title.
```

Figure 15.1

Figure 15.1—*Continued*

CHIEF SOURCE OF INFORMATION
(Title Page)   (Information on Verso)

TRANSFORMING SERIALS:
THE REVOLUTION CONTINUES

Proceedings of the
NORTH AMERICAN SERIALS
INTEREST GROUP, Inc.

17th Annual Conference
June 20-23, 2002
The College of William and Mary
Williamsburg, Virginia

Susan L. Scheiberg
Shelley Neville
Editors

The Haworth Information Press
An Imprint of
The Haworth Press, Inc.
New York • London • Oxford

Transforming Serials: The Revolution Continues has been co-published simultaneously as *The Serials Librarian*, Volume 44, Numbers 1/2 and 3/4 2003.

The development, preparation, and publication of this work has been undertaken with great care. However, the publisher, employees, editors, and agents of The Haworth Press and all imprints of The Haworth Press, Inc., including The Haworth Medical Press® and Pharmaceutical Products Press®, are not responsible for any errors contained herein or for consequences that may ensue from use of materials or information contained in this work. Opinions expressed by the author(s) are not necessarily those of The Haworth Press, Inc.

Cover design by Thomas J. Mayshock Jr.

Library of Congress Cataloging-in-Publication Data

North American Serials Interest Group. Conference (17th : 2002 : College of William and Mary)
     Transforming serials : the revolution continues : proceedings of the North American Serials Interest Group, Inc. 17th Annual Conference, June 20-23, 2002, the College of William and Mary, Williamsburg, Virginia / Susan L. Scheiberg, Shelley Neville, editors.
        p. cm.
"Co-published simultaneously as The serials librarian, v. 44, nos. 1/2 and 3/4 2003."
Includes bibliographical references and index.
     ISBN 0-7890-2281-8 (alk. paper) – ISBN 0-7890-2282-6 (pbk : alk. paper)
1. Serials librarianship–Congresses. 2. Libraries–Special collections–Electronic journals–Congresses. 3. Electronic journals–Congresses. I. Scheiberg, Susan L. II. Neville, Shelley. III. Serials librarian. IV. Title.
     Z692.S5N67 2002
     025.17'32–dc21   2003005542

- Sound recordings, films, or videos for which the responsible corporate body does more than just perform. Catalogers must judge when a performing group does something that qualifies as *more than mere performance,* that is, something qualifying as *creation.* The cataloger asks to what extent new content—such as music, words, movement—is present, something that is typical of improvisation. In classical music, improvisation is unusual; in popular or jazz music, the opposite is true. Thus, popular performing groups often earn main entries. The same is true with some videos and films. This rule applies to performers who act together as a group and have a name, such as the rock group Abba. It does not apply to individuals who happen to be on the same program for a recording date or a concert.
- A cartographic representation where the corporate body is responsible for more than publication. The National Geographic Society is an example. It sponsors expeditions to explore the territories it maps, hires and directs cartographers, and performs other functions as well. Therefore, the society is often chosen as main entry for the maps it publishes.

If an item emanates from a corporate body but does not fit into any of these categories, it is ineligible and is not given a corporate body main entry. Instead, either a personal creator or a title is selected as main entry, depending on what appears on the chief source of information.

According to AACR2-2005, once the possibility of corporate body main entry has been ruled out, the cataloger should name as the main entry "the personal author, the principal personal author, or the probable personal author."[3] Figures 15.2 and 15.3 illustrate instances when a personal author is chosen as the main entry.

The final option, title main entry, is applied when there is no known creator; when there are more than three creators sharing equal amounts of the same responsibility for the item, if their contributions are the same; when the item emanates from a corporate body but is not eligible for corporate body main entry and has no personal author; or when the material is a work is produced under editorial direction. Figures 15.4 through 15.6 illustrate materials given title main entries.

SELECTION DECISION TREE

The following questions and caveats form a useful decision tree for determining the main entry:

1. Does the item emanate from a corporate body? Yes? Go to question 2. No? Proceed to question 8. (If in doubt, assume that the answer is no and proceed to question 8.)
2. Is the item an administrative work dealing with the body itself? Yes? Assign a corporate body main entry. (If more than one corporate body is

```
This example is an illustration of:
     • single author
     • other title information
     • edition statement
     • bibliography and index note
     • Library of Congress subject headings
     • title added entry
     • 2nd level cataloging


Weinberger, David.
   Everything is miscellaneous : the power of the new digital
disorder / David Weinberger. -- 1st ed. -- New York : Times
Books, 2007.
   277 p. ; 24 cm.

   Includes bibliographical references and index.
   ISBN-13: 978-0-14-303825-2. -- ISBN-10: 0-8050-8043-0.

   1. Knowledge management.  2. Information technology --
Management.  3. Information technology -- Social aspects.
4. Personal information management.  5. Information resources
management.  6. Order.  I. Title.
```

Figure 15.2

Figure 15.2—*Continued*

CHIEF SOURCE OF INFORMATION
(Title Page)

(Information on Verso)

EVERYTHING IS MISCELLANEOUS

THE POWER OF THE NEW DIGITAL DISORDER

DAVID WEINBERGER

TIMES BOOKS
HENRY HOLT AND COMPANY ■ NEW YORK

Times Books
Henry Holt and Company, LLC
Publishers since 1866
175 Fifth Avenue
New York, New York 10010
www.henryholt.com

Henry Holt® is a registered trademark of
Henry Holt and Company, LLC.

Copyright © 2007 by David Weinberger
All rights reserved.
Distributed in Canada by H. B. Fenn and Company Ltd.

Library of Congress Cataloging-in-Publication Data is available.
ISBN-13: 978-0-8050-8043-8
ISBN-10: 0-8050-8043-0

Henry Holt books are available for special promotions and
premiums. For details contact: Director, Special Markets.

First Edition 2007

Designed by Kelly S. Too

Printed in the United States of America
1   3   5   7   9   10   8   6   4   2

involved, follow the rules for multiple personal authors in caveat 2.) No?
Go to question 3.

3. Is the item one of the designated types of works in rule 21.1B2b? Yes?
    Assign a corporate body main entry. (If more than one corporate body is
    involved, follow the rules for multiple personal authors in caveat 2.) No?
    Go to question 4.

4. Does the item record the collective thought of the body? Yes? Assign a
    corporate body main entry. (If more than one corporate body is involved,
    follow the rules for multiple personal authors in caveat 2.) No? Go to
    question 5.

5. Does the item record the collective activity of an event? Yes? Assign a
    corporate body main entry. (If more than one corporate body is involved,
    follow the rules for multiple personal authors in caveat 2.) No? Go to
    question 6.

6. Does the item result from the collective activity of a performing group
    as a whole that goes beyond mere performance? Yes? Assign a corporate
    body main entry. (If more than one corporate body is involved in the per-
    forming group, follow the rules for multiple personal authors in caveat 2.)
    No? Go to question 7.

This example is an illustration of:
- three authors
- main entry given to first named author
- bibliographic form of author's name from CIP data
- two places of publication
- publication date not listed, copyright date given
- detailed pagination
- bibliography and index note
- Library of Congress subject headings (note contrast with subject headings in British Library CIP)
- personal name added entries
- title added entry
- Dewey Decimal Classification (DDC)
- different bibliographic records in Library of Congress and British Library CIPs
- 2nd level cataloging

```
Matthews, Graham, 1953-
   Disaster management in archives, libraries and museums / Graham
Matthews, Yvonne Smith, Gemma Knowles. -- Farnham, England ;
Burlington VT : Ashgate Publishing, c2009.
   xv, 229 p. ; 24 cm.

   Includes bibliographical references and index.
   ISBN 978-0-7546-7273-9.

   1. Libraries -- Safety measures.  2. Libraries -- Great Britain
-- Safety measures.  3. Archives -- Safety measures.  4. Archives
-- Great Britain -- Safety measures.  5. Museums -- Safety
measures.  6. Museums -- Great Britain -- Safety measures.
7. Library materials -- Conservation and restoration.
8. Archival materials -- Conservation and restoration.
9. Cultural property -- Protection.  10. Emergency management.
I. Smith, Yvonne.  II. Knowles, Gemma.  III. Title.
```

Note the difference in the DDC assigned by the Library of Congress (025.8'2) and the DDC assigned by the British Library (027.00684) and the greater number of subject headings assigned by the Library of Congress.

CHIEF SOURCE OF INFORMATION (Title Page)	(Information on Verso)

(Information on Verso)

© Graham Matthews, Yvonne Smith and Gemma Knowles 2009

All rights reserved. No part of this publication may be reproduced, stored in a retrieval system or transmitted in any form or by any means, electronic, mechanical, photocopying, recording or otherwise without the prior permission of the publisher.

Graham Matthews, Yvonne Smith and Gemma Knowles have asserted their moral right under the Copyright, Designs and Patents Act, 1988, to be identified as the authors of this work.

Published by
Ashgate Publishing Limited   Ashgate Publishing Company
Wey Court East   Suite 420
Union Road   101 Cherry Street
Farnham   Burlington
Surrey, GU9 7PT   VT 05401-4405
England   USA

www.ashgate.com

British Library Cataloguing in Publication Data
Disaster management in archives, libraries and museums
   1. Libraries – Risk management 2. Museums – Management
   3. Emergency management
   I. Matthews, Graham, 1953- II. Smith, Yvonne III. Knowles, Gemma
   027.00684

Library of Congress Cataloging-in-Publication Data
Matthews, Graham, 1953–
   Disaster management in archives, libraries and museums / by Graham Matthews, Yvonne Smith, and Gemma Knowles.
      p. cm.
   Includes bibliographical references.
   ISBN 978-0-7546-7273-9
   1. Libraries--Safety measures. 2. Libraries--Great Britain--Safety measures. 3. Archives--Safety measures. 4. Archives--Great Britain--Safety measures. 5. Museums--Safety measures. 6. Museums--Great Britain--Safety measures. 7. Library materials--Conservation and restoration. 8. Archival materials--Conservation and restoration. 9. Cultural property--Protection. 10. Emergency management. I. Smith, Yvonne. II. Knowles, Gemma. III. Title.

   Z679.7.M38 2009
   025.8'2--dc22
                                                        2008045373
ISBN 978-0-7546-7273-9

Disaster Management in Archives, Libraries and Museums

GRAHAM MATTHEWS

YVONNE SMITH

GEMMA KNOWLES

Printed and bound in Great Britain by
MPG Books Ltd, Bodmin, Cornwall.

ASHGATE

Figure 15.3

7. Is the item cartographic and does the responsibility of the corporate body go beyond publication or distribution? Yes? Assign a corporate body main entry. (If more than one corporate body is involved, follow the rules for multiple personal authors in caveat 2.) No? Go to question 8.

8. Is the work by one or more persons? Yes? Go to question 9. No? Assign a title main entry.

9. Is one person the sole creator or principal creator of the work? Yes? Assign that person as the main entry. No? Go to question 10.

10. Are two or three persons equally responsible for the creation of the work? Yes? Assign the first-named person as the main entry and give added entries for the rest. No? Go to question 11.

11. Are more than three persons equally responsible for the creation of the work? Assign a title main entry.

```
This example is an illustration of:
     • title main entry; no statement of responsibility given
     • other title information (in 2nd level cataloging)
     • publishing date not listed; copyright date given
     • detailed pagination
     • bibliography and index note (in 2nd level cataloging)
     • ISBN qualified
     • Library of Congress and Sears subject headings compared
     • added entry for corporate body (form of name taken from
       the established form in the Library of Congress CIP)
     • Dewey Decimal and Library of Congress classifications
     • prime mark in Dewey Decimal Classificationn
     • two levels of cataloging
```

1st level cataloging

```
The film preservation guide. -- National Film Preservation
   Foundation, c2004.
   xi, 121 p.

   ISBN 0-9747099-0-5 (alk. paper).
```

2nd level cataloging

```
The film preservation guide : the basics for archives, libraries,
   and museums. -- San Francisco : National Film Preservation
   Foundation, c2004.
   xi, 121 p. : ill. ; 24 cm.

   Includes bibliographical references and index.
   ISBN 0-9747099-0-5 (alk. paper).
```

Tracing with Library of Congress subject heading:

```
   1. Motion picture film -- Preservation.  I. National Film
Preservation Foundation (U.S.).
```

Tracing with Sears subject heading:

```
   1. Motion pictures -- Preservation.  I. National Film
Preservation Foundation (U.S.).
```

Suggested DDC: 778.5'8
Suggested LCC: TR886.3 F58 2003

Figure 15.4

Figure 15.4—*Continued*

CHIEF SOURCE OF INFORMATION
(Title Page)

(Information on Verso)

National Film Preservation Foundation
870 Market Street, Suite 1113
San Francisco, CA 94102

THE FILM PRESERVATION GUIDE
THE BASICS FOR ARCHIVES, LIBRARIES, AND MUSEUMS

© 2004 by the National Film Preservation Foundation

Library of Congress Cataloging-in-Publication Data
   The film preservation guide : the basics for archives, libraries, and museums.
      p.   cm.
   Includes bibliographical references and index.
   ISBN 0-9747099-0-5 (alk. paper)
   1. Motion picture film—Preservation. I. National Film Preservation Foundation (U.S.)
TR886.3F58   2003
778.5'8—dc22

2003024032
CIP

This publication was made possible through a grant from The Andrew W. Mellon Foundation. It may be downloaded as a PDF file from the National Film Preservation Foundation Web site: www.filmpreservation.org.

Credits
Except as noted below, all photographs were provided by Barbara Galasso and the L. Jeffrey Selznick School of Film Preservation at George Eastman House. The following contributed illustrations and text material: American Museum of Natural History (94), Anonymous (67), California Pacific Medical Center (57), Chace Productions Inc. (12 center and right), Duke University (48 top), Estate of Edith Lutyens Bel Geddes and the Harry Ransom Humanities Research Center at the University of Texas at Austin (84), Florida Moving Image Archive (91), Image Permanence Institute at the Rochester Institute of Technology (10 top), Library of Congress (48 bottom, 51, 63, 87), Minnesota Historical Society (92), National Center for Jewish Film (90), Nebraska State Historical Society (69, 73, 74), Northeast Historic Film (back cover, 62 bottom, 76, 85), Oklahoma Historical Society (5), Pacific Film Archive at the University of California at Berkeley (back cover), Sabucat Productions (93), UCLA Film and Television Archive (86), University of Alaska Fairbanks (40), University of South Carolina Newsfilm Library (89), Visual Communications (58).

Typesetting by David Wells
Copyediting by Sylvia Tan
Printed in the USA by Great Impressions

National Film Preservation Foundation
San Francisco, California

Caveat 1: Questions 10 and 11 assume shared responsibility. Consult the special rules for mixed responsibility when there are different types of contributions.

Caveat 2: Apply a rule of thumb called the Rule of Three when more than one person or body is involved in either shared or mixed contributions. The Rule of Three says: If the number of persons exceeds three and none are predominant, assign title main entry.

Caveat 3: Editors are not creators of the works they edit. An edited work with contributions from one or more authors is considered the collective work of those authors, whether they are persons, corporate bodies, or both. But bibliography compilers are creators, even if the term applied to the compiler on the title page is "editor." For example *The Book of Quotes* is entered under the compiler in Figure 15.7.

ADDED ENTRIES

Once the main entry is chosen, it is time to consider choosing more access points, called "added entries," for the names of other people and bodies or other titles associated with the material. Some added entries are mandated by the rules for main entry,

This example is an illustration of:
- item with more than three authors entered under title
- other title information
- marks of omission
- edition statement
- detailed pagination statement
- index note
- ISBN qualified
- added entry for first author with bibliographic form of name
- Library of Congress subject headings
- Dewey Decimal and Library of Congress classifications
- Library and Archives Canada CIP
- 2nd level cataloging

```
The book of lists : the original compendium of curious
    information / by David Wallechinsky ... [et al.]. -- 1st
    Canadian ed. -- Toronto : Knopf, 2005.
    x, 518 p. : ill. ; 23 cm.

    Includes index.
    ISBN 0-676-97720-0 (pbk.).

    1. Handbooks, vade-mecums, etc.  2. Curiosities and wonders.
3. Curiosities and wonders -- Canada.  I. Wallechinsky, David,
1948-


    Suggested DDC: 031.02
    Suggested LCC: AG106.B66 2005
```

(Information on Verso)

CHIEF SOURCE OF INFORMATION
(Title Page)

PUBLISHED BY ALFRED A. KNOPF CANADA

Original edition copyright © 1977, 1980, 1983, 2004 David Wallechinsky and Amy Wallace
Canadian edition copyright © 2005 Ira Basen and Jane Farrow
Published by agreement with Canongate Books Ltd., Edinburgh, Scotland

All rights reserved under International and Pan-American Copyright Conventions. No part of this book may be reproduced in any form or by any electronic or mechanical means, including information storage and retrieval systems, without permission in writing from the publisher, except by a reviewer, who may quote brief passages in a review. Published in 2005 by Alfred A. Knopf Canada, a division of Random House of Canada Limited. Distributed by Random House of Canada Limited, Toronto.

Knopf Canada and colophon are trademarks.

www.randomhouse.ca

Photo Credits
Chapter 1–Copyright © *The People's Almanac* Photographic Archives; Chapter 2–Film still from *McKenna of the Mounted* ; Chapter 3–Library and Archives Canada/ Credit: Duncan Cameron (PA-180804); Chapter 4–Paul V. Galvin Library collection; Chapter 5–Library and Archives Canada/ Credit: Claude-Charles Bacqueville de La Potherie (CFC305 B326); Chapter 6–City of Vancouver Archives, CVA 1184–2559; Chapter 7–Copyright © Frank Micoletta/Getty Image; Chapter 8–Steve Patterson/Glaucomys.org; Chapter 9–Jeff Goode/*Toronto Star*; Chapter 10–Copyright © M. Ponomareff/PonoPresse; Chapter 11–Copyright © Brian Willer - Toronto; Chapter 12–J.H. Webster/Hudson's Bay Co. Archives/Archives of Manitoba (HBCA 1987/363-E-152/4); Chapter 13–Library and Archives Canada/Montreal Star collection (PA-209767); Chapter 14–Niagara Falls (Ont.) Public Library - Digital Collections - George Bailey; Chapter 15–Saskatchewan Archives Board (S-B4121)

Pages 506 to 507 constitute a continuation of the copyright page. Also included is a key to contributors.

LIBRARY AND ARCHIVES CANADA CATALOGUING IN PUBLICATION

The book of lists / David Wallechinsky ... [et al.]. — Canadian ed.

Includes index.
ISBN 0-676-97720-0

1. Handbooks, vade-mecums, etc. 2. Curiosities and wonders.
3. Curiosities and wonders—Canada. I. Wallechinsky, David, 1948– .

AG106.B66 2005   031.02   C2005-901023-1

Text design: CS Richardson

First Canadian Edition

Printed and bound in the United States of America

10 9 8 7 6 5 4 3 2 1

Figure 15.5

This example is an illustration of:
- work produced under editorial direction
- main entry under title
- two statements responsibility in correct order (compare with CIP)
- distributor
- two ISBNs qualified
- Library of Congress subject headings
- personal name added entries
- Dewey Decimal and Library of Congress classifications
- prime mark in Dewey Decimal Classification
- 2nd level cataloging

```
The company they kept : writers on unforgettable friendships /
    preface by Robert B. Silvers ; edited by Robert B. Silvers and
    Barbara Epstein. -- New York : New York Review of Books ;
    distributed by Random House, c2006.
    298 p. ; 22 cm.

    ISBN-13: 978-1-59017-203-2 (alk. paper). -- ISBN-10: 1-59017-
    203-5 (alk. paper).

    1. Celebrities -- Biography.  2. Authors -- Biography.
    3. Friendship.  4. Influence (Literary, artistic, etc.)
    5. Biography -- Twentieth century.  I. Silvers, Robert B.
    II. Epstein, Barbara, 1929-


Suggested DDC: 920.009'4
Suggested LCC: CT120.E55 2006
```

CHIEF SOURCE OF INFORMATION
(Title Page)

The Company They Kept

Writers on Unforgettable Friendships

PREFACE BY
Robert B. Silvers

EDITED BY
Robert B. Silvers and Barbara Epstein

NEW YORK REVIEW BOOKS

nyrb

New York

(Information on Verso)

THIS IS A NEW YORK REVIEW BOOK
PUBLISHED BY THE NEW YORK REVIEW OF BOOKS

THE COMPANY THEY KEPT:
WRITERS ON UNFORGETTABLE FRIENDSHIPS
Copyright © 2006 by The New York Review of Books
Preface © 2006 Robert B. Silvers
All pieces © by individual authors:
"On John Cheever" © 1983 by Saul Bellow. Reprinted with permission of The Wylie Agency, Inc.
"Francis Bacon (1909–1992)" © 1992 by Caroline Blackwood. Reprinted with permission.
Excerpt from "Isaiah Berlin at Eighty" © 1989 by Joseph Brodsky. Reprinted by permission of Farrar,
Straus and Giroux, LLC, on behalf of the Estate of Joseph Brodsky.
"My Life with Stravinsky" © 1982 by Robert Craft. Reprinted with permission.
"Knowing S.J. Perelman" © 1987 by Prudence Crowther. Reprinted with permission.
"Hart Crane" © 1966 by Edward Dahlberg. Reprinted with permission.
"E. W. (1895–1972)" © 1972 by Jason Epstein. Reprinted with permission.
"Visiting Gertrude and Alice" © 1986 by Maurice Grosser. Reprinted with permission.
"Mary McCarthy in New York" © 1992 by Elizabeth Hardwick. Reprinted with permission.
Preface to the book *There You Are: Writings on Irish and American Literature and History* by Thomas
Flanagan; preface by Seamus Heaney; edited and with an introduction by Christopher Cahill; published
by The New York Review of Books. Preface © 2004 by Seamus Heaney. Reprinted with permission.
"On Bruce Chatwin" © 1989 by Michael Ignatieff. Reprinted with permission.
"Josephine Herbst" © 1969 by Alfred Kazin. Reprinted with permission of The Wylie Agency, Inc.
"In Memory of Octavio Paz (1914–1998)" © 1998 by Enrique Krauze. Reprinted with permission.
"Theodore Roethke" © 1963 by Stanley Kunitz. Reprinted with permission on behalf of the author by
Darhansoff, Verrill, Feldman, Literary Agents.
"Anthony Hecht (1923–2004)" © 2004 by Brad Leithauser. Reprinted with permission.
"Randall Jarrell, 1914–1965" © 1965 by Robert Lowell. Reprinted with permission.
"Delmore Schwartz (1913–1966)" © 1966 by Dwight Macdonald. Reprinted with permission.
"F. W. Dupee (1904–1979)" © 1979 by Mary McCarthy. Reprinted with permission of
The Mary McCarthy Literary Trust.
"On the Road" © 2002 by Larry McMurtry. Reprinted with permission.
"On Albert Einstein" © 1966 by Robert Oppenheimer. Reprinted with permission.
"Sweet Evening Breeze" © 1984 by Darryl Pinckney. Reprinted with permission.
"Remembering Francis Crick" © 2005 by Oliver Sacks. Reprinted with permission of The Wylie Agency, Inc.
"On Jérôme Lindon, 1926–2001" © 2001 by Richard Seaver. Reprinted with permission.
"On Paul Goodman" © 1972 by Susan Sontag. Reprinted with permission of The Wylie Agency, Inc.
"On Joseph Brodsky (1940–1996)" © 1996 by Tatyana Tolstaya. Reprinted with permission of The Wylie
Agency, Inc. Translation © 1996 by Jamey Gambrell.
"On Robert Lowell" © 1984 by Derek Walcott. Reprinted with permission.

All rights reserved, which includes the right
to reproduce this book or portions thereof in any form whatsoever.
Published by The New York Review of Books, 1755 Broadway, New York, NY 10019
www.nyrb.com
Distributed in the United States by Random House

Library of Congress Cataloging-in-Publication Data
The company they kept : writers on unforgettable friendships / edited by Robert B. Silvers and Barbara
Epstein ; preface by Robert B. Silvers.
    p. cm.
    ISBN 1-59017-203-5 (hardcover : alk. paper) — ISBN 1-59017-204-3 (pbk. : alk. paper)
    1 Celebrities — Biography. 2. Authors — Biography. 3. Friendship. 4. Influence (Literary, artistic,
etc.) 5. Biography — 20th century.
    I. Silvers, Robert B. II. Epstein, Barbara, 1929–
    CT 120.E55 2006
    920.009'04 — dc22
                                                2005027598

Cover design: Louise Fili Ltd.
Printed in the United States of America on acid-free paper.

ISBN-13: 978-1-59017-203-2
ISBN-10: 1-59017-203-5
1 3 5 7 9 10 8 6 4 2

Figure 15.6

for example, a rule says, "Choose A as the main entry and make an added entry for B." Figure 15.8 illustrates the case.

Catalogers can make any added entries if they believe searchers will use them, so long as the names or titles are mentioned in the bibliographic description. The

```
This example is an illustration of:
    • entry under compiler
    • ISBN qualified
    • Sears and Library of Congress subject headings compared
    • title added entry
    • Dewey Decimal and Library of Congress classifications
    • 2nd level cataloging


Eckstrand, Tatyana.
    The librarian's book of quotes / compiled by Tatyana Eckstrand.
-- Chicago : American Library Association, 2009.
    116 p. ; 17 cm.

    ISBN 978-0-8389-0988-1 (alk. paper).


Tracing with Library of Congress subject headings
    1. Library science -- Quotations, maxims, etc.  2. Librarians
-- Quotations, maxims, etc.  3. Libraries -- Quotations, maxims,
etc.  I. Title.

Tracing with Sears subject headings
    1. Library science -- Quotations.  2. Librarians -- Quotations.
3. Libraries -- Quotations.  I. Title.


Suggested DDC: 020
Suggested LCC: PN6084.L52E25 2009
```

CHIEF SOURCE OF INFORMATION
(Title Page)

(Information on Verso)

The Librarian's Book of Quotes

COMPILED BY TATYANA ECKSTRAND

AMERICAN LIBRARY ASSOCIATION

CHICAGO   2009

September 14, 2009

While extensive effort has gone into ensuring the reliability of information appearing in this book, the publisher makes no warranty, express or implied, on the accuracy or reliability of the information, and does not assume and hereby disclaims any liability to any person for any loss or damage caused by errors or omissions in this publication.

The paper used in this publication meets the minimum requirements of American National Standard for Information Sciences—Permanence of Paper for Printed Library Materials, ANSI Z39.48-1992. ∞

Library of Congress Cataloging-in-Publication Data

Eckstrand, Tatyana.
    The librarian's book of quotes / compiled by Tatyana Eckstrand.
        p. cm.
    ISBN 978-0-8389-0988-1 (alk. paper)
    1. Library science—Quotations, maxims, etc. 2. Librarians—Quotations, maxims, etc. 3. Libraries—Quotations, maxims, etc. I. Title.

    PN6084.L52E25 2009
    020—dc22   009000557

Cover illustration ©2007 Oldrich Jelen (www.jeleni.net)

Book design by Karen Sheets de Gracia

Copyright ©2009 by the American Library Association. All rights reserved except those which may be granted by Sections 107 and 108 of the Copyright Revision Act of 1976.

ISBN-13: 978-0-8389-0988-1

Printed in the United States of America

13 12 11 10 09   5 4 3 2 1

Figure 15.7

This example is an illustration of:
- joint responsibility
- bibliographic form of author's name taken from Library of Congress CIP
- other title information statement (in 2nd level cataloging)
- edition statement (in 2nd level cataloging)
- publishing date not listed; copyright date given
- detailed pagination
- descriptive illustration statement (in 2nd level cataloging)
- index note (in 2nd level cataloging)
- personal name added entry
- title added entry
- Sears and Library of Congress subject headings compared
- Library of Congress CIP
- 2 levels of cataloging

1st level cataloging

Spielman, A. (Andrew).
   Mosquito / by Andrew Spielman and Michael D'Antonio. --
Hyperion, c2001.
   xix, 247 p., [8] p. of plates.

   ISBN 0-7868-6781-7.

2nd level cataloging

Spielman, A. (Andrew).
   Mosquito : a natural history of our most persistent and deadly
foe / by Andrew Spielman and Michael D'Antonio. -- 1st ed. -- New
York : Hyperion, c2001.
   xix, 247 p., [8] p. of plates : ill. (some col.), maps ; 22 cm.

   Includes index.
   ISBN 0-7868-6781-7.

Tracing with Sears subject headings:

   1. Mosquitos.   I. D'Antonio, Michael.   II. Title.

Tracing with Library of Congress subject headings:

   1. Mosquitos.   2. Mosquitos as carriers of disease.
I. D'Antonio, Michael.   II. Title.

Figure 15.8

Figure 15.8—*Continued*

CHIEF SOURCE OF INFORMATION
(Title Page)

(Information on Verso)

MOSQUITO

A NATURAL HISTORY OF OUR
MOST PERSISTENT AND DEADLY FOE

ANDREW SPIELMAN, Sc.D.,
AND MICHAEL D'ANTONIO

Copyright © 2001 Andrew Spielman, Sc.D., and Michael D'Antonio
Photographs by Leonard E. Munstermann, Yale School of Medicine and Yale Peabody Museum.
Maps by Paul J. Pugliese

All rights reserved. No part of this book may be used or reproduced in any manner whatsoever without the written permission of the Publisher. Printed in the United States of America. For information address: Hyperion, 77 W. 66th Street, New York, New York 10023-6298.

Library of Congress Cataloging-in-Publication Data

Spielman, A. (Andrew)
     Mosquito : a natural history of our most persistent and deadly foe / by Andrew Spielman and Michael D'Antonio.—1st ed.
        p.   cm.
     ISBN 0-7868-6781-7
     1. Mosquitoes.   2. Mosquitoes as carriers of disease.   I. D'Antonio, Michael.   II. Title.
     QL536.S65 2001
     595.77'2—dc21   2001016815

Book design by Casey Hampton

FIRST EDITION

10 9 8 7 6 5 4 3 2 1

reason for the added entry must be evident from the rest of the description. Notes are made about variant titles, titles of parts, and/or secondary statements of responsibility, so they may be selected as headings. Evidence is not necessary to document main entries. When an item is erroneously attributed on the chief source, but the cataloger knows who truly created it, the rules prescribe giving the main entry to its true creator (or its probable creator, if there is doubt).

Added entries are made routinely for the following:

- Joint creators
- People or bodies making other creative contributions, if they are named prominently on the item
- Titles proper
- Uniform titles not chosen as main entry
- Title variations found on the item
- Analytical titles
- Series titles.

A new type of added entry is an electronic resource's Uniform Resource Locator (URL). Many guidelines for cataloging Internet resources recommend adding it, preferably as a direct link.

NAME AND TITLE AUTHORITIES

What is a name authority or a title authority? It is a record of the way names and titles are formulated for use as access points in the catalog. Once they are chosen, the rules of AACR2-2005 provide numerous rules for putting them into authorized form. That form is expected to be the only one used for each name or title. This results in all the materials by a person or corporate body or bearing a unique title being gathered in one place in the catalog, even if the materials themselves display the names and titles in different forms.

Personal Names

Two principles underlie the rules in AACR2-2005 for creating the authorized form for a personal name access point: (1) the form should be the one most familiar to searchers, and, (2) in most instances, only one form is used for an individual, ensuring that all the person's works are brought together in one place in the catalog.

The first principle seems logical, but is the reverse of AACR1's principle, which required using the fullest form of a person's real name. AACR2-2005 follows Charles Cutter's idea that catalog headings should match what searchers are most likely to expect. It instructs catalogers to use the most commonly known form of a name and sometimes permits more than one form to be used simultaneously. AACR2-2005 also permits pseudonyms, initials, nicknames, and appellations to be authorized if they are how an individual is most commonly known. Following are authorized headings that illustrate these instances.

- The most commonly known name form consists of initials:

  - *IBM Academic Information Systems* [full name: International Business Machines Corporation Academic Information Systems]
  - *Unesco* [full name: United Nations Education, Scientific, and Cultural Organization]

- The most commonly known name form consists of initials (a qualifier that is part of the authorized form is added to the initials giving the full name):

  - *H.D. (Hilda Doolittle), 1886–1961*
  - *Eliot, T.S. (Thomas Stearns), 1888–1965*

- The most commonly known name form consists of a pseudonym:

  - *Orwell, George, 1903–1950* [real name: Eric Arthur Blair]
  - *Twain, Mark, 1835–1910* [real name: Samuel Langhorne Clemens]

- The most commonly known name form consists of a nickname:

  - *Carter, Jimmy, 1924–* [real name: James Earl Carter; this name form is used for his publications written as a private person, not as president of the United States]
  - *Gillespie, Dizzy* [real name: John Birks Gillespie]

Research is required to determine the most common name form. Catalogers are instructed to examine all the published works of a person or corporate body, counting the number of times each form appears on published materials and selecting the one that appears most often to be the authorized form. Some authors deliberately use more than one name on their publications, because they wish to have different types of materials associated with each name form. Catalogers call this establishing "multiple bibliographic identities." When this happens, AACR2-2005 allows catalogers to authorize the form associated with each type of material or, in the case of contemporary authors, whatever name that appears on each publication. Cross-references are made for unauthorized name forms (*see* references) and multiple name forms (*see also* references).

Most creators use only one name form. The form authorized when an individual's first publication is cataloged is usually the only access point needed for that person. National libraries and libraries that participate in national cooperative programs prepare files of the name forms they authorize for their catalogs, called "authority files." The forms they authorize are called "name authorities."

Title access points are a little different. Titles proper do not need authorization, because, by definition, they are transcribed exactly as they appear on published materials. Series titles, however, can differ from one publication to another, and uniform titles are created when the same content is published bearing different titles proper. These titles require an authorized form. AACR2-2005 has rules for establishing title access points, called "title authorities."

Catalogers can consult national library authority files and copy the name forms they authorize, thus avoiding the costly research of doing the work themselves. Different national libraries do not always select the same form for a person (see the cataloging-in-publication [CIP] information in Figure 15.9 for Jean Weihs). The Library of Congress (LC) and Library and Archives Canada (LAC) each have a formal policy for establishing the names of corporate bodies, but this agreement does not cover personal names.

AACR2-2005 rule 22.17 directs catalogers to add a person's dates (e.g., birth, death) to a heading if the heading is otherwise identical to another. It also allows the optional use of dates even when there is no need to distinguish people with the same names. Dates have been added to personal names in this book when they are found in the CIP record and for names that have long been established that way, for example, Bernard Shaw and Charles Darwin.

Corporate Bodies

The same principles that apply to personal names apply also to corporate body names. A single form is established for a corporate body, but when a corporate body changes its name, it may also become a new body. Changes are more likely to be substantive, resulting in the presence of more than one access point for a corporate body that has evolved over time.

Using the most commonly known form of name as the authoritative form holds for corporate bodies, but the application differs. The name used by the group on its stationery, official documents, and publications is the one selected. Problems occur when a body updates its image by changing its logo. Rules define substantive changes to a corporate body name to eliminate multiple headings for a body undergoing changes of this kind, which are merely cosmetic. Sometimes corporate bodies announce an intention to change names, for example, Trenton State College to College of New Jersey.[4] Multiple names are appropriate in that case.

When a corporate body is part of a larger body, catalogers must decide how to formulate an authorized name, either alone (called "direct" entry) or as a unit under the larger body (called "subordinate" entry). It is more difficult when multiple layers of bureaucracy separate the parent body and the subordinate unit; for example, the Committee on Cataloging: Description and Access (CC:DA)—the committee that governs

```
This example is an illustration of:
    • named conference
    • main entry under corporate body
    • other title information
    • multiple places of publication and publishers
    • detailed pagination
    • publishing note (in first record)
    • contents note
    • Library of Congress subject headings
    • additional title added entry
    • Library of Congress and Canadian CIPs
```

2nd level cataloging for a Canadian library

```
International Conference on the Principles and Future of AACR
      (1997 : Toronto, Ont.)
   The principles and future of AACR : proceedings of the
International Conference on the Principles and Future of AACR,
Toronto, Ontario, Canada, October 23-25, 1997 / Jean Weihs,
editor. -- Ottawa : Canadian Library Association, 1997.
   xi, 272 p. ; 28 cm.

   Co-published by American Library Association and Library
Association.
   Includes bibliographies and index.
   ISBN 0-88802-287-5.
```

2nd level cataloging for a U.S. library

```
International Conference on the Principles and Future of AACR
      (1997 : Toronto, Ont.)
   The principles and future of AACR : proceedings of the
International Conference on the Principles and Future of AACR,
Toronto, Ontario, Canada, October 23-25, 1997 / Jean Weihs,
editor. -- Ottawa : Canadian Library Association ; Chicago :
American Library Association, 1997.
   xi, 272 p. ; 28 cm.

   Includes bibliographies and index.
   ISBN 0-8389-3493-5.
```

Tracing for both

```
   1. Anglo-American cataloging rules -- Congresses.
2. Descriptive cataloging -- Congresses.  I. Weihs, Jean.
II. Title.  III. Title: Principles and future of Anglo-American
cataloguing rules.
```

Figure 15.9

Figure 15.9—*Continued*

CHIEF SOURCE OF INFORMATION
(Title Page)

The Principles and Future of AACR

Proceedings of the
International Conference
on the Principles
and Future Development
of AACR

Toronto, Ontario, Canada
October 23–25, 1997

JEAN WEIHS
Editor

CANADIAN LIBRARY ASSOCIATION / Ottawa
LIBRARY ASSOCIATION PUBLISHING / London
AMERICAN LIBRARY ASSOCIATION / Chicago
1998

(Information on Verso)

Published by
AMERICAN LIBRARY ASSOCIATION
50 East Huron Street, Chicago, Illinois 60611
CANADIAN LIBRARY ASSOCIATION
200 Elgin Street, Ottawa, Ontario K2P 1L5
LIBRARY ASSOCIATION PUBLISHING
7 Ridgmount Street, London WC1E 7AE
Library Association Publishing is wholly owned
by The Library Association

Library of Congress Cataloging-in-Publication Data
International Conference on the Principles and Future Development of
AACR (1997 : Toronto, Ontario, Canada)
    The principles and future of AACR / Jean Weihs, editor
        p.   cm.
    "Proceedings of the International Conference in the Principles and
Future Development of AACR, Toronto, Ontario, October 23-25, 1997
American Library Association, Chicago and London, 1999."
    Includes bibliographical references (p.   ) and index.
    ISBN 0-8389-3493-5
    1. Anglo-American cataloging rules—Congresses. 2. Descriptive
cataloging—United States—Rules—Congresses. 3. Descriptive
cataloging—Great Britain—Rules—Congresses. 4. Descriptive
cataloging—Canada—Rules—Congresses. 5. Descriptive cataloging —
Australia—Rules—Congresses. I. Weihs, Jean Riddle. II. Title.
III. Title: Principles and future of Anglo-American cataloguing rules.
Z694.15.A5155   1997
025.32—dc21   98-34562

Canadian Cataloguing in Publication Data
International Conference on the Principles and Future Development of
AACR (1997 : Toronto, Ont.)
    The principles and future of AACR : proceedings of the International
Conference on the Principles and Future Development of AACR.
Toronto, Ontario, Canada, October 23-25, 1997
    Co-published by American Library Association and Library Association
    Includes bibliographical references.
    ISBN 0-88802-287-5
    1. Anglo-American cataloging rules—Congresses. 2. Descriptive
cataloging—United States—Rules—Congresses. 3. Descriptive
cataloging—Great Britain—Rules—Congresses. 4. Descriptive
cataloging—Canada—Rules—Congresses. 5. Descriptive cataloging—
Australia—Rules—Congresses. I. Weihs, Jean, 1930- II. American
Library Association. III. Library Association. IV. Title. V. Title:
Principles and future of Anglo-American cataloguing rules.
Z694.15.A5158   1997   025.3'2   C98-901015.5

British Library Cataloguing-in-Publication Data
A catalogue record for this book is available from the British Library
    ISBN 1-85604-303-7

Copyright © 1998. American Library Association.
Canadian Library Association, and The Library Association

AACR2-2005 in the United States—has two intervening layers of hierarchy between its parent entity, the American Library Association (ALA), and the unit itself:

1. ALA (parent body)

    2. Association for Library Collections & Technical Services (ALCTS; subunit of the parent body, a division)

        3. Cataloging and Classification Section (subunit of the division, a section)

            4. CC:DA (subunit of the section, a committee)

When the name of a corporate body implies that it is a subordinate unit—clearly the case with committees, divisions, and sections—the name of the higher body is always included. In the case of a multilevel hierarchy, AACR2-2005 instructs catalogers to include the name of the lowest unit of hierarchy that can stand alone, provided it is a unique identification. For CC:DA, the only higher body that needs to be added is ALCTS. The authoritative name form for CC:DA is the following;

Association for Library Collections & Technical Services. Committee on Cataloging: Description and Access.

"Cataloging and Classification Section" is not used because it is subordinate and no other section of ALCTS has a committee by this name; therefore, the name is unique.

The Cataloging and Classification Section of ALCTS also has a Policy and Research Committee, but its authoritative heading would not be *Association for Library Collections & Technical Services. Policy and Research Committee,* because another section within ALCTS, the Serials Section, also has a committee by that name. Each of the two committees must be identified uniquely. The authoritative form of the Cataloging and Classification Section's Policy and Research Committee is *Association for Library Collections & Technical Services. Cataloging and Classification Section. Policy and Research Committee.*[5]

The best way to help searchers find what they are looking for is to make cross-references to any name form they might reasonably seek and to program online public access catalogs (OPACs) to match word combinations in corporate body headings to retrieve all sets that include the requested terms. Thousands of corporate bodies are listed in LC's *Name Authority File* and LAC's *Canadiana Authorities,* which are available for catalogers to adopt instead of establishing those names from scratch. Organizations at state and local levels sometimes provide lists of local corporate body authorities as a public service.[6]

Geographic Names

Geographic names are used in some access points in the catalog. It is easy to imagine the confusion that would result if different forms of name were used for the same geographic entity. For example, should Britain, Great Britain, or United Kingdom be used as the authoritative access point for the territory inhabited by our colleagues across the Atlantic? For places located in non–English-speaking countries, does the cataloger authorize the English or the vernacular name form (for example, Florence or Firenze, Milan or Milano)? What does the cataloger do about nonroman languages, such as Arabic, Chinese, and Russian?

AACR2-2005's Chapter 23 instructs catalogers to choose English name forms for places if such forms are in general use. When no English form is in general use, the vernacular form in the official language of the country is authorized. For example, Leghorn, the English name for Livorno, is not generally used in the English-speaking world; therefore, it is not chosen to be the authorized name of that Italian city. Instead, *Livorno,* the Italian (vernacular) name is chosen as the authorized form.

Place names change (for example, Russia to the Union of Soviet Socialist Republics and back to Russia). In these instances, catalogers are instructed to use as many name forms as are required to satisfy the rules in Chapter 24 for government names, additions to corporate and conference names, and other corporate body name access points. Because this means a single place can have more than one authorized name in the catalog, cross-references are used to clarify the relationships.

Sometimes a name is used for more than one place (for example, Cairo, which could identify the capital of Egypt or the city in Illinois). Additions to the name serve to distinguish them. Additions differ for some countries, with one group comprising Australia, Canada, Malaysia, the U.S.S.R., Yugoslavia, and the United States. Localities within these places are qualified by adding the name of the state, province, territory, and so on. The countries of the British Isles—England, Republic of Ireland,

Northern Ireland, Scotland, and Wales as well as the Isle of Man and the Channel Islands—are a second group, for which local place names[7] are augmented by the addition of a country or island name. This practice applies to other countries of the world as well.

Special rules cover places that require still more specific identification or special kinds of identification, for example, localities with identical headings even after additions are made (two places named Saint Anthony, Minnesota, one in Hennepin County and the other in Stearns County), communities within cities (Hyde Park in London, England, or Chicago, Illinois), or names of political jurisdictions. These rules and their interpretations can be consulted if material being cataloged requires those kinds of access points to be established. Like personal and corporate body names, geographic names are included in national and international authority files.

Uniform Titles

Most works are published once and bear one title. Their titles proper are the only title access points they need. Some works, however, are issued many times over the years and may not be given the same title proper by their publishers. This is common among world classics (*Alice in Wonderland* and *Alice's Adventures in Wonderland*), holy scriptures (different editions of Bibles, different spellings of Koran or Quran), translations, and so on. Works given different titles proper by their publishers would not be filed in the same place in the catalog, even though their content is the same. To solve the problem and gather them, such works are given a single agreed-upon title by catalogers, called a *uniform title,* under which they are filed together. Uniform titles serve another function: They are used to distinguish identical titles, such as musical works called "Symphony" or serials called "Journal."

The most widely used uniform titles are described in AACR2-2005's chapter 25, along with rules for creating and assigning uniform titles to works catalogers believe need one. Uniform titles are common among seven types of works:

- Classics
- Music
- Religious works
- Laws
- Works that are issued both complete and in parts, such as *Mother Goose*
- Works issued in multiple physical formats, such as *Gone With the Wind*
- Translations, if more than one version is in a library collection

When material being cataloged has a personal or corporate body author, the uniform title is displayed as an added entry in square brackets on a line inserted between the main entry and the title proper. If the material has no personal or corporate body author, the uniform title is given as the main entry and displayed in the usual position for main entries. Uniform titles are also found in added entries. Figures 15.10–15.14 demonstrate the use of uniform titles.

Uniform titles need not be made for every work that exists in multiple versions unless several are represented in a catalog or are likely to be added to it. Some, how-

```
This example is an illustration of:
     •  uniform title as main entry
     •  edition statement
     •  multiple places of publication
     •  all illustrations are colored
     •  edition and history note (in 2nd level cataloging)
     •  ISBN
     •  comparison of Dewey, Library of Congress, and Library of
        Congress children's subject headings
     •  personal name added entry with and without optional
        designation of function
     •  title added entry
     •  two levels of cataloging
```

2nd level cataloging for a U.S. library

```
Mother Goose.
  The real Mother Goose / illustrated by Blanche Fisher Wright.
-- Anniversary ed. -- New York : Scholastic, 2006.
  143 p. : col. ill. ; 24 cm.

  "Originally published in 1916"--T.p. verso.
  ISBN 0-439-85875-5.
```

Publication statement for a Canadian library:

```
New York ; Toronto : Scholastic, 2006.
```

1st level cataloging for libraries in both countries

```
Mother Goose.
  The real Mother Goose / illustrated by Blanche Fisher Wright.
-- Anniversary ed. -- Scholastic, 2006.
  143 p.

  ISBN 0-439-85875-5.
```

Tracing with Sears or Library of Congress subject headings

```
  1. Nursery rhymes.  2. Children's poetry.  I. Wright, Blanche
Fisher, ill.  II. Title.
```

Tracing with Library of Congress children's subject headings

```
  1. Nursery rhymes.  2. Poetry.  I. Wright, Blanche Fisher.
II. Title.
```

CHIEF SOURCE OF INFORMATION
(Title Page)

(Information on Verso)

Figure 15.10

```
This example is an illustration of:
    •   catalog records with and without a uniform title
    •   main entry/access point from title proper
    •   optional addition of dates to personal name
    •   subsidiary responsibility statement
    •   personal name added entry with optional designation of
        function
    •   title added entry
```

2nd level cataloging without a uniform title (suitable for general collections)

```
Shaw, Bernard, 1856-1950.
  The sayings of Bernard Shaw / edited by Joseph Spence. --
London : Duckworth, 1993.
  64 p. ; 20 cm.

  ISBN 0-7156-2491-1.

  I. Spence, Joseph, ed.   II. Title.
```

2nd level cataloging with a uniform title (suitable for large collections of Shaw's works)

```
Shaw, Bernard, 1856-1950.
  [Selections]
  The sayings of Bernard Shaw / edited by Joseph Spence. --
London : Duckworth, 1993.
  64 p. ; 20 cm.

  ISBN 0-7156-2491-1.

  I. Spence, Joseph, ed.   II. Title.
```

CHIEF SOURCE OF INFORMATION
(Title Page)

The Sayings of

BERNARD
SHAW

edited by

Joseph Spence

Duckworth

(Information on Verso)

This impression 2002
First published in 1993 by
Gerald Duckworth & Co. Ltd.
61 Frith Street, London W1D 3JL
Tel: 020 7434 4242
Fax: 020 7434 4420
inquiries@duckworth-publishers.co.uk
www.ducknet.co.uk

Quotations from the works of Bernard Shaw
© 1993 by The Trustees of the British Museum,
the Governors and Guardians of the National
Gallery of Ireland and Royal Academy
of Dramatic Art

Introduction and editorial arrangement
© 1993 by Joseph Spence

All rights reserved. No part of this publication
may be reproduced, stored in a retrieval system, or
transmitted, in any form or by any means, electronic,
mechanical, photocopying, recording or otherwise,
without the prior permission of the publisher.

A catalogue record for this book is available
from the British Library

ISBN 0 7156 2491 1

Printed in Great Britain by
Antony Rowe Ltd, Eastbourne

Figure 15.11

This example is an illustration of:
- catalog record for a translation
- optional addition of dates to personal name
- uniform title in second record
- subsidiary responsibility statement
- descriptive pagination
- series statement
- edition and history note in first record
- two ISBNs qualified
- Library of Congress subject heading
- personal name added entry
- title added entry
- CIP data not identified

2nd level cataloging without a uniform title (suitable for general collections)

Maupassant, Guy de, 1850-1893.
  Afloat / Guy de Maupassant ; translated from the French with an introduction by Douglas Parmée. -- New York : New York Review of Books, c2008.
  xx, 105 p. ; 20 cm. -- (New York Review of Books classic)

  Originally published in French as Sur l'eau.
  ISBN-13: 978-1-59017-259-9 (alk. paper). -- ISBN-10: 1-59017-259-) (alk. paper).

  1. Riviera (France) -- Description and travel. I. Parmée, Douglas. II. Title.

2nd level cataloging with a uniform title (suitable for a collection where some users read or know about books in French)

Maupassant, Guy de, 1850-1893.
  [Sur l'eau. English]
  Afloat / Guy de Maupassant ; translated from the French with an introduction by Douglas Parmée. -- New York : New York Review of Books, c2008.
  xx, 105 p. ; 20 cm. -- (New York Review of Books classic)

  ISBN-13: 978-1-59017-259-9 (alk. paper). -- ISBN-10: 1-59017-259-) (alk. paper).

  1. Riviera (France) -- Description and travel. I. Parmée, Douglas. II. Title.

CHIEF SOURCE OF INFORMATION
(Title Page)

(Information on Verso)

AFLOAT

GUY DE MAUPASSANT

Translated from the French and with an introduction by
DOUGLAS PARMÉE

THIS IS A NEW YORK REVIEW BOOK
PUBLISHED BY THE NEW YORK REVIEW OF BOOKS
435 Hudson Street, New York, NY 10014
www.nyrb.com

Translation, introduction, and notes copyright © 2008 by Douglas Parmée
All rights reserved.

Maupassant, Guy de, 1850-1893.
  [Sur l'eau. English]
  Afloat / by Guy de Maupassant ; translated and with an introduction by Douglas Parmée.
    p. cm. — (New York Review Books classics)
  ISBN-13: 978-1-59017-259-9 (alk. paper)
  ISBN-10: 1-59017-259-0 (alk. paper)
  1. Riviera (France)—Description and travel. I. Title.
PQ2350.S713 2008
848'.803—dc22

                    2007029777

ISBN 978-1-59017-259-9

Printed in the United States of America on acid-free paper.
10 9 8 7 6 5 4 3 2 1

NEW YORK REVIEW BOOKS

New York

Figure 15.12

```
This example is an illustration of:
   • sound recording (compact disc)
   • item without a collective title
   • uniform title
   • optional addition of dates to some personal names
   • general material designation
   • bibliographic forms of name different than those listed
     on item
   • phonogram date
   • specific material designation has optional term in common
     use
   • publisher's number given in optional placement as first
     note (in item cataloged as a unit): this option is
     applied in many libraries
   • performer note
   • accompanying materials listed in note area
   • with note for item cataloged as separate units
   • added entries for performers
   • added entry for second piece on item with a uniform title
     (in item cataloged as a unit)
   • 2nd level cataloging showing alternate methods of
     description
```

Item cataloged as one unit

```
Prokofiev, Sergey, 1891-1953.
  [Concertos, violin, orchestra, no. 2, op. 63, G minor]
  Violin concerto no. 2 in G minor, op. 63 [sound recording] /
Sergei Prokofiev. Violin concerto no. 2 in C sharp minor, op. 129
/ Dmitri Shostakovich. -- Hamburg : Teldec Classics, p1997.
  1 compact disc (62 min., 18 sec.) : digital ; 4 3/4 in.

  Teldec: 0630-13150-2.
  Maxim Vengerov, violin; London Symphony Orchestra, Mstislav
Rostropovich, conductor.
  Program notes in English, German, and French, by Christiane
Kuhnt.

  I. Vengerov, Maksim.  II. Rostropovich, Mstislav.
III. Shostakovich, Dmitrii Dmitrievich, 1906-1875. Concertos,
violin, orchestra, no. 2, op. 129, C# minor.  IV. London Symphony
Orchestra.
```

Item cataloged as separate units

```
Prokofiev, Sergey, 1891-1953.
  [Concertos, violin, orchestra, no. 2, op. 63, G minor]
  Violin concerto no. 2 in G minor, op. 63 [sound recording] /
Sergei Prokofiev. -- Hamburg : Teldec Classics, p1997.
  Part of 1 compact disc : digital ; 4 3/4 in.

  Maxim Vengerov, violin; London Symphony Orchestra, Mstislav
Rostropovich, conductor.


  Program notes in English, German, and French, by Christiane
Kuhnt.
  Teldec: 0630-13150-2.
  With: Concertos, violin, orchestra, no. 2, op. 129, C# minor /
Dmitri Shostakovich.

  I. Vengerov, Maksim.  II. Rostropovich, Mstislav.  III. London
Symphony Orchestra.


Shostakovich, Dmitrii Dmitrievich, 1906-1875.
  [Concertos, violin, orchestra, no. 2, op. 129, C# minor]
  Violin concerto no. 2 in C sharp minor, op. 129 [sound
recording] / Dmitri Shostakovich. -- Hamburg : Teldec Classics,
p1997.
  Part of 1 compact disc : digital ; 4 3/4 in.

  Maxim Vengerov, violin; London Symphony Orchestra, Mstislav
Rostropovich, conductor.
  Program notes in English, German, and French, by Christiane
Kuhnt.
  Teldec: 0630-13150-2.
  With: Concertos, violin, orchestra, no. 2, op. 63, G minor /
Sergei Prokofiev.

  I. Vengerov, Maksim.  II. Rostropovich, Mstislav.  III. London
Symphony Orchestra.
```

Figure 15.13

Figure 15.13—*Continued*

CHIEF SOURCE OF INFORMATION

(Information from Jacket)

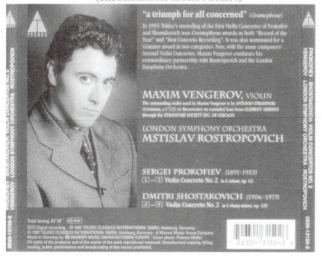

This example is an illustration of:
- religious work with uniform titles in added entries
- two other title information
- multiple reprinting dates; publication date given
- detailed pagination
- descriptive illustration statement
- language of item note
- bibliography note
- Library of Congress subject headings
- Dewey Decimal and Library of Congress classifications
- title added entry
- Library of Congress CIP
- 2nd level cataloging

Raphael, Chaim.
   A feast of history : the drama of Passover through the ages :
with a new translation of the Haggadah for use at the Seder /
Chaim Raphael. -- Washington, D.C. : B'nai B'rith Books, 1972.
   157, 159 p. : ill. (some col.), col. maps ; 26 cm.

   Text of Haggadah in Hebrew and English.
   English language pages run left to right; Hebrew language pages
have double numbering right to left and left to right.
   Includes bibliographical references.
   ISBN 0-910250-26-X.

   1. Haggadot -- Texts -- History and criticism. 2. Seder --
Liturgy -- Texts -- History and criticism. 3. Judaism -- Liturgy
-- Texts -- History and criticism. 4. Haggadah -- Illustrations.
5. Illumination of books and manuscripts, Jewish. 6. Haggadot --
Texts. 7. Seder -- Liturgy -- Texts. 8. Judaism Liturgy --
Texts. I. Haggadah. 1972. II. Haggadah. English. 1972.
III. Title.

Suggested DDC: 296.4'37 1993
Suggested LCC: BM674.79.R36

CHIEF SOURCE OF INFORMATION
(Title Page)

CHAIM RAPHAEL

A Feast of History

THE DRAMA OF PASSOVER
THROUGH THE AGES

with a new translation of the Haggadah
for use at the Seder

B'nai B'rith Books
Washington, D.C.

Jerusalem • London • Paris • Buenos Aires • East Sydney

(Information on Verso)

Copyright © 1972 by Chaim Raphael

First published in Great Britain in 1972 by
George Weidenfeld and Nicolson Ltd., Orion House
5 Upper St Martin's Lane, London WC2H 9EA

Reprinted 1978, 1981, 1984, 1993

All rights reserved.
No part of this book may be used or reproduced
in any manner whatsoever without written permission
except in the case of brief quotations embodied
in critical articles and reviews.

For information address the publisher.
Published and distributed by
B'nai B'rith Books
1640 Rhode Island Avenue, N.W.
Washington, D.C. 20036

Designed by Alex Berlyne
Picture research and selection by Irène Lewitt
Photographs by David Harris

Printed and bound in Italy

Library of Congress Cataloging-in-Publication Data

Raphael, Chaim.
A Feast of History: the drama of Passover through the ages:
with a new translation of the Haggadah for use at the Seder/
Chaim Raphael.
p.   cm.
Text of Haggadah in Hebrew and English.
Includes bibliographical references.
ISBN 0-910250-26-X
1. Haggadot—Texts—History and criticism.
2. Seder—Liturgy—Texts—History and criticism.
3. Judaism—Liturgy—Texts— History and criticism.
4. Haggadah—Illustations. 5. Illumination of books
and manuscripts, Jewish. 6. Haggadot—Texts.
7. Seder—Liturgy—Texts.
8. Judaism—Liturgy—Texts.
I. Haggadah. 1993.   II. Haggadah. English. 1993.
III. Title.
BM674.79.R36   1993
296.4'37—dc20   93-4770

Figure 15.14

ever, such as the Bible, require the addition of a uniform title to meet the requirements of cataloging networks, even though a library owns only one version.

SUMMARY

Charles Cutter's second object of the catalog—helping searchers select a desired work from among the works of an author held in a library's collection or a desired edition of a work held by the library in multiple editions—requires that the works of an author and the editions of a work be gathered together in the catalog. This is deemed the collocation object. To accomplish it, authors' names and titles of works cannot appear in multiple forms, even if that is how they appear on publications. It is the opposite of the first object of the catalog. Transcribing names and titles faithfully, which is what the rules of description require, helps accomplish that—namely, revealing what the library has by an author or if it holds a title, which is called the finding list function. On the other hand, collocating names and titles that appear in different form on publications requires selecting one form to serve as the gathering point for each name and each title.

Performing the work of selecting name and title forms is known as "authority work," because the resulting selections are authorized for use as access points in the catalog. It involves examining all the possible forms and selecting the most commonly known form, the one preferred by AACR2-2005, because that is the form searchers are most likely to request. The rules allow for multiple name forms to be used in instances when creators have gone out of their way to create separate bibliographic identities for different types of content, sometimes using a real name and a pseudonym or multiple pseudonyms. Rejected forms generally become cross-references leading to the authorized form, and when multiple forms are permitted, cross-references link them.

Records of authorized access points, cross-references, and the sources of information used to establish them are called *authority files.* National libraries and other large libraries doing a great deal of original cataloging maintain these files, but the work is costly and time-consuming. When faced with a new name, catalogers in North American libraries can benefit from the work of their national libraries by consulting LC's *Name Authority File* or the LAC's *Canadiana Authorities* for any of the following:

- Personal names
- Corporate body names
- Geographic names
- Series titles
- Uniform titles

Authority files are available directly from the two libraries, or indirectly as part of the services offered to customers of bibliographic networks, commercial cataloging services, and subscribers to LC's *Cataloger's Desktop.* The value of using only authorized names and titles as access points in the catalog is better patron service.

The rules of RDA add a great many details to the authority records for names. Its section 8, titled "General Guidelines on Recording Attributes of Persons, Families, and Corporate Bodies," is devoted to establishing authoritative name forms.

REVIEW QUESTIONS

1. Define mixed responsibility and give two examples.

2. When a person uses more than one name form on his or her published works, how do catalogers determine which one to authorize?

3. Explain the difference between direct entry and subordinate entry for corporate bodies.

4. Describe the three kinds of cross-references for which AACR2-2005 has rules.

5. What is a main entry and how does it differ from an added entry?

NOTES

The epigraph is from *Anglo-American Cataloguing Rules,* 2nd ed., 2002 revision, 2005 update. Prepared under the direction of the Joint Steering Committee for Revision of AACR. Chicago: American Library Association, 2005.

1. To qualify as a genuine corporate body, a group of people must work together as a unit and have a name. If either feature is lacking, the people are not considered a corporate body.

2. AACR2-2005, 21–27.

3. AACR2-2005, rule 21.1A2, 21–26.

4. "College of New Jersey" was the original name of the institution now known as Princeton University. Princeton changed to its current name in 1896. One hundred years later, in 1996, Trenton State College changed its name to College of New Jersey despite controversy over its adopting a name that had once belonged to a different university.

5. Note that the word "and" in the authorized name of the association is represented by an ampersand. That is the official spelling of the name in the Association's stationery, publications, etc. It is reasonable for some searchers to spell out "and," therefore it should be a cross-reference to the authorized form.

6. See, for example, a list of Maine corporate body names in the Name Authorities of Maine Agencies Web site, http://www.umpi.maine.edu/info/lib/namaume.htm.

7. In this context, "local" refers to cities, towns, and so on.

SUGGESTED READING

Authority Control in the 21st Century: An Invitational Conference, March 31–April, 1996. Dublin, OH: OCLC, 1996. http://www.oclc.org/oclc/man/authconf/confhome.htm.

Carlyle, Alyson. "Fulfilling the Second Objective in the Online Catalog: Schemes for Organizing Author and Work Records into Usable Displays." *Library Resources & Technical Services* 41, no. 2 (April 1997): 79–100.

The Future Is Now: Reconciling Change and Continuity in Authority Control: Proceedings of the OCLC Symposium, ALA Annual Conference, June 23, 1995. Dublin, OH: OCLC, 1995.

Koth, Michelle. *Uniform Titles for Music.* Music Library Association Technical Reports. no. 31. Lanham, MD: Scarecrow Press, 2008.

Maxwell, Robert L. *Maxwell's Guide to Authority Work.* Chicago, IL: American Library Association, 2002.

NACO Name Authority Cooperative Program of the PCC Web site. http://www.loc.gov/catdir/pcc/naco.

OCLC. WorldCat Identities Web site. http://www.worldcat.org/identities.

Taylor, Arlene G., and Daniel N. Joudrey. *The Organization of Information.* 3rd ed. Westport, CT: Libraries Unlimited, 2009.

Taylor, Arlene G., and Barbara B. Tillett, eds. *Authority Control in Organizing and Accessing Information: Definition and International Experience.* New York: Haworth Information Press, 2004.

Vellucci, Sherry L. "Metadata and Authority Control." *Library Resources & Technical Services* 44, no. 1 (January 2000): 33–43.

16

Subject Analysis

When our stock of information has been systematically arranged, and is available for use . . . it has gradually developed into the nucleus of an **intelligence department,** covering all the subjects and their ramifications within the scope of our activity. It has become a powerful base on the strength of which successful operations may be undertaken. But let there be no doubt about it: it is an instrument, we are its masters.

> —*Julius O. Kaiser,* Systematic Indexing
> *(emphasis in the original)*

Thus far we have covered bibliographic description and access. Bibliographic description enables catalogers to prepare a kind of super citation that identifies each resource in a library's collection so completely that it cannot be mistaken for any other resource. Access covers the process of selecting and formulating the names of people and groups associated with a resource as well as its title(s), which become access points by which the item can be retrieved. To use these descriptive access points, however, library users must know the name of the creator or the title of the material they want. What happens if they do not know either of these? Users often want to find a kind of material—something entertaining to take on a beach vacation, an exercise video, science experiments for children, dance music for a party, information about cataracts—without knowing exactly which item in the collection fits the need. They are looking for specific content, not for creators or titles. In cataloging, the representation of content is called *subject analysis*. Catalogers represent the content of materials in two ways: they assign *subject headings* that users can search in the catalog and *call numbers* that group materials with like content on the shelves. Representing the subject content of materials is sometimes referred to as providing *intellectual access* to materials.

The assignment of subject headings, which is a kind of indexing, is called *subject cataloging.* No single code of rules governs it, unlike description and access, which follow the *Anglo-American Cataloguing Rules,* second edition, 2002 revision, 2005 update (AACR2-2005) and will soon follow the rules of *Resource Description and Access.* Similarly, no single code governs the assignment of *classification numbers,* the category codes that are the basis of call numbers. Instead, catalogers adopt one of the available tools for subject cataloging and classification, and follow accepted practices in applying them.

Subject cataloging and classification both involve two steps: determining the subject content of the materials being cataloged and expressing it. Determining subject content is the same for both, but expressing it depends on the particular tools selected for the task. General principles of subject analysis are discussed in this chapter. Specific tools for subject cataloging, known as *subject authorities*, are discussed in chapter 17, and tools for classification in chapter 18.

DETERMINING SUBJECT MATTER

Representing the content of the materials being cataloged first requires catalogers to determine what the content covers—in other words, what the subject matter is. Describing how to go about doing it, however, is not so easy. Each cataloger brings his or her personal background, knowledge, and experience to the task of deciding what something is about and whether the approach taken to the material is relevant. Depending on how much a cataloger knows about a subject area, he or she might recognize different aspects of content in a particular item. This affects the determination of subject matter made for that item.

Typically, information derived directly from the items being cataloged helps reveal their contents, whether or not catalogers have special knowledge of those subject areas. Sometimes catalogers are assigned to do subject cataloging for a set of subjects, whether or not they know anything about them. If they are responsible for cataloging materials in unfamiliar subjects, they must study them enough to be able to handle them. In research libraries, catalogers may be expert in selected subject areas and/or languages. In most libraries and with most materials, however, the catalogers are expected only to be generally conversant with subjects.

Where can clues to the subject matter of materials be found? Four places are likely sources:

1. Titles, including alternative titles and subtitles
2. Tables of contents and their equivalents, such as menus and site maps
3. Indexes
4. Introductions, prefaces, "about" files, and their equivalents

Catalogers cannot read every word of a book or Web site, or view every inch of a video to ascertain its subject. Instead, material is read, heard, or viewed technically, which means a few key sources are examined carefully and subject matter, scope, and coverage are determined from them. Subtitles often reveal subject content better than main titles, which may be chosen for dramatic appeal. Chapter or segment titles add greater detail to information contained in titles, and suggest scope and coverage.

Introductions, prefaces, about files, and the like can describe an author's intended audience, important inclusions or exclusions, and other subject-related information. Back of the book indexes, Web site index terms, and similar internal finding aids offer evidence of the range of subtopics covered in an item. A quick scan of the rest of the item can answer questions that remain after a technical examination is completed.

If it is necessary to go beyond the material itself for information, descriptions of materials in publishers' or producers' catalogs and reviews of materials can provide helpful detail. These sources can augment catalogers' ideas or confirm conclusions about subject matter gleaned from the item itself when technical reading fails to reveal it clearly or completely. However, information taken from book jackets, album covers, and promotional blurbs is not always reliable and should be used cautiously. These are marketing tools aimed at enticing buyers and may not be strictly accurate.

An item's content can also be affected by the approach taken to the material. An item that gives an overview of the whole field of chemistry and an item that is solely a dictionary of terminology used in the field of chemistry are both about chemistry, but the dictionary approach merits recognition. It is different from an introductory overview of the subject. General coverage of the subject is assumed when catalogers say a book is about chemistry or a video is about exercise. If the approach is not general, catalogers usually identify it by specifying its form. A chemistry dictionary is about chemistry, but its form is that of a dictionary. An exercise video is about exercise, but its approach may be that of a lecture on the subject (general coverage) or an activity session in which the viewer is expected to participate (directed exercise), and the physical form of the item is an audiovisual presentation recorded on videotape. Thus, catalogers speak of subject and form, where form may be defined as a genre (e.g., dictionaries, biographies, bibliographies, essays), a physical format, or a specific type of approach to the subject.

Subject matter may be limited to one location or time period, and geographical and chronological specifications are often added to reflect those limitations. If a Web site about divorce is limited to Canada, catalogers want to express that explicitly, so that a searcher seeking information about divorce in Mexico or the United States would not think the item answers the person's need. Subject headings and classification sources provide for both geographic and chronological approaches to subjects.

ENUMERATION VERSUS FACETING

Subject headings and classification categories share other features, among them the way the headings or categories are formulated and displayed. Two ways of formulating and displaying subject headings are to establish complete headings and categories and list them—called *enumeration*—or to establish the parts from which headings and categories might be formed and allow the catalogers or the searchers to put the parts together as needed—called *faceting*. Because a faceted subject-heading system or classification requires synthesizing a heading or category from the parts, faceted systems are also called "synthetic." When using an enumerative system, catalogers find a desired subject heading or classification category in the listing. When using a faceted or synthetic system, catalogers combine available parts to create the desired subject heading or classification category.

Another way of looking at enumeration versus faceting is to ask if a subject heading or classification source provides prebuilt combinations of complex headings or categories or if catalogers are expected to do the work of building them. When the combinations are prepared in advance of use, the source is enumerative. These kinds of sources are also called "precoordinated." When the combinations are not prepared in advance of use, the source is faceted, also called "postcoordinated." Examples of enumerative systems include the *Sears List of Subject Headings*, *Library of Congress Subject Headings* (LCSH), Dewey Decimal Classification (DDC), and Library of Congress Classification (LCC). Faceted or synthetic systems include the keywords used in searching computer databases or the Internet. A keyword, although it might be used as a subject by itself, is likely to be combined with other keywords to represent complex subjects, thus behaving like a facet (or part) of the whole.

Searching a keyword such as "restaurants" in a huge database such as the Internet could retrieve tens of thousands of hits, but combining "restaurants" and "Boston" and "reviews" could whittle them down to a smaller group of reviews for Boston restaurants. Postcoordination permits the parts—location (Boston), approach (reviews), and topic (restaurants)—to be entered in any order to retrieve materials that contain them all. A precoordinated system would have a subject heading or classification category for reviews of food served in Boston restaurants that could look like one of the following (the list is not exhaustive—more combinations are possible):

BOSTON—RESTAURANTS—REVIEWS
RESTAURANTS—BOSTON—REVIEWS
RESTAURANT REVIEWS—BOSTON
REVIEWS, RESTAURANT—BOSTON

A precoordinated classification scheme might subordinate location and approach under the topic, restaurants, as in the second heading in the previous list. It might combine the topic and approach directly (restaurant reviews) or indirectly (reviews, restaurant) as in the third and fourth headings. Or, it might subordinate reviews of restaurants under the location, Boston, as in the first heading. What it would not do is allow more than one of those choices.

To succeed in searching a precoordinated index or classification, the cataloger needs to know the principle focus of the subject or where the topic is located in relation to other topics. The Dewey Decimal Classification appends an alphabetic index in which subject terms containing the word "water," such as "waterwheels" and "water spirits," are brought together for consultative purposes. In this way, classifiers can see that resources covering waterwheels are close to resources covering other mechanical devices in the call numbers for technology (621+) while those covering water spirits are near fairy tale creatures in call numbers for folklore (398+).

SUBJECT AUTHORITIES: SUBJECT HEADING VOCABULARIES

Subject cataloging is a type of indexing[1] done by catalogers for the materials they catalog. Indexing specialists do the same kind of work on the texts of individual books, for which they prepare back-of-the-book indexes. Indexers also work on journal articles, book chapters, research reports, Web sites, and similar documents, preparing ongoing periodical indexes, such as *Readers' Guide to Periodical Literature.* Like library catalogs, periodical indexes also list authors' names and article titles.

The same principles apply to all types of indexing, including subject cataloging, and the same search skills are needed to retrieve indexed material from catalogs, periodical indexes, and back-of-the-book indexes. The main differences among the types of indexing are the nature of the material being indexed and the degree of specificity of the indexing. Back-of-the-book indexers work on individual documents and prepare very specific indexes consisting of up to hundreds or even thousands of terms for one document. Periodical indexers work on articles appearing in magazines and journals (and article equivalents, such as book chapters), and they do broader indexing, consisting of a number of terms per article. Subject catalogers work on monographs and whole title runs, and they do very broad indexing, assigning a handful of terms to describe the contents of the documents at a summary level.

Words used to represent the subjects of materials listed in the catalog can be taken from different sources, depending on individual library policy. Standard terms come from published lists accepted by the library community for use as sources for subject headings in the catalog, called *subject authorities.* Subject authorities are much like the name authorities discussed in chapter 15. Because subject authorities effectively control which words can and cannot be used as subject headings, they are also known as *controlled vocabularies.* Libraries usually choose one standard subject authority. In recent years, however, some libraries have chosen to combine more than one subject authority in their catalogs, using a general subject authority for most materials and specialized authorities for a few disciplines, such as art or medicine.

An entirely different type of word list can be derived from keywords, for example, by compiling lists of important title words. (Articles such as "a," "an," and "the," and other words that do not reflect subject matter, are ignored.) Because no one controls the words authors choose for their titles, such word lists are referred to as *uncontrolled vocabularies.* Computer-based catalogs are frequently programmed to search title words. Individual words may also be searched when they are part of authorized subject headings. Thus, people speak of title keywords and subject keywords, which are not the same thing. Enabling both types of searching accomplishes two things simultaneously: subject headings from the controlled vocabulary provide precision in identifying relevant material; subject headings from the uncontrolled vocabulary increase the possibility that searchers' words match authors' title words, thus increasing the number of potential hits in answer to a search request. To maximize the possibility of finding desired materials, both types of subject terms can be used. Catalogers provide the authorized headings, while computer systems are programmed to find and retrieve materials containing the uncontrolled keywords.

PRINCIPLES OF SUBJECT CATALOGING

Two kinds of principles affect subject cataloging: those underlying the selection of words and phrases authorized as subject headings and those underlying the assignment of subject headings to materials. According to Cutter's "Objects," the catalog should serve as a finding list for subjects and should bring together all items on a subject, just as it does for authors, titles, and editions. But because subject headings are words, language issues arise, such as words with several possible meanings, words whose meanings change over time, and so on. The word "bridges," for example, could refer to dental bridges, structures that span bodies of water, bony ridges on people's noses, parts of stringed instruments, or the control rooms of ships. An example of evolving meaning is the word "lobby." Once it was interpreted as a noun meaning an entrance foyer of a building such as a hotel; now, it can also be interpreted as a verb that means to "try to influence legislation." Other linguistic issues include but are not limited to whether to use singular or plural nouns, which verb forms to use, whether to invert modified nouns or keep them in natural (direct) order, and how to formulate complex topics.

Similarly, decisions about the assignment of subject headings involve questions such as how much material on a subject must be present in a document to justify assigning a subject heading to it and in what order topical, geographic, and chronological elements in a complex subject should appear. While the assignment of subject headings is, essentially, a subjective activity, agreement on general principles can help make it less idiosyncratic.

Subject catalogs can be arranged alphabetically or in classified, or subject, order. Generally, catalogs that use verbal subject headings are arranged alphabetically, though they could be arranged in classified order. Classified catalogs are usually arranged according to classification numbers. (The library shelflist is an example of a classified catalog.) North Americans are familiar with alphabetical subject indexes because this is how their library catalogs usually are arranged. Classified catalogs may contain the same terms, but arranged in *subject* order, with the broadest topics given first, followed by related but narrower topics in a logical organization for each major subject division.

In a classified subject catalog, the entire catalog might be divided into a few main classes, for example, HUMANITIES, NATURAL SCIENCES, and SOCIAL SCIENCES. HUMANITIES is the broadest term in the first section and would be followed by individual humanities disciplines: ART, LITERATURE, MUSIC, RELIGION, and so forth. In turn, MUSIC would be followed by still smaller topics, such as VOCAL MUSIC and INSTRUMENTAL MUSIC. It is easy to see the contrast with an alphabetical, or dictionary, catalog such as those in most media centers and public libraries. There, the same topics would be arranged as follows: ART, HUMANITIES, INSTRUMENTAL MUSIC, LITERATURE, MUSIC, NATURAL SCIENCES, RELIGION, SOCIAL SCIENCES, and VOCAL MUSIC. HUMANITIES follows ART, which seems odd, and MUSIC follows INSTRUMENTAL MUSIC but precedes VOCAL MUSIC, which would seem peculiar to users of classified subject catalogs. A hybrid catalog, partly classified and partly alphabetical, was also devised, called an *alphabetico-classified* catalog. In this catalog, principal headings are in classified order, but headings at each level of hierarchy are arranged alphabetically (see Figure 16.1).

In the column on the left in Figure 16.1, levels of hierarchy are distinguished by indentations. Other ways of showing hierarchical levels include thumb tabs and guide cards if indentations are inconvenient to display, and they need not be identified at all. A knowledgeable searcher knows that MUSIC falls under HUMANITIES and that

Classified Order	Alphabetic Order
Humanities	Art
Art	Humanities
Literature	Instrumental music
Music	Literature
Instrumental music	Music
Vocal music	Natural sciences
Religion	Religion
Natural sciences	Social sciences
Social sciences	Vocal music

Figure 16.1. Subject-heading arrangements.

INSTRUMENTAL MUSIC and VOCAL MUSIC are at a narrower level than MUSIC in general.

Though the arrangements of terms can vary, the choice of terms and their assignment flow from one set of principles:

1. *Synonyms cannot be used simultaneously as headings in a catalog.* Librarians rely on subject authorities to avoid using two headings that mean the same thing, for example, AUTOMOBILES versus CARS. If both terms are likely to be searched, both may be listed, but only one is authorized for use; the other will refer to the term actually used.

2. *Words chosen as subject headings have clear and precise meanings.* Subject authorities avoid words with more than one meaning, or, when such words must be used, something is added that indicates the intended meaning, for example, BARS (DRINKING ESTABLISHMENTS), BARS (ENGINEERING), BARS (FURNITURE), and BARS (GEOMORPHOLOGY).

3. *Terms assigned as subject headings match the specificity of the topics they represent.* A term should not be broader or narrower (that is, more specific) than the topic it represents. For example, if CALCULATORS is a heading, it should be defined to exclude computers, which, although they also manipulate numbers, are a different type of machine. In *Library of Congress Subject Headings,* the scope note at CALCULATORS says: "Here are entered works on present-day calculators as well as on calculators and mechanical computers of pre-1945 vintage. Works on modern electronic computers first developed after 1945 are entered under Computers."[2]

4. *Each subject heading term is discrete with respect to all others.* Problems occur when overlaps in meaning occur between subject headings, particularly when they are all at the same level of hierarchy, such as

BIOLOGY, BIOCHEMISTRY, and CHEMISTRY. Where does BIOL-OGY end and BIOCHEMISTRY begin? Where does BIOCHEMISTRY end and CHEMISTRY begin? If all are used in the same catalog, each must cover discrete territory.

David Judson Haykin, a respected head of LC's subject division in the 1950s, codified the principles that apply to subject-heading assignment at LC. They are based, for the most part, on Cutter's ideas, and remain to this day the definitive expression of our basic assumptions about subject heading practice:

1. *The reader as the focus.* The primary consideration in choosing a word as a subject heading is that it is the one people are most likely to look for in the catalog.
2. *Unity.* A subject catalog must gather under one heading all the materials that deal with the subject, no matter what terms are used for it by authors, and whatever changing terms are used at different times. Catalogers choose the term with care and apply it uniformly to all materials on the subject.
3. *Usage.* The heading chosen is in common use.
4. *English versus foreign terms.* English-language terms are preferred unless a concept is foreign to Anglo-American experience, or when a foreign term is precise while its English counterpart is not.
5. *Specificity.* When assigned, headings should be as specific as the topics they cover, not broader or narrower. Rather than apply a broader heading, catalogers should use two specific headings that will approximately cover the topic.[3]

EVALUATING SUBJECT CATALOGS

Subject catalogs can be evaluated using at least six criteria: recall, relevance, precision, exhaustivity, ease of use, and cost. These are described in detail in this section.

Recall refers to the amount of material retrieved when a heading is used in a search. To be considered good, subject headings in the catalog should retrieve enough material to satisfy searchers but not overwhelm them. If every movie in a very large collection of videorecordings of made-for-television movies had a different subject heading, the recall would be one item per subject heading. If all the items were assigned TELEVISION MOVIES, the searcher would retrieve all of them with that heading. A balance is sought between these extremes. Someone using a subject heading should recall all items related to the subject but exclude unrelated items.

Relevance refers to how well materials retrieved using a subject heading match the searcher's needs. A good subject catalog earns high marks here. The more specific a search is, the more likely what is found will be relevant. If a searcher wants something about computer programming and uses the subject heading PROGRAMMING (ELECTRONIC COMPUTERS), he should recall every item in the collection about the subject. However, that heading is assigned only to items entirely about the topic, not to items with just a chapter about it. If the broader subject heading COMPUTERS were added to the original search, the searcher would retrieve items having a chapter or two about programming, but this larger batch of material would also contain material about hardware, computer architecture, network design, and other irrelevant subjects. Relevance tends to decrease as the amount of recall increases, so relevance and recall are said to have an *inverse relationship.*

Precision is the ability to specify exactly what is wanted, without using broader subject headings representing other things as well. Imagine that the searcher in the previous example was interested only in items about programming in BASIC, one programming language. The subject heading PROGRAMMING (ELECTRONIC COMPUTERS) retrieves material on all programming languages, including BASIC. If, however, the searcher used the subject heading BASIC (COMPUTER PROGRAM LANGUAGE), he or she would retrieve only materials covering BASIC programming. It allows for much more precision because it is narrower than either COMPUTERS or PROGRAMMING (ELECTRONIC COMPUTERS). Precision varies with subject heading specificity and is affected by the presence of overlapping and ambiguous terminology.

Exhaustivity refers to the amount (or depth) of subject cataloging. Some catalogers give each resource only one subject heading. Others may give up to three or five headings, both common practices, to cover the overall subject matter of each item. Some catalogers might wish to furnish more, for example, subject headings for each chapter of a book or each part of an electronic resource. This is a deeper level, furnishing greater exhaustivity. The highest marks for exhaustivity go to a catalog furnishing subject headings for every idea contained within an item, like a back-of-the-book index.

Ease of use is judged by catalogers who assign subject headings and ordinary people using the library who search the catalog to find material they want. The subject heading system should be easy for both kinds of people to use. Catalogers should be able to find the headings they want quickly and have straightforward rules to follow for assigning headings. Ordinary people should be able to retrieve relevant materials using familiar words and phrases. If the words they search do not retrieve any material, they should be assisted to try more productive alternatives.

Cost is an important factor to consider. The subject catalog must be affordable and should provide good service for the money spent on it. The dollars spent on producing and maintaining the subject catalog is one thing to consider. The faster subject cataloging work can be done, the lower the cost per unit cataloged. A system that allows computers or clerical staff to do the work generally is less costly than one that requires librarians to function. But cost alone is not the whole issue. In measuring the value received, another factor to consider is the impact of cataloging. If the catalog helps people find relevant material quickly and easily, the cost of subject cataloging may be justified. Cost is relative, and no standard measures for high- and low-cost cataloging exist. However, variations in cost and resulting service can be measured, if objective definitions of service are devised (e.g., better service = fewer requests for assistance with searches, or better service = an increase in use of materials with no more than a 2 percent increase in requests for assistance with searches). Once a definition of good service is established, experiments that balance cost and service can be done.

There are tradeoffs among cost, speed, and quality in producing and using subject catalogs. One criterion cannot measure a catalog's worth, and all the criteria just described need to be put into a reasonable balance to achieve good service at bearable cost. No magic formulas dictate how deeply to index or how many cross-references to make, but problems demand the attention of concerned practitioners.

PROBLEMS OF THE SUBJECT CATALOG

Problems occur when different terms are used to express the same topic (sometimes due to changes over time in the meaning and usage of words or among the works of different authors); when topics overlap; when the number of records recalled in an average search is too great or too small; and, perhaps most critical of all, when authorized headings and searchers' vocabularies do not match. A person using terms that are not present in the catalog as subject headings or cross-references will find nothing. To promote the identification feature of the subject catalog, words used by searchers and authors should be present as headings. But if this were done, how would works on a subject be brought together? To promote the collocating feature, synonymous and quasi-synonymous terms are combined in one or a few carefully defined terms, whose specificity results in reasonable numbers of relevant retrieved items.

These conflicts have no single resolution, but computers offer new possibilities. Computers enable catalog users to search the words found in titles, summaries, and other descriptive areas containing information about the content of works in "natural language" (that is, not in subject heading terminology) in addition to the designated subject headings. Computers permit searching any word of a subject heading (that is, a subject keyword), even if it is not the first word of a heading. Such searches were not possible in card catalogs, in which only the word in the filing position (called the "lead term") could be searched. New retrieval capabilities made possible when subject catalogs are computerized include the following:

- Searches with partial data (for example, if an asterisk stands for any letters, COMPUT* can retrieve both COMPUT*ERS* and COMPUT*ING,* and *COMPUT* can retrieve both of those plus *MICRO*COMPUT*ERS* and *MINI*COMPUT*ERS*).
- Search requests can be saved and used in more than one database or catalog file.
- More than one subject heading can be combined into complex requests, for example, COMPUTERS AND ART, or MUSIC AND POPULAR NOT JAZZ.
- A subject heading can be combined with other bibliographic elements in a single search, for example, SU = SYMPHONIES AND AU = MOZART.
- The catalog can be accessed from outside the library via the Internet.
- Local acquisition and circulation data, as well as catalog records, can be accessed so a searcher can determine an item's availability.

This list is not exhaustive. The boundaries between search capabilities that require use of a particular kind of subject vocabulary and those that only need a properly programmed computer system are blurring. The use of computers did not make controlled vocabularies obsolete, as some predicted in the 1980s. Instead, it led to intensified efforts to improve controlled vocabularies and develop new ways to search data elements likely to express subject content.

SUBJECT AUTHORITIES: NUMBERS FOR CLASSIFICATION

A second type of subject-related authority is the source from which numbers for classification are taken. The DDC and the LCC, two of the most popular classification systems, are discussed in chapter 18. Both systems consist mainly of lists of numbers, each number paired with a term for the subject matter it represents. Helpful information is often added to the list of numbers, such as introductions giving the history and background of the system, instructions on how to assign the numbers, and indexes (that is, lists of verbal terms) to the numbers. Individual numbers or groups of numbers, known as "number spans," may have scope notes explaining what they cover or exclude and, in the latter instance, suggested alternatives.

Libraries generally choose one classification to assign to their materials, although nothing prevents them from adopting multiple classifications simultaneously. In the United States and Canada, classification numbers are used mainly to arrange materials on library shelves, forming the basis of shelf addresses that group materials covering the same topics. In other parts of the world, classification numbers may be used to organize catalogs and bibliographies as well as to shelve materials. The *British National Bibliography* is an example of a bibliography arranged by Dewey numbers. North American libraries often maintain shelflists—catalogs arranged by call number—for inventory-control purposes. Traditionally, shelflists were separate card files accessible solely to library staff. Today, shelflists are part of computerized catalogs and may be accessed by the public and by library staff members.

Like subject vocabularies, classifications can be precoordinated/enumerative or postcoordinated/faceted/synthetic. Elements of pre- and postcoordination appear in DDC and LCC to different degrees. LCC is overwhelmingly precoordinated, enumerating hundreds of thousands of numbers for classifiers to assign to materials. Nevertheless, LCC also has tables listing specific aspects of topics to be added to numbers from the main list if classifiers want to limit or qualify a topic. DDC has fewer numbers in its enumeration. It also has six auxiliary tables listing aspects of topics that further specify them and instructions within number spans to apply subdivisions of one topic to other topics within the span. Tables and subdivision instructions add a measure of synthesis to the systems. They economize on the total number of enumerated classification numbers. Over time, DDC has grown from fewer than 50 pages to more than 3,000, and LCC consists of more than 40 volumes, so such economies are valuable both from practical and theoretical points of view.

Fully faceted classifications are not used very much in North America, but they have enjoyed popularity elsewhere in the world. Among the better-known faceted classifications are the Colon Classification, the Universal Decimal Classification, and the Bliss Classification. Colon Classification originated in the early part of the 20th century, devised by S. R. Ranganathan, an Indian librarian. It was adopted by a number of Indian libraries, though the number has dwindled in recent years. Colon

Classification divides the universe of knowledge into 41 main classes to which numbers for five facets are added to build complete numbers. Ranganathan called his five facet types Personality, Matter, Energy, Space, and Time. A complex system of letters from multiple alphabets, numbers, and symbols are used for the numbers.

The Universal Decimal Classification (UDC; see http://www.udcc.org), a transformation of DDC devised by Belgians Henri Otlet and Henri La Fontaine, internationalized DDC by translating it into French. UDC was also intended to accommodate automation. The United Nations Educational, Scientific, and Cultural Organization (UNESCO) adopted UDC, which uses Arabic numbers and a few symbols, and updated it in the latter part of the 20th century. Since then, it has been used in Europe to arrange bibliographies.

The Bliss Classification, devised by Henry Evelyn Bliss, librarian at the City College of New York, was used for many years in that library and a few libraries in England, but it did not develop a following. Bliss Classification uses capital letters and a few symbols. After Bliss's death, practical considerations in keeping the system up-to-date and teaching classifiers how to assign the numbers led the City College of New York library to switch to LCC. British librarians John Mills and Vanda Broughton continue to update the Bliss system, but its users remain a small group of libraries.[4]

The discussion of the kinds of characters and symbols used by various classifications raises the question of the choice of characters used to represent the categories. Known as the *notation,* classifications can use only one type or more than one; for example, letters only or letters and numbers. Single-character notation is called *pure notation,* and multiple-character notation is called *mixed notation.* DDC uses pure notation (Arabic numbers, punctuated once with a dot or point, hence the name "decimal"), whereas LCC uses a mixed notation consisting of capital letters and Arabic numbers, sometimes punctuated by a dot or point. The type of notation used results in longer or shorter combinations for very specific topics. In a pure notation system, the more specific a category is the longer the number representing it must be. A mixed notation system has greater flexibility to vary the types and positions of the characters in order to keep numbers short, even for very specific topics.

PRINCIPLES OF CLASSIFICATION

Classification systems use codes called "numbers" to identify the subject matter of materials, even when the numbers consist of characters other than digits. The use of numbers on the materials frees classification from many of the linguistic problems that affect subject headings and subject catalogs. Still, classifications have problems of their own and they are not completely free of language-related problems. The lists of classification numbers use words to identify the subject matter the numbers represent, but these words are not displayed to the public.

An issue of importance is the underlying philosophy of the classification, which dictates the method chosen to distinguish subjects from one another. A series of main classes is selected as the first analysis of knowledge into smaller components. Then, subsequent subdivisions may follow the same pattern or different patterns, and all subject areas may be treated alike or each subject area may be treated differently, according to ideas associated solely with that area. One might begin by dividing the universe of knowledge into animal, vegetable, and mineral. Or one might divide it into humanities, social sciences, and sciences. Some might divide it into earth, sky, fire, and water. Library classifications usually divide knowledge into disciplines familiar to academia. DDC begins with 10 main classes; LCC with 21; and Colon Classification with 41. None of these systems is good or bad, better or worse; none is right or wrong. They simply start from different perspectives and draw their boundaries differently.

A classification must cover all the subjects needed for the materials in the collection, which, for general libraries, means the entire universe of knowledge. A medical library might not need a classification that deals in detail with music and religion, but some subtopics related to these disciplines need to be covered, such as music therapy, medical problems unique to musicians, religious tenets pertaining to medicine and medical practice, and faith healing, among others. If there were no numbers in the classification for music and religion per se, these would have to be subsumed under other rubrics. To function over long periods of time, a classification must be open to the inclusion of new subjects not known when the classification originated—a feature of classification called "hospitality." It is difficult to predict where new topics and subtopics will emerge or whether changes will occur in the relationships among topics, but since knowledge in all subjects is constantly evolving, a classification must be able to handle the changes.

To be easily used, the system must follow logical, recognizable patterns, both for the people using its numbers to find materials and for library classifiers assigning its numbers to materials. Easily memorized notation is a feature that contributes to ease of use. Short numbers are more convenient than long ones, although in classifications that show the whole hierarchy preceding a very specific topic, the numbers can be very long.

DDC and LCC both employ the principle of relative location, which means that materials are shifted to accommodate new materials being added to a library's collection so the new items stand with others on the same subjects. Both also operate on the principle of classification by discipline, although they differ about what constitutes a discipline or main class. DDC has fewer main classes than LCC, even though both cover all subjects. Some (but not all) of the differences between the way the two systems divide knowledge include the following:

- DDC has one main class for all the social sciences (300); LCC has four that include H (e.g., sociology, demographics, economics, social problems), J (political science), K (law), and L (education).
- DDC makes medicine a subdivision of technology and applied science (612), while LCC makes medicine a main class (R).
- DDC divides language and literature into two separate main classes (400 and 800, respectively), whereas LCC combines them into one large main class (P).

The philosophies underlying DDC and LCC differ considerably. DDC is a natural or hierarchical classification of all knowledge in which each discipline starts with the broadest possible categories and proceeds through narrower categories until the most specific categories of the subject are represented. This principle of hierarchy facilitates browsing and discovery by less knowledgeable searchers. DDC has one set of rules for the entire classification and employs memory aids. LCC is designed only to arrange LC's materials on its shelves in a logical, subject-oriented order. LC's stacks are closed to the public and browsing is not an issue. LCC uses the same rules within a main class but permits different rules to apply between main classes.

Some classification systems do not reflect the subject content of materials and primarily provide shelf location, not subject access. One such system assigns numbers to materials sequentially as each item is added to a collection; for example, book 1 is the first book acquired, book 2 is the second, and so forth. This is called an "accession number" system and reflects the order of acquisition. In an accession number system, materials are not shifted when new items arrive. Once classified, materials remain in the same place for as long as they are held. Another system alphabetizes materials, shelving them by a chosen element, usually authors' names or title words. These systems are logical, follow recognizable patterns, and provide shelf addresses for materials, but they fail to reveal subject matter or group materials on a subject in one place on the shelves. Caution should be used before adopting these systems, because they make browsing difficult and are costly to change.

North American library classifications are used primarily for shelving and, therefore, are two dimensional or linear. The numbers start at the first one and proceed sequentially to the last one, for example, 001–999 for DDC or A-Z for LCC. Knowledge, however, does not behave in a linear fashion. Think of the topics mentioned previously: medicine, music, and religion. They are distinct disciplines, but they have cross-disciplinary meanings, such as music therapy and faith healing. Music therapy is also related to religious music and aromatherapy, and faith healing is related to faith-based charities and meditation chants, which can be involved in medical treatment. Topics do not follow one after the other in linear fashion but instead branch out helter-skelter in all directions. All the relationships cannot be maintained simultaneously in a linear system.

Faceted systems, which begin with the parts of subjects, behave differently. In a faceted system, related parts can be moved about to stand together, on request. For instance, faith-based charities and faith healing can be linked through a number that stands for "faith." Aromatherapy and music therapy can be linked via a number for "therapy." Faceted classification numbers can be permuted to link whatever common facets are present. When used for shelving, though, only some of the numbers can be used, because library shelves are linear and only accommodate a linear sequence of numbers. In a catalog or a bibliography, however, the numbers can be displayed as appropriate in different places to show each of the facets to a searcher, as shown in Figure 16.2. (Note the similarity to keyword searching.)

CALL NUMBERS

Classification numbers, as mentioned, are the basis for locating materials on library shelves. Numbers or alphabetic codes representing such elements as main entries, particular collections, dates of publication, titles, volumes, and so on, known collectively as shelf marks, are usually added to classification numbers to complete the addresses for materials. The entire combination, consisting of the classification number plus the shelf marks, is known as a *call number.*

In the DDC, Music = 780; Medicine = 610; and Religion = 200. If DDC were faceted, the topics discussed in this section could be expressed as follows:

Music therapy	= 780 + 610 (music + medical treatment)
Faith healing	= 200 + 610 (religion + medical treatment)
Religious music	= 200 + 700 (religion + music)

A catalog or a bibliography could list them as follows:

200 + 610	= Faith healing
200 + 780	= Religious music
610 + 200	= Healing by faith
610 + 780	= Healing by music
780 + 200	= Music in religion
780 + 610	= Music therapy

Rules for shelving can permit only one sequence, however, such as listing the facets from lower to higher numbers only. Each topic is shelved in one place, based on the six assigned numbers. The result is:

2006610	= Faith healing
200780	= Religious music
610780	= Music therapy

Figure 16.2. The DDC as a faceted scheme.

Librarians are not unanimous about assigning a different call number to each title in a library's collection. Large libraries often choose to assign a unique call number to each title. Small libraries that have no more than a few titles on most subjects have no problem when several different ones are shelved at the "same" address. (The word "same" is enclosed in quotations because two physical entities cannot occupy the same space; rather, it means all the titles that share the same call number may be randomly shelved at the designated location.)

The first shelf mark assigned after a document is classified usually is, by unofficial agreement, an alphanumeric code representing the main entry of the item called a *cutter number.* The name comes from the fact that Charles Cutter was the first to publish a list of these codes. Cutter's tables were later revised by a librarian named Margaret Sanborn and called Cutter-Sanborn tables.[5] LC synthesizes cutter numbers from a simple set of rules available free via its Web site.[6] Today cutter is spelled with a small "c" and is also a verb—librarians refer to assigning these numbers as "cuttering" them.

Small libraries and media centers sometimes substitute call letters for cutter numbers in call numbers because they are easier to apply. The first one, two, or three letters of the main entry are used as call letters. If the main entry is a title, the call letters are not taken from initial articles but from the word following them. Call letters may be expressed in all uppercase letters or both uppercase and lowercase letters. For example, a book by Jane Austen could be assigned the call letters A, AU, Au, AUS, or Aus, depending on the policy on call letters and preferred lettering style. This system does not always produce unique call numbers; for example, books on the same subject by two authors named Rose and Ross could have the same classification number and the same call letters. In a small collection this is not a problem and saves money in the classifier's time and the purchase of special cuttering tools.

Other shelf marks in call numbers may include one or more letters of the alphabet preceding the classification number for the particular collection to which an item belongs, such as "R" or "Ref," for reference materials or "J" for children's materials (standing for "Juvenile" materials). Alphabetic designations for biography (B/BIO/Bio), fiction (F/FIC/Fic), oversized items (O), and audiovisual materials (AV) are popular, also. Within particular collections, subcategories can be distinguished by the use of spine labels depicting icons for science fiction (an atom), mystery (a gun), westerns (a rearing horse), or Canadian items (a maple leaf). These labels describe content rather than location but can also be used for location.

A popular addition to cutter numbers symbolizing author main entries for authors who write more than one title is a letter or two from the first significant word in each title. This addition results in arranging the author's works on the shelf in alphabetical order by title without having to look beyond the call number. The method works, but it tends to lengthen call numbers and complicate them for classifiers and members of the public seeking desired items.

Dates added to call numbers are now frequently encountered in libraries. At first, LC added them primarily to distinguish editions of a title subsequent to the first edition. Thus, a copy of the 22nd edition of DDC shelved in the reference collection might have the complex LCC call number R/Z696/.D519/2003, meaning:

R = Reference collection
Z696 = LCC classification number for library classifications.
D519 = The cutter number for Dewey, the author main entry
2003 = Date of the edition

In recent years, dates are routinely added as shelf marks, following the cutter numbers.

The final shelf mark classifiers may add, as appropriate, are volume numbers. Volume numbers distinguish individual volumes of multivolume titles. For example, DDC is a four-volume document. All the volumes are assigned the same call number, so each individual volume also needs a volume number, following the date, to ensure that it is shelved in the proper order.

Complex call numbers containing many shelf marks are useful for staff in large libraries who shelve many items with similar call numbers, but they are hard for members of the public to remember when they go from the catalog to the shelf, and difficult to write down without making mistakes. Library policies governing small collections can simplify call numbers by mandating fewer shelf marks, thus making it easier for members of the public to retrieve (or request) materials. It might not make much difference in small libraries if several materials share the same call number.

EVALUATING CLASSIFICATIONS

Criteria similar to those used in evaluating subject catalogs can be applied to classifications. They include the level of specificity afforded by the system; the browsability it produces; its ease of use, including understandable notation, mnemonics, indexing, and simple rules for the assignment of numbers; its hospitality to new subjects; regular updating; and its cost.

The level of specificity should be appropriate to the size and distribution of the library's collections. If the classification has a few broad numbers, many items on diverse aspects of a topic will be classified in the same number. If it has a great many narrow numbers, very few items will be classified in the same number even if their content is closely related. A balance appropriate to the collection being classified should be sought. Sometimes, local adjustments to classification systems are made by libraries to accommodate their individual needs.

Browsability as a feature of classifications depends to a large degree on the subject relationships it presents. In most instances, progression from broader to narrower topics in a subject area enhances browsing. The logic of subject relationships should be clear to a searcher, making it possible to anticipate where to look for a desired subject or subdivision. The juxtaposition of subjects also affects browsability. Folklore and cannibalism—subjects most people do not consider closely related—are only a few numbers apart in DDC, whereas English language and English literature are several hundred numbers apart. Similarly, dance and drama are quite far apart in LCC (dance is in G; drama in P) even though many people think of them as closely related performing arts, whereas they are neighbors in DDC (dance is in the 790s; theater is in the 800s).

Ease of use depends on many factors, including an easily remembered, easily understood type of notation. The flexibility of the notation to handle numerous narrow categories while still being economical also affects the ease of use, as does mnemonic numbering (using the same number for a topic or subtopic wherever it appears). The presence of good indexes to the numbers is essential for classifiers and ordinary searchers. An asset for classifiers is the existence of relatively uncomplicated rules for assigning the numbers.

Regarding *hospitality,* classification systems cannot be expected to cover unknown subjects, but how new subjects are handled when they emerge is a matter of concern. Ideally, a hospitable system can incorporate them into the list of numbers in a way that retains appropriate relations with related subjects. Practically speaking, this can also mean having to revise related areas, as was the case when the subject of computers emerged. Classifications must be updated regularly to add or alter categories as knowledge of subjects and perceptions of their relationships change over the years.

The *cost* of using a classification is an important aspect of its total value. If a cataloger adopts the same classification as his or her peers and can share the burden of assigning numbers to commonly held materials, it is likely to be less costly than using a unique classification and doing all the work alone. Cost was a major factor in the decisions of college and university libraries that changed from other classifications to LCC after OCLC's shared cataloging database was established. Because LC's cataloging was the lion's share of the records in the network database in its early years, it was less costly for OCLC member libraries to copy its numbers and avoid the burden of classifying the same materials differently. The cost of the classification authority and related materials is another factor to be considered as well as the average time and necessary expertise required for assigning numbers to new materials.

Some features, such as browsability and ease of use, are difficult to measure. Doing so means translating them into concrete terms so they can be measured. It is worth making a serious effort to do so if changes in a library's classification practices are contemplated. Although savings might be achieved in some areas, new costs might be incurred in other areas. Sometimes the savings only benefit the library, whereas the searchers end up having to do more work to find what they want. The value of a classification should be figured as a total package that includes the amount of service provided as well as the total cost.

MAINTENANCE ISSUES

Maintaining subject catalogs and classifications involves making policy decisions. When card catalogs were the rule, libraries could choose whether to present one dictionary catalog containing name, title, and subject headings in one file or divide the file into two separate files: one for names and titles, and a second for subjects. Current computerized catalogs typically require that searchers select an index before entering a search term (subject, title, keyword, or name). This is the same as presenting several divided files. If their first attempts do not bring the desired results, searchers must remember to try other available files.

Another policy issue concerns cross-references. Keeping track of cross-references and changing them when necessary is a difficult and costly process. Cross-references branch out rapidly—one heading can have several cross-references, each of which has more of its own. Decisions must be made about how extensively these will be made. Searchers dislike cross-references that lead them to terms having no materials listed under them, called *blind references*. Policies for maintaining the cross-reference structure can prevent this from happening. Some librarians believe cross-references teach users about related subjects and that all references given in the subject authority should be present in the catalog whether or not they lead to any entries. (If such a policy is followed, catalogers can add notations to headings that lack materials explaining that the library has no holdings on those topics.) Others believe the cost of creating and maintaining a living cross-reference structure (called a *syndetic* structure) is unwarranted when it doesn't lead to use of materials.

Each library must weigh three alternatives—to include all, some, or no cross-references—and arrive at a viable policy for its catalog. Some decide about cross-references on a case-by-case basis, but it is more efficient to systematize the policy so that individual decisions are unnecessary.

The way subject headings are filed also has implications for maintenance. Two different arrangements of subject headings are furnished by the rules used by LC and those published by American Library Association (ALA).[7] The Library of Congress's filing rules distinguish between different subject heading forms and subdivision types. ALA's filing rules do not. Figure 16.3 illustrates how the use of each method would cause an identical group of headings to be arranged.

Maintaining the library's classification system also involves decisions. Foremost among these is how to incorporate updates to the system. Ideally, all changes to the numbers are adopted, which means the affected materials and their catalog records are reprocessed with new numbers and shelved in their new locations. In a less-than-

Filed by the ALA Filing Rules (1980)   Filed by the LC Filing Rules (1980)

```
Music -- Acoustics and physics     Music -- Acoustics and physics
Music and literature               Music -- Discography
Music appreciation                 Music -- History and criticism
Music -- Discography               Music -- Psychological aspects
Music festivals                    Music, Gospel USE Gospel music
Music, Gospel USE Gospel music     Music and literature
Music -- History and criticism     Music appreciation
Music -- Psychological aspects     Music festivals
```

Figure 16.3. Comparison of filing rules.

ideal world in which staff time is at a premium, following such a policy might mean allowing new materials to go unprocessed while staff members revise materials that have already been processed once. Librarians view such developments with displeasure and tend to resist adopting changes in classification numbers. The authors recommend adopting changes judiciously, over limited periods of time, enabling the library to benefit from the results without committing all its resources to making the changes at once.

Another matter of importance, especially for libraries with large collections, is the arrangement of the shelves. Choices include starting with the first number and following through to the last, all-in-one sequence, or grouping parts of the collection out of sequence in specially designated locations. Music and art are sometimes chosen to be set apart from the rest of the collection. Science and technology materials, medical materials, and law materials also may be grouped separately, sometimes in departments or buildings of their own. Reference works are usually deployed in a separate sequence or in special rooms to provide workspace for users. Children's materials are frequently set apart from adult materials, and material intended for teens may be set apart from both of those.

The age of materials may play a role, with older materials stored in less accessible locations and newer materials shelved in more accessible locations. Newly acquired materials, for example, are often placed in the most visible areas so users can find them easily. Exceptions to the regular shelving system can add extra time to a browser's task and to staff workload, but doing so may be justified if it is clear that most people using specific out-of-sequence materials focus solely on them and benefit from having them set apart from other collections. Studies have not been done to demonstrate this is the case, but lack of data has not influenced librarians who wish to adopt such arrangements.

SUBJECT ANALYSIS FOR LITERARY WORKS

Assigning subject headings and classification numbers to literary works (novels, plays, stories, poetry, and so on) also called works of imagination, should be considered carefully. For decades, policies at Library and Archives Canada (LAC), LC, and other large libraries limited the assignment of subject headings to nonfiction works unless they were collections of texts by more than one author, texts augmented by literary criticism, or historical or biographical works. People were thought to seek literary works in the catalog solely by their authors or titles, not by subject. Children and youth, however, often choose (or are guided by parents, teachers, media specialists, and librarians to choose) to learn about something by reading about it in stories. In the 1960s, in response to many requests from librarians and media specialists, LC established new policies for children's fiction providing both subject headings and summary notes. The LC Annotated Card Program, now called "Children's Subject Headings," is discussed more fully in chapter 17.

Searchers have come to expect subject headings for children's fiction. Many years ago, ALA's Subject Analysis Committee published guidelines for assigning them and lists of genre headings for various types of material.[8] Recently, practitioners have argued successfully for the assignment of genre headings for adult fiction in many media. LC experimented with the new genre headings, found them helpful, and encourages others to do the same. Local libraries need to establish policies for subject access to literary works based on estimates of searchers' need for them and the libraries' ability do the added work.

Similarly, many public libraries choose not to classify fiction and biography. They assume that people always seek these materials by an author's name or, in the case of biographies, a subject's name. One code such as F, FIC, or Fic, for fiction and B, BIO, or Bio, for biography is assigned and the materials are shelved in alphabetic order by author or subject. Academic libraries, on the other hand, tend to classify everything, including works of imagination, keeping them in the order prescribed by the classification scheme. This aids catalog searchers and should not hinder browsers at the shelf.

WHY USE STANDARD SYSTEMS?

A library might be tempted to dispense with standard subject headings and standard classification numbers. It might seem easier to make up appropriate headings and numbers than to buy expensive tools and be bound by the terms they offer. Why invest time and money in them? First, making up local subject headings and classification numbers puts the burden of keeping track of selected terms entirely on catalogers' shoulders. Catalogers must also decide how to define subject-heading terms and classification numbers and make up rules about how to apply them. In the case of subject headings, catalogers must also decide what cross-references should be made for each term. In the case of classification, a consistent notation must be constructed. It is time consuming to create and maintain subject and classification authorities, and requires a great deal of expertise to do properly. If other staff members do subject cataloging and classification, lists of headings and class numbers must be made available to them in a usable form. Even if all the work is done alone, a properly written list is needed for searchers to consult. All of this is extremely costly, and makes the cost of published lists conceived and maintained by LC, LAC, and others appear more reasonable.

Second, if catalogers use nonstandard subject headings and classification numbers, they cannot use the ones assigned by others or benefit from the work they do. If the library enters a network environment, the terms can be accommodated as locally defined headings and classification numbers, but no one else can use them.

Third, the catalog is an ongoing tool, not the individual expression of one collection at one point in time, managed by one librarian. Complete, explicit instructions on how headings or classification numbers have been chosen, used, and managed, and a complete list of terms, cross-references, or numbers must be provided to the cataloger's successors. Another librarian might not wish to continue the system or decide that it is not cost-effective and opt to change to a standard system. Then, the entire collection must be converted to standard systems. Establishing unique subject headings or classification numbers should be undertaken only after the library has assessed the alternatives and rejected them for good reasons. A nonstandard subject or classification authority could result in less effective service overall.

Some public libraries are experimenting with "reader interest" classifications, similar to the way that materials are arranged and displayed in bookstores, in place of DDC or LCC. While it is possible that reader interest systems can provide satisfactory service on-site, they preclude enabling the libraries to copy standard call numbers used by other libraries and can complicate browsing for off-site searchers. It remains to be seen whether reader interest classifications attract more followers.

SUMMARY

Subject analysis—describing the content of library materials and making it possible to find by people searching for material on particular subjects—is a matter of determining what the content is and representing it by means of subject headings and classification numbers. Catalogers learn to find clues to subject content via titles, tables of contents, indexes, and other introductory information. Once they are clear about the scope, coverage, and approach of the creator, catalogers can consult subject heading and classification authorities to find appropriate words and numbers for the material.

Two different ways of presenting subject headings and classification numbers are providing lists that enumerate them in their final form and lists of subject parts from which catalogers can build the headings and numbers. Fully formed headings and numbers are said to be precoordinated; parts that must be put together to form headings and numbers are said to be postcoordinated.

Subject heading and classification authorities are described in terms of their underlying principles, criteria for evaluating them, and an overview of their problems. Call numbers—the shelf addresses libraries use to place materials on the shelves—are formed by adding shelf marks to classification numbers.

The maintenance of subject catalogs and classification systems includes decisions on how to deploy the subject catalog's files, whether to have one sequence of shelving or several, and how to deal with updates and other changes in the subject authorities. The trend toward treating literary works (also known as works of imagination) like nonfiction materials by assigning subject headings and classifying them also requires making decisions at the local level about those services.

The chapter closes by asking why the use of standard systems is justified and exploring their value. The next two chapters examine standard subject heading lists and classification systems used by most libraries in North America: Chapter 17 covers *Sears List of Subject Headings* and *Library of Congress Subject Headings*. Chapter 18 covers DDC and LCC.

REVIEW QUESTIONS

1. Where do catalogers look for information about the subject content of materials?

2. What is the difference between precoordinated and postcoordinated subject authorities?

3. Give three examples of subject facets and show how they might be combined to form subject headings in as many ways as you can.

4. Describe how keywords differ from authorized subject headings.

5. Name three principles that underlie subject-heading authorities.

6. Define "shelf mark" and name three types of shelf marks.

7. How do North Americans and Europeans differ in their use of classifications?

8. Why do public libraries sometimes exclude fiction and biography from classification?

9. What does it mean to say that library classifications produce linear shelf arrangements?

10. Name three principles that underlie classification authorities.

NOTES

The epigraph is from Julius O. Kaiser, "Systematic Indexing," in *Theory of Subject Analysis: A Sourcebook*, ed. Lois Mai Chan et al. (Littleton, CO: Libraries Unlimited, 1985), 54–55.

1. Vanda Broughton defines indexing as "the act of determining the subject content of items and assigning appropriate subject indexing terms or notations." Vanda Broughton, *Essential Thesaurus Construction* (London: Facet 2006), 214.

2. See "Scope Note" for the subject heading CALCULATORS at the Library of Congress Web site: authorities.loc.gov/cgi-bin/Pwebrecon.cgi?GetScopeNotes=1&SEQ=20100808215 615&PID=7Xu694Q_81CvXGt-g3DylpqgWH6k.

3. David Judson Haykin, *Subject Headings: A Practical Guide* (Washington, D.C.: Government Printing Office, 1951), 7–9.

4. Bliss Classification Association, "BC2" in "The Bliss Bibliographic Classification: History & Description," http://www.blissclassification.org.uk/bchist.htm.

5. Charles Ammi Cutter, *Two-Figure Author Table* (Littleton, CO: Hargrave House, 1969–); Charles Ammi Cutter, *Three-Figure Author Table* (Littleton, CO: Hargrave House, 1969–);

Charles Ammi Cutter and Margaret Sanborn, *Cutter-Sanborn Three-Figure Author Table,* Swanson-Swift revision (Littleton, CO: Hargrave House, 1969). These tools and four-figure cutter tables are available online for subscribers to OCLC's Dewey Cutter Program.

6.   Library of Congress, Guidelines for Using the LC Online Shelflist and Formulating a Literary Author List, Cutter Table, 2008, http://www.loc.gov/catdir/pcc/053/table.html.

7.   John C. Rather, *Library of Congress Filing Rules* (Washington, D.C.: Library of Congress, 1980), and *ALA Filing Rules* (Chicago, IL: American Library Association, 1980).

8.   Association for Library Collections & Technical Services, Subject Analysis Committee, *Guidelines on Subject Access to Individual Works of Fiction, Drama, Etc.,* 2nd ed. (Chicago, IL: American Library Association, 2000).

SUGGESTED READING

Anderson, James D., and Melissa A. Hoffman. "A Fully Faceted Syntax for Library of Congress Subject Headings." *Cataloging & Classification Quarterly* 43, no. 1 (2006): 7–38.

Foskett, A. C. *The Subject Approach to Information.* 5th ed. London: Library Association Publishing, 1996. (Classic British text on subject theory.)

Google. *A Research Guide.* Chapter 15. A Virtual Library of Useful URLs Subject Headings Arranged by Dewey Decimal Classification: 000-999. http://www.aresearchguide.com/15urls.html.

Guidelines on Subject Access to Individual Works of Fiction, Drama, Etc. 2nd ed. Chicago, IL: American Library Association, 2000.

Hunter, Eric J. *Classification Made Simple: An Introduction to Knowledge Organisation and Information Retrieval.* Surrey, UK: Ashgate, 2009.

IFLA Working Group on FRSAR. *Functional Requirements for Subject Authority Data, 2010-07-03.* http://nkos.slis.kent.edu/FRSAR/index.html.

Library of Congress Working Group on the Future of Bibliographic Control. *On the Record: Report of the Library of Congress Working Group on the Future of Bibliographic Control.* http://www.loc.gov/bibliographic-future/news/lcwg-ontherecord-jan08-final.pdf.

LibraryThing Web site. Tagging. http://www.librarything.com/wiki/index.php/Tagging.

Mann, Thomas. "'On the Record' but Off the Track: A Review of the Report of The Library of Congress Working Group on The Future of Bibliographic Control With a Further Examination of Library of Congress Cataloging Tendencies." March 14, 2008. http://www.guild2910.org/WorkingGrpResponse2008.pdf.

Mann, Thomas. "Why LC Subject Headings Are More Important Than Ever." *American Libraries* (Oct. 2003): 52–54.

Mann, Thomas. "Will Google's Keyword Searching Eliminate the Need for LC Cataloging and Classification?" August 15, 2005. http://www.guild2910.org/searching.htm.

Olson, Hope A., and John J. Boll. *Subject Analysis in Online Catalogs.* 2nd ed. Englewood, CO: Libraries Unlimited, 2001.

Robare, Lori, Adam Schiff, and Rebecca Belford. *New Developments in Genre/Form Access.* Presented at the Oregon Library Association, April 2, 2009. http://www.nwcentral.org/files/Genre_Form_Access_Intro_Robare.pdf.

Rolla, Peter J. "User Tags versus Subject Headings: Can User-Supplied Data Improve Subject Access to Library Collections?" *Library Resources & Technical Services* 53, no. 3 (July 2009): 174–84.

Sauperl, Alenka. *Subject Determination During the Cataloging Process.* Lanham, MD: Scarecrow Press, 2002.

Schwartz, Candy. *Sorting Out the Web: Approaches to Subject Access.* Westport, CT: Ablex, 2001.

Scott, Mona L. *Conversion Tables: LC-Dewey; Dewey-LC; Subject Headings—LC and Dewey.* 2nd ed. Englewood, CO: Libraries Unlimited, 1999. (Available on disk.)

Taylor, Arlene G. *The Organization of Information.* 2nd ed. Westport, CT: Libraries Unlimited, 2004.

Subject Authorities

The difference between the right word and the almost right word is the difference between lightning and the lightning bug.

—Mark Twain

In this chapter, two published lists used as sources for subject headings—*Library of Congress Subject Headings* and *Sears List of Subject Headings*—are described. They are the most popular subject authorities used by libraries in Canada and the United States. Libraries beyond the borders of North America have also adopted them to reap the benefits of global shared cataloging and to save work, time, and money.

LIBRARY OF CONGRESS SUBJECT HEADINGS

Library of Congress Subject Headings (LCSH) began development in 1909, based on a list of subject headings compiled and issued by the American Library Association (ALA) called *The List of Subject Headings for Use in Dictionary Catalogs.* Subject specialists at the Library of Congress (LC) adopted many of the headings exactly as they appeared in the ALA list, modified others, and created new ones when they did not find what they needed on the list. In 1914, LC first published its work under the title *Subject Headings Used in the Dictionary Catalogues of the Library of Congress.* Subsequently, new editions of LCSH appeared about once every 10 years until 1988, when conversion to a computerized database was completed. At that time, printed editions began to be issued annually, and electronic versions were developed, first in CD-ROM and, later, online.

LCSH's vocabulary was initially established, grew, and continues to grow, based on the contents of items in the LC's collection. As a result, it lacks headings for topics not included in the collection. Moreover, it has not followed a consistent set of rules for creating new headings for the list during a century of growth. Subject headings were created according to the ideas of the heads of subject cataloging. Despite these drawbacks, LCSH is widely used in North America, United Kingdom, and elsewhere. Its appeal is attributable to three factors: (1) LC collects many more books in nearly all subjects than other general libraries and, therefore, it needs to establish subject headings for them; (2) it does a fine job of maintaining and distributing the ever-growing list of authorized subject headings and cross-references; and (3) it charges very reasonably for its work.

The Publication

An online version of LCSH is available by subscription from LC as part of its *Classification Web* product. Weekly lists of new and changed LCSH headings are part of LC's *Cataloger's Desktop* product. The LCSH introduction is also included there. Individual subject headings can be searched and browsed free of charge on LC's web site, in its authority files. Still, many libraries continue to buy LCSH in book form. The 32nd edition is current at this writing, although LC's Cataloging Distribution Service Web site states that the 31st edition is still in print. It contains approximately 308,000 authorized terms and cross-references, introductory and explanatory information, and supplementary material—including subdivisions, genre/form headings, and children's headings—bound into six massive volumes with distinctive red covers. Some libraries that purchase the online version of LCSH for the cataloging department also purchase the printed publication as a reference tool for library patrons, keeping it in the reference collection or near the public catalog. Paper updates to the printed LCSH are found in LC's *Cataloging Service Bulletin*, available from its Cataloging Distribution Service as a subscription issued twice a year.

Detailed instructions for applying LCSH are provided separately in *Subject Cataloging Manual: Subject Headings,* also available online in *Cataloger's Desktop* and in a four-volume loose-leaf publication that cumulates decisions and interpretations originally compiled for LC's subject catalogers. In response to requests from libraries using LCSH, LC began to publish the manual so all LCSH users could apply it more consistently. The manual covers general issues; treatment of many types of topics, such as biography, visual images, literary materials; and the appropriate use of a group of general subdivisions known as *free-floating subdivisions.* These are subdivision terms that can be added, with some limitations, to subject headings from the main list. The free-floating subdivisions appear in volume VI of the printed edition, titled *Supplementary Vocabularies,* as well as in *Cataloger's Desktop, Classification Web,* and a separate paper publication titled *Free-Floating Subdivisions: An Alphabetic Index.* Together, the subject heading list and subdivisions, manual, and updates constitute a complete LCSH subject-heading authority system.

Catalogers using LCSH are expected to coordinate their use of the list with other cataloging tools. Most LCSH headings and cross-references are topical terms. Some names appear in the list (see Figure 17.1), but LCSH does not control them. The same name authority file used to control descriptive headings (see chapter 15) is used to control the names of people, geographic locations, corporate bodies, and titles used as subject headings. Catalogers are directed to add name and title headings as needed. When the name authority file does not list a wanted name or title, catalogers establish it following the form prescribed by the *Anglo-American Cataloguing Rules,* second edition, 2002 revision, 2005 update (AACR2-2005). With a few exceptions, catalogers cannot add topical headings to LCSH. Instead, they are instructed to use the most appropriate authorized headings already present in the list and wait for the LC to add the desired new headings.

We (Cameroon people) *(May Subd Geog)*
  UF Kuwe (African people)
        Qué (African people)
        Wae (African people)
        We (African people)
          [Former heading]
  BT Ethnology—Cameroon
We (Côte d'Ivoire and Liberian people)
  (May Subd Geog)
  UF Wee (African people)
  BT Ethnology—Côte d'Ivoire
        Ethnology—Liberia
  NT Krahn (African people)
        Ngere (African people)
        Sapo (African people)
        Wobe (African people)
WE 32000 (Microprocessor) *(Not Subd Geog)*
  [QA76.8.W]
  BT Microprocessors
We-al-hus (Ariz.)
  USE Sierra Estrella (Ariz.)
We-en-de-quint Creek (Utah)
  USE Big Cottonwood Creek (Salt Lake
        County, Utah)
We masks (Côte d'Ivoire and Liberia)
  USE Masks, We (Côte d'Ivoire and Liberia)
Wea Indians *(May Subd Geog)*
  [E99.W45]
  BT Indians of North America—Indiana
        Indians of North America—Oklahoma
        Miami Indians
  —Missions *(May Subd Geog)*
  —Treaties
Weaber Plain (N.T.)
  BT Plains—Australia
Weackley family
  USE Weakley family
Wead family
  USE Weed family
Weager family
  USE Weger family
Weagley family
  USE Weigle family
Weagly family
  USE Weigle family
Weak Asplund spaces
  USE Asplund spaces
Weak interactions (Nuclear physics)
  [QC794.8.W4]
  BT Nuclear reactions
  NT Electroweak interactions
Weakes family
  USE Weeks family
Weakeyever River (Fla.)
  USE Wekiva River (Lake County-Orange
        County, Fla.)
Weakfield family
  USE Wakefield family
Weakfish
  USE Cynoscion regalis
Weakfish, Common
  USE Cynoscion regalis
Weakfish, Spotted
  USE Spotted seatrout
Weakfish fishing *(May Subd Geog)*
  [SH691.W4]
  UF Squeteague fishing
  BT Fishing
Weakfishes
  USE Cynoscion
Weakfishes (Menticirrhus)
  USE Menticirrhus
Weakland family
  USE Weaklend family
Weaklend family *(Not Subd Geog)*
  UF Weakland family
Weakley family *(Not Subd Geog)*
  UF Weackley family
        Weakly family
        Weekly family

Weakly family
  USE Weakley family
Weakness (Physiology)
  USE Asthenia
Weaks family
  USE Weeks family
Weal family
  USE Wailes family
Wealand family
  USE Whelan family
Weald, The (England)
  UF The Weald (England)
  BT Forests and forestry—England
  NT Weald of Kent (England)
Weald of Kent (England)
  UF Kentish Weald (England)
  BT Forests and forestry—England
        Weald, The (England)
Weales family
  USE Wailes family
Wealhtheow
  USE Wealhtheow (Legendary character)
Wealhtheow (Legendary character)
  (Not Subd Geog)
  UF Wealhtheow
          [Former heading]
        Wealhþēow (Legendary character)
        Wealtheow (Legendary character)
        Wealthow (Legendary character)
  BT Folklore—Great Britain
        Folklore—Scandinavia
Wealhþēow (Legendary character)
  USE Wealhtheow (Legendary character)
**Wealhtheow (Legendary character) in
  literature** *(Not Subd Geog)*
Weals family
  USE Wailes family
Wealth *(May Subd Geog)*
  [HB251 (Theory)]
  [HC79.W4 (Economic history)]
  UF Affluence
        Distribution of wealth
        Fortunes
        Riches
  BT Business
        Economics
        Finance
  RT Capital
        Money
        Property
        Well-being
  NT Cost and standard of living
        Distribution (Economic theory)
        Gross national product
        Income
        Luxury
        Poverty
        Profit
        Saving and investment
        Unearned increment
        Value
  —Biblical teaching *(Not Subd Geog)*
        BT Wealth—Religious aspects
  —Moral and ethical aspects
        (May Subd Geog)
        [HB835]
        UF Wealth, Ethics of
              [Former heading]
        RT Business ethics
        NT Avarice
              Distributive justice
  —Religious aspects
        NT Wealth—Biblical teaching
  ——Baptists, [Catholic Church, etc.]
  ——Buddhism, [Christianity, etc.]
Wealth, Ethics of
  USE Wealth—Moral and ethical aspects
Wealth in literature *(Not Subd Geog)*

Wealth tax *(May Subd Geog)*
  [HJ4101-HJ4129]
  UF Net worth tax
        Taxation of wealth
  BT Taxation
  NT Gifts—Taxation
        Property tax
  —Law and legislation *(May Subd Geog)*
Wealtheow (Legendary character)
  USE Wealhtheow (Legendary character)
Wealthow (Legendary character)
  USE Wealhtheow (Legendary character)
Wealthy children
  USE Children of the rich
Wealthy consumers
  USE Affluent consumers
Wealthy people
  USE Rich people
Weaning of infants
  USE Infants—Weaning
Weapon systems
  USE Weapons systems
Weapon X (Fictitious character)
  USE Wolverine (Fictitious character)
Weaponry
  USE Weapons
Weapons *(May Subd Geog)*
  [GN497-GN498 (Ethnology)]
  [NK6600-NK6699 (Decorative arts)]
  [U800-U897 (Military art and science)]
  UF Arms and armor
          [Former heading]
        Weaponry
        Weapons, Primitive
          [Former heading]
  BT Implements, utensils, etc.
        Tools
  RT Armor
  NT Battle-axes
        Blowguns
        Boomerangs
        Bow and arrow
        Children's weapons
        Daggers
        Firearms
        Indian weapons
        Martial arts weapons
        Military weapons
        Miniature weapons
        Ninjutsu weapons
        Nonlethal weapons
        Polearms
        Projectile points
        Slings
        Slingstones
        Spears
        Swords
        Throwing-sticks
  —Exhibitions
  —Law and legislation *(May Subd Geog)*
  —Marks
        USE Armorers' marks
  —Private collections *(May Subd Geog)*
  —Japan
  ——History
  **———Kamakura-Momoyama periods,
        1185-1600**
  ———Edo period, 1600-1868
  ———Meiji period, 1868-1912
  —United States
        NT Cherokee weapons
              Chumash weapons
              Miwok weapons
              Omaha weapons
Weapons, Ancient *(May Subd Geog)*
  UF Ancient weapons
        Arms and armor, Ancient
          [Former heading]
  —India
        NT Vájra (Weapons)
Weapons, Ancient, in art *(Not Subd Geog)*

Figure 17.1. Library of Congress subject headings.

Format of LCSH Entries

In the printed edition of LCSH, authorized headings are listed in bold print; unauthorized headings and cross-references in plain print. LCSH prints headings three columns to a page (see Figure 17.1).

When appropriate for a topic, an abbreviated instruction to subdivide it geographically appears immediately after the heading (explained later). Coded instructions for making cross-references (UF, BT, RT, SA, and NT, also explained later) appear with the subject headings to which they relate. Cross-references are given in that order and, within each category, in alphabetical order. If a subject heading's meaning might be in question, instructions in the form of scope notes are given about how to use it, beginning with the words "*Here are entered . . .*" The instructions are usually framed in positive language, but occasionally state what should *not* be entered under a particular heading and, sometimes, suggest alternatives for specific subject areas.

LC classification numbers are listed for many of the main headings and for some of the subdivided headings. These are merely suggestions and should not be assigned without consulting the full classification schedules directly. They are a useful shortcut alternative to consulting page after page of numbers in crowded portions of the schedules and can provide a guide to unfamiliar territory.

LCSH uses a variety of grammatical constructions for its headings from one-word headings to complex multiword headings. One-word headings usually are nouns or verb forms used like nouns, such as FISHING. Sometimes, the plural form of a noun is preferred, for example, FISHES is the authorized heading for these animals, not "fish." Different meanings can depend on whether a topical word is singular or plural, for example, BUILDING is used for the process of construction, while BUILDINGS is used for structures or edifices.

A noun modified by an adjective (or a second noun that functions like an adjective) is another grammatical type, for example, TELEVISION CAMERAS. LCSH sometimes reverses the order in which the words appear to bring the more important word to the filing position, for example, COSMOLOGY, ANCIENT. With computer-based keyword searching, the order of words does not matter, but in printed lists and card catalogs where only the initial word is searchable, it is important. Two- and three-word headings are also formulated as nouns with explanatory qualifiers to ensure their correct interpretation, such as EQUILIBRIUM (ECONOMICS) and EQUILIBRIUM (PHYSIOLOGY). The qualifiers may distinguish disciplines or other kinds of subject matter, for example, TRANSITIONS (RHETORIC), TRANSITIONS (LASER), TRANSITIONS (METAL-INSULATOR), and TRANSITIONS (PRESIDENTIAL).

Another form consists of two nouns connected by a conjunction, such as "AND," for example, ART AND BUSINESS. The nouns can represent similar things or opposites, for example, ART AND CAMOUFLAGE or GOOD AND EVIL. Complex headings in this category may include modified nouns, such as LANDSCAPE ARCHITECTURE AND ENERGY CONSERVATION. Prepositions are also used to link two nouns or modified nouns, for example, PRESENCE OF GOD and APPLICATIONS FOR POSITIONS.

More complex headings can involve both multiword concepts and combinations of concepts, such as RIGHT AND LEFT (POLITICAL SCIENCE) IN MUSIC. Sometimes complex headings are simplified from edition to edition, for example, ERRATA

(IN BOOKS) was changed to ERRATA, and CONVENTS AND NUNNERIES, BUDDHIST to BUDDHIST CONVENTS. In other instances, LCSH revisions add to headings to clarify them or expand their scope, for example, some years ago PETER'S DENIAL IN ART became JESUS CHRIST—DENIAL BY PETER—ART, and the one-word heading CLARET was changed to WINE AND WINE MAKING—FRANCE—BORDELAIS.

LCSH headings and subject-heading strings are filed according to a set of rules that facilitates computerized filing, devised by John C. Rather. The system files word by word with digits preceding alphabetic characters, and it treats letter combinations as they appear (for example, "Dr." files as "D-r-period," not "Doctor"). LC's filing rules distinguish between different kinds of subject heading forms and subdivisions, based on their computer coding. Recognition of heading and heading-and-subdivision forms is programmed into the computer systems that produce the printed LCSH. As a result, headings that consist of one word and this word plus subdivisions all appear before multiword headings beginning with the same word. Searchers need to know this because there can be many intervening headings (or pages of them in LCSH) between ART—THEMES, MOTIVES (a subdivided heading) and ART AND SCIENCE (a multiword heading). The filing system appears to give preference to subdivided headings over multiword main headings. In filing subdivided headings, chronological subdivisions are filed first, followed by topical subdivisions, and geographical subdivisions last.

Cross-References in LCSH

Six types of cross-references in LCSH are identified by standard mnemonic abbreviations mandated by the National Information Standards Organization:

1. BT (Broader Term)—one level higher in a hierarchy
2. RT (Related Term)—same level of hierarchy
3. NT (Narrower Term)—one level lower in a hierarchy
4. UF (Use For)—authorized term
5. SA (See Also)—reference to subject groups, not individual subject terms
6. USE—unauthorized term

LCSH does not specify the highest term in a subject hierarchy, identified as TT (Top Term), nor does it show the entire hierarchy of a subject area from the broadest to the narrowest term, such as can be found in the National Library of Medicine's *Medical Subject Headings.* Cross-references in LCSH show a maximum of three levels of hierarchy for a subject heading: one level broader (BT) and one level narrower (NT). In practical terms, however, catalogers are instructed to display only NT references in the catalog. The BT references are provided for consultation only. The RTs at the same level of hierarchy have reciprocal cross-references, and both are displayed in the catalog.

As the name implies, BTs lead from the heading at which they appear to broader headings in the same subject. This is called leading "upward." Similarly, NTs lead to narrower terms in the same subject, called leading "downward." RTs lead to headings at the same level of hierarchy in a related area, which might be part of the same subject or another subject associated with it. The relationships of these three types of cross-references to the heading at which they appear are clear from their names.

As shown in the previous list, SAs are references from the heading at which they appear to groups of headings, rather than individual headings. SAs may instruct catalogers to consult other headings or add headings and subdivisions that do not appear in the list. For example, at BOOKS, it says: "SA *headings beginning with the word* Book" and at COMMERCIAL PRODUCTS, it says, "SA *names of individual products*." Occasionally, catalogers are told to use the heading at which the SA appears as a subdivision under specific types of other headings, for example, at ART it says, "SA subdivision ART under names of individual persons who lived before 1400, under names of deities and mythological or legendary figures, and under headings of the type [TOPIC]—[SUBDIVISION] . . ." Typically, terms used as subject headings may not be used as subdivisions, and vice versa.

UF and USE are reciprocal; that is, wherever a UF is made leading to an authorized heading, a USE heading will appear at the target heading leading back to the original, unauthorized one. UFs appear at authorized headings, telling catalogers to make cross-references from unauthorized headings for a subject that searchers are likely to try. The reciprocal USE headings appear under the unauthorized headings and reveal which authorized headings to use instead for the subject. The two headings ACCELERATED EROSION (unauthorized) and SOIL EROSION (authorized) illustrate the point. ACCELERATED EROSION has a USE reference to SOIL EROSION; SOIL EROSION has a reciprocal UF for ACCELERATED EROSION. In practice, when the heading SOIL EROSION is first assigned, catalogers also make a cross-reference for the UF heading ACCELERATED EROSION. When a searcher looks up ACCELERATED EROSION, which is a common term for the subject not authorized by LCSH, he or she finds the cross-reference to the authorized heading, "USE SOIL EROSION." In the catalog display, the reference should look like this:

ACCELERATED EROSION. *Use* SOIL EROSION

The USE reference remains in the catalog until the last item on the subject SOIL EROSION is removed from the collection and that heading is removed. Accompanying the removal of SOIL EROSION, the cross-reference ACCELERATED EROSION, which would then be unnecessary, is also removed. Otherwise, the cross-reference leads to a heading with no materials under it, known as a *blind reference*. Blind references frustrate searchers because they fail to retrieve relevant materials.

Subdivisions in LCSH

LCSH has many subdivided headings throughout the list. Usually, one level of subdivision is sufficient to represent most topics in detail, but some headings require two, three, or even four levels of subdivision.

Subdivisions for a heading are listed following the cross-references for the heading. As with an unsubdivided heading, each entry for a subdivided heading may have scope notes, classification numbers, and cross-references that pertain to that particular subdivision. Subdivisions are indented and printed with long dashes preceding them to indicate that they are not to be used alone, but only as subdivisions of the headings under which they appear. When a subdivided heading is, itself, subdivided further, which is necessary for very large topics that have several kinds of subdivisions (e.g., topical, chronological, and geographic), it is indented further and given additional dashes, one for each subdivision. For example, a topic such as the history of Chinese calligraphy in the 20th century would be expressed by the LCSH heading CALLIG-RAPHY, CHINESE—HISTORY—20TH CENTURY, which is a two-level hierarchy; and a topic such as the attribution of Chinese calligraphy from the Sui dynasty would be expressed as CALLIGRAPHY, CHINESE—HISTORY—THREE KINGDOMS-SUI DYNASTY, 220-618—ATTRIBUTION, which is a three-level hierarchy. Figure 17.2 illustrates how they look in the printed LCSH.

Broad topics such as art, music, and science have numerous cross-references and subdivisions, some of which have their own subdivisions as well. This makes for confusion in locating a particular subdivided heading, because it can be many columns or even a few pages away from the main heading. LCSH includes all these subdivisions because it is used to organize large collections of materials on topics about which much has been and is still being written. Dividing a huge file of catalog records by narrowing the topic, which is what subdivisions do, makes it easier for searchers to zero in on exactly what they seek and, simultaneously, makes the file smaller and quicker to search.

Three types of subdivisions predominate in LCSH: topical, chronological, and geographical. A fourth type, form or genre subdivisions, is also present in the list, but these terms can be construed as a special type of topical subdivision. Subdivisions are indicated in the list in several ways, so catalogers must be alert to all of them. Individual subdivisions are assigned according to LC policies, given in *Subject Cataloging Manual: Subject Headings.* Beginning catalogers should be aware that two main headings cannot be combined in a heading-subdivision relationship, unless one is listed specifically as a subdivision under the other, or unless one heading functions both as a main heading and a subdivision and is permitted as a subdivision under the second heading. Catalogers should not assume that the absence of an instruction *not* to subdivide is permission to do it. On the contrary—if there is no clear indication of permission to subdivide a heading, it should not be subdivided. An important exception to the rule is the group of pattern headings listed in the preface to LCSH, discussed later.

Subdivisions for LCSH headings may be indicated in one of four ways:

1. The subdivision appears in the list under the heading
2. An instruction to subdivide is given with the heading in the list
3. The heading fits into a designated pattern heading and can be subdivided like it
4. The heading is a term to which free-floating subdivisions can be added

Appears in the list: The easiest and most straightforward method of providing for subdivisions is listing them under the headings to which they can be assigned, but doing so for all possible subdivisions would cause LCSH to expand far beyond its current size. Thus, although this method is used, alternatives are also used for reasons of economy and flexibility.

Instruction appears with the heading: When a heading can be subdivided geographically, this is usually noted by a parenthetic instruction (*May Subd Geog*) after

Calle Larga (Buenos Aires, Argentina)
    USE Avenida Montes de Oca (Buenos Aires,
            Argentina)
Calle Larga, Palacete de la (Jerez de la Frontera,
    Spain)
    USE Palacete de la Calle Larga (Jerez de la
            Frontera, Spain)
Calle Moneda (Mexico City, Mexico)
    This heading is not valid for use as a geographic
    subdivision.
    UF Calle de la Moneda (Mexico City,
            Mexico)
        Calle de Martín López (Mexico City,
            Mexico)
        Calle del Arzobispado (Mexico City,
            Mexico)
        Moneda Street (Mexico City, Mexico)
    BT Streets—Mexico
Calle Ordoño II (León, Spain)
    This heading is not valid for use as a geographic
    subdivision.
    UF Calle de Ordoño II (León, Spain)
        Ordoño II Street (León, Spain)
    BT Streets—Spain
Calle Piedras (Montevideo, Uruguay)
    This heading is not valid for use as a geographic
    subdivision.
    UF Piedras Street (Montevideo, Uruguay)
    BT Streets—Uruguay
Calle Reyes Católicos (Granada, Spain)
    This heading is not valid for use as a geographic
    subdivision.
    UF Reyes Católicos Street (Granada, Spain)
    BT Streets—Spain
Calle San Felipe (Guadalajara, Mexico)
    This heading is not valid for use as a geographic
    subdivision.
    UF Calle de San Felipe (Guadalajara,
            Mexico)
        San Felipe Street (Guadalajara, Mexico)
    BT Streets—Mexico
Calle Tristán Narvaja (Montevideo, Uruguay)
    This heading is not valid for use as a geographic
    subdivision.
    UF Calle de Tristán (Montevideo, Uruguay)
        Tristán Narvaja Street (Montevideo,
            Uruguay)
        Tristán Street (Montevideo, Uruguay)
    BT Streets—Uruguay
Calleham family
    USE Callahan family
Callejón de Huaylas (Peru)
    USE Huaylas, Callejón de (Peru)
Calendar House (Falkirk, Scotland)
    BT Dwellings—Scotland
Callenia
    USE Stromatolites
Callens family   *(Not Subd Geog)*
    UF Calens family
        Cales family
        Calis family
        Calles family
        Callis family
        Calliss family
    RT Collins family
Caller family
    USE Kahler family
Caller ID telephone service   *(May Subd Geog)*
    UF Automatic telephone number
            identification
        Caller identification telephone service
        Telephone—Caller ID
        Telephone—Caller identification
        Telephone number identification
    BT Telephone
    —Law and legislation   *(May Subd Geog)*
Caller identification telephone service
    USE Caller ID telephone service
Caller-paid telephone services
    USE Pay-per-call telephone services
Calles family
    USE Callens family

Callesen family   *(Not Subd Geog)*
    UF Callison family
Calleway family
    USE Callaway family
Calley family   *(Not Subd Geog)*
    UF Cally family
        Kaley family
    RT McCauley family
Callianassa californiensis
    USE Bay ghost shrimp
Callianassidae
    USE Ghost shrimps
Calliandra   *(May Subd Geog)*
    [QK495.M545 (Botany)]
    UF Powderpuffs (Plants)
    BT Mimosaceae
    NT Calliandra calothyrsus
Calliandra calothyrsus   *(May Subd Geog)*
    [QK495.L52 (Botany)]
    [SB317.C25 (Multipurpose plant)]
    [SD397.C333 (Forestry)]
    BT Calliandra
Calliarthron   *(May Subd Geog)*
    [QK569.C8]
    BT Coralline algae
Callicanthus
    USE Naso
Callicebus
    USE Titis (Mammals)
Callichone
    USE Colascione
Callichthyidae   *(May Subd Geog)*
    [QL638.C14]
    BT Catfishes
    NT Corydoras
Callicoat family
    USE Callicott family
Callicore
    USE Amaryllis (Genus)
Callicot family
    USE Callicott family
Callicott family   *(Not Subd Geog)*
    UF Calico family
        Callacot family
        Callicoat family
        Callicot family
        Callicotte family
        Callicutt family
        Collicott family
Callicotte family
    USE Callicott family
Callicutt family
    USE Callicott family
Callide Creek (Qld.)
    BT Rivers—Australia
Callide Creek Watershed (Qld.)
    BT Watersheds—Australia
Callidiellum   *(May Subd Geog)*
    [QL596.C4 (Zoology)]
    BT Cerambycidae
    NT Japanese cedar longhorn beetle
Callidiellum rufipenne
    USE Japanese cedar longhorn beetle
Callier family   *(Not Subd Geog)*
Calliergon   *(May Subd Geog)*
    [QK539.A6]
    BT Amblystegiaceae
Calligan Creek (Wash.)
    BT Rivers—Washington (State)
Calligan Lake (Wash.)
    BT Lakes—Washington (State)
Callignathus
    USE Kogia
Calligraphers   *(May Subd Geog)*
    UF Penmen
    BT Artists
    NT Copyists
        Muslim calligraphers
        Women calligraphers
    —Autographs

Calligraphers, Muslim
    USE Muslim calligraphers
Calligraphers' marks
    UF Marks, Calligraphers'
    BT Artists' marks
Calligraphic paintings
    USE Letter-pictures
Calligraphy   *(May Subd Geog)*
    [NK3600-NK3640 (Decorative arts)]
    [Z43-Z45 (Penmanship)]
    BT Decorative arts
        Penmanship
        Writing
    NT Buddhist calligraphy
        Finger calligraphy
        Islamic calligraphy
        Taoist calligraphy
        Writing, Copperplate
    —Attribution
        UF Attribution of calligraphy
            Calligraphy—Reattribution
        BT Calligraphy—Expertising
    —Copy-books
        USE Copybooks
    —Copying
        BT Copying
    —Exhibitions
    —Expertising   *(May Subd Geog)*
        NT Calligraphy—Attribution
    —Handbooks, manuals, etc.
        USE Copybooks
    —Reattribution
        USE Calligraphy—Attribution
Calligraphy, Arabic   *(May Subd Geog)*
    UF Arabic calligraphy
Calligraphy, Bengali   *(May Subd Geog)*
    UF Bengali calligraphy
Calligraphy, Buddhist
    USE Buddhist calligraphy
Calligraphy, Celtic   *(May Subd Geog)*
    UF Celtic calligraphy
Calligraphy, Chinese   *(May Subd Geog)*
    UF Chinese calligraphy
    —Sung-Yüan dynasties, 960-1368
        USE Calligraphy, Chinese—History—
            Song-Yuan dynasties, 960-1368
    —Appreciation   *(May Subd Geog)*
        UF Appreciation of Chinese
            calligraphy
        BT Art appreciation
    —Attribution
        UF Attribution of Chinese calligraphy
            Calligraphy, Chinese—
                Reattribution
        BT Calligraphy, Chinese—Expertising
    —Expertising   *(May Subd Geog)*
        NT Calligraphy, Chinese—Attribution
    —History
    ——To 221 B.C.
    ——Three kingdoms, six dynasties-Sui
        dynasty, 220-618
        USE Calligraphy, Chinese—History—
            Three kingdoms-Sui dynasty,
            220-618
    ——Three kingdoms-Sui dynasty, 220-618
        UF Calligraphy, Chinese—
            History—Three kingdoms, six
            dynasties-Sui dynasty, 220-618
            [Former heading]
    ———Attribution
        UF Attribution of Three
                kingdoms-Sui dynasty
                Chinese calligraphy
            Calligraphy, Chinese—
                History—Three kingdoms-
                Sui dynasty, 220-618—
                Reattribution
        BT Calligraphy, Chinese—
                History—Three kingdoms-
                Sui dynasty, 220-618—
                Expertising

1130

Figure 17.2. Subdivisions in LCSH.

the heading. If a subdivided heading can be further subdivided geographically, the same instruction will appear after the subdivision. The LC's preferred method of sub-dividing geographically is indirect. This means putting the name of a country after the heading being subdivided. Larger entities, such as continents or multicountry regions, are given the same way, but entities wholly within a country are preceded by the name of the country in which they are located. In the example that follows, headings and their geographic subdivisions assigned to books about agriculture in North and South America, the Amazon Region, the Andes Mountains, the Andes Mountains of Venezuela, Argentina, Germany, Israel, and the cities of Buenos Aires and Munich are filed as follows:

AGRICULTURE—AMAZON RIVER REGION
AGRICULTURE—ANDES REGION
AGRICULTURE—ARGENTINA
AGRICULTURE—ARGENTINA—BUENOS AIRES
AGRICULTURE—GERMANY
AGRICULTURE—GERMANY—MUNICH
AGRICULTURE—ISRAEL
AGRICULTURE—NORTH AMERICA
AGRICULTURE—SOUTH AMERICA
AGRICULTURE—VENEZUELA—ANDES REGION (VENEZUELA)

The resulting file gathers the geographic entities either at the country level or larger levels, but not at smaller levels, such as city or town levels. Localities can be browsed within their country files or found directly by requesting the desired place in a key-word search.

Three countries—the United States, Canada, and Great Britain—have special rules for indirect subdivision. (Although *United Kingdom* is the proper name of the country and should be used in place of Great Britain, LCSH uses Great Britain because of the difficulty of making the change.) For these countries, the names of states, provinces, and constituent countries, respectively, are used. Materials on agriculture in Iowa City, education in London, and advertising in Toronto would be assigned the following subject headings:

AGRICULTURE—IOWA—IOWA CITY
EDUCATION—ENGLAND—LONDON
ADVERTISING—ONTARIO—TORONTO

Policies for geographic subdivision have changed over the years, sometimes favoring direct subdivision, sometimes indirect, and sometimes accepting both depending on the country. New direct geographic subdivisions will not be established under the current policy, but older headings that were subdivided directly remain. The three exceptions gather records first at the state, province, or constituent country level before grouping them at the local level. Because much geographically distinctive material in libraries is about these countries, this strategy avoids gathering huge numbers of records at the country level.

Heading fits a designated pattern: Some topics serve as patterns for groups of related topics that can all be subdivided the same way. For example, PIANOS is the pattern for similar musical instruments. Any subdivision approved for PIANOS can be used to subdivide other keyboard instruments. Similarly, any subdivision approved for use with HEART can be assigned to other organs of the body. The list of topics designated as pattern headings is printed in the front matter of LCSH. (See additional details in the following section.)

Heading can be subdivided by free-floating subdivisions: LCSH has rules governing the types of subject headings to which its general subdivisions, known as "free-floating subdivisions," can be applied. Some of these general subdivisions are not appropriate under all possible main headings. If a main subject heading is of the type eligible for a particular free-floating subdivision, the subdivision can be added. For example, some free-floating subdivisions are approved for use with classes of persons and/or ethnic groups, others with places, still others with religions, and so on. Rules for free-floating subdivisions can be found in *Subject Cataloging Manual: Subject Headings* and *Cataloger's Desktop*. (See additional details in the following section.)

Other Subdivision Instructions

Embedded instructions: Instructions to use a particular topical heading as a subdivision under other descriptors may be given with the heading in the list. For example, in the scope note under RESEARCH, it says: "Works on research about a particular region, country, etc. are entered under the name of the region, country, etc. with the subdivision Research." This means catalogers can add the subdivision "—RESEARCH" at will to the names of regions, countries, or other geographic entities, as in the hypothetical heading NEW JERSEY—RESEARCH.

Pattern headings: LCSH's creators identify 23 groups of headings as *pattern headings*. Each member of a pattern-heading group might need the same set of subdivisions, but instead of repeating the whole set under each one, one heading is fully subdivided in the list and catalogers are instructed to use the same pattern for all the others in the same category. For example, all plants and crops can be subdivided with the same terms as those given under CORN and all sacred works can be subdivided exactly like BIBLE. For some heading groups, more than one pattern is provided; for example, subdivision of diseases may either follow the pattern under CANCER or the one under TUBERCULOSIS. Pattern headings are listed in the printed edition of LCSH.

Free-floating subdivisions: Some subdivisions—all topical terms, a number of them representing literary forms—are designated as *free-floating*. These have such widespread potential for use as subdivisions that it is difficult to anticipate and list them all. Instead, they can be assigned with a broad range of headings. The list of free-floating subdivisions appears in the 31st edition of LCSH, in the online version, and in a printed booklet. Detailed guidance on how to assign free-floating subdivision terms is given in the booklet and the *Subject Cataloging Manual: Subject Headings.*

Form/Genre subdivisions: Form and genre subdivisions, mentioned previously in connection with the list of free-floating terms, include terms that describe the format in which a work appears, such as "—CATALOGS". This group of terms also includes literary genres, such as "—DICTIONARIES" and "—BIOGRAPHIES". Most form subdivisions are free-floating. ALA's SAC committee and the LC have been expanding the use of form and genre subdivisions as well as form and genre headings. The trend is to be more liberal in establishing and assigning such headings and subdivisions, because users want them and computerized searching makes them practical to use.

Chronological subdivisions: Chronological subdivisions, most of which are not free-floating, are almost always given in the list of terms for those subject headings and subdivisions that may be subdivided by period. History is frequently subdivided by time period, and historical topics often are specific to particular places. The introductory explanations warn catalogers not to use the historical periods developed for one place under other places, for example, it would not be appropriate to use chronological periods for Japan under India or China. Each country, state, or province has its own chronological landmarks. However, general chronological periods that can apply to many topics, such as the names of the centuries, appear both as main headings and subdivisions that can be used under other headings.

Topical subdivisions: Topical subdivision is exactly what the name implies: a subdivision that represents a topic, such as COMPUTERS—CIRCUITS. CIRCUITS, the subdivision, does not represent a geographical, chronological, or form subdivision. It is a topical subdivision, but it cannot be used just anywhere, as the free-floating subdivisions can. If it were not listed as an authorized subdivision under COMPUTERS, catalogers could not create it. They would have to use COMPUTERS alone or use two headings to embody the concept.

Because subdivision is done only as LC directs, uniform strings of headings and subdivisions are created that can be combined in only one way. ARCHITECTURE—ARID REGIONS and ARID REGIONS—ARCHITECTURE may mean the same thing, but LCSH only authorizes the former as a subject heading. Catalogers examining both terms will find—ARID REGIONS listed as a subdivision under ARCHITECTURE but no listing for "—ARCHITECTURE" as a subdivision under ARID REGIONS. This happens because LCSH is *precoordinated.*

LCSH's Canadian Complement

The differences in the sociopolitical structure between Canada and the United States and an in-depth arrangement of Canadian history are obvious areas where subject headings suitable to a Canadian topic are needed. *Canadian Subject Headings* (CSH), published by the Library and Archives Canada (LAC), is a list of English-language subject headings, compatible with LCSH, that is used to access and express the subject content of documents on Canada and Canadian topics. It is no longer published in a paper format and has been superseded by *CSH on the Web,* a free, up-to-date listing of more than 6,000 English-language subject authority records (http://www.collectionscanada.ca/csh/index-e.html). The records are available in both the machine-readable cataloging (MARC 21) format and thesaurus display. (MARC formats will be discussed in chapter 19). There is a monthly list of new and revised headings and an alphabetical list of subdivisions. The database is updated monthly and provides a large number of references, scope notes, and instructions setting topics in their Canadian context. The list of subdivisions provides French-language equivalents and the database provides a link to *Répertoire de vedettes-matière* for equivalent French-language headings. Subject authority records for *Canadian Subject Headings* are also available in the AMICUS database. Registered AMICUS users can download CSH authority records in the MARC 21 format from AMICUS. (Although users must register to obtain entry to the AMICUS database, its use is free of charge.)

CSH is neither a comprehensive list nor a substitute for LCSH. It is to be used for items containing Canadian subject matter, whereas LCSH is to be applied to all other materials. CSH's headings and references expand and adapt LCSH where Canadian topics are not adequately covered or where LCSH headings are not acceptable in a

Canadian context. "MUMMERS" in Figure 14.15 on page 287 is an example of a subject heading not found in LCSH.

LAC may consult the Canadian Committee on Cataloguing and the cataloging community on major policy directions for CSH. In addition, LAC has been contributing new subject concepts identified in Canadian publications to LCSH since 1994. LC uses CSH as a basic source when considering new headings.

Problems with LCSH

Until recently, LCSH evolved very slowly. Critics, such as the late Sanford Berman, who spearheaded valuable initiatives to improve LC subject headings, claimed that LC policy makers were too stubborn in resisting needed changes in its spelling and terminology. In theory, LCSH is constantly being revised, and catalogers are able to propose new or altered headings at any time.

In any list this large, a slow pace of change is understandable. LC has many more items cataloged under any one heading than small libraries do; therefore, the number of operations needed to update LC records when a change is made to an existing heading is considerable, running into many thousands for headings also used as subdivisions. As a result, there is sometimes a reluctance to change headings. For example, for many years, subject catalogers at LC resisted eliminating the now obsolete heading NEGROES, even though they acknowledged that common usage had invested the word with pejorative connotations. Eventually, it was dropped in favor of AFRICAN AMERICANS and BLACKS (BLACKS refers to black people who are not American). Similarly, LC resisted changing MOVING PICTURES to MOTION PICTURES until 1989, which necessitated the change of many derivative headings following the form [TOPIC] IN MOTION PICTURES. In the 1990s, however, the conversion of LC's catalog records and authority files to online form was completed. This has speeded up the process of change. Greater flexibility in revising old headings and introducing new ones is an encouraging change in the status quo.

Selected problems of LCSH have been and are still being addressed by the Subject Analysis Committee (SAC), a standing committee of the Cataloging and Classification Section of the Association for Library Collections & Technical Services. The committee appoints and maintains subcommittees and task forces, each devoted to a particular problem or issue. Members are appointed on the basis of their interest and expertise, and their reports are instrumental in adding new headings to LCSH, changing older ones, or modifying its application policies. In the recent past, SAC lobbied LC successfully to revise terms with negative connotations and terms for groups of people that offended those they identified. SAC also has subcommittees charged with exploring faceted access and genre and form subject headings, several of which (e.g., those studying genre terms for maps and videorecordings) submitted reports while this chapter was being written that greatly expand the use of such headings.

Other groups have also successfully lobbied LC to create needed headings. Some have created their own thesauri to augment or supplement LCSH. The idea of using more than one subject authority in a library's catalog, once thought impossible, is an accepted option today. Terms from alternative thesauri are accommodated in the MARC encoding system.

LCSH has informative scope notes and instructions for the application of numerous subject headings and is adding more. Nonetheless, with so many headings appearing over such a long period of time, overlaps are inevitable, for example, CONFORMITY and COMPLIANCE; COMPUTERS, ELECTRONIC DIGITAL COMPUTERS, MINICOMPUTERS, and MICROCOMPUTERS (but no heading appears for "mainframes," not even as a cross-reference). LC makes fine distinctions between headings that can be missed by searchers unfamiliar with its terminology. For example, AFRICAN AMERICANS and BLACKS differ only in whether the specified people are American citizens or not. Specialists who work with LCSH are aware of the difference, but users searching the catalog may not be.

LC's Children's and Young Adults' Cataloging Program

In 1965, LC responded to requests on the part of librarians working with children and youth for subject-heading modifications for children's materials by initiating its Annotated Card (AC) program, now titled the Children's and Young Adults' Cataloging program. Four modifications were made to the materials treated under the program:

1. Subdivisions referring to age level, such as "—JUVENILE LITERATURE," were dropped.
2. Selected terms were added, revised, or simplified.
3. Subdivision practice was altered.
4. Summaries were added in the descriptive cataloging to inform searchers about the content of the materials (hence the term "annotated").

Examples of children's and young adults' cataloging headings that differ slightly from LCSH are ALPINE ANIMALS, which is used instead of LCSH's ALPINE FAUNA, and BEDWETTING, which is used instead of LCSH's ENURESIS. Clearly, "animals" and "bedwetting" are recognized and understood by youngsters more easily than "fauna" and "enuresis," respectively. In other instances, the modification is subtler; for example, ROBOTS is used in the CYACP program for materials about androids and other kinds of robots, while ANDROIDS is used for adult materials specifically about that particular type of robot. Two important modifications in subdivision practice are the use of "—BIOGRAPHY" for individual biographies in subject fields, where LCSH lacks the term for persons in the field, and "—FICTION," which can be added to all topical headings.

The list of Children's Subject Headings in the printed edition of LCSH immediately precedes the regular adult list and is similar to it, three columns to a page, with scope notes, cross-references, geographic subdivision instructions, and subdivisions, but without classification numbers. In cataloging-in-publication (CIP) data, CYACP headings are assigned in addition to, not in place of, adult headings. The headings appear in square brackets following the adult headings and the term "AC" is often noted at the end of the record. In online catalogs, CYACP headings are encoded differently than adult headings. Summaries appear in the note area of the descriptive cataloging. Figure 17.3 illustrates these differences.

```
This example is an illustration of:
    • other title information
    • subsidiary statement of responsibility
    • edition and history note
    • audience note
    • summary
    • two ISBNs
    • ISBN qualified
    • Library of Congress and Library of Congress Children's
      subject headings compared
    • title added entry
    • second level cataloging
```

```
Banks, Lynne Reid.
    Harry the poisonous centipede's big adventure : another story
to make you squirm / Lynne Banks Reid ; illustrated by Tony Ross.
-- 1st ed. -- New York : HarperCollins, 2001.
    179 p. : ill. ; 22 cm.

    Sequel to: Harry the poisonous centipede.
    For 8-12 year olds.
    Summary: Harry, a young centipede, faces danger and frustration
when he is captured by a hoo-min and placed in a jar.
    ISBN 0-06-029139-7. -- ISBN 0-06-029394-2 (lib. bdg.).
```

*Tracing with Library of Congress subject headings for an adult
collection*

```
    1. Centipedes -- Juvenile fiction.   I. Title.
```

*Tracing with Library of Congress Children's subject headings for
a young people's collection*

```
    1. Centipedes -- Fiction.   2. Insects -- Fiction.   I. Title.
```

CHIEF SOURCE OF INFORMATION (Title Page)	(Information on Dust Cover) Ages 8–12 (Information on Verso)

LYNNE REID BANKS

Illustrated by Tony Ross

Harry the Poisonous Centipede's Big Adventure:
Another Story to Make You Squirm
Copyright © 2001 by Lynne Reid Banks
Illustrations copyright © 2001 by Tony Ross
All rights reserved. No part of this book may be used or reproduced in any
manner whatsoever without written permission except in the case of brief
quotations embodied in critical articles and reviews. Printed in the United
States of America. For information address HarperCollins Publishers,
1350 Avenue of the Americas, New York, NY 10019.
www.harperchildrens.com

Library of Congress Cataloging-in-Publication Data
Banks, Lynne Reid, 1929–
    Harry the poisonous centipede's big adventure / Lynne Reid Banks.
        p.   cm.
    Sequel to: Harry the poisonous centipede.
    Summary: Harry, a young centipede, faces danger and frustration when he
is captured by a hoo-min and placed in a jar.
    ISBN 0-06-029139-7 — ISBN 0-06-029394-2 (lib. bdg.)
    1. Centipedes—Juvenile fiction.   [1. Centipedes—Fiction.   2. Insects—
Fiction.]   I. Title
PZ10.3.B2155 Hat   2001   00-38832
[Fic]—dc21   CIP
                                                                   AC

                    1 2 3 4 5 6 7 8 9 10
                              ❖
                         First Edition

▬ HarperCollins*Publishers*

Figure 17.3. Children's and Young Adults' Cataloging Program.

SEARS LIST OF SUBJECT HEADINGS

Sears List of Subject Headings (Sears) was initiated by its original compiler, Minnie Earl Sears, in response to requests from librarians for subject headings that were simpler to understand and assign than those in LCSH. Publisher H. W. Wilson, which printed and sold catalog cards to small school and public libraries at that time, first published the Sears list in 1923 under Ms. Sears editorship, and adopted Sears subject headings for its cards. This ensured that the Sears list would have a substantial market.

Minnie Earl Sears recognized the value of maintaining a uniform structure between LCSH and her list. That uniform structure made it possible to coordinate terms from both lists. If Sears lacked a heading wanted by a cataloger, he or she could turn to LCSH for it and add it without fear of conflict. If a small library grew large enough that the Sears headings were no longer effective, it could move to LCSH. Minnie Earl Sears did not find the LCSH structure unacceptable, but its terms tended to be too technical for novice searchers and too specific for smaller institutions with limited collections of materials. The small size and simple terminology of the Sears list appealed to catalogers who found LCSH difficult to learn to use. The similarities between Sears and LCSH are demonstrated in comparing the Sears subject headings WEALTH and WEAPONS in Figure 17.4 with those LCSH headings in Figure 17.1. A comparison of the subject heading CALLIGRAPHY in Figure 17.2 (LCSH) and in Figure 17.5 (Sears) demonstrates LCSH's greater range of specificity.

Although H. W. Wilson ended its commercial card-distribution service many years ago, it continues to update Sears for its customers. Until 1988, new editions of Sears appeared more often than new editions of LCSH. Since then, LCSH has become an annual whereas H. W. Wilson issues new editions of Sears less often, but more frequently than it did in the 20th century. For example, the two editions that preceded the 19th edition (Sears 19), published in 2007 and current at this writing, appeared in 2000 and 2004. Joseph Miller, the principal editor of the this edition, and his associate editor Barbara A. Bristow, are only the fifth and sixth persons in the series of editors who followed Minnie Earl Sears.

Sears List of Subject Headings: Canadian Companion, 6th edition, (CC6) edited by Lynne Lighthall[1] provides headings for items containing Canadian subject matter. A new edition of SearsCC has not been published because its editor believes there is not enough new material to warrant publication.

Libraries with significant collections of Canadian materials should continue to use CC6 and Sears 19 because some of the subject headings in Sears 19 have a U.S. orientation not suited to Canadian materials. For example Sears 19 uses the term "**Native Americans—Canada**" with a USE reference from "First Nations," the term Canadian Native peoples that are not Inuit have chosen for their name. Those libraries that wish to be politically correct should assign "**Native Americans—Canada**" only to works that deal with both the First Nations and Inuit peoples and assign the subject heading "**First Nations**" and the qualifier "**First Nations people,**" for example, "**Haida (First Nations people)**" to works that used to be listed under the discarded heading "Indians of North America—Canada."

Examples of other differences that reflect Canadian usage are "**French-speaking Canadians**" (CC6) rather than "**French Canadians**" (Sears 19) and "**Quebec**

Water supply—*Continued*
        Water fluoridation
        Water purification
  RT Water conservation
        Water resources development
        Wells
Water supply engineering (May subdiv. geog.) 628.1
  BT Civil engineering
        Engineering
  NT Drilling and boring (Earth and rocks)
  RT Hydraulic engineering
Water transportation
  USE Shipping
Watercolor painting (May subdiv. geog.) 751.42
  UF Watercolors
  BT Painting
Watercolors
  USE Watercolor painting
Watergate Affair, 1972-1974 973.924
  BT United States—History—1961-1974
Watering places
  USE Health resorts
Waterways (May subdiv. geog.) 386
  Use for materials on rivers, lakes, and canals used for transportation.
  BT Transportation
  NT Canals
        Lakes
        Rivers
  RT Inland navigation
Waterwise gardening
  USE Xeriscaping
Waterworks
  USE Water supply
Wave mechanics 530.12; 531
  BT Mechanics
        Quantum theory
        Waves
Waves 531
  BT Hydrodynamics
        Vibration
  NT Electric waves
        Ocean waves
        Radiation
        Sound waves
        Wave mechanics
Waves, Electromagnetic
  USE Electromagnetic waves

Waves, Ultrasonic
  USE Ultrasonic waves
Way (Chinese philosophy)
  USE Tao
Wealth (May subdiv. geog.) 330.1
  UF Distribution of wealth
        Fortunes
        Riches
  BT Economics
        Finance
  NT Cost and standard of living
        Economic conditions
        Gross national product
        Income
        Inheritance and succession
        Profit
        Saving and investment
        Success
  RT Capital
        Money
        Property
Wealthy people
  USE Rich
Weaponry
  USE Weapons
Weapons (May subdiv. geog.) 355.8; 623.4
  UF Arms and armor
        Weaponry
  SA types of weapons, e.g. Swords
        [to be added as needed]
  BT Tools
        Weapons
  NT Bow and arrow
        Firearms
        Knives
        Military weapons
        Swords
        Weapons
  RT Armor
        Military art and science
Weapons, Atomic
  USE Nuclear weapons
Weapons industry
  USE Defense industry
        Firearms industry
Weapons, Nuclear
  USE Nuclear weapons
Weapons, Space
  USE Space weapons

798

Figure 17.4. Sears subject headings for WEALTH and WEAPONS.

(Province)—Separatist movements" (CC6) rather than "**Quebec (Province)-History-Autonomy and independence movements**" (Sears 19). Sears 19 reflects the cross-border difference in attitude toward the War of 1812, which each side claims it won. The Sears 19's UF and BT references ignore Canada's role in the war despite the fact that there were battles on Canadian soil. Libraries with collections of Canadian materials should establish Canadian-oriented UFs and BTs. A different Dewey number (971.03) should be assigned in Canadian libraries and to those works about the War of 1812 written from a Canadian perspective that rather than the one in Sears 18 that applies to U.S. history (973.5).

The Publication

Sears subject headings are contained in one large volume. The headings and references are listed in 823 pages having two columns to a page (see Figure 17.5).

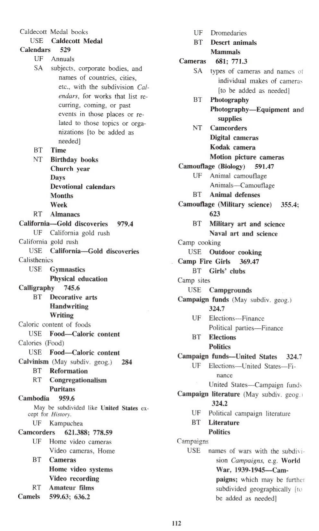

Caldecott Medal books
USE **Caldecott Medal**
Calendars   529
  UF Annuals
  SA subjects, corporate bodies, and names of countries, cities, etc., with the subdivision *Calendars*, for works that list recurring, coming, or past events in those places or related to those topics or organizations [to be added as needed]
  BT **Time**
  NT **Birthday books**
     Church year
     Days
     Devotional calendars
     Months
     Week
  RT **Almanacs**
California—Gold discoveries   979.4
  UF California gold rush
California gold rush
  USE **California—Gold discoveries**
Calisthenics
  USE **Gymnastics**
     Physical education
Calligraphy   745.6
  BT **Decorative arts**
     Handwriting
     Writing
Caloric content of foods
  USE **Food—Caloric content**
Calories (Food)
  USE **Food—Caloric content**
Calvinism (May subdiv. geog.)   **284**
  BT **Reformation**
  RT **Congregationalism**
     Puritans
Cambodia   959.6
  May be subdivided like **United States** except for *History.*
  UF Kampuchea
Camcorders   621.388; 778.59
  UF Home video cameras
     Video cameras, Home
  BT **Cameras**
     Home video systems
     Video recording
  RT **Amateur films**
Camels   599.63; 636.2

  UF Dromedaries
  BT **Desert animals**
     Mammals
Cameras   681; 771.3
  SA types of cameras and names of individual makes of cameras [to be added as needed]
  BT **Photography**
     Photography—Equipment and supplies
  NT **Camcorders**
     Digital cameras
     Kodak camera
     Motion picture cameras
Camouflage (Biology)   591.47
  UF Animal camouflage
     Animals—Camouflage
  BT **Animal defenses**
Camouflage (Military science)   355.4; 623
  BT **Military art and science**
     Naval art and science
Camp cooking
  USE **Outdoor cooking**
Camp Fire Girls   369.47
  BT **Girls' clubs**
Camp sites
  USE **Campgrounds**
Campaign funds (May subdiv. geog.)   **324.7**
  UF Elections—Finance
     Political parties—Finance
  BT **Elections**
     Politics
Campaign funds—United States   324.7
  UF Elections—United States—Finance
     United States—Campaign funds
Campaign literature (May subdiv. geog.)   **324.2**
  UF Political campaign literature
  BT **Literature**
     Politics
Campaigns
  USE names of wars with the subdivision *Campaigns,* e.g. **World War, 1939-1945—Campaigns;** which may be further subdivided geographically [to be added as needed]

112

Figure 17.5. Sears subject headings for CALLIGRAPHY.

The publisher describes Sears as having "more than 8,000 established subject terms and copious provisions for establishing further terms as needed," and more than 500 authorized subdivisions.[2]

Sears List of Subject Headings is available to subscribers online via WilsonWeb. At this writing, reports say that a 2009 update to the 19th edition of *Sears List of Subject Headings* is to be available for electronic users in MARC 21 authority format. New headings added in both the 2008 and the 2009 updates are included in the Sears database online and are to be included in the 20th edition.

Sears begins with an extensive introductory chapter giving a brief history, a description of the principles on which it is based, instructions for applying the headings, and a bibliography of basic sources for more information. Following this are explanations of headings to be added by the cataloger, key headings (equivalent to LCSH's pattern headings), and a list of canceled and replacement headings. The list of changed headings expedites identifying specific revisions that should be made in the catalog when adopting the new edition.

The 19th edition includes very few changes. Some of the changes are minor, such as the replacement of **Super Bowl** with **Super Bowl (Game)**. Others are more far-reaching, such as the replacement of **Native peoples** with **Indigenous peoples**. The former change involves only adding a qualifier to clarify the context of the term, whereas the latter change alters the words used for the concept and shifts the subject file from the "Ns" to the "Is." A few changes are still more extensive, such as the change from **Libraries and students** to **Students—Library services**. Though the heading still contains three words, the new heading is filed far from its previous location and its syntax has changed. Now the words are arranged in a "main heading—subdivision form" in place of two nouns connected by "and." The changed heading seems to reflect a shift in focus from institutions to people. This kind of conceptual shift was once difficult to implement, because of the time and cost of unfiling, altering, and refiling cards, but computerized catalogs minimize those practical problems.

A section titled "The Use of Subdivisions in the Sears List" introduces and briefly explains a flexible system of subdivision practice. It is followed by a list of all words used as subdivisions for which Sears has specific provisions. These terms also appear in the main list, where some are authorized for use both as main headings and subdivisions, and others are authorized for use solely as subdivisions. To find the instructions for a particular subdivision, catalogers must search it in the main list.

Format of the Entries

Authorized headings always appear in boldface type, whether they are main headings or cross-references under other main headings. Roman print is used for terms not authorized for use as headings but included as cross-references. For example, **Carnivorous plants** appears in boldface print as a main heading in the "Cs," while Insect-eating plants appears in roman print under it. In the "I" section, Insect-eating plants appears in the main list in roman print with the cross-reference instruction to "USE **Carnivorous plants**" following it in boldface.

In addition to the subject headings and cross-references, many of the headings have suggested classification numbers, taken from the 14th edition of *Abridged Dewey Decimal Classification and Relative Index* (DDC-Abridged). When a subject has more than one viewpoint, two or more classification numbers may be suggested for the topic, depending on which viewpoint is represented in an item. For example, **Files and filing** is given three numbers, 005.74, 025.3, and 651.5, depending on whether the focus is computers, library catalogs, or business management. The editors explain that Dewey numbers are not assigned to very general topics and are deliberately kept short, but can be extended using subdivision numbers in Dewey Decimal Classification tables. They also caution catalogers against using the numbers without first examining them in DDC-Abridged.

Some headings are followed by instructions on how to apply or subdivide them as well as how not to use them and what alternatives are acceptable. For instance, under the heading **Film adaptations**, the instruction states: "Use for individual works, collections, or materials about film adaptations of material from other media." Under **Drama**, it says "Use for general materials on drama, not for individual works.

Materials on the history and criticism of drama as literature are entered under **Drama—History and criticism.** Materials on the presentation of plays are entered under **Acting; Amateur theater;** or **Theater—Production and direction.** Collections of plays are entered under **Drama—Collections; American drama—Collections; English drama—Collections;** and so on and adds under the SA reference, "S[ee] A[lso] subjects, historical events, names of countries, cities, etc., ethnic groups, classes of persons, and names of individual persons with the subdivision *Drama,* to express the theme or subject content of collections of plays, e.g. **Easter—Drama; United States—History—1861–1865, Civil War—Drama; Napoleon I, Emperor of the French, 1769–1821—Drama;** etc. [to be added as needed]." The instructions may include information about when *not* to use a heading and furnish alternatives for similar works with different emphases.

Sears, like LCSH, does not list personal names and other proper nouns or the names of particular animals, plants, or diseases, and so on that would be difficult to anticipate and include in the list. Instructions allow catalogers to add these headings as needed.

Subject headings in Sears are arranged according to the 1980 edition of filing rules sponsored by ALA. These rules, based on the principle of filing subject headings as they appear and ignoring all punctuation, were simplified from a more complicated version published in 1968. The current rules facilitate automated filing in computerized catalogs. Subject headings are now filed word by word with digits preceding letters, and punctuation is ignored. Figure 17.6, shows a list of hypothetical subject headings filed by these rules.

All multiword headings appear in natural order, that is, in the order they would be spoken. Inverted terms were eliminated from Sears years ago. The few that still appear in the list, such as Children, Abnormal, are there solely as cross-references. The use of natural order and the rule of ignoring punctuation in filing disperses some headings more closely related to one another than to those filed next to them, but it is a boon to users who do not have to remember that different types of punctuation have special meanings.

Art
Art – 15th and 16th centuries
Art – 17th and 18th centuries
Art – 19th century
Art and mythology
Art and religion
Art appreciation
Art criticism
Art – Exhibitions
Art metalwork
Art museums
Art – Political aspects
Art – Themes
Art therapy

Figure 17.6. Terms filed by ALA rules.

Advantages and Disadvantages of Using Sears

Many of Sears' features are the same as or very similar to the features of LCSH. What advantages are to be gained from adopting it? What disadvantages must be considered in doing so?

The main advantage of adopting Sears derives from its vocabulary, which is smaller, simpler, and broader than the vocabulary of LCSH and, therefore, better tailored to the language levels and searching skills of young people and adults whose knowledge of subjects is general. Another advantage is that a larger number of materials are brought together by the broad headings in Sears than would be collocated using LCSH's narrower headings. Users of libraries and media centers with small collections benefit from the larger average number of retrievals Sears provides, which increases the possibility that searchers will find what they seek among them. When other members of a school district or public library group use Sears, conforming to that choice makes sense if the group shares a single catalog, orders cataloging from the same vendor, or offers shared products and services.

The main disadvantage of adopting Sears is that it limits the number of sources from which a local library or media center can derive its cataloging. One important source of cataloging copy for small agencies—CIP—does not provide Sears headings. Catalogers can use the LCSH headings in CIP as suggestions, but they must still look up and assign the Sears subject headings to all the materials they buy, not just materials that lack CIP. In addition, just because a larger number of titles can be retrieved using Sears headings does not mean all of them are equally relevant to the searcher. In subject areas where a library collects heavily, narrower headings that differentiate similar materials and group them into smaller sets might be more appropriate.

Striking a balance among competing goals—accommodating language needs, achieving optimal specificity, conforming to peer choices, minimizing costs, and maximizing potential sources for cataloging copy—is never easy. User needs should take priority, but practical matters cannot be ignored. Consulting with users, information service staff, and cataloging staff can help with these decisions.

SUMMARY

LCSH remains the subject heading list in widest use among U.S. and Canadian libraries despite its problems and idiosyncrasies. The general growth of collections in the past several decades has turned small libraries into larger ones, and that growth has generated a need for a larger list of more specific subject headings. In small libraries and media centers, Sears is used quite often. However, because CIP records always contain LCSH headings and network records almost always contain them, many librarians and media specialists have had to rethink their adherence to Sears. On the other hand, when all the small libraries in a group use Sears, it is logical to use it also.

There is no requirement that narrow headings be used when broader ones will do an acceptable job. If a library has only a few books on a subject, a cataloger can decide not to distinguish them and put them all under one broad heading. These decisions should be based on a clear idea of how the collection will grow in the future. If a library has small collections that are unlikely to grow much larger, Sears headings might be applied instead of LCSH, because they are broader.

Subject headings must gather enough material so that someone looking under a particular heading will find most of the holdings of the library or media center relevant to that topic. At the same time, they must not bring together too many items or the file is rendered useless to all but the most persistent searchers. If a library uses a cataloging network as its source for cataloging data, decisions must also weigh the cost of changing headings on derived cataloging against putting up with retrieval that is less than ideal. Maintaining a local subject authority file to manage unique practices has costs that generally outweigh the benefits.

The delicate balance between gathering and distinguishing materials by subject shifts according to the needs of individual groups of materials and individual searchers. The best the cataloger can do is to try to please *most* of the searchers *most* of the time, while working toward an ideal subject catalog in which all users find exactly what they need under whatever headings they use.

REVIEW QUESTIONS

1. How are authorized headings identified in LCSH and Sears?

2. What is a free-floating subdivision and how is it assigned?

3. Explain how pattern headings are applied in practice.

4. Explain the main difference in the arrangement of subject headings filed by the ALA and the LC rules.

5. What is the difference between direct and indirect geographic subdivision?

6. Describe two benefits of adopting LCSH and two benefits of adopting Sears.

7. What are reciprocal cross-references?

8. Why do catalogers make references from a subject heading to the narrower term cross-references listed with it in the subject authority, but not to the broader term cross-references listed with it?

9. Name two kinds of terms used as subject headings that are not listed in subject authorities.

10. What is the generally accepted policy for assigning subject headings to individual works of fiction? Why do libraries accept the policy?

NOTES

The epigraph is from *21st Century Dictionary of Quotations*, ed. The Princeton Language Institute (New York: Laurel, 1993), 470.

1. *Sears List of Subject Headings Canadian Companion,* ed. Lynne Isberg Lighthall (New York: H.W. Wilson, 2001).

2. *Sears List of Subject Headings*, 19th ed., ed. Joseph Miller and Barbara A. Bristow (New York: H.W. Wilson, 2007), back cover.

SUGGESTED READING

Anderson, James D., and Melissa A. Hoffman. "A Fully Faceted Syntax for Library of Congress Subject Headings." *Cataloging & Classification Quarterly* 43, no. 1 (2006): 7–38.

Chan, Lois Mai. *Library of Congress Subject Headings: Principles and Application.* 4th ed. Westport, CT: Libraries Unlimited, 2005.

DeZelar-Tiedman, Christine. "Subject Access to Fiction: An Application of the Guidelines." *Library Resources & Technical Services* 40, no. 3 (July 1996): 203–10.

Drabenstott, Karen M., et al. "End User Understanding of Subject Headings in Library Catalogs." *Library Resources & Technical Services* 43, no. 3 (July 1999): 140–60.

Google. *A Research Guide.* Chapter 15: A Virtual Library of Useful URLs Subject Headings Arranged by Dewey Decimal Classification: 000-999. http://www.aresearchguide.com/15urls.html.

Guidelines on Subject Access to Individual Works of Fiction, Drama, Etc. 2nd ed. Chicago, IL: American Library Association, 2000.

Haykin, David Judson. *Subject Headings: A Practical Guide.* Washington, D.C.: Government Printing Office, 1951.

Holley, Robert P. "Subject Access Tools in English for Canadian Topics: Canadian Extensions to U.S. Subject Access Tools." *Library Resources & Technical Services* 52, no. 2 (April 2008): 29–43.

IFLA Working Group on FRSAR. *Functional Requirements for Subject Authority Data, 2010-07-03.* http://nkos.slis.kent.edu/FRSAR/index.html.

Kornegay, Rebecca S., Heidi E. Buchanan, and Hildegard B. Morgan. *Magic Search: Getting the Best Results From Your Catalog and Beyond.* Chicago, IL: American Library Association, 2009.

Library of Congress Working Group on the Future of Bibliographic Control. *On the Record: Report of the Library of Congress Working Group on the Future of Bibliographic Control.* http://www.loc.gov/bibliographic-future/news/lcwg-ontherecord-jan08-final.pdf.

LibraryThing Web site. Tagging. http://www.librarything.com/wiki/index.php/Tagging.

Mann, Thomas. "'On the Record' but Off the Track: A Review of the Report of The Library of Congress Working Group on The Future of Bibliographic Control With a Further Examination of Library of Congress Cataloging Tendencies." March 14, 2008. http://www.guild2910.org/WorkingGrpResponse2008.pdf.

Mann, Thomas. "Why LC Subject Headings Are More Important Than Ever." *American Libraries* (Oct. 2003): 52–54.

Mann, Thomas. "Will Google's Keyword Searching Eliminate the Need for LC Cataloging and Classification?" August 15, 2005. http://www.guild2910.org/searching.htm.

OCLC CatCD for Windows: LC Subject Authorities. Dublin, OH: OCLC, 1996–.

Olson, Hope A., and John J. Boll. *Subject Analysis in Online Catalogs.* 2nd ed. Englewood, CO: Libraries Unlimited, 2001.

Robare, Lori, Adam Schiff, and Rebecca Belford. *New Developments in Genre/Form Access.* Presented at the Oregon Library Association, April 2, 2009. Available at http://www.nwcentral.org/files/Genre_Form_Access_Intro_Robare.pdf.

Rolla, Peter J. "User Tags versus Subject Headings: Can User-Supplied Data Improve Subject Access to Library Collections?" *Library Resources & Technical Services* 53, no. 3 (July 2009): 174–84.

Satija, M. P., and Elizabeth Haynes. *User's Guide to Sears List of Subject Headings.* Lanham, MD: Scarecrow Press, 2008.

Sauperl, Alenka. *Subject Determination During the Cataloging Process.* Lanham, MD: Scarecrow Press, 2002.

Schwartz, Candy. *Sorting Out the Web: Approaches to Subject Access.* Westport, CT: Ablex, 2001.

Scott, Mona L. *Conversion Tables: LC-Dewey; Dewey-LC; Subject Headings—LC and Dewey.* 2nd ed. Englewood, CO: Libraries Unlimited, 1999. (Available on disk.)

Stone, Alva T. "The LCSH Century: A Brief History of the Library of Congress Subject Headings, and Introduction to the Centennial Essays." *Cataloging & Classification Quarterly* 29, nos. 1/2 (2000). (Theme issue about LCSH.)

Taylor, Arlene G., and Daniel N. Joudrey. *The Organization of Information.* 3rd ed. Westport, CT: Libraries Unlimited, 2009.

Chapter

Classification Systems

A place for everything and everything in its place.

—Isabella Mary Beeton

To arrange a library is to practice / in a quiet and modest way / the art of criticism.

—Jorge Luis Borges

The two most popular classification systems used in North America to arrange library materials on the shelves are the Dewey Decimal Classification (DDC) and the Library of Congress Classification (LCC). They are described in this chapter, along with the National Library of Medicine Classification (NLMC), a specialized system that is used in practice with LCC. The classification numbers assigned to materials are the part of their call numbers that reflects the subject content of the materials. By assigning the same or similar classification numbers to material on a topic, browsers find them gathered together on the shelves for easy access.

DEWEY DECIMAL CLASSIFICATION

The DDC is a universal, enumerative, hierarchical classification system. Its publisher, OCLC/Forest Press, claims it is the most popular classification system in the world. DDC is widely used in public and school libraries in the United States and Canada, and by these and other types of libraries in more than 100 other countries. The Library and Archives Canada (LAC) uses DDC to classify its collection. It is the basis for arrangement of the *British National Bibliography* and other national bibliographic agencies in the Commonwealth and elsewhere.

Seven principles underlie the organization and structure of DDC:

1. *Decimal division.* Division by 10s is the primary method used by DDC. All knowledge is first divided into 10 main classes. Each main class is subsequently subdivided into 10 more subclasses, and so on, theoretically, ad infinitum. It is a simple, familiar, and useful method of dividing—something people think of as round numbers. At the same time, this form of division is at the root of some of the system's most troubling limitations.

2. *Classification by discipline.* The primary attribute applied in dividing knowledge is subject discipline, represented by the 10 main classes. That may seem natural to readers of this book, because it is so familiar to most librarians, but it is not the only possibility. Knowledge could, for instance, be divided first by a different element, such as time period or geographic location, and only after that, by discipline, genre, or form, and other attributes.

3. *Hierarchy.* The principle of moving from broad categories to narrower ones and from these to still narrower ones until reaching the narrowest one possible is often encountered in classification, but DDC emphasizes it and uses it in creating complex numbers. Ideally, the hierarchy built into DDC numbers identifies topics at the same level and clarifies which are broader and narrower merely by counting the total number of digits in the class. In practice, this works only part of the time, because all topical areas do not divide neatly into 10 elements. In areas such as literature, a number with three digits (e.g., 813, American fiction) can be at the same level as a number with five (e.g., Russian fiction, 891.43) or more.

4. *Mnemonics.* Melvil Dewey liked time-saving devices and incorporated as many as he could into his classification. Specific groups of numbers may represent the same topic in many places in the classification. An example is the number "-73," which stands for United States in geography (917.3), cookery (641.5973), political parties (324.273), etc. However, it doesn't always work; for example, the number 730 stands for sculpture.

5. *Literary warrant.* This principle dictates that classes are created only after materials exist that require them. The DDC purports to be a classification of all knowledge, and it does an outstanding job of including topics. However, no classification of limited size can anticipate or list all topics. When new knowledge emerges, new numbers are created to accommodate them. "Computers" is a good example of a topic that was added when the need for it became clear. In the 19th and earlier editions of DDC, computers occupied a tiny category (001.64) under the larger topic of "Research" (001). In the 20th edition, computers expanded to occupy three newly established sections of their own (004–006).

6. *Enumeration.* This principle dictates listing complete class numbers in contrast to listing components (facets) of numbers that must be put together (or synthesized) to build complex topics. Enumeration generally guides DDC, but recent editions incorporate more instances of number

building because it is more economical of page space and allows for greater flexibility. Expansion of many subject areas in recent years would require many more enumerated numbers to represent them, whereas instructions to copy existing expansion techniques does not.

7. *Relative location.* At one time in the United States, Canada, and elsewhere, library books were shelved in fixed locations. Once an item was given its place on the shelves, it was never moved, no matter what new materials were added to the collection. The DDC assumes that as new books are added and shelved, existing items will be moved to maintain their subject relationships. The DDC number merely identifies a place relative to other items in the collection.

None of these principles operates perfectly throughout DDC. They are observed as far as possible when they do not conflict, create unwanted juxtapositions of subjects, or interfere with practical considerations. Enumeration is abandoned to save space, mnemonics are superseded, and other principles may be modified when it is important to do so. Nevertheless, the principles govern many of the decisions made by DDC's editors with regard to class numbers and relationships.

An eighth principle—integrity of numbers—was promised by Melvil Dewey to DDC users in the classification's early days. Numbers assigned to represent a particular topic were expected to remain stable and not change. Number changes create work in a library keeping all of its materials shelved in a consistent, up-to-date manner. At the least, call-number labels and markings in or on materials must be changed, catalog records must be altered to display new call numbers, and materials must be moved to their new locations. However, as knowledge grows and changes over time, maintaining accurate relationships among subjects requires changing the existing numbers despite the promise. From time to time, entire spans of numbers have been altered to reflect profound changes in a subject area in a practice called "phoenixing." A phoenixed schedule was one that was discarded and rebuilt from scratch (rising from its ashes, like the mythical bird). At some points in DDC's history, users have rebelled at having to absorb too many changes, so in recent years, DDC's editors have used the milder term "complete revision" for revised number spans, and the practice was modified, though not entirely abandoned. In recent years, to provide as much stability as possible, complete revisions have been kept to a minimum and revised schedules have been given extensive testing before being published.

Format of DDC

The DDC may be purchased in book form in full or abridged editions, or as an online subscription. An outline of the classification, consisting of its three summaries (10 main classes, 100 divisions, and 1,000 sections), which appears at the beginning of the second volume of the unabridged print edition, is available free of charge on the DDC Web site, www.oclc.org/dewey.

At the time of this writing, the printed version of unabridged DDC is in its 22nd edition. The book version is in four volumes totaling more than 4,000 pages.[1] The first volume includes the usual introductory information: a brief background of the classification, a list of numbers that have changed from the previous edition, a user manual to guide classifiers in assigning numbers, and six auxiliary tables of subdivisions to be added to numbers from the main schedules. The schedules themselves are enumerated in the second and third volumes. The Relative Index appears in the fourth volume.

The online version of DDC, called WebDewey (www.oclc.org/dewey/versions/webdewey), includes all the content from DDC 22 as well as ongoing quarterly updates (new developments, new "built" numbers, and additional electronic index terms), updated mappings to Edition 22 numbers in the areas of computer science and law, thousands of headings from *Library of Congress Subject Headings* (LCSH) that have been statistically mapped to DDC numbers from records in the OCLC Online Union Catalog, thousands of Relative Index terms and built numbers not available in print, links from mapped LCSH to the LCSH authority records, and selected mappings from the National Library of Medicine's *Medical Subject Headings* (MeSH). WebDewey also includes optional Dewey Cutter Software that automatically provides cutter numbers from the OCLC Four-Figure Cutter Tables (Cutter Four-Figure Table and Cutter-Sanborn Four-Figure Table).

The principal advantages of the electronic version over the book version, aside from computerized retrieval, are the inclusion of frequently used LCSH subject headings associated with a classification number; the ability to verify a classification number assignment by sampling a catalog record that uses the number drawn from the OCLC database; a popular, easy-to-use "windowed" user interface; cut-and-paste functions that help minimize keying; online help screens; and an introductory tutorial.

The Relative Index was Melvil Dewey's original contribution to classification. Its great value lies in bringing together all aspects of a topic under the term used to represent it no matter where the topic would be classified. For example, topics relating to music are located in the music schedule (780–789), but music therapy is found in medicine (610s), music in literature is in the 800s, and music in art is in the 700s (but not 780–789). The Relative Index does more than just list topics in alphabetical order with their associated class numbers. It brings together the different contexts in which a single topical term might be used and the different disciplines in which a single topic might be found.

The DDC abridged edition[2] is suitable for very small general collections, defined by OCLC-Forest Press as collections totaling 20,000 volumes or less. The abridged edition contains about one-tenth as many numbers as the unabridged edition, rarely displaying numbers longer than five digits. At the time of this writing, the abridged version is in its 14th edition, published in one volume of approximately 1,000 pages. Numbers in the abridged edition, while broader in meaning and shorter in length, are compatible with those in the unabridged edition.

The Schedules

The DDC's main classes, based to some degree on an inversion of Sir Francis Bacon's classification of knowledge (philosophy, expanded to cover most of the modern disciplines, poetry, and history), include the following:

000 = Generalities
100 = Philosophy
200 = Religion

300 = Social Sciences
400 = Language
500 = Pure Science
600 = Technology
700 = Arts
800 = Literature
900 = Geography and History

By covering knowledge in only 10 main classes, DDC forces some odd companions into a single class. For example, in the 100s, philosophy, psychology, and the occult are grouped together. Statistics, etiquette, commerce, and war share the 300s with sociology, economics, political science, law, and education. The 700s, primarily covering the arts, also include sports and games. Geography and history are grouped together in the 900s in one huge main class, even though they are quite different topics. One might expect to find library science with the social sciences or education, but instead it is located in the 000s (read this as *zero hundreds*) along with research, publishing, and other generalities.

At the start of the second volume are three summaries of all the numbers: the 10 main classes, the 100 divisions, and the 1,000 sections. They are a good place to begin when trying to assign a Dewey number for an unfamiliar topic. After deciding about the topic to be represented, choose an appropriate main class, based on the emphasis of the material. For example, it would be easy if there were only one place to put a book on computers, but if the book emphasizes the machinery, it is classified with other books on machinery in the 600s, applied science and technology. If it emphasizes computer programs and applications, it is classed nearer to research in the 000s. A video about trucks might emphasize the truck as a type of vehicle (600s), or it might emphasize transportation via truck (300s).

In some cases, a classification number is chosen to reflect the interests of library users. For example, Figure 18.1 shows a book about the free-trade agreement between Canada and the United States. Depending on the library, either 382.971073, stressing Canada's agreements with the United States, or 382.973071, stressing U.S. agreements with Canada, is equally correct. In both cases, assigning the full nine-digit number enables the classification to reflect an item involving both countries, no matter which comes first.

DDC allows options in classification for some topics. Biography is one of these. The preferred method is to place a biography with the topic for which the person is known. The biography of Lincoln Hall (see Figure 18.2), for example, is classified in mountaineering.

However, DDC provides an alternate series of numbers in the 920s for libraries that wish to shelve all biographies together. The following options are suggested:

- Use the 920–928 schedule, for example, 923.871 (biography of Canadian persons in commerce, communication, transportation)
- Use 92 for individual biographies
- Use B (indicating Biography) for individual biographies
- Use 920.71 for biographies of men, 920.72 for biographies of women

This example is an illustration of:
- joint authors
- other title information listed on title page before title proper
- detailed pagination
- bibliography and index note
- Library of Congress subject headings
- joint author added entry
- two title added entries
- difference in Dewey Decimal Classification number according to emphasis desired
- 2nd level cataloging

```
Doern, G. Bruce.
  Faith & fear : the free trade story / G. Bruce Doern & Brian W.
Tomlin. -- Toronto : Stoddart, 1991.
  xi, 340 p. ; 24 cm.

  Includes references (p.319-333) and index.
  ISBN 0-7737-2534-2.

  1. Free trade -- Canada.  2. Free trade -- United States.  3. Canada
-- Commercial policy.  4. United States -- Commercial policy.  5. Canada
-- Commerce -- United States.  6. United States -- Commerce -- Canada.
I. Tomlin, Brian W.  II. Title.  III. Title: Faith & fear
```

Recommended DDC: 382.971073 (for Canadian emphasis)
                   or
                   382.973071 (for U.S. emphasis)

CHIEF SOURCE OF INFORMATION
(Title Page)

(Information on Verso)

THE FREE TRADE STORY

FAITH
&FEAR

G. BRUCE DOERN & BRIAN W. TOMLIN

Stoddart

Copyright © 1991 by G. Bruce Doern and Brian W. Tomlin

All rights reserved. No part of this publication may be reproduced or transmitted in any form or by any means, electronic or mechanical, including photocopy, recording, or any information storage and retrieval system, without permission in writing from the publisher.

First published in 1991 by
Stoddart Publishing Co. Limited
34 Lesmill Road
Toronto, Canada
M3B 2T6

ISBN 0-7737-2534-2

Cover Design: Leslie Styles
Typesetting: Tony Gordon Ltd.

Printed and bound in the United States of America

Figure 18.1. Varying classification numbers.

This example is an illustration of:
- other title information
- probable publishing date
- detailed pagination statement
- descriptive illustration statement
- edition and history note
- bibliography and index note
- library's holdings note
- Library of Congress subject headings
- Dewey Decimal Classification with prime mark
- Library of Congress Cataloging in Publication (CIP)
- 2nd level cataloging

```
Hall, Lincoln, 1955-
   Dead lucky : life after death on Mount Everest / Lincoln Hall.
-- New York : Jeremy P. Tarcher/Penguin, [2008?].
   xx, 307 p., [16] p. of plates : ill.(some col.) ; 24 cm.

   Originally published in Australia by Random House, 2007.
   Includes bibliographical references (p. [277]-281) and index.
   Library's copy signed by author.
   ISBN 978-1-58542-646-1.

   1. Hall, Lincoln, 1955-  2. Mountaineers -- Australia --
Biography.  3. Mountaineering accidents -- Everest, Mount (China
and Nepal).  4. Mountaineering -- Everest, Mount (China and
Nepal.  I. Title.
```

Recommended DDC: 796.522'092

Publication statement in a Canadian library would be:

New York ; Toronto : Jeremy P. Tarcher/Penguin, [2008?].

DEAD LUCKY

LIFE AFTER DEATH ON MOUNT EVEREST

Lincoln Hall

JEREMY P. TARCHER/PENGUIN
a member of Penguin Group (USA) Inc.
New York

(Information on Verso)

JEREMY P. TARCHER/PENGUIN
Published by the Penguin Group
Penguin Group (USA) Inc., 375 Hudson Street, New York, New York 10014, USA ·
Penguin Group (Canada), 90 Eglinton Avenue East, Suite 700, Toronto,
Ontario M4P 2Y3, Canada (a division of Pearson Canada Inc.) ·
Penguin Books Ltd, 80 Strand, London WC2R 0RL, England · Penguin Ireland,
25 St Stephen's Green, Dublin 2, Ireland (a division of Penguin Books Ltd) ·
Penguin Group (Australia), 250 Camberwell Road, Camberwell, Victoria 3124, Australia
(a division of Pearson Australia Group Pty Ltd) · Penguin Books India Pvt Ltd,
11 Community Centre, Panchsheel Park, New Delhi–110 017, India · Penguin
Group (NZ), 67 Apollo Drive, Rosedale, North Shore 0632, New Zealand
(a division of Pearson New Zealand Ltd) · Penguin Books (South Africa) (Pty) Ltd,
24 Sturdee Avenue, Rosebank Johannesburg 2196, South Africa

Penguin Books Ltd, Registered Offices:
80 Strand, London WC2R 0RL, England

Originally published in Australia by Random House 2007

Copyright © 2007 by Lincoln Hall
Interior illustrations © 2007 by Ken Beatty
All rights reserved. No part of this book may be reproduced, scanned,
or distributed in any printed or electronic form without permission. Please do not
participate in or encourage piracy of copyrighted materials in violation
of the author's rights. Purchase only authorized editions.
Published simultaneously in Canada

Most Tarcher/Penguin books are available at special quantity discounts for bulk
purchase for sales promotions, premiums, fund-raising, and educational needs.
Special books or book excerpts also can be created to fit specific needs. For details,
write Penguin Group (USA) Inc. Special Markets,
375 Hudson Street, New York, NY 10014.

Library of Congress Cataloging-in-Publication Data

Hall, Lincoln.
Dead lucky : life after death on Mount Everest / Lincoln Hall.
p.   cm.
Originally published in Australia by Random House in 2007;
published simultaneously in Canada.
Includes index.
ISBN 978-1-58542-646-1
1. Hall, Lincoln, date. 2. Mountaineers—Australia—Biography.
3. Mountaineering accidents—Everest, Mount (China and Nepal).
4. Mountaineering—Everest, Mount (China and Nepal) I. Title.
GV199.92.H3235A3   2008   2008006676
796.522092—dc22
[B]

Printed in the United States of America
1 3 5 7 9 10 8 6 4 2

BOOK DESIGN BY AMANDA DEWEY

While the author has made every effort to provide accurate telephone numbers and Internet addresses at the time of publication, neither the publisher nor the author assumes any
responsibility for errors, or for changes that occur after publication. Further, the publisher
does not have any control over and does not assume any responsibility for author or third-
party websites or their content.

Figure 18.2. Options for Biography in DDC.

In addition, some libraries use 920 for collected biographies and 921 for individual biographies.

A good rule of thumb to remember about classification is that it aims to bring related works together. To do this, a cataloger can look in the shelflist or on the shelves to see what kinds of materials were assigned the number being considered. If the materials do not appear to be related to the work in hand, the cataloger should look elsewhere for an appropriate classification number.

Throughout the schedules, selected numbers are left blank (or "unoccupied") to allow for future expansion without disturbing the existing numbers. In the 000s, for example, 007–009, 013, 024, and 040–049 are unoccupied. Although many areas of the 500s and 600s are very crowded, and there are categories bearing numbers of seven or more digits, some sections in these classes remain unoccupied.

A Closer Look at the Schedules

DDC's main classes are explored here in greater detail, noting the subjects each typically includes; however, no attempt is made to list all subjects in any of the main classes. Familiarity with the schedules is best acquired by using them, together with a library's shelflist and common sense.

000s: Generalities includes works about knowledge in general; research; communication in general; computer science, updated to accommodate recent topics such as the World Wide Web, virtual reality, and markup languages; controversial knowledge, such as UFOs, the Loch Ness monster, and the Bermuda Triangle; reference materials, such as bibliographies and catalogs; library and information science, including reading in general; encyclopedias; organizations; publishing; and collections that cover many topics.

100s: Philosophy, Paranormal Phenomena, and Psychology includes concepts and schools of thought in detail, as well as the occult, the entire field of psychology, logic, and ethics.

200s: Religion deals solely with this one subject area. Changes begun in the 21st edition to address a long-standing criticism of Christian bias were completed in the current edition. That bias—traceable to literary warrant in 19th-century U.S. college libraries, where collecting was largely confined to books about the Christian religion—persisted into the 21st century. Although non-Christian religions still tend to have long numbers, many new developments have increased the level of detail available for materials about these religions, including Judaism, Islam, Bahaism, Black African religions, and American native religions.

300s: Social Sciences, in keeping with its label, covers sociology, political science, economics, law, public administration, and social problems. It also includes statistics (demographic statistics, not probabilities, which is located in mathematics); military science; education; commerce; and an odd group of topics headed "Customs, Etiquette, and Folklore," under which subtopics such as marriage, death, war, holidays, chivalry, suicide, and cannibalism are subsumed. The 22nd edition includes revisions in the numbers for social groups (305–306) and law (340s).

400s: Language is a straightforward class. It begins with language in general (i.e., linguistics) and follows with numbers for individual languages beginning with English and other Western European languages. Preferential positioning of English and European languages probably is due to literary warrant and the fact that this is an American scheme, but the schedules include an instruction explaining how classifiers can give local emphasis to any other language of their choice.

500s: Natural Sciences and Mathematics includes mathematics, which was revised substantially in the 22nd edition; astronomy; chemistry, also revised in the 22nd edition; physics; geology; the sciences of the ancient world, paleontology and paleozoology; and the life sciences, first in general and, then, the separate subjects of plants and animals.

600s: Technology (Applied Sciences) includes medicine and health, revised in the 22nd edition; engineering; agriculture (raising plant crops and animal husbandry); management; manufacturing; and buildings (but not architecture, which is found in the next main class, fine arts); and home economics and family living. Popular topics found here include parenting, pets, cookbooks, gardening, electronics, and automobiles. Many fine distinctions must be made between pure and applied sciences, necessitating careful examination of other works in the collection to bring together related items, for example, distinguishing between botany (580) and horticulture (630), or between immunity in animals (591.29) and immunity in human beings (616.079).

700s: The Arts, Fine and Decorative Arts, as previously mentioned, combines the familiar topics of art in general; architecture; painting; sculpture; crafts; and music; with performing and recreational arts. One finds circuses, movies, and television at 791, titled generically "Public performances"; theater, vaudeville, and ballet, called "Stage presentations," at 792; while other kinds of dancing are grouped at 793 as "Indoor games and amusements," along with puzzles, riddles, magic, and so on. The characterization of television as a "public performance" and folk dancing as an "indoor amusement" reflect the perceptions of earlier times. Today, people tend to think of television as an indoor amusement, while in some small towns folk dances are held outdoors as public events even if they are not paid public performances. Games of skill, including computer games and chess, are classed in 794, but games of chance (where some might prefer putting computer games) are in 795. Bowling is classed as an "indoor game of skill," in 794, while baseball and football are at 796 with other "Athletic and outdoor sports and games." The distinctions are, perhaps, transparent to those who watch all three sports and more on their television sets. "Aquatic and air sports" are at 797; outdoor sports that bring people close to nature—horseback riding, animal racing, hunting, and fishing—are found at 798 and 799. An interesting placement in the 700s is photography. One might expect photographic art and techniques would be found under different main classes in the same way computer software and hardware are separated, but an entire division, 770–779, is devoted to the art of photography, its techniques, and its processes. Specialists who see film and television art as a subset of photographic arts in general might be critical of these placements. The music schedule (780–789), although it resembles other schedules in outward appearance, was revised completely in the 20th edition, and is actually a faceted scheme based on the British Classification for Music.

800s: Literature (Belles-Lettres) and Rhetoric in general is followed in this class by the individual literatures of different countries, beginning, as one might expect, with American literature in English. An instruction here similar to the one for languages enables the literature of a different nation or language to be assigned the preferential position, if desired. English literature in English and Anglo-Saxon literature is followed by European literatures, including Latin and Greek, both ancient and modern, consuming all but the final ten sections, 890–899. These last few numbers cover all of Asian, Middle Eastern, and African literature as well as Russian, Polish, and other languages less familiar to North Americans. Shakespeare is the only author with his own number, 822.33. A citation order is strictly observed in the 800s: country/language first, followed by genre and time period. All individual literatures do not have defined time periods— only popularly collected literatures have them. Three tables for literature (see the "A closer look at the tables" section in this chapter) augment these topics.

900s: Geography, History, and Auxiliary Disciplines, the final class, begins with three divisions for general works on both geography and history (900–909); general works on geography alone, including travel books (910–919); and biography (920–929). Regarding biography, application policies given in the manual and used at the Library of Congress's (LC) Decimal Classification Office recommend using the 920s solely for collective biographies and classing the life stories of individuals in the subjects with which each is associated. Thus, biographies of mathematicians Carl Friedrich Gauss and Nikolai Lobachevski who pioneered non-Euclidean geometry, would be in 516.9 with that subject, and a biography of Sigmund Freud would be in 150, with other works on psychology. The other seven divisions (930–999) are devoted to history alone, begin-ning with a division for the ancient world and followed by one each for the continents of Europe, Asia, Africa, North America, and South America. All other countries and regions are grouped into the final division, including the final section, 999, for extrater-restrial worlds. The 22nd edition includes an expansion of numbers for the Holocaust at 940.5318.

A Closer Look at the Tables

Because creating coextensive class numbers requires use of the tables, a closer look at them is warranted. Each number in the tables is preceded by a dash to show that it may not be used alone, but must be attached to a number from the schedules. The tables are preceded by a table of precedence directing classifiers how to assign multiple subdivi-sions when more than one subdivision is applicable.

Table 1, Standard Subdivisions: Table 1 is used most frequently, because applying it does not require an explicit instruction in the schedules. If the base number in the schedules to which the subdivision is being applied has instructions to apply standard subdivisions in special ways, they must be heeded. These explicit instructions super-sede unlimited application of numbers from Table 1. The DDC's mnemonics are rec-ognizable to a great degree in the standard subdivisions. The philosophy of a subject is designated -01, just as the 100s represent that field; -06 is the standard subdivision for organizations and management, just as the 650s stand for management; -09 stands for historical and geographic treatment, just as the 900s stand for those fields. The analogies are not complete, however: -05 stands for serial publications, not scientific aspects; -08 stands for history and description of a subject among groups of persons, not literary treatments; and so forth. A new number for racism was established in -08 in the 22nd edition.

Table 2, Geographic Areas, Historical Periods, Persons: Table 2 can be applied only when an explicit instruction directs classifiers to do so. Table 2 gives numbers for geographic areas, beginning with general areas such as frigid zones at -11 (-113 if they are north of the equator and -116 if they are south of it), or land and landforms at –14. Locations in the ancient world are identified by -3 in this table; those in the modern world are assigned numbers between -4 and -9. Some locales, particularly in the United States, have their own numbers; for example, the number for New York City's borough of Manhattan is -7471. Size is not the issue that decides whether a special number is established, however. All of Antarctica is classified at -989, and all extraterrestrial worlds are classified at -99. The issue is how much material is published about the place. Table 2 has another major application: Standard subdivision -09 instructs classifiers to go to Table 2 for a number for a specific geographical area to which a topic is limited, and to add it to -09. For example, an item about forest lands in France is classified 333.75'09'44. (The meaning of the prime marks that appear after the 5 and 9 in this number is explained later.) The first five digits (333.75) represents forest lands in general, the addition of -09 from Table 1 represents limited geographical treatment, and, following the instruction there, the addition of -44 from Table 2 represents France. Major changes to this table in the 22nd edition and subsequent updates address political changes affecting jurisdictions and boundaries.

Table 3, Subdivisions for the Arts, for Individual Literatures, for Specific Literary Forms: Numbers from Table 3 are applied only when explicit instructions direct classifiers to do so. Table 3 is made up of three subordinate tables: Table 3-A, "Subdivisions for Works by or about Individual Authors"; Table 3-B, "Subdivisions for Works by or about More than One Author"; and Table 3-C, "Notation to Be Added Where Instructed in Table 3-B, 700.4, 791.4, and 808–809." In Tables 3-A and 3-B, the general categories of genre and criticism are subdivided finely for arranging very large collections of literary materials about authors. In Table 3-C, different categories with their subdivisions are found, such as literary qualities or themes, to be used for arranging very large collections of general literary criticism.

Table 4, Subdivisions of Individual Languages and Language Families: Table 4 contains subdivision numbers to be added to base numbers for individual languages (420–490) from the main schedules. Frequently used numbers from this table include -3, which represents dictionaries, and -86, which stands for readers in a language. The numbers in this table include other characteristics of language materials and publication form; for example, -5 is "Grammar of the standard form of the language."

Table 5, Ethnic and National Groups: Table 5 contains numbers for racial, ethnic, and national groups, organized more or less by geographic origin; for example, -1 stands for North Americans, -2 for people of the British Isles, -3 for Nordics, and so on. Some interesting divisions occur in this table; for example, Modern Latins (-4) includes French, Walloons, and Catalans. It does not include Italians, Romanians, and related groups, who have their own numbers beginning -5, or Spanish and Portuguese peoples, whose numbers begin with -6. The -6s include all Spanish-Americans at (-68) as well as Brazilians, subsumed under Portuguese-speaking peoples at -69. The number for groups not previously given their own numbers, -9, includes Semites, North Africans, Asians, Africans, and indigenous peoples of America and Australia. Individual peoples within this large group also have their own numbers; for example, Sri Lankans are at -91413. An option in Table 5 allows classifiers to put a group other than North Americans at -1 if local emphasis is desired for that group.

Table 6, Languages: Table 6 contains numbers for subdividing languages of the world, but they are not intended to be added to base numbers from the 400s. The table provides for the language characteristics of materials classed in the other schedules.

If, for example, a translation of the Bible into Dutch is being classified, the notation for Dutch language from Table 6 (-3931) is added to the base number for the Bible (220.5) to form a coextensive number for Dutch-language Bibles, 220.53931. Here, as in the 400s, 800s, and elsewhere, an option allows users to put a language other than English first. DDC gives preference to English (-2) and European languages (-3 to -8). The languages of the rest of the world follow in -9. Table 6 is a tiny encyclopedia of the world's languages, enumerated in a few pages.

New classifiers are reminded to go to Tables 2 through 6 only when explicitly instructed to do so. Table 1's numbers (standard subdivisions) are the only ones that may be applied without specific instructions. At the same time, classifiers must be alert to instructions limiting or changing the normal pattern for standard subdivisions. They may be directed to use -001 to -009 in place of the usual -01 to -09; or they may be instructed to use -03 to -09, which means the first two standard subdivisions (-01 and -02) cannot be used for the particular number or number span to which the instruction applies. Situations sometimes arise for which there are no instructions in either the schedule or the manual, but, more often, the editors give needed guidance about the way subdivisions should be assigned.

LIBRARY OF CONGRESS CLASSIFICATION

LCC is the result of applying practical solutions to practical problems. When LC's collections were destroyed by fire during the War of 1812, Thomas Jefferson sold Congress his personal library, then numbering about 7,000 volumes, as the basis for building a new collection. Along with the materials came Jefferson's own classification system, which remained in place until the turn of the 20th century. Herbert Putnam, then the new Librarian of Congress, implemented many changes at LC, including the launching of a new classification. The choice was not an easy one. The DDC was in its fifth edition at the time, and Cutter's Expansive Classification, a popular rival, was in its sixth. However, after consideration of these and other alternatives, Putnam and Charles Martel, LC's chief cataloger, decided to devise a new and different scheme having as its primary objective solely the orderly arrangement of LC's current and future holdings. They wanted to avoid adopting an existing scheme into which LC's holdings would have to be fitted.

One result of the main objective—organizing LC's holdings for effective retrieval—was to release LC from any obligation to a higher authority, such as the DDC's editors. LC has total control over the classification. Another was to permit literary warrant to govern the scheme, which evolved into a loose federation of schedules, each fitting a particular subject area according to what LC owned and expected to collect in the years to come. Although several overarching principles are found throughout LCC, each schedule is an individual entity in which the breakdown and organization of the subjects need not relate to any other schedule. Thus, some schedules are in their fourth, fifth, or later editions, and the most recently developed law schedules are still in their first editions. (At the end of the 20th century, LC abandoned numbered editions in favor of dated editions.)

LCC is updated continuously. Decisions on new or revised classification numbers are disseminated online via LC's Web site and in its *Classification Plus* product.

A printed newsletter titled *Additions and Changes,* which once published the changes in a printed version, ended publication in 2002.

Other aids to using LCC for original classifying include LCSH (for general guidance only; numbers listed there should never be used without consulting the schedules themselves), the *Classification and Shelflisting Manual; LC Classification Outline; LC Pocket Guide;* and *JZ and KZ: Historical Notes & Introduction to Application.* The most complete guide to LCC is *A Guide to the Library of Congress Classification* by Lois Mai Chan.[3]

Principles Underlying LCC

Nine principles underlie the organization and structure of LCC:

1. *Classification by discipline.* Like DDC, LCC divides knowledge first into disciplines, but there are 21 rather than 10, and the concept of what constitutes a discipline differs considerably from Dewey. For example, DDC's interpretation of the discipline of social sciences (300s) includes political science, law, and education, whereas LCC's interpretation does not, making each of those subject areas a separate discipline (J, K, and L, respectively).

2. *Literary warrant.* This principle, which dictates that classes be created only when materials exist that require them, operates much more prominently in LCC than it does in DDC. In DDC, literary warrant acts more as a priority check, because DDC attempts to classify all knowledge, not just the knowledge covered by existing documents. (Even DDC does not include all potential subjects, because to do so would require an infinite number of classes.) LCC aims only to classify all of LC's holdings, not all knowledge. As a result, the classification does not need to anticipate and accommodate topics outside LC's collecting interests. The experts who devised the original schedule created numbers for existing holdings and for those topical areas in which they believed publication would flourish *and* that LC would continue collecting.

3. *Geographical arrangement.* In the course of legislative research, inquiries often involve particular places; therefore, subdivision by geographical location is often preferred over subdivision by other characteristics geared to a subject's natural hierarchy.

4. *Alphabetical arrangement.* A second subdivision technique used by LCC is cutter numbers, which alphabetize when they are applied. LCC uses cutter numbers for many elements throughout the schedules, including geographic names, topical terms, and personal names. Although cutter numbers are thought of as mnemonic devices, they do not assist memory very much in LCC, because they are applied differently in different parts of the schedules. There is no guarantee that the same term, if it appears in different parts of the schedules, will be cuttered the same way; or, conversely, that the same cutter number will represent the same word or name in different parts of the classification. At times the cutter number does not represent a name or word, but stands for a topical subdivision.

5. *Economy of notation.* The LCC uses mixed notation, employing both alphabetic and numeric characters. It can represent extremely narrow topics with fewer characters than DDC uses for topics at the same level of specificity.

6. *Close classification.* The LCC originated at a time when LC's collection contained more than one million books. It was devised to handle not only this many items but also an ever-growing total. Thus, it reflects a deep specificity that DDC does not, even though DDC can be extended to accommodate equally narrow topics. In LCC, classifiers are more likely to find an established number that matches the topic of an item being classified than they are if they use DDC—provided, of course, that LC collects in the subject area.

7. *Enumeration.* Similar to DDC, LCC enumerates a very large proportion of the categories it provides and minimizes the use of number-building devices that allow classifiers to synthesize their own classes. The enormous size of LCC (40-plus volumes) is evidence of its heavy reliance on enumeration.

8. *Relative location.* Like DDC, LCC uses the principle of relative location, although its use of geographic and alphabetic subdivisions tends to fragment materials related to one another in a topical hierarchy.

9. *Stability of numbers.* Although not explicitly stated, LC numbers, once established, rarely change. Very few schedules have changed radically, although it has happened. For example, the JX schedule (International law) was eliminated in 1997 and its topics relocated in other schedules; and, much earlier, numbers originally established within various schedules for legal aspects of subjects were eliminated and different numbers for these topics were developed as part of new law (K) schedules.

Like DDC, none of LCC's principles operate perfectly throughout the entire classification, but they are observed as long as they do not conflict, create unwanted juxtapositions of subjects, or interfere with practical considerations. For example, enumeration is sometimes abandoned to save space; choices between geographic, alphabetic, and topical subarrangements may be forced; and other principles may be modified as LC's management desires. Nevertheless, the operation of the principles can be observed throughout the schedules.

In addition to the nine principles, the following seven-point intellectual structure devised by Charles Martel is seen in the arrangement of materials within classes and subclasses. Current policies have abandoned it, so it is not found in newer numbers.

1. *Form.* The first few numbers of classes and subclasses are allocated to general form subdivisions, including periodicals, often linked with society publications, yearbooks, congresses, documents, exhibitions and museums, and directories.

2. *Theory and philosophy.*

3. *History and biography.*

4. *Treatises and general works.*

5. *Law.* Until the K classes were completed, legal materials for a subject were classed with the subject; for example, building codes were classed in TH219 with building construction, TH9500 with fire prevention, and so on. Since the publication of separate law classes, these numbers have been deleted and relocated within the law schedules (K).

6. *Education.* Materials dealing with study, teaching, and research on a subject, as well as textbooks on that subject, are included in this section.

7. *Specific subjects and subdivisions.* These numbers are the bulk of each schedule.

Martel's seven-point structure applied to topics at each level of hierarchy. For example, TH1 is "Periodicals and societies" for building construction as a whole; TH1061 is "Periodicals, societies, etc." for systems of building construction; and TH2430 is "Periodicals, societies, congresses, etc." for roofing. Every topic does not have a number for periodicals; for example, floors and flooring, the topic following roofing, does not. Development of special numbers for periodicals depends on the likelihood that periodicals covering a subject are published and that LC collects and classifies them. Note that the phrase used differs in each of the three instances in the example, combining different types of publications.

Format of LCC

Forty-three separate volumes of enumerated numbers make up LCC at the time of this writing, and it is also available as an online product, *Classification Web,* which is available by subscription from LC's Cataloging Distribution Service. In the print edition, some disciplines occupy a whole volume (e.g., A, C, J, L, M, N); two share a volume (E-F); others are divided among several volumes (B, K, P). Class P, languages and literatures, is contained in 11 volumes plus a separate volume of tables. Each volume contains some or all of the following parts:

1. *Preface.* Gives a brief history of the schedule and its editions.

2. *Synopsis.* Lists the primary divisions of the class (or subclass) of the volume.

3. *Outline.* Summarizes the main subdivisions of the class. A combination of all of these outlines, which used to be published from time to time as a paper pamphlet, is available now online at LC's Web site.

4. *Schedule.* This is the body of the volume. It enumerates all the numbers in the subclasses.

5. *Tables.* Includes tables intended for use throughout the schedule. LCC has three interschedule or auxiliary tables: cutter numbers for countries of the world, U.S. states and Canadian provinces, and cities. The auxiliary tables are not printed in all volumes but appear in H, T, and Z. Other tables, such as those used with the P schedules, are published separately from the schedules.

6. *Index.* Provides access to terms used in the volume.

The lack of a combined index to LCC is a serious drawback. Also troublesome for classifiers is the lack of coordination between LCSH and LCC. Terminology for a topic differs between the two tools, and the LCC numbers provided in LCSH are not prescribed, merely suggested. Scope notes and helpful instructions are sporadic in LCC schedules, although some appear. For example, at VM20, Shipbuilding in the 20th century, it says, "For individual companies, shipyards, etc., see VM301.A-Z."

Printed volumes of LCC have neat, attractive pages bound in paper covers. Libraries often rebind them to ensure that they remain in good condition despite heavy use. The online version is more convenient to store, search, and use. It is updated daily, offers numerous ways to search for class numbers, can be browsed, displays subject headings and DDC numbers that correspond to particular LCC numbers, automatically calculates table numbers, and can be linked to local online cataloging systems. The product includes LCSH and LCC. The Cataloging Distribution Service offers free trials and tutorials for new users, making it attractive for libraries that do a great deal of original classifying to switch from buying the printed volumes to the online version. The cost of a subscription depends on the number of users within an institution, but it seems reasonable.

Main Classes of LCC

Main classes in LCC are designated by letters of the alphabet. Depending on how one counts, one or two letters may define a main class. For example, if a cataloger takes the broad view, P stands for languages and literatures, PR is English literature, and PS is American and Canadian literature. The same idea is applicable to B (Philosophy and Religion), H (Social Science), and K (Law), which may be seen broadly as three individual classes or narrowly as several classes each. The other classes are all given one letter, with the exception of history, which encompasses four single letters (C, D, E, and F). An outline of LCC appears in Figure 18.3.

A	= General Works	M	= Music
B	= Philosophy and Religion	N	= Fine Arts
C	= Auxiliary Sciences of History	P	= Literature
D	= Old World History	Q	= Science
E/F	= New World History	R	= Medicine
G	= Geography	S	= Agriculture
H	= Social Sciences	T	= Technology
J	= Political Science	U	= Military Science
K	= Law	V	= Naval Science
L	= Education	Z	= Bibliography

Figure 18.3. LCC Outline.

The outline reveals several differences between the overall structures of LCC and DDC. First, several subjects grouped together in DDC are given their own schedules in LCC: Agriculture and Medicine are not part of Technology, and each has its own schedule; Education, Political Science, Law, and Military and Naval Sciences are not part of Social Sciences, and each has its own schedule; Generalities and Bibliography/Library Science are distinguished into two separate classes, A and Z, respectively, that are as far apart in the alphabet as possible. Second, DDC's wide divergence between Language and Literature (400s and 800s) is absent from LCC. Both subject areas are combined in P. Third, in LCC, Music (M) and Fine Arts (N) each has its own schedule, separate from Recreation. Recreation is found in the Arts class in DDC but is located at the end of the Geography (G) schedule in LCC. Finally, History and Geography, separated into several different schedules, are located toward the beginning of the scheme, immediately after Religion, instead of at the end of the classification as they are in DDC. History and Law are among LC's largest groups of holdings, so it is understandable that between them these two subject areas cover 15 printed volumes, or nearly one-third of the scheme.

LC does not use the two schedules developed by LAC for materials relating to Canadian history and literature: FC (Canadian history) and PS8000 (Canadian literature). Canadian libraries aiming to assign more specific classification numbers to Canadian topics may prefer to use derived records from LAC rather than LC for those subject areas. Figure 18.4 illustrates the difference in classification schedules for Canadian history.

```
This example is an illustration of:
     • edition statement taken from outside prescribed sources
       (many libraries place such an edition statement in the
       note area, sometimes as a quoted note)
     • publishing date not listed, copyright date given
     • detailed pagination
     • edition and history note
     • bibliography and index note
     • Canadian subject headings
     • author/title added entries
     • additional title added entries
     • comparison between Library of Congress and National
       Library of Canada classification
     • comparison between Library of Congress, Library and
       Archives Canada, and Dewey decimal classifications
     • Canadian CIP data
     • 2nd level cataloging

Donaldson, Gordon.
   The Prime Ministers of Canada / Gordon Donaldson. -- [4th ed.].
-- Toronto : Doubleday, c1994.
   x, 380 p. ; 22 cm.

   Previous eds. published as: Fifteen men (1969), Sixteen men
(1975), Eighteen men (1985).
   Includes bibliography (p. 370-373) and index.
   ISBN 0-385-25454-7.

   1. Prime ministers -- Canada -- Biography. 2. Canada --
Politics and government. I. Donaldson, Gordon. Fifteen men. II.
Donaldson, Gordon. Sixteen men. III. Donaldson, Gordon. Eighteen
men. IV. Title. V. Title: Fifteen men. VI. Title: Sixteen men.
VII. Title: Eighteen men.

Recommended DDC: 971.00922
Recommended LCC: F1005.D65 1994
Recommended NLC classification: FC26.P7D65 1994
```

Figure 18.4. Classification of Canadian history.

Figure 18.4—*Continued*

CHIEF SOURCE OF INFORMATION
(Title Page)

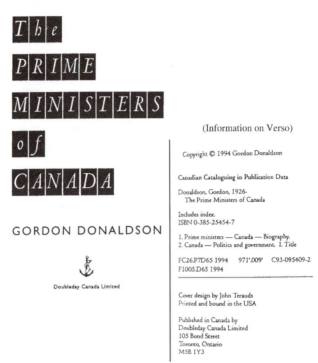

GORDON DONALDSON

Doubleday Canada Limited

(Information on Verso)

Copyright © 1994 Gordon Donaldson

Canadian Cataloguing in Publication Data

Donaldson, Gordon, 1926-
    The Prime Ministers of Canada

Includes index.
ISBN 0-385-25454-7

1. Prime ministers — Canada — Biography.
2. Canada — Politics and government. I. Title

FC26.P7D65 1994   971'.009'   C93-095409-2
F1005.D65 1994

Cover design by John Terauds
Printed and bound in the USA

Published in Canada by
Doubleday Canada Limited
105 Bond Street
Toronto, Ontario
M5B 1Y3

Preface

This is a revised and extended version of *Fifteen Men*, which first appeared in 1969, was updated in 1975, and became *Sixteen Men*, and then *Eighteen Men*. *Twenty Persons* didn't have the same ring to it, hence the new genderless title.

Subdivision in LCC

The use of geographical location to subdivide a topic is frequently encountered in LCC. Geographic subdivisions may be arranged alphabetically or by area, and the latter arrangements often give preference to the United States and/or the countries of Europe and the Western Hemisphere. An example of this arrangement can be found at "Exploitation of timber trees" (S434–534). After a number for general works, the topic is further subdivided by country, beginning with the United States and followed by the rest of the Americas, Europe, Africa, Australia, New Zealand, the Atlantic Islands, and, finally, the Pacific Islands. Elsewhere, the countries are listed in alphabetical order, as can be seen in the next part of the schedule at "Plant culture: study and teaching" (SB51–52). In this case, SB51 is used for general works and SB52 is used to further subdivide the topic geographically with the instruction to add a cutter number "by region or country, A-Z." This means that every country is assigned a cutter number using the initial letter of its name and one or more digits to represent a subsequent letter or letters, thus producing an alphabetical arrangement.

Topical subdivisions under each geographic locality are sometimes represented by designated number spans for different countries and sometimes by a different letter-and-number device resembling a cutter number. To subdivide the topic "Regulation, inspection, etc. of seeds" (SB114), a cataloger uses .A1 for the publications of societies, .A3 for general works, and .A4-Z for specific regions or countries. Although the first two subdivisions resemble cutter numbers, they do not represent words or names as ordinary cutters do. The United States has a special cutter number under the .A4-Z portion: .U6–7, where .U6 represents general works and .U7 is further subdivided by state, A–W. According to this instruction, a work about the inspection of seeds in the state of Georgia would be SB114.U7G+. (An additional level of subdivision allows the classifier to add a third cutter number to represent a specific locality within each state.)

Topical subdivisions of a subject unrelated to geographic locations can also be arranged alphabetically by means of cuttering. The S schedule is particularly rich in lists of cuttered subtopics, such as different types of crops, ornamental plants, plant diseases, and trees. In the list of trees, some of the cuttering goes to five digits beyond the initial letter. Topical subdivisions can also be represented by a sequence of whole numbers. For example, in the HV schedule (Social Pathology):

HV6085 = general works on the language of criminals;
HV6089 = prison psychology;
HV6093 = general works on intellectual and aesthetic characteristics of criminals;
HV6097 = prison literature, wall inscriptions;
HV6098 = tattooing; and
HV6099 = other forms of intellectual and aesthetic expression among criminals.

Differing treatments for similar topical arrangements makes for an extremely complicated scheme. In addition, the lack of effective aids to its application makes LCC difficult to implement for original classification outside of LC. Libraries that adopt LCC expect to do little, if any, original classification. They are under the impression they can find all or nearly all of the materials they buy already classified. If this is true, they are well satisfied.

Use of cutter numbers as part of the classification is one of the disadvantages of LCC for libraries other than LC; no one but LC can assign an official cutter number for anything—a location, a topic, or a shelf mark. Other libraries must wait until LC classifies an item requiring the appropriate cutter number before it is officially established. A cataloger might encounter a book on a particular type of tree that is not in the list given under SD397. To classify it, the cataloger must guess at which numbers LC will use in the numeric portion of the cutter, and if there is any doubt about the proper name of the tree, the initial letter as well. (Imagine the following hypothetical example: A cataloger is assigning cutters for different types of people who receive discount fares on public transit. Would that cataloger call student recipients "students" or "educational recipients"? Would older people be identified as "seniors," "aged," or "elderly"? Would civil servants be lumped into one group, or divided into "police," "transit workers," "firefighters," and so on?)

```
1. After initial vowels
        for the 2nd letter:  b   d   l,m   n    p    r   s,t   u,y
              use number:  2   3    4    5    6    7    8     9
2. After the initial letter S
        for the 2nd letter:  a   ch   e   h,i   m-p    t     u
              use number:  2    3    4    5      6    7-8    9
3. After the initial letters Qu
        for the 2nd letter:  a   e   i   o   r   y
              use number:  3   4   5   6   7   9
     for names beginning Qa-Qt
                   use:  2-29
4. After other initial consonants
        for the 2nd letter:  a   e   i   o   r   u   y
              use number:  3   4   5   6   7   8   9
5. When an additional number is preferred
        for the 3rd letter:  a-d  e-h  i-l   m   n-q   r-t   u-w   x-z
              use number:   2*   3    4    5    6     7     8     9
(*optional for 3rd letter a or b)
```

Figure 18.5. LC rules for creating cutter numbers.

LC establishes new cutter numbers after consulting its shelflist to see what already has been assigned. In doing so, its classifiers sometimes decide to depart from their usual pattern, a simple formula with just a few rules (see Figure 18.5), because of a unique problem, or because of their expectation about future assignments likely to affect few libraries outside of LC. The first element in an LC cutter number consists of the initial letter of the word to be represented, combined with one or more Arabic numerals chosen according to the rules shown in Figure 18.5. A publication titled *Classification and Shelflisting Manual,* which combines two earlier manuals titled *Subject Cataloging Manual: Classification* and *Subject Cataloging Manual: Shelflisting,* offers guidance on how to assign LCC numbers and create call numbers for materials.[4]

Note the different cutter numbers in the two Cataloging-in-Publication (CIP) items on the verso of Figure 15.9 on page 318: A5155 from LC and A5158 from LAC (then National Library of Canada). LC and LAC have assigned slightly different cutters because of the items they already have in their collections.

Comparison of DDC and LCC

LCC has many more numbers and many more specific classes than DDC in which to place very narrowly defined topics. For instance, LCC has individual numbers for most 19th-century English and American authors, and some individual numbers for each of their works. Contemporary U.S. authors are assigned classification numbers according to the first letter of their surname and cutter numbers according to the second letter of their surname. The difference is made clear by an example: In DDC, Kurt Vonnegut would join most of his contemporaries at 813.54 (U.S. writers of fiction working after 1945); in LCC, he would join only those U.S. writers working after 1961 whose surnames begin with "V" at PS3572. That is a large difference in specificity. The desire for specificity is one reason large libraries such as the Boston Public Library and many university libraries turned to LCC. LCC's stability of numbers is another.

Small libraries that made the change to LCC did not always do so to achieve greater specificity but to take advantage of the larger proportion of titles classified according to LCC by LC and other major originators of cataloging copy, freeing them from having to do as much original classification. Small or medium-sized college libraries using OCLC thought they would save a great deal of time (and, therefore, money) by copying the LCC numbers found online instead of doing original classification.

Another contrast is the nature of the classification number produced by each scheme. LCC numbers usually are shorter for topics of the same specificity, but their combination of alphabetic characters and numbers is not necessarily easier to remember or use. Some people may find the alphanumerics more understandable and logical, but others prefer the purely numerical system of DDC, particularly when libraries add cutter numbers as shelf marks and other marks in various alphanumerical sequences to the classification number to give each item a unique shelf location. This can result in very complicated combinations of all sorts of characters, including upper- and lowercase letters, whole and decimal numbers, and punctuation. To accommodate all of this information on books with narrow spines, libraries often break up the arrangement of the classification number into several lines. It is sometimes hard to tell where the classification number ends and shelf marks begin, or what follows what; for example, should JX1977.8.C53q1984 come before or after JX1977.D5b1987? (In the Simmons College library, it came after, although the JX numbers are now obsolete; thus, these books were either reclassified or discarded.)

The general use of cutter numbers in all libraries as shelf marks becomes confusing when they are also part of the classification numbers. It is especially confusing when an item has several cutter numbers, perhaps with one denoting geographic location, another denoting a topic subdivision, and a third for the shelf mark. The LCC's methods of subdividing are quite different from DDC's. One of LCC's favorites, shown in the previous examples, is to add cutter numbers for subtopics or geographical subdivisions (or, sometimes, for both). LCC also uses numerical expansions to subdivide topics, but they are added differently. When DDC instructs classifiers to add to a number, it means that some other number from a table or another section of the schedule will be tacked on to a base number from the schedules, which is known as concatenating the numbers. For example, to expand the number for cooking, 641.5, to French cooking, one adds 9, representing geographic focus, and 44, for France, to obtain 641.5944. In LCC, the instruction to add a number from a table to a base number in the schedules may mean to add the two numbers arithmetically. For example, to expand the number for classical art in countries other than Greece and Italy (N5801–5896), one adds a number from a designated table to the base number N5800. Using the number 13 for Canada, one adds it to 5800 to get N5813, representing classical art in Canada. Sometimes, when whole numbers are lacking to subdivide a topic as desired, LCC uses decimal numbers. In the previous example, to subdivide classical art in the United States for the colonial period, one adds 03.5 to 5800, to arrive at N5803.5. LCC occasionally contains instructions to subdivide (or, as they deem it, subarrange) a topic like another class number in the schedule, but this is done far less frequently than in DDC. Rather, LCC simply lists various subarrangements in the schedules, and most differ from one another.

The degree of browsability that results from using LCC or DDC is an important consideration. Because of its principle of hierarchy, DDC produces arrangements that tend to be more satisfying to browse from a subject searcher's point of view. Use of alphabetical instead of hierarchical subarrangements, which LCC does by means of cuttering, tends to scatter materials on related topics and bring together topics at different levels of hierarchy. Even geographical subarrangement may be less browsable, despite its logic, for subject searchers who are more interested in topics than locations.

Finally, the difference in cost of the two tools is a practical matter that bears mention, although in the long run it may be the least important matter. DDC's four printed volumes (or the subscription to WebDewey) are a great deal less expensive than LCC's 40-plus volumes (or the subscription to *Classification Plus*), even though individual LC schedules are good value for the price.

NATIONAL LIBRARY OF MEDICINE CLASSIFICATION

LCC includes class R for Medicine. It is considered adequate for general libraries that collect small numbers of materials in that field. However, the U.S. National Library of Medicine (NLM), which collects far larger numbers of health-related materials on more specific topics than do most general libraries, did not find class R suitable for arranging its materials. Instead, NLM developed its own highly specialized classification system. The NLM classification, abbreviated here NLMC, was designed to coordinate with LCC for two reasons: (1) so that LCC could be used successfully in conjunction with it to classify materials held in its collection falling outside of the field of medicine (e.g., materials on malpractice law); and (2) so that LCC numbers could be used for health-related fields of study deemed preclinical. Such fields of study, while related to medicine, actually fall outside the realm of medical practice (e.g., anatomy and biochemistry).

Background and Development

The NLM began before the U.S. Civil War as the library of the Surgeon General of the U.S. Army and was known then as the Army Medical Library.[5] It remained under the authority of the Army until 1956, when control was demilitarized and transferred to the Public Health Service unit of the Department of Health, Education and Welfare. At that time, the library's name was changed to NLM. It moved to its current home in Bethesda, Maryland, on the campus of the National Institutes of Health in 1962.

As early as 1944, an Army survey recommended that the collection should be classified by a system like that of LC. In response to the recommendation, a classification committee, chaired by Keyes Metcalf, was formed to design the system. The classification committee, working with medical consultants, produced a preliminary edition of the new medical classification in 1948. This edition was revised over the next several years and published in 1951 under the title *U.S. Army Medical Library Classification*. The designers adopted the alphanumeric notation of LCC, using the letter W, which was not defined in LCC. A second letter defined the principal schedules within W, including the physiological system, various specialties connected with them, regions of the body involved, and subordinate related fields (see Figure 18.6). They

Medicine and Related Subjects

W	General Medicine. Health Professions
WA	Public Health
WB	Practice of Medicine
WC	Communicable Diseases
WD	Disorders of Systemic, Metabolic or Environmental Origin, etc.
WE	Musculoskeletal System
WF	Respiratory System
WG	Cardiovascular System
WH	Hemic and Lymphatic Systems
WI	Digestive System
WJ	Urogenital System
WK	Endocrine System
WL	Nervous System
WM	Psychiatry
WN	Radiology. Diagnostic Imaging
WO	Surgery
WP	Gynecology
WQ	Obstetrics
WR	Dermatology
WS	Pediatrics
WT	Geriatrics. Chronic Disease
WU	Dentistry. Oral Surgery
WV	Otolaryngology
WW	Ophthalmology
WX	Hospitals and Other Health Facilities
WY	Nursing
WZ	History of Medicine. Medical Miscellany

Source: http://www.nlm.gov/class//OutlineofNLMClassificationSchedule.html.

Figure 18.6. Outline of NLMC.

also adopted Charles Martel's system of starting each schedule within W with form numbers for specific publication types.

NLMC has two important features that differ from LCC. First, it uses the same controlled vocabulary—MeSH—that is used by NLM to index the medical literature. As a result, MeSH is an effective index to NLMC. Second, it maintains the MeSH hierarchy of subjects, called "tree structures," that leads searchers from the broadest subject areas to the most specific topics falling under them. Thus, there is a synergy between the two tools that makes it much easier for librarians and researchers to navigate between MeSH and NLMC.

Format of NLMC

NLMC is available solely in electronic form, although, since 2006, it can be downloaded as a pdf file and printed should a library wish to do so. The NLM was an early pioneer in bibliographic data processing, establishing the Medline database of medical literature in the 1960s and 1970s. NLMC was issued in sequentially numbered editions until 1999, when the fifth revised edition was the last one to be issued in print.

NLM states: "The online environment offers many advantages to users including hyperlinks between class numbers in the index and the schedules, and between terms within the index and direct links from these to the MeSH record itself under the MeSH Browser."[6] NLMC is updated annually in conjunction with MeSH. The close relation between the two subject analysis tools is a great help to searchers.

Main Classes and Subdivisions

NLMC is divided into 33 basic subclasses (see Figure 18.6) in contrast to LCC's 17 basic subclasses of medicine (see Figure 18.7). The preclinical subclasses that precede them include six schedules from LCC's class Q:

1. QS Human anatomy
2. QU Biochemistry
3. QV Pharmacology
4. QW Microbiology/immunology
5. QY Clinical pathology
6. QZ Pathology

Most of the numbers in NLMC are intended to be assigned to monographs. Serially issued publications are mainly classified by form in W1, with some exceptions. The exceptions are government and hospital reports and statistics, classified at W2; directories, handbooks, and similar publications, classified in other form numbers (W3–39), used also for monographs; and bibliographies and indexes, which are classed in ZW, Z plus the NLMC number for specific topics, or other Z numbers from LCC.[7]

Medicine:	
R	Medicine
RA	Public aspects of medicine
RB	Pathology
RC	Internal medicine
RD	Surgery
RE	Ophthalmology
RF	Otorhinolaryngology
RG	Gynecology and obstetrics
RJ	Pediatrics
RK	Dentistry
RL	Dermatology
RM	Therapeutics. Pharmacology
RS	Pharmacy and material medica
RT	Nursing
RV	Botanic, Thomsonian, and eclectic medicine
RX	Homeopathy
RZ	Other systems of medicine

Source: www.loc.gov/catdir/cpso/lcco/lcco_r.pdf.

Figure 18.7. Outline of LCC Schedule R.

The level of specificity in NLMC's class W is much greater than that found in LCC's class R. This is to be expected, since the principle of literary warrant dictates that numbers are not created unless LC has literature that requires them. The NLM collects more medical literature than LC and a considerable amount of it is on narrower topics aimed at the specialists who conduct medical research.

Note in Figure 18.6 that classes WL, Nervous system, and WM, Psychiatry, cover aspects of neurological and mental illnesses likely to overlap with psychology. NLMC concerns itself with the medical issues, which is entirely appropriate given that psychiatry is a subdivision of medicine and psychiatrists are medical doctors. Generally, psychologists are PhDs, not MDs. Materials intended for psychologists are classified in LCC class BF, although some materials classed in BF as well as pharmacology information in LCC QV is likely to be of interest to both psychologists and psychiatrists.

NLMC also has tables. One covers geographic subdivisions and is called Table G. It consists of nine capital letters signifying nine countries or regions, beginning with A for the United States. Few countries are subdivided further, with the exception of the United States, Great Britain, and Australia. When a country or region is subdivided, a second letter is added, to which whole numbers may also be added to obtain smaller locations. Table G has numbers for the U.S. military services and other federal departments related to medicine.

NLMC in Libraries

The NLM catalogs more than 20,000 items annually, assigning MeSH subject headings and NLMC numbers to them. If a book is a CIP publication, the record is available in the NLM's Locator Plus database (http://locatorplus.gov/). Machine-readable cataloging (MARC) records for NLM's preliminary records are identified by an NLMC call number in the 060 field and/or data coded in the local 999 field. If the 999 field says "CIP," it means the NLM intends to acquire the book. If NLM does not intend to acquire the book, the 999 field says NOC. When a preliminary record is completed, the 999 field says AUTH.

It is safe to assume that medical libraries prefer accepting and using NLMC call numbers for their materials. General university research libraries, however, acquire medical materials for their collections, the rest of which are arranged by LCC call numbers. Those libraries must decide how to arrange their medical materials. The materials may bear both LCC and NLMC call numbers, one or the other, or neither. In all events, some acquired materials are bound to lack the desired call number type and require original classifying, which is costly and time consuming.

General libraries can opt to keep all medical materials in one place—R or W—or they can use both types of call numbers, preferring one type when both are present. If medical materials are shelved together, users benefit by having only one place to look for medical materials. However, this is the more costly option. Materials that contain only the wrong type of call number and those with no call number at all have to be classified originally.

To minimize the amount of original classifying that must be done, libraries can opt to shelve medical materials in two places—at R and at W. Doing this, however, causes materials on like topics to be fragmented, makes browsing difficult, and requires users and librarians to look up every item they seek in the catalog to determine where it is located. The advantage to using both types of call numbers is that it is faster and less costly, because it requires less work. If either type of call number appears in a CIP or online catalog record for newly acquired materials, it can be accepted. Only materials having no CIP and no source records from which to copy call numbers, discussed more fully in the next section, have to be classified from scratch.

"COPY" CLASSIFICATION

Catalogers often use the DDC and LCC numbers provided by LC in the CIP information located on the verso of the title pages of books, or they find classification numbers in computer network records, such as OCLC. If so, conventions followed by larger institutions should be understood. For DDC numbers, the most important of these is the method used to show where numbers have been expanded. An apostrophe (also called a *prime* or *hash* mark) is placed at the end of the basic number and again after each complete expansion of a number (see Figure 18.2 for an example of a prime mark.)

Some agencies using DDC prefer that numbers not become too long and institute policies to limit them. Such policies should involve the addition or omission of expansions, for example, to limit a classification number to the basic number, or to one or more expansions beyond the basic number. They should not dictate a maximum number of digits, because for some numbers, the meaning would be lost. For example, the correct DDC number for slavery in ancient Athens is 306.3620385. This is a very long number that would only be necessary if a library has (or expects to have) many items about slavery in the ancient world in its collection. But the basic number for slavery has six digits, so, if library policy dictated stopping after a maximum of five, that basic meaning would be lost. The meaning of the entire number is as follows:

306	culture and institutions
306.3	economic institutions
306.36	systems of labor
306.362	slavery
306.36203	slavery in the ancient world
306.362038	slavery in ancient Greece
306.3620385	slavery in ancient Athens

Some libraries, including LC, furnish more than the class number, adding shelf marks to it. When using another library's catalog records, shelf marks should be ignored unless it is a local policy to follow these practices. If so, the cataloger must be careful about *whose* practices are followed. In some places, the initial letter of the main entry is used in place of a cutter number. In others, two-, three-, or four-digit cutters are used. It might be confusing to adopt all of these practices simultaneously.

SUMMARY

DDC is widely used all over the world. It is the basis for the Universal Decimal Classification and some national classifications as well (for example, in Korea and Japan). Its popularity in the United Kingdom is ensured by its use in the *British*

National Bibliography and all the British Library's authoritative online cataloging. Its flexibility is sufficient to serve many purposes, and its ease of use is enhanced by the mnemonics, the Relative Index, and its easily grasped overall logic.

LCC is widely used among academic libraries in the United States and, because of the likelihood that LC numbers are used in bibliographic network records, by some libraries outside of the United States as well. LCC is much larger and more complex than DDC. Its overall arrangement of subjects is, perhaps, more logical and better organized for contemporary use than DDC is, particularly in the fields of science and history. Using it to classify materials from scratch, however, is difficult for librarians outside of LC, because it is controlled entirely by LC and devoted to the arrangement of LC's own collections.

LCC requires less number building than DDC does and provides shorter classification numbers than does DDC (although they are made up of letters and numbers) for subjects of the same specificity. LCC seems more hospitable to new topics and allows for far greater subdivision of topics. In addition, it avoids trying to force differing disciplines into a single mold and allows every subject area to have the arrangement most natural to its literature.

The bias of LCC toward the United States, its neighbors, and traditional allies is, perhaps, even more pervasive than DDC's, but more understandable. LCC does not try to be a universal classification of knowledge, but only an orderly arrangement of LC's books. The difficulty of applying LCC to nonbook materials is probably no greater than applying DDC. Both schemes were developed to arrange books. In LCC's favor is the fact that there are more opportunities for close classification, a useful attribute because nonbook items may have very narrowly defined topics.

The specialized NLMC is patterned after LCC and is used in conjunction with LCC by medical libraries. In addition to numbers starting with the letter W, NLMC uses six schedules in LCC class Q for preclinical fields such as anatomy and pharmacology. NLMC uses mixed notation and has several tables for further specifying topics, including Table G for geographic locations.

LC and other libraries using LCC are unlikely to change to DDC. LCC is equally unlikely to become ubiquitous in North America or anywhere else. Rather, the dichotomy in the classification of library materials between DDC and LCC is likely to continue, with the choice depending on an agency's traditions, size, and orientation toward a particular source of cataloging and classification data. Heightened awareness of the workings of each system and an understanding of their differences and implications for use are valuable both for librarians and patrons.

Before going on, readers may want to try assigning DDC and/or LCC numbers to the following examples. The answers are on page 409 at the end of this chapter.

CLASSIFICATION EXERCISES

1.   TITLE: *The library: an illustrated history*
         SUMMARY: A history of libraries from prehistoric times to the present day.
         DDC: _____ LCC: _____

2.   TITLE: *Pursuing giraffe; a 1950s adventure*
SUMMARY: The account of a young zoologist traveling and doing research in Southern and East Africa
DDC: _____ LCC: _____

3.   TITLE: *Her story: women from Canada's past*
SUMMARY: Profiles of women from all walks of life and various ethnic backgrounds, from pioneers to 20th-century political activists
DDC: _____ LCC: _____

4.   TITLE: *The mother tongue: English and how it got that way*
SUMMARY: The history, eccentricities, resilience, and sheer fun of the English language
DDC: _____ LCC: _____

5.   TITLE: *Travel in the ancient world*
SUMMARY: A comprehensive review of ancient travel from the first recorded voyage to Egypt's Old Kingdom through Greek and Roman times to the Christian pilgrimages of the fourth century CE
DDC: _____ LCC: _____

6.   TITLE: *Writers & company*
SUMMARY: A collection of radio interviews with important writers from various countries
DDC: _____ LCC: _____

7.   TITLE: *The indoor plant primer: selection, care, and landscaping*
SUMMARY: An illustrated guide to flowering and foliage plants for home or office
DDC: _____ LCC: _____

8.   TITLE: *Videohound's world cinema: the adventurer's guide to movie watching*
SUMMARY: A catalog of more than 800 films produced outside the United States
DDC: _____ LCC: _____

9.   TITLE: *The art of Emily Carr*
SUMMARY: A profusely illustrated book that discusses the art of this British Columbia painter
DDC: _____ LCC: _____

10.   TITLE: *The rest of God: restoring your soul by restoring the Sabbath*
SUMMARY: A plea about removing commercialism from religious days
DDC: _____ LCC: _____

REVIEW QUESTIONS

1. Describe the difference between pure and mixed notation. What kind of notation is used by DDC? What kind of notation is used by LCC?

2. What is a mnemonic device? Give an example of a mnemonic device in DDC.

3. Identify two advantages for library patrons of arranging materials according to DDC.

4. Why have some libraries switched from DDC to LCC?

5. Name two principles shared by both DDC and LCC.

6. What is the result of applying cutter numbers to library materials?

7. Describe one principal difference between hierarchical and nonhierarchical classification. Which do you believe gives better service to library patrons?

8. What is the difference between an enumerative classification and a faceted or synthetic classification? Which do you believe gives better service to library patrons?

NOTES

The epigraphs are from *21st Century Dictionary of Quotations*, ed. The Princeton Language Institute (New York: Laurel, 1993), 322 and 259, respectively.

1. Melvil Dewey, *Dewey Decimal Classification and Relative Index,* 22nd ed., ed. Joan S. Mitchell, Julianne Beall, and Giles Martin (Dublin, OH: OCLC-Forest Press, 2003).

2. Melvil Dewey, *Abridged Dewey Decimal Classification and Relative Index,* 14th ed., ed. Joan S. Mitchell, Julianne Beall, and Giles Martin (Dublin, OH: OCLC-Forest Press, 2004).

3. Lois Mai Chan, *A Guide to the Library of Congress Classification,* 5th ed. (Westport, CT: Libraries Unlimited, 1999).

4. *Classification and Shelflisting Manual* (Washington, D.C.: Library of Congress, Policy and Standards Division, 2008); also available in *Cataloger's Desktop.*

5. Information in this section is taken from the NLM classification Web site: "Historical Development," in *Introduction to the National Library of Medicine Classification 2009,* www.nlm.nih.gov/class/.

6. Ibid.

7. National Library of Medicine, "NLM Classification Practices," http://www.nlm.nih.gov/class/nlmclassprac.html.

SUGGESTED READING

General

Hunter, Eric J. *Classification Made Simple: An Introduction to Knowledge Organisation and Information Retrieval,* 3rd ed. Farnham, UK: Ashgate, 2009.

DDC

025.431: The Dewey Blog. http://ddc.typepad.com.

Dewey Cutter Program. www.oclc.org/DEWEY/support/program.

Dewey Decimal Classification. http://www.purl.org/oclc/fp.

Holley, Robert P. "Subject Access Tools in English for Canadian Topics: Canadian Extensions to U.S. Subject Access Tools." *Library Resources & Technical Services* 52, no. 2 (April 2008): 29–43.

Mortimer, Mary. *Learn Dewey Decimal Classification (Edition 22)*. Santa Barbara, CA: Linworth/ABC-Clio, 2006.

Neigel, Christina, ed. *Workbook for DDC 22: Dewey Decimal Classification Edition 22*. Ottawa: Canadian Library Association, 2006.

Satija, M.P. *The Theory and Practice of the Dewey Decimal Classification System*. Oxford, UK: Chandos Publishing, 2007.

Scott, Mona L. *Dewey Decimal Classification 22nd Edition: A Study Manual and Number Building Guide*. Santa Barbara, CA: Libraries Unlimited/ABC Clio, 2004.

Wiegand, Wayne. *Irrepressible Reformer: A Biography of Melvil Dewey*. Chicago, IL: American Library Association, 1996.

LCC

C.A. Cutter's Three-Figure Author Tables [on CD-ROM]. Englewood, CO: Libraries Unlimited, 1995.

C.A. Cutter's Two-Figure Author Tables [on CD-ROM]. Englewood, CO: Libraries Unlimited, 1995.

Chan, Lois Mai. *Immroth's A Guide to the Library of Congress Classification*. 5th ed. Englewood, CO: Libraries Unlimited, 1999. (This text is somewhat dated, but still offers the most comprehensive guide to LCC.)

Dittmann, Helena, and Jane Hardy. *Learn Library of Congress Classification*. 2nd ed. San Diego, CA: TotalRecall, 2007.

FC: A Classification for Canadian Literature. 2nd ed. http://staff.library.mun.ca/staff/toolbox/tables/PS8000.htm.

Holley, Robert P. "Subject Access Tools in English for Canadian Topics: Canadian Extensions to U.S. Subject Access Tools." *Library Resources & Technical Services* 52, no. 2 (April 2008): 29–43.

Library of Congress. Subject Cataloging Division. Processing Services. *LC Classification Outline*. Washington, D.C.: Library of Congress, 1995–. http://www.loc.gov/catdir/cpso/cpso.html.

Robare, Lori, et al., eds. *Fundamentals of Library of Congress Classification: Trainee Manual*. Washington, D.C.: Library of Congress Cataloging Distribution Service, 2008.

Smiraglia, Richard P. *Shelflisting Music: Guidelines for Use with the Library of Congress Classification: M, 2nd edition*. Lanham, MD: Scarecrow Press, 2007.

NLM

National Library of Medicine. *Fundamentals of the NLM Classification.* http://www.nlm.nih. gov/tsd/cataloging/trainingcourses/classification/index.html.

ANSWERS TO THE CLASSIFICATION EXERCISES

1. DDC: 027.009   LCC: Z721
2. DDC: 590.92   LCC: QL31
3. DDC: 305.4'092'271   LCC: FC26.W6 (from LAC)
                         LCC: CT3270 (from LC)
4. DDC: 420'9   LCC: PE1072
5. DDC: 913.04   LCC: G88
6. DDC: 809.04   LCC: PN453
7. DDC: 635.9'65   LCC: SB419
8. DDC: 016.79143'75   LCC: PN1995.9.F67
9. DDC: 759.11   LCC: ND249.C3
10. DDC: 263'.2   LCC: BV4597.55

MARC Format and Metadata

Online cataloging has greatly enhanced the usability of catalogs, thanks to the rise of MAchine Readable Cataloging (MARC standards).

—New World Encyclopedia

Metadata is a generic term applied to the information created to identify, describe, and manage digital documents. However, definitions for metadata (and there are many, explored later in this chapter), can also be used to define library cataloging, which is the process of creating the information used to identify, describe, and manage library materials—both digital and analog documents. This chapter explains how cataloging data are prepared or marked up for entry into computerized databases. It also covers machine-readable cataloging (MARC), the library standard for digitizing bibliographic data, as well as other systems for accomplishing the same purposes used by librarians and members of communities beyond the library world.

MACHINE-READABLE CATALOGING

The MARC formats are a set of markup protocols for five kinds of information: bibliographic; authority; classification; holdings; and community entities, activities, and events. Adding MARC protocols to the information puts it into a form that can be understood and used by properly programmed computers. MARC is similar in principle to SGML, HTML, and other markup languages used for transmitting textual electronic resources.

The MARC formats are *communications* formats. Once data are marked up as a MARC-formatted record, a computer can transmit the data to another computer. The term *bibliographic data* applies to all of the elements of a bibliographic record that have been described in this book so far: descriptions, access points, subject headings, and call numbers. *Authority data* cover all of the elements of an authority record for names, titles, or subject descriptors, including the authorized form of the name or topic, cross-references to other name forms or topical terms, and references to the source material used in creating the authority record. *Holdings data* are the specific data relating to any item in a library's collection, including its copy number, cost, acquisition source, holding unit (such as a main library or branch library), or collection within a library or information center, and so forth. A fourth MARC format was developed for *classification data* and used to automate the Library of Congress (LC) classification. The fifth format is for *community information*, such as local officials, agencies, and lists of activities and events.

LC worked with automation pioneers—including such peers as the Library and Archives Canada (LAC) and the British Library; large research libraries, such as the University of Toronto, Stanford University, and New York Public Library, and other interested parties—in the development of the MARC formats. The ongoing evolution of MARC continues to be a cooperative endeavor, now of global proportions, shared by national libraries and major cataloging institutions, professional associations, and bibliographic networks. This chapter concentrates on the format for bibliographic data.

HISTORY AND BACKGROUND

The first MARC format was devised for the bibliographic data of books (printed monographs) in the 1960s. It went through several revisions before being published as a national standard in the 1970s by the National Information Standards Organization. Before long, a MARC format for serials was devised, followed by MARC formats for other types of materials for which LC produced bibliographies. After many years during which the number of separate MARC formats continued to grow, an integrated MARC format was implemented during the 1990s in which all fields were made uniform across all the physical forms of materials collected by libraries. All fields and codes are still not applicable to every type of material, but if they do apply, their meanings are the same, thereby simplifying the processes of learning and using the system of MARC protocols.

Individual bibliographic networks have issued manuals containing versions of MARC intended for use by their participants. Selected fields have been defined in unique ways by an individual network; for example, the coded version of the basic features of a document are known in the OCLC as *fixed fields* and in MARC 21 as field 008, shown in Figure 19.1.

Between 1994 and 1997, LC and LAC worked with their user communities through national MARC committees to reconcile the differences between the official Canadian and U.S. formats, known as CAN/MARC and USMARC, respectively. The result is MARC 21. MARC 21 is not a new format; it is a new name for the merged formats. MARC 21 consists of the five communications formats described previously: bibliographic data, authority data, holdings data, classification data, and community information. There also are concise formats for each of these.

Individual countries using the MARC formats had their own official versions, including the United Kingdom's UKMARC (MARC 21 superseded UKMARC in 2004); a generalized or universal version was also developed, called UNIMARC.

MARC 21 008 Field Character Positions

00-05 - Date entered on file

06 -   Type of date/Publication status

07-10 - Date 1

11-14 - Date 2

15-17 - Place of publication, production, or execution

18-34 - Coding for specific types of materials

35-37 - Language

38-   Modified record

39-   Cataloging source

OCLC Fixed Fields

Type:	ELvl:	Srce:	Audn:	Ctrl:	Lang:
BLvl:m	Form:	Conf:	Biog:	MRec:	Ctry:
	Cont:	GPub:	LitF:	Indx:	
Desc:	Ills:	Fest:	DtSt:	Dates:	

Figure 19.1. MARC 008 field.

Minor differences appeared among the versions of MARC formats, but their fundamental structure is identical and the same principles apply to them all. It is important to know what the MARC formats are *not*. They are not a set of cataloging rules or a cataloging code. Instead, they are designed for use with data created by applying the standard cataloging rules, subject headings, and classifications discussed in previous chapters. Some accommodations are made for local data, but there are limits to how far the formats can be stretched. For example, the bibliographic format is geared to the *Anglo-American Cataloguing Rules,* second edition (AACR2), so a library that does not follow it will find itself having to create AACR-compatible records anyway in order to code descriptive data successfully.

The MARC formats are not catalogs either. They are intended to be used *in* computerized catalogs as templates for record structures, but MARC, by itself, is not an information storage and retrieval system. Additional programming is required to use the MARC protocols for information storage and retrieval systems.

Ultimate authority over the MARC 21 formats rests with LC and LAC, though other groups in the two countries play consultative roles. In the United States, a major influence is an American Library Association interdivisional committee known as MARBI, which stands for Machine Readable Bibliographic Information. The participants are the Association for Library Collections & Technical Services, the Library and Information Technology Association, and the Reference and User Services Association. MARBI's counterpart in Canada is the Canadian Committee on MARC, a committee with representatives from the English- and French-speaking national library associations, the Canadian Library Association and l'Association pour l'avancement des sciences et des techniques de la documentation, respectively. Bibliographic networks, such as OCLC in the United States and A-G Canada (described later in this chapter), also contribute important advice. The MARC Editorial Office at LC and MARC Office at LAC make and publish the final decisions.

The MARC formats look very complicated because they must include everything needed to identify every detail of a record to a computer that cannot understand any part of it by itself. However, they are really mechanical in nature—a template for information produced by the application of content standards.

ELEMENTS OF A MARC RECORD

MARC records consist of a set of elements that include variable fields, fixed fields, and other control fields as well as protocols marking record beginnings and endings, and so on. The fields consist of tags, indicators, and subfields, each given numeric values, symbols, and alphanumeric codes, known generically as content designators. Adding the marks that identify record parts is called content designation. All of this is discussed in greater detail in this section.

Fields

Computer data generally are divided into parts called *fields,* and each field is further subdivided into *subfields.* Bibliographic (catalog) records are made up of fields that correspond to each area of the catalog record (e.g., call numbers, primary headings, titles, editions, publication information, subject headings, secondary headings). The subfields in each field, in turn, correspond to particular elements of the area; for example, subfields in the physical description field include one each for the extent, other physical details, dimensions, and accompanying materials; subfields in the Dewey Decimal call-number field correspond to the classification number, the shelf marks, and the edition of Dewey used.

Every MARC record has two kinds of information in it, contained in two kinds of fields: fixed and variable. The kind of information discussed in the previous paragraph is variable in nature. The names of personal authors are an example. A person's name may consist of a forename alone (Homer), a forename and a surname (William Shakespeare), a forename and a compound surname (Walter de la Mare or Sir Alec Frederick Douglas-Home), or a family name (Adams family). It may be another variant, such as initials or descriptive phrases. The name may have 7, 17, or 27 letters. It could require the inclusion of numbers, frequently encountered for royalty (Elizabeth II or Louis XVI). Titles, too, may be short or long; may contain letters, numbers, and/or symbols; and may have one word or many. Such data must be contained in fields that are flexible enough to admit all these possibilities. These fields have variable lengths and are called, appropriately, *variable fields.* Variable fields contain almost all of the data covered in this book thus far.

Some information in entries does not vary but is always entered the same way, either because the information is naturally invariant or because it is intentionally coded to eliminate variation. An example of naturally occurring invariable bibliographic data is the International Standard Book Number (ISBN). It always appears in the same form and sequence (10 characters for materials published before 2007 and 13 characters for those published later, all digits or with a final "X," representing the number 10). An example of information deliberately coded in an invariant form is the geographic focus of a title. Geographic locations are reduced to seven characters representing the applicable continent, country, and locale. These kinds of information are contained in invariable or *fixed fields*.

Information from the variable fields is sometimes duplicated in fixed fields in coded form so a programmer or a computer system can use it more efficiently. One such type of information relates to the physical description of materials. The physical description for nonbook materials is a good example. Different types of nonbook media have their own physical details. Films, videos, photographs, and electronic resources may have color or be in black and white. Sound recordings may be monophonic, stereophonic, or quadrophonic. Microforms may be reduced to several reduction ratios. In each instance, the number of possibilities is limited, making it easy to use a few letters or numbers to reduce them to short, invariable codes and then add these codes to the computerized record. Thus, it is useful to code elements such as the language of the item, its country of origin, the presence or absence of illustrations, and a host of other important aspects of an item, some of which may not appear in the eye-readable portions of catalog records. They are given, in fixed and unchanging form, in the fixed fields.

The order of elements in the MARC format (see Figure 19.2) is very similar to the order of elements in a catalog record. The main exception is that call numbers, standard numbers, and other coded elements, called *control fields,* appear first. Some of these elements would not display to the public in library online public access catalogs (OPACs). They are put first in computerized records because they generally identify the record and/or the item and, as such, are more efficiently utilized if they are read first. Generally, they are in coded form, such as a single character or a short string of characters in fixed order, and are not understandable until they are translated. Therefore, it is better to have them at the start of the record and not in the middle, where the coding would interrupt the bibliographic fields, or at the end, where a computer processor would have to scan through the first part of the record to reach them.

Subfields

Subfields are parts of fields. Each field is divided into parts corresponding to the parts within an element of a whole area of description, an entire subject heading, or a complete call number. For example, the title area in a bibliographic description is usually made up of four subelements: title proper, general material designation, other title information, and statement of responsibility. The title field corresponds to the title area as a whole, and each of the four subelements corresponds to a specific subfield within the title field. The title proper subfield, subfield a, is the first subfield in the title field; the general material designation is the second subfield, subfield h; other title information is the third subelement, subfield b; and the statement of responsibility is the fourth subelement, subfield c. Similarly, the date is usually the third subelement in the publication/distribution field, subfield c, following two subfields for the place (subfield a) and name (subfield b) of the publisher and/or distributor. These are

007   *coded physical description; use for selected nonprint materials, not for books*

010   *Library of Congress Control Number*

020   *ISBN*

050 __ *Library of Congress call number*

082 __ *Dewey Decimal call number*

1__ _ *Main entry*

245 __ *Title & statement of responsibility*

250   *Edition statement*

260   *Publication, distribution information*

300   *Physical description*

490 _ *Series statement (indicator shows tracing or no tracing)*

5XX   *Notes: many notes have their own tags, as follows:*
    500   *General note (use for index note not combined with bibliog. note)*
    504   *Bibliography note (use for a combined bibliog. & index note)*
    505   *Contents note*
    511   *Cast note*
    508   *Credits note (cast comes first even though 511 follows 508)*
    520   *Summary*
    538   *Physical description note (use for "Compact disc," "VHS," etc.)*

6XX   *Subject headings (use as many 6XX fields as necessary, 1 per heading)*

7XX   *Added entry headings (use as many 7XX fields as necessary, 1 per heading)*

830   *Series uniform title (use this always with 490, indicator 1 = different tracing)*

Figure 19.2. Order of MARC tags.

examples of descriptive field subelements. Following are examples of subject and call number field subelements.

1. If a subject heading for the novel *Gone With the Wind* is UNITED STATES—HISTORY—CIVIL WAR, 1860-1865—FICTION, it consists of a main heading and three subdivisions, one topical, one chronological, and one a literary genre. In the MARC format, the heading is coded as follows:
   651 0 $a United States $x History $y Civil War, 1860–1865 $v Fiction.
2. If the LC call number for a cookbook featuring French cuisine titled *Everyday Cooking with Jacques Pépin* is TX719.P458 and the Dewey Decimal call number for this book is 641.5944.P458, they would be coded in the MARC format as follows, respectively:
   050   4 $a TX719 $b .P458
   082 04 $a 641.5944 $b P458 $2 22

In both of the previous call-number examples, the classification number appears in subfield $a; the shelf marks appear in $b. The Dewey call number has an additional subelement coded $2, representing the edition number of the classification, which, in this example is the 22nd edition.

Indicators

Between the field names (that is, the tags) and the start of data in the field are places for two numerical characters known as *indicators*. One or both of the indicators may be defined for a field, or neither may be defined. When only one indicator is defined it may be in either the first or the second position. For the most part, indicators are values that instruct computer systems how to treat the data within the field to which they are assigned. For example, indicators in selected fields dictate how to index character strings, whether or not to display the data in the field, and whether or not to create an access point for the data in the field. For example, in fields in which personal names are entered, the indicator conveys information about whether the name is a surname followed by a forename (coded 1 = Einstein, Albert), a name with the forename first (coded 0 = Leonardo, da Vinci), or the name of a family (coded 3 = Kennedy family).[1] The computer system needs this information to index the names properly.

The most important thing to remember about indicators is that their meaning differs for each field in which they are used. Originally, they were a vital element in printing catalog cards from computerized data, and they are equally useful to computer programmers working with online systems, who use them to specify screen displays.

CONTENT DESIGNATION

Each field and subfield in a MARC record must be identified by a name, known as a *content designator*. In the MARC format, fields are identified by three-digit codes called *tags,* and subfields are identified by a symbol, called a *delimiter*, that identifies what follows as a subfield and a single letter, number, or, occasionally, a symbol, all called *subfield codes.* In the OCLC network, the delimiter appears as a double dagger, in the A-G Canada system it appears as a dollar sign, and in the LC system it appears as a vertical bar. In this book, the dollar sign is preferred, although any of these symbols could be reproduced. However it appears, the function of the delimiter is the same—to identify subfields—even when various keyboards and printers interpret it in different ways.

Content designation is defined as the application of appropriate tags and subfield codes to cataloging data. Content designation is frequently called *tagging and coding* a record, or sometimes just *tagging* or just *coding* it. All these terms, as well as the term *encoding a record,* mean the same thing: that the protocols of the MARC format are being applied to cataloging data for entry into a computer system programmed to use it.

Fixed fields are usually among the first fields in a record. In OCLC, they are identified by mnemonic prefixes, beginning with "Type," meaning "type of material," and ending with "Dates." In the LC, they are tagged field 008. Fixed fields are followed by other control fields, which include but are not limited to inventory control numbers, product numbers, call numbers, holding library designations, and so on. Control fields bear tags beginning with 0 (zero). Primary access points, which follow the control fields, usually have tags beginning with 1. Title-proper primary access points are the exception. They are identified in the 245 field by means of an indicator.

Following the primary access point, fields relating to the descriptive elements have tags beginning with 2, 3, 4, and 5, in a numeric sequence that follows the order of the areas of description. One exception to this sequence is the tag for standard numbers, area 8, which, because it represents inventory control numbers, begins with 0. Subject headings bearing tags that begin with a 6 and secondary descriptive access points bearing tags that begin with 7 or 8 complete the record. A few MARC fields beginning with 9 are defined for use, representing local links of various kinds.

Figure 13.2 on page 255 demonstrates a MARC record and some of the screen displays that can be generated from the MARC record.

MARC DISPLAYS

Figures 19.3 and 19.4 show bibliographic records for the same book as they appear in two national bibliographic networks, with their tags, indicators, delimiters, and subfield codes. Both are MARC records, although there are recognizable differences in the way they look. Some of the differences occur because of the differing capabilities of various printers, and some occur because of the differing procedures followed by each network.

```
***** Record 2  Length: 1824   "01824cam  2200361 a 4500"
<001>  CANA18466061
<003>  CPomAG
<005>  20080116081019.0
<008>  070709s2007    nyuaf    b    001 0beng
<091>  $aWPL-CANA$bCaMW
<010>  $a  2007028365
<020>  $a9780345485410 (acid-free paper)
<020>  $a0345485416 (acid-free paper)
<035>  $a(OCoLC)154678413$z(OCoLC)154799670
<040>  $aDLC$cDLC$dBAKER$dBTCTA$dYDXCP$dUPZ$dC#P$dDLC
<043>  $ae-uk---
<050>00$aDA335.B65$bF69 2007
<082>00$a942.05/2092$aB$222
<100>1 $aFox, Julia.
<245>10$aJane Boleyn :$bthe true story of the infamous Lady Rochford /$cJulia Fox.
<250>  $a1st ed.
<260>  $aNew York :$bBallantine Books,$cc2007.
<300>  $axviii, 379 p., [16] p. of plates :$bill. (chiefly col.) ;$c25 cm.
<504>  $aIncludes bibliographical references (p. [351]-361) and index.
<520>  $aExposes the inner sanctum of court life during the reign of Henry VIII
through the eyes and ears of Jane Boleyn, wife of George Boleyn and sister-in-law to
Queen Anne Boleyn. Jane emerges as a courageous spirit, a modern woman forced by
circumstances to fend for herself in a privileged but vicious world.--From source
other than Library of Congress.
<600>10$aBoleyn, Jane,$cViscountess Rochford,$dd. 1542.
<650> 0$aLadies-in-waiting$zGreat Britain$vBiography.
<651> 0$aGreat Britain$xCourt and courtiers$vBiography.
<651> 0$aGreat Britain$xHistory$yHenry VIII, 1509-1547.
<852>  $aWPL-CANA
<856>42$3Contributor biographical information
$uhttp://www.loc.gov/catdir/enhancements/fy0808/2007028365-b.html
<856>42$3Publisher description
$uhttp://www.loc.gov/catdir/enhancements/fy0808/2007028365-d.html
<856>41$3Sample text$uhttp://www.loc.gov/catdir/enhancements/fy0808/2007028365-
s.html
```

Figure 19.3. A-G Canada MARC record.

Figures 19.5, 19.6, and 19.7 show records from the LC authority files for a personal name, a corporate body name, and a *Library of Congress Subject Headings* (LCSH) subject descriptor, respectively. Differences in the meanings of tags and subfield codes are obvious in these records when they are compared with the bibliographic records.

WorldCat: Jane Boleyn

OCLC	316871121		No holdings in UTF - 4 other holdings					
Books	**Rec Stat** n		**Entered** 20090324		**Replaced** 20090324145527.8			
Type a		**ELvl** I	**Srce** d	**Audn**	**Ctrl**		**Lang** eng	
BLvl m		**Form**	**Conf** 0	**Biog** b	**MRec**		**Ctry** nyu	
		Cont b	**GPub**	**LitF** 0	**Indx** 1			
Desc a		**Ills** af	**Fest** 0	**DtSt** r	**Dates** 2009,2007			

040		BKL ‡c BKL
020		034551078X (pbk.) : ‡c $16.00
020		9780345510785 (pbk.) : ‡c $16.00
090		
049		UTFL
100	1_	Fox, Julia.
245	10	Jane Boleyn : ‡b the true story of the infamous Lady Rochford / ‡c Julia Fox.
250		Ballantine Books trade pbk ed.
260		New York : ‡b Ballantine Books, ‡c 2009.
300		392 p., [16] p. of plates : ‡b ill. (chiefly col.) ; ‡c 21 cm.
500		Originally published: 2007.
504		Includes bibliographical references (p. [351]-361) and index.
600	10	Boleyn, Jane, ‡c Viscountess Rochford, ‡d d. 1542.
651	_0	Great Britain ‡x Court and courtiers ‡v Biography.
651	_0	Great Britain ‡x History ‡y Henry VIII, 1509-1547.
650	_0	Ladies-in-waiting ‡z Great Britain ‡v Biography.

Figure 19.4. OCLC MARC record.

LC Control Number: n 84048778
HEADING: Intner, Sheila S.

```
000 00504cz a2200145n450
001 111496
005 19860703135455.4
008 840524n| acannaab |n aaa
010 __ |a n 84048778
035 __ |a (DLC)n 84048778
040 __ |a DLC |c DLC |d DLC
100 10 |a Intner, Sheila S.
670 __ |a Her Access to nonprint materials, 1984: |b CIP t.p. (Sheila S. Intner)
670 __ |a Her Circulation policy in academic, public, and school libraries, c1986:
        |b CIP t.p. (Sheila S. Intner) data sheet (b. 1935)
953 __ |a bt10 |b bd15
```

Figure 19.5. Library of Congress personal name authority record.

```
LC Control Number: n 82220766
        HEADING: Toronto Public Library
            000 00766cz a2200205n 450
            001 2878636
            005 20000202154254.0
            008 830413n| acannaab |a ana
            010 __ |a n 82220766
            035 __ |a (DLC)n 82220766
            040 __ |a DLC |c DLC
            110 2_ |a Toronto Public Library
            410 2_ |a Public Library, Toronto
            410 1_ |a Toronto (Ont.). |b Public Library
            410 2_ |a T.P.L.
            410 2_ |a TPL
            510 2_ |a Toronto Public Libraries
            670 __ |a Its Catalogue of the J. Ross Robertson Collection in the Historical Room
                of the Public Library, Toronto, 1912: |b t.p. (Public Library, Toronto)
            670 __ |a NLC 1/83 |b (AACR 2: Toronto Public Library. Name changed in 1968
                to Toronto Public Libraries and changed back to Toronto Public Library in
                1978)
            953 __ |a vj50
```

Figure 19.6. Library of Congress corporate name authority record.

```
LC Control Number: sh 96008124
        HEADING: Humanitarian assistance
            000 00580cz a2200205n 450
            001 4880597
            005 20001017114041.0
            008 960725i| anannbabn |a ana
            035 __ |a (DLC)sh 96008124
            906 __ |t 9634 |u te04 |v 0
            010 __ |a sh 96008124
            040 __ |a DLC |c DLC
            150 __ |a Humanitarian assistance
            450 __ |a Humanitarian aid
            550 __ |w g |a International relief
            670 __ |a UNBIS.
            670 __ |a LC database, 7/25/96 |b (humanitarian assistance; humanitarian aid)
            952 __ |a 16 bib. record(s) to be changed
            952 __ |a LC pattern: Economic assistance
            953 __ |a ta21
```

Figure 19.7. Library of Congress subject authority record.

BIBLIOGRAPHIC NETWORKS AND SHARED CATALOGING

An important feature common to library bibliographic networks such as OCLC is their use of the MARC format to enter and transmit their data. This acceptance of the MARC format by the networks helped make it an international standard. Nevertheless, each network adapts MARC in ways that aid its users. Some have altered the appearance and entry style of the 008 control field to make it easier to code; for example, OCLC provides mnemonic prefixes in place of delimiters and subfield codes. Local fields unique to a network have been defined that are not part of the official format. Generally, however, MARC records are interchangeable and easily recognized.

Networks incorporate national library cataloging. LC's MARC records formed the nucleus and lion's share of all network databases when they started and were a majority of records for a number of years. The balance between LC and member-contributed original cataloging shifted during the 1980s and, since then, the proportion of LC and national library records has been shrinking. In the 1990s, LC began using the original cataloging of network member libraries as the basis for its own cataloging. This change put real meaning into the phrase "cooperative cataloging," which was formerly defined as everybody else copying LC's original cataloging.

METADATA

Definitions of metadata range from the most basic—data about data—to one that is both more complex and more useful—"information used to find, access, use, and manage information resources primarily in a digital environment."[2] Library cataloging is information about all kinds of informational materials, analog and digital, making it possible to include it in most definitions of metadata.

Experts recognize five types of metadata depending on the functions being supported:

- *Administrative metadata*, including acquisition information, rights and reproduction tracking, legal access requirements, location information, selection criteria for digitization, and version control
- *Descriptive metadata*, including cataloging records, finding aids, specialized indexes, hyperlinked relationships between resources, and annotations by users
- *Preservation metadata*, including physical condition data and documentation of actions taken, such as data refreshing and migration
- *Technical metadata*, including hardware and software documentation, digitization, tracking response times, and authentication and security data (for example, passwords and encryption keys)
- *Use metadata*, such as exhibition records, use and user tracking, content reuse, and multiple versions.

The metadata itself can be made part of the resource itself, called *embedded* metadata; or it can be carried by a separate electronic record, similar to a library catalog record, called *associated* metadata. Embedded metadata is advantageous because it is created by the same people who create the resource. Authors should know more about the resources they create than anyone else and, therefore, are uniquely qualified to create good metadata for them. In addition, if an electronic resource has embedded metadata, it is instantly available to searchers as soon as the resource is posted. There is no waiting period while someone else prepares and mounts the metadata, as is the case with associated metadata. Associated metadata, however, can be managed more efficiently within a system and is unlikely to be lost if the resource is moved from one system to another. Embedded metadata sometimes gets stripped away and lost during such transactions.

Metadata systems (or schema) may be general or subject specific. Members of some disciplines have developed their own metadata systems instead of using generalized systems, mainly because they wanted to include certain kinds of information that were not in the generalized systems. One of the most popular generalized metadata systems among libraries is the Dublin Core, developed collaboratively by librarians and network experts from outside the library field. It is described in the next section. Two generalized metadata systems that provide greater specificity than Dublin Core (DC) are the Metadata Encoding and Transmission Standard (METS) and Metadata Object Description Schema (MODS). These are discussed in the sections that follow.

DUBLIN CORE

The aim of DC was to simplify metadata creation by requiring fewer elements than library cataloging, eliminating nearly all of the complicated rules about how to arrange the elements and what information is put into them, and using eye-readable tags in place of MARC-style content designators. DC's simplicity is both an asset and a liability. On the positive side, it means that anyone can create metadata records with a minimum of training. At the same time, it allows for a great deal of ambiguity. Two DC records for the same resource could look very different; and two identical records might actually describe different resources.

DC takes two forms: simple and qualified. All DC elements are optional and repeatable, and they can be modified by adding qualifiers. Very few rules govern the data that go into an element. Simple DC has 15 elements relating to a document's content, intellectual property, and instantiation, as follows:

- *Content* (seven elements): Title, Subject, Description, Type, Source, Relation, and Coverage
- *Intellectual property* (four elements): Creator, Publisher, Contributor, and Rights
- *Instantiation* (four elements): Date, Format, Identifier, and Language

Users for whom these 15 elements are not sufficient can use qualified DC, which includes three more elements—Audience, Provenance, and Rights holder—as well as numerous element refinements that modify them all.

Details for the DC elements—definitions, where the metadata creator should go to find the data, how elements should be input, guidelines on how to input them, and limits on their values—can be viewed at the Dublin Core Metadata Initiative Web site (http://dublincore.org/documents/dces). For example, the Contributor element is the entity responsible for making contributions to the content of the resource. The DC tagger is told to obtain the information from the item, the browser title, or other sources as appropriate and to enter the information as found on the item, including capitalization and punctuation. No controlled values are given. The Type element is defined as the nature or genre of the content of the item. The DC tagger is directed to determine type from the item itself. Type has controlled values: the definitions for 10 types, such as collection, dataset, image, software, sound, text, and so on.

Element refinements narrow the meaning of an element, making it more specific. For example, instead of just plain Date, DC taggers can give Date.issued, Date.created, Date.available, and so on. Qualifiers allow the identification of specific schemes; for example, for the Subject element, these include Subject.class.DDC, Subject.topical.LCSH, Subject.class.LCC, Subject.class.SuDoc, and so on.

A debate continues between DC users who prize its simplicity and those who want it altered to support more elements of data and greater detail in the data. In addition to the advantage of its simplicity, which means taggers do not need extensive training, DC is flexible within its range of elements and can be mapped to MARC and other metadata schemas. Even with the added refinements and qualifiers, DC is far simpler than MARC. It is an economical alternative to full MARC cataloging for large numbers of electronic resources, especially if those resources are perceived as having short shelf lives.

METADATA ENCODING AND TRANSMISSION STANDARD

According to Cantara, "The Metadata Encoding and Transmission Standard (METS) is a data communication standard for encoding descriptive, administrative, and structural metadata regarding objects within a digital library, expressed using the XML Schema Language of the World Wide Web Consortium."[3] The first part of the definition sounds exactly like MARC, but the use of XML differentiates it from that library standard. METS was developed by a group of U.S. research libraries, including Cornell University, the New York Public Library, and Penn State University on the East Coast, and Stanford University and the University of California at Berkeley on the West Coast. METS features emphasize interoperability, scalability, and the preservation of the objects in the digital library.

METS documents can have seven parts—a header and six sections—as follows:

- Descriptive metadata
- Administrative metadata
- File group (an inventory of files)
- Structural map (outlines the object's hierarchical structure and links elements of that structure to its content)
- Structural map linking (documents hyperlinks between any two links in the previous section)
- Behavior (associates executable behaviors with content in a METS object).

The only required section is the structural map section, which is known as the heart of a METS document. In addition, as a well-formed XML document, a METS document has one root element (<mets>) with five optional attributes of its own: XML identifier (ID), object identifier (OBJID), type (TYPE), label (LABEL—the title of the object), and profile (PROFILE).

METS is governed by an international editorial board and is maintained at LC by its Network Development and MARC Standards Office. METS allows for greater detail than DC, making it possible for different institutions to share the contents of their digital repositories.

A brief outline of METS with excellent examples of METS sections and full documents is available at the MPDL Media Wiki Web site (http://colab.mpdl.mpg.de/mediawiki/Metadata_Encoding_and_Transmission_Standard).

METADATA OBJECT DESCRIPTION SCHEMA

Metadata Object Description Schema (MODS), developed at LC, is a subset of 19 MARC elements expressed in XML format. It was developed to expedite the tagging of electronic resources. Instead of the numeric tags used in the MARC format, MODS elements are identified by language-based tags, as follows:

* titleInfo	* name	* typeOfResource
* genre	* originInfo	* language
* physicalDescription	* abstract	* tableofContents
* targetAudience	* note	* subject
* classification	* relatedItem	* identifier
* location	* accessCondition	* extension
* recordInfo		

Most of the MODS elements have equivalents in MARC 21, although in some cases, multiple MARC elements were combined into a single element in the MODS schema. For example, the several linking entry elements identified by MARC tags 76X–78X are covered by a single MODS element: relatedItem. However, type attributes can be added to relatedItem to express relationships of different kinds.

All MARC values are not duplicated in MODS, but MODS has a richer descriptive potential than DC. DC has 15 or 16 top-level elements, depending on whether it is simple or qualified DC. In contrast, MODS has 19 top-level elements. DC has 28 additional subelements; MODS has 47. MARC records can be converted to MODS successfully, but once converted, the records are not reversible. Data are lost in the conversion from MARC to MODS; therefore, the MODS records cannot be returned to their original MARC forms.

MODS appears to be a compromise between very simple and very complex metadata tagging systems. As such, it is likely to be successful in meeting the needs of users trying to find speedily produced metadata with more detail than minimalist schemas such as DC are currently able to provide.

SUMMARY

At the time of this writing, the MARC format is the library-wide standard for digitizing bibliographic information. Developed at LC and adopted first by North American bibliographic networks and later by major cataloging institutions around the world, it is used as the basis for integrated library systems. MARC has been criticized as being too complicated and difficult to learn, but it has exhibited a remarkable ability to change with the times and accommodate many kinds of data.

Newer markup systems, such as DC, METS, and MODS, were developed to provide simpler and speedier ways of digitizing bibliographic data for electronic resources. Although MARC can be used for electronic resources, its complexity requires a lengthy learning process and its application is time consuming. DC, the simplest of the metadata schemas described in this chapter, has many fewer fields than MARC and uses words rather than numeric tags, so almost anyone can use it with very little training. METS and MODS both have more fields and can express added detail, making them more attractive to librarians who want more precision.

LC and OCLC have been at the forefront of metadata development, along with research libraries pioneering in building digital repositories. Libraries have a vested interest in the success of these endeavors as they take on important roles in burgeoning global information systems.

REVIEW QUESTIONS

1. What does the acronym MARC stand for? Define MARC briefly.

2. Name the five types of MARC formats and explain briefly what each one covers.

3. Who developed the MARC format and how is it governed?

4. Define the term "content designator" and name three types of content designators.

5. What is a control field? A fixed field? A variable field?

6. What advantages accrue to libraries that belong to networks?

7. Name two metadata schemas and describe each one briefly.

8. Why is the MARC format considered difficult to use for electronic resources?

NOTES

The epigraph is from "Online Catalogs," *New World Encyclopedia*, http://www.new worldencyclopedia.org/entry;Library_catalog.

1. Indicator value 2 for personal name headings is obsolete. At one time, it stood for compound surnames, such as Smith-Jones, Jean. Since it became obsolete, compound surnames are given the same value—1—as single surnames.

2. John Feather and Paul Sturges, eds., *International Encyclopedia of Information and Library Science* (London: Routledge, 2003), 384.

3. Linda Cantara, "METS: The Metadata Encoding and Transmission Standard," in *Metadata: A Cataloger's Primer,* ed. Richard P. Smiraglia (New York: Haworth Information Press, 2005), 237.

SUGGESTED READING

MARC

Fritz, Deborah A. *Cataloging with AACR2R and USMARC for Books, Computer Files, Serials, Sound Recordings, and Videorecordings.* 2nd ed., 2006 cumulation. Chicago, IL: American Library Association, 2007.

Furrie, Betty. *Understanding MARC: Bibliographic: Machine-Readable Cataloging.* 6th ed. Washington, D.C.: Cataloging Distribution Service, Library of Congress, 2000–, http://www.loc.gov/marc/umb.

Library of Congress. MARC Home page. Washington, D.C.: Library of Congress, 2000–. http://www.loc.gov/marc/marc.html.

Library of Congress. Network Development and MARC Standards Office, in cooperation with Standards and Support, Library and Archives Canada. *MARC 21 Format for Bibliographic Data Including Guidelines for Content Designation.* http://lcweb.loc.gov/marc/bibliographic/. (Formats for authorities, holdings, classification, and community information data are available from LC and LAC; concise versions are available on their Web sites.)

MarcEdit. http://people.oregonstate.edu/~reeset/marcedit/html/downloads.html#current.

Weitz, Jay. *Music Coding and Tagging: MARC 21 Content Designation for Scores and Sound Recordings.* 2nd ed. Lake Crystal, MN: Soldier Creek Press, 2001.

Metadata Schemas

Caplan, Priscilla. *Metadata Fundamentals for All Librarians.* Chicago, IL: American Library Association, 2003.

Coleman, Anita. "From Cataloging to Metadata: Dublin Core Records for the Library Catalog." *Cataloging & Classification Quarterly* 4, no. 3 (2005): 153–81.

Hillmann, Diane E., and Elaine L. Westbrooks, eds. *Metadata in Practice.* Chicago, IL: American Library Association, 2004.

Intner, Sheila S., Susan S. Lazinger, and Jean Weihs. *Metadata and Its Impact on Libraries.* Westport, CT: Libraries Unlimited, 2006.

Jones, Wayne, et al. *Cataloging the Web: METADATA, AACR, and MARC 21.* Lanham, MD: Scarecrow Press, 2002.

Lagoze, Carl. "Keeping Dublin Core Simple: Cross-Domain Discovery or Resource Description?" *D-Lib Magazine* 7, no. 1 (Jan. 2001), http://www.dlib.org/dlib/january01/lagoze/01lagoze.html.

Smiraglia, Richard P., ed. *Metadata: A Cataloger's Primer.* New York, NY: Haworth Information Press, 2005.

Zeng, Marcia Lei, and Jian Qin. Metadata Web site. http://www.metadataetc.org/book-website.

Chapter

20   Copy Cataloging

You receive . . . into your library every year some twenty thousand volumes, or something like that. Why, if you had a printed catalogue dropped down from Heaven to you at this moment perfect, this day twelve-month[s hence,] twenty thousand interlineations would spoil the simplicity of that catalogue.

—the Right Honourable J. W. Croker

Copy cataloging is the name given to operations that use existing catalog records as data sources for materials being cataloged, editing the records in accordance with local policies so they can be incorporated into local catalogs. It is an appropriate name because the local catalogers are, essentially, *copying* relevant information from the source records they use instead of building entirely new records from scratch by transcribing information directly from the materials. Another name for copy cataloging is *derived cataloging,* because local library records are *derived* from preexisting source records. This chapter uses the term *copy cataloging*.

Copy cataloging has two principal goals: saving time and saving money. A third goal can be ensuring the quality of the records entered into the local library catalog, but achieving this goal depends on the likelihood that the source records are of better quality than the agency would achieve if its staff prepared an entirely new record without relying on existing records, generally called "original" cataloging. Copying poor-quality records cannot provide a good local catalog.

- *Saving time:* The idea behind copy cataloging is that, in order to produce a finished catalog record, local catalogers need not spend the time it takes to transcribe data carefully from materials to create bibliographic descriptions, determine descriptive access points, determine and assign subject headings, perform authority-control activities, classify the material, add shelf marks to create call numbers, and enter all the data into the catalog. Instead, the process is as fast as 1-2-3: (1) find a source record to copy; (2) make certain it matches the material being cataloged, and (3) change only those few elements that vary locally, such as call numbers. Voilà! The work is done. Instead of taking as much as 40 minutes to an hour for one book, copy cataloging might be done in 10 minutes or less.

- *Saving money:* Because the largest proportion of cataloging cost is paying for catalogers' time, speeding up the cataloging process enables local libraries to save money in addition to time, even though they may have to pay to gain access to source records, for example, to join a bibliographic network. On balance, the cost of access to the source records is believed to be less than the cost of original cataloging for all materials a library acquires for its collections.

- *Ensuring quality:* As already mentioned, the quality of copy cataloging depends on the quality of its sources. Records appearing in Cataloging In Publication (CIP) that originate at the Library of Congress and the national libraries of Canada and the United Kingdom provide the highest-quality data available and are only rarely incorrect. Catalogers should be particularly careful in checking unlabeled CIPs because some publishers provide their own CIPs, which may be done by untrained staff, thus reducing their publication costs. However, copying records that do not match the material being cataloged, copying records that match but lack needed data, or copying records that match but are created by people who do not conform to cataloging standards or are careless about transcription and data entry introduces errors or other problems into local catalogs, which cause retrieval problems for the patrons who search them. Source quality is discussed further in the next section.

POLICY ISSUES

To save the most time and money, library administrators may erroneously assume that source records can be accepted and used in local catalogs "as is," without any further work. Though ideal, this is rarely the case, because selected elements from outside local libraries do not apply to the local situations. In particular, call numbers are likely to be different from those of the source libraries, but call numbers are not the only problems. Five policy areas usually have to be considered: acceptability of sources, record fullness, errors in the source copy, call numbers, and tracings.

1. Acceptability of Sources

Copy catalogers recognize that all source records are not equally good. Sometimes source records lack needed data and sometimes they contain errors. Using them without adding the missing data or correcting errors debases the local catalog and makes it a less effective search tool for local patrons. Doing the work to upgrade poor-quality source records takes time and costs the local library money. Thus, although network contracts usually require that existing records be used if they match the materials being cataloged, the provision is hard to enforce. Copy catalogers might not recognize matches due to errors or omissions. To ensure that they avoid wasting time and work only with quality records, copy cataloging supervisors develop lists of preferred, acceptable, and unacceptable sources.

Catalogers recognize a hierarchy of quality that rates national libraries at the top, providing the best-quality records; followed by records created by trained members of the Program for Cooperative Cataloging (PCC), which are known to meet current national standards; records created by large research libraries that maintain knowledgeable cataloging staffs; and records created by catalogers working in a selection of other libraries known to do good cataloging. A great many contributors to shared cataloging databases recognize the importance of full and accurate data, and do their best to enter good-quality original cataloging into the database.

For many of the books a general library buys, preliminary catalog records appear on the verso of the title page as CIP. These data are authoritative and include access points that conform to name, title, and subject authorities as well as officially assigned Dewey Decimal Classification numbers and full Library of Congress call numbers. The principal disadvantage of using CIP records is their lack of full descriptive data, missing because the records are created before the books are published and, thus, cannot be determined. As a result, the data in the CIP record must be checked for accuracy and the missing data supplied, such as pagination and other physical descriptions. While CIP is generally accurate, sometimes the absence of the published book causes even the best cataloger to make mistakes that appear in the printed CIP. Figure 20.1 shows a CIP record containing erroneous data that is likely to have occurred because the correct information was not available at the time the preliminary record was created. A second disadvantage of relying solely on CIP for source data is that some books still do not provide it, and it is generally not available for materials other than books.

```
This example is an illustration of:
    • two other title information statements
    • subsidiary responsibility
    • detailed pagination
    • descriptive illustration statement
    • index note
    • two International Standard Book Numbers (ISBNs) qualified
    • personal name added entry
    • title added entry
    • Library of Congress subject headings
    • Library and Archives of Canada CIP with incorrect other title
      information
    • 2nd level cataloging


Ebadi, Shirin.
   Iran awakening : from prison to peace prize : one woman's struggle at
the crossroads of history / Shirin Ebadi ; with Azadeh Moaveni. --
Toronto : Knopf, 2006.
   xvi, 232 p. : ill., maps, ports. ; 25 cm.

   Includes index.
   ISBN-13: 978-0-676-97802-5 (bound). --   ISBN-10: 0-676-97802-9
(bound).

   1. Ebadi, Shirin.  2. Women human rights workers -- Iran.  3. Women
lawyers -- Iran.  4. Women -- Iran -- Social conditions.  5. Iran --
Politics and government -- 1979-1997.  I. Moaveni, Azadeh.  II. Title.

Note: The publication, distribution statement for this book in a U.S
library would be:

Toronto : Knopf ; New York : Random House, 2006.
```

Figure 20.1 Incorrect CIP.

Figure 20.1—*Continued*

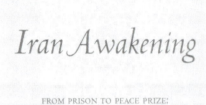

Iran Awakening

FROM PRISON TO PEACE PRIZE:

ONE WOMAN'S STRUGGLE AT THE

CROSSROADS OF HISTORY

SHIRIN EBADI

Winner of the Nobel Peace Prize

WITH AZADEH MOAVENI

Alfred A. Knopf Canada

PUBLISHED BY ALFRED A. KNOPF CANADA

Copyright © 2006 Shirin Ebadi

All rights reserved under International and Pan-American Copyright Conventions. No part of this book may be reproduced in any form or by any electronic or mechanical means, including information storage and retrieval systems, without permission in writing from the publisher, except by a reviewer, who may quote brief passages in a review. Published in 2006 by Alfred A. Knopf Canada, a division of Random House of Canada Limited, and simultaneously in the United States of America by Random House, an imprint of The Random House Publishing Group, a division of Random House, Inc., New York, and in Great Britain by Rider & Co., an imprint of The Random House Publishing Group, London. Distributed by Random House of Canada Limited, Toronto.

Knopf Canada and colophon are trademarks.

www.randomhouse.ca

Library and Archives Canada Cataloguing in Publication

Ebadi, Shirin
Iran awakening : a memoir of revolution and hope / Shirin Ebadi ; with Azadeh Moaveni.

Includes index.

ISBN-13: 978-0-676-97802-5
ISBN-10: 0-676-97802-9

1. Ebadi, Shirin. 2. Women human rights workers—Iran. 3. Women lawyers—Iran. 4. Women—Iran—Social conditions. 5. Iran—Politics and government—1979–1997. 6. Iran—Politics and government—1997– . I. Moaveni, Azadeh, 1976– . II. Title.

DS318.84.E22A3 2006   323'.092   C2005-905736-X

4 6 8 9 7 5 3

Equally authoritative and generally more complete than CIP is the cataloging in the machine-readable cataloging (MARC) database. These MARC records are prepared by catalogers at the Library of Congress and selected partners, including the Library and Archives Canada, the British Library, and members of the PCC trained to meet national library standards. Records entered initially as preliminary CIP records are later updated when the finished products are received. In addition, cataloging for materials other than books is included. MARC records are transferred electronically to the major bibliographic networks and become part of network databases, or the MARC database can be purchased from the Library of Congress or another national library to be added to local databases.

Bibliographic networks, such as OCLC, Inc. (the acronym stands for Online Computer Library Center, founded in 1967–1968), provide their members and other subscribers with services for shared cataloging. Early in their history, the Library of Congress's

MARC database, still part of network databases, made up the largest share of catalog records, but members' original cataloging soon outstripped it and continues increasing in proportion to national library contributions. In addition to providing network members with shared cataloging, many libraries are served by networks indirectly when they purchase their cataloging from cooperative or commercial suppliers that obtain the data they sell from the networks. The quality of cataloging obtained from networks varies depending on the quality of the original contributions and the level of quality control imposed by the network. Generally, efforts are made to ensure that standards are met, but in a great many instances compliance is voluntary and no real enforcement mechanisms are in place.

Commercial companies may offer only catalog records for library customers or they may offer many products and services, such as supplying materials to libraries, processing materials and/or selling the processing products, and designing and selling computer software for catalogs, circulation control, and so on. Companies may purchase cataloging data from bibliographic networks and/or generate original cataloging themselves. Quality standards at levels designated by customers can usually be guaranteed. Commercial companies offer customized catalog records for a price, adding value to the data they buy from outside sources and enabling customers to function as they wish without hiring specialized staff or reprocessing network records themselves.

2. Record Fullness

Local policies concerning bibliographic levels govern the amount of information provided in original cataloging. The second edition of the *Anglo-American Cataloguing Rules* and all its subsequent versions provided for three levels of fullness (see chapter 13, pages 245–51). Bibliographic level 1 omits some data elements that are important for libraries with large collections, whose patrons depend on catalogs for research. Even when level 2 is the norm, optional elements can be omitted on a routine basis. Some libraries opt for minimal-level cataloging (such as OCLC K level or PCC core records) for some materials given original cataloging, especially if they face a combination of heavy workloads and shrinking resources. A long-time debate continues over the relative value of less-than-full cataloging versus no cataloging at all. The chart in Figure 20.2 shows the difference between OCLC K and I level records.

Despite cataloging rules and network contract obligations, some libraries omit data they do not use, such as notes, standard numbers, added entries, and numerous subject headings. (One of the authors worked in a library that filed only title added entries, but no others. Among her tasks was crossing out the unwanted added entries from Library of Congress unit cards.) Some libraries assign no more than one or two subject headings to nonfiction materials, do not check authority files, and establish new headings as they appear on materials without worrying about using only authorized name forms or potential conflicts.

3. Errors

Catalog records prepared and processed by human beings are bound to contain some errors, despite quality control procedures and other efforts to keep network databases clean. The policy issue is what to do about errors found in source copy. Should

Element	Full-Level	Minimal-Level
ELvl	♭,, I, L	K, 2, 5, 7, M
Fixed field	Code fully on every record	Default values
020, 022, 028	Supply full available information	Subfield ‡a if present on item
042	Include as program requires	Omit
050, 082, 086, etc.	One number from a recognized scheme if available	Optional
1xx	Include/establish if applicable	Include/establish if applicable
240	Include/establish if applicable	Optional
245–300	Include all applicable elements	Include all applicable elements
4xx	Transcribe series if present. Trace according to LC practice	Transcribe if present
5xx	All applicable notes according to the latest revision of AACR2 and LCRIs	Enter the following notes if applicable: • Field 501 • Field 502 • Field 533
6xx	Subject headings at appropriate level of specificity from an established thesaurus or subject heading system if available	Optional
7xx	Full added entry coverage according to the latest revision of AACR2 and LCRIs	Express primary added entry relationships and important title access information
8xx (Established form of series if different from that in field 490)	If series is traced, use as appropriate	Optional
856	Optional	Optional

AACR2 = *Anglo-American Cataloging Rules,* 2nd edition; LCRI = *Library of Congress Rule Interpretations.*

Figure 20.2. Required fields for OCLC K- and I-level records.

they be allowed to remain, or should they be corrected? Three choices are possible: correct all errors, correct no errors, or correct selected errors. The first choice is the most costly, and policy makers should be certain that having an error-free catalog is worth the expense before taking that option. The second choice contributes most to loss of quality and presents the most problems for local patrons trying to search in the catalog. The third choice is a compromise solution that tries to balance cost and quality.

Catalogers generally divide errors into those that affect retrieval, such as misspelled titles, names, or subject headings, and those that do not, such as misspelled notes or incorrect punctuation. Knowing that it costs the library money to correct errors that do not affect retrieval and are unlikely to cause problems for searchers, local libraries may choose not to correct them. In that event, rules must be devised that clearly identify the "must correct" errors for data entry staff. Also, library staff must be prepared for patrons to see the uncorrected errors on their screens and, possibly, complain about them.

4. Call Numbers

Of all the elements of a standard catalog entry, the call number is most likely to vary from one library to another. A call number is a shelf address in a local library collection. There is little to be gained from making it conform to the shelf address of any other library, including the Library of Congress. Local classification and shelf-marking policies may mandate differences from recommendations of standard tools and the practices of leading libraries. Typical examples include the following:

- Not classifying fiction; instead, arranging it alphabetically by authors' surnames in a separate Fiction section; or, classifying fiction by genre into a number of sections such as General Fiction, Short Stories, Westerns, Science Fiction, Romances, and Mysteries.
- Not classifying periodicals; instead, arranging them alphabetically by title in a separate Periodicals section.
- Not classifying individual biographies; instead, arranging them alphabetically by the subjects' surnames in a separate Biography section.
- Using cutter letters instead of cutter numbers.
- Obtaining cutter numbers from Cutter tables instead of synthesizing them from the Library of Congress's cuttering rules.

5. *Tracings* (Subject Headings and Added Entries/Access Points)

General libraries with small collections catering mainly to students, novices, and casual readers may find that numerous tracings—long lists of subject headings and added entries—offer information that is unlikely to be of use to their patrons. Instead of making the local catalog a better and more informative research tool, the unwanted tracings clutter it up and make searches more confusing. Eliminating unwanted tracings requires editing, but it slows down the growth of the catalog. Alternatively, a library could provide the ability to look up the MARC record where all tracings are included.

Decisions about these and other matters dictate what should and should not be included in local catalog records and how the information should appear. These decisions are important to make before choosing a source database and starting to do copy cataloging. Local variations that cannot be shown to have clear and tangible benefits for patrons should be avoided, because they take more editing time and, therefore, add to the cost a local library ends up paying for its cataloging.

OVERVIEW OF THE OPERATION

Copy cataloging begins with choosing the source or sources for cataloging copy. Once the source(s) are chosen, operations involve five steps: (1) searching and retrieving records to copy from source databases, (2) confirming the record matches with the material to be cataloged, (3) editing data from the source records, (4) entering local data, and (5) producing the records.

Choosing the Source(s)

As discussed earlier, source data may originate as CIP information, records in national library databases, and/or records in bibliographic network databases. (Libraries that buy from commercial sources usually buy completed catalog records, not source data from which catalog records can be derived.) One immediate advantage of CIP is that it appears in the books being cataloged. A copy cataloger does not have to go beyond the material itself to find the CIP, although in some books the CIP record is not reproduced in full and only a record number is given. As mentioned, another advantage is that CIP information is prepared by extremely knowledgeable catalogers and classifiers at the Library and Archives Canada, the Library of Congress, or the British Library. The disadvantage of CIP is that it does not appear in most nonbook materials, including digital materials. A library that relies on CIP alone must do original cataloging for all other types of material.

1. Searching and Retrieving Records to Copy from Source Databases

Copy catalogers are bound both by network contracts and by duty to search thoroughly for existing records that match their materials before entering new catalog records. The idea is to find existing records to copy. Good search techniques save more time than almost any other step of the copy cataloging process.

The best search request is one likely to match only one desired title and no others. This type of element is called a "unique identifier," and several of these are given routinely in catalog records, among them International Standard Book Numbers (ISBNs) and Library of Congress Control Numbers (LCCNs). Sometimes searching unique identifiers retrieves multiple records. This can occur because of errors or because several records are stored in the database for the same material.

When unique identifiers are absent from material being cataloged, or when they fail to return matching records, other search options must be tried. These include titles, the names of personal and corporate body authors, and series titles. Of these options, titles proper are most efficient, followed by the names of authors or series titles. Uniform titles might be necessary to search if the material being cataloged has one. Combinations of names and titles are better than titles alone or names alone. However, all of these elements can be expected to match multiple titles in the database and are less efficient than unique identifiers.

2. Confirming Record Matches and Selecting a Source Record

Once one or more source records are identified as possible matches, the copy cataloger must confirm an appropriate match. For example, if one is working with the OCLC database, the elements to be checked against the material in hand include the "Type" fixed field (for the format), "Date" fixed field, title statement, edition, publisher, and physical description. If all of these match the material, the record is likely to be a good match. If more than one record is a full match to these fields, the best source record should be selected, which is defined as the one most likely to contain full, high-quality data (a national library record, a PCC library record, or a well-reputed network member, in that order).

Multiple matches sometimes include more than one national library record. In this event, prefer the record contributed by the one in the cataloger's home country.

Sometimes incomplete matches are still useful. If a partial match contains the correct headings and title statements (for example, if the record is for a different edition of the same book) or differs in one or a few subelements (for example, if the record has the same title statement but names a different publisher), it can still be chosen and edited to correct the data that differ from the material in hand. When a partial match is finally produced, however, the copy cataloger must know whether the edited record should be designated a new record (permissible if it is, indeed, a record for a different material) or merely added to the original source record.

3. Editing Data from the Source Records

Ideally, all data in the source record that does not match the material being cataloged should be edited. As a practical matter, however, not all data elements are equally important, and some elements might be allowed to remain as they appear in the source record, especially if they occur in the notes or in fields that do not display to members of the public. Data elements most likely to require editing include the following:

- *Call numbers.* Some local libraries routinely assign their own call numbers, using the source data merely for guidance. If local library policy is to accept national library classification numbers, shelf marks may still have to be edited, unless they are also accepted as assigned. Library of Congress records do not provide shelf marks for Dewey call numbers, for example, so these must be added. (Some libraries copy the shelf marks appearing in subfield b of the Library of Congress call number field.) Small libraries using Dewey call numbers might accept only the basic classification number but no expansions, or might accept only one expansion. Copy catalogers should be clear about policies governing both classification numbers and shelf marks.
- *Standard numbers and binding data.* This information in source records might differ from materials being cataloged if, for example, the source record was for a hardcover version of a title and the material in hand is a paperback, or *vice versa*. Both kinds of information may appear in the source record, but

the local library chooses to accept only the data that match its material. In either instance, copy catalogers must edit the appropriate field.

- *Missing data.* Information missing from source records entered as CIP, minimal-level cataloging, or order records can be added. Sometimes this means only adding data in the physical description field, but at other times more is needed, including subject headings and added entries. If standard numbers, subtitles, statements of responsibility, series, important notes, and other useful data are missing from the source record, local library policies can be to add or ignore them. Editing policy should state clearly which fields should be added, if the information is available, and which should be ignored.

- *Errors.* Similarly, errors in the source records can be corrected. Some level of error can be tolerated in the interests of speeding up the process and saving money, but data used by local library patrons should be corrected the first time the record is used, not at a later time after problems occur. It is less expensive to make desired changes at once than to wait and revise records later. Editing policy should state clearly which fields should be corrected, if information in source records is wrong. At the very least, it seems sensible to correct errors in headings and other searchable fields as well as in the edition statement, material specific details, and publication, distribution element.

4. Entering Local Data

In addition to call numbers, other local information relating to newly acquired materials needs to be added before the records can be considered complete. A note about a strictly local matter might be added to notes or tracings, for example, the fact that an author was the town's mayor from 1955 to 1958, or that a particular chapter contains information about the town's history (a note and added subject heading). A whole category of library-specific data includes acquisitions data (e.g., vendors from whom materials are purchased, prices, dates of order and delivery, funds to which they are charged, names of requesters) and circulation data (e.g., the call numbers, copy numbers, loan types). Much of this data is copy-specific and does not normally display on public catalog screen displays for patrons, although staff members can request it.

5. Producing the Records

The final step in the process is producing completed records containing all the edited information desired by the local library for its catalog and other bibliographic files. When local records are uploaded to the database, the local libraries' identifications are added to the lists of holding libraries to show they own copies of the materials the records represent. This facilitates interlibrary loans.

Unless a local library is permitted to make permanent changes to the records contributed by other libraries, the local edits do not alter or update source records when the local record is produced. If corrections are needed for the source records, copy catalogers are expected to file reports with the source database quality-control group that is responsible for updating the source records.

SUMMARY

This chapter has covered the policies and procedures involved in cataloging materials by using existing catalog records as source copy, instead of starting from scratch and building a complete new record for each material acquired by the library. Many catalogers, particularly in those libraries buying mainstream materials likely to be cataloged before publication by national libraries, are accustomed to using CIP as source copy. This is the most basic kind of copy cataloging. It is one step further to use other types of source copy, such as the catalog records contributed by members to bibliographic network databases.

CIP records are also part of bibliographic network databases, where, in time, they are routinely upgraded with data that cannot be obtained before publication, such as the number of pages in a book or the number and types of illustrations a book contains. National library records are a valuable source of cataloging copy and are part of network databases as well as being available directly in the MARC database. In addition, many librarians use records that are contributed to network databases by members doing original cataloging in their local libraries. Bibliographic networks also share data among themselves, tape-loading batches of records from a variety of sources into the databases. With tape loads data may be lost in the transfer process and, as a result, may furnish less complete records than those contributed by means of direct uploads from libraries doing the cataloging.

Issues that bear careful consideration are the sources a library accepts, the kind of editing done, and the amount of editing source records require before data can be entered into the local library catalog. A whole range of options exists, from no editing to complete editing of every element that differs from data that would have been recorded had the local library done original cataloging. The trade-off in setting local policies is that doing no editing is quickest and cheapest, but it maximizes the number of errors in the local catalog. In contrast, doing complete editing takes longest and is most expensive, but it maximizes the accuracy of the local catalog.

Most catalogers make decisions that strike a compromise between no editing and perfect editing—for example, editing only those fields likely to affect retrieval or cause major confusion for searchers. At the same time, they try to find the best possible records to copy, which are contributed by libraries known for doing high-quality original work. The best safeguard for a local library's catalog is having knowledgeable copy catalogers who recognize the difference between major and minor issues, and who, themselves, do high-quality copy cataloging.

REVIEW QUESTIONS

1. Discuss how copy cataloging saves libraries time and money.
2. Identify three sources for cataloging source copy and describe the main advantages of each.
3. Name the five steps of the copy cataloging operation and discuss how they are accomplished.

NOTE

The epigraph is from Charles Coffin Jewett in his "On the Construction of Catalogues . . ." in which he proposed the first U.S. union catalog project at the Smithsonian Institution. See Charles C. Jewett, "Smithsonian Catalogue System," in *Foundations of Cataloging: A Sourcebook*, ed. Michael Carpenter and Elaine Svenonius (Littleton, CO: Libraries Unlimited, 1985), 52.

SUGGESTED READING

AUTOCAT Cataloging Listserv. http://www.AUTOCAT@listserv.syr.edu/.

Differences Between, Changes Within. Chicago, IL: Association for Library Collections & Technical Services, 2004.

Fritz, Deborah A. "Copy Cataloging Correctly." In *Cataloging Correctly for Kids,* 5th ed., ed. Sheila S. Intner, Joanna F. Fountain, and Jean Weihs, 49–72. (Chicago, IL: American Library Association, 2010).

Northwestern University Libraries. *MARC Responsibilities: Copy Cataloging Process.* http://www.staffweb.library.northwestern.edu/arc/catproc.html.

OCLC. "When to Make a New Record." In *(OCLC) Bibliographic Formats and Standards*, 4th ed.. http://www.oclc.org/us/en/bibformats/en/input/default.shtm.

OCLC. *OCLC CatExpress: A Simple-to Use Copy Cataloging Tool.* http://www.oclc.org/catexpress.

OCLC. OCLC Online Computer Library Center, Inc. Web site. http://www.oclc.org.

Program for Cooperative Cataloging. About the PCC. Library of Congress Web site. http://www.loc.gov/catdir/pcc/2001pcc.html.

Saffady, William. "Commercial Sources of Cataloging Data: Bibliographic Utilities and Other Vendors." *Library Technology Reports* vol. 34. no. 3 (May/June 1998): 281–432.

Taylor, Arlene G., with the assistance of Rosanna M. O'Neil. *Cataloging with Copy: A Decision-Maker's Handbook,* 2nd ed. Englewood, CO: Libraries Unlimited, 1988.

Yale University Libraries. *SML Copy Cataloging Workflow.* http://www.library.yale.edu/cataloging/Orbis2Manual/SML.

Processing Materials

Sharing is sometimes more demanding than giving.

—*Mary Catherine Bateson*

After analog materials—that is, materials whose physical formats consist of tangible objects such as books, videos, sound recordings, maps—have been cataloged and classified, they are prepared for use. The preparation involves a set of procedures called "processing."[1] Processing has two purposes—adding needed information to the materials and preserving them so they can be used for as long as the library wishes to do so. Generally, three kinds of information, which will be discussed in more detail later in this chapter, need to be added to the materials:

1. Evidence of ownership
2. Location information
3. A way to record and track use.

Some processing, such as putting clear plastic covers over the dustcovers of hardcover books, reinforcing or rebinding paperbacks, placing maps and pictures between sheets of plastic (called "encapsulating"), is done to protect the materials from damage and lengthen their shelf lives. This work can be done in-house or it can be outsourced to wholesalers from whom the library buys its materials.

Materials that come in unusual shapes and sizes sometimes require repackaging to facilitate storage and use. Because information agencies of all kinds consist largely of books and/or book-like materials, book stacks are the standard storage method. This makes it difficult to handle materials that come in formats other than books. And, even when different kinds of storage units (e.g., cabinets, oversize drawers) are made available for oddly shaped or sized materials, they still need the same kinds of identification and usage data added. Special packaging for nonbook formats such as discs and reels has improved since these kinds of materials began to be collected by libraries and media centers in the mid-20th century, but satisfactory processing still takes creativity.

Processing involves making physical additions and/or changes to the materials. Therefore, when processing decisions are made, librarians and media specialists should be sensitive to possible unintended consequences of their actions. There are trade-offs between actions that achieve the desired goals with minimal invasiveness but are easy to alter, and actions that are irreversible but possibly hasten the physical deterioration of the materials over time. Processing decisions need to balance the desire to maintain the integrity of materials and extend their longevity with the desire for clear identification and substantial security.

EVIDENCE OF LIBRARY OWNERSHIP

Ownership marks and other strategies for identifying owners of books typically include one (or sometimes more than one) of the following:

1. Stamping the owner's name in the books, usually in indelible ink
2. Pasting bookplates inside the books
3. Pasting other kinds of labels bearing the owner's name inside the books
4. Embossing pages in the books with an ownership mark.

Stamping names on books is extremely common. The favorite places to stamp are inside the covers of books and pamphlets, user guides, and so on; on the edges of the pages (known as edge-stamping); and on title pages. Sometimes, a randomly selected page within a book is also stamped as added insurance against theft. Because title pages and covers can be removed with relative ease and doing so does not affect the main texts, edge-stamping tends to be favored. Readers don't see the stamp while they are reading, and most or all of the textblock bears the evidence (see Figure 21.1), making it more difficult for a thief to obscure or remove it. Depending on the chemical composition of the ink used for the imprints, stamps are more or less harmful to the materials on which they are used.

Figure 21.1. Edge-stamped book.

Pasting library or school media center bookplates into books and book-like materials is another method of declaring ownership (see Figure 21.2). In earlier times, bookplates might be works of art, carefully designed to embellish and beautify the owner's name, sometimes hand painted and highly ornamented. Even in the 21st century, bookplates bearing classic designs are manufactured and sold to book lovers (or libraries) wishing to mark their materials in an aesthetically pleasing fashion. Bookplates may be ordered with preprinted names or with blank spaces where names can be added (see Figure 21.3). Bookplates generally are better looking than stamps and carry on a genteel tradition of establishing ownership. It is not uncommon for research libraries to use bookplates to identify specific collections funded by respected donors, who are rewarded for their generosity by having their names associated for all time with the objects of scholarship they fund. Depending on the chemical composition of the adhesives used to paste bookplates to materials, they may be more or less harmful for the materials on which they are used.

Because bookplates can be costly and are relatively large, some libraries and media centers may find them impractical to use on all their materials, especially on small objects such as paperback books, DVDs and CDs, sound tapes, and the like. For many years, library suppliers have offered smaller labels bearing an agency's name for such materials or all materials if the agency chose to use them (see Figure 21.4). Small labels come in different shapes and many sizes—some of them only a centimeter (or less) in width or diameter.

Another strategy for identifying printed materials—especially books—as library property is embossing a library name or institutional logo on one or more of the pages. These marks, while invasive and irreversible, are less obvious than stamps or

Figure 21.2. Library bookplate.

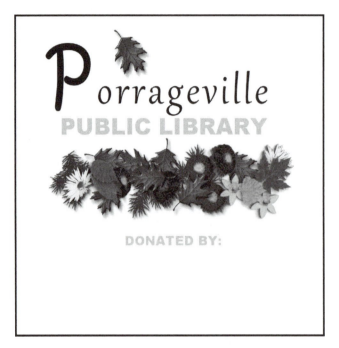

Figure 21.3. Library donor bookplate.

Figure 21.4. Core label.

bookplates and may even be considered aesthetically attractive. They have the added advantage of using no inks or adhesives. Libraries in colleges and universities sometimes use their institutional seal for this purpose, but at other times a special image is created that includes words to the effect that the embossed item belongs to Library X or Media Center Y. The principal drawback to embossing pages is that they are easily removed if a person is scheming to steal the material.

Still another strategy for displaying ownership is marking materials with indelible markers. For example, Cornell University Library's processing guidelines state: "DVDs and CDs should be processed according to each library's requirements. The call number should be written on the label side of one sided (one side silver and one side with label) CDs and DVDs with a permanent marker and a specially designed CD security strip applied to the disc on the label side. For two sided discs, do not write on the disc itself; the call number should be written on the inner circular area. Do not tattletape. A computer-generated label is applied to the spine of the case, preferably, if not, to the upper left side of the front of the case."[2]

Overall, some sort of ownership evidence is needed. It is unusual for libraries or media centers to allow materials to circulate that bear no markings or labels to show who owns them. Sometimes, several methods are used simultaneously.

LOCATION INFORMATION

Information about where material is stored within the library's collections is as important as evidence that it belongs to the library. This means putting call numbers in visible places on the materials so they can be shelved in the right locations. Labels imprinted with call numbers are typically affixed to the spines of books, bound volumes of periodicals, and materials in other formats that have the space for them. Labels imprinted with call numbers are also made in different sizes and shapes intended for use with nonbook materials. These can be purchased from library supply houses and applied to materials in-house; or, for a small fee, wholesalers can arrange to label the materials before they are delivered to the library.

One problem that occurs is the call-number labels placed on the outer spines of books wear out at the edges and start to peel off before the material's usefulness to patrons is over. Many libraries reinforce the spine labels of books before putting them out on the shelves by covering them with clear tape. This cannot be done so easily with certain types of nonbook materials, such as sound recordings on CD and videorecordings on DVD, but specialized labels for such materials are not subjected to the same kinds of wear and tear from shelving and reshelving, or movements of the spine as books are opened and shut.

A different problem occurs when book spines are too narrow to hold standard sized spine labels.[3] In this event, labels usually are placed on the outside of the front cover. Again, protective clear tape may be applied over the label to secure it. The call number label cannot be read unless the book is pulled out of its place on the shelf, which subjects it to added wear and, depending on where on the cover the label is placed, more or less manipulation to see it. The lower left-hand corner requires the smallest amount of removal from the shelf, but the right-hand corners—both upper and lower—are where the eye typically focuses when the book is used.

Like books with narrow spines, the jewel cases in which CDs and DVDs are stored are too narrow to support standard spine labels, but these can be placed on the front of the case. Some libraries arrange the jewel cases like books; others put them in wide bins, proportioned so the cases can be stacked facing out. When the latter is the storage venue, call number labels on the front of the jewel case are the best choice.

Books-on-tape tend to be packaged by their publishers as if they were books and do not present special spine-label problems, but individual cassette tapes in small plastic boxes need a different label. Videorecordings on cassettes are also packaged in boxes wide enough to take a standard-sized book label and present no special labeling problems. Maps and drawings are often stored in oversized drawers in large cabinets so the materials can be laid flat without folding. If this is how they are stored, call-number labels can be affixed to the individual sheets.

Boxed games and kits that consist of numerous pieces in various shapes and sizes present a unique problem: whether to label all the pieces or just the container in which they are packaged. Decisions may be made on a case-by-case basis, depending on the number of pieces, their sizes and shapes, and the cost of replacing lost pieces. For example, a 500-piece jigsaw puzzle might be labeled only on the box, but a board game consisting of a small number of pieces might put call numbers on the individual pieces and on the box. Sometimes, the pieces of multipart materials that are received without adequate packaging are repackaged in boxes, folders, or bags, and call number labels are affixed to those containers.

Adding call numbers to materials is routine for most materials, but materials that depart from the norm pose challenges. The most important skills processors can have are flexibility and creativity in dealing with the variety of materials collected by libraries as well as a practical eye.

RECORDING AND TRACKING USE

The advent of computers in libraries enabled circulation departments to automate recording and tracking the use of library materials. During processing, barcodes are placed on materials to identify each separate item and the bibliographic and item data recorded in a database. Each person who wishes to borrow materials must have a library card bearing a barcode that identifies him as an eligible borrower. When the person borrows materials, the material and user barcodes are linked to create borrowing transactions in a transaction database. Transaction data remain active until the materials are returned. At that time, the links between the barcodes are marked for deletion. Additional programs to erase or overwrite the data may be required as well, but for all intents and purposes, the transactions are ended and the links between the material barcodes and the borrower barcodes are broken. Some libraries have introduced an automated easy-to-use system where borrowers can check out materials without the intervention of library staff.

Systems using barcodes have many advantages:

- All the data—about the materials, borrowers, and transactions—are always available to everyone with access to the database
- The computer automatically notifies circulation staff when materials are overdue

- Limits on borrowing eligibility can be programmed by the library into their computers; this automatically rejects those who exceed the limits
- Barcodes, being much smaller than cards and pockets or slips of paper, can be used successfully not only on books and book-like materials, but also on a variety of smaller nonbook materials.

New digital technology goes beyond barcodes by providing protection against theft as well as borrowing and tracking information. Called radio-frequency identification (RFID) systems, tags combine microchip and radio frequency technologies to identify and track analog materials within and outside of library buildings.[4] RFID systems involve putting tiny tracking devices on materials (the tags) that function the same way as bugs used by police, spies, and private detectives in crime fiction, movies, and television shows.

Pre-computer methods of recording and tracking use included putting cards and pockets labeled with identifying data in or on the materials. Borrowing transactions were recorded on the cards, which were, usually, filed in the library. Borrowers took away cards stamped with the due dates to remind them when to return the materials. Some systems stamped borrower information and due dates on a card that also identified the material. Some systems identified the borrowers by numbers rather than names. Doing so, however, meant the library had to keep a file of borrower numbers in addition to transaction files. Some systems microfilmed the borrower card, material card, and transaction date. The library retained the images, which produced a list of identifying numbers and dates, and the borrower was given a due date card. When materials were returned, transaction numbers were crossed off the filmed list. Some systems did without cards and pockets altogether, gluing in slips of paper that could be stamped with due dates instead.

Computerized circulation systems are much less costly now than they were in the late 20th century, but some libraries still use noncomputerized methods. They must decide how to record borrowing data and provide due dates to borrowers. Once those decisions are made, they must decide whether to purchase the supplies and do the processing in-house or contract with an outside supplier to complete the procedures on the library's behalf. Similarly, libraries using computerized systems using barcodes or RFID systems can purchase the supplies and do the work of affixing barcodes or tags and entering data in-house, or contract with an outside supplier to do it for them.

No matter what system is used to record and track the data, and no matter how the processing is done, users need to know when to return the materials they borrow. Some automated systems supply slips on which due dates are printed. However, not long ago, a circulation librarian remarked to one of the authors that even though her library had a high-tech circulation system involving fancy electronics, the people at the circulation desk still relied on a "dinosaur"—the date-due stamp—to tell borrowers when their materials were to be returned.

PRESERVATION AND SECURITY

Two more topics warrant consideration in processing: preservation and security. Preserving library materials, particularly books and other paper-based materials, involves minimizing the stresses that cause them to deteriorate. At the same time processors work to provide clear evidence of library ownership, location, and usage, they can use products and procedures that cause the least stress on the materials. Important considerations are

- avoiding potentially corrosive inks, glues, tapes, and inserts made of acidic paper;
- making sure that markings and labels do not obscure information on the inside covers of books, blurbs and descriptions on boxes, and so on; and
- choosing the least invasive and obtrusive methods of accomplishing processing goals.

Some stresses on materials are environmental, such as excessive heat and/or humidity, large swings in temperature and humidity, the presence of pests and air pollutants, exposure to ultraviolet light, and storing materials on shelves made of materials that give off acids. Processing cannot do much about these matters. People cause other stresses, such as damage to books, warped and broken plastic discs, and lost pieces from kits and games. Processors can do a few things to address those problems, such as putting clear plastic sleeves on books, mentioned earlier in this chapter, to keep them clean.

Another aid to preserving materials that one of the authors has seen in practice falls under the heading of user education. In one library she visited, processors put labels on CD and DVD folders instructing borrowers how to handle the materials, such as not leaving the recordings in the sun or in a closed car on a hot day, not putting them on a radiator in cold weather, and—important for digital materials—keeping them out of strong magnetic fields. Cautions to keep books, maps, printed music, and similar paper-based materials dry in rainy weather are also added to the due dates stamped on bookmarks used by this library.

An important thing processors can do is to keep their stamps, labels, markings, barcodes, and so on as neat as possible, thereby setting a good example for everybody who sees them. Sloppy processing that looks as if things were slapped on materials in a hurry give off an image of carelessness, as if the library has no interest how materials are treated. If the library does not care, why should the borrowers?

Keeping materials in good condition for as long as possible includes preventing them from being stolen. Processing for security is usually done by inserting security strips in hidden places within the spines or gutters of books and printed periodicals. The strips emit electromagnetic frequencies that can set off alarms if they pass through a security gate without being desensitized. A similar, but more advanced technology is the RFID tag, discussed earlier. When activated, RFID tags can be monitored electronically wherever they are. When the tags are placed on library materials, library computers can track them continuously until the materials are brought back and the tags shut off and removed.

A small survey conducted in 2006[5] suggests that security strips and gates are used often, but some libraries do not use them fully. Others deploy security gates but do not insert the strips in their materials. They reason that library users do not know the strips are missing. Borrowers think alarms will sound at the gate, so they take the materials to the circulation desk where desk clerks go through the motions of desensitizing them. Some of the survey responders said they were considering switching to RFID technology.

SUMMARY

This chapter examined the goals of physical processing and selected methods libraries use to accomplish them. Goals include providing clear evidence of libraries' ownership of materials, location information, and usage data such as borrower and transaction information. Establishing policies to guide these functions and supervising staff that carry them out are among a technical services manager's duties.

Standard methods are generally geared toward dealing with books and materials packaged like books—materials that can stand on shelves in book stacks. Processing nonbook materials that come in unusual shapes and sizes takes creativity and ingenuity flavored with a large pinch of practicality.

Two other issues merit the processor's attention, namely, preservation and security. Preservation measures include using the least-damaging processing products and procedures, doing processing work neatly, and adding instructions about handling materials properly. Security measures typically include placing electromagnetic security strips inside materials that set off alarms if they are not desensitized before borrowers walk through a security gate to exit the library building. RFID, a newer digital technology, is beginning to supersede security strips and gates. Once activated, the tags of RFID systems give off radio frequencies that can be continuously monitored.

Processing usually is the final step before materials are made available to members of the public. If it is done well, the materials can be used for long periods of time, yet remain in good condition. Should damage occur, materials are sometimes returned to the processing staff for repair, rebinding, repackaging, and reprocessing.

REVIEW QUESTIONS

1. Describe three methods libraries use to show that they own materials and discuss the advantages and disadvantages of each method.

2. What function do barcodes serve?

3. If processors aim to extend the length of time that materials are usable, what kinds of measures can they take to preserve them?

4. What environmental conditions contribute to the deterioration of books and other printed materials?

5. What is RFID and how does it work to protect library materials?

NOTES

The epigraph is from *21st Century Dictionary of Quotations*, ed. The Princeton Language Institute (New York: Laurel, 1993), 407.

1. The functions of cataloging and processing are so closely related in practice that some departments are actually named "Cataloging and Processing," not simply "Cataloging," or "Cataloging and Classification."

2. Cornell University Library, "Special Formats Processing," Physical Processing Procedure, http://lts.library.cornell.edu/lts/pp/dam/physproc104#D.

3.   For an entertaining explanation of why this happens, see Michael Gorman's "The Longer the Number the Narrower the Spine," *American Libraries* 12, no. 8 (September 1981): 498–99.

4.   See, for example, descriptions of RFID options promoted by the Minitex Library Network: "3M Library Security: Tattle-Tapes, RFID Tags, Red Tag Disc Protection," https://www.minitex.umn.edu/Products/3M/Rfid.aspx.

5.   Claudine Perrault, *Library Materials Security,* http://www.lrs.org/documents/field_stats/materials_security.pdf.

SUGGESTED READING

Cornell University Library. *Physical Processing Procedure.* http://lts.library.cornell.edu/lts/pp/dam/physproc104#D.

Dale, Robin, et al. *Audio Preservation: A Selective Annotated Bibliography and Brief Summary of Current Practices.* Chicago, IL: American Library Association, 1998.

Dreissen, Karen, and Sheila A. Smyth. *A Library Manager's Guide to the Physical Processing of Nonprint Materials.* Westport, CT: Libraries Unlimited, 1995.

Fogler Library. University of Maine. *Processing Newly Cataloged Books.* http://library.umaine.edu/techserv/Cataloging/processing.htm.

Olson, Nancy B., et al. *Cataloging of Audiovisual Materials and Other Special Materials: A Manual Based on AACR2 and MARC 21.* 5th ed. Westport, CT: Libraries Unlimited, 2008. (See selected pages, listed in the index.)

Chapter

22

Leading the
Catalog Department

A leader is a dealer in hope.

—Napoleon I

The real leader has no need to lead—he is content to point the way.

—Henry Miller

Responsibility for the catalog department may rest with a department manager, with a group of people forming a management team or committee, or, in some instances, with self-governing individuals. In a large measure, the size of the catalog department and its composition defines how it is led. In addition, the traditions of the library in which the department operates influence the form that its management takes. Authority and responsibility for setting policies, organizing and directing operations, monitoring outputs, evaluating the work, and reporting the results to the library's administration needs to be undertaken and carried out on an ongoing basis.

Large libraries that do a great deal of new cataloging and employ many catalogers at different staff levels often assign management tasks to one person—typically a degree-holding librarian—as his or her primary job. In some libraries, the catalog department is organized into one or more teams, where each team is given decision-making powers over its part of the whole operation. In small libraries and media centers, the role of manager is more likely to be assumed by the same person responsible for managing other functions and services. No matter what form department management takes, however, the ultimate aim is the same: to ensure that cataloging and classification operations are performed properly and in a timely manner, and that they follow established policies and produce the expected results.

MANAGEMENT TASKS

The tasks described in this section are required of the catalog department manager, the management team, or the individuals managing a portion of the department's work. They have less to do with cataloging and classification than with managing the library as a whole, or, for that matter, managing operations of any kind. They include the following:

1. *Staffing*—recruiting personnel, training and integrating them into the staff, supervising their work, and evaluating both the work and each staff member's overall performance (such as reliability, promptness, adaptability) for the purposes of salary determination, promotion, and so forth.
2. *Budgeting*—preparing budgets periodically, monitoring expenditures, and supplying the library or media center director with a financial report at the end of the budget period (usually a year).
3. *Planning*—proposing departmental goals and objectives and how departmental operations should proceed; devising workflow routines and all procedures for accomplishing the work of the department; and, when necessary, thinking up and trying new methods for getting the work done.
4. *Decision making*—taking the risk of choosing among alternative goals and objectives, potential plans or proposals, policies, strategies, procedures, suppliers, staff members and staff assignments, budgets, and so forth for the department, and ensuring that all decisions made are consistent with the policies set by those who govern the media center or library.
5. *Directing*—taking charge, assigning tasks, arranging for things to be done properly, ensuring that people are functioning effectively, and providing leadership for the department
6. *Evaluating*—reviewing activities and measuring production, with special attention to quality, speed, and costs
7. *Reporting*—writing reports about department activities, production, staff, and budgets, and sending them to the appropriate administrative supervisor(s)

NEEDED SKILLS

Knowledge of cataloging and classification is essential for a department manager to perform the tasks listed earlier. Other skills that are needed do not involve bibliographic information. These include communication skills, political skills, financial skills, and leadership skills.

Communication skills—both speaking and writing—are important to convey one's ideas to staff members, peers, superiors, and others. Members of the cataloging department need training to do their work, especially when they are first hired. Even if new catalogers are skilled at cataloging and classification, the local situation must be explained and any special rules and procedures described. This will be particularly important if the person has come from a different type of library. All department employees need to know what is expected of them, the meaning of policies, and how to follow local procedures.

When a search for a new cataloger is conducted, the department manager may be expected to write, edit, or contribute to the wording of the job description. When selected candidates are brought to the institution for on-site interviews, the department manager is often (or should be) a major participant, describing the work of the department and asking questions to determine the candidate's knowledge and suitability for the job. Once hired, the manager is often the one who helps the person get settled and learn to operate comfortably and effectively in the job.

The department manager must be able discuss the work of the department with the heads of other library departments, with administrators, and with peers at other libraries. Often he or she must speak and write to suppliers, computer system vendors, and a variety of outsiders on whom the department depends for everything from paper and printer cartridges to contracts for access to online tools such as *Cataloger's Desktop* and *WebDewey*. The department manager is responsible for gathering statistics and writing reports, evaluating staff and operations, writing and submitting proposals for new equipment, gaining approval for new policies, designing improved procedures, and keeping up correspondence for the department within and outside of the organization.

Political skills are defined here as the skills needed to get things done through people, and they are important for the cataloging department manager. By exercising political skills, the manager can succeed in getting administrators to recognize the department's needs and approve its programs and budgets. These skills encompass being persuasive, putting forth ideas in ways that will appeal to decision makers, and being good at gaining support for new proposals.

Political skills help the department manager build consensus within the department on its goals and objectives and establish and maintain an esprit de corps that helps the department run smoothly and gives its members a sense of satisfaction. Political skills are important in enabling the manager to play a leadership role—putting forth ideas that can improve output; enhance the workplace environment; result in higher quality, more rapidly prepared, and/or less costly products—and implement the ideas in a timely manner. Political skills are critical in avoiding conflicts when members of the department are challenged or criticized, or when problems involving the department must be addressed.

Political skills have come under a cloud to some degree because of the selfish and unsavory machinations of some professional politicians and political operatives. But the positive aspects of being skillful at politics—working agreeably with people, persuading them to bring good programs to fruition, and helping them achieve good results for the benefit of others, not just the politician—are important to good management.

Leadership skills, as mentioned earlier, combine envisioning goals for the department, imbuing others with the vision, and risking the decisions that make progress possible toward those goals. Any decision could prove to be right or wrong, and the person who makes decisions risks failure. If the cataloging department is to grow and change, develop and achieve, it must have leadership willing to take on the risks of making changes and trying new things. Management teams spread the obligation and the risk of leadership among the members of the team, but they do not eliminate them. Some teams are better prepared and more willing to take risks than individual managers; some are more reluctant to change the status quo.

Financial skills are necessary for planning the department's budget, defending it successfully before higher authorities within the organization, monitoring expenditures, and evaluating the results at the end of the budget cycle. Even when managers do not create budgets, the task of overseeing department expenditures is always part of their jobs. Computer software is available to assist with the statistical work, but even the best software cannot substitute for an understanding of basic financial management processes and techniques. The cataloging department manager should be able to determine the true costs and evaluate the total value of alternative expenditures, not just to learn the price of things.

DEPARTMENT POLICIES AND PROCEDURES

A written record of the policy decisions that govern cataloging and classification of materials and the library's bibliographic services is essential for a number of reasons. First, such a record ensures continuity when members of the department change due to retirements and new hires. Second, the written record is available to consult when someone is not sure about how to proceed. An up-to-date, well-written manual can be the cornerstone of a library's cataloging and classification operations. Developing such a manual takes time and effort, but the result is a valuable document that is helpful for all staff members, whether they perform cataloging and classification tasks or merely use bibliographic services to help patrons find what they want. A departmental manual can also help to highlight the way the mission of the library is served by its cataloging and bibliographic services.

A bibliographic policy manual should begin with a brief description of the library's community, school, or organization being served; an official mission statement; and a summary of its facilities, staff, collections, and patrons. Putting these elements at the beginning clarifies the setting and context in which the policies operate. Any obvious discrepancies observed at this point between the setting, its mission, and the policies contained in the document need to be resolved before continuing to describe the details.

Next, a section for each part of the bibliographic system, arranged in any order that seems logical to the staff, should include the decisions pertaining to that part along with a brief explanation of when and why they were made. There is no one right way to organize policy documents. Popular arrangements are chronological, by material format, and functional. In a chronological arrangement, policies cover the steps of the workflow, from the receipt of materials in the department, through the steps of cataloging, classification, processing, shelving, and deacquisition. In a manual organized by material format, policies cover books, videos, databases, maps, serials, and so on. Functionally organized manuals divide the policies into those that concern original and copy cataloging, with appropriate sections about bibliographic description and access, the assignment of subject descriptors, classification and shelflisting, and processing.

The local library manual is probably best organized by the kind of workflow used in the department. If the first step when materials are received is to choose whether to send them to a department's books, audiovisuals, or serials cataloging unit, format-related organization makes sense. Sections for each format can cover the policy decisions related to those materials. Videos might require being scanned for important bibliographic elements, subject matter, etc., whereas sound recordings might require only filling in data from labels and accompanying materials. Books lacking Cataloging in Publication (CIP) or network records might be cataloged immediately or put in a queue to be searched again after a brief waiting period in hopes of locating an existing record to copy. Serials-control software might require very different policies involving ongoing procedures.

If all materials follow the same path through the department, chronological order makes sense. Following the library's standard operating procedures from start to finish and documenting the policy decisions for each step seems like the best way to handle this type of workflow. Small libraries are most likely to have this kind of workflow, not large ones in which specializations in cataloging one type of material format seems more likely. Small general libraries buying mainstream materials probably do copy cataloging for most of their materials, with, perhaps, only a small percentage of local history or local-interest materials requiring original cataloging.

If the first decision when materials are received is whether to go to original or copy cataloging, policies governing that choice become the manual's first section. Methods of searching, matching, capturing, and editing existing records from a source database are outlined. Because every change made to a derived record adds cost, policy decisions should guide the use of bibliographic records as is to the greatest extent possible. Mandated changes written into the policy should be scrutinized periodically to ensure that their benefits exceed their costs.

The section on original cataloging might begin with descriptive cataloging, specifying the level of description for various types of materials, the authority control system, the way items that are part of a series will be treated (that is, cataloged and classified separately or as a collection at the series level), whether some or all series titles will be traced, if or when multipart items will be analyzed (that is, provided with separate catalog records for each part), and when uniform titles will be adopted. Catalogers might decide to furnish analytic records for electronic resources in which the individual files may be used singly, but only one overall record for electronic resources in which the files are used in concert. Different descriptive treatments for each material format might be specified; for example, collections of tests or college catalogs might be given first-level descriptions, while reference and research materials might be given second-level descriptions. Policy decisions about optional identifying data, the addition or deletion of descriptive access points, and so forth should be documented.

The next section might deal with subject headings, starting with the sources for descriptors, the number of descriptors typically assigned, the desired depth of indexing, and any special treatments accorded to particular materials. For example, if broad headings are desired for a small collection, *Library of Congress Subject Headings* might be adopted as the source list for descriptors, but subdivisions (that is, subheadings) might be omitted for all but a few subject areas in which holdings are relatively abundant. Some materials might be indexed analytically, with descriptors assigned for each part of a multipart item, each chapter of a book, or each cut on a sound recording.

The section on classification might indicate the chosen system used, the level of complexity within the system, and the way hard-to-classify materials such as periodicals and databases are treated. The method of assigning cutter letters or numbers and styles of adding these and other shelf marks to the classification number to complete the call number should be described. The choice between creating unique call numbers for each item or allowing more than one item to share the same call number needs to be documented here. Desired anomalies in the shelving arrangement should be noted, such as keeping new acquisitions in a prominent display for a month or two; housing oversized books on special shelves; or dividing materials by instructor, grade level, class, and so on.

Explanations for the decisions recorded in the policy document enable new members of the department to understand the reasoning behind them and, as conditions change, to recognize when it is time to make changes.

Every manual needs regular review to determine whether the policies it mandates should be changed. Annual or biennial policy reviews might seem unnecessary when new policies are instituted, but they are a wise measure. Frequent reviews head off crises caused by following outmoded policies. If the reviewers take this responsibility seriously and examine every part of the document thoroughly—from the prefatory descriptions, through each section of the main text, to the closing amendment process—they have a chance of anticipating needed changes before a crisis occurs.

Adding descriptions of procedures to the statements of policy decisions is optional, but can be useful, especially if department management is decentralized among members of a team or individual catalogers and classifiers. Explanations of procedures, often in one or more separate manuals, are no substitute for a policy manual. The procedures manual needs only to spell out the steps of departmental operations, but not the policy decisions that underlie them or the reasons why those decisions were made. Nonmanagement workers need to know what to do, but they may or may not have to know why they do it. Depending on the composition of the staff and the numbers of people involved, combining policies and procedures into one manual makes sense. While managers do not want to overload staff members with extraneous information they do not need to do their jobs, understanding the overall goals and reasoning behind the tasks can make their work more meaningful and satisfying.

Procedures seem best when they follow the chronological order of steps involved, but there is no reason why separate processes can't be arranged in any order. One way to arrange the procedures manual is by physical medium, another is by bibliographic function, and a third is simply to put the procedures in alphabetical order by name. Procedures can also be arranged together with the policies to which they relate. No matter what the arrangement of the procedures manual, it should be possible to locate an individual procedure easily. Thus, if the manual is arranged by function, it should have an alphabetic index by title; and if it is arranged alphabetically by the names of the procedures or by physical medium, there should be a functionally organized list of contents provided as well.

WHEN CATALOGING STANDARDS CHANGE

An important set of decisions that should be included in the policy manual is the response to changes in the cataloging tools used by the library. When new rules for descriptive cataloging and new subject and classification authorities appear, how will they be adopted and implemented? Such changes occur regularly, because all cataloging tools follow policies of continuous revision, so it should be acknowledged and strategies developed for their implementation. Among several possible responses are the following:

1. *Make all required changes for all holdings immediately.* This is the most desirable option for keeping the entire collection together in one style of organization and completely up to date, but it is the most costly alternative, both in terms of dollars and cents and the amount of staff time it will consume in the short run.

2. *Make no changes in existing holdings, but implement the changes for new materials immediately.* This is the strategy followed by many librarians, because it seems to be the best that can be done with limited resources. The problem with this strategy is that over time, even just a few years, the organization of the library starts to break down. What emerges is not one unified collection, but several fragmented collections, each following different rules. This was the strategy of choice for many libraries when they automated; when it finally became necessary to incorporate the older holdings into the automated system, it was a huge job that cost much more than had been anticipated.

3. *Make all changes over a limited period of time.* This strategy seems to be the most reasonable when circumstances don't permit the first approach, because all the materials remain in one unified organizational structure, even though the structure will take on different aspects as various changes are implemented. It probably has the best payoff in the long run, because it will ultimately result in the same organizational effectiveness as the first option but will not require as large an investment at once; however, it usually ends up costing more than implementing all the changes immediately.

4. *Make changes selectively.* This strategy also is popular with practitioners and can be the best overall strategy when changes in cataloging rules, subject descriptors, and classification schemes do not affect local library holdings to a great extent. For example, some years ago when numbers in the Dewey classification's music schedule changed radically, a library that did not buy many items about music and whose music holdings consisted solely of a few works about music appreciation, might have decided not to implement the changes that appeared in the 20th edition. This strategy can lead to future problems, however, should the discrepancies become more significant over time or should the local library begin to collect music materials in larger quantities. Still, if a greatly enlarged music collection is established, the decision can be made to implement the newer Dewey numbers at the same time.

5. *Make no changes and continue using older editions of tools.* This strategy is deceptively simple, easy, and cheap. Sooner or later, however, it breaks down completely because it lacks the capacity to keep up with changes in materials, subject matter, and user needs. Moreover, it causes the local library to grow further and further out of step with the rest of the library community. When the moment finally arrives that librarians realize that something must be done, it will cost a great deal more to address

the changes and implement new policies than when the changes first occurred.

Each of these alternatives—and they are not the only ones possible—has advantages and disadvantages, and each will have a different result both in the short term and
over the long run. The first option seems like an ideal response, but it is the most costly;
and although the last option is the least costly in the short run, it probably will result
in the least effective service to patrons, even though the problems might not become
apparent for some time. The other options fall somewhere between these extremes,
and libraries must weigh the alternatives in terms of their individual situations and the
impact on budgets, staff, and patron services.

WRITING A POLICY MANUAL

No matter how a department's management is configured, one person should be
tapped to write the manual. This minimizes the possibility that individual differences in
style and language will produce sections using different words for the same concepts,
using the same words for different concepts, and other potentially confusing language
problems. Over time, more than one person may write and/or edit sections of the manual, but at any one time, one person should be assigned this responsibility.

A good way to begin preparing the policy manual is to draw up a table of contents
and circulate it among staff for suggestions about additions or changes to be made. It
might be wise to indicate that just because suggestions are solicited does not mean they
will automatically be followed. If major differences arise, negotiation can produce an
acceptable solution so that the manual is a source of agreement, not contention. The
table of contents, once defined, establishes the scope of the manual and identifies the
way the whole bibliographic system will be divided and addressed.

Writing the manual might begin by listing all the decisions and operations to be
covered within each section and circulating the list for input from other department
members. For example, decisions relating to materials issued in series could be listed
under "Descriptive Cataloging," "Tracing Practice," "Indexing," and "Classification," if
the manual is divided functionally, or under "Series" or "Monographic Series," if it is
divided by types of material. Either way, all the decisions relating to the handling of
series must be covered somewhere in the manual. For the user's convenience, an index
can bring together related information that falls into different sections or chapters (that
is, to bring together all the descriptive cataloging decisions when the division is by material type, or all the decisions relating to series when the division is by function). Word
processing software enables indexes to be created automatically, making this a relatively
easy task. When the manual combines policies and procedures, similar handling of procedures also has to be done.

When the decisions (and operations) to be covered are listed, but before actual
writing begins, questions about the style of the presentation should be asked and answered. Some are as simple as whether one or both sides of a page should be used;
whether sources will be cited at the bottom of pages or as endnotes; and whether illustrative examples, flowcharts, tables, and so forth will be given within text or as separate
pages or sections. These decisions might sound trivial, but they affect the ease with

which the manual can be updated; the size of the completed document ("document" is used as a generic term here; the manual need not be a book—it could be a database); the ease with which it can be consulted, excerpted, or duplicated; its applicability to the task of training new staff; and similar issues. Other decisions include the approach to describing operations, as step-by-step procedures or straight narratives; the amount and types of illustration; the inclusion or exclusion of supporting material (such as quoting Library of Congress rule interpretations in full or citing the page in a different document on which the interpretation appears); and so forth.

Once the questions are answered and the content, approach, and style are clearly defined, writing can begin. If the designated author is knowledgeable in all the areas covered by the manual, he or she can begin writing each part, section, and chapter, completing them according to an agreed-upon schedule. If the manual includes policies or procedures that the writer does not know well, these should be written jointly with a knowledgeable guide, or another person should submit a draft to the writer, who puts it into final format. Either way, as each part is written, it is wise to circulate drafts among staff members who are expected to use them, or who actually perform the tasks, to be certain the text is clear and understandable. The writer should expect to edit the work not only to account for solicited feedback from staff members, but also to enhance, clarify, sharpen, and polish the text, based on her own re-readings.

When enough of the manual is completed to warrant its distribution, the first few months (or longer) of its use should be considered a test run to see how well it functions. It might be issued in chapters or sections, or only after completion of the whole. With actual use, however, unanticipated problems can arise, which usually must be resolved by revising the language, examples or illustrations, finding aids, and so on. Occasionally, enough difficulty is encountered to prompt reconsidering the basic organization, format, or style, and to suggest doing a major overhaul. If this happens, it is best to weigh the true need for a total revision versus continuing to try making the existing manual work. The first version of a manual need not be the last, but the difficulties should be evaluated carefully and estimates made that changes in style or approach can achieve the desired improvement before discarding an existing document. It is realistic to expect several months of revision to follow issuing any new manual to discover and work out all its bugs. The problems are no one's fault. Revision is inherent in the process of obtaining an effective manual.

ADOPTING THE POLICY MANUAL

When the policy manual is complete and satisfies department staff members, one more step is necessary before it is adopted. It is essential that administrators affirm the manual and the policies it presents. It will do little good to decide to put a bibliographic policy in place if those responsible for the library are unwilling to support its ideas, fund its implementation, and appreciate its value to the organization being served. Surprisingly, even when library management and boards of directors are the ones to make the decisions, seeing those decisions incorporated into a departmental manual sometimes prompts objections. Perhaps the thinking of the people involved has changed. Perhaps the interpretation seems to have changed in the manual's text. Whatever the reasons behind the objections, they must be resolved and official approval obtained before the manual can be adopted.

In connection with seeking administrative approval for policies, librarians must be prepared to document the goals and priorities served by particular policies, know their costs, and defend the expenditures. Whether or not a costly change is being considered, it is fair for an administrator to expect cataloging department managers to answer questions about the costs and benefits of bibliographic policies, to argue persuasively on behalf of proposed policies, and to negotiate compromise positions, when necessary.

CURRENT ISSUES

For several decades starting in the 1970s, the greatest challenge facing cataloging department managers was introducing computers into their operations and upgrading them as new hardware and software became available. Far from being a better producer of catalog cards, automation soon required reorganizing the workflow, retraining the staff, and incorporating all previous bibliographic data into the new computer-based systems being implemented. Among the profound changes that resulted are new patron services made possible by linking catalogs electronically. If a library or media center catalog is linked to the Internet, searchers can go beyond local library holdings to seemingly limitless resources located all around the world. Internet services began in the 1990s and have increased exponentially since then.

Locally, a computerized catalog can be linked to other internal information files within the organization, such as order files and circulation files, enabling searchers to determine the exact status of a desired title or when it is due to be returned if it is out on loan to a borrower. Because of this linkage, online public access catalogs, called OPACs for short, finally are able to answer library users' most basic question: Can I have this item?

As electronic resources become more sophisticated, the challenge to make optimal use of them has increased, putting pressure on library managers to continue making changes in the way locally managed holdings are cataloged, indexed, classified, and processed. Demand for high-quality cataloging continues unabated, but the digital revolution has prompted the development of metadata—cataloging of electronic resources stored in digital libraries. Hiring specialists who can prepare metadata to support local projects and can initiate, manage, and market digital library projects is not easy. Candidates with the requisite computer knowledge and library expertise are a small cohort, and libraries rarely offer enough compensation to woo them away from the business world. This and other computer-related issues continue to occupy cataloging department managers' attention, mainly concerning the implementation of new releases for local library software and/or the purchase of newer integrated library systems, both of which involve implementation plans, including training department staff members, other library staff, and users in use of the new systems.

Another important issue is deciding whether maintaining an in-house cataloging operation is as effective as contracting with an outside service to provide the library with cataloging for new acquisitions and to maintain the catalog system. Called *out-sourcing,* outside contracting has attracted much attention and prompted intense debate. Deciding whether to contract with cataloging sources outside the library or have the cataloging done by library employees requires careful consideration of many factors, including the cost, speed, and quality of the products, as well as control over local operations and the availability of bibliographic expertise on the library's staff. Options for outsourcing include commercial firms offering services based on ever-larger network databases, access to network databases, cataloging software, and hiring consultants on a project-by-project basis for collections requiring original cataloging.

What too many library directors fail to realize is the impact on the library of the potential loss of expertise that results from closing down cataloging departments and dispersing staff members having special bibliographic knowledge. The specialization that has developed over more than a century of library growth seems to have removed cataloging from all the services for which it is the foundation. Reference and information services do not exist in a vacuum, divorced from cataloging. The catalog remains the primary reference tool for most people using local libraries, yet some librarians perceive it as just another database. When cataloging is obtained from outside sources, someone should be monitoring it on behalf of the library—someone who has knowledge of both the local population and the local catalog. If this supervision disappears, control over local catalogs, which is greatly diminished by outsourcing, disappears entirely.

In the last decade, development of genre headings continued to the point that they are now assigned to many materials as a matter of course. Catalogs that use multiple subject authorities instead of just one are now common, especially among large libraries catering to a broad range of searchers, including offsite users. These changes have augmented the vocabulary available to searchers for retrieving materials, especially nonbook materials, and have also encouraged catalogers to increase the number of headings they assign. Similarly, work has continued on revising and improving core standards for catalog records that offer less data, but equally high-quality data as in full records. Adopting core records for segments of the collection enables managers to stretch the output of understaffed departments. The goal of cataloging everything acquired by the library and avoiding backlogs is still merely an ideal in a good many places.

The difficulty of recruiting well-trained catalogers persists and is unlikely to change unless libraries with large cataloging departments offer meaningful incentives to attract more new professionals to the specialty. The mistaken notion that computers are doing original cataloging all by themselves, without human intervention, also persists, putting a damper on the likelihood that such incentives will soon appear. It may be just a matter of time until expert systems incorporating cataloging tools can create full standard records automatically, but it has not happened yet. In this book's previous edition, the authors suggested that publishers could develop such expert systems and use them to add full cataloging to every item they issue as part of the publishing process, like CIP, but with greater control and accuracy. To date, they have not done so, nor have they even offered embedded metadata in their products other than CIP. Observers cannot help but hope the situation will change, perhaps in reaction to a burst of new electronic books and their readers.

Automating time-consuming cataloging processes can make it possible for catalogers to spend more time helping searchers find what they want, either in person or via online bibliographic services. User service is, after all, the object of cataloging. In the meantime, cataloging department managers must endeavor to employ computing and electronic access to accomplish the work that catalogers have performed in different ways since Callimachus classified texts in ancient times for the great library at Alexandria, currently rebuilt, refurbished, and reopened in 2009 as an exemplary 21st-century institution.

TEN HINTS FOR LEADERSHIP

Much of the advice in this chapter can be distilled into brief guidelines that cataloging department managers would do well to heed. They include the following:

1. Make basic decisions about bibliographic control policies, write them down, and stick to them until annual reviews give evidence that they need to be changed. When considering alternatives, keep in mind the needs of users, obligations to the network, and available budget and staffing.

2. Trade-offs between quality and quantity require balancing doing the best job with doing the whole job. Allowing backlogs to grow while the department's resources are invested in doing more complex work than necessary should be absolutely forbidden.

3. Have the tools to do a good job of cataloging. Acquiring an expensive reference tool pays off in the long run in the form of higher-quality cataloging with less effort.

4. Write down local rule interpretations and subject applications, and use them for all other cases of the same kind.

5. Work on making copy cataloging true to its name. Examine what is being edited and updated as well as what materials are being cataloged from scratch and try to expedite the work. If given the opportunity to outsource some or all of the cataloging to a reliable vendor, be objective in analyzing the costs and benefits of doing so.

6. Face problems and experiment with solutions. Own up to mistakes quickly and honestly, then move on to more successful options. Try not to promise output that perhaps cannot be delivered.

7. Develop a support system, and work at both using it and contributing to it. Join the cataloging group in the state, provincial, regional, or national professional association, and be active in it. Befriend colleagues in the library, in peer libraries, and in nearby libraries of all types; network partners and network representatives; and cataloging experts. Write for help to us and other authors of cataloging texts, user group and association leaders, cataloging educators, and others. Professional education is an ongoing obligation, so do it.

8. Be informed. Cataloging rules and tools are dynamic and are constantly accommodating new decisions. Read the literature, keep up with revisions, and take advantage of continuing education opportunities.

9. Inform those who use the library and public-service staff members of decisions and procedures, and seek their input before making changes.

10. *Trust yourself!* Undoubtedly, no one in the organization knows more about bibliographic issues than you do. When in doubt, consult your network, but listen to your instincts about your library and its users.

PATRON SERVICE FIRST AND FOREMOST

Service to patrons is the ultimate object of all bibliographic policies and procedures, and should be the main goal of department managers and all of their operations. Standard tools and processes are recommended in this book because the authors believe they furnish good service and benefit patrons. One of their greatest advantages is that they enable local libraries to share the work of their peers and participate in systems that reach far beyond their immediate territory.

Librarians can benefit by developing a positive attitude toward change and a better grasp of how to implement new and creative ideas involving new technologies and methods. It behooves cataloging managers to realize that, ultimately, cataloging is a public service, and must be measured according to how well it performs for its users.

REVIEW QUESTIONS

1. Identify three tasks that fall to the cataloging department manager and discuss the skills needed to accomplish them.

2. Describe different types of department management and the advantages of each one.

3. What budget responsibilities are part of the department manager's job in most libraries? What budget responsibilities might also be assigned to the department manager?

4. How should policy decisions be handled in the department?

5. Describe the difference between policies and procedures.

6. Who should write the department policy manual and how should that person obtain feedback from the rest of the members of the department?

7. What responsibilities does the department manager have in the recruiting and hiring of new department staff members?

8. When should department activities be evaluated?

SUGGESTED READING

Eden, Bradford Lee, ed. *More Innovative Redesign and Reorganization of Library Technical Services.* Santa Barbara, CA: ABC-CLIO/Libraries Unlimited, 2008.

Evans, G. Edward, and Patricia Layzell Ward. Management *Basics for Information Professionals,* 2nd ed. New York: Neal-Schuman, 2007.

Giesecke, Joan, and Beth McNeil. *Fundamentals of Library Supervision.* 2nd ed. Chicago, IL: American Library Association, 2010.

Laughlin, Sara, Denise Sisco Shockley, and Ray W. Wilson. *The Library's Continuous Improvement Fieldbook: 29 Ready-to-Use Tools.* Chicago, IL: American Library Association, 2003.

Matthews, Joseph R. *The Evaluation and Measurement of Library Services.* Santa Barbara, CA: ABC-CLIO/Libraries Unlimited, 2007.

Matthews, Joseph R. *Strategic Planning and Management for Library Managers.* Santa Barbara, CA: ABC-CLIO/Libraries Unlimited, 2005.

McKinlay, James, and Vicki Williamson. *The Art of People Management in Libraries: Tips for Managing Your Most Vital Resource.* Abingdon, UK: Chandos Publishing, 2010.

Poll, Roswitha, Phillip Ramsdale, and Michael Hansen. *Financial Management in Libraries.* London: Facet Publishing, 2010.

Indexes

The three indexes that follow provide a detailed guide to the contents of the book. The first index is a topical guide to the text followed by an index of both personal and corporate names. The third index accommodates those who wish to study the figures and examples more systematically, and is divided into four subsections: Type of Media, Access Points, Description, and Classification.

TOPICAL INDEX TO THE TEXT

INDEX TO NAMES

INDEX TO FIGURES

Type of Media

Access Points

Author/Creator Main Entry

Title Main Entry

Added Entry

Subject Headings

Description

Title and Statement of Responsibility Area (Area 1)

Edition Area (Area 2)

Material Specific Details Area (Area 3)

Publication, Distribution, Etc., Area (Area 4)

Physical Description Area (Area 5)

Series Area (Area 6)

Note Area (Area 7)

Standard Number and Terms of Availability Area (Area 8)

CLASSIFICATION

About the Authors

DR. G. EDWARD EVANS is semiretired after a career of more than 50 years in librarianship. (Currently he looks after the Harold S. Colton Memorial Library and Archives at the Museum of Northern Arizona.) Academically, he holds graduate degrees in both anthropology and librarianship. He started his career as a student worker in the reserve room of the University of Minnesota Library and spent the past 25 years as a library director. His last full-time position was as Associate Academic Vice President for Scholarly Resources at Loyola Marymount University. He has taught librarianship courses as a practicing librarian and completed the faculty "academic ladder" (moving from assistant professor to full professor) while at the University of California, Los Angeles. Evans's practical experience was in both public and private academic library environments. He has held both National Science Foundation and Fulbright fellowships during his career and has been active in statewide and national library associations. He currently has eight books in print, covering a range of library-related topics including management, collection development, public services, and technical services.

SHEILA S. INTNER is Professor Emeritus at Simmons College's Graduate School of Library and Information Science, where she taught cataloging and collection development for 21 years. She earned a B.A. from Northwestern University, an M.L.S. from Queens College of the City of New York, and a D.L.S. from Columbia University. Retired in 2006, Sheila was the founding director of Simmons' MLS program at Mount Holyoke College, South Hadley, MA. Sheila served as an ALA Councilor-at-large, President of the Association for Library Collections & Technical Services, Chair of its Cataloging and Classification Section, Chair of Online Audiovisual Catalogers, editor of *Library Resources & Technical Services* and *Technicalities*, and serves now on the ALA Editions Advisory Committee. She is the author or editor of more than 30 books, among them *Beginning Cataloging* (with Jean Weihs), *Standard Cataloging for*

School and Public Libraries, 4th edition (also with Jean Weihs), *Fundamentals of Technical Services Management* (with Peggy Johnson) and *Cataloging Correctly for Kids*, 5th edition (with Joanna Fountain and Jean Weihs). She is the editor of two scholarly series, *Third Millennium Cataloging* (with Susan S. Lazinger) and *Frontiers of Access to Library Materials*. She received the Margaret Mann Citation Award, the Distinguished Alumna Award of Queens College's Graduate School of Library and Information Science, annual awards of Online Audiovisual Catalogers and New England Technical Services Librarians. In addition, she presented papers in cities across the United States as well as in China, Japan, Germany, the Marshall Islands, and Canada. She taught as a Fulbright Scholar (Israel) and as a member of the U.S. State Department Speakers Bureau (Indonesia; the Republic of Georgia). Sheila continues teaching cataloging and classification part-time at Rutgers' School of Communications and Information.

JEAN WEIHS has worked in university, public, school, and special libraries as a reference librarian, a bibliographer, and a school librarian. However, most of her career has been involved in cataloguing, both as a practitioner and a teacher of librarians, library technicians, and school librarians in Canada and as a visiting professor in the United States. She represented the Canadian Committee on Cataloguing for nine years on the Joint Steering Committee for Revision of AACR, five of these as JSC Chair. *Nonbook Materials: The Organization of Integrated Collections* (written with Shirley Lewis and Janet Macdonald, in consultation with the CLA/ALA/AECT/AMTEC Advisory Committee on the Cataloguing of Nonbook Materials) was one of the bases for the development of the present rules in AACR2. She has been the recipient of fourteen national and international awards including the Margaret Mann Citation in Cataloging and Classification, the Queen's Jubilee Medal (given by the Governor General of Canada, nominated by the Canadian Library Association), and was the first recipient of the John Comaromi Lectureship. She has held 45 positions on national and international committees and has written or co-written 19 books, 5 separately-published pamphlets/documents, 14 chapters in books edited by others, and over 150 articles and book reviews in professional journals.